the penguin good

wineguide

2009

Nick Stock is one of Australia's most respected and prolific wine critics. His deep involvement in wine stretches well beyond wine-writing to show-judging, educating, broadcasting and winemaking. His wealth of knowledge extends to all corners of the wine world and this, combined with his frank and fearless style, has made him one of the most popular and widely read Australian wine writers. He engages all – from the most sophisticated and involved collector right through to the enthusiast and novice wine drinker – with his savvy, informed and user-friendly style. He makes this highly complex and detailed subject enjoyable and intriguing, an approach that has earned him international acclaim. Nick was awarded Best Drinks Journalist at the 2007 Le Cordon Bleu World Food Media Awards.

the penguin good australian

wineguide
2009

nick stock

Penguin Books

PENGUIN BOOKS

Published by the Penguin Group
Penguin Group (Australia)
250 Camberwell Road, Camberwell, Victoria 3124, Australia
(a division of Pearson Australia Group Pty Ltd)
Penguin Group (USA) Inc.
375 Hudson Street, New York, New York 10014, USA
Penguin Group (Canada)
90 Eglinton Avenue East, Suite 700, Toronto, Canada ON M4P 2Y3
(a division of Pearson Penguin Canada Inc.)
Penguin Books Ltd
80 Strand, London WC2R 0RL England
Penguin Ireland
25 St Stephen's Green, Dublin 2, Ireland
(a division of Penguin Books Ltd)
Penguin Books India Pvt Ltd
11 Community Centre, Panchsheel Park, New Delhi – 110 017, India
Penguin Group (NZ)
67 Apollo Drive, Rosedale, North Shore 0632, New Zealand
(a division of Pearson New Zealand Ltd)
Penguin Books (South Africa) (Pty) Ltd
24 Sturdee Avenue, Rosebank, Johannesburg 2196, South Africa

Penguin Books Ltd, Registered Offices: 80 Strand, London, WC2R 0RL, England

First published by Penguin Group (Australia), a division of Pearson Australia Group Pty Ltd, 2008

10 9 8 7 6 5 4 3 2 1

Copyright © Penguin Group (Australia) 2008

Cover illustration by Danie Pout © Penguin Group (Australia)
Text design by Marina Messiha © Penguin Group (Australia)
Author photograph by Tim de Neefe
Typeset in Stone Sans by Post Pre-Press Group, Brisbane, Queensland
Printed and bound in Australia by McPherson's Printing Group, Maryborough, Victoria

ISBN 9780143008330

penguin.com.au

For

Harold James North

&

Frank Stock

Contents

Acknowledgements	viii
Introducing the 2009 *Guide*	1
The Penguin rating system	4
Penguin wine awards 2009	7
Five-star wines – the best of the best	16
Best of the rest	20
Best-value wines $25 and under	27
Vintage report 2008	40
State of play	43
Sparkling wines	47
Champagne	56
Sauvignon blanc	64
Sauvignon blanc NZ	73
Semillon	83
Semillon sauvignon blanc blends	88
Riesling and gewürztraminer	96
Pinot gris and pinot grigio	107
Emerging white wines	116
Viognier, marsanne and roussanne	119
Chardonnay	126
Imported white wines	150

Rosé   153
Pinot noir   160
Pinot noir NZ   184
Italian varietals   202
Emerging red wines   209
Grenache, shiraz, mataro and blends   218
Shiraz   233
Shiraz cabernet blends   270
Cabernet sauvignon   276
Cabernet merlot blends   288
Merlot and blends   298
Imported red wines   305
Sweet wines   311
Fortified wines   314

Wine terms   320
Tasting terms   324
Principal wine regions   326
Regional guide   328
Directory of wineries   350
Index   382

Acknowledgements

Putting the *Guide* together is a mammoth task and I will never forget the wry smiles of past authors Huon Hooke and Ralph Kyte-Powell as they handed me the torch. They, along with the late Mark Shield, have left me an inspiring legacy.

Having cut my early wine teeth on this very book, it's both a labour of love and a great honour to be steering the *Guide* and charting its course through the ever-expanding world of great wine.

This book would not exist without the patience and support of many colleagues, editors, friends and family. My deepest gratitude to Kerry Ryan, whose friendship, intellect and assistance with this year's *Guide* have been invaluable.

Introducing the 2009 *Guide*

It's an exciting time to be writing about wine in Australia and, having cut my teeth on *The Penguin Good Australian Wine Guide* many years ago, it's a privilege to be taking over the reins. Wine quality has never been better, Australia's vineyards keep maturing, the variety and diversity is unparalleled and there is more good wine on our shelves than ever before.

This makes the process of tasting wine a vital one. There's an endless flow of new wine and it's virtually impossible to keep up with, but we've done the hard yards to bring you, the wine lover, the very best of what's on offer. The tasting notes get straight to the point; each description aims to give you a feel for the essence of the wine listed, what its strengths are and what to expect should you choose to track it down and investigate for yourself.

Australia's winemaking community is vibrant and full of inspirational people doing the very best they can – many are keen to stand tall on the world wine stage. The *Guide* brings their efforts to light in a global context but also places a strong emphasis on where they stand in regional terms.

A new generation of better travelled, tasted, informed, resourced and technically supported winemakers is taking shape at the heart of the Australian industry. The leaders and the young guns are working furiously at the cutting edge, the legends continue to inspire and there's a growing emphasis on making wine that is truly distinctive – wine that stands out from the pack.

NEW ZEALAND WINES

Australians have developed a taste for the wines of our Pacific neighbour. The New Zealand industry is a little sheepish about just how much we're drinking for fear of giving us a cultural – and economic – fright. Needless to say, we're their major export market, and it's driven by sauvignon blanc. Almost half of the $400 million dollar growth in the value of Australian retail wine sales over the last five years is attributable to an increase in sales of NZ sauvignon blanc – a staggering $180 million dollars. In Australia at the moment, the number one selling table wine is a sauvignon blanc from Marlborough, and the top-selling wine by dollar value is an Oyster Bay sauvignon blanc (source: AC Nielsen).

Our demand for New Zealand pinot noir is also stepping up, as is our regard for their wines. They have made a big splash on the global stage with pinot and their focus on quality is one to be envied.

So, for the first time in the *Guide*'s history, there are dedicated chapters for New Zealand sauvignon blanc and pinot noir. You'll also find a selection of NZ chardonnay, riesling, cabernet and syrah (shiraz) dotted throughout the regular chapters, but the strength and interest that pinot and sauvignon are garnering earned them their very own place in this year's re-vamped edition.

CHAMPAGNE

Our love of wine with bubbles is seemingly unquenchable. The United Kingdom is still the number one export destination for fine French fizz, with its population guzzling an impressive 39 million bottles per annum. But Australian consumption has now reached the 3.3 million bottles per annum mark, placing this country in the world's top-10 markets for champagne. So, the 2009 *Guide* includes a champagne chapter to help you navigate this growing category.

Currently, a total of 150 million bottles of champagne are exported each year to over 190 countries. This is three times the volume that was traded in the 1980s, putting intense pressure on production and future supplies. The Champagne region is looking to extend its borders to cope with the projected growth in demand – a controversial topic among the region's vignerons.

IMPORTED WINES

Another addition to the *Guide* this year is the inclusion of two chapters dedicated to imported wines. The previous *Guide* authors, Huon Hooke and Ralph Kyte-Powell, made mention of Australia's rising interest in imported wines in the 2007 edition, and the rise has continued unabated since then.

Several factors have contributed to this phenomenon. The world of wine has become a globally connected sphere: winemakers and wine drinkers travel more and have developed a wider experience and appreciation of wine. We are maturing as a wine-drinking nation, and in the search for quality and interesting wines we are looking beyond our own excellent home-grown choices. Eclectic wine varieties, styles and influences are appearing on the shelves to satisfy this demand.

A committed band of importers have been growing their portfolios, some newer players are exploring their personal passions, and the two largest national retailers, Woolworths and Coles, are shipping vast amounts of wine directly to our shores. The range and the quality of well-priced European wines – not just the established top end – are improving, and their impact on Australian wine styles is increasing all the time.

HOW THE WINES ARE TASTED

The tasting, rating and selection process for inclusion in this book is a major exercise in logistics and organisation. Wines are arranged in variety or style and broken down into smaller groups according to region, then vintage. This means that wines of a similar style and origin are all tasted together, allowing the top-quality wines to shine above their peers. The identity of each wine is unknown until after the tasting and once the rating has been completed, creating a level playing field and the fairest, most objective assessment of quality. It's a massive undertaking with more than 5000 wines tasted in order to select the pick of the crop for readers of the *Guide*.

Happy drinking!

The Penguin rating system

With an increasingly global wine market, *The Penguin Good Australian Wine Guide* first used the 100-point rating system in 2007. This system has become the most commonly used rating scale around the world and is now the international benchmark for wine ratings. The US market has led the charge with intense importance placed on points in recent years; this points-driven culture is now maturing along with their market and their palates.

Ultimately, however, you are the judge of the wines. The descriptions are still the most reliable guide to the style and quality of each wine. Reading a review should give you a feel for what it's like to drink that wine, not simply an arms-length breakdown that uses unfamiliar technical language and conjures up images of lab coats and clipboards.

Points provide a quick reference as you flick through the *Guide*. The score out of 100 is then equated to a simplified five-star scale, which allows wines to be grouped into broader categories of quality.

Rating	Quality	What it means
96–100	★★★★★	It simply doesn't get any better. A benchmark for the style and of world-beating quality.
93–95	★★★★ ʲ	Seriously great wine with all aspects of style and quality in top form. Well ahead of the pack.
90–92	★★★★	This is where serious quality starts to kick in. Greater concentration and purity, superior in every aspect.
87–89	★★★ ʲ	Good wine that is defined by high-quality fruit, quality winemaking and impressive balance.
84–86	★★★	A simple thumbs up; this wine is soundly made and will deliver reliably enjoyable drinking.

It is important to consider the rating on the 100-point scale against the price of the wine in question. A $20 wine with a rating of 90 points is a very good result, whereas a $200 wine with a rating of 90 points would be considered an underperformer. The value symbol ✓ is a handy guide to quickly assessing wines that offer quality at a good price (see opposite). Unless specified, all wines in the *Guide* are 750 ml bottles.

Preview scores (90–92)

In order to bring you the most up-to-date selection of the best wines available, I have tasted an extensive selection of unwooded whites from the 2008 vintage, both in Australia and New Zealand. A small number of wines have been tasted right on deadline.

As these wines are tasted in finished but unbottled form, they are scored within a range (indicated in brackets, as above), allowing for an exact score to be awarded when they are released into the market. Given the popularity of many of these wines, it's good to have the inside running on the most up-to-date vintages. Only wines from reliable producers with an established track record have been included. Inexpensive wines aren't always good value just because they're cheap, and expensive wines frequently don't deliver the quality their price tag suggests.

✓ Good value

In the past the *Guide* has rated each wine on a five-star score for value. This has now been simplified to a simple tick placed next to the price of the wine – an indication that the wine represents good value for money. A range of wines – at a full range of price-points – that outperform similarly priced competition exhibit this tick. Sometimes an outstanding result can be achieved by spending a few more dollars; sometimes you'll find better wine at a lower price.

🍃 Organics, biodynamics and generally doing the right thing

Certain wines in this year's *Guide* are marked with a leaf motif. Wine is made from organic material – grapes – and it's important to recognise those people who are striving for sustainable farming alongside making the best wines possible. The best wines are not always those with the least non-organic input; however, there is a growing sentiment that makes a strong case for biodynamic practices. Whilst the science behind Rudolph Steiner's teachings is difficult to unravel and explain, the basic premise of health and balance in the vineyard does translate into the quality of the grapes grown and the wine produced.

The leaf motif indicates producers who are making an effort towards sustainable practices in the winery and the vineyard – through organics or biodynamics or both. The symbol is a flag for your reference, nothing more. If you are interested in more detail, then you can get in touch with the producer directly and source the information from the horse's mouth, so to speak.

The process of certification in organics and biodynamics is fraught with politics and inconsistency. As one producer put it to me, 'The people who do use chemicals should be the ones certified, not the people who don't.' Certification is an industry in its own right, and many producers I speak with are disenchanted by the process. I'm opening it up for discussion; the issue is not done and dusted and will not be for years, perhaps decades. In the meantime, I want to encourage those doing the right thing and not exclude environmentally responsible producers on technicalities. I hope that readers who are interested might find the leaf motif useful in choosing wine.

A note on pricing

As any keen Australian wine buyer will know, the competition on retail shelves has been a feature of recent years, for better or for worse. It's a battlefield of discounting and ruthless deals that have been a boon for bargain hunters and a storm to weather for many of our smaller brands. Due to a rapidly changing landscape of Australian wine retailing, I've dispensed with attempting to identify wines that are likely to be sold on promotion and discount, in the name of reliability. Therefore, the prices in this year's *Guide* are calculated on a standard retail margin.

If you have the inclination to pursue the best prices, shop around and peruse the Internet. Most retailers will match the prices of their competition, although smaller businesses will struggle to compete with the national big-box retailers. Some stores are more heavily geared towards discounting than others, so make a note of these and keep a keen eye on their stock.

When to drink?

The system for when to drink the wines in the *Guide* has been simplified. Drink 'Now' means that the wine needs no time to settle down and is ready to go. Where a year is indicated, this is a guide to when the wine will be reaching the period of optimum drinking. How long it remains at its peak will depend on cellaring conditions. With many full-bodied red wines being released very early on in their evolution, it's worth considering that cellaring will enhance the experience of drinking.

The recommended year is calculated with ideal cellaring conditions in mind. This will therefore be a moving target, for wines not stored in ideal conditions will mature more rapidly. As a collector, you'll have an idea of the pace of maturation in your wine cellar, so factor this into your own calculations.

Penguin wine awards 2009

Following the initial tasting of more than 5000 bottles, I revisited these wines – sometimes more than twice – to arrive at what proved to be some very difficult decisions. Hence there are two joint awards this year, as the choice came down to either varietal and/or regional bias, rather than which wine was better than the other.

Each award is not simply handed to the wine that scores the highest points in its category. It's a process of looking at the whole picture and singling out wines that epitomise the very best that is possible for that style. Price, or value, and availability are also factored into the decision.

You'll note that points for the top wines are higher for some varieties and styles than others. All grape varieties and styles are not created equal, and their inherent strengths and weakness are reflected in the spread of points. Congratulations to this year's award winners.

WINERY OF THE YEAR

Spinifex

Pete Schell and Magali Gely win not only on the strength of their wines but also for the region in which they are excelling. Competition at the top in the Barossa Valley is fierce and Spinifex takes the essence of this great region and fuses a wealth of history and vineyard resources with refined skill and insightful vision.

BEST NEW WINERY

Collector Wines

Former winemaker at Hardy's (now defunct) Kamberra Winery, Alex McKay has had his eye on the cool-climate prize for a while. He's already snapping at the heels of the established cool-climate heroes and is a name to keep a close eye on.

WINEMAKER OF THE YEAR

Tim Kirk – Clonakilla

Tim needs little introduction to readers of the *Guide*, having been awarded here in past years. His commitment and dedication to the cause of great Australian wine is unwavering and, had some of the wines not been in such short supply (due to a frosted 2007 vintage), he would have won even more awards this year.

WINE OF THE YEAR & BEST GSM BLEND

2006 Spinifex Esprit

A seamlessly woven Barossa blend, perfectly interpreting the vintage, the multiple varieties and the essence of the Barossa Valley, this wine succeeds where many others fail. And at a price that puts it well within the reach of Australian wine lovers. (See page 229.)

BEST-VALUE SPARKLING WINE

2006 Taltarni Vintage Brut

There's a fierce competition to dominate the lucrative and fast-growing sparkling wine category. Taltarni has made the most of Tasmanian and Victorian resources to craft a bottle-fermented beauty, beating many higher-priced competitors, hands down. (See page 55.)

BEST-VALUE RED WINE

2007 Josef Chromy Pepik Pinot Noir
2006 Penley Estate Phoenix Cabernet Sauvignon

Impossible to separate these two sub-$20 reds as they both deliver so far ahead of the competition. The 2007 Pepik Pinot Noir lights the way for Tasmanian pinot to break into the mainstream and Kym Tolley's 2006 Penley Estate Phoenix Cabernet Sauvignon shows all the class of truly elegant Coonawarra cabernet. (See pages 168 and 283.)

BEST-VALUE WHITE WINE

2006 Forest Hill Chardonnay

Chardonnay is back with a vengeance and this Western Australian wine shows exactly why this grape is held in such high regard. Where once this kind of intensity and purity could only be found at ultra premium prices, this heralds the new face of contemporary Australian chardonnay. (See page 132.)

BEST NON-VINTAGE SPARKLING WINE

NV Brown Brothers Pinot Noir Chardonnay Pinot Meunier

A bottle-fermented bargain that offers a complete set of fruit and winemaking characters, savoury complexity and impeccable balance. Lovely texture too and unbeatable at the price. (See page 48.)

BEST VINTAGE SPARKLING WINE

2002 Arras

The flagship of the Hardy Wine Company's formidable arsenal of sparkling superstars, Arras leads the way with piercing focus, concentration and complexity. It holds its own amongst many a great champagne. (See page 47.)

BEST NON-VINTAGE CHAMPAGNE

NV Pierre Gimmonet Cuis 1er cru

It's rare to find a lower-priced NV champagne that delivers this kind of purity, focus, refinement and class. A smaller producer that punches well above its weight. (See page 61.)

BEST VINTAGE CHAMPAGNE

2002 Louis Roederer Cristal

When Cristal is on form it's very hard to beat and in 2002 it's right in the zone. Rapier-like acid drive, impossibly intense – its best years are ahead. (See page 60.)

BEST SAUVIGNON BLANC

2007 De Bortoli Yarra Valley Reserve Release Sauvignon

This is exactly the kind of wine that we can expect to see a lot more of from both Australian and New Zealand winemakers. Refined, focused, sophisticated and cool. (See page 66.)

BEST NEW ZEALAND SAUVIGNON BLANC

2008 Giesen Marlborough Sauvignon Blanc

Giesen wins this award on the basis of consistency, volume and price-point. They make a substantial quality of this wine in a consistent style year after year, delivering exactly what's required. It's no wonder they have such a loyal following. (See page 77.)

BEST SEMILLON

2007 Andrew Thomas Braemore Semillon

Andrew Thomas has decoded the secret of great Hunter semillon and delivers outstanding quality almost at will. Terrific value too, when compared to the more established Hunter icons. (See page 83.)

BEST SEMILLON SAUVIGNON BLANC BLEND

2006 Cape Mentelle Wallcliffe Vineyard Sauvignon Blanc Semillon

Truly sophisticated winemaking meets intensely concentrated fruit and delivers a dry white blend that wins on all fronts; balance, complexity and power. (See page 88.)

BEST RIESLING

2008 O'Leary Walker Polish Hill River Riesling

Although this hits the shelves as a wine in motion (one of the first new-season whites every year), it's already looking the part; 2008 has well and truly delivered in this part of the Clare Valley. (See page 102.)

BEST PINOT GRIS AND PINOT GRIGIO

2007 Mount Difficulty Pinot Gris (NZ)

There's more character and interest in this stunning Central Otago pinot gris than ten others put together – proof that the right location plus vision and inspiration are a winning combination. (See page 110.)

BEST VIOGNIER, MARSANNE AND ROUSSANNE

2007 Fairbank Viognier

An inspired rendition of complex viognier that harnesses the texture and exotic allure of this sometimes elusive grape. Pitched to perfection, intense and convincing. (See page 121.)

BEST CHARDONNAY

2006 Bindi Quartz Chardonnay

If the future of great Australian chardonnay looks like this we're in for one hell of a ride. Piercing intensity, site-driven purity and refined textural quality. This cuts closer to the nerve than any Australian chardonnay has managed yet. (See page 127.)

BEST IMPORTED WHITE WINE

2006 Martin Codax Albariño

This grape variety is gaining a keen interest amongst Australian winemakers. Here's a well-priced, well-made version that shows exactly what this variety is all about at a price that doesn't intimidate. (See page 151.)

BEST ROSÉ

2008 Charles Melton Rose of Virginia

Charlie Melton's rosé delivers beautifully in 2008, taking the gloss of an early vintage and delivering vivaciously on its promise. (See page 154.)

BEST PINOT NOIR

2006 By Farr Sangreal Pinot Noir

Great pinot should be captivating; Gary Farr has made a wine that showcases his wealth of experience and all that makes this variety so sought after. A true pinot lover's masterpiece! (See page 163.)

BEST NEW ZEALAND PINOT NOIR

2007 Felton Road Pinot Noir

A hotly contested race that Felton Road won in more than three separate tastings. Central Otago's most consistently complete and sophisticated pinot noir, lighting the way forward. (See page 188.)

BEST ITALIAN VARIETAL

2007 Coriole Sangiovese

The competition is heating up for Italian varieties in Australia and Coriole's commitment to sangiovese, as well as an innate understanding of how the style works and is consumed, singles them out for this year's award. (See page 204.)

BEST EMERGING RED WINE

2007 Hardys The Sage Shiraz Sangiovese

Sangiovese can certainly stand alone in Australia (as Coriole has proved), yet there's a convincing argument that it delivers most reliably when partnered with another, more familiar red variety. This is a showstopper and very nearly trumped the Best-Value Red award. (See page 212.)

BEST SHIRAZ

2007 Clonakilla Shiraz Viognier

Easily the most highly contested award in this year's *Guide* and the hardest to judge; shiraz in Australia delivers such vastly different styles. Here, with the judicious hand of experience and, at times, divine inspiration, Tim Kirk has wrought greater concentration and complexity and set it more deeply into his flagship wine than ever before. Made in tiny amounts due to frost, do not rest until you've found even one precious bottle! (See page 237.)

BEST SHIRAZ CABERNET BLEND

2004 Mildara Coonawarra Cabernet Shiraz

A modern Australian classic, this two-play between shiraz and cabernet works superbly in Coonawarra, delivered here with convincing power and grace. Winemaker Andrew Hale is a talent indeed! (See page 272.)

BEST CABERNET SAUVIGNON

2006 Balnaves The Tally Reserve Cabernet Sauvignon

2004 Cape Mentelle Cabernet Sauvignon

Two deserving winners that each represent the pinnacle of their respective regions. Cabernet in Australia is reaching new heights of refined style and polish; these are both regally crafted. (See pages 276 and 277.)

BEST CABERNET MERLOT BLEND

2004 Voyager Estate Cabernet Merlot

A wine that precisely treads the balance beam between these two varieties; it doesn't fall back on oak or hide behind a shroud of winemaking to succeed. Just beautifully pitched, balanced and soulful red – the epitome of elegance and finesse. (See page 296.)

BEST MERLOT AND BLENDS

2006 Penley Estate Gryphon Merlot

Kym Tolley delivers exactly the kind of wine that merlot is, can and should produce. Quality fruit, respected in the winery, delivered with skill and not trying to punch above its weight. (See page 302.)

BEST IMPORTED RED WINE

2005 Guigal Côtes du Rhône

Easily the best edition of this enduringly popular red that we've seen for a few years. Resoundingly good, it showcases the strength of the Rhone Valley in a great year. (See page 307.)

BEST SWEET WINE

2007 Heggies Botrytis Riesling

The world of sweet Australian wine is better for this champion riesling. Hedonistic richness and luscious appeal. Textural and balanced, it speaks uniquely of the Eden Valley and holds its own among the world's great sweet wines. (See page 312.)

BEST FORTIFIED WINE

NV Chambers Grand Muscat

Celebrating 150 years in the business, making some of Australia's greatest fortified wines, Chambers' treasured elixir is a national treasure. Touched by generations of family hands and crafted by time and dedication, every home should have just one small bottle on hand. (See page 315.)

Five-star wines – the best of the best

In order to achieve a five-star rating, a wine must score 96 points or higher. This rating is extremely hard to achieve, and deliberately so; these wines are singled out as the very best. They are the benchmarks to which other producers aspire and represent an elite group of the very finest Australian wines available.

Wine	Price	Score
SPARKLING WINES		
Arras 2002	$55.00	97
Hanging Rock Cuvée VII LD (NV)	$110.00	97
Jansz Vintage Cuvée 2003	$38.00	96
Radenti Chardonnay Pinot Noir 1999	$65.00	96
Yarrabank LD Sauvage 1999	$45.00	96
CHAMPAGNE		
Billecart Cuvée Nicholas Francois-Billecart 1998	$180.00	96
Dom Perignon 2000	$285.00	96
Louis Roederer Cristal 2002	$350.00	97
Salon Cuvées Blanc de Blancs 1996	$500.00	100
Taittinger Comtes de Champagne 1998	$240.00	96
SEMILLON		
Mount Pleasant Lovedale Semillon 2006	$38.00	96
RIESLING AND GEWÜRZTRAMINER		
Clonakilla Riesling 2008	$30.00	96
Frankland Estate Isolation Ridge Vineyard Riesling 2007	$27.00	96
Freycinet Riesling 2007	$27.00	96
Pegasus Bay Riesling 2007	$33.00	96
Pikes The Merle Reserve Riesling 2008	$36.00	96

VIOGNIER, MARSANNE AND ROUSSANNE

Clonakilla Viognier 2007	$50.00	96

CHARDONNAY

Bindi Quartz Chardonnay 2006	$70.00	96
Coldstream Hills Chardonnay 2007	$49.00	96
Forest Hill Block 8 Chardonnay 2006	$38.00	96
Freycinet Chardonnay 2007	$38.00	96
Giaconda Chardonnay 2006	$120.00	96
Kooyong Farrago Chardonnay 2006	$65.00	96
Kumeu River Maté's Vineyard Chardonnay 2006	$65.00	96
Oakridge 864 Chardonnay 2006	$60.00	97
TarraWarra Reserve Chardonnay 2005	$50.00	96
Voyager Estate Chardonnay 2006	$42.00	96

PINOT NOIR

Bannockburn Stuart Pinot Noir 2006	$65.00	96
Bindi Block 5 Pinot Noir 2006	$95.00	96
By Farr Sangreal Pinot Noir 2006	$65.00	96
Freycinet Vineyard Pinot Noir 2005	$65.00	96
Kooyong Ferrous Pinot Noir 2006	$65.00	96
Pirie Estate Pinot Noir 2006	$39.00	96
Stefano Lubiana Estate Pinot Noir 2006	$45.00	96

PINOT NOIR NZ

Felton Road Pinot Noir 2007	$70.00	96
Felton Road Pinot Noir Block 3 2007	$120.00	(96–98)
Pegasus Bay Prima Donna Pinot Noir 2005	$110.00	97
Pyramid Valley Growers Collection Calvert Vineyard Pinot Noir 2007	$70.00	96
Pyramid Valley Growers Collection Eaton Family Vineyard Pinot Noir 2007	$70.00	96
Quartz Reef Bendigo Estate Vineyard Pinot Noir 2006	$95.00	96
Rippon Pinot Noir 2006	$75.00	96

FIVE-STAR WINES – THE BEST OF THE BEST

GRENACHE, SHIRAZ, MATARO AND BLENDS

d'Arenberg The Ironstone Pressings 2006	$65.00	96
Hewitson Old Garden Mourvèdre 2006	$50.00	96
Kalleske Old Vine Grenache 2006	$45.00	96
S.C. Pannell Grenache 2006	$55.00	96
Spinifex Esprit 2006	$28.00	96

SHIRAZ

Brokenwood Graveyard Vineyard Shiraz 2006	$125.00	96
Clonakilla Shiraz Viognier 2007	$90.00	97
Clonakilla Syrah 2006	$80.00	96
De Bortoli Reserve Release Syrah 2006	$55.00	96
Giaconda Warner Vineyard Shiraz 2006	$96.00	96
Henschke Hill of Grace Shiraz 2004	$550.00	96
Henschke Mount Edelstone Shiraz 2005	$90.00	96
Hewitson The Mad Hatter Shiraz 2006	$50.00	96
John Duval Eligo Shiraz 2005	$105.00	96
Penfolds RWT Shiraz 2005	$160.00	96
Penfolds St Henri Shiraz 2004	$90.00	96
Seppelt St Peters Grampians Shiraz 2006	$60.00	96
Torbreck Run Rig 2005	$240.00	96
Torbreck The Struie 2006	$45.00	96
Trinity Hill Homage Syrah 2006	$120.00	96

SHIRAZ CABERNET BLENDS

Mildara Coonawarra Cabernet Shiraz 2004	$29.00	96

CABERNET SAUVIGNON

Balnaves The Tally Reserve Cabernet Sauvignon 2006	$95.00	96
Cape Mentelle Cabernet Sauvignon 2004	$80.00	96
Henschke Cyril Cabernet Sauvignon 2005	$110.00	96
Stonehaven Father Woods Cabernet Sauvignon 2006	$55.00	96

CABERNET MERLOT BLENDS

Te Mata Estate Coleraine 2006	$90.00	96
Voyager Estate Cabernet Merlot 2004	$60.00	96

SWEET WINES

De Bortoli Noble One Botrytis Semillon 2006	$65.00 (375 ml)	96
Heggies Botrytis Riesling 2007	$27.00 (375 ml)	97
Josef Chromy Botrytis Riesling 2007	$24.00 (375ml)	96

FORTIFIED WINES

Chambers Grand Muscat NV	$50.00 (375 ml)	98
Chambers Old Vine Muscadelle NV	$40.00 (375 ml)	96
Dutschke 'The Tawny' 22 Year Old NV	$35.00 (375 ml)	96
Grant Burge 20 Year Old Tawny NV	$62.00	96
Kalleske J.M.K. Shiraz VP 2006	$24.00 (375 ml)	96
Morris of Rutherglen Old Premium Liqueur Muscat NV	$70.00 (500 ml)	96
Morris of Rutherglen Old Premium Liqueur Tokay NV	$70.00 (500 ml)	97
Seppelt DP63 Grand Muscat NV	$30.00	96
Stanton & Killeen Grand Muscat NV	$75.00 (500 ml)	96
Stanton & Killeen Vintage Fortified 2003	$27.00	96

Best of the rest (★★★★→)

Below the elite ranks of the five-star wines, there are many wines that stand out from the pack but slide in just under the top ranking. A wine may be held back for a simple reason, such as a challenging vintage, or it may be a new champion on the rise; whatever the reason, the following wines deserve to be singled out for special recognition.

Wine	Price	Score
SPARKLING WINES		
Bay of Fires Tigress Rosé NV	$27.00	94
Bindi Macedon Cuvée V NV	$45.00	94
Croser 2005	$35.00	94
Hanging Rock Rosé Brut NV	$27.00	94
Sir James Pinot Noir Chardonnay 2003	$26.00	94
Sir James Tumbarumba Cuvée 2000	$30.00	94
Taltarni Vintage Brut 2006	$24.00	94
CHAMPAGNE		
Ayala Rosé Nature NV	$100.00	94
Charles Heidsieck Blanc des Millénaires 1995	$180.00	95
Dom Perignon 1999	$285.00	95
Mumm de Cremant NV	$150.00	94
Perrier-Jouet Epoque Blanc 1998	$250.00	95
Pommery Grand Cru Vintage 1999	$98.00	94
Ruinart Blanc de Blancs NV	$130.00	94
SAUVIGNON BLANC		
De Bortoli Yarra Valley Reserve Release Sauvignon 2007	$38.00	94

SAUVIGNON BLANC NZ

Craggy Range Te Muna Road Vineyard Sauvignon Blanc 2007	$32.00	94
Dog Point Section 94 2006	$34.00	94

SEMILLON

Andrew Thomas Braemore Semillon 2007	$25.00	94
Juniper Estate Semillon 2006	$27.00	94

SEMILLON SAUVIGNON BLANC BLENDS

Cape Mentelle Wallcliffe Vineyard Sauvignon Blanc Semillon 2006	$38.00	95
Cullen Vineyard Sauvignon Blanc Semillon 2007	$35.00	94
Hay Shed Hill Block 1 Semillon Sauvignon Blanc 2007	$28.00	94
Pegasus Bay Sauvignon Semillon 2007	$33.00	94

RIESLING AND GEWÜRZTRAMINER

Bay of Fires Riesling 2007	$30.00	94
Grosset Polish Hill Riesling 2008	$46.00	(93–95)
Kanta Riesling 2007	$31.00	94
Leo Buring Leopold Riesling 2007	$40.00	94
Mitchell McNicoll Riesling 2005	$32.00	94
Mount Horrocks Watervale Riesling 2008	$28.00	(93–95)
O'Leary Walker Polish Hill River Riesling 2008	$19.00	94
Pegasus Bay Dry Riesling 2007	$32.00	94
Peter Lehmann Wigan Eden Valley Riesling 2003	$40.00	94
Pewsey Vale Prima Riesling 2007	$25.00	94
Radford Dale Eden Valley Riesling 2007	$24.00	95

PINOT GRIS AND PINOT GRIGIO

Mount Difficulty Pinot Gris 2007	$30.00	94

VIOGNIER, MARSANNE AND ROUSSANNE

By Farr Viognier 2005	$55.00	94
De Bortoli Viognier 2007	$25.00	94
Fairbank Viognier 2007	$30.00	95
The Lane Viognier 2007	$39.00	94

CHARDONNAY

Bannockburn Chardonnay 2006	$50.00	94
Forest Hill Chardonnay 2006	$23.00	94
Juniper Estate Chardonnay 2007	$34.00	94
Kooyong Estate Chardonnay 2007	$45.00	95
Kumeu River Estate Chardonnay 2006	$48.00	94
Leeuwin Estate Art Series Chardonnay 2005	$96.00	95
Oakridge Chardonnay 2006	$32.00	95
Pierro Chardonnay 2006	$70.00	94
Pirie Estate Chardonnay 2006	$39.00	94
Punch Lance's Vineyard Chardonnay 2006	$44.00	94
Seppelt Jaluka Chardonnay 2007	$30.00	94
Tapanappa Tiers Vineyard Chardonnay 2006	$75.00	95
Ten Minutes By Tractor Wallis Vineyard Chardonnay 2006	$55.00	94
Toolangi Reserve Chardonnay 2005	$75.00	94
Vasse Felix Heytesbury Chardonnay 2006	$45.00	94

PINOT NOIR

Ashton Hills Estate Pinot Noir 2007	$49.50	94
Bannockburn Serré Pinot Noir 2005	$105.00	94
Bass Phillip 21 Pinot Noir 2006	$75.00	94
Bay of Fires Pinot Noir 2007	$38.00	94
By Farr Pinot Noir 2006	$65.00	95
Clyde Park Pinot Noir 2006	$35.00	94
De Bortoli Estate Grown Pinot Noir 2006	$38.00	94
De Bortoli Reserve Release Pinot Noir 2006	$60.00	95
Freycinet Louis Pinot Noir 2005	$38.00	94
Giaconda Nantua Vineyard Pinot Noir 2006	$90.00	94
Giant Steps Tarraford Vineyard Pinot Noir 2006	$40.00	94
Kooyong Estate Pinot Noir 2006	$42.00	94
Kooyong Meres Pinot Noir 2006	$55.00	95
Lillydale Estate Pinot Noir 2006	$27.00	94
Mac Forbes Coldstream Pinot Noir 2006	$38.00	94
Mac Forbes Woori Yallock Pinot Noir 2006	$46.00	95
Mayer Bloody Hill Pinot Noir 2007	$30.00	94
Mayer Pinot Noir 2007	$38.00	94

Oakridge Pinot Noir 2006	$32.00	94
Paringa Estate Reserve Pinot Noir 2006	$90.00	95
Punch Lance's Vineyard Close Planted Pinot Noir 2006	$90.00	95
St Huberts Pinot Noir 2006	$26.00	94
Ten Minutes By Tractor McCutcheon Vineyard		
Pinot Noir 2006	$70.00	95
William Downie Mornington Peninsula Pinot Noir 2006	$45.00	95

PINOT NOIR NZ

Alana Estate Pinot Noir 2006	$60.00	94
Carrick Pinot Noir 2006	$50.00	94
Clos Henri Marlborough Pinot Noir 2007	$56.00	94
Dog Point Pinot Noir 2006	$45.00	95
Gibbston Valley Central Otago Pinot Noir 2007	$45.00	94
Felton Road Pinot Noir Calvert Vineyard 2007	$85.00	(93–95)
Felton Road Pinot Noir Cornish Point 2007	$85.00	(93–95)
Neudorf Moutere Pinot Noir 2006	$65.00	95
Pegasus Bay Pinot Noir 2006	$65.00	95
Peregrine Pinot Noir 2007	$55.00	94
Te Mania Nelson Pinot Noir Reserve 2007	$35.00	94
Villa Maria Cellar Selection Pinot Noir 2007	$46.00	94
Villa Maria Single Vineyard Taylors Pass Pinot Noir 2006	$46.00	95

ITALIAN VARIETALS

Joseph Nebbiolo 2006	$75.00	95
Pizzini Nebbiolo 2003	$56.00	95

EMERGING RED WINES

Hewitson Cellar Reserve Tempranillo 2006	$70.00	94

GRENACHE, SHIRAZ, MATARO AND BLENDS

Australian Old Vine Collection Grenache 2006	$110.00	94
Deisen Grenache 2006	$40.00	94
Deisen Mataro 2006	$40.00	94
Rudderless Grenache 2005	$40.00	94
Rudderless Grenache Shiraz Mataro 2005	$40.00	94

Torbreck The Pict Mataro 2005	$200.00	95
Turkey Flat Mourvèdre 2006	$35.00	94

SHIRAZ

Australian Old Vine Collection Barossa Shiraz 2005	$110.00	95
Brokenwood Verona Vineyard Shiraz 2006	$45.00	94
By Farr Shiraz 2006	$60.00	94
Clonakilla O'Riada Shiraz 2007	$40.00	94
Collector Reserve Shiraz 2006	$46.00	94
Craggy Range Le Sol 2005	$97.00	94
d'Arenberg Dead Arm Shiraz 2006	$60.00	94
Dutschke Oscar Semmler 2006	$50.00	94
Eden Road V06 Shiraz 2006	$200.00	94
First Drop Fat Of The Land Ebenezer Shiraz 2005	$75.00	94
Giant Steps Miller Vineyard Shiraz 2006	$32.00	94
Glaetzer Amon-Ra Shiraz 2006	$90.00	94
Grove Estate The Cellar Block Shiraz Viognier 2007	$36.00	94
Kaesler The Bogan Shiraz 2006	$50.00	95
Kalleske Greenock Shiraz 2006	$40.00	94
Kalleske Johann Georg Old Vine Shiraz 2006	$100.00	95
Maverick Greenock Rise Shiraz 2006	$55.00	94
Maverick Trial Hill Eden Valley Shiraz 2005	$57.00	94
Meerea Park Hell Hole Shiraz 2006	$55.00	94
Pikes EWP Reserve Shiraz 2005	$65.00	94
Radford Dale Eden Valley Shiraz 2005	$32.00	94
Ravenswood Lane Shiraz 2007	$39.00	94
S.C. Pannell Shiraz 2006	$65.00	94
Seppelt Benno Bendigo Shiraz 2006	$55.00	94
Shaw and Smith Shiraz 2006	$38.00	94
Sutton Grange Estate Syrah 2005	$50.00	95
Torbreck Descendant 2006	$120.00	94
Torbreck The Gask 2006	$80.00	94
Water Wheel Bendigo Shiraz 2006	$19.00	94
Wirra Wirra RSW Shiraz 2006	$60.00	94
Yering Station Reserve Shiraz Viognier 2006	$75.00	94

SHIRAZ CABERNET BLENDS

Tapanappa Cabernet Shiraz 2005	$78.00	94

CABERNET SAUVIGNON

Balnaves Cabernet Sauvignon 2006	$35.00	94
Bowen Estate Cabernet Sauvignon 2006	$30.00	94
David Franz Georgie's Walk Cabernet Sauvignon 1998	$120.00	94
Grant Burge Shadrach Cabernet Sauvignon 2005	$55.00	94
Hay Shed Hill Cabernet Sauvignon 2005	$23.00	94
Juniper Estate Cabernet Sauvignon 2004	$36.00	94
Mac Forbes 'Hugh' Cabernet Sauvignon 2006	$40.00	94
Parker Coonawarra Estate Terra Rossa First Growth 2005	$110.00	94
Penfolds Bin 707 Cabernet Sauvignon 2005	$175.00	94
Sandalford Prendiville Reserve Cabernet Sauvignon 2005	$89.00	94
Suckfizzle Cabernet Sauvignon 2005	$50.00	94
Vasse Felix Cabernet Sauvignon 2005	$35.00	94
Vasse Felix Heytesbury Cabernet Sauvignon 2005	$75.00	95
Woodside Baudin Cabernet Sauvignon 2005	$56.00	94
Wynns John Riddoch Cabernet Sauvignon 2005	$75.00	94

CABERNET MERLOT BLENDS

Clonakilla Ballinderry 2006	$40.00	94
Petaluma Coonawarra 2005	$60.00	95
Te Mata Estate Awatea Cabernet Merlot 2006	$46.00	94

MERLOT AND BLENDS

Craggy Range Sophia 2005	$70.00	94
Penley Estate Gryphon Merlot 2006	$19.00	94

IMPORTED RED WINES

Tábula Ribera del Duero 2004	$67.00	94
Viette Perbacco Nebbiolo 2005	$45.00	94

BEST OF THE REST (★★★★⁺)

SWEET WINES

Brown Brothers Patricia Botrytis Riesling 2006	$35.00 (375 ml)	94
Craggy Range Noble 2006	$51.00 (375 ml)	94
Pegasus Bay Aria Riesling 2007	$48.00	95

FORTIFIED WINES

De Bortoli Show Liqueur Muscat NV	$18.00	94
Noon Winery VP 2006	$18.00 (500 ml)	95
Pondalowie Vintage Port 2003	$30.00 (500 ml)	94
Stanton & Killeen Classic Rutherglen Tawny Port NV	$27.00 (500 ml)	95

Best-value wines $25 and under

Value exists across the whole range of price-points; this is a selection of wines that reach into high-quality territory yet still maintain a price-point below the $25 mark. Some of these bottles are astounding; it's a credit to their makers that they attain the stylish ranks and still remain accessible to virtually every wine lover's budget.

Wine	Price	Score
SPARKLING WINES		
Brown Brothers Pinot Noir Chardonnay		
Pinot Meunier NV	$20.00	93
Chandon Brut NV	$25.00	92
De Bortoli Emeri Pink Moscato NV	$12.00	89
De Bortoli Rococo Blanc de Blancs NV	$19.00	91
De Bortoli Sacred Hill Brut Cuvée NV	$7.00	86
De Bortoli Windy Peak Pinot Noir Chardonnay NV	$15.00	89
Innocent Bystander Moscato 2008	$12.50	90
Jansz Premium Cuvée NV	$25.00	91
Jansz Premium Rosé NV	$25.00	92
Seppelt Fleur de Lys NV	$12.00	87
Taltarni Brut Taché 2006	$24.00	93
Taltarni T Series Chardonnay Pinot Noir		
Pinot Meunier NV	$15.00	91
Taltarni Vintage Brut 2006	$24.00	94
Yarra Burn Pinot Noir Chardonnay Pinot Meunier 2006	$20.00	93
SAUVIGNON BLANC		
Alkoomi Sauvignon Blanc 2007	$20.00	90
Alta Sauvignon Blanc 2007	$20.00	93
Bannockburn Sauvignon Blanc 2007	$25.00	93
Barwang Sauvignon Blanc 2007	$19.00	92

BEST-VALUE WINES $25 AND UNDER

Capel Vale Pemberton Sauvignon Blanc 2007	$23.00	91
Cockatoo Ridge Sauvignon Blanc 2008	$10.00	88
Cuttaway Hill Sauvignon Blanc 2007	$18.00	92
Dominique Portet Sauvignon Blanc 2007	$24.00	91
Henschke Coralinga Sauvignon Blanc 2007	$20.00	92
Katnook Estate Sauvignon Blanc 2007	$23.00	91
Mantra Sauvignon Blanc 2007	$20.00	91
Mount Trio Sauvignon Blanc 2007	$16.00	88
O'Leary Walker Sauvignon Blanc 2008	$20.00	91
Paracombe Sauvignon Blanc 2007	$21.00	92
Paracombe Sauvignon Blanc 2008	$21.00	93
Pike & Joyce Sauvignon Blanc 2007	$22.00	91
Ravenswood Lane Sauvignon Blanc 2007	$25.00	92
Riposte The Foil Sauvignon Blanc 2007	$19.00	92
Rymill Sauvignon Blanc 2008	$17.00	89
Shelmerdine Sauvignon 2007	$24.00	92
Smithbrook Sauvignon Blanc 2007	$19.00	91
Stella Bella Sauvignon Blanc 2007	$20.00	91

SAUVIGNON BLANC NZ

Catalina Sounds Sauvignon Blanc 2007	$22.00	91
Churton Sauvignon Blanc 2007	$25.00	91
The Crossings Marlborough Sauvignon Blanc 2007	$17.00	91
Dog Point Sauvignon Blanc 2007	$24.00	93
Forrest Estate Sauvignon Blanc 2007	$23.00	91
Giesen Marlborough Sauvignon Blanc 2008	$18.00	91
Greystone Sauvignon Blanc 2008	$23.00	92
Jackson Estate Sauvignon Blanc 2007	$24.00	92
Lawson's Dry Hills Sauvignon Blanc 2007	$22.00	90
Mahi Marlborough Sauvignon Blanc 2007	$22.00	93
Matua Valley Hawkes Bay Sauvignon Blanc 2008	$17.00	(90–92)
Old Coach Road Sauvignon Blanc 2008	$19.00	88
Palliser Estate Sauvignon Blanc 2007	$25.00	91
Pencarrow Sauvignon Blanc 2007	$22.50	90
Staete Landt Estate Grown Marlborough Sauvignon 2007	$25.00	91

SEMILLON

Andrew Thomas Braemore Semillon 2007	$25.00	94
Andrew Thomas The O.C. Semillon 2007	$20.00	93
Bethany Semillon 2005	$18.00	93
Cockfighter's Ghost Semillon 2007	$19.00	92
Glenguin Estate The Old Broke Block Semillon 2007	$20.00	93
Krinklewood Semillon 2007	$20.00	93
Meerea Park Epoch Semillon 2007	$19.00	92
Mistletoe Reserve Semillon 2007	$22.00	93
Mount Pleasant Cellar Release Elizabeth Semillon 2003	$17.00	93
Peter Lehmann Semillon 2006	$13.50	91
St Hallett Semillon 2004	$19.00	92
Vasse Felix Semillon 2007	$25.00	93`

SEMILLON SAUVIGNON BLANC BLENDS

Capel Vale Regional Series Semillon Sauvignon Blanc 2007	$23.00	91
Cartwheel Semillon Sauvignon Blanc 2007	$23.00	91
Clairault Semillon Sauvignon Blanc 2007	$22.00	93
Cuttaway Hill Semillon Sauvignon Blanc 2007	$18.00	90
Devil's Lair Fifth Leg White 2007	$16.00	88
Dividing Range Sauvignon Blanc Colombard Chardonnay 2007	$10.00	85
Frog Rock Semillon Sauvignon Blanc 2007	$15.00	89
Gapstead Valley Selection Sauvignon Blanc Semillon 2007	$16.00	87
Grant Burge Zerk Semillon Viognier 2006	$21.00	89
Hamelin Bay Rampant White 2007	$18.00	90
Hay Shed Hill Sauvignon Blanc Semillon 2007	$20.00	90
Hazard Hill Semillon Sauvignon Blanc 2007	$12.00	89
Henschke Tilly's Vineyard 2007	$18.00	90
Kalleske Clarry's White 2007	$15.00	89
Leaping Lizard Semillon Sauvignon Blanc 2007	$15.00	88
Leeuwin Estate Siblings Sauvignon Blanc Semillon 2007	$23.00	91

O'Leary Walker Blue Cutting Road Semillon

Sauvignon Blanc 2008	$14.00	89
Peter Lehmann Clancy's 2008	$15.00	89
Sandalford Estate Reserve Sauvignon Blanc Semillon 2007	$19.00	92
Schild Estate Semillon Sauvignon Blanc 2008	$15.00	88
Seven Hill White Spider Semillon Chardonnay 2007	$15.00	89
Stella Bella Semillon Sauvignon Blanc 2007	$21.00	90

RIESLING AND GEWÜRZTRAMINER

Alkoomi Riesling 2007	$21.00	92
Bannockburn Riesling 2007	$23.00	92
Ferngrove Cossack Riesling 2008	$21.00	91
Flaxman Riesling 2007	$25.00	91
Hewitson Gun Metal 2007	$22.00	92
Kilikanoon Mort's Block Riesling 2008	$23.00	(92–94)
Mac Forbes Riesling rs9 2006	$24.00	93
Mount Majura Riesling 2007	$16.00	91
O'Leary Walker Polish Hill River Riesling 2008	$19.00	94
O'Leary Walker Watervale Riesling 2008	$17.50	92
Peter Lehmann Eden Valley Riesling 2007	$16.00	93
Pewsey Vale Eden Valley Riesling 2007	$20.00	93
Pewsey Vale Prima Riesling 2007	$25.00	94
Pfeiffer The Carson Gewürztraminer 2008	$17.00	90
Pirie South Riesling 2007	$22.00	91
Radford Dale Eden Valley Riesling 2007	$24.00	95
Seven Hill Riesling 2008	$19.00	(91–93)
St Hallett Eden Valley Riesling 2007	$21.00	93
Tamar Ridge Gewürztraminer 2007	$22.00	91

PINOT GRIS AND PINOT GRIGIO

David Hook The Gorge Pinot Grigio 2008	$18.00	90
De Bortoli Windy Peak Pinot Grigio 2008	$15.00	91
Devil's Corner Pinot Grigio 2007	$17.00	89
Leabrook Estate Pinot Gris 2007	$25.00	92
Mountadam Pinot Gris 2007	$24.00	93
Nazaaray Pinot Gris 2007	$25.00	90

Nepenthe Pinot Gris 2007	$23.00	90
Ninth Island Pinot Grigio 2007	$21.00	92
Over The Shoulder Pinot Grigio 2007	$20.00	91
Paracombe Pinot Gris 2007	$19.00	92
Pike & Joyce Pinot Gris 2007	$22.00	91
Pirie South Pinot Gris 2007	$22.00	92

EMERGING WHITE WINES

d'Arenberg The Stump Jump White 2007	$12.00	88
Fox Gordon Princess Fiano 2007	$24.00	90
Gapsted Petit Manseng 2006	$21.00	89
Krinklewood Verdelho 2007	$20.00	91
Krinklewood Wild White 2007	$15.00	90

VIOGNIER, MARSANNE AND ROUSSANNE

Angove's Nine Vines Viognier 2007	$15.00	87
d'Arenberg The Hermit Crab Viognier Marsanne 2007	$17.00	90
d'Arenberg The Last Ditch Viognier 2007	$20.00	91
d'Arenberg The Money Spider Roussanne 2007	$20.00	92
De Bortoli Viognier 2007	$25.00	94
Fox Gordon Abby Viognier 2007	$20.00	93
Grove Estate The Wombat Way Viognier 2007	$20.00	90
Langmeil SWH Viognier 2007	$19.50	91
Massena The Surly Muse Viognier 2007	$20.00	93
McHenry Hohnen 3 Amigos Marsanne Chardonnay Roussanne 2006	$22.00	93
Meerea Park Viognier 2007	$23.00	93
Mitchelton Viognier 2007	$20.00	90
Rutherglen Estates Marsanne Viognier 2007	$16.00	88
Terra Felix Viognier 2007	$17.00	91
Turkey Flat Butcher's Block Marsanne Viognier 2007	$23.00	92

CHARDONNAY

Audrey Wilkinson Chardonnay 2007	$18.00	91
Barwang Chardonnay 2007	$19.00	90
Bridgewater Mill Chardonnay 2006	$23.00	90

Crittenden Geppetto Chardonnay 2006	$16.00	89
Element Chardonnay 2007	$13.00	88
Ferngrove Diamond Chardonnay 2007	$24.00	91
Forest Hill Chardonnay 2006	$23.00	94
Frankland Estate Isolation Ridge Vineyard Chardonnay 2006	$25.00	93
Fraser Gallop Estate Chardonnay 2007	$25.00	93
The Growers' Reward Chardonnay 2007	$19.00	90
Hay Shed Hill Chardonnay 2007	$25.00	91
Hoddles Creek Chardonnay 2007	$19.00	90
Innocent Bystander Chardonnay 2006	$20.00	90
Juniper Crossing Chardonnay 2006	$22.00	91
Kumeu River Village Chardonnay 2006	$22.00	90
Lillydale Estate Chardonnay 2007	$20.00	90
Logan Apple Tree Flat Chardonnay 2006	$11.00	89
Logan Chardonnay 2007	$20.00	92
Mt Trio Chardonnay 2007	$16.00	89
Over The Shoulder Chardonnay 2007	$20.00	92
Paracombe Chardonnay 2006	$21.00	91
Pirie South Chardonnay 2007	$24.00	91
Pitchfork Chardonnay 2007	$17.00	89
Sandalford Estate Reserve Chardonnay 2006	$24.00	92
Seppelt Grampians Chardonnay 2007	$20.00	90
Thorn-Clarke Sandpiper Chardonnay 2007	$15.00	87
Thorn-Clarke Shotfire Chardonnay 2007	$20.00	88
Toolangi Chardonnay 2006	$25.00	92
Windowrie Estate Deep River Chardonnay 2007	$14.00	90
Xanadu Chardonnay 2007	$25.00	91
Yalumba FDW[7c] Chardonnay 2007	$24.00	93
Yering Station Chardonnay 2006	$24.00	91

IMPORTED WHITE WINES

Basa Verdejo 2006	$23.00	90
Cascineta Vietti Moscato d'Asti 2007	$22.00	93
Hugel Pinot Blanc 2005	$23.00	90
Martin Codax Burgans Albariño 2006	$17.00	90
Tiefenbrunner Pinot Grigio 2007	$25.00	91

ROSÉ

Barratt Picadilly Sunrise Rosé 2007	$21.00	90
Chapel Hill il Vescovo Sangiovese Rosé 2007	$14.00	89
Charles Melton Rose of Virginia 2008	$24.00	93
Coriole Nebbiolo Rosé 2007	$18.00	91
Dominique Portet Fontaine Rosé 2007	$20.00	90
Krinklewood Francesca Rosé 2007	$20.00	91
Loose End Rosé 2007	$18.00	92
Old Mill Estate Rosé 2007	$20.00	90
Pikes The Bleedings Pinot Noir Rosé 2007	$22.00	91
Rosé McLaren Vale Cabernet Sauvignon Rosé 2007	$19.00	90
Seven Hill Lost Boot Rosé 2007	$15.00	88
Sorriso Rosé 2007	$15.00	89

PINOT NOIR

Breheny Vineyards Brown Magpie Pinot Noir 2006	$22.00	91
Coldstream Hills Pinot Noir 2007	$25.00	92
De Bortoli Windy Peak Pinot Noir 2007	$15.00	90
Devil's Corner Pinot Noir 2007	$19.00	92
Hat Rock Pinot Noir 2006	$24.00	91
Hoddles Creek Estate Pinot Noir 2006	$18.00	92
Innocent Bystander Pinot Noir 2006	$20.00	90
Josef Chromy Pepik Pinot Noir 2007	$19.00	93
Magnetic Hill Pinot Noir 2006	$25.00	91
Moorooduc Estate Devil Bend Creek Pinot Noir 2007	$25.00	91
Mount Majura Pinot Noir 2007	$20.00	90
Ninth Island Pinot Noir 2007	$24.00	91
Paracombe Pinot Noir 2006	$21.00	90
Punt Road Pinot Noir 2006	$25.00	91
Scotchmans Hill Swan Bay Pinot Noir 2007	$19.00	91
South Pinot Noir 2007	$25.00	93
Toolangi Pinot Noir 2006	$25.00	93
Treehouse Pinot Noir 2006	$22.00	91
Weemala Pinot Noir 2007	$16.00	90
The Wine Society Pinot Noir 2007	$20.00	93

PINOT NOIR NZ

Braided River Marlborough Pinot Noir 2007	$19.00	89
Dashwood Pinot Noir 2007	$20.00	89
Delta Vineyard Pinot Noir 2007	$23.00	91
Mud House Pinot Noir 2007	$22.00	91
Trinity Hill Hawkes Bay Pinot Noir 2007	$19.00	92

ITALIAN VARIETALS

Acrobat Sangiovese Shiraz 2006	$10.00	89
Chapel Hill il Vescovo Sangiovese 2006	$20.00	90
Coriole Sangiovese 2007	$22.00	93
Margan Barbera 2006	$25.00	92
Primo Estate Il Briccone Shiraz Sangiovese 2006	$22.00	90
Ravensworth Sangiovese 2007	$24.00	93
Tar & Roses Sangiovese 2007	$23.00	92
Zilzie Sangiovese 2007	$16.00	90
Zonte's Footstep Sangiovese Barbera 2007	$18.00	91

EMERGING RED WINES

All Saints Estate Durif 2006	$23.00	91
Bleasdale Malbec 2005	$15.00	90
Brown Brothers Durif 2006	$20.00	90
Brown Brothers Graciano 2006	$20.00	90
Cascabel Tempranillo 2007	$21.00	92
Fox Gordon By George Cabernet Tempranillo 2006	$20.00	93
Gemtree Bloodstone Tempranillo 2007	$25.00	92
Hardy's The Sage Shiraz Sangiovese 2007	$13.00	90
Hare's Chase Tempranillo 2006	$20.00	90
Hastwell & Lightfoot Cabernet Franc 2005	$22.00	91
Juniper Crossing Tempranillo 2007	$18.00	90
Kirrihill Companions Tempranillo Garnacha 2007	$15.00	90
Morris Rutherglen Durif 2004	$21.00	91
Mount Trio Tempranillo 2007	$16.00	89
Nashwauk Tempranillo 2006	$25.00	92
Pondalowie MT Tempranillo 2006	$25.00	93
Rutherglen Estates Red Shiraz Durif 2006	$13.00	90
Westend 3 Bridges Durif 2006	$20.00	89

GRENACHE, SHIRAZ, MATARO AND BLENDS

Blackbilly GSM 2006	$22.00	90
Cape Barren Native Goose GSM 2006	$25.00	91
Cape Mentelle Marmaduke Shiraz Grenache 2006	$19.50	91
Chapel Hill Shiraz Grenache 2006	$20.00	91
Coriole The Dancing Fig Shiraz Mourvèdre 2006	$22.00	92
d'Arenberg d'Arry's Original Shiraz Grenache 2006	$20.00	92
d'Arenberg The Cadenzia GSM 2006	$25.00	93
d'Arenberg The Custodian Grenache 2006	$20.00	91
d'Arenberg The Stump Jump 2006	$12.00	88
Dirty Bliss Grenache Shiraz 2006	$20.00	92
Domain Barossa Toddler GSM 2007	$22.00	91
Gilligan Shiraz Grenache Mourvèdre 2006	$23.00	92
Glaetzer Wallace 2006	$20.00	90
Hanging Rock Shiraz Grenache Mourvèdre Pinot Noir 2005	$14.00	89
Hewitson Miss Harry Grenache Shiraz Mourvèdre 2006	$22.00	91
Jamabro Bush Vine Grenache 2005	$25.00	91
John Hongell Old Vine Grenache Shiraz 2006	$19.00	93
Kaesler Stonehorse Grenache Shiraz Mourvèdre 2006	$18.00	92
Kalleske Clarry's Red 2007	$18.00	91
La Curio The Nubile Grenache Shiraz 2006	$22.00	90
Massena The Moonlight Run 2006	$25.00	92
McHenry Hohnen 3 Amigos Shiraz		
Grenache Mourvèdre 2006	$22.00	91
McPherson Basilisk Shiraz Mourvèdre 2006	$18.00	90
Paxton AAA Shiraz Grenache 2007	$23.00	92
Pertaringa Two Gentlemens Grenache 2006	$20.00	92
Rosemount Show Reserve GSM 2005	$20.00	91
Ross Estate Old Vine Grenache 2006	$19.00	90
S.C. Pannell Pronto 2006	$20.00	90
Schild Estate GMS 2007	$16.00	90
Spinifex Papillon 2007	$22.50	92
St Hallett Gamekeeper's Reserve 2007	$15.00	89
St John's Road A Motley Bunch 2006	$24.00	92
Te-aro Estate GSM 2006	$20.00	92
Winter Creek Second Eleven Blend 2005	$19.00	91

SHIRAZ

Acrobat Shiraz 2006	$10.00	88
Battle of Bosworth Shiraz Viognier 2006	$24.00	93
Bremerton Selkirk Shiraz 2006	$22.00	88
CR Ebenezer Shiraz 2006	$25.00	92
Dutschke GHR Shiraz 2006	$25.00	91
Fairbank Syrah 2005	$25.00	92
Gemtree Uncut Shiraz 2006	$20.00	91
Hesketh The Protagonist Shiraz 2005	$25.00	91
Hewitson Ned & Henry's Shiraz 2006	$24.00	91
Innocent Bystander Shiraz Viognier 2006	$20.00	90
John Hongell Shiraz 2005	$20.00	90
Kirrihill Baile an Gharrai Shiraz 2006	$20.00	92
Kirrihill Estates Langhorne Creek Shiraz 2005	$20.00	91
Lloyd Brothers Shiraz 2006	$22.00	92
Marius Simpatico Shiraz 2006	$24.00	91
Meerea Park Shiraz 2007	$15.00	91
Michael Unwin One Goat Shiraz 2005	$14.00	91
Mistletoe Shiraz 2006	$20.00	93
Mount Majura Shiraz 2006	$25.00	93
Oakridge Over The Shoulder Shiraz Viognier 2007	$22.00	91
Off The Leash Max Shiraz Viognier 2006	$25.00	93
Paracombe Shiraz Viognier 2005	$21.00	91
Pertaringa Undercover Shiraz 2006	$20.00	91
Rolling Shiraz 2005	$17.00	91
Taltarni T Series Shiraz 2005	$15.00	90
Thorn-Clarke Shotfire Shiraz 2006	$20.00	90
Trevor Jones Boots Shiraz 2006	$18.00	89
Tyrrell's Rufus Stone Heathcote Shiraz 2006	$24.00	91
Water Wheel Bendigo Shiraz 2006	$19.00	94
Yering Station Shiraz Viognier 2006	$24.00	91

SHIRAZ CABERNET BLENDS

Bremerton Tamblyn Cabernet Shiraz Malbec Merlot 2006	$19.00	90
Dutschke Willow Bend Shiraz Merlot		
Cabernet Sauvignon 2006	$20.00	93

Hare's Chase Red Blend 2005	$15.00	90
Hentley Farm Fool's Bay Beached Shiraz Cabernet 2006	$14.00	90
Hollick Shiraz Cabernet 2005	$21.00	91
Lake Breeze Bernoota Shiraz Cabernet 2005	$22.00	90
Penfolds Koonunga Hill Shiraz Cabernet 2006	$15.00	89
Penley Estate Condor Coonawarra Shiraz Cabernet 2006	$19.00	90
Tatachilla Partners Cabernet Shiraz 2006	$11.00	89
Te-aro Estate Shiraz Cabernet 2006	$18.00	92
Thorn-Clarke Sandpiper The Blend 2006	$15.00	89
Water Wheel Memsie 2006	$12.00	92
Wirra Wirra Church Block 2006	$20.00	89
Wynns Coonawarra Estate Cabernet Shiraz Merlot 2006	$18.00	91

CABERNET SAUVIGNON

Capel Vale Regional Series Cabernet Sauvignon 2005	$23.00	93
Evil Cabernet Sauvignon 2006	$12.00	89
Hay Shed Hill Cabernet Sauvignon 2005	$23.00	94
Kirrihill Tulach Mor Cabernet Sauvignon 2005	$20.00	92
Little r Cabernet Sauvignon 2006	$15.00	91
Penley Estate Phoenix Cabernet Sauvignon 2006	$19.00	93
Punt Road Cabernet Sauvignon 2005	$25.00	92
Yering Station Cabernet Sauvignon 2006	$24.00	91
Zema Estate Cabernet Sauvignon 2005	$25.00	91

CABERNET MERLOT BLENDS

Balnaves Cabernet Merlot 2006	$24.00	92
Balnaves The Blend 2006	$19.00	91
Dividing Range Cabernet Merlot 2006	$10.00	87
Ferngrove Symbols Cabernet Merlot 2007	$16.00	89
Fire Gully Cabernet Sauvignon Merlot 2005	$25.00	90
Flying Fish Cabernet Merlot 2007	$22.00	90
Gemtree Tatty Road 2006	$18.00	90
Happs Cabernet Merlot 2005	$22.00	91
Higher Plane Cabernet Merlot 2006	$22.00	91
Jacob's Creek Cabernet Merlot 2005	$11.00	88
Juniper Crossing Cabernet Sauvignon Merlot 2005	$20.00	93

BEST-VALUE WINES $25 AND UNDER

Kirrihill Companions Cabernet Merlot 2006	$15.00	90
Over The Shoulder Cabernet Merlot 2005	$20.00	92
Paracombe The Reuben 2004	$21.00	91
Philip Shaw No.17 Merlot Cabernet Franc Cabernet 2006	$25.00	92
Reschke Bull Trader Cabernet Merlot 2004	$18.00	91
Rymill MC^2 2004	$17.00	91
Shaw Vineyard Estate Cabernet Merlot 2004	$22.00	90
Taltarni 3 Monks Cabernet Merlot 2005	$22.00	91
Te Mata Estate Merlot Cabernet 2006	$25.00	91
Thorn-Clarke Quartage 2006	$20.00	92
Voyager Estate Girt By Sea Cabernet Merlot 2006	$24.00	91
Wine By Brad Cabernet Merlot 2005	$18.00	90
Xabregas Cabernet Merlot 2004	$15.00	91

MERLOT AND BLENDS

Brand's Laira Merlot 2005	$23.00	92
Burnbrae Merlot 2005	$23.00	92
Ferngrove Merlot 2007	$19.00	91
Jones The Winemaker Merlot 2005	$20.00	91
Juniper Crossing Merlot 2006	$20.00	92
Logan Weemala Merlot 2006	$16.00	90
McWilliam's Hanwood Estate Merlot 2006	$13.00	90
Millamolong Isabelle's Ghost Merlot 2007	$20.00	91
Murdock Merlot 2005	$23.00	91
Penley Estate Gryphon Merlot 2006	$19.00	94
Prince Hill Merlot 2006	$25.00	92
Printhie Merlot 2006	$17.00	91
Wild Rock Gravel Pit Red 2006	$22.00	89

IMPORTED RED WINES

Cerro del Masso Chianti 2006	$25.00	90
Concha Y Toro Casillero del Diablo Cabernet Sauvignon 2006	$15.00	89
Concha Y Toro Casillero del Diablo Carmenere 2006	$15.00	90
Cosme Palacio Rioja Cosecha 2005	$21.00	93
Fattoria Zerbina Ceregio Sangiovese Di Romagna 2006	$24.00	92

Guigal Côtes Du Rhône 2004	$25.00	92
La Braccesca Sabazio Rosso di Montepulciano 2005	$22.00	91
LZ Tempranillo Rioja D.O. 2006	$25.00	92
Poliziano Chianti 2006	$24.00	90
Prunotto Barbera d'Alba 2006	$22.00	90
Saint Cosme Côtes Du Rhône 2006	$17.00	92

SWEET WINES

d'Arenberg The Noble Riesling 2007	$25.00 (375 ml)	92
Lou Miranda Leone Botrytis Semillon 2006	$17.00 (375 ml)	90

FORTIFIED WINES

De Bortoli Show Liqueur Muscat NV	$18.00	94
Kalleske J.M.K. Shiraz VP 2006	$24.00 (375 ml)	96
Noon Winery VP 2006	$18.00 (500 ml)	95
Pfeiffer Old Distillery Classic Rutherglen Tokay NV	$24.00 (500 ml)	91
Stanton & Killeen Ruby Port NV	$16.50 (500 ml)	91

Vintage report 2008

Many of the wines from the 2008 vintage are still under construction, so this is a guide only to what you might expect. It is a brief summary of many visits, tastings, conversations, telephone calls and emails with winemakers – from the smallest artisans to the biggest players. As many 2008 vintage unwooded whites as possible (plus the odd rosé) have been included in the book, given the inevitable lead time involved in publishing the *Guide*.

In a broad assessment, the harvest volume was well up on the predicted overall tonnage. The pre-vintage estimate was in the order of 1.2 million tonnes, based on average yields, and the latest Winemakers Federation of Australia estimate on the actual crush was sitting at 1.83 million tonnes, as this year's *Guide* goes to print. Suffice to say, we have a lot more grapes than we were expecting.

Due to the heatwave and an abnormally early and compressed harvest, there was a great deal of pressure on wineries to deal with a vast amount of fruit across a range of varieties, all ripening on top of each other. Grapes matured early, and flavours developed early in the ripening cycle. Some out-standing chardonnay has been made, Margaret River cabernet could well be among the best we've seen in a decade or more, and Victorian shiraz is outstanding.

The biggest story, though, was the heat. It crossed South Australia in early March and continued over many days, battering vineyards with relent-less temperatures. Grapes had to come off, and they had to come off fast to prevent them from being ruined. There are stories of pickers being lured away from vineyards by other growers with handfuls of cash. Cooling plants went down in many wineries, unable to handle the capacity. The wineries with the most space for fermentation were therefore in the best position to deal with the onslaught of these intense pressure-cooker conditions.

In heat-affected areas, there will be two kinds of wines – those picked before the heat and those picked after. Winemakers with enough wine in the winery before the heat will be able to hide some later-picked stuff on the blending bench. Most measuring equipment is unable to measure fruit with a potential alcohol in the high 20s, but there were anecdotal measurements that these kinds of levels were seen in some regions following this season's extreme and sustained heat. What yeast can operate under those conditions is still being tested as wines struggle to finish fermentation. Machines and techniques do exist to bring these wines back to a more manageable alcohol level, but as Barossa legend Grant Burge said after harvest this year, 'You don't really want to take your fruit down that road, it really knocks it around and you'll end up with much lower-grade wine.'

WESTERN AUSTRALIA

Margaret River: An Indian summer, it looks great for shiraz, cabernet and chardonnay; aromatic whites (semillon sauvignon blancs) are outstanding.
Pemberton: Great for semillon sauvignon blancs; chardonnay is good.
Frankland River: Great year for shiraz and some cabernet is looking good.
Mount Barker: Very good riesling and shiraz.
Swan Valley: Excellent for chenin blanc and verdelho, both at their juicy and simplistic best.

SOUTH AUSTRALIA

McLaren Vale: The early (pre-heatwave) fruit is looking good; the later, heat-affected fruit is not.
Barossa Valley: A tale of two vintages: the fruit harvested before the heatwave in early March is excellent; the fruit harvested after or during is severely diminished in quality. Eden Valley rieslings are looking very promising.
Adelaide Hills: Better for whites than reds.
Clare Valley: Outstanding shiraz and riesling.
Coonawarra: If harvested before the heat, the cabernet is good; later fruit was stressed.
Limestone Coast/Wrattonbully: In general not too bad, given the heat.
Langhorne Creek: Similar tale of those who harvested before the heat compared with those who did not.
Padthaway: Similar to the Limestone Coast, decent quality given the heat.
Riverland: Very good for the early-picked varieties of chardonnay and shiraz, showing freshness.

TASMANIA

Good-quality sparkling pinot noir, riesling and pinot gris, and fine chardonnay. A large and early vintage, with even ripeness.

VICTORIA

Yarra Valley: Good-quality chardonnay, early flavour; pinot noir is good for lower-priced wines.

Mornington Peninsula: A strong vintage for pinot gris, chardonnay and pinot noir, with early flavour development favouring an early harvest.

Heathcote/Bendigo: Very high-quality vintage, superb ripeness and depth; a great year for shiraz.

Macedon Ranges: An early vintage with some good quality despite the heat pressure.

Pyrenees: Very good shiraz.

Gippsland: Looked promising before the heat; expect some good wines, despite the weather at harvest.

Grampians: Very good vintage with excellent depth and intensity.

Rutherglen: Moderate quality.

Geelong: An early vintage with moderate quality for pinot noir and chardonnay; shiraz looking promising.

NEW SOUTH WALES

Hunter Valley: One of the wettest seasons on record. Miracles will be needed to make great wines.

Tumbarumba: A very good year for sparkling fruit.

Orange/Hilltops: Chardonnay and reds from here are looking to be among the best of the NSW crop.

Canberra: A good year on the back of the severely frost-affected 2007 vintage.

Mudgee: A very challenging year due to rain and some late hail.

Cowra: Some good-quality chardonnay, with more restrained fruit characters, was harvested.

Riverina: Good access to water via the Snowy Mountains Hydro-electric Scheme ensured decent crops.

State of play

There's a lot of talk within the Australian wine trade that we are approaching times of great challenge; but it seems that we have the same conversation, of sorts, every year. Making wine – in particular, great wine – and running a successful business is a constant battle for Australian winemakers. There are easier ways to make money, but perhaps live a less satisfying life – well, maybe.

Mother Nature has dealt some cruel blows in recent years in the form of severe frosts and extensive bushfires. The drought is unrelenting; water is in short supply and expensive to buy – in many cases prohibitively so; vintages are becoming earlier; and grape varieties seem to be ripening in closer proximity to each other than ever before, placing pressure on resources at harvest. It's soul-testing to make the stuff – let alone sell it.

For all the talk of low crops and no water in our inland irrigation-dependent regions, the 2008 harvest delivered a much bigger crop than expected (see the Vintage Report 2008 on page 40) and the $2 cleanskin has quickly returned to our shelves. It's a worry that our peak industry body can get it wrong by 600 000 tonnes, roughly one-third of the actual total!

We've got plenty of wine to sell and the soaring value of the Australian dollar against the US dollar has started to dent trade to the lucrative American market. Just one year ago (year ended July 2007), the industry was crowing about reaching $3 billion dollars in exports for the first time. We sailed through the $2 billion mark in July 2002 and $1 billion had been passed back in July 1999. The latest figures, however, have seen a decline in both value and volume, and there's fear of a further slide.

On the positive side, while exports are down, quality is up – there's more great Australian wine out there than ever before. Our success at making cheap, simple wine has become a liability and we're now desperately trying to tell the world that we make great wine too. There's no doubt we do – just flip through the ensuing pages – but it seems we're just a bit too good at the bulk end of the business.

What remains to be seen is whether Australia convinces the rest of the world that we can produce both quality and quantity. We might still have plenty of wine, but truly great wines are never around for long!

CLOSURE ON CLOSURES

Although we've all gotten used to seeing screwcaps and other newer closures on wine bottles, there is still much debate, speculation and conjecture about the performance of the various seals: how wines will age and what the right answer is. Well, there really isn't one single closure that provides the definitive answer. We're a long way from closure.

Nothing kills a party quicker than a conversation about corks, screwcaps and their effects on wine, but it's worth considering this simple philosophy: when you buy and drink a wine, it should reach you in good condition. You should experience the wine as the winemaker intended; a closure should not add, remove or alter the character of the wine once it is in bottle.

So, choosing a closure is a winemaking decision because each type of closure will interact differently with the wine, just like the choice of oak, yeast type, fermentation temperature and so on. A good winemaker has the closure type in mind from early in the winemaking process, and factors it into their technique and decisions as they move through making and bottling the wine.

Unquestionably, the march of the screwcap is an unstoppable force and, of the 5000-odd wines tasted for this year's *Guide*, a staggering number – by far and away the majority – are now sealed under screwcap. This style of closure has proven to be reliable, consistent and neutral – suitable to all types of wines. It allows wine to age, with multiple bottles ageing at an even pace, providing consistent development from one bottle to the next.

Crown seals (like beer bottle tops) are being used on some sparkling wines, and are well received for exactly the same reasons as screwcap on still wine – they don't taint the wine and act as a more reliable and consistent seal.

Vinolok, a glass stopper closure pitched at premium territory, is making its first tentative steps, embraced by some famous names already. The early results look promising for much the same reasons as screwcaps, although the Vinolok definitely has a more prestige feel than the humble screwcap.

Diam is a proprietary technical cork product in which natural cork is milled and then treated with gas to remove cork taint characters. The particles are bound together with a polymer into a cork shape, and used in the same way as a natural cork. This closure has polarised opinion – many believe it imparts a character into the wine, others cite variable performance over time. A number of winemakers who have trialled this closure say it subtly scalps the wine of delicate aromatics and hardens the palate texture.

Procork, another proprietary cork product, has a small plastic coating on the cork end designed to prevent contact with the wine while still allowing maturation conditions similar to a natural cork. Consistency is the big issue, however, and a number of wines sealed under Procork and tasted this year showed evidence of cork taint.

Synthetic corks and agglomerate corks are almost obsolete at the quality level of the wines reviewed in the *Guide*, as there have been various problems over the years with wines taking on aromas and flavours from synthetic cork seals.

A good natural cork is a fine closure and will present a wine in terrific condition. The difficulty here is that natural corks have a highly varied performance record. Taint is not the biggest issue – it's the variable performance of each cork, which really starts to show the longer wines are left in bottle.

ALCOHOL AND BALANCE

In the last five or so years, there has been an upward swing in the alcohol level of Australian wines, as well as an interest in these rising levels. This upward trend is not unique to Australia; it's a global phenomenon, and there are many factors involved.

The US market has been a substantial export destination for Australian wine in the past decade, and the successes indicate that riper wines, predominantly reds, garner big interest. Climate change is a vexing topic and there's little doubt in most Australian winemakers' minds that grapes seem to be ripening earlier. The enduring drought conditions have also created substantial pressure on viticulture.

Then there's fashion – a force in wine as it is in just about every aspect of consumer activity. Tastings of a single-vineyard wine spanning back through the 1990s, the '80s and '70s often reveal a marked pattern in style: ripe wines in the 1970s; a trend for early-picked grapes in the 1980s, delivering lower alcohols; and then a return to riper wines through the '90s and into this decade.

So what does all this mean? Balance is the issue – the ultimate test of a wine. Some grape varieties need to reach higher maturity on the vine in order to deliver the desired aromas, flavours and textures. The same grape variety grown in different regions will reach different levels of ripeness, and average levels of finished alcohols will vary from region to region. Some wines carry higher alcohol levels than others; it's simply a part of the overall style of the wine. Acidity, sweetness, alcohol and tannin (in reds) are the major contributors to wine texture and all have an interrelated effect on each other.

So, although the finished alcohol for each wine is listed, don't simply look at the numbers; consider the style, the variety/ies and the origin of the wine, and remember that balance is the key to enjoyable drinking, no matter what style you're into.

SWEET SPOTS AND PRICE THRESHOLDS: WHERE'S THE *REAL* VALUE?

Having tasted in excess of 5000 bottles to bring you these recommended wines, it's patently clear there are price-points that represent considerable value. Between $20 and $25 is where quality starts to reliably kick in: better fruit quality, better winemaking, oak barrels rather than planks or oak chips, and decent packaging.

Step up to $30 and there are many wines showing balance and quality that outstrip higher-priced competitors. As you move up the scale from here, consistency actually tapers off and value is more difficult to identify and justify. Taken on a world stage, the average $30 bottle of Australian wine is very hard to beat for quality and consistency.

Sparkling wines

Australian sparkling wine covers a big range of stylistic options. The quality-oriented makers gravitate to the coolest corners of the country to make the finest styles. Non-vintage (NV) wines provide the greatest consistency from year to year and follow a set house style. Vintage wines capture each season's unique conditions and are usually made only in the years in which fruit quality is considered to be first rate. The bigger companies have thrown some impressive weight behind sparkling wine and the results are spectacular; there's incredible value out there too. FOOD: Think about the effervescence and the acidity. These will dictate either a delicate dish that reflects the mouth-watering freshness of the wine or a subtly rich dish that is counter-balanced by the bubbles. Oysters in season and soft raw-milk cheese are two simple options.

2002 **Arras**   *Score* **97**

TASMANIA	
Price	$55.00 ✓
Quality	★ ★ ★ ★ ★
Alc./Vol.	12.5%
Drink	2011
Closure	Cork

From a substantial company commitment and Ed Carr's insightful, committed approach, great things come. Add in a super-cool vintage like 2002 and you'll find yourself at the pinnacle of Australian sparkling wine. This bottle-fermented chardonnay pinot noir shows plenty of youthful cool-climate citrus fruits, really intense grapefruit and nectarine, pure and restrained with plenty of power. The palate pins itself down with bright acidity, citrus fruits here too, nectarines, some white peach and honeysuckle; Arras ripples with youthful intensity, fading to grilled nuts at the finish. A masterful sparkling. As Arras has proved in previous vintages, it'll keep improving with age.

PENGUIN BEST VINTAGE SPARKLING WINE

2003 **Bay of Fires Pinot Noir Chardonnay**   *Score* **93**

TASMANIA	
Price	$37.00
Quality	★ ★ ★ ★ ⟩
Alc./Vol.	12.5%
Drink	Now
Closure	Cork

The first port of call here is that this looks the part in the glass – ticking away with a fine stream of small bubbles that holds its bead nicely. Aromas are of dried fruits, intense and savoury, with plenty of well-crafted complexity. Impressive precision and texture on the palate, it unfolds in fine layers, classy stuff and truly elegant.

NV Bay of Fires Tigress Pinot Noir Chardonnay

Score 90

TASMANIA	
Price	$27.00
Quality	★★★★
Alc./Vol.	12.5%
Drink	Now
Closure	Cork

Bright, lively and direct, from one of the biggest and best producers of Australian sparkling comes this Tassie Tigress. It's a cool-climate beast, finely tuned and neatly structured, a terrific party drink to keep the guests refreshed. Fresh citrus and berry fruit aromas, softly textured and boasting just enough yeasty complexity, it's superbly balanced.

NV Bay of Fires Tigress Rosé

Score 94

TASMANIA	
Price	$27.00 ✓
Quality	★★★★ ⅃
Alc./Vol.	12.5%
Drink	Now
Closure	Cork

Superbly fresh and elegant primary fruits reflect the cool-climate origins of this handy pink sparkler: cut strawberry and some chalky mineral aromas, very fine, in the clean-cut Bay of Fires style. Super-smooth and precise palate too, bringing more strawberry fruit flavour amid smooth texture and a vibrant lifted finish. This is a class act.

NV Bindi Macedon Cuvée V

Score 94

MACEDON RANGES	
Price	$45.00
Quality	★★★★ ⅃
Alc./Vol.	12.5%
Drink	Now
Closure	Diam

Bindi's small but uncompromisingly excellent production of sparkling is well worth the hunt. Drawing on the cool potential of the region to create this intense and complex wine, Michael Dhillon weaves freshness and complexity neatly together with aromas of fresh-baked brioche, honey and grilled nuts. A similarly savoury, rich and intense palate. An assertive style.

 ## NV Brown Brothers Pinot Noir Chardonnay Pinot Meunier

Score 93

VICTORIA	
Price	$20.00 ✓
Quality	★★★★ ⅃
Alc./Vol.	12.5%
Drink	Now
Closure	Cork

This bottle-fermented NV sits in a richer style and has all the trimmings of toasty development with plenty of pinot noir's savoury red fruits, pinot meunier's earthy notes and just the right amount of sourdough bready complexity. The palate brings the chardonnay fruit to the fore, before rich yeasty autolysis takes over, adding woody notes and baking spices. Charming creamy texture, rich, even and long.

PENGUIN BEST NON-VINTAGE SPARKLING WINE

NV Brown Brothers Zibibbo Rosa

Score 88

SOUTH EASTERN AUSTRALIA	
Price	$15.00
Quality	★★★ ⅃
Alc./Vol.	8%
Drink	Now
Closure	Cork

It may sound like the latest and greatest Italian motor scooter to hit our shores, but this pink sparkling is a light, refreshing and low-alcohol wine made with Muscat of Alexandria (aka zibibbo). Smells super fresh, like fresh grape juice, with some floral musky perfume; it's sweet, refreshing and a tidy 8% alcohol.

NV Chandon Brut

Score **92**

MULTI-REGIONAL	
Price	$25.00 ✓
Quality	★★★★
Alc./Vol.	12.5%
Drink	Now
Closure	Cork

This chardonnay-pinot noir blend has impressively complex and authentic bottle-fermented sparkling wine characters. We're talking yeast autolysis while still retaining fresh fruits, pears and apples mostly. The palate has a smoothly integrated texture, rich pinot noir flavours and brighter citrusy chardonnay with some biscuity complexity.

2005 Croser

Score **94**

ADELAIDE HILLS	
Price	$35.00 ✓
Quality	★★★★ ┤
Alc./Vol.	13%
Drink	2011
Closure	Cork

This pinot-dominant blend is sourced from the home turf of Adelaide Hills pioneer, Petaluma. The savoury pinot fruits and subtle spicy complexity mean serious sparkling business, backed by attractive yeasty nuances and some ripe red-skinned apple aromas. Fine and piercing palate, plenty of savoury yeasty flavour, red fruits and nectarines. Still youthful, it will build in bottle for a while yet.

NV De Bortoli Emeri Pink Moscato

Score **89**

MULTI-REGIONAL	
Price	$12.00 ✓
Quality	★★★ ┤
Alc./Vol.	8%
Drink	Now
Closure	Diam

Packaged up like a princess, this light, refreshing moscato-style sparkling is alive with fresh pink grape juice aromas and a little spicy twist that catches extra attention. It fills the mouth with sweet musk-stick flavours, rolling soft and easy down the hatch and tastes every bit as pretty as it looks.

NV De Bortoli Rococo Blanc de Blancs

Score **91**

YARRA VALLEY	
Price	$19.00 ✓
Quality	★★★★
Alc./Vol.	12%
Drink	Now
Closure	Diam

Looking to really play ball, De Bortoli's new Yarra sparkling has 100% barrel-fermented chardonnay with a secondary fermentation in tank and plenty of lees contact. Punchy chardonnay aromas with some yeasty/fresh bread complexity, citrus and peach blossom. Attractive finely textured apple-flavoured palate. Balance, length, it's got it all.

NV De Bortoli Sacred Hill Brut Cuvée

Score **86**

RIVERINA	
Price	$7.00 ✓
Quality	★★★
Alc./Vol.	11%
Drink	Now
Closure	Cork

It's hard to imagine we can keep making wine this good and this cheap from the Riverland. Enjoy it while you can. Attractive richness and ripeness to the fore, lemon candy and cool fruit-salad aromas, and faint savoury/yeasty complexity. The palate carries ripe fruit flavour and sweetness in balance, there's crunchy fresh acidity backing it all and a hint of honey through the finish. Ridiculous value!

NV De Bortoli Windy Peak Pinot Noir Chardonnay — Score 89

VICTORIA	
Price	$15.00 ✓
Quality	★★★ ꜰ
Alc./Vol.	11.5%
Drink	Now
Closure	Cork

The striking blushed bronze-pink colour is mesmerising as this sits bubbling away finely in the glass. Bright pinot noir fragrance follows: some red flowers, it's quite savoury, dried red berries and almost chalky minerals. The palate rolls out ripe fruits, sweeter pinot noir flavours here, more dried red berries and fragrant lift through the finish, fanning out and up. Good balance and a more forward, easy-drinking style.

2006 Delatite Polly Sparkling Gewürztraminer — Score 92

CENTRAL VICTORIA	
Price	$29.00
Quality	★★★★
Alc./Vol.	12%
Drink	Now
Closure	Crown

You can pick this variety at 20 paces, whether it has bubbles or not. Here there's an exotic saffron-scented edge to traminer's lychee and roses. The palate is dry, full of flavour amid some rich textural swing and crunchy acid, leaving a wake of lychee fruit through the finish, balanced and even. Refreshingly different.

NV Hanging Rock Cuvée VII LD — Score 97

MACEDON RANGES	
Price	$110.00
Quality	★★★★★
Alc./Vol.	12%
Drink	Now
Closure	Diam

Hanging Rock won two special awards with this late disgorged cuvee: the prize for longest-lees maturation (10 years) and the award for the most expensive Australian sparkling wine. Easily the best Hanging Rock sparkling I've tasted, it's mostly material from the 1996 vintage and has a deeper golden hue borne of age. Everything's fitted together in mellow, harmonious form, plenty of earthy complexity and pinot noir spice, some slow-roasted nuts and hints of citrus still in place. The texture's the thing though, softened with time and gracefully structured, the bead is fine and consistent; there's plenty of acidity, it fades smoothly from still-fresh fruit characters to cashew nuts, finishing slow and dry. Mission accomplished, well done!

NV Hanging Rock Macedon Cuvée XII — Score 93

MACEDON RANGES	
Price	$49.00
Quality	★★★★ ꜰ
Alc./Vol.	12%
Drink	2010
Closure	Diam

The Hanging Rock style is built around winemaker John Ellis's favourite champagne, Bollinger. This means he's worked layers of complexity into every corner of this pinot-driven wine. Starts out with smoky-spicy flavours and then builds into more biscuity, bread dough territory, fulsome texture and no-holds-barred power. It's a well-rehearsed offering; this edition is based on the 2000 and 2001 vintages with smaller amounts of older reserves.

NV Hanging Rock Rosé Brut

Score 94

MACEDON RANGES	
Price	$27.00 ✓
Quality	★★★★ ⅃
Alc./Vol.	12.5%
Drink	Now
Closure	Diam

A rosé that reflects the distinctive Hanging Rock style, showing plenty of spicy cool-climate pinot noir complexity; it's 100% pinot, in fact, and savoury as a result. Some barrel-derived complexity, the palate is richly styled with intense pinot fruit flavour, red fruits and spices, long berry aftertaste. Ideally served at meal times.

2008 Innocent Bystander Moscato

Score 90

VICTORIA 🖋	
Price	$12.50 ✓ (375 ml)
Quality	★★★★
Alc./Vol.	5.5%
Drink	Right now
Closure	Crown

One of the most popular recent trends to arrive in the crossover between wine and beverage marketing, no refrigerator should be without a couple of these stacked cold in the door. Smells of lifted pink muscat perfume and packs plenty of sweet fresh grape flavour, it is low in alcohol and about as refreshing as wine can get.

2000 Jansz Brut LD

Score 93

TASMANIA	
Price	$45.00
Quality	★★★★ ⅃
Alc./Vol.	13%
Drink	Now
Closure	Cork

If you like the richness and savoury appeal of bottle-developed characters, then this is the wine for you. Complex aromas are present, it shows the whole array of nougat aromas, nutty but still fresh. The palate follows in the same rich vein of nougat and green almonds; those lees have been working away for seven years, adding a rich toasty twist to the finish, grilled hazelnut flavours. A terrific food wine.

NV Jansz Premium Cuvée

Score 91

TASMANIA	
Price	$25.00 ✓
Quality	★★★★
Alc./Vol.	12.5%
Drink	Now
Closure	Cork

Jansz is a chardonnay-dominant house making an excellent array of Tasmanian sparkling wines; this basic NV now receives added time on cork to settle down. Made with all the care and attention to detail of wines twice the price, it is bright and fragrant, offering citrus, stone fruits and berry notes below. A supple and refined palate, with a clever mix of creamy fruit texture and clean-cut acidity.

NV Jansz Premium Rosé

Score 92

TASMANIA	
Price	$25.00 ✓
Quality	★★★★
Alc./Vol.	15%
Drink	Now
Closure	Cork

This pinot noir-dominant NV rosé hits a sweet spot on the sparkling radar. It offers plenty of ripe red fruit aromas, smells sweet and attractive, with some savoury lees complexity. The palate gets straight to the pinot-flavoured point, juicy, almost meaty, yet glossed up with a fine creamy texture, finishing with a yeasty lick of savoury/malty flavour.

2004 Jansz Premium Vintage Rosé   Score 93

TASMANIA	
Price	$38.00
Quality	★★★★ ┤
Alc./Vol.	12.5%
Drink	Now
Closure	Cork

Only the second edition of this style released from Jansz, yet no less successful than their tried-and-tested cuvées. This is a complex and toasty rosé, more savoury and symphonic with plenty of red fruits and toasty, yeasty complexity. Impressive length and weight, acidity breathes life and lightness into a berry-flavoured palate before the finish fans out in rich style.

2003 Jansz Vintage Cuvée   Score 96

TASMANIA	
Price	$38.00 ✓
Quality	★★★★★
Alc./Vol.	12.5%
Drink	Now
Closure	Cork

Their flagship wine, with four years ageing on yeast lees, moves into majestic, complex territory. A stylish bouquet of citrus blossom, red fruits, some minerals at the edge and gentle lees-derived undertones. Love the drive and lift across the palate, this is bright, pure and restrained, moving through red fruit flavours and some savoury spice laces the finish. Dare I say it, champagne-like!

NV Joseph Sparkling Red   Score 93

MULTI-REGIONAL	
Price	$55.00
Quality	★★★★ ┤
Alc./Vol.	13.5%
Drink	Now
Closure	Cork

It's a winning combination when Joe Grilli's approach to wine is as much about its consumption as its provenance. A consistently great sparkling red and easy to spot in its tall slender bottle. Shiraz, cabernet, merlot, a few really old wines and fortifieds are folded together to deliver richness, complexity and smiles to all who partake.

NV Lindemans Premier Selection Brut Cuvée   Score 85

MULTI-REGIONAL	
Price	$6.00
Quality	★★★
Alc./Vol.	11.5%
Drink	Now
Closure	Cork

What to expect for a six-buck bottle of sparkling? Well, it fizzes up in the glass, veritably foams, and there's even a yeasty hint of complexity mixed in with lemony citrus aromas. Flavours of candied fruits fill the mouth with some musky notes through the finish; not too sweet, an easygoing all-rounder.

NV Minchinbury Private Cuvée Brut de Brut   Score 85

MULTI-REGIONAL	
Price	$8.00
Quality	★★★
Alc./Vol.	11%
Drink	Now
Closure	Cork

An old favourite for some, this is the driest (brut de brut) Minchinbury but still easygoing. Offering a clean, well-presented vinous nose – not quite a super-model – it just smells like a decent bottle of fizz. The palate's fullish and actually sweeter than the brut-de-brut labelling suggests, but it balances out and makes a clean exit.

1999 Radenti Chardonnay Pinot Noir

Score 96

TASMANIA	
Price	$65.00
Quality	★★★★★
Alc./Vol.	12%
Drink	Now
Closure	Cork

This sparkling masterpiece comes from the highly regarded Freycinet camp in Biceno. Astoundingly pure chardonnay aromas lead the wine out, limes, stone fruits and citrus oils; some of pinot's woody spices mix in richly through time on lees. A smouldering palate, led by chardonnay's powerful peach and nectarine fruits, twists through to complex savoury yeasty flavours at the finish. Long and bold, an uncompromising cool-climate triumph.

NV Seaview Brut de Brut

Score 86

MULTI-REGIONAL	
Price	$8.00
Quality	★★★
Alc./Vol.	11.5%
Drink	Now
Closure	Cork

This is the driest of all the Seaview sparklers and has a distinctly savoury/bread dough aroma, as if it's looking to shake it up with the *serious* sparkling wines. The palate has a slightly finer and drier profile than its stablemates and, depending on how long it's been in bottle, will leave a nice nougat-flavoured finish.

NV Seppelt Fleur de Lys

Score 87

SOUTH EASTERN AUSTRALIA	
Price	$12.00 ✓
Quality	★★★ ┤
Alc./Vol.	12%
Drink	Now
Closure	Cork

As old as boy scouts and girl guides, this NV Fleur de Lys remains a bottle-fermented bargain. A simple creamy fruit nose, it has riper fruit characters with glazed peaches and toffee apples, simple and appealing. The palate has the same richness and ripeness too, a straightforward wine with a bread-doughy twist through the finish. Safe as houses.

2003 Sir James Pinot Noir Chardonnay

Score 94

VICTORIA & TASMANIA	
Price	$26.00 ✓
Quality	★★★★ ┤
Alc./Vol.	12.5%
Drink	Now
Closure	Cork

Covered in wine-show bling, this vintage wine truly looks the part, boasting cool-climate style sourced from vineyards in Victoria and Tasmania. Honeysuckle and sweet white flowers on the nose, crisp acidity, a fine creamy texture and the right price all hit the sweet spot. Brilliant.

2000 Sir James Tumbarumba Cuvée
Score **94**

TUMBARUMBA	
Price	$30.00 ✓
Quality	★★★★⌐
Alc./Vol.	13%
Drink	2010
Closure	Cork

From the cool climes of the new(ish) Tumbarumba region, this pinot noir-chardonnay blend shows some sweet honey and nougat development here (thanks to an impressive five and a half years on lees). Fruit characters assertively reflect their cool-climate origins. Finely cut with plenty of chardonnay's grapefruity richness, the palate shows terrific structure, long with biscuity flavour through the middle and grilled nuts at the finish.

2002 Starvedog Lane Adelaide Hills Chardonnay Pinot Noir Pinot Meunier
Score **91**

ADELAIDE HILLS	
Price	$26.00
Quality	★★★★
Alc./Vol.	12.5%
Drink	2010
Closure	Cork

The cool '02 vintage delivered a triumph in the form of this sparkling gem. It opens with plenty of bright stone fruits, typical of Hills chardonnay, add to that a little nutty complexity and there's a lot going on in the glass. They've crafted a charming supple, smooth texture that carries rich ripe flavour and savoury complexity, which will grow in bottle if that's what you're after.

2006 Taltarni Brut Taché
Score **93**

VICTORIA & TASMANIA	
Price	$24.00 ✓
Quality	★★★★⌐
Alc./Vol.	13%
Drink	Now
Closure	Diam

Well, pink sparkling is all the rage and here's a very good reason why. Irresistible red fruit aromas, floral and perfumed, really pristine wild strawberry and yeasty complexity, creamy and fresh. The palate is zesty and packed with wild red berry flavours, finishing crisp and balanced. A very smart wine.

NV Taltarni T Series Chardonnay Pinot Noir Pinot Meunier
Score **91**

VICTORIA & TASMANIA	
Price	$15.00 ✓
Quality	★★★★
Alc./Vol.	12.5%
Drink	Now
Closure	Cork

From one of Australia's legendary good-value sparkling makers, this entry-level NV is bottle fermented and shows attractive complex fruit characters: fresh stone fruits and melon aromas, some citrus and red fruits too. Pinot noir and pinot meunier really drive the palate, bringing plenty of red fruit flavour and earthy/savoury richness.

2006 Taltarni Vintage Brut
Score **94**

VICTORIA & TASMANIA

Price	$24.00 ✓
Quality	★★★★﹜
Alc./Vol.	13%
Drink	2011
Closure	Diam

A proper grown-up bottle-fermented chardonnay-pinot noir blend wagering attractive ripe red fruit aromas, sweet spices and floral lift against stone fruits and the beginnings of biscuity complexity. The palate is packed with flavour, rich and ripe: the stone fruits dominate here, followed by waves of pinot flavour and assertive acidity that really stretches the fruit impact and red apple aftertaste.

PENGUIN BEST-VALUE SPARKLING WINE

2006 Yarra Burn Pinot Noir Chardonnay Pinot Meunier
Score **93**

YARRA VALLEY

Price	$20.00 ✓
Quality	★★★★﹜
Alc./Vol.	12.5%
Drink	2012
Closure	Cork

This bottle-fermented flagship still sits squarely in value territory; with Pink Lady apple aromas, it's a restrained and compact, cool-smelling wine. The palate ripples with piercing youthful intensity thanks to a racy acid backbone, supporting red fruit and citrus flavours, fragrant and subtle grilled cashew to finish. Classic Yarra Valley power and balance.

NV Yarra Burn Third Light Pinot Noir Chardonnay
Score **89**

VICTORIA

Price	$12.00
Quality	★★★﹜
Alc./Vol.	12.5%
Drink	Now
Closure	Cork

Sourced from Victorian vineyards, not just the home turf Yarra Valley, this is a foray into price-competitive territory offering an all-round set of sparkling wine characters, made to a fresh early-drinking style. Shows citrus, melon and stone fruit aromas, and sweet florals too; the palate brings in some yeasty complexity, like freshly kneaded bread dough, all nicely tuned together.

1999 Yarrabank LD Sauvage
Score **96**

VICTORIA

Price	$45.00 ✓
Quality	★★★★★
Alc./Vol.	12.5%
Drink	2011
Closure	Diam

With eight years on yeast lees, Yarrabank took second place in the sparkling wine longest-lees maturation award. They wisely decided not to add any sweetening dosage (hence the sauvage), letting the savoury characters lead this scintillating wine. Fine lemon- and lime-zest aromas, it's still really restrained and tightly integrated, with honeysuckle and nectarines and peaches too, some savoury toasty notes, roasted nuts and spices. Very complex. The palate's fine texture mixes elegance with power; it's linear and focused with a super-fine bead and a harmonious, zesty lemon toast finish.

Champagne

The champagne trade is alive and well – the best it's been, in fact – and the wines are in brilliant form. Global consumption has surged, there's even talk of extending the official boundary of the region to keep up with demand. Although the mention of champagne conjures up a single notion of wine with bubbles (and a party!), there is an array of styles to choose from. This chapter covers them all, from the non-vintage stalwarts, through to rosé and blanc de blancs, all the way into fantasy territory – the prestige cuvée wines. FOOD: Much the same rules apply for champagne as for Australian sparking wines, although many champagnes carry more powerful fruit, higher acidity and greater savoury complexity. Any time is a good time for champagne!

NV Ayala Rosé Nature   Score 94

CHAMPAGNE	
Price	$100.00
Quality	★★★★ ┤
Alc./Vol.	12.5%
Drink	Now
Closure	Cork

Salmon pink and billed as a low-dosage rosé, plenty of bright red fruits and red florals, dried rose petals; romantic and sophisticated. Confident flavoursome palate, fine cherry fruit flavour, it takes the rosé genre into a refined, balanced place.

NV Ayala ZD   Score 93

CHAMPAGNE	
Price	$89.00
Quality	★★★★ ┤
Alc./Vol.	12.5%
Drink	Now
Closure	Cork

Ayala is being marketed off the back of its new owners Bollinger but this stuff truly stands alone. Superb champagne, dry and crisp (ZD = zero dosage), it's an ideal aperitif style. Refreshing and flavoursome fizz, edgy, complete and balanced.

NV Billecart Brut Rosé   Score 91

CHAMPAGNE	
Price	$135.00
Quality	★★★★
Alc./Vol.	12.5%
Drink	Now
Closure	Cork

Billecart's NV Rosé has built up a loyal following over the last ten years. It tastes as good as it looks, sporting fresh ripe strawberry aromas and musky complexity. The palate is all red fruits, really juicy and direct, this certainly doesn't disappoint.

1998 Billecart Cuvée Nicholas François–Billecart

Score **96**

CHAMPAGNE	
Price	$180.00
Quality	★★★★★
Alc./Vol.	12.5%
Drink	2010
Closure	Cork

Very convincing champagne, showing harmony and integration, poise and complexity. Some early mushroom and savoury characters rise through fine chalky minerals and fresh brioche. Stone fruit flavours, some citrus, yeasty complexity, balanced and beautiful.

NV Boizel Blanc de Blancs

Score **91**

CHAMPAGNE	
Price	$110.00
Quality	★★★★
Alc./Vol.	12.5%
Drink	Now
Closure	Cork

Boizel is a house with immense history, and the quality is much higher than the prices would suggest. Great value! Plenty of toasty chardonnay citrus complexity, the palate brings honey into play with terrific drive and length.

1999 Bollinger La Grande Année

Score **93**

CHAMPAGNE	
Price	$230.00
Quality	★★★★⁺
Alc./Vol.	12.5%
Drink	Now
Closure	Cork

The Bollinger house style is in full effect here; edgy and complex yeasty characters, sweet and sour citrus fruits, freshly rolled bread dough, really fresh. The palate is a ball of intense fruit supplemented with woody spices, finishing with taut fresh acidity; this will age handsomely.

NV Cattier

Score **89**

CHAMPAGNE	
Price	$40.00 ✓
Quality	★★★⁺
Alc./Vol.	12%
Drink	Now
Closure	Cork

Super elegant with savoury light soy aromas, yeasty influence and fine stony mineral smells, gentle pinot spice here; simple, singular and fresh. A good core of flavour that drives punchy and deep, yeasty notes through the finish.

1995 Charles Heidsieck Blanc des Millénaires

Score **95**

CHAMPAGNE	
Price	$180.00
Quality	★★★★⁺
Alc./Vol.	12.5%
Drink	Now
Closure	Cork

One of the star blanc de blancs, showing plenty of finesse as well as complex rich characters growing in bottle. Symphonic and impressive palate, deep and swirling layers of flavour, delicate creamy mousse, zesty citrus lingers fresh and precise.

NV Charles Heidsieck Brut Reserve   *Score* 93

CHAMPAGNE	
Price	$80.00
Quality	★★★★ ┤
Alc./Vol.	12.5%
Drink	Now
Closure	Cork

The *mis en cave* concept is a system of marking NV bottlings, so don't be fooled by the year on the back – that's when it was put down for ageing in the Heidsieck cellar. One hell of an NV: rich, complex, balanced, consistently impressive champagne. Delicious!

1999 Charles Heidsieck Rosé   *Score* 93

CHAMPAGNE	
Price	$160.00
Quality	★★★★ ┤
Alc./Vol.	12.5%
Drink	Now
Closure	Cork

This is one of the best rosé styles available on the Australian market: rich, complex and spicy, intense red fruits and some toast beginning to show. Deep pinot flavour, impressive weight, richness and persistence.

NV Delamotte Blanc de Blancs   *Score* 93

CHAMPAGNE	
Price	$98.00
Quality	★★★★ ┤
Alc./Vol.	12.5%
Drink	Now
Closure	Cork

Made under the same management as the scintillatingly perfect Salon, this is a complex and balanced blanc de blancs, superbly structured and phrased. It's perfectly suited to pre-anything drinks and has the balance and structure to take through to dinner.

NV Delamotte Brut   *Score* 92

CHAMPAGNE	
Price	$69.00
Quality	★★★★
Alc./Vol.	12.5%
Drink	Now
Closure	Cork

The entry-level Delamotte is as good an NV as you'll find around town. Quite a modern, well-made nose, ripe grapefruit and chalky Champagne terroir. Stylishly arranged on the palate, layers of fruit flavour, fine, long and utterly delicious!

NV Devaux Cuvée D   *Score* 91

CHAMPAGNE	
Price	$95.00
Quality	★★★★
Alc./Vol.	12.5%
Drink	Now
Closure	Cork

Devaux's flagship cuvée is a richly fruited assembly of pinot noir and chardonnay from a large cooperative group in the south of the region. Lemon citrus and florals, a vinous and forthright style with power and sweet wood spice.

1999 **Dom Perignon**
Score **95**

CHAMPAGNE	
Price	$285.00
Quality	★★★★ ┦
Alc./Vol.	12.5%
Drink	Now
Closure	Cork

Plenty of intensity and richness here, ripe chardonnay characters, stone fruit, nectarines and peaches, attractive lemon and some toasty autolysis complexity. Gentle reduction gives the impression of chalky minerals, very strong core of anchored aromatics. Super-bright acidity and drive, has some creamy almondine nuts and savoury characters; very, very fine, precise and long, nutty almond finish, super-fine bead and crisp chalky/savoury texture, rolls long and deep. Lowest ever dosage – 6 gm.

2000 **Dom Perignon**
Score **96**

CHAMPAGNE	
Price	$285.00
Quality	★★★★★
Alc./Vol.	12.5%
Drink	2010
Closure	Cork

A bright, rich and precise 2000; classic Dom with all the boxes ticked. It's straight-laced, with an intense sturdy core of lemony citrus and a complete set of complex characters. Superb palate, really bright, young and upbeat, with breezy primary citrus characters, good density, reductive minerally edges and a long fine finish. Forthright fruit pushes texture out in fine, confident style.

NV **Gosset Brut Excellence**
Score **91**

CHAMPAGNE	
Price	$69.00
Quality	★★★★
Alc./Vol.	12.5%
Drink	Now
Closure	Cork

Certainly one of THE stars of the base-level NV in Australia. Gosset brings plenty of experience as one of the oldest houses in the Champagne region. Loads of subtle red fruit influence, structured and sturdy with good concentration pulled together with finesse and grace.

NV **Gosset Grande Reserve**
Score **93**

CHAMPAGNE	
Price	$89.00
Quality	★★★★ ┦
Alc./Vol.	12.5%
Drink	Now
Closure	Cork

This is where Gosset really starts to draw away from the pack; richness and power, layers of aroma and flavour, beautifully arranged. Focused red fruits, bright precise acidity and a dusting of spice threaded neatly through the palate.

NV **Henriot Blanc de Blancs**
Score **90**

CHAMPAGNE	
Price	$95.00
Quality	★★★★
Alc./Vol.	12.5%
Drink	Now
Closure	Cork

The blanc de blancs are where this house really excels, capturing finesse and precision, the chardonnay-only cuvée moderates richness, etching a finer line across the palate. Ripe yellow stone fruits, a little toast, all balancing neatly through the finish.

1996 **Jacquesson Rosé**

Score **93**

CHAMPAGNE
Price $179.00
Quality   ★★★★∤
Alc./Vol.   12.5%
Drink   Now
Closure   Cork

Jacquesson has produced a couple of stunning wines from the outstanding 1996 vintage, this rosé makes a strong cherry-scented impact, fresh, neat and pure. It has drive and intensity in the mouth, savoury cherries, impressive weight, just made for the dining table.

 2002 **Louis Roederer Cristal**

Score **97**

CHAMPAGNE
Price $350.00
Quality   ★★★★★
Alc./Vol.   12.5%
Drink   2013
Closure   Cork

This is easily the best we've seen since the scintillating 1996 Cristal! Intensity and fine concentration are the hallmarks of this exquisite champagne; chalky aromas, fine citrus and tight minerally restraint. The palate is needle-like in its precision, piercing acidity and fine floral notes, clean and long. Not one to be missed.

PENGUIN BEST VINTAGE CHAMPAGNE

2000 **Moët et Chandon Grand Vintage**

Score **93**

CHAMPAGNE
Price $100.00
Quality   ★★★★∤
Alc./Vol.   12.5%
Drink   Now
Closure   Cork

With new livery and a new name, the folks in Epernay have also tweaked the style into ever-more refined shape. This looks terrific, little white flowers, toasted hazelnuts and grapefruity citrus. Fine yet rich in the mouth, smartly structured, dynamic and precise.

NV **Mumm de Cremant**

Score **94**

CHAMPAGNE
Price $150.00
Quality   ★★★★∤
Alc./Vol.   12.5%
Drink   Now
Closure   Cork

This is certainly the ace in Mumm's champagne deck, it really sits out on its own as a cut above. Cremant is a commune in the Champagne vineyards, here it brings fine floral aromas, fresh fruit and minerals. Etches a fine line on the palate, elegant and intense. Terrific!

1998 **Perrier–Jouet Belle Epoque Blanc**

Score **95**

CHAMPAGNE
Price $250.00
Quality   ★★★★∤
Alc./Vol.   12.5%
Drink   2012
Closure   Cork

Perhaps the most instantly recognisable champagne bottle in the world, yet how many have sipped this special fizz? It's a stunner in the glass, symphonic and layered, restrained, refined and pure chardonnay aromas. Sizzles with intensity in the mouth, cutting precise lines of flavour.

NV Perrier-Jouet Grand Brut

Score **91**

CHAMPAGNE	
Price	$89.00
Quality	★★★★
Alc./Vol.	12.5%
Drink	Now
Closure	Cork

PJ has a reputation built on the iconic painted glass of its flagship, but this NV is a real star in the pack. It mixes up some bright, assertive primary fruit with cleverly placed complexity, bright fruits run through to Champagne's chalky soil-driven characters. Really smart.

NV Pierre Gimonnet Cuis 1er Cru

Score **92**

CHAMPAGNE	
Price	$50.00 ✓
Quality	★★★★
Alc./Vol.	12%
Drink	Now
Closure	Cork

From the village of Cuis, this blanc de blancs is all chardonnay: fine lemon and mineral aromas, really elegant and direct – terrific focus and gentle bready complexity. The palate packs decent acidity and cut, some smooth cashew nut flavour and balanced dosage, this is terrific value. Rich and elegant.

PENGUIN BEST NON-VINTAGE CHAMPAGNE

1998 Pol Roger Blanc de Blancs

Score **93**

CHAMPAGNE	
Price	$120.00
Quality	★★★★ ᛣ
Alc./Vol.	12.5%
Drink	Now
Closure	Cork

The combination of Pol's generous house style and the restraint of 100% chardonnay is a killer. Light toast, dried citrus zest, nuts and biscuits all smell delicious. The proof is in the palate, pristine lemon zest, depth and drive, concentrated and stylishly fine.

1998 Pol Roger Brut Vintage

Score **92**

CHAMPAGNE	
Price	$105.00
Quality	★★★★
Alc./Vol.	12.5%
Drink	Now
Closure	Cork

Long loved by the Brits, Pol is in staggeringly good shape these days; this vintage wine is one of the best value on offer. Richness and classic Pol toasty notes, some bright fresh yellow fruits, creamy fine mousse, depth and length.

NV Pommery Brut Royal

Score **92**

CHAMPAGNE	
Price	$70.00
Quality	★★★★
Alc./Vol.	12.5%
Drink	Now
Closure	Cork

This NV Pommery delivers admirably, plenty of richness and complexity without sacrificing fresh appeal. Lemons, chalk and bright citrus blossom fragrance, fresh autolysis characters. Well-pitched palate with fine bead, clean crisp texture and an elegant fresh oyster shell and soft, creamy citrus finish.

1999 Pommery Grand Cru Vintage

Score **94**

CHAMPAGNE	
Price	$98.00
Quality	★★★★ᛃ
Alc./Vol.	15%
Drink	2010
Closure	Cork

A more powerful and intensely focused nose here, piercing chalky lemon and lime citrus fruits, bright apple fruits and freshly kneaded bread dough. Superb finesse and crisp, restrained palate, apple and gentle chalk through the finish.

2000 Roederer Blanc de Blancs

Score **93**

CHAMPAGNE	
Price	$110.00
Quality	★★★★ᛃ
Alc./Vol.	12.5%
Drink	2011
Closure	Cork

Lovely precision here, showing plenty of ripe chardonnay fruits, and some reliably flavoursome yet fine house styling. There's fine citrus, lemon toast, focus and precision on the nose. Terrific acid crunch, grapefruit, nectarine and melon all sing in tune.

NV Roederer Brut Premier

Score **91**

CHAMPAGNE	
Price	$89.00
Quality	★★★★
Alc./Vol.	12.5%
Drink	Now
Closure	Cork

Roederer have a knack of bringing finesse and flavour into harmony, and this, their standard NV, has developed a loyal following in restaurants and beyond. Plenty of pinot fruit character, some toast and well-built complexity. Fine mousse, finishing savoury and tidy.

2000 Roederer Brut Vintage

Score **92**

CHAMPAGNE	
Price	$110.00
Quality	★★★★
Alc./Vol.	12.5%
Drink	2011
Closure	Cork

This is a bronzed, more masculine wine in the Roederer line-up, and it has some impressive richness in 2000. Super toasty with savoury spices, dried fruits and plenty of all-round ripeness and richness, toasted almonds and bright lemony acidity.

NV Ruinart Blanc de Blancs

Score **94**

CHAMPAGNE	
Price	$130.00
Quality	★★★★ᛃ
Alc./Vol.	12.5%
Drink	Now
Closure	Cork

Handsomely packaged, this little blanc de blancs cuts a mean shape. Superbly precise champagne, refreshing and intense, subtle toast and honey complexity woven through pure chardonnay fruits. Engaging, finely textured bubbles, oozes class and style.

NV Ruinart R de Ruinart

Score **92**

CHAMPAGNE	
Price	$85.00
Quality	★★★★
Alc./Vol.	12.5%
Drink	Now
Closure	Cork

Now under the substantial wing of LVMH, this historic house is well worth investigating. Plenty of clever complexing, assertive fruit and handy depth. The palate is taut and layered with smoky mineral flavour laced through pristine fruit. This will impress.

1996 Salon Cuvées Blanc de Blancs

Score **100**

CHAMPAGNE	
Price	$500.00
Quality	★★★★★
Alc./Vol.	12.5%
Drink	2012
Closure	Cork

It really doesn't get much better than this. Salon is the world's most sought-after champagne. Super-precise, restrained and powerful, Salon's purity and grace are what sets it apart from the pack; no one cuts this close to perfection! A demanding powerhouse of a champagne.

1998 Taittinger Comtes de Champagne

Score **96**

CHAMPAGNE	
Price	$240.00
Quality	★★★★★
Alc./Vol.	12.5%
Drink	2010
Closure	Cork

Taittinger's prestige cuvée blanc de blancs is regularly at the very top of the champagne tree. Impossibly intense, subtle bready complexity and fine minerals at the edge. Commanding yet precise, this sails across the palate leaving a brisk wake of fresh lingering flavour.

Sauvignon blanc

Cue the music! No other grape in recent times has even come close to charting such a meteoric rise in popularity. The best examples come from cooler regions and are more reserved, showing grassy characters, herbaceous notes, gooseberry, passionfruit and citrus. These wines have nicely balanced acids and some have a steely, mineral character worked into their wines. For the most part they are made without maturation in oak, although subtle barrel fermentation and oak maturation is used to enrich complexity and beef up the wine's texture. FOOD: Lighter flavoured foods, such as delicate seafood, mild young cheeses (especially goats cheese), green leafy vegetables and salads are all terrific matches for sauvignon.

2007 Alkoomi Sauvignon Blanc — Score 90

FRANKLAND RIVER	
Price	$20.00 ✓
Quality	★★★★
Alc./Vol.	13.5%
Drink	Now
Closure	Screwcap

Nice crisp fresh citrus fruit aromas and some cool grassy edges, tropicals sit gently behind. The palate is led by zesty lemon flavour, some richer tropical fruits – passionfruit, guava, mango and pineapple – finishing crisp and bright.

2007 Alta Sauvignon Blanc — Score 93

ADELAIDE HILLS	
Price	$20.00 ✓
Quality	★★★★♪
Alc./Vol.	12.5%
Drink	Now
Closure	Screwcap

Named for its altitude not attitude, Alta is one of the most enticing sauvignons around. It has super-sweet fragrant notes, heady frangipani perfume and tropical fruit aromas – really stands out in a crowd. Fabulous palate intensity with plenty of fine acid to keep it straight and true, sweet tropical fruits and a zesty balanced finish.

2007 Bannockburn Sauvignon Blanc — Score 93

GEELONG	
Price	$25.00 ✓
Quality	★★★★♪
Alc./Vol.	13.5%
Drink	Now
Closure	Cork

This barrel-fermented style is an amazing wine for reasons of sheer concentration alone. Intense orange citrus and grapefruit aromas are married into rich French oak. The palate packs superb concentration and creamy texture, orange zest and nutmeg flavours, measured power through the finish.

2007 Barwang Sauvignon Blanc

Score **92**

TUMBARUMBA	
Price	$19.00 ✓
Quality	★★★★
Alc./Vol.	11.5%
Drink	Now
Closure	Screwcap

McWilliams uses the Barwang label for its cooler- climate sourced wines and this Tumbarumba sauvignon is a fine, restrained example. If you find those over-the-top gooseberry and really pungent styles all a bit much, then you'll love this more delicate tropical and citrus fruit. Gently aromatic and a fine, crisp palate make for refreshing stuff. Bravo!

2007 Blackbilly Sauvignon Blanc

Score **88**

ADELAIDE HILLS	
Price	$20.00
Quality	★★★ ᛃ
Alc./Vol.	12%
Drink	Now
Closure	Screwcap

A bright, light lemon-and-lime style that has some fine crisp citrusy appeal, just faint tropical fruits – the restraint is refreshing. The palate has tart, lemon citrus flavour and a little grip through the finish; smart enough for now.

2007 Capel Vale Pemberton Sauvignon Blanc

Score **91**

PEMBERTON	
Price	$23.00 ✓
Quality	★★★★
Alc./Vol.	12.5%
Drink	Now
Closure	Screwcap

This smells and tastes every bit as elegant as it looks, showing fresh snow pea and gravel, some restrained tropical florals. The palate's crisp and vibrant, has a gentle tickle of fizz to it, delivering flinty/savoury flavour along cool acid lines.

2008 Cockatoo Ridge Sauvignon Blanc

Score **88**

RIVERLAND	
Price	$10.00 ✓
Quality	★★★ ᛃ
Alc./Vol.	10.5%
Drink	Now
Closure	Screwcap

At or around the $10 mark, this is one of the best examples on the market. It leads with bright ripe tropical fruits and sweet aromatic perfume; smells great. The palate has soft, delicate citrus and tropical flavour, smooth easy-drinking balance. Quite a polished result.

2007 Coombend Sauvignon Blanc

Score **91**

TASMANIA	
Price	$25.00
Quality	★★★★
Alc./Vol.	13.5%
Drink	Now
Closure	Screwcap

This hails from the east coast of Tasmania, and shows really vibrant tropical and citrus fruit aromas, quite heady and exotic. Some grassy flavours on entry, then straight into smooth-textured tropicals, heading to more savoury crispness through the finish. Did somebody say oysters?

2007 Cuttaway Hill Sauvignon Blanc

Score **92**

SOUTHERN HIGHLANDS
Price $18.00 ✓
Quality   ★★★★
Alc./Vol. 12.5%
Drink   Now
Closure   Screwcap

Some cool restraint here, all neatly sweet and ripe on the nose, smooth aromatics, nothing out of place. Tropical fruits, sure, but they're in the gooseberry spectrum, mouth-watering freshness and a crisp, finely honed palate. Superb.

2007 De Bortoli Estate Grown Sauvignon

Score **92**

YARRA VALLEY
Price $32.00
Quality   ★★★★
Alc./Vol. 12%
Drink   Now
Closure   Screwcap

A trademark complex nose, inspired by classic French sauvignons: plenty of barrel-derived complexity, the fruit has been teased into savoury territory, crafted not disfigured, edgy tropicals and flint. The palate has gentle, creamy/savoury characters, winemaking fits smoothly into the equation, balanced and crisp.

2007 De Bortoli Yarra Valley Reserve Release Sauvignon

Score **94**

YARRA VALLEY
Price $38.00
Quality   ★★★★ ┤
Alc./Vol. 12.5%
Drink   Now
Closure   Screwcap

This flagship De Bortoli sauvignon shows refined cool gooseberry fruits and fresh sliced cucumber aromas, gentle oak toast appears here too, and some smoky edges. The palate takes the same tack; fine tropical fruits are woven smoothly through gentle texture. Nicely balanced; a great effort.

PENGUIN BEST SAUVIGNON BLANC

2007 Devil's Lair Sauvignon Blanc

Score **89**

MARGARET RIVER
Price $27.00
Quality   ★★★ ┤
Alc./Vol. 13.5%
Drink   Now
Closure   Screwcap

A handy premium-pitched Margaret River sauvignon blanc that deploys clever winemaking to heighten the aromatics. Ripe passionfruit and guava, some regional grassy notes and plenty of palate richness. Fuller than most, a little raw and punchy through the finish.

2007 Dominique Portet Sauvignon Blanc

Score **91**

YARRA VALLEY
Price $24.00 ✓
Quality   ★★★★
Alc./Vol. 13.5%
Drink   Now
Closure   Screwcap

Dominique Portet has a knack for making superb, elegant wines with informed style. This cool sauvignon blanc is concentrated, fresh and has attractive complexity. A small portion (15%) of the fruit receives barrel fermentation, building complexity and texture into the equation – plenty of ripe citrus and tropical fruits, fine chalky finish.

2007 Gembrook Hill Sauvignon Blanc *Score* **90**

YARRA VALLEY
Price $33.00
Quality ★★★★
Alc./Vol. 13%
Drink   Now
Closure Screwcap

Some fine fragrant aromatics and direct passionfruit tropical notes, straight to the point sauvignon character – quite pure. Moves into stone fruits and zesty tropical flavours on the palate, guava and pawpaw; the texture has been gently enhanced, crisp acid pulls it all through the finish in fresh, zesty shape.

2007 Hanging Rock The Jim Jim Sauvignon Blanc *Score* **92**

MACEDON RANGES
Price $27.00
Quality ★★★★
Alc./Vol. 12%
Drink   Now
Closure Screwcap

A consistent performer from the cool Macedon region, it shows very bright primary fruits, tropical aromas and some cooler mineral edges, fine flinty lift and cool-regional character. The palate has greener fleshed fruits, melon and pear flavours, very subtle herbs and a fine line of crisp, direct acidity.

2007 Henschke Coralinga Sauvignon Blanc *Score* **92**

ADELAIDE HILLS
Price $20.00 ✓
Quality ★★★★
Alc./Vol. 12.5%
Drink   Now
Closure Screwcap

This Henschke take on sauvignon shows rich ripe fruits – almost tinned stone fruits – and some tropical notes; very direct and primary. The palate has a fullish texture too; it starts out rich and then slots into zesty acid-driven crunch, finishing fresh and clean.

2007 Jacob's Creek Reserve Sauvignon Blanc *Score* **89**

SOUTH AUSTRALIA
Price $17.00
Quality ★★★ ⅃
Alc./Vol. 13.5%
Drink   Now
Closure Screwcap

This label stretches the reserve concept away from the traditional idea, but the wine is a steady performer. Plenty of bright passionfruity tropical aromas, appealing aromatic lift. The palate is crisp and bright, citrus and more tropicals, balanced crisp finish.

2007 Katnook Estate Founder's Block Sauvignon Blanc *Score* **89**

COONAWARRA
Price $19.00
Quality ★★★ ⅃
Alc./Vol. 13%
Drink   Now
Closure Screwcap

A straight shooting passionfruit sauvignon blanc style, showing plenty of crisp guava and more restrained citrusy fruits. The palate has lemony verve, really direct, some white musky nuances through the finish, green mango to close.

2007 Katnook Estate Sauvignon Blanc

Score **91**

COONAWARRA
Price $23.00 ✓
Quality ★★★★
Alc./Vol. 13.5%
Drink Now
Closure Screwcap

Katnook has chipped away at sauvignon for many years, I can still remember bottles of the golden '86 vintage on the top shelves of bottle-shop fridges. This estate wine has some impressive focus, bright aromatics and citrus/tropical fruits. The palate is gently balanced and carries plenty of flavour, restrained and minerally.

2007 Lalla Gully Sauvignon Blanc

Score **90**

TASMANIA
Price $27.00
Quality ★★★★
Alc./Vol. 12.5%
Drink Now
Closure Screwcap

This reserved, fine sauvignon blanc shows some gentle winemaking complexity laced through restrained tropical fruit aromas. The palate is bright, tight and even, drawn together around a core of fine acidity; there's a savoury/flinty twist through the finish.

2007 Leeuwin Estate Art Series Sauvignon Blanc

Score **92**

MARGARET RIVER
Price $32.00
Quality ★★★★
Alc./Vol. 13%
Drink Now
Closure Screwcap

This impresses with its gentle charming tropical fruit aromas, really restrained and elegant, gently fragrant. The palate has the same bright elegance: starts out really fine and then gathers chirpy tropical flavours towards the finish; terrific build. A class act.

2007 Mantra Sauvignon Blanc

Score **91**

MARGARET RIVER
Price $20.00 ✓
Quality ★★★★
Alc./Vol. 13%
Drink Now
Closure Screwcap

This is a vivacious version of Margaret River sauvignon, really ripe and tropical, mango and guava, some passionfruit too. Bright, crisp acidity snaps the wine straight into gear, plenty of passionfruit flavour and a zesty, fresh finish. Bracing and delicious.

2007 Mount Trio Sauvignon Blanc

Score **88**

GREAT SOUTHERN
Price $16.00 ✓
Quality ★★★⫟
Alc./Vol. 12.5%
Drink Now
Closure Screwcap

This has some lively appeal that's sure to spark up any occasion. Bright, fresh and fragrant, the fruit delivers tropical aromas, adding citrus flavour through the palate, really crisp, with some grassy notes chiming in through the finish.

2007 Nepenthe Sauvignon Blanc

Score **89**

ADELAIDE HILLS	
Price	$23.00
Quality	★★★ ♪
Alc./Vol.	14%
Drink	Now
Closure	Screwcap

Nepenthe delivered one of the most successful Adelaide Hills sauvignons in 2007; it smells attractive, ripe and concentrated. Tropical fruit is the order of the day and it shines throughout this wine. The palate's richer than most (alcohol is up a little) with some real weight and drive, carrying plenty of flavour right the way through.

2007 Oakridge Over The Shoulder Sauvignon Blanc

Score **87**

YARRA VALLEY	
Price	$22.00
Quality	★★★ ♪
Alc./Vol.	11.5%
Drink	Now
Closure	Screwcap

Shows decent richness and faint smoky aromas from the fires of 2007. The overall impression is of cool-region, restrained aromas, greener fleshed fruits, kiwifruit and some fine minerals. The palate has a distinct smoky flavour, straightforward texture and a hint of spice.

2008 O'Leary Walker Sauvignon Blanc

Score **91**

YARRA VALLEY	
Price	$20.00 ✓
Quality	★★★★
Alc./Vol.	12.5%
Drink	Now
Closure	Screwcap

Gee, this is looking the part with its ripe tropical fruits and fresh grassy characters. There's plenty of passionfruit, some mango skin and guava on the palate, all crisply presented amid bright chirpy Adelaide Hills acidity; balanced up and ready to please.

2007 Paracombe Sauvignon Blanc

Score **92**

ADELAIDE HILLS	
Price	$21.00 ✓
Quality	★★★★
Alc./Vol.	12.5%
Drink	Now
Closure	Screwcap

Paul and Kathy Drogemuller have crafted a fine bright sauvignon; there's real brightness here, lifting out of the glass with sweet tropical fruits and some ripe apple aromas. Flavours follow suit, more clean-cut tropicals and apples, the texture is fine and crisp and flavour lingers long and clean through the finish.

2008 Paracombe Sauvignon Blanc

Score **93**

ADELAIDE HILLS	
Price	$21.00 ✓
Quality	★★★★ ♪
Alc./Vol.	13.5%
Drink	Now
Closure	Screwcap

Super-bright and zesty tropical and citrus fruit aromas here, really lifted and attractive; this has clarity and intensity – a consistent performer. The palate packs plenty of passionfruit flavour and bright zesty texture; the Drogemullers have nailed it again!

2007 **Philip Shaw No. 19 Sauvignon Blanc** *Score* **90**

ORANGE
Price $23.00
Quality   ★★★★
Alc./Vol. 13.8%
Drink   Now
Closure   Screwcap

Philip Shaw's take on Orange sauvignon is all about altitude, showing restrained tropical fruits, some lighter sweet fruit perfume and orange citrus oil. The palate plays rich texture against bristling acidity, really zesty and intense, melon-flavoured finish.

2007 **Pike & Joyce Sauvignon Blanc** *Score* **91**

ADELAIDE HILLS
Price $22.00 ✓
Quality   ★★★★
Alc./Vol. 13%
Drink   Now
Closure   Screwcap

Showing a few layers of complexity on the nose, this looks like it has been gently worked in the winery by Clare Valley riesling master, Neil Pike. Plenty of light, bright fragrance and perfumed lift, crisp acid crunch and a fine flavoursome palate. Attractive for its restraint.

2007 **Ravenswood Lane Sauvignon Blanc** *Score* **92**

ADELAIDE HILLS
Price $25.00 ✓
Quality   ★★★★
Alc./Vol. 14%
Drink   Now
Closure   Screwcap

The phoenix-like John Edwards has delivered a beaut '07 savvy. Bright tropical fruits, fine sweet ripe fragrance, plenty of clear passionfruit aromas and some strident lift. The palate is supple, soft and even, lovely balance, smooth texture and a fine flavoursome finish that lingers ever so sweetly.

2007 **Reschke Fumé Sauvignon Blanc** *Score* **91**

COONAWARRA
Price $18.00
Quality   ★★★★
Alc./Vol. 13%
Drink   Now
Closure   Vino-lok

Fumé refers to the style or approach that's been taken with this Coonawarra savvy, some oak is deployed to add complexity to all facets. Not overdone, this has gently savoury aromas sitting in beside soft tropicals. The palate is carrying additional texture and it works well, fine light tropical flavours and a gently savoury finish.

2007 **Riposte The Foil Sauvignon Blanc** *Score* **92**

ADELAIDE HILLS
Price $19.00 ✓
Quality   ★★★★
Alc./Vol. 13%
Drink   Now
Closure   Screwcap

Tim Knappstein has produced some stunning sauvignon over the years, and this is right on the mark with passionfruit and ripe green herbs. The palate drops a ball of tropical flavour, really impressive concentration, some musky texture and cleansing acid all add up to easy enjoyment.

2008 Rymill Sauvignon Blanc
Score **89**

COONAWARRA
Price $17.00 ✓
Quality ★★★ ↓
Alc./Vol. 12%
Drink Now
Closure Screwcap

Coonawarra produces some terrific sauvignon blanc thanks to a mild climate, and Rymill have really settled into stride with theirs. Cool, restrained aromas of citrus, snow peas and some tropical fruits – the palate is all juicy, crisp and flavoursome, finishing with clean musky freshness.

2007 Scotchmans Hill Sauvignon Blanc
Score **88**

GEELONG
Price $24.00
Quality ★★★ ↓
Alc./Vol. 14%
Drink Now
Closure Screwcap

A cool, grassy expression of Geelong sauvignon blanc here, showing herbaceous maritime influence. The palate has plenty of flavour, some grassy lantana and herbs, citrus fruits and crisp acid crunch.

2008 Shaw & Smith Sauvignon Blanc
Score **92**

ADELAIDE HILLS
Price $27.00
Quality ★★★★ ↓
Alc./Vol. 13%
Drink Now
Closure Screwcap

Right on the money here again for these reliable Adelaide Hills makers: passionfruit, gooseberry, gentle citrus and cut grass. Elegant wild herb and passionfruit flavours, crisply textured and tangy, this is right in the zone.

2007 Shelmerdine Sauvignon Blanc
Score **92**

YARRA VALLEY
Price $24.00 ✓
Quality ★★★★
Alc./Vol. 12.5%
Drink Now
Closure Screwcap

Made under the stewardship of De Bortoli, this is a complex rendition with some distinctly toasty, almost meaty characters. The oak is worked deep into ripe fruit aromas. The palate is crisp and zesty, with some bright apple and savoury citrus flavours. Struts through the finish with style.

2008 Shottesbrooke Adelaide Hills Sauvignon Blanc
Score **90**

ADELAIDE HILLS
Price $20.00
Quality ★★★★
Alc./Vol. 13.5%
Drink Now
Closure Screwcap

Another savvy McLaren Vale producer heads to the Hills to source cooler-grown white wine. This shows classic grass and citrus fruits, not too tropical or abrasive; it has some measure and is neatly ripened. The palate's driven by fresh piercing lemony acidity, elegant and lightweight. Good summer drinking.

2007 Shottesbrooke Sauvignon Blanc · *Score* **90**

ADELAIDE HILLS	
Price	$20.00
Quality	★★★★
Alc./Vol.	13.5%
Drink	Now
Closure	Screw

Some decent fragrance and lift, fine tropical aromas with some bath-powdery notes too; very direct. A good dollop of tropical fruit flavour, trademark Adelaide Hills passionfruit, sits along a well-balanced palate, finishing clean and neat.

2007 Smithbrook Sauvignon Blanc · *Score* **91**

PEMBERTON	
Price	$19.00 ✓
Quality	★★★★
Alc./Vol.	13%
Drink	Now
Closure	Screwcap

Pemberton certainly does deliver some impressive, restrained and minerally sauvignon blanc wines; here it's nice and flinty, and sporting some concentrated tropical fruits. The palate, more savoury than most, really flinty and elegant, has poise and refined style.

2007 Stella Bella Sauvignon Blanc · *Score* **91**

MARGARET RIVER	
Price	$20.00 ✓
Quality	★★★★
Alc./Vol.	13%
Drink	Now
Closure	Screwcap

This Margaret River savvy sports the region's trademark brazen grassy aromas, really bright and fresh fruit appeal, some tropicals emerging. The palate pushes more distinctly into passionfruit territory and there's some smooth textural charm. Neat balance, nice and fresh.

Sauvignon blanc NZ

New Zealand leads the global march of sauvignon blanc, making a huge splash in all the major markets. The style agenda has been set by the wines of Marlborough, at the top of the South Island, where the gravelly river terrace soils produce generous crops with generous flavours. The trademark sweet/sour palate is a strong feature of New Zealand savvy, the intense passionfruit and sweaty aromas are hard to miss. Plantings are increasing at a feverish rate and this along with aggressive discounting and fierce competition means that some well-known names are likely to head below the $10 mark. FOOD: Very similar to the Australian sauvignon food matchings. The main difference between the New Zealand sauvignons and their Australian counterparts (apart from popularity!) is their acidity – New Zealand typically achieves higher acids in their savvy, sometimes countered with a little sugar. Factor this into your food choices.

2007 Alana Estate Sauvignon Blanc   *Score* 90

MARTINBOROUGH	This Martinborough terrace estate delivers a mix of grassy, herbaceous aromas and some restrained tropicals, true to region with gravelly/savoury complexity. The palate delivers richer tropical fruits and lime juice flavours; a sweet, ripe finish.
Price $29.00	
Quality ★★★★	
Alc./Vol. 13%	
Drink Now	
Closure Screwcap	

2007 Amisfield Sauvignon Blanc   *Score* 90

CENTRAL OTAGO	Central Otago ain't the first stop for savvy but Amisfield has made a good fist of this savoury, flinty style. Preserved lemons and spice, lots of flinty minerals and some roundness through the palate, nice textural work and balanced melon fruit finish.
Price $30.00	
Quality ★★★★	
Alc./Vol. 13%	
Drink Now	
Closure Screwcap	

2007 Bell Echo Marlborough Sauvignon Blanc   *Score* 91

MARLBOROUGH	The junior label for the Henri Bourgeois project has an approachable style and gentle savoury mineral complexity. The palate delivers intense fruit flavour, really bright tropicals that are backed in by savoury minerals; dry, finishes long – a benchmark in the making.
Price $29.00	
Quality ★★★★	
Alc./Vol. 13.5%	
Drink Now	
Closure Screwcap	

2007 Blind River Sauvignon Blanc

Score **90**

MARLBOROUGH
Price $25.00
Quality   ★★★★
Alc./Vol. 13%
Drink   Now
Closure   Screwcap

Shows textbook Marlborough passionfruit and big aromatic punch – you won't miss this in a line-up. From the Awatere River Valley, there are gravelly minerals that carry through to the palate, ditto for the tropical fruits; nice balance, flinty finish.

2007 Catalina Sounds Sauvignon Blanc

Score **91**

MARLBOROUGH
Price $22.00 ✓
Quality   ★★★★
Alc./Vol. 13.5%
Drink   Now
Closure   Screwcap

This has attractive complexity; gently tweaked tropical fruits are delivered in intense form, really fresh and memorable. The palate packs similar impact and pungent ripe tropical flavours, plenty of cleansing acid crunch and lingering passionfruit flavour. Bright as a button, it will please the entire party.

2007 Churton Sauvignon Blanc

Score **91**

MARLBOROUGH 🍃
Price $25.00 ✓
Quality   ★★★★
Alc./Vol. 13.5%
Drink   Now
Closure   Cork

A smaller operation with a focus on quality, this is quite intense and has some savoury grassy aromas ahead of gentle, refined tropical fruits – an engaging style. The palate texture is full and focused, balance is a hallmark and there's plenty of long, fine tropical fruit flavour. Superb.

2007 Clos Henri Sauvignon Blanc

Score **93**

MARLBOROUGH
Price $39.00
Quality   ★★★★┥
Alc./Vol. 13.6%
Drink   Now
Closure   Screwcap

A southern hemisphere outpost for the Sancerre producer, Henri Bourgeois, close-planted and Euro-inspired. The fruit has some savoury complexity here, flinty and spicy, tropicals are on show. Terrific texture and weight, balanced, complex and layered palate; impressive wine, driving dry finish.

2007 Craggy Range Avery Vineyard Sauvignon Blanc

Score **92**

MARLBOROUGH
Price $32.00 ✓
Quality   ★★★★┥
Alc./Vol. 13%
Drink   Now
Closure   Screwcap

The Avery vineyard sits in Marlborough's stony river-bed soils. This has intense river pebble and savoury herb aromas, really distinctive. The palate is the most luscious of the Craggy sauvignons, showing rounder passionfruit and guava flavour, soft flesh through the middle and a peach-skin finish.

2007 Craggy Range Old Renwick Vineyard Sauvignon Blanc   *Score* **93**

MARLBOROUGH
Price $32.00 ✓
Quality   ★★★★ ⅃
Alc./Vol.   13%
Drink   Now
Closure   Screwcap

The Old Renwick Vineyard produces a powerful style of Marlborough sauvignon; an intense floral, almost honeysuckle aroma, and some sweet kiwifruit too. There's plenty of crisp acidity beneath dense savoury minerals and green papaya and peach fruit flavour. Really distinctive, shows lovely finesse.

2007 Craggy Range Te Muna Road Vineyard Sauvignon Blanc   *Score* **94**

MARTINBOROUGH
Price $32.00 ✓
Quality   ★★★★ ⅃
Alc./Vol.   13.5%
Drink   Now
Closure   Screwcap

This single-vineyard wine is always one of the highlights of the New Zealand sauvignon blanc brigade, it's more restrained and almost riesling-like, refreshingly understated, yet still amazingly intense. Aromas are super fine and there's a strong thread of lime citrus throughout, some just ripe nectarine and bracing mineral drive through the finish. Brilliant purity and convincing length.

2007 The Crossings Marlborough Sauvignon Blanc   *Score* **91**

MARLBOROUGH
Price $17.00 ✓
Quality   ★★★★
Alc./Vol.   13.5%
Drink   Now
Closure   Screwcap

A more fragrant, savoury and restrained savvy from the stunning Awatere Valley in Marlborough. Fresh citrus, stone fruits and some tropicals too, there's gentle leafy complexity and gravelly river pebble aromas. The palate packs zesty acidity, nectarine, white peach and citrus flavours. Delicious stuff!

2007 Crowded House Sauvignon Blanc   *Score* **89**

MARLBOROUGH 🖋
Price $18.00
Quality   ★★★ ⅃
Alc./Vol.   13%
Drink   Now
Closure   Screwcap

Crowded House, sauvignon blanc and New Zealand make a handy trifecta, and all in the one bottle – amazing! You can't help but smile at the cheeky cachet of the name; the wine's a sound, grassy array of tropical fruits and bright crisp acid crunch. An easy, melodic style.

2007 Dog Point Sauvignon Blanc   *Score* **93**

MARLBOROUGH
Price $24.00 ✓
Quality   ★★★★ ⅃
Alc./Vol.   13.5%
Drink   Now
Closure   Screwcap

One of the more restrained Marlborough savvies, this shies away from the overt tropical territory and into melons, apple, grapefruit and white peach. There's an innate sense of balance and focus in this wine that shines out from the pack. Sauvignon with class.

2006 Dog Point Section 94   *Score* **94**

MARLBOROUGH 🖋
Price $34.00 ✓
Quality   ★★★★ ⫯
Alc./Vol. 13.5%
Drink   2009
Closure   Cork

This is one of the smartest, most complex sauvignons on the market, showing fully worked, barrel-matured complexity. It's not all smoke and mirrors though, the fruit behind is piercing and intense. Ripe citrus and nectarine fruits, some more exotic tropical notes, the palate sizzles with intensity and cleverly balanced lees-derived richness. All class.

2008 Fairhall Downs Single Vineyard Sauvignon Blanc   *Score* **88**

MARLBOROUGH
Price $19.00
Quality   ★★★ ⫯
Alc./Vol. 13.5%
Drink   Now
Closure   Screwcap

A straight-shooting mix of tropical and citrus fruit aromas, this smells fresh and bright, very much in the pungent Marlborough style. The palate is all about the passionfruit, really juicy intense pulpy flavour and relatively soft texture. Easy-drinking style.

2007 Falveys Sauvignon Blanc   *Score* **89**

MARLBOROUGH
Price $24.00
Quality   ★★★ ⫯
Alc./Vol. 13.5%
Drink   Now
Closure   Screwcap

This Omaka Valley estate wine has attractive flinty complexity, spices and grassy, grapefruit aromas. The palate is full and rolls through on a ripe textural slide, plenty of rich stone fruit flavours, a soft finish.

2007 Forrest Estate Sauvignon Blanc   *Score* **91**

MARLBOROUGH
Price $23.00 ✓
Quality   ★★★★
Alc./Vol. 14%
Drink   Now
Closure   Screwcap

Big John Forrest has delivered a cracking '07 Marlborough sauvignon, plenty of bright ripe tropical fruits, mango, passionfruit, pawpaw – you name it, some herbs in the background too. The palate's ripe and rich, it really strikes fine acid balance and flavours linger long through the finish.

2007 Framingham Sauvignon Blanc   *Score* **90**

MARLBOROUGH
Price $21.00
Quality   ★★★★
Alc./Vol. 13%
Drink   Now
Closure   Screwcap

This is a straight-down-the-line Marlborough sauvignon blanc, with plenty of ripe lifted tropical fruit aromas and bright aromatics. The palate is full and rich, acidity cuts into the fruit delivering balance and a zesty sparkling tropical-flavoured finish.

2008 Giesen Marlborough Sauvignon Blanc

Score **91**

MARLBOROUGH	
Price	$18.00 ✓
Quality	★★★★
Alc./Vol.	13%
Drink	Now
Closure	Screwcap

Fresh and exotic, this has some betel leaf and shaved fennel, fresh zesty citrus fruit aromas and lime juice. The palate delivers all the tropical fruit you could ever wish for, intense passionfruit flavour; they've struck the right deal between acidity and sugar, long fruit finish.

PENGUIN BEST NEW ZEALAND SAUVIGNON BLANC

2008 Greystone Sauvignon Blanc

Score **92**

WAIPARA	
Price	$23.00 ✓
Quality	★★★★
Alc./Vol.	13%
Drink	Now
Closure	Screwcap

Intense pear fruits, sweet fragrant aromatics and impressive intensity, this is a striking style emanating from the Waipara region near Canterbury. The palate has decent chew and cut, there's plenty of acidity to back up rich stone fruit and pear flavours, gentle tropical finish.

2007 Herzog Sauvignon Blanc

Score **93**

MARLBOROUGH	
Price	$53.00
Quality	★★★★ ⌐
Alc./Vol.	13.5%
Drink	Now
Closure	Cork

Well, you'd want a few extras thrown in for this relatively high price tag. Hans Herzog has given us low yields, barrel fermentation in the finest of French wood and some stirring of the yeast lees to enrich texture – it's more a complex white than a sauvignon blanc. Certainly registers on the nose: ripe tropical fruits beneath punchy French oak aromas, some grapefruit citrus and superior complexity. The palate texture is superb and the intensity of fruit is there to carry all the complexity; creamy flavours and a spicy toasted nutmeg finish. Orchestral.

2007 Hesketh Hidden Garden Sauvignon Blanc

Score **88**

MARLBOROUGH	
Price	$20.00
Quality	★★★ ⌐
Alc./Vol.	13%
Drink	Now
Closure	Screwcap

John Hesketh is parlaying wines from several countries and regions into one banner, aiming at a global wine enterprise. Some oyster shell minerals on the nose, green apples and zesty tropical notes. The palate's crisp, more apples, not super concentrated but nicely balanced all the same.

2007 Hunter's Sauvignon Blanc

Score **89**

MARLBOROUGH
Price $23.00
Quality   ★★★⌐
Alc./Vol. 13%
Drink   Now
Closure   Screwcap

Essentially a family-owned smaller Marlborough operation and one of the pioneers of the region's sauvignon trade. Attractive lime juice, tropical fruits and grassy aromas here, the palate runs a balanced line of sweetness and acidity, finishing fresh with lime zest and passionfruit flavour.

2007 Isabel Estate Sauvignon Blanc

Score **88**

MARLBOROUGH
Price $25.00
Quality   ★★★⌐
Alc./Vol. 13.5%
Drink   Now
Closure   Screwcap

If you like them in a bigger style, this Marlborough sauvignon has plenty of winemaking boost. Quite a honeyed leesy nose, some grass and citrus fruit aromas. The palate moves in big sweeping layers, very worked-up texture, full tropical flavours and a stony mineral finish.

2007 Jackson Estate Sauvignon Blanc

Score **92**

MARLBOROUGH
Price $24.00 ✓
Quality   ★★★★
Alc./Vol. 13.5%
Drink   Now
Closure   Screwcap

This estate is one of the best farmed and most savvy of savvy producers, it makes a style deeply linked into their Marlborough terroir – the varietal character is on song. Limes and bright fine tropical edges, really precise, some minerals dance at the edges, fine and long.

2007 Lawson's Dry Hills Sauvignon Blanc

Score **90**

MARLBOROUGH
Price $22.00 ✓
Quality   ★★★★
Alc./Vol. 13%
Drink   Now
Closure   Screwcap

This small winery has its eye on the quality end of the spectrum. Subtle gravelly/savoury minerals and fine citrusy fruits here. The texture is subtly enhanced by French oak and the flavours emerge with fragrance and bright tropical appeal.

2007 Mahi Marlborough Sauvignon Blanc

Score **93**

MARLBOROUGH
Price $22.00 ✓
Quality   ★★★★⌐
Alc./Vol. 13.5%
Drink   Now
Closure   Screwcap

Mahi make a complex, lime and lemon grass style; there's restraint, and it's a welcome break from the pungent Marlborough assault. The use of wild yeast and partial barrel fermentation works well, the texture is complete and supple, there's some gentle creamy flavour and grassy/savoury elements, finishing with passionfruit and a nutty French oak twist. A triumph!

2007 Main Divide Sauvignon Blanc

Score **89**

MARLBOROUGH	
Price	$22.00
Quality	★★★ ⟊
Alc./Vol.	13%
Drink	Now
Closure	Screwcap

A bright, fresh savvy from the Pegasus Bay crew; sourcing fruit from outside their home region, this has softer minerally aromatics, not pungent or obtuse, smells attractive and gently tropical scented. The palate's carrying some sweetness, more tropical fruits here, even and supple.

2007 Martinborough Vineyards Te Tera Sauvignon Blanc

Score **91**

MARTINBOROUGH	
Price	$29.00
Quality	★★★★
Alc./Vol.	13%
Drink	Now
Closure	Screwcap

This is a zesty, lime and kiwifruit style of savvy, super fresh and bright, attractive grassy characters, there's plenty to enjoy here. The palate has decent richness and flavoursome appeal, more in the tropical fruit spectrum, passionfruit flavours, gentle balance.

2008 Matua Valley Hawkes Bay Sauvignon Blanc

Score **(90–92)**

HAWKES BAY	
Price	$17.00 ✓
Quality	★★★★ ⟊
Alc./Vol.	12%
Drink	Now
Closure	Screwcap

This has clean grassy aromas, citrus and guava, some passionfruit and mango in there too; really tropical. The palate blazes passionfruit flavour, pure and singular, neatly balanced with some softness through the finish – approachable and easy.

2007 Mount Nelson Sauvignon Blanc

Score **88**

MARLBOROUGH	
Price	$22.00
Quality	★★★ ⟊
Alc./Vol.	12.8%
Drink	Now
Closure	Screwcap

A famous Super-Tuscan, Lodovico Antinori, has planted a foot in Marlborough and is making a clean, dry, savoury style of Marlborough sauvignon. Grassy with some tropical notes, there's a hint of grapefruit and passionfruit through the finish.

2007 Mud House Sauvignon Blanc

Score **87**

MARLBOROUGH	
Price	$22.00
Quality	★★★ ⟊
Alc./Vol.	13%
Drink	Now
Closure	Screwcap

Leafy and gravel-scented wine, it has some wild mountain herbs too. The palate is rich, this has juicy ripeness, plenty of tropical fruits and looks a bit thick and heavy, needs a good chill to tighten it up.

2007 Neudorf Sauvignon Blanc
Score 93

NELSON
Price $28.00
Quality ★★★★ ⅃
Alc./Vol. 13.5%
Drink Now
Closure Screwcap

One of the later release sauvignon wines, this is left on lees for a little longer to work some texture into the equation. Classic passionfruit, some fine mineral notes, gravelly and savoury too. The palate texture is superb with flinty crisp flavour and soft, rounded edges. Great acidity and convincing length.

2008 Old Coach Road Sauvignon Blanc
Score 88

NELSON
Price $19.00 ✓
Quality ★★★ ⅃
Alc./Vol. 12.5%
Drink Now
Closure Screwcap

This has a spicy side: fennel and anise aromas, really striking and a step out of the ordinary. The palate is full, quite rich and juicy, has some textural roundness and slippery mouthfeel, nectarine and tropical fruit flavours, a smooth balanced finish.

2007 Overstone Sauvignon Blanc
Score 88

HAWKES BAY
Price $13.00
Quality ★★★ ⅃
Alc./Vol. 13%
Drink Now
Closure Screwcap

Minerally/gravelly aromas here, subtle herbs and citrus blossom, quite restrained, some faint honeysuckle too – really steps away from the tropicals. The palate weighs in with juicy, bright citrus flavour, gentle tropicals make an appearance, neatly balanced.

2007 Palliser Estate Sauvignon Blanc
Score 91

MARTINBOROUGH
Price $25.00 ✓
Quality ★★★★
Alc./Vol. 13.5%
Drink Now
Closure Screwcap

Palliser's 2007 sauvignon sits very much in the regional grass and gravel style, with bright citrus and tropical fruits rolled through. The palate heads into tropical territory with passionfruit pulp and lime juice flavours; plenty to enjoy, neat balance.

2007 Pencarrow Sauvignon Blanc
Score 90

MARTINBOROUGH
Price $22.50 ✓
Quality ★★★★
Alc./Vol. 13%
Drink Now
Closure Screwcap

The junior label from Palliser Estate; this is a grassy and unmistakably New Zealand savvy with bright aromatics, herbs and snow peas. Intense passionfruit flavour on the palate and bracing acidity, a little chalky texture through the finish – long on flavour and great value.

2008 Richmond Plains Nelson Sauvignon Blanc   *Score* (88–90)

NELSON	Super fresh and built on sweet aromatics, this has
Price $23.00	passionfruit, guava, some gooseberry and mango; there's
Quality ★★★⫶–★★★★	a grassy side there too. The palate has decent weight
Alc./Vol. 13%	and some textural richness, plenty of passionfruit and
Drink Now	gooseberry flavour, finishing fresh.
Closure Screwcap	

2007 Saint Clair Pioneer Block 4 Sawcut Sauvignon Blanc   *Score* 92

MARLBOROUGH	This is a grassy and herbaceaous style, quite gravelly and
Price $29.00	infinitely more savoury on the nose. It has a piercing
Quality ★★★★	quality and fine savoury minerals that drive through
Alc./Vol. 13.5%	tropical and citrus flavours; attractive for its combined
Drink Now	elegance and sheer intensity.
Closure Screwcap	

2007 Saint Clair Pioneer Block 2 Swamp Sauvignon Blanc   *Score* 93

MARLBOROUGH	Sourced from a plot near Cloudy Bay – the place not the
Price $29.00	winery, a cooler location in the scheme of the Marlborough
Quality ★★★★⫶	region – this delivers added fruit intensity. Plenty of
Alc./Vol. 13%	richness is evident on both the nose and the palate;
Drink Now	pungent passionfruit and gooseberry, juicy, textural and
Closure Screwcap	smoothly balanced.

2007 Saint Clair Sauvignon Blanc   *Score* 90

MARLBOROUGH	Superb varietal and regional integrity here, this is one
Price $21.50	big glass of ripe tropical fruit that's oozing with intensity
Quality ★★★★	and richness. The palate's smoothly trimmed, crisp and
Alc./Vol. 13%	flavoursome, it delivers more than the average, with
Drink Now	balanced impact.
Closure Screwcap	

2008 Secret Stone Sauvignon Blanc   *Score* (88–90)

MARLBOROUGH	Matua's Secret Stone has delivered reliably again in 2008;
Price $21.00	this has some fennel and betel leaf aromas, gentle methoxy
Quality ★★★⫶–★★★★	here too. The palate is crisp with some sweaty flavour, lime
Alc./Vol. 13%	juice citrus and bright crisp acidity. Finishes really fresh.
Drink Now	
Closure Screwcap	

2007 **Spy Valley Sauvignon Blanc**

Score **89**

MARLBOROUGH
Price $22.00
Quality   ★★★ ┤
Alc./Vol. 13%
Drink   Now
Closure   Screwcap

Some bright tropical fruits and leafy, grassy aromas here, plenty of ripeness and a real focus on fresh fruit fragrance. The palate has pleasant richness and textural roundness, packed with passionfruit flavour and a soft approachable balance. Big on drinkability.

2007 **Staete Landt Estate Grown Marlborough Sauvignon**

Score **91**

MARLBOROUGH
Price $25.00 ✓
Quality   ★★★★
Alc./Vol. 13.5%
Drink   Now
Closure   Screwcap

This small operation has a prime piece of Marlborough real estate and works with attention to detail. No surprise then that the wine is excellent! There are fragrant, savoury minerals driving the nose; the palate has charming texture and rich tropical fruit flavours, a flinty, smoky finish.

2007 **Stoneleigh Sauvignon Blanc**

Score **89**

MARLBOROUGH
Price $21.00
Quality   ★★★ ┤
Alc./Vol. 13%
Drink   Now
Closure   Screwcap

Something of a catch-all style, made to encompass everything that's great about the Marlborough region/ sauvignon blanc combination. Intense, ripe passionfruit aromas, very fragrant and intense; there's some really punchy flavours dealt out here, tropical delight from start to finish.

Semillon

The most esteemed semillon in Australia belongs to the Hunter Valley. There, the early ripening, low-alcohol fruit produces wines that are in their youth typically piercing, full of fine lemon flavour and even slightly grassy. Hunter semillons are revered for their capacity to age, evolving through the full array of lemon possibilities, eventually becoming toasty and delicate. They also represent extremely good value and are readily available as both young and old wines. The Barossa Valley has a long history with semillon, making a richer, riper style with cut straw as well as lemon character. Some Barossa producers wood-age their wines, while others prefer the unwooded styles, the latter being more suited to ageing. The Clare Valley has a number of excellent examples, and over in Margaret River the coastal conditions produce distinctly grassy semillon wines, pungent and easily distinguished. The common thread is that of value. FOOD: For the leaner Hunter semillons, think of simple steamed fish and crisp crunchy salads; tomato is great too, gazpacho in warmer weather. Aged examples and the richer Barossa styles complement chicken, grilled fish and some richer sauces.

2007 Andrew Thomas Braemore Semillon — *Score* **94**

HUNTER VALLEY	
Price	$25.00 ✓
Quality	★★★★ ┤
Alc./Vol.	11%
Drink	2013
Closure	Screwcap

The Braemore vineyard has a handy reputation among Hunter winemakers. Thomas crafts the restrained intense fruit into a traditional style: the nose sparkles with focused, pristine lemon fruit aromas, some dry straw in there too. Superb cut and brilliant sparkle on the palate, an unwavering line of lemon flavour, serious acidity to protect its future.

PENGUIN BEST SEMILLON

2007 Andrew Thomas The O.C. Semillon — *Score* **93**

HUNTER VALLEY	
Price	$20.00 ✓
Quality	★★★★ ┤
Alc./Vol.	12%
Drink	Now
Closure	Screwcap

One of the great modern Hunter semillon wines of the last few years. Andrew Thomas captures a rich, flavoursome expression of ripe lemon fruit and waxy/savoury complexity. The palate has some weight and richness, delivered with elegant style, the acidity sails out through the finish, crisp and clean. Approachable, superb.

2005 Bethany Semillon
Score **93**

BAROSSA VALLEY
Price $18.00 ✓
Quality ★★★★ᵻ
Alc./Vol. 13.5%
Drink Now
Closure Screwcap

Bethany has worked a treat with this barrel-fermented '05, it's built attractive toasty complexity, some bottle-derived savoury notes too, lemon butter – smells terrific. The palate has superb richness: lemon sherbet to start, fleshy texture through the middle and a toasty, nutty twist through the finish. Complex and complete.

2007 Cockfighter's Ghost Semillon
Score **92**

HUNTER VALLEY
Price $19.00 ✓
Quality ★★★★
Alc./Vol. 11.6%
Drink 2010
Closure Screwcap

A restrained, herbs-and-wax Hunter semillon, some lemon pithy smells and dried herb notes. Terrific balance and crisp lemony appeal, the palate carries decent weight and richness through the finish. Plenty to enjoy now and the promise of even more in the future.

2007 David Hook Old Vines Semillon
Score **88**

HUNTER VALLEY
Price $25.00
Quality ★★★ᵻ
Alc./Vol. 10.5%
Drink 2012
Closure Screwcap

A distinct straw and honeysuckle set of aromas, sweet lemon peel, citrus oil and savoury essence. There's decent power and drive on the palate, more savoury cut straw and dry citrus fruits; these old vines provide some cleansing acid bite.

2007 Glenguin Estate The Old Broke Block Semillon
Score **93**

HUNTER VALLEY
Price $20.00 ✓
Quality ★★★★ᵻ
Alc./Vol. 11%
Drink 2012
Closure Screwcap

Smells like a classic Hunter: lemon pith and savoury dry cut straw, some gentle herbs running behind. The palate has superbly stated elegance and searing acidity that drives fine lemony flavour along a sharp line through the finish. Brilliant.

2007 Henschke Louis Semillon
Score **92**

EDEN VALLEY 🍷
Price $28.00
Quality ★★★★
Alc./Vol. 12.5%
Drink 2011
Closure Screwcap

The Eden Valley makes a fine, restrained style of semillon; there's even some flinty regional accents too, and pristine lime oils. Supple fruit palate – really smoothly textured and elegant; these old vines (50 years) deliver innate balance. Guaranteed to age superbly.

2006 Juniper Estate Semillon
Score **94**

MARGARET RIVER
Price $27.00 ✓
Quality ★★★★ ┤
Alc./Vol. 12.5%
Drink Now
Closure Screwcap

Juniper give their semillon some work in the winery, it emerges with handsome barrel-fermented complexity built around savoury lemon and grassy varietal characters. The palate texture is elegant yet complex, lemon peel and nutty French oak; beautifully judged.

2007 Krinklewood Semillon
Score **93**

HUNTER VALLEY 🔖
Price $20.00 ✓
Quality ★★★★ ┤
Alc./Vol. 10.2%
Drink Now
Closure Screwcap

Really rich aromas here for Hunter semillon, heading into tropical territory, almost guava and passionfruit – mouth-watering stuff. The palate carries the same passionfruit flavour, some lime and lemon too, rich and zesty, full of flavoursome appeal, finishing dry and juicy.

2007 Meerea Park Epoch Semillon
Score **92**

HUNTER VALLEY
Price $19.00 ✓
Quality ★★★★
Alc./Vol. 11%
Drink 2011
Closure Screwcap

Aromas of savoury lemon grass and fine dry chalk, really restrained and pure, delicate hints of cut straw. The palate is super fine, really precise and polished, some lime and lemon citrus fruits, fine acidity and a soft, delicate texture.

2008 Meerea Park Hell Hole Semillon
Score **91**

HUNTER VALLEY
Price $25.00
Quality ★★★★
Alc./Vol. 10.5%
Drink 2010
Closure Screwcap

A pristine lemon and grass expression here, really bright and effusive savoury citrus notes. The palate brings some crisp green lemon and faint tropical fruits in the background, fine acidity, super fresh and tidy through the finish.

2008 Mistletoe Home Vineyard Semillon
Score **89**

HUNTER VALLEY
Price $18.00
Quality ★★★ ┤
Alc./Vol. 9.5%
Drink 2010
Closure Screwcap

A youthful and super-grassy semillon with restrained early-picked characters, it smells of lemon-scented gum leaves. The palate is super zesty and has bracing acid crunch, tingles away with restrained waxy lemon flavour, crisp finish.

2007 Mistletoe Reserve Semillon
Score 93

HUNTER VALLEY	
Price	$22.00 ✓
Quality	★★★★ ↓
Alc./Vol.	10%
Drink	2014
Closure	Screwcap

It's well worth stepping up to this bargain reserve-level bottling; there's super-fresh lemon citrus and some really concentrated lemon oil smells – impressive nose. The palate's a savoury, crisp crunchy acid style, pristine flavours stop for nothing, riding fast and long on racy acidity. Brilliant!

2007 Mitchell Semillon
Score 90

CLARE VALLEY	
Price	$21.00
Quality	★★★★
Alc./Vol.	13.5%
Drink	Now
Closure	Screwcap

This Watervale semillon is as fresh as a crisp spring morning in the Clare Valley, really delicate and elegant; soft citrus aromas are gently sweetened by some well-applied oak. It's elegant on the palate too, with a chalky smooth texture and brisk lemon flavour, gentle oak spice through the finish.

2008 Molly Morgan Semillon
Score 90

HUNTER VALLEY	
Price	$20.00
Quality	★★★★
Alc./Vol.	11.5%
Drink	2009
Closure	Screwcap

Super-bright lemon zest aromas – really fresh and primary – and hints of lemon grass; this is all about the fruit and they've done well to get it this fresh in 2008. Supple and approachable palate is an attractive mix of citrus and tropical flavours, all pulled into shape by a crisp line of acid through the finish.

2007 Mount Horrocks Semillon
Score 92

CLARE VALLEY	
Price	$27.00
Quality	★★★★
Alc./Vol.	13.5%
Drink	2011
Closure	Screwcap

One of the Clare Valley's semillon champions, this has trademark savoury French oak influence, bright ripe lemons and lighter, more fragrant fruit aromas across the top. The palate packs some weight and chew, the oak adds attractive spice and structure to lemon fruit flavours and some toast to the crunchy youthful finish.

2003 Mount Pleasant Cellar Release Elizabeth Semillon
Score 93

HUNTER VALLEY	
Price	$17.00 ✓
Quality	★★★★ ↓
Alc./Vol.	11.5%
Drink	Now
Closure	Cork

The days of buying these phenomenal wines at these prices must be well and truly numbered. Scintillating lemon drop and gentle toast build in this classic Hunter semillon. The palate has enriched with some time in bottle, lemon citrus flavours sit fresh, some lanolin through the finish, pinned into place with bracing acidity; gentle toast as it fades.

2006 Mount Pleasant Lovedale Semillon — *Score* **96**

HUNTER VALLEY	
Price	$38.00 ✓
Quality	★★★★★
Alc./Vol.	10.5%
Drink	2012
Closure	Screwcap

Lovedale under screwcap is a beautiful thing! The fine McWilliams style is perfectly presented, lemon and lime blossom, super-restrained and pristine citrus fruit. There's a superb play between intensity and restraint, fine citrus flavour and a spear of crisp acidity, edgy and engaging.

2006 Peter Lehmann Semillon — *Score* **91**

BAROSSA VALLEY	
Price	$13.50 ✓
Quality	★★★★
Alc./Vol.	12%
Drink	Now
Closure	Screwcap

One of THE great-value white wines; made in significant volume with reliable quality, this '06 has plenty of the Barossa straw bale and lanolin, some lemon blossom, honey will come in time. The palate is in scintillatingly fresh, clean-cut shape, superbly balanced and set to age like a charm.

2007 Ravensworth Semillon — *Score* **90**

HUNTER VALLEY	
Price	$18.00
Quality	★★★★
Alc./Vol.	10%
Drink	2010
Closure	Screwcap

Bryan Martin's inaugural take on Hunter semillon delivers a mix of savoury dried herbs, lemon grass and gentle waxy green apple notes. There's a richness running through the palate, plenty of waxy flavour and lemon-scented herbs, finishing dry and clean.

2004 St Hallett Semillon — *Score* **92**

BAROSSA VALLEY	
Price	$19.00 ✓
Quality	★★★★
Alc./Vol.	11.5%
Drink	Now
Closure	Screwcap

It's a boon that this aged example is available, especially at the sub-$20 price. Lemon balm, wax and honeysuckle, some pristine freshness still intact. The palate carries the same mix of characters, smoky oak toast evident too, bright crisp acid – years of further complexity ahead, for those who wait.

2007 Vasse Felix Semillon — *Score* **93**

MARGARET RIVER	
Price	$25.00 ✓
Quality	★★★★ ┤
Alc./Vol.	12.5%
Drink	Now
Closure	Screwcap

A tidy lemon grass, herb and citrus style of semillon, and right in the regional groove, showing subtle barrel-ferment texture and complexity. It's gently worked, honed in on acidity, and finishes fresh, long and convincing.

Semillon sauvignon blanc blends

Inspired by the great white wines of Bordeaux, blends of semillon and sauvignon blanc, in either order, have enjoyed great success in Australia. Vibrant, crisp, light- to medium-bodied white wines, made in an early-drinking style. Western Australia has developed a keen following for the dual blend, and for wines with other varieties added, coining the Classic Dry White. The grassy semillon grown in Western Australia lends itself to the tropical sauvignon blanc, adding structure and intensity to the blend. Many other regions have followed suit and you'll find good examples anywhere these two varieties are grown. The majority are made in stainless steel, although some producers add French oak and additional winemaking for a more complex, textured style. FOOD: These wines are super versatile, so the main factor in getting the food-matching on track is to understand which variety has the upper hand. Certain foods will draw semillon's citrusy characters out of the wine, particularly citrus-based dressings on fresh summer salads; and don't be afraid of seafood either, it will be a handy partner to these easygoing whites.

2007 Burnbrae Sauvignon Blanc Semillon   Score 87

ORANGE/MUDGEE	Roughly two-thirds sauvignon blanc from Orange and one-third semillon from Mudgee, this has some cool-climate restraint. Grassy tropical fruits and lemony citrus flavours, neatly balanced and zesty through the finish.
Price $18.00	
Quality ★★★ ↑	
Alc./Vol. 11.5%	
Drink Now	
Closure Screwcap	

2006 Cape Mentelle Wallcliffe Vineyard Sauvignon Blanc Semillon   Score 95

MARGARET RIVER 🍃	The Wallcliffe vineyard – a southerly outcrop on Margaret River's rugged coastal country – has old (1970) vines; this all adds up to extra intensity in the wine. Showing youthful assertive lemon and lime fruits, some richer tropical aromas, winemaking and French oak complexity. The palate has impressive shape and thrust, really powerful and textural, long citrus and tight tropical flavours with piercing acid drive. Will age superbly too.
Price $38.00	
Quality ★★★★ ↑	
Alc./Vol. 12.5%	
Drink 2010	
Closure Screwcap	

PENGUIN BEST SEMILLON SAUVIGNON BLANC BLEND

2007 Capel Vale Regional Series Semillon Sauvignon Blanc *Score* 91

PEMBERTON
Price $23.00 ✓
Quality ★★★★
Alc./Vol. 12.5%
Drink   Now
Closure Screwcap

This shows some Pemberton coolness, still nice and ripe though, with tropical sauvignon blanc aromas, citrusy semillon fruits and grassy complexity, bright and light. The palate delivers a fine line of soft tropical fruit flavour, gentle precise acidity and terrific balance. Winning drinkability.

2007 Cartwheel Semillon Sauvignon Blanc *Score* 91

MARGARET RIVER
Price $23.00 ✓
Quality ★★★★
Alc./Vol. 13%
Drink   Now
Closure Screwcap

A punchy regional statement, plenty of grassy semillon leading the charge really pins it to the Margaret River region. Some tropicals fall in behind, this is super fresh and pure. The palate brings more passionfruit sauvignon flavour into play, backed by citrusy semillon, finishing crisp and dry.

2007 Clairault Semillon Sauvignon Blanc *Score* 93

MARGARET RIVER
Price $22.00 ✓
Quality ★★★★ ⁴
Alc./Vol. 13%
Drink   Now
Closure Screwcap

This has had some impressive success on the wine show rounds, and it's easy to see why. Stunning concentration and aromatic intensity, bright tropical fruits and gravelly/savoury complexity. The palate is piercing and direct, impressive grassy cut through lighter juicy tropical flavour. Great length and presence.

2007 Cullen Mangan Vineyard Semillon Sauvignon Blanc *Score* 93

MARGARET RIVER 🖎
Price $35.00
Quality ★★★★ ⁴
Alc./Vol. 13.5%
Drink   2010
Closure Screwcap

The family's Mangan vineyard brings brighter, more flippant, lifted fruit to the semillon-sauvignon blend. Just tropical fruits, grassy semillon, melons and citrus fruits here, with a nice savoury spiced oak overlay. The palate has intense passionfruit and lemon flavour, balanced and upbeat, finishes super fresh.

2007 Cullen Vineyard Sauvignon Blanc Semillon *Score* 94

MARGARET RIVER 🖎
Price $35.00 ✓
Quality ★★★★ ⁴
Alc./Vol. 13%
Drink   2011
Closure Screwcap

From the home vineyard, lovely depth and ripeness, some gravelly complexity, flinty, bright citrus, ripe grassy herbs too – all superbly integrated. Piercing, direct palate, bright citrus flavours and a smooth nutty-oak overlay, harmonious texture and balance, long and fresh.

2007 Cuttaway Hill Semillon Sauvignon Blanc   *Score* **90**

SOUTHERN HIGHLANDS
Price $18.00 ✓
Quality   ★★★★
Alc./Vol. 10.5%
Drink   Now
Closure   Screwcap

This cool-climate beauty has passionfruit pulp aromas, really fresh and delicate, some minerals in there, too, and waxy lemon grass. Super-fine palate: lemons and gentle tropicals, really crisp and elegant, soft fine acidity holds it up nice and fresh. Balanced and even.

2007 Devil's Lair Fifth Leg White   *Score* **88**

WESTERN AUSTRALIA
Price $16.00 ✓
Quality   ★★★ ┤
Alc./Vol. 13%
Drink   Now
Closure   Screwcap

This flippant white blend calls on chardonnay to lend a hand to sauvignon blanc and semillon, filling out the wine and broadening its appeal. The nose is bright and matches melons with ripe tropical fruits. The palate is soft and easy, chardonnay rounds out the texture, fruit salad flavour and gently balanced.

2007 Dividing Range Sauvignon Blanc Colombard Chardonnay *Score* **85**

SOUTH EASTERN AUSTRALIA
Price $10.00 ✓
Quality   ★★★
Alc./Vol. 12.5%
Drink   Now
Closure   Screwcap

Plenty of wine here for 10 bucks: mixed melons and tropical fruit aromas, very straight-up-the-line primary fruits. Pineapple flavoured palate, crisp tropicals, even and well blended.

2007 Evans & Tate Classic   *Score* **89**

MARGARET RIVER
Price $19.00
Quality   ★★★ ┤
Alc./Vol. 13%
Drink   Now
Closure   Screwcap

Once E & T's super brand, this semillon sauvignon blanc is a classic (sorry) mix of tropical passionfruit and gentle grassy herbal notes. The palate's in super-smooth, crisp shape with plenty of zesty flavour, sweetness and acidity play out through the finish to impressive effect.

2007 Ferngrove Symbols Sauvignon Blanc Semillon   *Score* **88**

WESTERN AUSTRALIA
Price $16.00
Quality   ★★★ ┤
Alc./Vol. 14%
Drink   Now
Closure   Screwcap

This entry-level Ferngrove cheapie has some cool southern style to it, plenty of gravelly herbal notes, green capsicum and some passionfruit. It all works well together. Lovely sweet-fruited palate with an abundance of fresh passionfruit pulp; sugar and alcohol just smudge the finish though.

2007 Fire Gully Sauvignon Blanc Semillon

Score 92

MARGARET RIVER	
Price	$28.00
Quality	★ ★ ★ ★
Alc./Vol.	14%
Drink	Now
Closure	Screwcap

Pierro's stylish second-tier wine is a cool, restrained Margaret River blend, showing bright tropical and melon fruits, gentle grassy notes too. The palate's crisp and sports impressive focus and textural class often missing in these blends; lingering, sizzling acidity keeps lemon and green mango flavours burning long through the finish.

2007 Frog Rock Semillon Sauvignon Blanc

Score 89

MUDGEE	
Price	$15.00 ✓
Quality	★ ★ ★ ┤
Alc./Vol.	11%
Drink	Now
Closure	Screwcap

From a cool outpost in Mudgee, this little gem has a compact, elegant understated style – a classic crisp dry white. The nose is waxy and lemon-scented, some tropical fragrance in the background. A fine low-alcohol palate, lemons and cut straw, savoury through the finish.

2007 Gapstead Valley Selection Sauvignon Blanc Semillon

Score 87

SOUTH EASTERN AUSTRALIA	
Price	$16.00 ✓
Quality	★ ★ ★ ┤
Alc./Vol.	12%
Drink	Now
Closure	Screwcap

A 50/50 blend with fruit coming from Gundagai, the Adelaide Hills and around Victoria. It has classic bright sauvignon aromatics, passionfruit and pineapple aromas and flavours, and a tidy, crisp balance.

2006 Grant Burge Zerk Semillon Viognier

Score 89

BAROSSA VALLEY	
Price	$21.00 ✓
Quality	★ ★ ★ ┤
Alc./Vol.	13%
Drink	Now
Closure	Screwcap

Pretty much unique, this was once a straight semillon (and a good one at that); it leads with semillon's bright lemon juice aromas, some straw and orange citrus. The palate rides on semillon's sturdy core of citrus fruit, viognier adds apricot and other stone fruit flesh at the sides. Works well.

2007 Hamelin Bay Rampant White

Score 90

MARGARET RIVER	
Price	$18.00 ✓
Quality	★ ★ ★ ★
Alc./Vol.	13%
Drink	Now
Closure	Screwcap

Made in the same style as the Devil's Lair Fifth Leg White: adding chardonnay to the classic semillon-sauvignon repertoire. Enter stone fruits amid the passionfruit and lemon grass semillon aromas, all rolled together neatly on the palate, soft texture and easy balance.

2007 Hay Shed Hill Block 1 Semillon Sauvignon Blanc — Score 94

MARGARET RIVER
Price $28.00 ✓
Quality ★★★★ ⅃
Alc./Vol. 12%
Drink 2010
Closure Screwcap

This single site, Block 1, comes from old vines and has the power to prove it. Made in the complex style drawing on barrel fermentation, there's preserved lemons and subtle spices, some bush herbs in the mix. The palate has terrific concentration and length, scintillating acidity and fine lemon zest flavour. Brilliant!

2007 Hay Shed Hill Sauvignon Blanc Semillon — Score 90

MARGARET RIVER
Price $20.00 ✓
Quality ★★★★
Alc./Vol. 12.4%
Drink Now
Closure Screwcap

The regular estate-level wine from Hay Shed is a straight-shooting sauvignon blanc semillon with plenty of bright tropical fruit aromas, lemon oil and herbs. The palate is super fresh, filled with passionfruit and fresh lemon flavours, finishing clean, soft and beautifully balanced.

2007 Hazard Hill Semillon Sauvignon Blanc — Score 89

WESTERN AUSTRALIA
Price $12.00 ✓
Quality ★★★ ⅃
Alc./Vol. 13%
Drink Now
Closure Screwcap

This shows some bright tropical aromas, the sauvignon's brash fruity lift climbs out over the semillon, passionfruit and lemons sit below. Bright and tight palate, more passionfruit and zesty apples, citrus too; crisp and easy.

2007 Henschke Tilly's Vineyard — Score 90

BAROSSA VALLEY/
ADELAIDE HILLS 🍃
Price $18.00 ✓
Quality ★★★★
Alc./Vol. 12.5%
Drink Now
Closure Screwcap

Named as a tribute to Great Auntie Tilly, this is one of the most reliable whites on the market for under 20 bucks. Made with sauvignon blanc and semillon from the Barossa and the Adelaide Hills, it shows restrained cool melons and tropical fruits, gentle citrus too. The palate is crisp and crunchy, bright citrus and melon, some apples here too; balanced and delicious. A drink-now style, it'll also age well for five to six years.

2007 Kalleske Clarry's White — Score 89

BAROSSA VALLEY 🍃
Price $15.00 ✓
Quality ★★★ ⅃
Alc./Vol. 12%
Drink Now
Closure Screwcap

A 50/50 semillon-chenin blanc blend that has distinctive Barossa regional character, ripe waxy lemon citrus fruits and attractive newly cut hay. The palate's fresh: lemon and apple flavour, very crisp; gentle sweetness balances chenin's savoury finish.

SEMILLON SAUVIGNON BLANC BLENDS

2007 Leaping Lizard Semillon Sauvignon Blanc

Score **88**

MARGARET RIVER
Price $15.00 ✓
Quality ★★★ ┦
Alc./Vol. 14%
Drink Now
Closure Screwcap

Pitching right into the heart of commercial territory, this is a soft mix of tropicals and ripe citrus fruits; they've taken the semillon to full maturity. The palate is soft, carrying plenty of tropical flavour, some sugar and slightly higher alcohol work a richer texture.

2007 Leeuwin Estate Siblings Sauvignon Blanc Semillon

Score **91**

MARGARET RIVER
Price $23.00 ✓
Quality ★★★★
Alc./Vol. 12.5%
Drink Now
Closure Screwcap

Named in tribute to the second generation of family entering the fray at Leeuwin; this has classic grassy/savoury semillon aromas, herbs and leaves, the sauvignon also sits more savoury in this blend. Bright and compact palate, terrific integration and balance, more tropicals here, finishing soft and clean.

2008 Moss Brothers Jane Moss Semillon Sauvignon Blanc

Score **90**

MARGARET RIVER 🖋
Price $22.00
Quality ★★★★
Alc./Vol. 13%
Drink Now
Closure Screwcap

Stunning intensity here, rich ripe passionfruit and some grassy semillon in the background, superbly aromatic and super fresh. The palate's a bright slippery amalgam of more tropical passionfruit, papaya and some grassy semillon. Juicy and balanced.

2008 O'Leary Walker Blue Cutting Road Semillon Sauvignon Blanc

Score **89**

CLARE VALLEY/ADELAIDE HILLS
Price $14.00 ✓
Quality ★★★ ┦
Alc./Vol. 11.5%
Drink Now
Closure Screwcap

Semillon from the Clare Valley is joined here by Adelaide Hills sauvignon blanc and, hey presto, it's a crisp classic dry white! Bush grasses and waxy lemon citrus aromas; the palate's lively and fresh with plenty of acidity and a lip-smacking finish.

2007 Pegasus Bay Sauvignon Semillon

Score **94**

WAIPARA, NZ 🖋
Price $33.00 ✓
Quality ★★★★ ┦
Alc./Vol. 14%
Drink Now
Closure Screwcap

This is a polished wine with well-rehearsed winemaking adding to intense fruit characters. Cloudy juice (full of grape solids), fermented with natural yeast and partially in older French wood, brings background savoury aromas; still, the pungent green mango and passionfruit sails out in spades. The texture is enriched and there are some subtle oak flavours, terrific bright fruit presence, and long zesty passionfruit flavours. Stunning!

2008 Peter Lehmann Clancy's

Score **89**

BAROSSA VALLEY	
Price	$15.00 ✓
Quality	★★★ ⌐
Alc./Vol.	11.5%
Drink	Now
Closure	Screwcap

This sprightly semillon-sauvignon blanc blend is a fresh starter and terrific value; some tropical passionfruits added to semillon's waxy lemons. Bright acidity and plenty of juicy flesh, passionfruit, nectarine and lemon flavours; direct, crisp and built for pleasure.

2007 Pitchfork Semillon Sauvignon Blanc

Score **89**

MARGARET RIVER	
Price	$17.00
Quality	★★★ ⌐
Alc./Vol.	12%
Drink	Now
Closure	Screwcap

Michael Kerrigan has worked some fresh magic at Hay Shed Hill, delivering this handy little semillon-sauvignon blend: well balanced between citrus, grassy and tropical characters. Stays crisp and fresh, the bright acidity keeps the mouth watering for more.

2007 Ravenswood Lane Semillon Sauvignon Blanc

Score **90**

ADELAIDE HILLS	
Price	$30.00
Quality	★★★★
Alc./Vol.	14%
Drink	Now
Closure	Screwcap

A stylish dry, white blend from the Adelaide Hills: restrained tropical fruits and fine fragrant citrus blossom, faint grassy herbs in there too. The palate is crisp, cool lemon-pith flavours, bright acid crunch – quite savoury – finishes strong.

2007 Sandalford Estate Reserve Sauvignon Blanc Semillon

Score **92**

MARGARET RIVER	
Price	$19.00 ✓
Quality	★★★★
Alc./Vol.	12.5%
Drink	Now
Closure	Screwcap

A light, fragrant, elegant take on the Margaret River SBS blend: pristine lifted tropicals, some lemon sherbet aromas sparkle away below – gets the mouth watering! Lovely pitch into ripe tropical fruit flavours and sweet juicy presence through the middle-palate, finishing with crisp sizzling acidity.

2008 Schild Estate Semillon Sauvignon Blanc

Score **88**

BAROSSA VALLEY/	
ADELAIDE HILLS	
Price	$15.00 ✓
Quality	★★★ ⌐
Alc./Vol.	12.5%
Drink	Now
Closure	Screw

Bright grassy herbs, tropical fruits and lemon citrus make for a fresh-smelling blend. This is bright and attractive and it's interesting to see Barossa producers following whites up into the cool Adelaide hills for freshness. Sweet ripe tropical fruit flavours rule the palate.

2007 Seven Hill White Spider Semillon Chardonnay

Score **89**

CLARE VALLEY
Price $15.00 ✓
Quality ★★★ ┤
Alc./Vol. 12%
Drink Now
Closure Screwcap

Named not after the flesh-destroying arachnid but a rare orchid found on the Jesuit property, this is a modern take on things. Ripe stone fruits and lemon citrus notes, some creamy complexity; the palate's juicy and rich, hangs together on brisk acidity, peach and apricot flavours linger.

2007 Smithbrook The Yilgarn Blanc

Score **92**

PEMBERTON
Price $28.00
Quality ★★★★
Alc./Vol. 13%
Drink Now
Closure Screwcap

A complex, rich barrel-fermented sauvignon blanc-semillon blend, showing intense tropical fruits, guava and passionfruit, some finer lemon grassy semillon below, and gentle oak spice. The oak impact on the palate weighs in on entry, deepening through the middle with preserved lemon and nutty/savoury complexity, finishing fine and dry.

2007 Stella Bella Semillon Sauvignon Blanc

Score **90**

MARGARET RIVER
Price $21.00 ✓
Quality ★★★★
Alc./Vol. 13%
Drink Now
Closure Screwcap

Attractive and savoury with regional grassy lemon-scented semillon leading the charge, gravelly green and grey aromas too. The palate is super smooth and balanced – terrific blending – passionfruit emerges here, bright from top to toe.

2005 Suckfizzle Sauvignon Blanc Semillon

Score **93**

MARGARET RIVER
Price $45.00
Quality ★★★★ ┤
Alc./Vol. 13%
Drink Now
Closure Screwcap

This southerly outcrop delivers a reliable cool style: plenty of ripe herbs and grass, some green capsicum and nicely handled winemaking complexity, building tropical fragrance with air. The palate has terrific style, savoury restraint and understated intensity, cleverly massaged into complex territory.

2007 Wine By Brad Semillon Sauvignon Blanc

Score **88**

MARGARET RIVER
Price $18.00
Quality ★★★ ┤
Alc./Vol. 13%
Drink Now
Closure Screwcap

Leads with textbook grassy Margaret River semillon fruit aromas, sweeter sauvignon tropicals waft in the background. The palate's well weighted and offers crisp easy-drinking appeal; a little sweet but there's enough zesty acid to keep it honest, finishes with lemon and guava.

Riesling and gewürztraminer

Dry Australian riesling has a long and esteemed history. It's an amazing grape variety that garners respect throughout the world of fine wine, and it's also one of *the* great-value wines on our shelves. Yet sales remain unaccountably slow. Riesling tastes and smells like the place it comes from – it's a prism for terroir, highly expressive and very pure. Styles in Australia are opening up and we're seeing some compelling and diverse examples from the biggest to the smallest players. Riesling's exotic cousin, gewürztraminer, remains an elusive variety for the most part with just a few local benchmarks on offer. FOOD: Riesling's diverse flavour profile and assertive acidity make it a standout wine for food, and an ideal foil for heat and spice; Japanese, Thai, Vietnamese and Indian cuisines are all excellent options. Ditto for gewürztraminer, although be mindful of higher alcohol and thicker texture – as it's a rich fragrant wine.

2007 Alkoomi Riesling
Score **92**

FRANKLAND RIVER	Intense citrus blossom here, some really attractive finesse
Price $21.00 ✓	and elegance on the nose, ripe lime and lemon butter too.
Quality ★★★★	The palate is delicate and restrained, it has elegance and
Alc./Vol. 13.5%	approachable fine acidity, lovely balance, grapefruit finish.
Drink 2010	
Closure Screwcap	

2007 Bannockburn Riesling
Score **92**

GEELONG	This is well and truly in the sweeter end of the spectrum
Price $23.00 ✓	with rich creamed honeysuckle aromas, fragrance and
Quality ★★★★	gentle minerals below. The palate's all lined up by some
Alc./Vol. 9%	assertive acidity, chalky apple and pear drop flavour, more
Drink Now	honey and a smooth textural glide; citrus to close.
Closure Cork	

2007 Bay of Fires Riesling
Score **94**

TASMANIA	This scintillating Tasmanian riesling has intensity and verve,
Price $30.00	super-pure citrus and mineral aromas, steely restraint too;
Quality ★★★★ ⌐	very intense. In the mouth it's built around a solid spine of
Alc./Vol. 11.4%	brisk acidity, driving citrus and stone fruit flavours long and
Drink 2014	deep, finishing flinty with zesty punch.
Closure Screwcap	

2008 Clonakilla Riesling
Score **96**

CANBERRA DISTRICT	
Price	$30.00 ✓
Quality	★★★★★
Alc./Vol.	12.5%
Drink	2014
Closure	Screwcap

A very distinctive style, this '08 Clonakilla smoulders with flint and deep aromatics. Ripe green apples and fine lime citrus aromas, it shows terrific lift and definition. The palate sets out in fine delicate form then gathers weight and richness, cut into shape by a flurry of acidity and savoury minerals. A stylish cool-climate masterpiece.

2008 Crabtree Watervale Riesling
Score **(92–94)**

CLARE VALLEY	
Price	$22.00
Quality	★★★★–★★★★↓
Alc./Vol.	12.5%
Drink	2014
Closure	Screwcap

This Watervale riesling is showing plenty of intensity here in 2008. The nose is all finesse and sports restrained citrus aromas. Really even across the palate, nicely honed texture, austere and piercing drive.

2007 Craggy Range Fletcher Vineyard Riesling
Score **92**

MARLBOROUGH	
Price	$32.00
Quality	★★★★
Alc./Vol.	12.3%
Drink	2013
Closure	Screwcap

The Fletcher family's vineyard is out in the Wairau River Valley, where the young stony river terrace soils deliver bright fine citrus blossom aromas in this restrained, fragrant riesling. The palate moves into richer territory with some stone fruits and tropical flavours, gentle sweetness balances intense acidity; superbly judged.

2008 Ferngrove Cossack Riesling
Score **91**

FRANKLAND RIVER	
Price	$21.00 ✓
Quality	★★★★
Alc./Vol.	12.5%
Drink	2011
Closure	Screwcap

A fine young riesling from one of WA's most consistent producers, this shows Frankland River elegance and power, sweet lime citrus aromas and gentle spice. The palate is brightly pitched into grapefruit territory, very pure and approachable, finishes savoury, crisp and dry.

2007 Flaxman Riesling
Score **91**

EDEN VALLEY	
Price	$25.00 ✓
Quality	★★★★
Alc./Vol.	12.5%
Drink	2015
Closure	Screwcap

One of the happiest new riesling discoveries of recent tastings, this savoury Eden Valley offers a bright flash of regional gunmetal. The palate pushes dry and savoury through crisp lime juice and mineral flavours; soft, chalky and smooth.

2007 Forest Hill Block 1 Riesling   Score 93

MOUNT BARKER
Price $35.00
Quality   ★★★★⸴
Alc./Vol.   12.8%
Drink   2012
Closure   Screwcap

A distinctive and defined riesling from down at Mount Barker, showing restrained lime and mineral accents, finely fragrant spice and flint. Intense palate, uncompromising steely resolve and linear shape, super-fine lime flavours, clean and elegant. Made to age with grace.

2007 Frankland Estate Isolation Ridge Vineyard Riesling   Score 96

FRANKLAND RIVER 🖉
Price $27.00 ✓
Quality   ★★★★★
Alc./Vol.   12%
Drink   2019
Closure   Screwcap

This, from the original vineyard established in 1988, is one heck of a riesling! Rippling with power and intensity, it sports lime juice and savoury spice aromas, stock in trade for this isolated outcrop of vines. The palate is precise, filled with pristine freshly squeezed lime juice flavour and innate terroir-driven minerally complexity, richly flavoured and tautly structured, full of nerve and power.

2007 Freycinet Riesling   Score 96

TASMANIA
Price $27.00 ✓
Quality   ★★★★★
Alc./Vol.   13%
Drink   2016
Closure   Screwcap

One of the star Tasmanian rieslings, this runs about as close to the essence of minerally restraint and sheer power as you could wish for. Savoury/quartzy mineral aromas, gun flint and fine lemon/lime zest. Crunchy smooth palate with a soft delicate core of citrus and apple flavour, turning savoury through the finish. Superb now, even better in time.

2008 Grosset Polish Hill Riesling   Score (93–95)

CLARE VALLEY
Price $46.00
Quality   ★★★★⸴
Alc./Vol.   13%
Drink   2016
Closure   Screwcap

The 2008 vintage has wrought definition and fineness into the rieslings of Clare, and Grosset's Polish Hill is filled with slate minerals and fine fragrance. Really zesty and flavoursome palate, lime juice flavour, elegant and precise. One of the stars of the vintage.

2007 Henschke Joseph Hill Gewürztraminer   Score 93

EDEN VALLEY 🖉
Price $35.00
Quality   ★★★★⸴
Alc./Vol.   13%
Drink   Now
Closure   Screwcap

Where many others fail to extract the exotic complexity of this distinctive grape, Henschke draw out every last fragrance and flavour without losing the all-important balance. There's opulence and delicacy with sweet musk and lychee aromas, fine and defined, some leaner citrus notes and minerally fine-cut Eden Valley quartz.

2007 Henschke Julius Riesling

Score **93**

EDEN VALLEY 🖋	
Price	$26.00 ✓
Quality	★★★★ ╉
Alc./Vol.	12.5%
Drink	2013
Closure	Screwcap

The signature Henschke riesling bottling has fine zesty lime fragrance, classic quartzy minerals and bright pure appeal – a powerful yet refined Eden Valley riesling. The palate is cast on a savoury quartz base, lime flavours on top and acidity bind them together. Superbly balanced.

2007 Hewitson Gun Metal

Score **92**

EDEN VALLEY	
Price	$22.00 ✓
Quality	★★★★
Alc./Vol.	12.5%
Drink	2013
Closure	Screwcap

Hewitson has made one of the leading '07 Eden rieslings: fine flinty/quartzy fragrance, lime, precise, lifted and fresh. The palate moves in the same savoury mineral zone; flinty lime flavour, taut, balanced and savoury.

2007 Jacob's Creek Steingarten Riesling

Score **93**

EDEN VALLEY	
Price	$32.00
Quality	★★★★ ╉
Alc./Vol.	12.5%
Drink	2016
Closure	Screwcap

It may have switched badges (it was formerly bottled as an Orlando wine) but it's still the same old riesling. Superb precision and purity, fragrant lime-scented lift, truly regional, quite bracing. The palate is savoury and intense, crisp, long and even, finishes with resounding balance.

2007 Jim Barry Lodge Hill Riesling

Score **90**

CLARE VALLEY	
Price	$19.50
Quality	★★★★
Alc./Vol.	13%
Drink	Now
Closure	Screwcap

Sourced from the vineyard by the same name, at 480 metres above sea level it is one of the highest in the Clare Valley. This has some bright fragrance, grassy herbal edges and green citrus fruits. Drives a deep fleshy groove through the middle palate, finishes with good weight, nicely balanced.

2007 Kanta Riesling

Score **94**

ADELAIDE HILLS	
Price	$31.00
Quality	★★★★ ╉
Alc./Vol.	13.4%
Drink	2012
Closure	Screwcap

The Adelaide Hills is fast becoming the next hotbed of riesling, offering some diverse and exploratory styles, like this rich, complex style. Bath salts and green apples, some sweet floral perfume – plenty of interest here. Bracing acidity shoots through intense lime and apple flavours, a musky shroud at the edges; fine, long and compelling.

2008 Kilikanoon Mort's Block Riesling *Score* (92–94)

CLARE VALLEY
Price $23.00 ✓
Quality   ★★★★–★★★★ ⅃
Alc./Vol. 12.5%
Drink   2014
Closure   Screwcap

Kilikanoon's Mort's Block is a regular fixture among the top Watervale rieslings – very fragrant and quite ripe in 2008 with some tropical notes, guava and lime, a little spice too. Complex fruits and assertive acidity make this an engaging young proposition.

2008 KT & The Falcon Watervale Riesling *Score* 93

CLARE VALLEY 🥬
Price $35.00
Quality   ★★★★ ⅃
Alc./Vol. 12%
Drink   2012
Closure   Screwcap

Sourced from the Peglidis Vineyard, an east-facing red loam slope over a limestone base, these sweet florals are typical Watervale. Very fragrant, some gentle chalky notes, pulpy citrus flavours and fine crisp acidity. Finishes dry and resolved; great length, line and balance.

2008 Leasingham Classic Clare Riesling *Score* (90–92)

CLARE VALLEY
Price $39.00
Quality   ★★★★
Alc./Vol. 12%
Drink   2013
Closure   Screwcap

The top rung of Leasingham's riesling range offers some intriguing spices, shaved fennel and anise. It's bright and aromatic in the mouth with some finely tuned texture, finishing with soft spiced lime fruit.

2007 Leo Buring Eden Valley Leonay *Score* 93

EDEN VALLEY
Price $40.00
Quality   ★★★★ ⅃
Alc./Vol. 11.5%
Drink   2013
Closure   Screwcap

Leonay is one of the more savoury Eden rieslings, showing fine spice aromas, a little pepper, river stones and fine lime fruit. It has superb palate texture, super clean, with bright lemon sherbet flavour; a long, pure finish.

2008 Leo Buring Eden Valley Leonay *Score* (92–94)

EDEN VALLEY
Price $40.00
Quality   ★★★★ ⅃
Alc./Vol. 11.5%
Drink   2015
Closure   Screwcap

A very handy Eden Valley Leonay from 2008 (there's also an '08 Clare Valley Leonay) showing plenty of fragrance and sweet lime juice florals, softer acidity and mellow spice. Superb fine flinty regional accent, finishing with restraint and measure.

2007 Leo Buring Leopold Riesling

Score **94**

TASMANIA
Price $40.00
Quality ★★★★⌐
Alc./Vol. 12%
Drink   2011
Closure Screwcap

A distinct contrast to the traditional Leonay wines, this Leopold edition is all about investigating a new approach, clearly European-inspired. Tasmanian cool-climate fruit that packs real intensity is given some texture and complexity, delivering a fresh sturdy style with plenty of ageing potential.

2006 Mac Forbes Riesling rs9

Score **93**

STRATHBOGIE RANGES
Price $24.00 ✓
Quality ★★★★⌐
Alc./Vol. 12%
Drink   Now
Closure Screwcap

Train spotters will know that the 'rs9' stands for '9 grams of residual sugar', tipping this into gently sweet territory, only just. The most striking thing is the mandarin and cumquat citrus aromas of this wine, some flinty minerals in there too. The palate is juicy and rich, the sugar enhances flavours and there's enough acidity to keep it honest. Insightful style.

2005 Mitchell McNicoll Riesling

Score **94**

CLARE VALLEY
Price $32.00 ✓
Quality ★★★★⌐
Alc./Vol. 13.5%
Drink   Now
Closure Screwcap

It's terrific that the Mitchells thought to put some of this stunning vintage aside for later release in 2008. There's some handy early development building in bottle, gentle lime toast and very complex minerals, pure and concentrated. The palate is founded on crisp acidity and candied lime flavour, showing the beginnings of creamy development and a neat savoury twist.

2008 Mount Horrocks Watervale Riesling

Score **(93–95)**

CLARE VALLEY
Price $28.00
Quality ★★★★⌐
Alc./Vol. 13%
Drink   2014
Closure Screwcap

Stephanie Toole has her eye on the prize with her stunning 2008 Watervale riesling, it shows super-fine lime juice aromas, very fragrant and precise. The palate is stacked with ripe sweet lime fruits and musk; superbly balanced, very intense.

2007 Mount Majura Riesling

Score **91**

CANBERRA DISTRICT
Price $16.00 ✓
Quality ★★★★
Alc./Vol. 11.1%
Drink   Now
Closure Screwcap

A bright and compact lemon and lime juice style that shows attractive cool-region restraint and hints of savoury minerals. Starts with soft fruit flavour and gathers intensity through the palate, building to a gently toasty, juicy finish. Approachable as a youngster.

2007 Neudorf Brightwater Riesling

Score **91**

NELSON, NZ

Price $30.00

Quality ★★★★

Alc./Vol. 11%

Drink Now

Closure Screwcap

Bright by name and nature, this has some chalky fine fragrant notes, lovely freshness; there's apple and stone fruit, fine lime citrus and mineral aromas. The palate's fine, supple and wields intense acidity, green apple and lime flavours, subtle balancing, sweetness rounds fruit flavour out.

2007 Neudorf Moutere Riesling

Score **93**

NELSON, NZ

Price $42.00

Quality ★★★★⌐

Alc./Vol. 10%

Drink Now

Closure Screwcap

This signature Neudorf riesling is in the off-dry style, much richer and more concentrated than the Brightwater, it has more savoury spice and restrained yet powerful characters. Terrific power, richness and weight on the palate, luscious and intense, zesty and balanced.

2008 O'Leary Walker Polish Hill River Riesling

Score **94**

CLARE VALLEY

Price $19.00 ✓

Quality ★★★★⌐

Alc./Vol. 12%

Drink 2014

Closure Screwcap

O'Leary Walker's 2008 Polish Hill Riesling is in scintillating form, full of piercing intent. Bright and crisp, it smells of slate and lime juice – really pure and focused. Intense fresh acidity runs straight through the palate, finishing with lip-smacking flavour and wet mineral cut.

PENGUIN BEST RIESLING

2008 O'Leary Walker Watervale Riesling

Score **92**

CLARE VALLEY

Price $17.50 ✓

Quality ★★★★

Alc./Vol. 12%

Drink 2010

Closure Screwcap

The Watervale sibling of the Polish Hill is a less dramatic style – pulled back from the knife edge – showing more fragrant, delicate characters. The palate is quite savoury and elegant, with candied lime flavours and a lingering mellow finish. Lovely balance, instantly approachable.

2007 Pegasus Bay Dry Riesling

Score **94**

WAIPARA, NZ

Price $32.00

Quality ★★★★⌐

Alc./Vol. 14%

Drink Now

Closure Screwcap

Matt Donaldson and Lynette Hudson, the talent behind winemaking at Pegasus Bay, were inspired by a star-studded line-up of dry Rieslings they encountered at an Australian get-together. So they made their own. It shows superb florals and sweet perfume, bright lifted aromatics and impressive precision and concentration. Mandarin citrus flavours, typical of the Waipara region, some sugar registers (just under 6 grams), very long, complex and complete with ripe acid sizzle.

2007 Pegasus Bay Riesling

Score 96

WAIPARA, NZ
Price $33.00 ✓
Quality ★ ★ ★ ★ ★
Alc./Vol. 11%
Drink 2009
Closure Screwcap

Outstanding purity and mandarin citrus; piercing, clear and intense. Fine zesty palate, very powerful, very crisp and very aromatic – long and fine, superb. Pegasus Bay's signature style is in the off-dry zone at 31 grams of sugar, yet beautifully balanced. Sourced from the gifted river gravel soils of the Waipara region, it is one heck of an endorsement for the region and New Zealand riesling in general.

2007 Penfolds Bin 51 Riesling

Score 93

EDEN VALLEY
Price $32.00 ✓
Quality ★ ★ ★ ★ ┤
Alc./Vol. 12.5%
Drink 2014
Closure Screwcap

Essentially made by the same entity, the Penfolds Eden Valley riesling has more intense lime fruit than the 2007 Buring wines – fruitier and richer. The palate delivers fine acid cut, stunning purity and assertive acidity, finishes savoury; will cellar superbly.

2008 Penfolds Bin 51 Riesling

Score (91–93)

EDEN VALLEY
Price $32.00
Quality ★ ★ ★ ★ ┤
Alc./Vol. 11.5%
Drink 2013
Closure Screwcap

Although it wields plenty of acid cut, there's also a richer, punchier side to this style. Shows plenty of lime citrus fruit aromas and flavours, and some savoury stony soil-derived notes; impressive drive through the palate, finishing with lime and lemon oils.

2007 Peter Lehmann Eden Valley Riesling

Score 93

EDEN VALLEY
Price $16.00 ✓
Quality ★ ★ ★ ★ ┤
Alc./Vol. 11.5%
Drink 2013
Closure Screwcap

Lovely lifted floral aromatics, Lehmann's Eden Valley Riesling is always restrained and compact, there are very fine citrus characters, lemon barley and lemon sherbet. The palate is beautifully cut by precise acidity and smooth even texture, savoury lemon to close. Outrageous value here.

2003 Peter Lehmann Wigan Eden Valley Riesling

Score 94

EDEN VALLEY
Price $40.00
Quality ★ ★ ★ ★ ┤
Alc./Vol. 11%
Drink Now
Closure Screwcap

Named in honour of Andrew 'Wig' Wigan who has been a faithful Lehmann riesling maker since the outset, helping establish their position at the top of the league. There's some ripeness here from a warmer season but this has a classic, smooth palate shape and delicate lemon/lime flavour, just showing the early development of some toasty bottle-age. Superb drinking, released in its prime.

2003 Pewsey Vale Contours Riesling   Score 93

EDEN VALLEY
Price $27.00
Quality   ★★★★ ∢
Alc./Vol. 12.5%
Drink   2010
Closure   Screwcap

A superb aged release from this legendary riesling vineyard shows big, ripe lime aromas, lime oils and some almost tropical notes. The palate is rich, riper than usual in this '03 vintage, but has a core of sturdy acid pinning it together, balanced and supple and right in the zone.

2007 Pewsey Vale Eden Valley Gewürztraminer   Score 93

EDEN VALLEY
Price $27.00
Quality   ★★★★ ∢
Alc./Vol. 13.5%
Drink   Now
Closure   Screwcap

It's stunning to see how much vineyard character travels through all the Pewsey Vale aromatic whites, from young riesling to old riesling, off-dry riesling and this minerally gewürz. Smoky flint and fine savoury mineral aromas lead the style, very powdery minerals. The palate has intensity with restrained savoury mineral flavours, some gentle tropical fruits, very measured, very fine.

2007 Pewsey Vale Eden Valley Riesling   Score 93

EDEN VALLEY
Price $20.00 ✓
Quality   ★★★★ ∢
Alc./Vol. 13%
Drink   2014
Closure   Screwcap

One of the standout rieslings from the Eden Valley in 2007, this shows fine lime juice aromas and very precise fragrant notes; it's finer than just about any other '07. Beautifully resolved as a young wine, it's super fresh and fragrant, elegant and distinctive. The palate fuses power and grace with concentrated pure lime juice flavour, quite ripe and long, building richness through the finish.

2007 Pewsey Vale Prima Riesling   Score 94

EDEN VALLEY
Price $25.00 ✓
Quality   ★★★★ ∢
Alc./Vol. 9.5%
Drink   2010
Closure   Vino-lok

This off-dry project adds another facet to the repertoire of this stunning terraced vineyard perched up high in the Eden Valley. Made from the first grapes to be harvested, it's pinned to the map by strong regional character, crisp minerals and quartzy lime juice, some lime sherbet too. The palate has a terrific balance of sugar and acidity, making a mouth-watering impression through long fine lines of flavour. Superb balance.

2008 Pfeiffer The Carson Gewürztraminer   Score 90

KING VALLEY
Price $17.00 ✓
Quality   ★★★★
Alc./Vol. 13%
Drink   Now
Closure   Screwcap

This zesty fresh King Valley traminer is a tidy, clean and refreshing style, nicely ripened and delivered with skill. Aromas are musky and lifted, with flint and sweet floral perfume. Musk flavours follow suit, this is soft, supple and custom-made for spicy Asian cuisine.

2008 Pikes The Merle Reserve Riesling　　　*Score* **96**

CLARE VALLEY	
Price	$36.00 ✓
Quality	★★★★★
Alc./Vol.	12%
Drink	2016
Closure	Screwcap

This 2008 reserve riesling has made a transition into new territory with a portion of natural yeast fermentation adding texture and enriching the intensity of the Polish Hill terroir. Intense, pure and fine citrus fruit aromas, the palate travels on bright acid lines, finishing strong with slatey minerals and show-stopping intensity.

2006 Pirie Estate Gewürztraminer　　　*Score* **92**

TASMANIA	
Price	$31.00
Quality	★★★★
Alc./Vol.	13%
Drink	Now
Closure	Screwcap

Andrew Pirie is one of those rare individuals who really digs this exotic, full-bodied stuff, and working in the super-cool climes of Tasmania allows him to push this variety's pungent aromatics right to the edge. Intense ripe lychee fruits, bath powder and musk, the texture is deep and juicy.

2007 Pirie South Riesling　　　*Score* **91**

TASMANIA	
Price	$22.00 ✓
Quality	★★★★
Alc./Vol.	13%
Drink	Now
Closure	Screwcap

Sensational value and a canny balance between approachability and resolve, this has some bath powder aromatics and fine lime citrus aromas, really fresh and attractive. The palate has a core of juicy rich flavour, sweet and musky through the finish, no sharp edges, just flavoursome enjoyment.

2007 Radford Dale Eden Valley Riesling　　　*Score* **95**

EDEN VALLEY	
Price	$24.00 ✓
Quality	★★★★ ⌐
Alc./Vol.	11.5%
Drink	2014
Closure	Screwcap

The Radford Dale riesling is given plenty of time and space to settle into stride, bottled later and better for it. Fine savoury aromatics, citrus and minerals; it shows loads of stony regional character. Softer corners in the mouth, supple and fine, superb integration and lime flavour.

2008 Seven Hill Riesling　　　*Score* **(91–93)**

CLARE VALLEY	
Price	$19.00 ✓
Quality	★★★★ ⌐
Alc./Vol.	12.5%
Drink	2014
Closure	Screwcap

Starts out with savoury slate aromas and builds some rich orange citrus into the mix, it has a sense of purity and precision. The palate is packing concentrated flavours: grapefruit and citrus peel, some apple and an intense juicy texture.

2007 St Hallett Eden Valley Riesling

Score **93**

EDEN VALLEY
Price $21.00 ✓
Quality ★★★★┩
Alc./Vol. 12.5%
Drink 2012
Closure Screwcap

Super-fine aromatics and lift here, this has attractive brightness and fine fragrance, St Hallett make this stuff in their sleep these days. The palate is cut in clean lines with lemon zesty flavour, regional minerals, a savoury talc finish; it's just a baby.

2007 Tamar Ridge Gewürztraminer

Score **91**

TASMANIA
Price $22.00 ✓
Quality ★★★★
Alc./Vol. 14%
Drink Now
Closure Screwcap

Tasmania is an ideal place for this variety to flourish and develop a full array of rich exotic characters. Here there's intense lychee fruit, distinctive and super-attractive, pristine; some lighter rose petal perfume too. Gentle honeysuckle and rosewater flavours; acidity sizzles below.

2008 Taylors Gewürztraminer

Score **(90–92)**

CLARE VALLEY
Price $19.00
Quality ★★★★
Alc./Vol. 13.5%
Drink Now
Closure Screwcap

Musky rose petals and impeccable fragrant lychee fruits, these exotic varietal characters have been beautifully captured by the folks at Taylors. The palate delivers Turkish delight flavour and plenty of rich fruit weight, all balanced out to an elegant conclusion.

Pinot gris and pinot grigio

One grape variety – two wine styles. The names have their origins in other parts of the world and are used as style reference points for Australian producers. Pinot gris originates in Alsace, France, where the wines are typically rich and full-bodied, often carrying residual sugar, some botrytis and low acidity. Australian examples are more richly textured, filled with pears, spiced apple and stone fruit flavours. Pinot grigio refers to the northern Italian style, crisper, lighter, drier and generally higher in acidity, and unoaked. Grigio is citrusy with lighter apple notes, very fresh and fragrant. Both styles are enjoying growing popularity in Australia; New Zealand also makes some handy sweeter, richer gris styles. FOOD: The ideal food match depends heavily upon which style you're looking at. Grigio suits delicate seafood dishes like salt and pepper squid, steamed fish or tuna tartare; gris has a wider scope and is fantastic with Asian dishes like crispy quail and pork san choi bow.

2007 **Alta Pinot Grigio**
Score **90**

ADELAIDE HILLS
Price $24.00
Quality ★★★★
Alc./Vol. 13%
Drink Now
Closure Screwcap

The tall bottle suits the name. It looks like a stylish northern Italian package: plenty of ripe pears and exotic tropical fruits, gentle spicy fragrance, some fine minerals too. Upbeat freshness in the mouth, bright acidity twists the flavours towards citrus fruits, finishing with a balanced tangy crunch.

2007 **Coldstone Pinot Grigio**
Score **87**

VICTORIA
Price $13.00
Quality ★★★ ⁊
Alc./Vol. 12.5%
Drink Now
Closure Screwcap

A slightly muddled nose: pears and apples, gentle fragrance and sweet florals, not giving too much away. The palate is a straight-shooting, slightly tropical-flavoured affair, a little thicker and sweeter through the finish.

2007 **Crowded House Pinot Gris**
Score **89**

NELSON, NZ
Price $22.00
Quality ★★★ ⁊
Alc./Vol. 13%
Drink Now
Closure Screwcap

No relation to the band but a handy name for a New Zealand winery to run with. This is a rich, honeyed style, some sweet pear fruits and yeasty complexity. The palate has plenty of texture and ripe fleshy pear flavour, finishes dry and tidy.

2007 Cuttaway Hill Pinot Gris

Score **89**

SOUTHERN HIGHLANDS
Price $22.00
Quality   ★★★ ┩
Alc./Vol. 13%
Drink   Now
Closure   Screwcap

This smells of provincial flowers, fields full of them, strong honeysuckle and lavender, with pear in behind; charming. The palate is delicate and elegant: fine pear fruits, soft, polite texture and quiet balance.

2008 David Hook The Gorge Pinot Grigio

Score **90**

HUNTER VALLEY
Price $18.00 ✓
Quality   ★★★★
Alc./Vol. 11%
Drink   Now
Closure   Screwcap

The Hunter ain't exactly synonymous with pinot grigio but this has all the hallmarks of the variety. Bright light pear and stone fruit aromas and sweet floral spices. Same story on the palate, fresh pears and neat elegant balance. Lovely.

2008 De Bortoli Windy Peak Pinot Grigio

Score **91**

VICTORIA
Price $15.00 ✓
Quality   ★★★★
Alc./Vol. 12.5%
Drink   Now
Closure   Screwcap

This youthful, well-made grigio is stocked full of stone fruit aromas, very fresh, some tropicals and bright estery fragrance. The palate delivers plenty of ripe stone fruit richness and has some passionfruit pulp, smooth, soft and balanced. Great value.

2007 Devil's Corner Pinot Grigio

Score **89**

TASMANIA
Price $17.00 ✓
Quality   ★★★ ┩
Alc./Vol. 13%
Drink   Now
Closure   Screwcap

Tasmania works well for the crisp, fresh grigio style, retaining its freshness and building aroma and flavour. A full tropical fruit salad and some spiced pear aromas – very fresh. Cleverly assembled palate, pitching sweetness and acidity together to extend flavours, finishing crisp and clean.

2007 Frog Rock Pinot Gris

Score **91**

MUDGEE
Price $27.00
Quality   ★★★★
Alc./Vol. 13.5%
Drink   Now
Closure   Screwcap

The extreme elevation (1000 metres) of this Rylestone vineyard brings restraint and pure fruit freshness, straightforward cool grapefruit and pear flavours. Acidity is a feature of the palate, rolling through from start to finish, keeping the wine pinned to the line; finishes super fresh.

2007 Galli Estate Artigiano Pinot Grigio
Score **89**

SUNBURY
Price $20.00
Quality ★★★ ⸾
Alc./Vol. 14%
Drink Now
Closure Screwcap

Lovely bright stone fruits, lemon zest and pears, smells fresh and attractive, white musk. The palate has some richness and texture, not too challenging, finishing softer with a gentle wash of sugar through the back.

2007 Grant Burge East Argyle Pinot Gris
Score **88**

EDEN VALLEY
Price $21.00
Quality ★★★ ⸾
Alc./Vol. 13%
Drink Now
Closure Screwcap

Named after a small section of Glen Para where this fruit is sourced, it's a fairly neutral affair; the melon fruits are simple and fresh. The palate is ripe and fleshy, more in the poached apple spectrum, some honey and sweet chalk to finish.

2007 Hanging Rock The Jim Jim Pinot Gris
Score **91**

MACEDON RANGES
Price $27.00
Quality ★★★★
Alc./Vol. 12%
Drink Now
Closure Screwcap

This cool Macedon Ranges gris nails the pure varietal essence of pears and spiced apple fruits, hard baking spices and savoury lees aromas. The palate builds textural richness and biscuity/savoury character around a core of brisk acidity, finishing dry and crisp.

2007 Henschke Innes Vineyard Pinot Gris
Score **92**

ADELAIDE HILLS
Price $34.00
Quality ★★★★
Alc./Vol. 14%
Drink 2009
Closure Screwcap

Sourced from the Innes vineyard in Littlehampton, this has some very restrained beurre bosc pear fruits – elegant, clean and fresh. The palate is a fine-tuned affair, really linear and precise, crisp apples and pears with a zesty acid crunch.

2007 Innocent Bystander Pinot Gris
Score **89**

YARRA VALLEY
Price $20.00
Quality ★★★ ⸾
Alc./Vol. 13.5%
Drink Now
Closure Screwcap

Pinot gris is often more about lack of aroma and flavour than it is about the striking intensity of fruits. Here there's spiced apples and pears, straight-shooting flavour that's balled up neatly on the palate, decent acidity sharpens the texture, not unlike biting into a green pear. Some gently flinty edges through the finish, simple and direct.

PINOT GRIS AND PINOT GRIGIO

2007 **Kooyong Pinot Gris**
Score 91

MORNINGTON PENINSULA	Kooyong has weighed into the gris debate with bright
Price $32.00	tropical notes, really lifted and sprightly aromas, and just
Quality ★★★★	an edge of cooler almost grassy notes – very much a fruit-
Alc./Vol. 13.5%	forward style. The palate delivers crunchy rich fruits, citrus
Drink Now	and tropical flavours and a full but balanced texture.
Closure Diam	

2007 **Lalla Gully Pinot Gris**
Score 90

TASMANIA	From a little amphitheatre vineyard in the Pipers region
Price $23.00	of Tasmania, this has classic poached pears, apple fruit lift
Quality ★★★★	and sweet honeyed florals. Plays the sweetness game to
Alc./Vol. 13%	great effect, crisp ripe apple flavours, some presence and
Drink Now	texture – neat.
Closure Screwcap	

2007 **Leabrook Estate Pinot Gris**
Score 92

ADELAIDE HILLS	Colin Best gets his gris to full ripeness, delivering heady
Price $25.00 ✓	rich pear and melon fruits with a twist of guava. The palate
Quality ★★★★	texture is soft and swirling, gentle spices thread through
Alc./Vol. 12.6%	super-ripe apple flavours, mouth-watering richness.
Drink Now	Superb!
Closure Screwcap	

2007 **Mount Difficulty Pinot Gris**
Score 94

CENTRAL OTAGO, NZ	Almost too good to be true, this is a watershed wine –
Price $30.00	Australian and NZ producers take note! Cascading aromas
Quality ★★★★⁺	of poached pears and precise ripeness, the very best of the
Alc./Vol. 14.5%	variety is on show with a gently savoury winemaking edge.
Drink Now	A creamy palate, intensely flavoured with yellow peach and
Closure Screwcap	ripe nectarines, the concentration is reminiscent of Alsace,
	the sweetness discreet, finishing with long peach flavour.
	One of the best examples going.
	PENGUIN BEST PINOT GRIS AND PINOT GRIGIO

2007 **Mountadam Pinot Gris**
Score 93

EDEN VALLEY	With an esteemed track record for scintillating riesling,
Price $24.00 ✓	this is a natural addition to the Mountadam range. Plenty
Quality ★★★★⁺	of strong varietal character and spiced pear fruits, pure
Alc./Vol. 13.8%	and concentrated – right in the varietal zone. The palate
Drink Now	balances gentle sweetness with brisk acidity, spiced pears
Closure Screwcap	and apples; it all stacks up neatly through the finish.

2007 Nazaaray Pinot Gris

Score 90

MORNINGTON PENINSULA
Price $25.00 ✓
Quality ★★★★
Alc./Vol. 14.5%
Drink Now
Closure Screwcap

This sits in the big, rich Mornington Peninsula style, plenty of ripe pears and honey aromas, some minerals too. The palate has fresh acidity to boost along rich pear, melon and tropical flavours, bright acidity and fine dry balance through the finish.

2007 Nepenthe Pinot Gris

Score 90

ADELAIDE HILLS
Price $23.00 ✓
Quality ★★★★
Alc./Vol. 14%
Drink Now
Closure Screwcap

It's a varietal triumph: sweet candied fruits here, with gentle creamy honeysuckle and pear, like the gentle spices too. In the mouth it delivers straight down the line pears and sweet spices, musky and honeyed through the finish – nicely balanced.

2007 Ninth Island Pinot Grigio

Score 92

TASMANIA
Price $21.00 ✓
Quality ★★★★
Alc./Vol. 13.5%
Drink Now
Closure Screwcap

Bright and breezy Tassie grigio with some fine aromatic notes, cool apple and melon fruits and Epsom salts. It delivers much more ripeness on the palate: apples, stone fruits – almost tropical – bananas and musk, pinned in place with crisp acidity, finishing with harmony and freshness. Plenty of appeal.

2006 Ocean Eight Pinot Gris

Score 90

MORNINGTON PENINSULA
Price $28.00
Quality ★★★★
Alc./Vol. 13.5%
Drink Now
Closure Diam

One of young Mike Aylward's first wines to make it to the market; his family established Kooyong and has now set this little label into play. Showing plenty of ripe fruits, a little spice, fragrant notes and savoury winemaking characters on the nose; rich texture, nutty pear compote and mealy oak-derived flavours. A true gris style.

2007 Over The Shoulder Pinot Grigio

Score 91

YARRA VALLEY
Price $20.00 ✓
Quality ★★★★
Alc./Vol. 12.5%
Drink Now
Closure Screwcap

This shows winemaker David Bicknell's classic burgundian touch over some bruised apple and ripe chalky pear fruits; a light coat of winemaking complexity adds grapefruity/struck-match character – it works. Smooth and supple on the palate, the flavours sit in crisp cider/pear spectrum, some leesy texture smooths out the finish nicely. Finishes crisp and dry.

2006 Palliser Estate Pinot Gris

Score 92

MARTINBOROUGH, NZ

Price	$30.00
Quality	★★★★
Alc./Vol.	13.5%
Drink	Now
Closure	Screwcap

Full-bore richness and ripeness, this has gathered a little puppy fat in bottle and sits in the exotic end of the spectrum, pears and guava, some gravelly complexity too. Sweet tropical fruit flavours and glossy texture, sweet honeycomb finish.

2007 Paracombe Pinot Gris

Score 92

ADELAIDE HILLS

Price	$19.00 ✓
Quality	★★★★
Alc./Vol.	13%
Drink	Now
Closure	Screwcap

Quite an exotic take on the gris theme, plenty of guava and sweet fragrant aromas, really intense and fresh. The palate has instant weight and richness, striking density and texture, ripe apple and guava flavours, smoothly balanced and fresh.

2008 Paxton PG Pinot Gris

Score 88

McLAREN VALE

Price	$23.00
Quality	★★★⫟
Alc./Vol.	13.5%
Drink	Now
Closure	Screwcap

McLaren Vale is an unlikely home for pinot gris, but the Paxton crew has worked magic in this ripe apple-scented wine, plenty of flavour too, some grip through the finish. Not a bad result at all.

2007 Pike & Joyce Pinot Gris

Score 91

ADELAIDE HILLS

Price	$22.00 ✓
Quality	★★★★
Alc./Vol.	13%
Drink	Now
Closure	Screwcap

Has a slight high-toned lift, ripe honeysuckle and pear, all the right characters; a little fuzzy at the edges, fragrant. The palate is where it wins: nicely pitched texture and mouth-feel, there's more green apple here and the finish is tidy and dry. Gentle minerals too.

2007 Pirie South Pinot Gris

Score 92

TASMANIA

Price	$22.00 ✓
Quality	★★★★
Alc./Vol.	13.5%
Drink	Now
Closure	Screwcap

This holds more aromatic interest than most of its competitors, smelling almost like sauvignon with ripe passionfruit aromas, pears and poached quince. The palate uses bright acidity to clip flavour on every facet, more pears here and gentle spice, drives with forthright style across the palate and balances neatly.

2007 Punt Road Pinot Gris

Score **88**

YARRA VALLEY
Price $23.00
Quality ★★★ ┤
Alc./Vol. 13.5%
Drink Now
Closure Screwcap

A super-restrained and almost elusive wine on the nose: fine fragrant notes and some young pear fruits. Very youthful. The palate delivers simple fresh crunchy appeal and gentle spiced pear flavour, finishing crisp.

2007 Quartz Reef Pinot Gris

Score **91**

CENTRAL OTAGO, NZ
Price $30.00
Quality ★★★★
Alc./Vol. 14.5%
Drink Now
Closure Screwcap

Rudi Bauer has a strong handle on getting the best from his Central Otago grapes. His pinot gris is right in the zone of honey and baked pears, some pastry too. The palate is rich and soft, loaded with pear and apple flavour, finishing with a leesy drizzle of honey, balanced fine acid finish.

2007 Ravenswood Lane Pinot Gris

Score **87**

ADELAIDE HILLS
Price $30.00
Quality ★★★ ┤
Alc./Vol. 13.5%
Drink Now
Closure Screwcap

Pinot gris can be a bit insipid and this treads that line. It has plenty of not much on the nose, cloaked in invisible fruit character; no, wait . . . there is some stone fruit. Yes, apricot! The palate is beefed up with sugar to create a fuller impression; could use a flavour injection.

2007 Richmond Grove Pinot Grigio

Score **89**

ADELAIDE HILLS
Price $19.00
Quality ★★★ ┤
Alc./Vol. 12.5%
Drink Now
Closure Screwcap

A nice cool interpretation of the grigio style has some trademark pear fruits and fresh apples, a little fragrance and some spice too. The palate is simply phrased and admirably balanced, it's a white wine all-rounder without too much to challenge. It slides down easy as.

2007 Scorpo Pinot Gris

Score **93**

MORNINGTON PENINSULA
Price $33.00 ✓
Quality ★★★★ ┤
Alc./Vol. 13.5%
Drink Now
Closure Diam

Right on form in '07. Looking decidedly like it's been modelled on Alsace: intriguing ripe stone fruits, cumquat too, rich and honeyed. The palate has plenty of fruit and some really smooth texture, a smoky, flinty edge, finishing rich and savoury.

2007 Seppelt Coborra Pinot Gris

Score **93**

HENTY
Price $31.00
Quality ★★★★ ·
Alc./Vol. 14%
Drink Now
Closure Screwcap

From the Drumborg vineyard, this captures classic pear fruits and some brilliant purity. The palate is cleverly textured and has a smooth textural ride on pear and apple flavours, finishing with chalky sweetness.

2007 T'Gallant Grace Pinot Grigio

Score **89**

MORNINGTON PENINSULA
Price $22.00
Quality ★★★ ·
Alc./Vol. 12.5%
Drink Now
Closure Screwcap

This shows attractive ripe fruit aromas, some honeyed pears, gentle spice and just a hint of later-picked, almost botrytis-style influence. The palate feels a little wavy, lacking real soul and focus, but it's a nice enough drink.

2007 Tamar Ridge Pinot Gris

Score **91**

TASMANIA
Price $25.00
Quality ★★★★
Alc./Vol. 14%
Drink Now
Closure Screwcap

Tamar's take on pinot gris is very tidily presented: fine fragrance, cider apples and pears, very fresh and primary. The palate is pitched to fleshy shape, more apples here, and a bright crisp finish.

2007 Tar & Roses Pinot Grigio

Score **88**

STRATHBOGIE RANGES
Price $17.00
Quality ★★★ ·
Alc./Vol. 13%
Drink Now
Closure Screwcap

A cleverly made grigio with bright minerally fragrance and some carefully weighted winemaking influence to lift the impression. The palate is quite savoury, some spiced nashi pear fruits and gentle acid balance, finishes dry.

2007 Ten Minutes By Tractor 10X Pinot Gris

Score **88**

MORNINGTON PENINSULA
Price $28.00
Quality ★★★ ·
Alc./Vol. 14%
Drink Now
Closure Screwcap

More a rich retro-styled take on pinot gris: plenty of buttery gloss across the fruit, some ripe baked peach and toffee too. The texture is full and smooth with creamy richness, some butterscotch and pear toast flavour to close.

2007 Thorn-Clarke Shotfire Pinot Gris

Score **89**

EDEN VALLEY
Price $20.00
Quality ★★★ ꜱ
Alc./Vol. 13.5%
Drink Now
Closure Screwcap

This Eden Valley gris has some oak influence from fermentation in old French barrels, it works well. Some mealy nutty complexity and riper pear fruits, the palate texture is smooth and rich, finishes with quartzy minerals.

2007 Zonte's Footstep Pinot Grigio

Score **88**

LANGHORNE CREEK
Price $18.00
Quality ★★★ ꜱ
Alc./Vol. 12.5%
Drink Now
Closure Screwcap

This has a deeper colour picked up from the bronze gris grapes, which have some Langhorne Creek richness and weight. Ripe pears and green melon aromas, the palate is dense and smooth, finishes crisp with plenty of flavour.

Emerging white wines

These wines provide colour and movement in the world of white wine – a refreshing break from the usual suspects, offering some familiar qualities that you'll find in the more popular varieties. 'Emerging' refers in a politically correct manner to the new and fledgling varieties yet to establish a category in their own right, as well as those that have been around for longer but have not firmly gripped the hearts and minds of wine drinkers. They can be full of excitement, running the cutting edge of the wine trade or tracing the passions of winemakers and viticulturalists. Chenin blanc, verdelho, fiano, albariño – there's an ever-increasing fold of fledglings; some will remain in obscurity and others will be picked up and planted in greater numbers. FOOD: This is a diverse group so grab a couple of bottles, a couple of friends and start experimenting with a variety of dishes. Keep a bottle of your favourite white alongside for comparison and have fun.

2006 By Farr Farrago   Score 93

GEELONG	Neither viognier nor chardonnay but a straight down the
Price $55.00	line 50/50 blend of the two, often seen in the innovative
Quality ★★★★┦	Languedoc area in the south of France. Works a charm,
Alc./Vol. 13.5%	peach and apricot fruits here, there's terrific winemaking
Drink Now	laid across the top. Superior palate texture, rich and
Closure Cork	swirling, nutmeg and baking spices to close. Perfect for
	poultry with a truffle sauce.

2005 Coriole The Optimist Reserve Chenin Blanc   Score 91

McLAREN VALE	Well, the name says it all; Coriole has been chipping away
Price $28.00	at this lesser-known white for some time and it works in
Quality ★★★★	McLaren Vale as a full(ish)-bodied white that holds on to
Alc./Vol. 13%	its acidity. Lemon barley and gentle honeysuckle, plenty
Drink Now	of rich texture and flesh, balanced and clean through the
Closure Cork	finish. Great antipasto wine.

2007 d'Arenberg The Stump Jump White   *Score* **88**

McLAREN VALE/
ADELAIDE HILLS
Price $12.00 ✓
Quality   ★★★ ⅃
Alc./Vol. 13%
Drink   Now
Closure   Screwcap

An all-in blend of just about everything in the shed at d'Arenberg, it smells of citrus and tropical fruits, some gentle spice too. Plenty of texture in the mouth, well balanced, persistent lemon and tropical fruit flavours; good drinking.

2007 Domain Day Garganega   *Score* **89**

BAROSSA
Price $20.00
Quality   ★★★ ⅃
Alc./Vol. 12.5%
Drink   Now
Closure   Screwcap

To say garganega doesn't sound all that elegant but it's the white grape responsible for all those crisp, steely soave wines from the north of Italy. This is gently fragrant with crisp pear, grass and minerals, plenty of bright acidity, super crisp!

2007 Fox Gordon Princess Fiano   *Score* **90**

ADELAIDE HILLS
Price $24.00 ✓
Quality   ★★★★
Alc./Vol. 13%
Drink   Now
Closure   Screwcap

Nice clarity and ripe apple aromas here, some melons too, gentle spice and fragrance, bit of citrus, very grigio-like wine – it suits the Adelaide Hills region. Like the palate texture and the weight of the wine, apples and melons here too, acidity holds it all in line and finishes with some chalky/savoury apple-skin notes.

2007 Freeman Fortuna   *Score* **92**

HILLTOPS
Price $30.00
Quality   ★★★★
Alc./Vol. 14%
Drink   Now
Closure   Screwcap

A superbly appealing white blend that leads with pinot gris ahead of riesling, sauvignon blanc, chardonnay and aleatico. It's a veritable fruit salad: stone fruits and pears, ripe concentrated aromas, some citrus too, full of varietal complexity (which you'd expect given the array of grapes). Harking into richer territory on the palate: fleshy banana and pear fruit, a swathe of acidity runs below and really draws the palate together, a long finish.

2006 Gapsted Petit Manseng   *Score* **89**

ALPINE VALLEYS
Price $21.00 ✓
Quality   ★★★ ⅃
Alc./Vol. 13%
Drink   Now
Closure   Screwcap

This variety hails from the south-west of France and seems well at home in Victoria's King Valley. Hints of bright apple and melon fruits, quite ripe characters here, almost tropical. Nice thread of density through the palate; pears, melons and some grip through the finish.

2007 **Krinklewood Verdelho**

Score **91**

HUNTER VALLEY 🍃
Price $20.00 ✓
Quality   ★★★★
Alc./Vol.   13.5%
Drink   Now
Closure   Screwcap

One of the best examples around: attractive fine fragrant tropical fruit aromas, some stone fruits too, really lifted, appealing and restrained; direct and varietal. Lovely rolling texture and medium-weight, balanced and even, tropical fruits from top to toe, a crisp finish.

2007 **Krinklewood Wild White**

Score **90**

HUNTER VALLEY 🍃
Price $15.00 ✓
Quality   ★★★★
Alc./Vol.   13.5%
Drink   Now
Closure   Screwcap

A commercial off-dry white (mostly verdelho with a touch of chardonnay) made with an artisan's touch! Sweet tropical fruit aromas, guava, some stone fruits too. Bright zesty passionfruit flavour, smooth texture and plenty of juicy sweet fruit that lingers on balancing acidity.

2007 **Tamar Ridge Research Series Albariño**

Score **92**

TASMANIA
Price $25.00
Quality   ★★★★
Alc./Vol.   13%
Drink   Now
Closure   Screwcap

Looks like this research has paid off handsomely! This Tasmanian albariño (originally from north-west coastal Spain) is sweetly fragrant with ripe stone fruits and some tropical edges. Superb purity and elegant palate shape, this shows concentration and bright cool-climate acidity. Citrus finish – excellent!

2007 **Windowrie Estate The Mill Verdelho**

Score **89**

COWRA
Price $15.00
Quality   ★★★ ┤
Alc./Vol.   14.5%
Drink   Now
Closure   Screwcap

From a cool Cowra outcrop, this shows some almost fragrant aromas of cucumber and apple – smells fresh and lively. There is some fruit character (which makes a pleasant change for this innocuous variety), nice ripe sweet tropical fruit flavour, fleshy texture and some apple-skin bite at the finish.

2007 **YarraLoch Arneis**

Score **90**

YARRA VALLEY
Price $25.00
Quality   ★★★★
Alc./Vol.   12.5%
Drink   Now
Closure   Screwcap

Arneis makes crisp, delicate and fragrant white in the north-east of Italy. This Yarra Valley example is right in the zone with crisp fragrant pear and wet stone aromas. The palate's packing some texture and weight, really nicely balanced and twisting savoury through the finish.

Viognier, marsanne and roussanne

These three white Rhône Valley varieties are relatively unfamiliar. Although marsanne has been in Australia for a long time, and there are a couple of well-loved examples, it has never become a mainstream white. Lemony in its youth, marsanne has the potential to age for many years, heading into toasty, honeyed territory. Roussanne, a cousin of marsanne, also has a long history of production. It is often blended with marsanne and, higher in acid, brings a more intense flavour and deeper presence to the wine. The newcomer of the trio, viognier has made considerable inroads with a range of styles on offer: an elegant, fragrant style or a hedonistic, luscious full-bodied style. Great viognier captures citrus, apricots, ginger and perfumed florals. Oak adds richness to the palate texture as well as nutty complexity that complements the apricots beautifully. FOOD: White poultry and spicy dishes are particularly strong matches for viognier. All three grapes are pretty resilient, handling heat, richness and texture with ease.

2006 All Saints Chardonnay Viognier   Score 90

ADELAIDE HILLS	Although this leads with chardonnay fruit aromas the viognier makes a strong impact, they marry well. Labelled under the estate livery, the fruit's actually from the Adelaide Hills, quite fragrant, almost tropical, ripe stone fruits, finishes with fresh apricot. Neat balance.
Price $20.00	
Quality ★★★★	
Alc./Vol. 13.5%	
Drink Now	
Closure Screwcap	

2006 All Saints Family Cellar Marsanne   Score 91

RUTHERGLEN	A rich deep-golden colour in the glass with plenty of candied lime peel and honeyed lemons, it has a sense of both richness and brightness, some gentle nutty oak complexity. The palate's a complex affair with two distinct stages: lemon fruit to start and savoury cashewy/mealy fade through the finish.
Price $28.00	
Quality ★★★★	
Alc./Vol. 13.5%	
Drink Now	
Closure Screwcap	

2007 **Angoves Nine Vines Viognier**
Score **87**

RIVERLAND (SOUTH AUSTRALIA)	Ripe Riverland fruit characters: zesty orange citrus and ripe
Price $15.00 ✓	apricots, it moves into tropical mango notes, still lifted and
Quality ★★★ ⃒	fresh. The richly textured and supple palate is filled with
Alc./Vol. 14.5%	sweet fruit flavours, a punchy combination of fruit weight
Drink Now	and structural depth.
Closure Screwcap	

2005 **By Farr Viognier**
Score **94**

GEELONG	Beautiful ripeness and classic, rich apricot fruits here,
Price $55.00	there's a light fragrant aromatic side, some orange oil and
Quality ★★★★ ⃒	savoury/nutty complexity. Impressive. Super-rich fruits,
Alc./Vol. 14%	concentrated through the middle palate, acidity holding
Drink Now	through the back before a strip of toasty afterburn. Bloody
Closure Cork	terrific!

2007 **Capel Vale Cellar Exclusive Viognier**
Score **92**

GEOGRAPHE	Lovely rich, ripe concentrated fruits here, really impressive
Price $27.00	musk and apricot aromas; a superb varietal snapshot. The
Quality ★★★★	palate packs rich texture and some smoky complexity,
Alc./Vol. 14.5%	varietal grip through the finish. Fires on all cylinders!
Drink Now	
Closure Screwcap	

2007 **Clonakilla Viognier**
Score **96**

CANBERRA DISTRICT	This shows some classic ginger and gentle apricot fruit
Price $50.00 ✓	aromas, there's a fine musk perfume lift and concentrated
Quality ★★★★★	fresh apricot fruits. The palate is scintillating: plenty of
Alc./Vol. 13.5%	spice, white pepper almost, ripe fine apricot fruits and a
Drink Now	zesty acid rush. Terrific balance and concentration.
Closure Screwcap	

2007 **d'Arenberg The Hermit Crab Viognier Marsanne**
Score **90**

McLAREN VALE/ADELAIDE HILLS	Terrific value drinking, this smells of orange zest, white
Price $17.00 ✓	peaches and apricots, quite floral too; really attractive and
Quality ★★★★	tending towards exotic territory. The palate has creamy
Alc./Vol. 13.5%	richness right throughout, there's plenty of apricot flavour
Drink Now	here, softly balanced.
Closure Screwcap	

2007 d'Arenberg The Last Ditch Viognier

Score 91

ADELAIDE HILLS/McLAREN VALE	
Price	$20.00 ✓
Quality	★★★★
Alc./Vol.	13.5%
Drink	Now
Closure	Screwcap

A punchy, ripe viognier with plenty of rich, ripe orange fruits and warm fresh-picked apricot aromas. The palate has almost tropical flavours, mango and pawpaw, slippery rich texture and some warmth through the finish. A bigger style.

2007 d'Arenberg The Money Spider Roussanne

Score 92

McLAREN VALE	
Price	$20.00 ✓
Quality	★★★★
Alc./Vol.	13.5%
Drink	Now
Closure	Screwcap

This rare bird has a restrained, spicy nose, some peppery nuances, fine fresh green melon and lifted leafy fragrance. Distinctive. The palate starts out with impressive weight and richness, supple, sweet melony fruit flavour that lingers, long and ripe through the finish.

2007 De Bortoli Viognier

Score 94

YARRA VALLEY 📖	
Price	$25.00 ✓
Quality	★★★★ ┤
Alc./Vol.	13%
Drink	Now
Closure	Screwcap

A symphony of viogner's alluring aromatic characters: musk, really ripe and rich apricot kernel and nutty complexity, ripe fruit – apricot syrup. The palate's supple and swirling texture carries ripe, rich stone fruit flavour – has density and grace, thanks to impeccable balance.

🐧 *2007* Fairbank Viognier

Score 95

BENDIGO 📖	
Price	$30.00 ✓
Quality	★★★★ ┤
Alc./Vol.	14%
Drink	Now
Closure	Screwcap

Striking primary fruit character of rich, ripe grapefruit and lime, cleverly worked solids and yeast lees complexity here, musk. Outstanding. The palate is layered in rich waves, while terrific acidity and sweetness build through the finish. Crisp, clean and superbly crafted.

PENGUIN BEST VIOGNIER, MARSANNE AND ROUSSANNE

2007 Fox Gordon Abby Viognier

Score 93

ADELAIDE HILLS	
Price	$20.00 ✓
Quality	★★★★ ┤
Alc./Vol.	13%
Drink	Now
Closure	Screwcap

This gives an instant impression of coolness, stepping back into nectarine and citrus territory, cumquat and candied orange rind; really piercing. More peach and nectarine stone fruit flavours, complex varietal characters, nice textural slip and balance.

2007 Galli Estate Artigiano Viognier
Score **90**

HEATHCOTE
Price $22.00
Quality ★★★★
Alc./Vol. 14%
Drink Now
Closure Screwcap

This has all the charming aromatics that good viognier should deliver: apricot fruits, musk and peach blossom, very sweet perfume. The acidity sits out a little from the fruit on the palate but holds some musky orange fruit tingle. Medium-weight.

2007 Grove Estate The Wombat Way Viognier
Score **90**

HILLTOPS
Price $20.00 ✓
Quality ★★★★
Alc./Vol. 14.5%
Drink Now
Closure Screwcap

The first viognier release from this Hilltops producer is a waxy, soft stone fruit affair, with cooler ginger at the edges and attractive apricot fruits. The palate heads straight down the middle line of richness and balance, some grippy phenolics through the finish and plenty of savoury complexity.

2007 The Lane Viognier
Score **94**

ADELAIDE HILLS
Price $39.00
Quality ★★★★┥
Alc./Vol. 13.5%
Drink Now
Closure Screwcap

Beautifully ripe apricot fruits, with intensity and richness, some ginger fragrance here too – this nails the variety precisely. The palate is supple, fine musk and apricot flavoured, plenty of nutty apricot kernel flavour, swirling, rich and ripe. Sensational!

2007 Langmeil GWH Viognier
Score **91**

BAROSSA VALLEY
Price $19.50 ✓
Quality ★★★★
Alc./Vol. 13.5%
Drink Now
Closure Screwcap

Super-concentrated grapefruit and some tropical fruit aromas, really exotic and complex, orange citrus. The palate is ripe, full with some waxy orange and apricot flavour, slight sulphur blow-back and an apricot kernel finish.

2006 McHenry Hohnen 3 Amigos Marsanne Chardonnay Roussanne
Score **93**

MARGARET RIVER
Price $22.00 ✓
Quality ★★★★┥
Alc./Vol. 13.5%
Drink Now
Closure Screwcap

Essentially a new complex fruit style of wine. There's rich tropical fruits and stone fruit appeal, smells sweet and fruit driven, some gravelly notes too. The palate reveals measured winemaking texture and bright vivacious acidity, superb balance. Understated and feels natural.

2006 McIvor Estate Marsanne Roussanne
Score **90**

HEATHCOTE
Price $25.00
Quality ★★★★
Alc./Vol. 13%
Drink Now
Closure Diam

This little duo has weathered the Heathcote heat, making some aromatic headway in the glass, waxy lemons and honeysuckle notes. The palate is decidedly off-dry, but it seems to work well for this style, adding textural richness; citrus, honey and apricot flavours linger through the finish.

2007 Massena The Surly Muse Viognier
Score **93**

BAROSSA VALLEY
Price $20.00 ✓
Quality ★★★★ ›
Alc./Vol. 13.5%
Drink Now
Closure Screwcap

A stunning, clear apricot style, superb ripeness and intensity, some ginger and musk too; this is a show-stopper. Creamy palate, with well-placed oak adding texture and spice, long creamy stone fruit flavours, balanced and complete.

2007 Meerea Park Viognier
Score **93**

HUNTER VALLEY
Price $23.00 ✓
Quality ★★★★ ›
Alc./Vol. 14%
Drink Now
Closure Screwcap

This has striking concentration, some apricot kernel aromas and nicely matched oak and fruit characters, baked peach too. The palate is thick but balanced – acidity keeps punching through the finish, more apricot kernel flavour. Drinking superbly.

2006 Mitchelton Airstrip Marsanne Viognier Roussanne
Score **92**

CENTRAL VICTORIA
Price $26.00 ✓
Quality ★★★★
Alc./Vol. 14%
Drink Now
Closure Screwcap

This rich, barrel-fermented style is a complex savoury blend, marsanne has the upper hand with waxy lemon citrus fruits, nutty oak and honeysuckle. Complex texture too, bright acidity and some decent weight, orange citrus, nougat and a grilled cashew nut finish.

2007 Mitchelton Viognier
Score **90**

CENTRAL VICTORIA
Price $20.00 ✓
Quality ★★★★
Alc./Vol. 14%
Drink Now
Closure Screwcap

This youthful style has bright ripe orange blossom fruits and plenty of fragrant lift, ripe peaches and apricots. The palate sits up brightly and weighs in with punchy acidity, ripe stone fruit flavours and an orange zesty finish.

2007 Ravensworth Viognier

Score **90**

CANBERRA DISTRICT
Price $25.00
Quality ★★★★
Alc./Vol. 14.5%
Drink Now
Closure Screwcap

Bryan Martin has transformed this into a rich, ripe savoury barrel-fermented style, adding nutty appeal to the waxy gingerbread fruit characters. Rich savoury palate follows suit, more ginger biscuits and honeysuckle.

2007 Rutherglen Estates Marsanne Viognier

Score **88**

RUTHERGLEN
Price $16.00 ✓
Quality ★★★↷
Alc./Vol. 13.5%
Drink Now
Closure Screwcap

This little blended white takes the structure and resolve of marsanne and applies the fragrance and fruit appeal of viognier. Some waxy citrus and stone fruit aromas, no oak here. The palate's sporting the same fruit characters, supple and fresh, medium-weight and soft.

2006 St Huberts Roussanne

Score **91**

YARRA VALLEY
Price $29.00
Quality ★★★★
Alc./Vol. 13%
Drink Now
Closure Screwcap

With the chic hunting lodge label, this stalwart has weathered an unfashionable storm. Straight roussanne from the Yarra, it has savoury waxy melon aromas, dried hay and lemon. The palate is an exercise in texture, bright acid too, there's lemony melon flavour and some nutty build through the finish. *Vive la différence!*

2007 Tamar Ridge Research Series 83–1 Viognier

Score **91**

TASMANIA
Price $28.00
Quality ★★★★
Alc./Vol. 14.5%
Drink Now
Closure Screwcap

This research-series bottling is priced in the finished wine territory, and it's interesting to see viognier taken to ripeness in such a cool place. Edgy apricot blossom, ginger and musk fragrance, very aromatic. The palate packs plenty of acidity, juicy fruit and some nutty/savoury notes to finish.

2007 Te Mata Woodthorpe Vineyard Viognier

Score **92**

HAWKES BAY, NZ 🏷
Price $35.00
Quality ★★★★
Alc./Vol. 14%
Drink Now
Closure Screwcap

This cool-as-a-cucumber Hawkes Bay viognier is understated and reserved, elegant and succinct with ginger, white peach and musk aromas. The palate is elegant, tight and fine, gently nutty and peach flavoured, bright acid balance.

2007 Terra Felix Viognier
Score **91**

CENTRAL VICTORIA
Price $17.00 ✓
Quality ★★★★
Alc./Vol. 14.2%
Drink   Now
Closure Screwcap

This, a first release for Terra Felix, is measured and understated in style, some gingerbread, honeysuckle and stone fruit aromas. The palate has a springy, bright texture and orange fruit flavours, finishing with musk and gentle varietal grip.

2007 Tim Smith Viognier
Score **91**

ADELAIDE HILLS
Price $27.00
Quality ★★★★
Alc./Vol. 14%
Drink   Now
Closure Screwcap

Very fragrant and aromatic nose, almost sauvignon-like, opens with air to classic apricot stone fruits, primary and direct. A commercially savvy style. Sparkling palate, bright and unobtrusive with plenty of acidity and some good hearty flavour, slightly tropical passionfruit finish.

2007 Turkey Flat Butcher's Block Marsanne Viognier
Score **92**

BAROSSA VALLEY
Price $23.00 ✓
Quality ★★★★
Alc./Vol. 13.5%
Drink   Now
Closure Screwcap

This Barossa take on the Rhône white theme smells of ripe lemon and straw, really waxy and zesty, with lemon oil and faint stone fruits. The palate has superb even-handed flavour and texture, really assertive fresh fruit, viognier's apricots peek out on the finish.

2007 Watershed Viognier
Score **90**

MARGARET RIVER
Price $25.00
Quality ★★★★
Alc./Vol. 14%
Drink   Now
Closure Screwcap

A ripe, well-made style showing intense varietal stone fruits, sweet musky fragrance and some savoury complexity behind. Plenty of smooth ripe texture, quite soft with creamy tropical fruit flavours, glazed stone fruits and custard spices.

2007 Yalumba The Virgilius Viognier
Score **93**

EDEN VALLEY
Price $50.00
Quality ★★★★ ┤
Alc./Vol. 14.5%
Drink   Now
Closure Screwcap

Not only Yalumba's flagship viognier but their flagship white wine. This '07 shows classic ripe, rich ginger and apricot-stone fruit aromas, with subtle mealy barrel-derived complexity; concentrated with a glow of minerals below the fruit. Plenty of texture and weight, a savoury and seriously structured viognier with no punches pulled; richness and power are tightly fitted together, bright acid line.

Chardonnay

Australia's most widely planted white grape, chardonnay has had its challenges in the market but is bouncing back with a vengeance. Hot inland irrigated regions are on notice from the big companies to stop churning out tropical fruit juice, while the cooler climates are forging ahead with very smart wines at value prices. It's a great time to be a chardonnay drinker in Australia! Winemakers are polishing their techniques and selecting the right soils, sites and climates to grow more restrained, edgy and downright sexy chardonnay. Complexity, restraint and intensely focused wines are where it's at, and you can find them at lower prices than ever before. FOOD: Climate and winemaking play the biggest part in deciding what food to pair with versatile chardonnay. If you're drinking a ripe, rich style with oak flavour, then meat dishes such as roast chook with farmer's market root vegetables would be a direction to take. Cross over to seafood if you have a leaner version with mineral and lemon-peel flavours; try pan-fried King George whiting with fresh herbs and a squeeze of lemon.

2007 Alkoomi Unwooded Chardonnay   Score 87

FRANKLAND RIVER	Trades on the brightness of the unwooded, elegant lighter style. Fruit salad aromas, rolling through figs and some gentle honey in the background. The palate packs plenty of poached stone fruit flavour and gentle grip through the finish. Good times.
Price $16.00	
Quality ★★★↓	
Alc./Vol. 13%	
Drink Now	
Closure Screwcap	

2007 Audrey Wilkinson Chardonnay   Score 91

HUNTER VALLEY	Attractive bright and lifted stone fruit fragrance, some peach blossom, citrus and fresh cut melon fruits, hints of lemon drop too. The palate has density and drive, plenty of rich tropical fruit flavours and some canny sweet oak along the finish, twisting through savoury cashew nuts, balanced and even.
Price $18.00 ✓	
Quality ★★★★	
Alc./Vol. 13.5%	
Drink Now	
Closure Screwcap	

2006 Bannockburn Chardonnay

Score **94**

GEELONG	
Price	$50.00
Quality	★★★★ ⅃
Alc./Vol.	13.5%
Drink	2010
Closure	Cork

Bannockburn's '06 is complex and beguiling; there's plenty of winemaking gently fused to intense citrus fruits, honeysuckle and impressive restraint. The palate tells the full story: intense stone fruit and citrus flavours are laced up with savoury/nutty oak. Complex textures play between piercing acidity, attractive peach-skin grip and smooth-rolled flesh in between.

2005 Barratt Piccadilly Valley Chardonnay

Score **93**

ADELAIDE HILLS	
Price	$31.00
Quality	★★★★ ⅃
Alc./Vol.	13.5%
Drink	2011
Closure	Screwcap

Cooler Piccadilly aromas, minerally, with some sweet floral perfume, ripe and lively. The oak sits in behind concentrated stone fruit flavours, classic Hills chardonnay with nectarine and peach, a long zesty acid finish and just a hint of grilled nuts. Well-made wine.

2007 Barwang Chardonnay

Score **90**

TUMBARUMBA	
Price	$19.00 ✓
Quality	★★★★
Alc./Vol.	14%
Drink	Now
Closure	Screwcap

This cool-climate beauty has fine fragrance, bright citrus and nectarine fruits, the oak sits in neat and tight. The palate starts taut and savoury, ripe melon and peach fruits, bright French oak influence and assertive, punchy acidity. Finishes as it starts, with savoury almond flavour.

2007 Bindi Composition Chardonnay

Score **93**

MACEDON RANGES 🍃	
Price	$45.00
Quality	★★★★ ⅃
Alc./Vol.	14%
Drink	2010
Closure	Diam

A challenging vintage of drought has been negotiated with success. It bounces out with ripe stone fruit and melon aromas, plenty of mealy complexity too. The palate is approachable and supple, like the texture, acidity is fine but forgiving and there's a flurry of savoury/mealy complexity bringing it home.

2006 Bindi Quartz Chardonnay

Score **97**

MACEDON RANGES 🍃	
Price	$70.00
Quality	★★★★★
Alc./Vol.	13.5%
Drink	2012
Closure	Diam

The cool, quartz-crusted Bindi vineyard produces stunning, defined and intense chardonnay, crafted into superb shape by the winemaker's winemaker, Michael Dhillon. Fine citrus and nectarine fruits, and striking minerality; the winemaking serves to finesse the inherent fruit character. Ripples with intensity, refined, long and powerful.

PENGUIN BEST CHARDONNAY

2006 Bridgewater Mill Chardonnay   *Score* **90**

ADELAIDE HILLS
Price $23.00 ✓
Quality   ★★★★
Alc./Vol.   14%
Drink   Now
Closure   Screwcap

Fresh packaging and bright contents, it's certainly worth revisiting this junior Petaluma wine if you've been grazing in other fields. Trademark Adelaide Hills nectarines and peaches, some honeysuckle, the oak is in check. The palate delivers ripe peach flavour and some slippery smooth texture. Plenty here to enjoy.

2006 Brokenwood Indigo Vineyard Chardonnay   *Score* **93**

BEECHWORTH
Price $30.00 ✓
Quality   ★★★★ ⌐
Alc./Vol.   14%
Drink   2010
Closure   Screwcap

Perched up at the feet of Alpine country, this vineyard delivers melon and cool peach fruit aromas; really vital and fresh, nice ripeness, some honeysuckle and gentle winemaking complexity. Impressive density and finesse in the mouth, rich flavour, some nougat and a flinty line of acidity that holds it all in place.

2004 Brookland Valley Reserve Chardonnay   *Score* **92**

MARGARET RIVER
Price $62.00
Quality   ★★★★
Alc./Vol.   13%
Drink   Now
Closure   Cork

Plenty of richness and ripeness here. There's a lot of wine and winemaking in this bottle: figs and really ripe chardonnay fruits, some toasty nuts and savoury background mealy notes. Old-school richness is cut with a clean Burgundian line of savoury/solidsy lees-derived chew. Well done indeed!

2006 By Farr Chardonnay   *Score* **92**

GEELONG
Price $58.00
Quality   ★★★★
Alc./Vol.   13.5%
Drink   2011
Closure   Cork

Not far from the mark. Attractive restraint and elegance with some savoury oak, there's a bit of integrating to come but the fruit and wood are nicely paired up. The palate's supple and even, crisp acid crunch and some oak sitting proud; needs some time yet.

2007 Cape Mentelle Chardonnay   *Score* **93**

MARGARET RIVER
Price $40.00
Quality   ★★★★ ⌐
Alc./Vol.   13%
Drink   2009
Closure   Screwcap

A rich, heady style that comes out of the glass firing on all cylinders, spiced stone fruit aromas, some citrusy complexity, the oak is neatly cut in. The palate is taut and compact, quite restrained and crisp, nice density through the middle and zesty acidity; toasty oak, spiced melon and nectarine flavours linger through the finish.

2006 Chandon Barrel Selection Chardonnay
Score 93

YARRA VALLEY
Price $44.00
Quality ★★★★ ⌐
Alc./Vol. 13%
Drink 2010
Closure Screwcap

A prime parcel of cool-fruited chardonnay was selected for this revised reserve wine; peach and passionfruit, freshly sliced cucumber, delicate spice, pristine and restrained. The palate is wound in nice and tight, really compact with hints of exotic complexity starting to build; bright acidity brings balance and finesse.

2007 Clairault Chardonnay
Score 89

MARGARET RIVER
Price $24.00
Quality ★★★ ⌐
Alc./Vol. 13%
Drink Now
Closure Screwcap

A workable Margaret River chardonnay that deals in more general terms, some pear and faint peach fruit aromas with a tropical edge. Simple tinned fruit flavours in the mouth, some leesy richness builds texture and weight, balanced and easy.

2006 Clairault Estate Chardonnay
Score 92

MARGARET RIVER
Price $35.00
Quality ★★★★
Alc./Vol. 14%
Drink 2009
Closure Screwcap

Has spicy complex reduction on the nose, the winemaker is going for some savoury funk and complexity here, melon rind and white peach fruits. Nice crisp zesty acidity underpinning fine ripe stone fruit flavours that stretch right across the palate in even shape, savoury toasted nuts to close.

2007 Coldstream Hills Chardonnay
Score 92

YARRA VALLEY
Price $30.00 ✓
Quality ★★★★
Alc./Vol. 13%
Drink 2009
Closure Screwcap

Coldstream is one of the key players in the new Yarra chardonnay pack, making a reliably elegant and concentrated, complex style. This '07 has plenty of grapefruit citrus and winemaking complexity, flinty and intense. The oak is still settling in and this will be an even better drink in a year or so.

2006 Coldstream Hills Reserve Chardonnay
Score 96

YARRA VALLEY
Price $49.00 ✓
Quality ★★★★★
Alc./Vol. 14%
Drink 2010
Closure Screwcap

This superb modern 'old world meets new world' chardonnay is on fire with its intense cool fruit characters. Complex winemaking is layered into citrus and nectarine fruit aromas and the oak is stitched in deep. Citrus fruit palate – edgy, complex and concentrated; oak and fruit travel in formation along a fine acid spine. Superb cut and drive, toasty afterglow.

2007 Craggy Range C3 Kidnappers Vineyard Chardonnay   *Score* 93

HAWKES BAY, NZ
Price $32.00 ✓
Quality   ★★★★ ↲
Alc./Vol. 14%
Drink   2010
Closure   Screwcap

A lovely restrained, savoury – almost chalky – nose, fine steely edges, and some stone fruits, all neatly integrated. Really tightly wound palate, compact and savoury, with restrained melony fruits, bright acidity and a steely/chalky finish. Chablis-like, delicious.

2006 Crittenden Geppetto Chardonnay   *Score* 89

MORNINGTON PENINSULA
Price $16.00 ✓
Quality   ★★★ ↲
Alc./Vol. 13.5%
Drink   Now
Closure   Screwcap

A straight-shooting fruit-forward style, showing melon aromas, some grapefruit and tropical fruits, direct and primary. The palate places attractive bright acidity amid ripe fruit flavour and texture; simple, light and bright.

2006 De Bortoli Reserve Release Chardonnay   *Score* 93

McLAREN VALE
Price $45.00
Quality   ★★★★ ↲
Alc./Vol. 13%
Drink   2011
Closure   Screwcap

The nose is bound up tightly in winemaking: restrained and citrusy, some faint stone fruit and melon, mealy lees-derived complexity and smoky oak folded through. In the mouth it shows similar savoury, fine and restrained shape, pared back and elegant, nashi pear fruit and a crisp, clean finish.

2007 Devil's Corner Chardonnay   *Score* 89

KAYENA
Price $19.00
Quality   ★★★ ↲
Alc./Vol. 13%
Drink   Now
Closure   Screwcap

Pear fruits, quite cool and restrained, some vanillin and background spices, varietal and clean-cut. The palate has simple pear and apple flavours, subtle honeysuckle, plenty of keen Tasmanian acidity and enough texture to balance it all through the finish.

2006 Devil's Lair Chardonnay   *Score* 93

MARGARET RIVER
Price $45.00
Quality   ★★★★ ↲
Alc./Vol. 13.5%
Drink   2012
Closure   Screwcap

Some bottle cramp here, it needs some air to open up, building to stylish complex chardonnay with restrained flinty fruits, citrus zest, grilled nuts and nectarines. Lovely rich yet restrained palate, there's plenty of life in this flavoursome chardonnay, supportive acidity, beautifully pitched oak complexity, spices and nougat to close.

2007 **Element Chardonnay**

WESTERN AUSTRALIA	
Price	$13.00 ✓
Quality	★★★ ╕
Alc./Vol.	13.5%
Drink	Now
Closure	Screwcap

Certainly at the richer end of the spectrum, this WA blend draws primarily on Margaret River fruit with some fig and gently creamy lees complexity. The palate moves between fig and stone fruit flavours, gently textured, bright and crisp, finishing with sweet rich fruit flavour; decent whack of fruit throughout.

2006 **Even Keel Chardonnay**

TUMBARUMBA	
Price	$27.00
Quality	★★★★
Alc./Vol.	13.6%
Drink	Now
Closure	Screwcap

This smart little cool-climate chardonnay has some nut and spice complexity across its pear fruit aromas; it all sits up nice and bright on the nose. The palate's a crisp and restrained shape, plenty of pear fruit flavour and some savoury oak through the finish.

2007 **Evoi Reserve Chardonnay**

MARGARET RIVER	
Price	$49.00
Quality	★★★★
Alc./Vol.	14%
Drink	2010
Closure	Screwcap

A ripe, brassy nose with a good serve of fine French timber (100% new) on show, nutty and direct, some complexity and bright, ripe rich stone fruits. The palate is similarly framed in savoury oak, plenty of flesh through the middle, stays elegant though, figs and peach, toasted nuts to close.

2007 **Ferngrove Diamond Chardonnay**

FRANKLAND RIVER	
Price	$24.00 ✓
Quality	★★★★
Alc./Vol.	14.5%
Drink	Now
Closure	Screwcap

Sourced from their isolated Frankland River posting, this has bright lifted fragrance, really pristine, some orange oil, ripe melon fruits and cashew nuts. The palate is supple and swirling, rich not thick, decent fruit drive and custard spices to finish. They've used the oak to good effect, creating a richer opulent style.

2006 **Forest Hill Block 8 Chardonnay**

MOUNT BARKER	
Price	$38.00 ✓
Quality	★★★★★
Alc./Vol.	13.5%
Drink	2009
Closure	Screwcap

Sourced from a select vineyard parcel, this is a super-fine and intense chardonnay, has fresh citrus oil aromas and zesty minerals, nectarines too; very restrained, the oak is tightly wound in. The palate is fine and tight, there's a juicy core of nectarine and young peach flavour, finishing crisp and taut.

2006 **Forest Hill Chardonnay**   *Score* **94**

GREAT SOUTHERN	Fine and striking pristine citrus fruits, nectarines and fresh
Price $23.00 ✓	fine precise lift, perfect ripeness and clever winemaking –
Quality ★★★★⸴	oozes class. Crisp zesty fruit palate, really intense and edgy,
Alc./Vol. 13.8%	drives an unwavering line from start to mouth-watering
Drink 2010	finish. Superb!
Closure Screwcap	**PENGUIN BEST-VALUE WHITE WINE**

2006 **Frankland Estate Isolation Ridge Vineyard Chardonnay**   *Score* **93**

FRANKLAND RIVER	This is striking for its intensity, precision and focus, bright
Price $25.00 ✓	yellow peach and smoky complexity, struck match and
Quality ★★★★⸴	grilled nuts – the winemaking is right in tune. Mixing
Alc./Vol. 13.5%	fineness and power to great effect on the palate, it's
Drink 2011	compact and structured; the acidity supports the wine
Closure Screwcap	in its quest for sophisticated complex appeal.

2007 **Fraser Gallop Estate Chardonnay**   *Score* **93**

MARGARET RIVER	Etched by the esteemed hands of winemaker Clive Otto,
Price $25.00 ✓	this is a well-priced complex Margaret River chardonnay
Quality ★★★★⸴	that has all the trimmings of greatness. The full array of
Alc./Vol. 13.7%	stone fruits is dressed in stylish French oak; there's plenty of
Drink 2010	brisk acidity and an attractive play between elegance and
Closure Screwcap	power.

2007 **Freycinet Chardonnay**   *Score* **96**

TASMANIA	This is a powerful cool-climate style, showing plenty of
Price $38.00	baking spices and rich creamed stone fruits below, some
Quality ★★★★★	citrus too. The palate is bright and crisp, with just a hint of
Alc./Vol. 13.5%	buttery complexity in the background, rich and dense, fine
Drink 2010	classy style, poached pear flavour. Balanced, long and taut.
Closure Screwcap	Superb.

2005 **Gembrook Hill Chardonnay**   *Score* **91**

YARRA VALLEY	Plenty of ripe melon and fig fruits, sweet baking spices and
Price $35.00	creamy/savoury complexity. The palate sits fresh and lively,
Quality ★★★★	bright stone fruit and ripe apple flavours, a flicker of crisp
Alc./Vol. 13%	acidity, the oak is well integrated, all balanced at the richer
Drink Now	end of the spectrum.
Closure Diam	

2006 Giaconda Chardonnay

Score **96**

BEECHWORTH
Price $120.00
Quality ★★★★★
Alc./Vol. 13.9%
Drink 2012
Closure Cork

This sits right in Giaconda's trademark opulent style, established over an impressive track record: baking spices and creamed custard aromas, ripe banana and stone fruits, plenty of savoury oak and some chalky notes below. Swathed in rich texture, really swirling and mouth-filling, nougat, poached peach and a burst of acid through the finish, long and opulent.

2007 Giant Steps Sexton Vineyard Chardonnay

Score **90**

YARRA VALLEY
Price $35.00
Quality ★★★★
Alc./Vol. 14%
Drink Now
Closure Screwcap

The Sexton Vineyard chardonnay has really attractive ripe yellow-flesh peach and rich honey-scented fruits. The palate has some juicy peach flavour, more grilled nuts and cashewy, honeyed flavour through the finish. Balanced and even – simple and direct.

2007 Giant Steps Tarraford Vineyard Chardonnay

Score **91**

YARRA VALLEY
Price $40.00
Quality ★★★★
Alc./Vol. 13.5%
Drink Now
Closure Screwcap

Faint yeasty complexity, the Tarraford Vineyard makes a straightforward stone fruit impression with gently added winemaking complexity, some fresh cashew and honey. The palate is fine, just a little stunted, ripe simple tropical and stone fruits, honey and nougat to close. Good result in a horror season.

2007 The Growers' Reward Chardonnay

Score **90**

MARGARET RIVER
Price $19.00 ✓
Quality ★★★★
Alc./Vol. 13.5%
Drink Now
Closure Screwcap

Sparkling clarity and bright fruit appeal, this lifts through grapefruit and lemon citrus fruits, bright and concentrated. The palate is tight-knit and complete, offering plenty of medium-weight texture and melon citrus flavours, balanced and fresh.

2006 Hamelin Bay Five Ashes Vineyard Chardonnay

Score **88**

MARGARET RIVER
Price $26.00
Quality ★★★ ⌐
Alc./Vol. 13%
Drink Now
Closure Screwcap

Sweet ripe peach blossom, melons and some toasty brassy oak, looks well assembled though; rich and nicely ripened in a super-cool year. The palate is keenly honed, integrated and balanced, plenty of flesh, creamy through the finish, cashews to close.

2007 Hay Shed Hill Block 6 Chardonnay   *Score* 92

MARGARET RIVER
Price $35.00 ✓
Quality   ★★★★
Alc./Vol. 12.8%
Drink   Now
Closure   Screwcap

A super-ripe, almost tropical, fruit salad style with plenty of rich fruit; some mango, guava and tinned peach all smell attractive and get the mouth watering. Richness on the palate is wound in by crunchy acid, carrying the same array of ripe tropical flavours, some mango here too; powerful.

2007 Hay Shed Hill Chardonnay   *Score* 91

MARGARET RIVER
Price $25.00 ✓
Quality   ★★★★
Alc./Vol. 12.8%
Drink   Now
Closure   Screwcap

Very ripe peach and orange citrus fruits, some fig too, there's Margaret River power on show here. The palate has regional sweet/sour interplay, tropical-meets-citrus flavours and subtle savoury notes through the finish. Really juicy.

2007 Henschke Croft Chardonnay   *Score* 92

ADELAIDE HILLS
Price $45.00
Quality   ★★★★
Alc./Vol. 13%
Drink   2010
Closure   Screwcap

This is the full bells and whistles Henschke chardonnay and it's worked into impressive shape in the winery. Ripe peach aromas are dressed in French oak spice and creamy winemaking influence. The palate's rolled up into a ripe crisp ball of stone fruit flavour, finishes clean and fresh.

2007 Hoddles Creek Chardonnay   *Score* 90

YARRA VALLEY
Price $19.00 ✓
Quality   ★★★★
Alc./Vol. 13.2%
Drink   Now
Closure   Screwcap

A knockabout Yarra chardonnay that rides on the region's innate talent for producing flavour and balance. Ripe peach and honeysuckle aromas, the smoothly textured palate is gently savoury, finishing with cleansing acid crunch.

2006 Howard Park Chardonnay   *Score* 93

MARGARET RIVER 🍃
Price $38.00
Quality   ★★★★┤
Alc./Vol. 13%
Drink   2010
Closure   Screwcap

The cool 2006 vintage played into the hands of Margaret River's whites and this is a powerhouse of intense nectarine aromas, smoky oak-derived complexity, grilled nuts and gravelly complexity. The palate delivers real richness and concentration, plenty of peach fruit marked out along a line of crisp acidity, cashew nuts to close.

2006 Innocent Bystander Chardonnay   *Score* **90**

YARRA VALLEY 🌿
Price $20.00 ✓
Quality   ★★★★
Alc./Vol. 14%
Drink   Now
Closure   Screwcap

Admirable for its directness and simplicity, a cleansing, refreshing chardonnay with little human intervention. Fine and precise lemon and nectarine aromas, some richer tropical fruit flavours – really bright and fresh, cool and elegant.

2006 Juniper Crossing Chardonnay   *Score* **91**

MARGARET RIVER
Price $22.00 ✓
Quality   ★★★★
Alc./Vol. 13.5%
Drink   Now
Closure   Screwcap

This has some exotic fruit characters, ripe and juicy, the oak makes a sweeter impression wrapped snug around the fruit. On the palate it's all melons and nectarines, assertive and direct, finishing with fresh nutty almond flavours and sweet spice. Made for up-front enjoyment.

2007 Juniper Estate Chardonnay   *Score* **94**

MARGARET RIVER
Price $34.00 ✓
Quality   ★★★★ ⟩
Alc./Vol. 13.5%
Drink   2009
Closure   Screwcap

A complex, rich array of aromas, showing astute winemaking: the finest French timber, and fruit ranging from grapefruit citrus through nectarine and into soft sweet figs, savoury almonds too; super-intense. The palate tells the same story: very punchy fruit flavour, richness and acid crunch, some cashew, nougat and tart stone fruit flavours, sweet spices and melon rind to finish. Brilliant!

2007 Kooyong Clonale Chardonnay   *Score* **92**

MORNINGTON PENINSULA
Price $28.00 ✓
Quality   ★★★★
Alc./Vol. 13%
Drink   Now
Closure   Diam

Kooyong's entry-level offering plays attractive grapefruit character and bright fruit lift against savoury, yeasty/bread dough complexity, some fresh herbs too. The palate has a sizzling entry, very fine and intense, brisk acidity, stone fruit flavour and gentle yeasty influence. Great value.

2007 Kooyong Estate Chardonnay   *Score* **95**

MORNINGTON PENINSULA
Price $45.00
Quality   ★★★★ ⟩
Alc./Vol. 13%
Drink   2010
Closure   Diam

Careful refinement of this estate-level wine has brought chablis-like chalky savoury notes, fruit sits in the peach spectrum with subtle spicy oak in the background; really clean-cut and precise. The palate sizzles with bright acid cut, weighing in with serious density, very long, fine and intense. Uncompromising.

2006 **Kooyong Farrago Chardonnay** *Score* **96**

MORNINGTON PENINSULA	The most refined and piercing of the Kooyong chardonnay
Price $65.00	collection, crisp and clean-smelling wine with forthright
Quality ★★★★★	grapefruit citrus aromas and gentle honeysuckle
Alc./Vol. 13.5%	complexity. The palate is fine and intense, really restrained
Drink 2010	stone fruit flavour, it trades on fruit intensity and acid cut.
Closure Diam	Captivating and edgy.

2006 **Kooyong Faultline Chardonnay** *Score* **93**

MORNINGTON PENINSULA	A fulsome ripe expression of single-vineyard Mornington
Price $65.00	Peninsula chardonnay: stone fruits, verging on tropical
Quality ★★★★┥	characters, restrained oak and some biscuity complexity.
Alc./Vol. 13.5%	The palate balances richness with refined acid crunch,
Drink 2009	plenty of savoury oak toast and grilled nut flavours; just
Closure Diam	lacks the intensity through the back palate.

2006 **Kumeu River Estate Chardonnay** *Score* **94**

KUMEU, NZ	Michael Brajkovich has moved into a new gear with his
Price $48.00	chardonnay, and that's saying something – he was almost
Quality ★★★★┥	unmatched beforehand. Superbly refined and piercing
Alc./Vol. 13.5%	fruit, bright citrus aromas, lemon blossom, oak toast and
Drink 2009	flinty winemaking complexity. The palate moves at a
Closure Screwcap	brisk, clean-cut pace, ripe pear fruits and a stunning crisp
	grapefruity finish.

2006 **Kumeu River Maté's Vineyard Chardonnay** *Score* **96**

KUMEU, NZ	This is the established centrepiece of the Kumeu River
Price $65.00	winery and produces a consistently refined, intense
Quality ★★★★★	chardonnay that can stand the test of time. Complex
Alc./Vol. 13.5%	flinty aromas and ripe pear fruits, the palate has a textural
Drink 2010	richness that plays against intense fine citrusy flavour and
Closure Screwcap	strong acid drive; balanced and masterful.

2006 **Kumeu River Village Chardonnay** *Score* **90**

KUMEU, NZ	The name reveals the burgundian influence up front; this
Price $22.00 ✓	has complexity and fruit richness with plenty of match
Quality ★★★★	strike, gentle nutty notes too – showing all the Kumeu
Alc./Vol. 13%	River cleverness when it comes to chardonnay. Terrific fruit
Drink Now	intensity and soft-edged palate structure, taut acidity and a
Closure Screwcap	savoury cashew finish.

2005 Leeuwin Estate Art Series Chardonnay
Score **95**

MARGARET RIVER	
Price	$96.00
Quality	★★★★ ┤
Alc./Vol.	14.5%
Drink	2013
Closure	Screwcap

The 2005 Leeuwin makes a heady, opulent impression, some match strike, ripe open melon and peach fruits, deeply layered complexity and supportive oak below. The palate starts out creamy and rich, mouth-filling, really draws wide, before heading to a fine spine of acid structure, gentle citrus notes and some savoury punch through the finish. Will develop neatly, always does.

2006 Leeuwin Estate Prelude Chardonnay
Score **91**

MARGARET RIVER	
Price	$33.00 ✓
Quality	★★★★
Alc./Vol.	14%
Drink	Now
Closure	Screwcap

Plenty of richness and ripeness here in the baby Leeuwin chardonnay: figs and stone fruits, cut pineapple, quite opulent with a line of cooler restraint running below, oak isn't too punchy. Supple smooth palate, rich tropical and stone fruit flavours, figs through the back, balanced and approachable.

2007 Lillydale Estate Chardonnay
Score **90**

YARRA VALLEY	
Price	$20.00 ✓
Quality	★★★★
Alc./Vol.	13%
Drink	Now
Closure	Screwcap

One of the Yarra's smart modern bunch, it shows melon and stone fruits, saffron, some yeasty complexity and up-front fruit. Direct fruit flavours on the palate too, lemon citrus tang, zesty acidity, young and bright.

2006 Little Rebel Chardonnay
Score **87**

YARRA VALLEY	
Price	$17.00
Quality	★★★ ┤
Alc./Vol.	13%
Drink	Now
Closure	Screwcap

Plenty of charm here – a gentle rebellion. Fine bright stone fruit aromas, subtly placed winemaking adds interest at the edges, it pretty much rests on simple direct fruit characters. The palate is a succinct, crisp snapshot of chardonnay fruit with some nutty cashew flavours to close.

2006 Logan Apple Tree Flat Chardonnay
Score **89**

MUDGEE/ORANGE	
Price	$11.00 ✓
Quality	★★★ ┤
Alc./Vol.	14%
Drink	Now
Closure	Screwcap

Logan is on fire with this bargain, restrained chardonnay. Plenty of apple and crab apple fruits, gentle, smooth cool-climate texture, grapefruit and pears too. Superb value and balanced appeal, this is a cracker!

2007 Logan Chardonnay
Score 92

ORANGE	
Price	$20.00 ✓
Quality	★★★★
Alc./Vol.	13.5%
Drink	2010
Closure	Screwcap

This really looks at home up in Orange. Cool, refined, almost fragrant aromas, fine citrus oils, discreet and site-driven intensity. The palate ripples with concentration and has a core of compact pear-flavoured fruit, fine chalky texture – almost chablis-like, some cucumber and brilliant cut.

2007 Mayer Bloody Hill Chardonnay
Score 92

YARRA VALLEY	
Price	$30.00
Quality	★★★★
Alc./Vol.	13.5%
Drink	Now
Closure	Diam

The name pays homage to the site of this Yarra Valley vineyard. It opens with grilled nuts and peach fruits, some honey and spice, ripe and complex. The palate delivers similar nougat-like flavour and supple zesty fruit; melons and peaches, bright acidity and cashews to close.

2007 McHenry Hohnen Calgardup Brook Chardonnay
Score 93

MARGARET RIVER 🌿	
Price	$35.00
Quality	★★★★★ ⅃
Alc./Vol.	13.5%
Drink	2010
Closure	Screwcap

Sourced from the south of the region, this shows restrained and reserved style, some flinty stone fruits and melon-rind aromas, the oak sits up a little at this stage – give it time to settle. The palate is compact and taut, has some nutty bite, crisp melon and peach flavour, the acidity is a feature. Refreshing finish, the fruit takes centre stage.

2006 Mountadam Estate Chardonnay
Score 91

EDEN VALLEY	
Price	$35.00
Quality	★★★★
Alc./Vol.	13.5%
Drink	2009
Closure	Screwcap

The wine that time forgot is moving forward again and showing some of its trademark richness: ripe peach fruits, some flinty edges and toasty oak. The palate is richly textured, quite full on entry, but tightens and hones in on the finish, pulling flavour and texture together into a toasty after-burn.

2007 Mt Trio Chardonnay
Score 89

GREAT SOUTHERN 🌿	
Price	$16.00 ✓
Quality	★★★ ⅃
Alc./Vol.	13%
Drink	Now
Closure	Screwcap

Gavin Berry and Gill Graham's home project has a distinct passionfruit aroma, not unlike sauvignon blanc, some greener tropical fruits, fresh and simple. Cooler flavours than expected, pears and peaches, bright and fruit driven.

2006 Neudorf Moutere Chardonnay

Score 92

NELSON	
Price	$68.00
Quality	★★★★
Alc./Vol.	14.5%
Drink	2010
Closure	Screwcap

This heavy-hitting Kiwi is a very savoury interpretation: loads of nuts and mineral aromas, smells tight and minerally. The palate has impressive power, it's all about texture and chew; plenty of grapefruity solids influence, very powerful and muscular. It's stacked with future promise.

2006 Ninth Island Chardonnay

Score 88

TASMANIA	
Price	$23.00
Quality	★★★ ↓
Alc./Vol.	13.5%
Drink	Now
Closure	Screwcap

Classic chardonnay fruit characters; it looks rich and fragrant, ripe peach and stone fruits, very ripe, some rockmelon here too. The palate has some cool-climate acid verve, plenty of ripe flavours in the stone fruit spectrum, simple and intense.

2006 Oakridge Chardonnay

Score 95

YARRA VALLEY	
Price	$32.00 ✓
Quality	★★★★ ↓
Alc./Vol.	13%
Drink	2009
Closure	Screwcap

It's hard to think of another winemaker that's making better chardonnay with greater consistency than David Bicknell. This has the kind of X-factor appeal that means everything is exactly judged – and there's plenty going on. Lemon oils, fine fragrant oak, grapefruit peel, fine minerally sulphides, peach and melon fruits; superb complexity. Finely woven fruit and oak flavour, complex-layered texture and edgy citrusy acidity all pin the palate along a precise line from start to lingering finish. Intense, stylish and one to marvel at.

2006 Oakridge 864 Chardonnay

Score 97

YARRA VALLEY	
Price	$60.00 ✓
Quality	★★★★★
Alc./Vol.	13.5%
Drink	2011
Closure	Screwcap

Attractive winemaking complexity here, very much inspired by great white burgundy; flinty struck-match complexity, fine piercing grapefruit citrus and sizzling minerals in the background. Taut. The palate makes an assertive, restrained and uncompromisingly intense impression; fine citrus and melon flavours, edgy and precise, bright acidity flies through the finish, leaving a smoky trail. One of the greatest Australian chardonnays of all time.

2006 Ocean Eight Grande Chardonnay
Score **93**

MORNINGTON PENINSULA
Price $38.00
Quality ★★★★┤
Alc./Vol. 13.5%
Drink 2010
Closure Diam

This is the heavy hitter of the Ocean Eight range, showing ripe fruit with controlled reduction, and oak brings custard spice, savoury stuff. The palate unfolds with citrusy restraint, the oak sits up across fine acidity and gentle richness – it trades on savoury acidity and raw nervy power. Shows promise.

2006 Ocean Eight Verve Chardonnay
Score **91**

MORNINGTON PENINSULA
Price $32.00
Quality ★★★★
Alc./Vol. 13.5%
Drink 2010
Closure Diam

Showing older wood and savoury/yeast-leesy complexity, it opens with air to ripe tropical fruit, some flinty citrus rind too. The palate's quite brisk, plenty of bright acid here and finer fragrant citrus blossom notes; precise, long and intense.

2007 Over The Shoulder Chardonnay
Score **92**

YARRA VALLEY
Price $20.00 ✓
Quality ★★★★
Alc./Vol. 12%
Drink Now
Closure Screwcap

It's a great time to be an Australian chardonnay drinker; Oakridge has dropped this gem in our laps and it aces many wines at more than twice the price. Fragrant, steely and restrained, there's complexity in the form of spice and savoury/yeasty notes. The palate is pinned together with crisp acidity, packing flavour and pitching a perfectly balanced line from start to finish. World-beating quality and value, this is exactly the sort of wine Australia should be making.

2006 Paracombe Chardonnay
Score **91**

ADELAIDE HILLS
Price $21.00 ✓
Quality ★★★★
Alc./Vol. 13%
Drink Now
Closure Screwcap

Perched up in the cool Adelaide Hills, Paracombe have delivered a complex yet restrained chardonnay that has terrific balance. Some gently flinty aromas, citrus and nectarine fruits, the oak works in beautifully. The palate plays savoury against fruit flavour in superb form in this fresh everyday wine – terrific all-round appeal.

2006 Petaluma Chardonnay
Score **93**

ADELAIDE HILLS
Price $45.00
Quality ★★★★┤
Alc./Vol. 13.5%
Drink 2011
Closure Screwcap

A classic complex chardonnay – the full package. It shows strident oak influence, creamy and spiced, plenty of work has been added to concentrated nectarine fruit. The palate travels down the same smoothly fruited path, long and even, plenty of white peach and spice, rich toasty oak and great power through the finish.

2006 **Pierro Chardonnay**
Score **94**

MARGARET RIVER
Price $70.00
Quality ★ ★ ★ ★ ┤
Alc./Vol. 13.5%
Drink   Now
Closure Screwcap

Pierro has a knack for restraint and beautifully folded complexity. This cool vintage brings citrus oil and reserved savoury/chalky notes, smart French oak is nicely matched. The palate tells the same story, layered flavours and texture, soulful peach and citrus fruits, subtle savoury lees and oak-derived complexity. Smooth fading finish.

2005 **Pipers Brook Chardonnay**
Score **91**

TASMANIA
Price $34.00
Quality ★ ★ ★ ★
Alc./Vol. 13.5%
Drink   2009
Closure Screwcap

Although it hails from cool Tasmanian soils, this sits right out in the ripe spectrum with almost candied fruit aromas, rich stone fruits and some grainy oak. The palate has some acid cut through ripe fruit texture and flavour, tropical guava and biscuity oak rolls through the finish. A big wine.

2006 **Pirie Estate Chardonnay**
Score **94**

TAMAR VALLEY
Price $39.00 ✓
Quality ★ ★ ★ ★ ┤
Alc./Vol. 14%
Drink   Now
Closure Screwcap

A classy Tassie chardonnay from one of the masters shows astute, modern chardonnay winemaking: nice complexity and intensity, lemon and grapefruit, almond meal and nectarine; really fresh. Piercing richness and intensity, ripe stone fruit flavours here, the oak sits in well, fairly pinned to the palate in savoury fashion by bright zesty acidity; long cashew nut finish.

2007 **Pirie South Chardonnay**
Score **91**

TAMAR VALLEY
Price $24.00 ✓
Quality ★ ★ ★ ★
Alc./Vol. 13.5%
Drink   Now
Closure Screwcap

This approachable junior wine has some nicely dealt complexity and creamy/yeasty notes, ripe bananas and restrained nashi pear aromas. Baked pear flavours run on steely mineral lines through the palate, gently creamed lees influence through the finish. Nicely pitched and balanced.

2007 **Pitchfork Chardonnay**
Score **89**

MARGARET RIVER
Price $17.00 ✓
Quality ★ ★ ★ ┤
Alc./Vol. 12.5%
Drink   Now
Closure Screwcap

Hay Shed Hill's junior label shows fine peach and melon aromas, some attractive, delicate fragrance and handy lift; it's a simple wine with direct fruity appeal. Soft and fluffy palate, really easy stone fruit flavours and a drop of sherbet-like acidity to hold the freshness.

2007 Port Phillip Estate Chardonnay *Score* **93**

MORNINGTON PENINSULA	
Price	$40.00
Quality	★★★★ ꜰ
Alc./Vol.	13%
Drink	2011
Closure	Diam

Another cool and restrained wine from the Mornington Peninsula: melon rind and grapefruit citrus fruits, shadows of savoury winemaking adding complexity. Juicy, fresh and intense palate, more citrus here too, subtle layered texture and a savoury, dry, zesty finish.

2006 Punch Lance's Vineyard Chardonnay *Score* **94**

YARRA VALLEY	
Price	$44.00
Quality	★★★★ ꜰ
Alc./Vol.	13%
Drink	2010
Closure	Screwcap

Stunning clarity on the nose here, some stone fruits, nectarine and peach, gently savoury soil-derived characters emerge with air. The palate is pinned to a delicate line of bright crisp acidity, fine and detailed, really even and balanced, finishes cool, dry and fresh. Superb.

2006 Punt Road Chardonnay *Score* **89**

YARRA VALLEY	
Price	$23.00
Quality	★★★ ꜰ
Alc./Vol.	13%
Drink	Now
Closure	Screwcap

With simple poached stone-fruit aromas and nutty oak, this adds up to a decent drinkable Yarra chardonnay; a safer, less edgy style than most of its competitors. There's restraint and balance, finishing just a little thick; needs a good chill to tighten it up.

2007 Ravenswood Lane Chardonnay *Score* **90**

ADELAIDE HILLS	
Price	$30.00
Quality	★★★★
Alc./Vol.	13%
Drink	Now
Closure	Screwcap

A single-vineyard wine at a decent price, it shows some of the wooly ripe aromas of the '07 vintage and forward tropical notes. Guava and mango flavour, almost retro chardonnay that thickens through the finish; a simple and approachable, fruit-driven style.

2006 Red Claw Chardonnay *Score* **88**

MORNINGTON PENINSULA	
Price	$24.00
Quality	★★★ ꜰ
Alc./Vol.	13%
Drink	Now
Closure	Screwcap

This Yabby Lake cheapie heads off the beaten track and into riper fruit salad territory. Pitched for instant appeal with an early-drinking forward style, there's some zesty lift, assertive and varietal, finishing with peach kernel flavour. Like most Yabby Lake wines, this would stack up if it was a few dollars cheaper.

2007 Salitage Treehouse Chardonnay

Score **89**

PEMBERTON
Price $18.00
Quality ★★★┤
Alc./Vol. 14%
Drink Now
Closure Screwcap

This Salitage-made chardonnay is composed of fruit taken from around the Pemberton region. Sports cool spicy stone fruits ahead of restrained melons and musky fragrance. The palate bristles with spritzy acid freshness, mango and guava flavours, crisp and balanced. Well made; drink up.

2006 Sandalford Estate Reserve Chardonnay

Score **92**

MARGARET RIVER
Price $24.00 ✓
Quality ★★★★
Alc./Vol. 13.5%
Drink Now
Closure Screwcap

This covers a broad spectrum of bright, ripe chardonnay fruit characters, from citrus through melon and into stone fruit territory, oak is placed in behind. Ripe and juicy palate, some crisp acidity runs through fig fruit flavours and fresh cashew nuts, flavoursome and balanced finish.

2007 Scorpo Aubaine Chardonnay

Score **90**

MORNINGTON PENINSULA
Price $28.00
Quality ★★★★
Alc./Vol. 13.5%
Drink Now
Closure Diam

Scorpo chardonnays are inevitably very savoury and boldly structured – just like this junior wine, which takes in a range of fruit sources. Stone fruits and savoury nutty oak, simple melon flavour; savoury complexity and yeast-driven texture.

2006 Scorpo Chardonnay

Score **93**

MORNINGTON PENINSULA
Price $39.00
Quality ★★★★┤
Alc./Vol. 14%
Drink 2009
Closure Diam

Sourced from the Merricks North estate block, this attractive, complex chardonnay has bright lifted fruit aromas, some melon rind, nuts and nougat, fine and cool. The palate has finesse and precision, stylishly restrained; it moves on smooth clean lines, concise and direct.

2007 Seppelt Jaluka Chardonnay

Score **94**

HENTY
Price $30.00 ✓
Quality ★★★★┤
Alc./Vol. 13%
Drink 2010
Closure Screwcap

This fruit is sourced from Seppelts Drumborg vineyard, where many a stunning chardonnay has originated. Cool fruits sit in the citrus and pear spectrum, some lime blossom, with chalky mineral accents. The palate has impressive restraint, pears and cucumber flavour, clean and crisp – super-fresh finish.

2007 Seppelt Grampians Chardonnay *Score* **90**

GRAMPIANS
Price $20.00 ✓
Quality ★★★★
Alc./Vol. 12.5%
Drink Now
Closure Screwcap

A special bottling for the Vintage Cellars stores. For the humble $20 you'll pay this is a sophisticated chardonnay, stone fruits, lemony citrus and trading on fruit appeal. Supple, smooth, balanced palate, melon and nectarine flavour, bright acidity – strong on drinkability.

2007 Shaw & Smith M3 Chardonnay *Score* **92**

ADELAIDE HILLS
Price $38.00
Quality ★★★★
Alc./Vol. 13%
Drink Now
Closure Screwcap

This has pristine fruit aromas, pears and peach, some peach blossom and lightly toasted nuts, sweet baking spices faintly behind, the oak is in check. Nice clear palate entry, bright acidity, savoury and even. Closing with grilled nuts, balanced and reasonable persistence; impressive restraint given the season.

2006 Shelmerdine Chardonnay *Score* **93**

YARRA VALLEY
Price $28.00
Quality ★★★★½
Alc./Vol. 13.5%
Drink 2009
Closure Screwcap

A happy marriage of cool pear fruits and some poaching spices, flinty complexity and a twist of clever winemaking influence; plenty of fruit impact here. The palate folds out attractive rich fruit flavour and juicy stone fruits, the oak sits in nicely; it looks balanced and complete.

2006 St Huberts Chardonnay *Score* **93**

YARRA VALLEY
Price $25.00
Quality ★★★★½
Alc./Vol. 13.5%
Drink 2009
Closure Screwcap

This shows some clever complexity and winemaking across cool restrained fruit, citrus and stone fruits – very fine, elegant. Plenty of zesty ripe flavour, lemon and lime fruits are really concentrated and compact. A clever wine, great value and a leading example of our new wave chardonnay.

2006 Stella Bella Chardonnay *Score* **92**

MARGARET RIVER
Price $28.00
Quality ★★★★
Alc./Vol. 12.5%
Drink 2010
Closure Screwcap

Stellar indeed, this has some enticing barrel-derived complexity, spices and struck-match aromas, fresh cashew nuts and restrained citrus fruits, nervy and complete – chardonnay dressed to kill. The palate has savoury appeal and smooth charming texture, terrific intensity, smoothly polished and appealing.

2007 Stonier Chardonnay

Score **90**

MORNINGTON PENINSULA
Price $25.00
Quality ★★★★
Alc./Vol. 14%
Drink Now
Closure Screwcap

This has the Stonier trademark of ripe creamy fruit aromas, plenty of baking spices, custard apple, nuts and spice glaze. The palate sits up straighter than the nose suggests and is filled with creamy peach fruit flavour. A more retro style of chardonnay.

2006 Tapanappa Tiers Vineyard Chardonnay

Score **95**

ADELAIDE HILLS
Price $75.00
Quality ★★★★┤
Alc./Vol. 13.5%
Drink 2012
Closure Cork

From Brian Croser's cherished Piccadilly vineyard, this shows complex honeysuckle and grilled nut aromas, cool and restrained, some fragrant but savoury oak lifts fine stone fruit and melon fruits, hints of citrus oil too. Lovely chalky mineral palate really bristles with bright acid and crunchy melon fruit flavour, finishing savoury and taut, fine and long. Terrific elemental appeal.

2005 TarraWarra Reserve Chardonnay

Score **96**

YARRA VALLEY
Price $50.00 ✓
Quality ★★★★★
Alc./Vol. 13.5%
Drink 2010
Closure Screwcap

A welcome return to top form for TarraWarra's top-flight chardonnay. Really complex, smelling zesty and intense: fragrant oak lift and bright cool citrus fruits, peach sherbet. The palate works in majestic layers: powerfully rich nectarine and peach flavour, acidity sizzles below and oak rolls through delivering a twist of savoury toasted nuts. Firing on all cylinders!

2007 Te Mata Elston Chardonnay

Score **90**

HAWKES BAY, NZ 🗹
Price $52.00
Quality ★★★★
Alc./Vol. 14%
Drink Now
Closure Screwcap

Te Mata's full-bore, oak-influenced style, harking into retro-chardonnay territory almost: buttery nougat, smoky complexity and grilled banana. The palate has some structured restraint and compact richness, vanillin and nougat, grilled peaches and banana; it finishes nice and dry.

2006 Ten Minutes By Tractor 10X Chardonnay

Score **93**

MORNINGTON PENINSULA
Price $30.00 ✓
Quality ★★★★┤
Alc./Vol. 13.5%
Drink 2009
Closure Screwcap

This is one heck of a flash chardonnay. It has all the trimmings of complex well-made wine; the fruit is pristine, sizzling with zesty citrus fruit and savoury/yeasty complexity – thoroughly engaging! Terrific density on the palate, punchy fresh grapefruit flavour, some fresh cashew and great length.

2006 Ten Minutes By Tractor Wallis Vineyard Chardonnay   *Score* 94

MORNINGTON PENINSULA
Price $55.00
Quality   ★★★★ ⌐
Alc./Vol. 13.5%
Drink   2010
Closure   Screwcap

Plenty of creamy richness and well-placed artefact here; hazelnut brittle and vanillin, the wine is cloaked with complexity. The palate starts out smooth, gently creamy with intense stone fruit flavour, ripe and concentrated with chablis-like chalky intensity; long, fine and precise.

2007 Thorn–Clarke Sandpiper Chardonnay   *Score* 87

EDEN VALLEY
Price $15.00 ✓
Quality   ★★★ ⌐
Alc./Vol. 13.5%
Drink   Now
Closure   Screwcap

Tropical and exotic fruits here in this inexpensive single-vineyard Barossa chardonnay; really ripe and rich, straightforward primary wine. The palate is simple and heads into the tropical fruit spectrum, straight edges and finishes sweetish but clean.

2007 Thorn–Clarke Shotfire Chardonnay   *Score* 88

EDEN VALLEY
Price $20.00 ✓
Quality   ★★★ ⌐
Alc./Vol. 13%
Drink   Now
Closure   Twin top

Plenty of winemaking tossed into the mix. An intricate set of aromas: ripe stone fruits and melons, some toasty complexity and lifted spicy oak too. The palate is balanced with more elegant flavour than most, just finishes a little sweet – needs a good chill to balance.

2006 Toolangi Chardonnay   *Score* 92

YARRA VALLEY
Price $25.00 ✓
Quality   ★★★★
Alc./Vol. 13.5%
Drink   Now
Closure   Screwcap

Looking good and right in the regional Yarra style, sweet lemon blossom, stone fruits and melon, just the right amount of savoury complexity curled around the fruit. The palate has a core of juicy fruit flavour, some oak spice, cashews and lines of bright acidity, running from start to mouth-watering finish.

2005 Toolangi Estate Chardonnay   *Score* 93

YARRA VALLEY
Price $38.00
Quality   ★★★★ ⌐
Alc./Vol. 13.5%
Drink   2009
Closure   Screwcap

These Toolangi chardonnays are right on form, showing cryptic savoury aromas, some green melon and fine oak-derived complexity – cool and youthful. In the mouth it's zesty and crisp with bright acid crunch, smooth nutty complexity; well dressed in complex winemaking, fine and long. Looks sharp.

2005 Toolangi Reserve Chardonnay
Score **94**

YARRA VALLEY
Price $75.00
Quality ★★★★ ⌐
Alc./Vol. 14.2%
Drink 2010
Closure Screwcap

It's business time! Funky complex and well-judged heady winemaking influence, the oak is wedged in tight, some flinty struck-match aromas sit across cool reserved grapefruit aromas. The palate's long and enticing, zesty flavours punch in a straight line of smooth rich stone fruits, some nougat and a smoky after-burn.

2006 24 Karat Chardonnay
Score **92**

MARGARET RIVER
Price $29.00
Quality ★★★★
Alc./Vol. 13%
Drink 2011
Closure Screwcap

Bling bling! Some toasty struck-match complexity here, the oak is dealt in cleverly beside the fruit, adding depth and interest, creamy nuts and stone fruits. Savvy winemaking. The texture and balance is impeccable from the very outset, terrific complexity and build, supple, integrated and complete. Ripe but restrained stone fruit flavours. A polished act.

2006 Tyrrell's Belford Chardonnay
Score **90**

HUNTER VALLEY
Price $35.00
Quality ★★★★
Alc./Vol. 13.5%
Drink 2010
Closure Screwcap

This speaks in both regional and Tyrrell's house-style voice, some lemon barley aromas, fine fruits and well-judged savoury oak influence. The palate rides on bright acidity and taut chewy stone fruit flavours, finishes bright and dry.

2006 Tyrrell's Vat 47 Chardonnay
Score **92**

HUNTER VALLEY
Price $50.00
Quality ★★★★
Alc./Vol. 12.5%
Drink Now
Closure Screwcap

The one and only Hunter chardonnay of consistent repute, here it has some flint edges and ripe but restrained fruits, lemons and ripe peaches; the oak sits in neatly. The palate is young and direct, sporting orange citrus flavours, crisp acidity and straightforward appeal. Will age nicely.

2006 Vasse Felix Heytesbury Chardonnay
Score **94**

MARGARET RIVER
Price $45.00
Quality ★★★★ ⌐
Alc./Vol. 13%
Drink 2012
Closure Screwcap

This, the flagship white wine of Vasse Felix, opens with plenty of swanky complexity, really quite burgundian, with cooler vintage white peach and pear fruits, punchy but stylish. The palate ripples with tightly woven flavour and structure, fine acidity lines up through the middle of the wine, savoury oak through the back, finishing balanced and stylish.

2006 Voyager Estate Chardonnay   Score 96

MARGARET RIVER
Price $42.00 ✓
Quality   ★★★★★
Alc./Vol. 13.3%
Drink   2011
Closure   Screwcap

Stylish and intense cool citrus fruit aromas with some cashew and grilled nut complexity; super restrained, it moves in savoury shadows and cool mineral tones. The palate really flows dense, bright and deep with crisp pear and ripe grapefruit citrus, spiced grilled cashew builds through the finish, rippling with intensity and missile-like precision.

2007 West Cape Howe Styx Gully Chardonnay   Score 90

GREAT SOUTHERN
Price $24.00
Quality   ★★★★
Alc./Vol. 13%
Drink   Now
Closure   Screwcap

A cool-handed southern WA wine showing rich ripe nectarine fruit with a citrusy orange edge, mango too, and some gravelly undertones. Pronounced acidity on the palate, orange and peach flavour here, some smoky complexity, rich and opulent but tightly strung with a firmish finish.

2007 Windowrie Estate Deep River Chardonnay   Score 90

COWRA
Price $14.00 ✓
Quality   ★★★★
Alc./Vol. 14%
Drink   Now
Closure   Screwcap

Attractive fine melon and restrained varietal fruits, melons and stone fruits, some savoury oak and nutty marzipan notes. The palate has well-weighted bright acidity and melon fruit flavour, spritely and fresh, gently nutty finish, a balanced, early drinking style.

2007 Xanadu Chardonnay   Score 91

MARGARET RIVER
Price $25.00 ✓
Quality   ★★★★
Alc./Vol. 13.5%
Drink   2010
Closure   Screwcap

A complex and understated style, fruits are ripe but not over the top, some stone fruits and figs, winemaking delivers a gentle overlay of grilled nuts and creamy lees characters. The palate is smoothly layered and understated, fig flavours and sweet spices, finishing with a toasty after-burn. There's plenty on offer here.

2007 Yalumba FDW[7c] Chardonnay   Score 93

ADELAIDE HILLS
Price $24.00 ✓
Quality   ★★★★┧
Alc./Vol. 13%
Drink   Now
Closure   Screwcap

True to its cool Adelaide Hills origins, this shows fine fragrance, really elegant, with bright nectarine and peach fruits, a little oak cream, and spice and savoury minerals. The palate has a nutty/savoury thread that runs right the way through (they've worked with the latest-greatest burgundian clones that tend to bend more savoury), it unleashes phenomenal rich tangy melon and peach flavour, toasty to close. A lot of wine for the money.

2006 Yering Station Chardonnay   *Score* **91**

YARRA VALLEY	
Price	$24.00 ✓
Quality	★★★★
Alc./Vol.	13%
Drink	Now
Closure	Screwcap

Sporting some attractive subtle complexity, this basic Yering chardonnay shows gentle grilled nuts, bright stone fruits, citrus and solids-derived complexity. The palate is very savoury, held tight with fine lemony acidity, some chalky minerals and grilled nuts across the finish.

2006 Yering Station Reserve Chardonnay   *Score* **92**

YARRA VALLEY	
Price	$75.00
Quality	★★★★
Alc./Vol.	13%
Drink	2010
Closure	Screwcap

This has had the full winemaking toolkit thrown at it and the resilient fruit carries it off with style. Grilled nuts and nougat, nectarines and creamy spiced peach; complex, attractive and ripe. The palate is richly flavoured with stone fruits, melons and gentle smoky complexity sits behind. Balanced and flavoursome, finishing with restraint.

2006 Yeringberg Chardonnay   *Score* **93**

YARRA VALLEY	
Price	$40.00
Quality	★★★★ ꜒
Alc./Vol.	13.5%
Drink	2010
Closure	Diam

Yeringberg's '06 chardonnay is a distinctive wine with fine citrus aromas, some riper pear and stone fruits, flinty winemaking complexity, honeysuckle and gentle oak spice. The palate texture is creamy yet savoury, it swirls around on entry before a brisk acid drive takes it through its paces; impressive intensity.

Imported white wines

The world of imported whites offers an expanding horizon of new wines from a increasing range of regions, as well as some of the established classics – next to chablis and sancerre, there's albariño and verdejo. As a sweeping overview, to have the equivalent level of quality in imported red wine, you'll need to spend more on white. The good news is that quality is improving at lower price points thanks to some technical improvements and attention to detail, and importers are being adventurous in finding the best value as well as the best quality. FOOD: This category casts a broad net over many different styles and countries, but generally the wines from Europe have a more savoury style and less fruity characters, making them an ideal accompaniment to dining.

2006 **Basa Verdejo**   *Score* **90**

D.O. RUEDA, SPAIN
Price $23.00 ✓
Quality   ★★★★
Alc./Vol. 12.5%
Drink   Now
Closure   Cork

This wine has built a strong following in Australia with its crisp, zesty tropical fruits. It comes from Rueda, just to the north-west of Madrid, and packs impressive freshness, plenty of tart tropical flavour and a soft, easy texture. Makes a handy alternative to NZ sauvignon blanc.

2007 **Cascineta Vietti Moscato d'Asti**   *Score* **93**

PIEDMONT, ITALY
Price $22.00 ✓ (375 ml)
Quality   ★★★★⁺
Alc./Vol. 5.5%
Drink   Now
Closure   Cork

A wine this pure must be tasted to be believed, smells of super-fresh apples and fresh fragrant grape juice, sweet honey, slightly creamy. Honeysuckle flavours roll over pear and apple fruits, amazing sense of refreshment; it's not overtly sweet and finishes fresh, flinty and clean.

2006 **Domaine Zind Humbrecht Riesling Turckheim**   *Score* **91**

ALSACE, FRANCE 🍃
Price $52.00
Quality   ★★★★
Alc./Vol. 14%
Drink   Now
Closure   Cork

A classic Alsace riesling with the producer's stamp all over it. Very ripe aromas, right in the stone fruits and spiced-apple spectrum, strong botrytis influence too, adding darker colour already. The palate is richly textured, swirling and full, plenty of ripe orange citrus flavour, a spine of acid shines through, finishing with peach skin and sweet balance.

2006 Henry Pellé Menetou-Salon

Score **90**

LOIRE VALLEY, FRANCE	
Price	$25.00
Quality	★★★★
Alc./Vol.	13%
Drink	Now
Closure	Cork

This commune sits just to the west of Sancerre and this wine, in particular, offers sensational value. A racy crisp sauvignon blanc with ripe tropical fruits, it plays some chalky/stony complexity against pristine fruit, finishing with crisp, chalky acid crunch.

2005 Hugel Pinot Blanc

Score **90**

ALSACE, FRANCE	
Price	$23.00 ✓
Quality	★★★★
Alc./Vol.	13%
Drink	Now
Closure	Cork

This, the most humble of all Alsatian white grapes, is an easy-drinking white all-rounder with some additional texture and weight. In 2005 it brings ripe stone fruits and some savoury regional edges, crisp and balanced and priced for quaffing.

2006 Louis Jadot Saint-Veran

Score **90**

BURGUNDY, FRANCE	
Price	$35.00
Quality	★★★★
Alc./Vol.	15%
Drink	Now
Closure	Cork

This region sits at the southern end of Burgundy and straddles several communes; chardonnay is made in a ripe, direct style and priced to sell. Jadot's '06 is terrific, showing melon and ripe stone fruits, some chalky notes below, plenty of brisk acidity and hints of honeysuckle. A superb crisp chardonnay.

2006 Martin Codax Burgans Albariño

Score **90**

D.O. RIAS BAIXAS, SPAIN	
Price	$17.00 ✓
Quality	★★★★
Alc./Vol.	12.5%
Drink	Now
Closure	Screwcap

Albariño is a lighter fragrant white from the north-west coast of Spain, just above Portugal. Bright and breezy, it smells of melon fruits and sea spray. The palate's easy, crisp and refreshing, honeysuckle and stone-fruit flavours, dry and refreshing.

PENGUIN BEST IMPORTED WHITE WINE

2007 Pascal Jolivet Sancerre

Score **92**

LOIRE VALLEY, FRANCE	
Price	$40.00
Quality	★★★★
Alc./Vol.	12.5%
Drink	2009
Closure	Cork

Sancerre is a wine for enthusiasts. Those who love the stuff tend to drink it with great gusto, and with a wine like this it's easy to see why. Terrific complex minerals and citrus fruits, the palate's cut in with steely acidity and restrained mouth-watering tropical and citrus flavours, finishing with zesty dry punch.

2006 Philippe Portier Quincy

Score 91

LOIRE VALLEY, FRANCE
Price $35.00
Quality   ★★★★
Alc./Vol. 12.5%
Drink   Now
Closure   Cork

This packs a bit more punch and weight than the wines from neighbouring Sancerre, but there's still the same core of stony minerals that make these sauvignon blancs truly captivating. Smooth tropical fruit flavours, some creamy textural richness and a chalky soft finish; very tidy indeed!

2006 Quinta do Ameal Loureiro

Score 91

D.O.C. VINHOS VERDES, PORTUGAL
Price $28.00
Quality   ★★★★
Alc./Vol. 11.5%
Drink   Now
Closure   Cork

This white brings new meaning to the idea of refreshing, showing light lemon blossom, honeysuckle and finer flinty complexity; really pure and aromatic. The palate's an intense ride amid zesty dry lemon peel flavours, superb smooth cut and almost glossy through the finish. Distinctive, bracing dry white wine.

2007 Tiefenbrunner Pinot Grigio

Score 91

ALTO ADIGE, ITALY
Price $25.00 ✓
Quality   ★★★★
Alc./Vol. 13%
Drink   Now
Closure   Screwcap

This crisp, easy white grows in the Alto Adige region of Italy's north where it retains mountain freshness and sweet fragrance. Musky spiced pear fruits and light white florals, the palate's impressive for its concentrated pear flavour, slippery smooth texture and its polished, balanced finish. This is well ahead of the competition.

2007 Vietti Roero Arneis

Score 93

PIEDMONT, ITALY
Price $43.00
Quality   ★★★★ ⸱
Alc./Vol. 13%
Drink   Now
Closure   Cork

A white wine of some noble standing from the revered Piedmont region in the north-west of Italy, this shows classic pears and minerals, super fresh and very elegant. Fills the palate with pears, apples and feijoa fruits, supple texture through the middle and a stylish, dry, white musk-flavoured finish. Impeccable.

2006 William Fevre Chablis

Score 90

CHABLIS, FRANCE
Price $38.00
Quality   ★★★★
Alc./Vol. 12.5%
Drink   2010
Closure   Cork

Fevre makes this chablis in a steely, pure unoaked style, so it glistens with bright citrus fruits and plenty of stony, oyster-shell minerals. The palate delivers attractive peach and citrus fruits, pristine and direct, underscored with brisk acid cut and finely judged balance.

Rosé

In Australia, just about every red wine grape has produced a rosé-style wine, and aside from varietal nuances the major distinguishing character of our local rosé is sweetness or residual sugar. Almost every winery has one, sometimes two or more; the pink drink has increased in popularity and makes an interesting alternative to drinking white wine. Australia has a strong culture of grenache-based rosé, usually made in a sweeter style, darker in colour, full of red fruits and vibrant youthful exuberance. Of the drier styles, pinot makes a number of good examples, showcasing elegance and savoury complexity. You'll find shiraz, cabernet, sangiovese, nebbiolo and many other grapes can do the job; balance and texture are the key features of truly great rosé. Most wines are best consumed cool, and as a general rule, the sweeter the wine the cooler it should be served. FOOD: Can't decide if you feel like white or red? Hedge your bets and go with rosé. Salmon, ocean trout and fish stew are all good for rosé – it's adaptable when it comes to food, and spicy dishes are ideal.

2007 Alta for Elsie
Score **89**

ADELAIDE HILLS	Lovely bright pinot noir berry fruits here, this has bright striking freshness and rose petal fragrance. Red fruits, some strawberry flavour, the palate is soft and light, lifts musky off the finish, some creamy texture and cherry skin through the finish, really charming, just like the name.
Price $18.00	
Quality ★★★ ⌐	
Alc./Vol. 13%	
Drink Now	
Closure Screwcap	

2007 Barratt Piccadilly Sunrise Rosé
Score **90**

ADELAIDE HILLS	Named after the Adelaide Hills sunrises that winemaker Lindsay Barratt sees plenty of times during vintage, it's bright as a button in the glass. Ripe red apple and some creamy notes, toffee apples and fine musky fragrance. The palate is supple, has tart red fruit flavour and juicy crunch through the finish. Really balanced and snappy.
Price $21.00 ✓	
Quality ★★★★	
Alc./Vol. 13.5%	
Drink Now	
Closure Screwcap	

2007 **Chapel Hill il Vescovo Sangiovese Rosé**
Score **89**

McLAREN VALE
Price $14.00 ✓
Quality ★★★ ┤
Alc./Vol. 13.5%
Drink Now
Closure Screwcap

Light reddish orange colour, very bright fruits and some smoky wafts here, just showing a twist of sangiovese spices. Very supple palate, savoury red fruits, a soft foamy texture and light musk lift off the finish. Gentle and easy, feminine.

2008 **Charles Melton Rose of Virginia**
Score **93**

BAROSSA VALLEY
Price $24.00 ✓
Quality ★★★★ ┤
Alc./Vol. 13%
Drink Now
Closure Screwcap

Charlie Melton delivers this rosé with Jedi-like precision every year. Deeper colour, light purple almost, really vibrant attractive brambly grenache aromas, very bright, no lumps or bumps, just ripe berry fruits and red apples; mouth-watering. The palate is juicy dense and flavoursome, unmatched for its vivacious, delicious drinkability.
PENGUIN BEST ROSÉ

2007 **Coriole Nebbiolo Rosé**
Score **91**

McLAREN VALE
Price $18.00 ✓
Quality ★★★★
Alc./Vol. 13%
Drink Now
Closure Screwcap

The orange colour is a distinctive nebbiolo hue, a little lift of soft rose petal perfume here, trademark stuff, then some tarry red cherry smells. Yum! Nice richness in the mouth and some really intense cherry and redcurrant flavours, bright acid crunch and a dry finish. Likes food, this one!

2006 **David Franz Red Rosé**
Score **88**

BAROSSA VALLEY
Price $23.00
Quality ★★★ ┤
Alc./Vol. 12.2%
Drink Now
Closure Screwcap

One of the darkest rosé wines, looks like pinot. A unique blend of shiraz, white frontignac, grenache, riesling and mataro, this has sweet musky red fruits, the frontignac and riesling add floral lift, has some briary fragrant notes too. The palate is gently sweet and very soft, simple glossy red fruit flavours and just a hint of grip.

2007 **Devil's Lair Fifth Leg Rosé**
Score **88**

MARGARET RIVER
Price $18.00
Quality ★★★ ┤
Alc./Vol. 13.5%
Drink Now
Closure Screwcap

This well-made merlot/cabernet/shiraz rosé has bright creamy red fruits and musk, it casts a wide net of appeal over anyone who likes to drink the pink. The palate is a simple mouthful of red berry flavour, musky after that, finishing soft, sweetly balanced and clean.

2007 Dominique Portet Fontaine Rosé

Score **90**

YARRA VALLEY
Price $20.00 ✓
Quality ★★★★
Alc./Vol. 13.5%
Drink Now
Closure Screwcap

There's no doubt about him, Dominique makes a brilliant rosé year in, year out. Using cabernet, merlot and shiraz, he's captured some more savoury notes, cherries and spice here, it really piques the interest. The palate is soft; it flies across low and even, more savoury spiced cherry fruit here too, terrific balance.

2006 Farr Rising Saignée

Score **90**

GEELONG
Price $25.00
Quality ★★★★
Alc./Vol. 14%
Drink Now
Closure Diam

A standout in the lineup because there's a good whack of oak dealt into this free-run pinot juice. Some spiced red fruits sit just below, it's decidedly savoury. The palate is a densely textured, savoury and complex affair, not a simple beverage style, complex and chewy, finishes dry with red fruits and nutty oak to close.

2006 Jacob's Creek Reserve Shiraz Rosé

Score **89**

SOUTH EASTERN AUSTRALIA
Price $17.00
Quality ★★★ ┤
Alc./Vol. 13%
Drink Now
Closure Screwcap

Reserve rosé bottlings are few and far between, the notion kinda raises a smile. Mid-red colour, has some complex sulphides, making the wine more interesting, sitting atop bright red fruits. The palate has really tight concentrated red berry flavours, fine acid and some spritzy tingle. Tidy style.

2007 Krinklewood Francesca Rosé

Score **91**

HUNTER VALLEY 🌿
Price $20.00 ✓
Quality ★★★★
Alc./Vol. 12.3%
Drink Now
Closure Screwcap

This light-coloured mourvèdre rosé is a dead ringer for the quaffable southern French seaside rosé wines of Bandol and Cassis. Berry fruit aromas, subtle spices and fresh acid crunch are rolled up in smoothly balanced texture. Serve well chilled and drink it like a white with bouillabaisse.

2006 Liebich Tempranillo Rosé

Score **89**

BAROSSA VALLEY
Price $19.00
Quality ★★★ ┤
Alc./Vol. 12.8%
Drink Now
Closure Screwcap

Liebich's first shot at a rosé and they've already got their eye in. Pale red in the glass, with attractive fragrant red fruit aromas, the palate is fine and dry, really delicate red fruit flavours, some chirpy tempranillo cherry skin and delicate acid-driven balance. Finishes crisp and fresh.

2007 Loose End Rosé

Score **92**

BAROSSA VALLEY
Price $18.00 ✓
Quality ★★★★
Alc./Vol. 13%
Drink Now
Closure Screwcap

This draws on the natural affinity of grenache's red fruits and fragrant perfume, really bright and lifted, right in the sweet spot of easy-drinking appeal. The palate pitches plenty of fruit flavour with some sweet appeal, lovely balance and freshness. Nicely pitched!

2007 Massena Rosé

Score **89**

BAROSSA VALLEY
Price $20.00
Quality ★★★ꜭ
Alc./Vol. 13.5%
Drink Now
Closure Screwcap

The Massena boys have a keen eye for splicing wines together with a range of varieties on offer. This calls on grenache, mataro, cinsault and petite syrah; it shows brambly fruit aromas and some gravelly notes, the palate is super bright and musky, with some nice lift and bright fruit presence, gentle acid spike and neat balance. Well judged.

2007 Mitolo Jester Rosé

Score **90**

McLAREN VALE
Price $22.00
Quality ★★★★
Alc./Vol. 15%
Drink Now
Closure Screwcap

The light red colour is a beacon for good times; surely this was the Jester's favourite drink of all? Following a short spell on skins, sangiovese's red cherries and berries are in full swing. Flavours are all red fruits and fragrant musk, the texture is smooth and it handles a good chill, cherry-pip finish.

2007 Mount Majura Rosé

Score **90**

CANBERRA DISTRICT
Price $16.00
Quality ★★★★
Alc./Vol. 11.9%
Drink Now
Closure Screwcap

A handy merlot rosé from this hillside vineyard with a darker hue than many. Has some herb, cherry and briary berry fruit aromas, a little complexity, bright and super fragrant. The palate is a nicely weighted and balanced affair, really briary, they've used the acidity to good effect, finishes with crisp cherry berry flavours. Long and balanced.

2007 Old Mill Estate Rosé

Score **90**

LANGHORNE CREEK
Price $20.00 ✓
Quality ★★★★
Alc./Vol. 12%
Drink Now
Closure Screwcap

Peter and Vicki Widdop have a handy knack with this pink made from touriga naçional. Light red fruits, some jammy ripe red fruit aromas here, nice lift and fragrance. The palate is supple, with really juicy light red fruit flavours and some understated savoury edges. Nice balance and very easy to drink.

2007 Penley Estate Over The Moon Rosé
Score **88**

COONAWARRA	
Price	$15.00
Quality	★★★ ⌐
Alc./Vol.	13.5%
Drink	Now
Closure	Screwcap

Another winner from Kym Tolley down in Coonawarra, just 24 hours' skin contact gives this rosé a light bright red, almost iridescent in the glass. Quite striking, ripe red fruit aromas, nice and attractive, the palate is super soft, pillowy red fruit flavours, raspberries and decent balance.

2007 Pikes The Bleedings Pinot Noir Rosé
Score **91**

ADELAIDE HILLS	
Price	$22.00 ✓
Quality	★★★★
Alc./Vol.	13.5%
Drink	Now
Closure	Screwcap

Pale salmon colour, light berry fruit aromas here, some strawberry and cherry, with some savoury edges. Quite a savoury palate, raspberry and red cherry flavour, structured and even, it's best not to chill this too hard to get the most out of the texture. Food-friendly style.

2007 Pitchfork Pink
Score **88**

MARGARET RIVER	
Price	$17.00
Quality	★★★ ⌐
Alc./Vol.	12.6%
Drink	Now
Closure	Screwcap

Made from cabernet juice, this has some lifted bright fragrance, sour cherries, apples and some more savoury regional cabernet accents. The palate is a bright but demanding affair with plenty of taut acid crunch and dense texture, just sweetens through the finish.

2007 Pizzini Rosetta
Score **88**

VICTORIA	
Price	$17.00
Quality	★★★ ⌐
Alc./Vol.	13.5%
Drink	Now
Closure	Screwcap

Attractive bright light red colour, this well-made sangiovese rosé has plenty of bright brambly red fruits, hints of smoky spice, really attractive, clean and lifted. The palate is an easy-drinking proposition with sweet red fruits through the middle and slightly smoky edges. It finishes dry and juicy.

2007 R osé McLaren Vale Cabernet Sauvignon Rosé
Score **90**

McLAREN VALE	
Price	$19.00 ✓
Quality	★★★★
Alc./Vol.	13%
Drink	Now
Closure	Screwcap

Bright ripe cabernet fruits here and some really attractive brambly red berries and leafy complexity. There's enough sweet and savoury to attract just about everyone; a little chew through the finish leaving savoury red fruit flavours. Inspired by Provençal living, delivered with dinki-di Aussie style.

2007 Seven Hill Lost Boot Rosé

Score **88**

CLARE VALLEY
Price $15.00 ✓
Quality ★★★ ↻
Alc./Vol. 14%
Drink Now
Closure Screwcap

The Jesuits found a 130-year-old boot in the wall of one of their historic buildings, in case you were wondering. It's one of the darker rosé wines in a line-up, some really piercing red grenache fruit aromas here. The palate runs with intensity, direct raspberry fruits and soft, easy berry flavours tumble through the finish. Decent balance too.

2007 Sorriso Rosé

Score **89**

BAROSSA VALLEY
Price $15.00 ✓
Quality ★★★ ↻
Alc./Vol. 12.5%
Drink Now
Closure Screwcap

Thorn-Clark has approached rosé with cabernet and nebbiolo, throwing one of the darker hues in the line-up, some decent ripe berry aromas and a bright concentrated spice and rose impression. The palate pushes quite wide, really juicy with musky red flavours, finishing soft.

2007 St Hallett Rosé

Score **90**

BAROSSA VALLEY
Price $18.00
Quality ★★★★
Alc./Vol. 12.5%
Drink Now
Closure Screwcap

You'll have to make it to the cellar door to get your hands on a bottle of this juicy Barossa pink, but it's well worth the detour. Bright attractive brambly berries, one of the darker coloured rosés, it has plenty of juicy supple fruits and doesn't rely on sugar to boost it along; nice savoury finish.

2007 Stella Bella Pink Muscat

Score **92**

MARGARET RIVER
Price $19.00 (375 ml)
Quality ★★★★
Alc./Vol. 7.5%
Drink Now
Closure Screwcap

Mid-salmon colour and the faintest visible bubbles on pouring, this is a classic moscato-style, smells of grapes, honeysuckle and red apples, a little Turkish delight, spritzy on the tongue and nicely balanced, not too sweet, leaves rose water flavour through the finish, ideal for summer. Refreshing and not cloying.

2007 Sutton Grange Estate Rosé

Score **92**

CENTRAL VICTORIA
Price $32.00
Quality ★★★★
Alc./Vol. 13.5%
Drink Now
Closure Diam

This is complex and lees-influenced, there's a distinct rose petal aroma too, really perfumed and cryptic, some honey and sweet wattle perfume. Terrific texture and balance, makes a bright complex impression, layered texture, gently creamy and finishing with a nutty savoury twist. Grown-up rosé.

2007 Sutton Grange Fairbank Rosé — *Score* 90

CENTRAL VICTORIA
Price $20.00
Quality ★★★★
Alc./Vol. 13%
Drink Now
Closure Screwcap

This needs some air to come clean, stays savoury though, really restrained red earthy fruits, gentle perfume and minerals. The palate texture is superb, really smooth, supple and gently caressing, has some dense, savoury red fruit flavours, neatly balanced. A blend of syrah, cabernet and merlot.

2008 Turkey Flat Rosé — *Score* 90

BAROSSA VALLEY
Price $23.00
Quality ★★★★
Alc./Vol. 15%
Drink Now
Closure Screwcap

Nice bright pinkish-red. Some really bright lifted fragrance here, florals, almost muscat-like, fragrance, some briary cassis-like berry aromas too, like the musky flavours, attractive and balanced, sweetness used to fine tune.

2007 YarraLoch Rosé — *Score* 89

YARRA VALLEY
Price $20.00
Quality ★★★↓
Alc./Vol. 12%
Drink Now
Closure Screwcap

A complex cabernet rosé that's utilised natural yeast and French oak fermentation to build intrigue and texture. Just a lightly stained salmon colour, some ripe berry fruit aromas, strawberry and cherries, some spice in there too. The palate is really savoury and carries off some nutty savoury oak influence, finishing with striking nutmeg spice. One for the dining table.

Pinot noir

Pinot has quickly become one of the most talked about red wines in Australia; it has hit the big time – in a very big way. The days of highly priced, inconsistent wines are behind us and quality has arrived at almost previously unthinkable price points, with reliability. The pinot grape has winemakers the world over chasing the Holy Grail; it has wine collectors worked up by its aura of rarity. Pinot makes more of a splash on the dining table than almost any other red wine, and its beguiling, complex personality demands a big shaped glass. FOOD: Lighter body, fine tannins, lower alcohol levels, fragrant aromas and layered flavours make pinot a good match for game meats and a range of cuisines, from French to Chinese. Duck is the banker.

2006 Apsley Gorge Pinot Noir — Score 92

TASMANIA	From the Bicheno area on the east coast of the island, this shows deep-seated ripe pinot fruits, dark cherries, undergrowth and scents of spiced earth. Plenty of flesh through the palate, juicy red fruits, musky lift and convincing weight through the finish. Richly bodied and keenly balanced.
Price $56.00	
Quality ★★★★	
Alc./Vol. 14%	
Drink 2010	
Closure Screwcap	

2007 Ashton Hills Estate Pinot Noir — Score 94

ADELAIDE HILLS	Stephen George is the unchallenged king of Adelaide Hills pinot. This is an unfiltered, complex wine with superb varietal character, ripe cherries, orange peel, spices, subtle oak toast and a big hit of fragrance. The palate's soft and dense, musky perfume lifts right across spicy cherry and strawberry flavours, tannins layer away below and it all launches the finish in style.
Price $49.50	
Quality ★★★★★ ⌐	
Alc./Vol. 14%	
Drink 2010	
Closure Screwcap	

2007 Ashton Hills Piccadilly Valley Pinot Noir — Score 91

ADELAIDE HILLS	This is the entry-level from Ashton and it's a safe bet for authentic pinot character, plenty of cherry fruits and cool earthy undergrowth. The palate delivers impressive concentration and fruit density, fairly solid texture on a bed of light tannins – cherry fruits from start to finish.
Price $34.00	
Quality ★★★★	
Alc./Vol. 13.5%	
Drink Now	
Closure Screwcap	

2005 Bannockburn Pinot Noir

Score 93

GEELONG	
Price	$55.00
Quality	★ ★ ★ ★ ┤
Alc./Vol.	13.5%
Drink	Now
Closure	Cork

The light cherry-red colour gives little clue about the concentration and complexity at work here. Plenty of fragrant spice, sweetened with swish French oak across cherry fruits. The palate is supple and toned, tannins add definition to ripe fruit flavours, heading into some savoury territory through the finish.

2006 Bannockburn Pinot Noir

Score 93

GEELONG	
Price	$60.00
Quality	★ ★ ★ ★ ┤
Alc./Vol.	12.5%
Drink	2012
Closure	Cork

Bright, lifted and super-spicy pinot nose, sweet cinnamon and some added French oak richness pushing from behind. The palate's all about silky tannin and finesse, some baking spices and rich cherry fruits, compact and concentrated. Superb balance and, cork willing, a fine future ahead.

2005 Bannockburn Serré Pinot Noir

Score 94

GEELONG	
Price	$105.00
Quality	★ ★ ★ ★ ┤
Alc./Vol.	13.5%
Drink	2013
Closure	Cork

This patch of the Bannockburn vineyard always delivers additional depth and darker fruits, rich cherry and spice, some undergrowthy complexity and gentle oak toast. The palate's built with intensity and depth, plenty of meaty/cherry flavour and toasted spices; brooding and impressive.

2006 Bannockburn Stuart Pinot Noir

Score 96

GEELONG	
Price	$65.00 ✓
Quality	★ ★ ★ ★ ★
Alc./Vol.	12.5%
Drink	2010
Closure	Cork

This Stuart pinot is differentiated by the method of fermenting only whole bunches of pinot grapes; that's right, 100%. It brings an upwards spiral of complex aromatics to the nose, hard baking spices and cherry fruits. The palate's where it all unfolds, amazing textural density, super-soft, pillow-like flesh and fine long dense tannins sweep through the finish. Superb.

2006 Barratt The Bonython Pinot Noir

Score 90

ADELAIDE HILLS	
Price	$27.00
Quality	★ ★ ★ ★
Alc./Vol.	14%
Drink	Now
Closure	Screwcap

Sourced from the cool saddle of the Piccadilly Valley, this has bold primary, almost raw, fruit characters, blue fruits, strawberry jam and forest floor. Delivers plenty of strawberry flavour on the palate, some cool herbs and approachable tannins.

2007 Barwick Estate The Collectables Pinot Noir
Score **92**

PEMBERTON
Price $30.00
Quality ★★★★
Alc./Vol. 14%
Drink 2010
Closure Screwcap

A more savoury/earthy take on the pinot theme, typical of the cool coastal Pemberton region. Plenty of sweet spices and bright cherry fruit aromas, some earthy notes, brambly red berries and cedary oak. The palate has plenty of ripe bright cherry flavour, fine sweeping tannins and an alluring supple musky lift through the finish.

2006 Bass Phillip 21 Pinot Noir
Score **94**

GIPPSLAND
Price $75.00
Quality ★★★★ ⅃
Alc./Vol. 12.8%
Drink 2012
Closure Diam

The one and only 2006 release, an amalgam of all material spared from frost. It shows that typical Bass Phillip unfiltered hue in the glass, complex soft cherry fruit aromas, smoked spices and earthy undergrowth too; breathes to life with air. The palate is swathed in supple fleshy texture and has engaging density, tannins are evenly distributed, bright spiced red cherry flavour, flinty mineral notes and a spear of acid. Switches earthy through the finish. A superb statement of variety, region and producer.

2007 Bay of Fires Pinot Noir
Score **94**

TASMANIA
Price $38.00 ✓
Quality ★★★★ ⅃
Alc./Vol. 13.5%
Drink 2009
Closure Screwcap

This stylish and well-priced Tasmanian pinot has intense spices, almost shiraz-like, very peppery and cool, plenty of complex winemaking laid across the top of briary/brambly fruit. The palate's smoothly textured, finely structured and coated in deep cherry flavour. It's very much about the variety and winemaker, with terrific spicy lift launching through the finish.

2006 Bindi Block 5 Pinot Noir
Score **96**

MACEDON RANGES
Price $95.00
Quality ★★★★★
Alc./Vol. 13.5%
Drink 2011
Closure Diam

A wine with striking fragrance and fine musky perfume that conjures up pinot planted to quartzy soils, restrained and defined, superbly elegant. The palate has terrific density and weight, driving flavours fine and deep, the oak smoulders away behind bright dense cherry fruit. Long, even, regal and complete, crafted with impeccable balance. A rippling masterpiece!

2007 **Bindi Composition Pinot Noir**   *Score* **93**

MACEDON RANGES	
Price	$50.00
Quality	★★★★ ⌐
Alc./Vol.	13.5%
Drink	2010
Closure	Diam

Winemaker Michael Dhillon is pleasantly surprised with his '07 Composition pinot given the challenge of the season. It's looking fragrant and darn attractive, bright cherry fruits and some sweet cinnamon spice. The palate's supple and even, elegant and filled with soft rounded tannins, finishing with musky lift and fine savoury minerals.

2006 **Breheny Vineyards Brown Magpie Pinot Noir**   *Score* **91**

GEELONG	
Price	$22.00 ✓
Quality	★★★★
Alc./Vol.	14%
Drink	Now
Closure	Screwcap

A juicy approachable pinot with direct fruit characters, dried spiced cherry and some earthy notes too. Oak is of little importance, this is all about fruit. Lively juicy cherry and raspberry fruit palate, acidity lifts it high; tannins are soft and supportive, leaving a musky trail. A great everyday pinot.

2006 **By Farr Pinot Noir**   *Score* **95**

GEELONG	
Price	$65.00
Quality	★★★★ ⌐
Alc./Vol.	14%
Drink	2011
Closure	Cork

Winemaker Gary Farr could probably make great pinot in his sleep these days and there's no mistaking this for the real deal. The oak sits up when first poured but fruit swirls smoothly into action, offering bright cherry and whole-bunch aromatics in impressive concentration. The palate's smoky and dense, drawn on fine, sturdy tannins; it's a solid wine, yet a charming pinot. Balanced and resolved, the godfather is on form with this '06.

2006 **By Farr Sangreal Pinot Noir**   *Score* **96**

GEELONG	
Price	$65.00
Quality	★★★★★
Alc./Vol.	13.5%
Drink	2012
Closure	Cork

This smoky, complex pinot is Gary Farr's top bottling. Sweet roasted meat and rich dark cherry fruit aromas, terrific ripeness and engaging, lifted whole-bunch fragrance – cleverly pitched. Superb depth and smooth-flowing palate shape with cherry and chocolate flavour, regal smoky oak, deep charming tannins; it's precisely structured and impeccably balanced. Delicious drinking now, it will reward time in bottle.

PENGUIN BEST PINOT NOIR

2006 Clair de Lune Pinot Noir

Score **92**

GIPPSLAND
Price $30.00
Quality   ★★★★
Alc./Vol. 12.5%
Drink   Now
Closure   Diam

Named after Claude Debussy's astoundingly beautiful music, this is from one of Gippsland's smallest producers. It shows plenty of dark spice and toasty oak, ripe and complex, some earthy chocolate smells. Supple, smooth palate and fluid tannins, a terrific balance between sweet fruit and savoury structure, the oak paints a toasty stripe across the finish. Won the pinot trophy at the 2008 Gippsland Wine Show.

2006 Clyde Park Pinot Noir

Score **94**

GEELONG
Price $35.00 ✓
Quality   ★★★★ ⟩
Alc./Vol. 13.5%
Drink   2010
Closure   Screwcap

Another Geelong name that's hit a purple patch recently, here showing upbeat musky, red floral pinot aromas and impressive complexity. Lovely breadth and subtle savoury layering, bright strawberry flavour and a fine core of tannin that pins flavour right around the palate. Subtle and engaging.

2007 Coldstream Hills Pinot Noir

Score **92**

YARRA VALLEY
Price $25.00 ✓
Quality   ★★★★
Alc./Vol. 13%
Drink   Now
Closure   Screwcap

This Yarra blend shows striking strawberry fruits with sweet florals mixed throughout, whole bunches in the mix bring additional lift, also savoury oak and spice. A supple and fleshy palate is already building smoky oak-derived complexity. Plenty to offer and great value to boot.

2006 Crittenden Estate Geppetto Pinot Noir

Score **89**

PORT PHILLIP
Price $20.00
Quality   ★★★ ⟩
Alc./Vol. 13.5%
Drink   Now
Closure   Screwcap

The Peninsula puppeteer, Garry Crittenden, has sourced pinot from further afield, showing ripe dark cherry fruit, assertive oak and savoury complexity. Decent fruit weight on the palate and just enough flesh on the bones to carry it through, some oak char and savoury edges cross the finish.

2007 Darling Park Pinot Noir

Score **88**

MORNINGTON PENINSULA
Price $30.00
Quality   ★★★ ⟩
Alc./Vol. 14.3%
Drink   Now
Closure   Screwcap

Attractive complexity in this regional blend, drawing fruit from both high and low vineyard sites on the Peninsula. Shows foresty dark fruits and some savoury/meaty aromas, direct and fragrant too. The palate is elegant and juicy, lively red cherry fruit flavours and sprightly acidity.

2006 De Bortoli Estate Grown Pinot Noir

Score 94

YARRA VALLEY 📖
Price $38.00 ✓
Quality   ★ ★ ★ ★ ⊰
Alc./Vol.   13%
Drink   2012
Closure   Screwcap

Plenty of new wood here, brassy and a little raw on the nose, the fruit has been wrapped in savoury winemaker's clothing for the moment. The palate tells the real story, built with layers of flavour and finely ground tannin, smooth and savoury, it makes a balanced impression from start to finish.

2006 De Bortoli Reserve Release Pinot Noir

Score 95

YARRA VALLEY
Price $60.00
Quality   ★ ★ ★ ★ ⊰
Alc./Vol.   13%
Drink   2011
Closure   Screwcap

This leads with savoury/earthy characters on the nose, slowly unfurling cherry fruit freshness and accentuated spice characters, oak plays a strictly supporting role. Mouth-filling supple tannins and fresh wild strawberry fruit flavours, really attractive and delicate, soft and curvaceous, some game meats and a flurry of complexity through the finish. Impressive depth and drive.

2007 De Bortoli Windy Peak Pinot Noir

Score 90

VICTORIA
Price $15.00 ✓
Quality   ★ ★ ★ ★
Alc./Vol.   13%
Drink   Now
Closure   Screwcap

Windy Peak offers tremendous value, particularly in the pinot stakes. Youthful and direct, wild berry fruits are dressed in toasty oak, there's musky appeal and brightness. Has a straight-shooting upright palate, tannins are sturdy yet supple, balanced and even.

2007 Devil's Corner Pinot Noir

Score 92

KAYENA
Price $19.00 ✓
Quality   ★ ★ ★ ★
Alc./Vol.   13.5%
Drink   2011
Closure   Screwcap

Outrageously good pinot for the money and a ringing endorsement for big-picture Tasmanian terroir. Super-fine strawberry and fresh wild raspberry fruit aromas, terrific lift and life, primary and fine. The palate moves in a similar vein, sliding along fine fresh acid-etched lines, precise and harmonious, red fruit flavours running elegant and long.

2006 Farr Rising Geelong Pinot Noir

Score 91

GEELONG
Price $40.00
Quality   ★ ★ ★ ★
Alc./Vol.   13.5%
Drink   2011
Closure   Screwcap

With a few vintages under the belt now, Nick Farr has settled into the regional groove. He's dropped plenty of oak across this Geelong bottling, some sweet spices and earthy complexity, ripe red fruits working out from below. The palate's all lined up with fine tannin, impressive structure, the wood is bedded in nicely – some savoury/grippy chew through the cherry cola finish.

2005 Freycinet Louis Pinot Noir

Score **94**

NORTHERN TASMANIA	
Price	$38.00 ✓
Quality	★★★★ ↓
Alc./Vol.	13.5%
Drink	2009
Closure	Screwcap

This, the most affordable Freycinet pinot, punches well above its weight. Cool, calm and compact aromas; red cherry fruits, gently smoked meats, strawberry and fine French oak. Superbly concentrated ripe cherry flavour, bright acidity and neatly shaped tannins. Balanced, fresh and vital.

2005 Freycinet Vineyard Pinot Noir

Score **96**

NORTHERN TASMANIA	
Price	$65.00
Quality	★★★★★
Alc./Vol.	14%
Drink	2010
Closure	Screwcap

Plenty of heady pinot fragrance that's deeply anchored in the ripe dark cherry spectrum, with some nutty oak behind; it's knit tightly together and building some game meat complexity. Gripping depth and intensity, very polished tannins, complex cherry and spice flavours, finishing with faultless length and balance.

2006 Gembrook Hill Pinot Noir

Score **91**

YARRA VALLEY	
Price	$48.00
Quality	★★★★
Alc./Vol.	13%
Drink	Now
Closure	Diam

Very much in the light, airy style with bright sappy strawberry fruits, pale colour; it's certainly seen some whole bunches in fermentation and is building smoky complexity, ahead of a swathe of sulphide. Bright cherry and berry flavours, fine light tannins and prickly acid crunch.

2006 Giaconda Nantua Vineyard Pinot Noir

Score **94**

BEECHWORTH 🖉	
Price	$90.00
Quality	★★★★ ↓
Alc./Vol.	13.5%
Drink	2015
Closure	Screwcap

Showing discreet complexity and subtle toasty oak, cool-handed restraint and fine minerally fragrance; it opens smoothly with air. Rick Kinzbrunner has crafted a beauty in '06. Superior texture and density, great length, it drives a fine line of precise acidity, fine tannin and long cherry flavour. Will develop nicely.

2006 Giant Steps Sexton Vineyard Pinot Noir

Score **93**

YARRA VALLEY 🖉	
Price	$35.00
Quality	★★★★ ↓
Alc./Vol.	13.5%
Drink	2010
Closure	Screwcap

Perched on a sloping site around the hill from Yarra Yering et al, the '06 Sexton vineyard pinot is spicy and broodingly dense, offering savoury/stony characters and sour cherry fruits, some cassis flavours too. A handsome marriage of detail, finesse and power; site driven and distinctive.

2006 Giant Steps Tarraford Vineyard Pinot Noir

Score **94**

YARRA VALLEY
Price $40.00 ✓
Quality ★★★★⁺
Alc./Vol. 13%
Drink 2012
Closure Screwcap

This is the finer and more delicate pinot of the Giant Steps single vineyards: bright pristine red cherry fruits, attractive fragrance, some vanilla and sweet spices. The palate rolls in fine layers, good build and shape, sweet spices and fine savoury tannins. An elegant, precise pinot with a bright future.

2006 Hat Rock Pinot Noir

Score **91**

GEELONG
Price $24.00 ✓
Quality ★★★★
Alc./Vol. 13.5%
Drink Now
Closure Screwcap

A riper, richer and more developed 2006 pinot, showing red fruits and brambly notes, some finer fragrance too, supportive oak sits in behind. The palate has thickness and weight, really juicy through the middle, finishing soft and balanced. Drink up!

2006 Henschke Giles Pinot Noir

Score **91**

ADELAIDE HILLS
Price $46.00
Quality ★★★★
Alc./Vol. 13.5%
Drink 2009
Closure Screwcap

From the cool and elevated Lenswood district of the Hills, this shows bright red cherry fruits, peppery spice and fine cedary oak; plenty of savoury brambly notes too. The palate has cool resolve, elegant red berry flavours, fine but concentrated, finishing with a softer edge.

2006 Hoddles Creek Estate Pinot Noir

Score **92**

YARRA VALLEY
Price $18.00 ✓
Quality ★★★★⁺
Alc./Vol. 13.2%
Drink Now
Closure Screwcap

This has an earthy/undergrowthy style, some forest-floor and bright red cherry fruit aromas with oak neatly integrated into the mix. The palate has impressive weight and richness: tannins fold neatly around the fruit, bringing length, balance and a cherry pie finish.

2006 Innocent Bystander Pinot Noir

Score **90**

YARRA VALLEY
Price $20.00 ✓
Quality ★★★★
Alc./Vol. 13.5%
Drink Now
Closure Screwcap

From the Giant Steps fun factory in Healesville, here's a come-and-get-it red fruits pinot with straightforward pure cherry and raspberry aromas. It slips lightly across the palate, bringing strawberry and musk flavour, flippant and very easy to take.

2007 Josef Chromy Pepik Pinot Noir — Score 93

TASMANIA
Price $19.00 ✓
Quality ★★★★ ⟩
Alc./Vol. 12.5%
Drink Now
Closure Screwcap

One of the highlights of the *Guide* this year was discovering this ripper from Tasmania. It's hard to fathom that you can get this great pinot noir for under $20. Plenty of cool resolve, fragrant dark cherry and strawberry fruits, bright and lifted. The palate rolls through in charming shape: smooth, fleshy and impeccably balanced. Grab it while you can!

PENGUIN BEST-VALUE RED WINE

2006 Kooyong Estate Pinot Noir — Score 94

MORNINGTON PENINSULA
Price $42.00
Quality ★★★★ ⟩
Alc./Vol. 13.5%
Drink 2011
Closure Diam

One of the most charming Kooyong pinots to date, showing plenty of ripe cherry fruits and attractive savoury oak; the house style is developing depth and richness. It's supple from start to finish, velveteen tannins unfurl and roll along the palate, punchy acidity keeps the palate juicy and balanced.

2006 Kooyong Ferrous Pinot Noir — Score 96

MORNINGTON PENINSULA
Price $65.00
Quality ★★★★★
Alc./Vol. 14%
Drink 2013
Closure Diam

It's not a competition but this is the pick of the '06 Kooyong single-vineyard wines; richly coloured, it shows spicy complexity across ripe dark cherry fruits, orange zest and Eastern spices. Impressive depth and palate weight, the oak is in check, allowing some finer red fruits, cherries and musk to show through. It's a structured and commanding pinot, fusing power, definition and balance.

2006 Kooyong Haven Pinot Noir — Score 93

MORNINGTON PENINSULA
Price $65.00
Quality ★★★★ ⟩
Alc./Vol. 13%
Drink 2010
Closure Diam

The biggest and most obvious of the Kooyong single-vineyard pinots, Haven shows classic sweet cherry fruits, very primary, smells warm and round. An assertive mix of red fruits and savoury flavours, the oak is worked in behind soft dense fruit tannins, painted in broader brushstrokes.

2007 Kooyong Massale Pinot Noir — Score 91

MORNINGTON PENINSULA
Price $27.00
Quality ★★★★
Alc./Vol. 13%
Drink 2009
Closure Diam

Sweet musky fragrance and hints of roasting herbs place this outside the repertoire of estate-sourced pinot. Red fruits and bright fragrant lift, appealing perfume and earthy edges. The wine sits up on the palate, delivering smart smoky pinot flavour and fine light sheets of tannin.

2006 **Kooyong Meres Pinot Noir**   *Score* **95**

MORNINGTON PENINSULA	The finest and most elegant of the single-vineyard trio,
Price $55.00	but deceptively powerful and intense. Cedary oak rolls
Quality ★★★★⁺	through cherry-scented fruits, bridged by fragrant sweet
Alc./Vol. 13.5%	spice. Smoky complexity runs through the palate, plenty of
Drink 2012	ripe red cherry fruit flavour, supple tannin, savoury oak and
Closure Diam	bright acid crunch that sizzles through the finish.

2006 **Lark Hill Pinot Noir**   *Score* **92**

CANBERRA DISTRICT 🍃	This biodynamic Canberra District veteran makes pinot
Price $30.00	in a decidedly cool hue: fragrant wild cherries, some
Quality ★★★★	blueberries, brushy herbs and attractive fragrance. The
Alc./Vol. 13.5%	palate rolls convincing texture right throughout, earthy
Drink 2011	cherry flavour and astute oak twirled playfully through
Closure Screwcap	ripe tannin.

2006 **Lethbridge Pinot Noir**   *Score* **93**

GEELONG 🍃	Ray Nadeson's estate bottling is deep and perfumed: ripe
Price $32.00 ✓	dark cherry fruits, impressive concentration and richness,
Quality ★★★★⁺	while the oak forms a savoury backdrop. The palate
Alc./Vol. 13.5%	builds weight in layers across fine tannins and hearty
Drink 2009	fruit presence, finishing upbeat and fragrant.
Closure Diam	

2007 **Lillydale Estate Pinot Noir**   *Score* **91**

YARRA VALLEY	Straightforward red cherry fruit, this has even-handed
Price $26.00 ✓	pinot character, plenty of supporting wood, all in balance
Quality ★★★★	and some spice here too. Spritzy palate, raw vinous dark
Alc./Vol. 13.5%	cherry flavour with the oak wedged in tight; there's earthy
Drink Now	complexity, ripe dark cherries and some smoky '07 vintage
Closure Screwcap	character through the finish.

2006 **Lillydale Estate Pinot Noir**   *Score* **94**

YARRA VALLEY	Another winning take on the Yarra pinot theme: deep
Price $27.00 ✓	brambly fruits with charry oak and meaty spices rolling
Quality ★★★★⁺	through the background. It starts out fine and silky on
Alc./Vol. 14.5%	the palate, building richness and density in layers, turning
Drink 2010	bold and powerful; the tannins fold in dark velvet layers,
Closure Screwcap	finishing long and balanced.

2006 Little Rebel Pinot Noir   Score 89

YARRA VALLEY

Price $17.00

Quality ★★★ ⁴

Alc./Vol. 13%

Drink Now

Closure Screwcap

This bargain-basement Yarra pinot has a slightly shy nose, regional red fruits and some older oak providing nutty/savoury complexity; it takes time to warm up in the glass. Strawberry and raspberry fruit flavours, simple and ripe, finishing musky and upbeat.

2007 Logan Pinot Noir   Score 91

ORANGE

Price $35.00

Quality ★★★★ ⁴

Alc./Vol. 14%

Drink 2009

Closure Screwcap

Bright violet fruits and blueberry pinot in its new folksy livery, attractive freshness and varietal purity with some alluring background oak spice. The palate's direct primary fruit gets straight down to cherry flavour and musky tannin, finishing fresh and clean.

2006 Mac Forbes Coldstream Pinot Noir   Score 94

YARRA VALLEY

Price $38.00 ✓

Quality ★★★★ ⁴

Alc./Vol. 13.5%

Drink 2010

Closure Screwcap

A clever mix of sweet and savoury characters, fine fragrance, delicate supple red fruits, ripe strawberry and sweet spices – all make an attractive proposition. The palate is well structured and evenly paced, super fine and precise, pristine musky cherry fruits, fine tannins and bright savoury/sappy chew. Delicious, elegant pinot.

2006 Mac Forbes Woori Yallock Pinot Noir   Score 95

YARRA VALLEY

Price $46.00 ✓

Quality ★★★★ ⁴

Alc./Vol. 13%

Drink 2012

Closure Screwcap

This is the alpha pinot in the Mac Forbes pack: trademark meaty complexity and edgy intense fruit with raw appeal, savoury and earthy pinot noir characters, fragrant floral notes, red cherries and fine savoury spices. The palate texture is dense yet elegant, it makes a solid impression; classic iron fist in velvet glove stuff. Long cherry flavour, very very good.

2006 Mac Forbes Yarra Valley Pinot Noir   Score 92

YARRA VALLEY

Price $28.00 ✓

Quality ★★★★

Alc./Vol. 12.5%

Drink 2011

Closure Screwcap

Mac Forbes has a knack for working meaty barrel-derived complexity into his pinots. There's a lot going on: charcuterie, sausage meats and smoked cherry fruits, complex stuff indeed! Ripe cherries and some briary complexity on the palate, cedary oak, plenty of soft chewy tannin, and a supple alluring finish. A serious regional wine.

2006 Magnetic Hill Pinot Noir

Score **91**

MACEDON RANGES
Price $25.00 ✓
Quality ★★★★
Alc./Vol. 13.5%
Drink Now
Closure Screwcap

From a small estate, this has classic bright red cherry fruits, really pristine and lifted, shows real promise and cool elegant style, the oak is dealt in behind fruit and there's a fine mineral fragrance. The chirpy palate places red cherry fruit up high. Taut acid, fresh, very youthful and crisp; light tannins, elegant and precise.

2006 Main Ridge Half Acre Pinot Noir

Score **93**

MORNINGTON PENINSULA
Price $60.00
Quality ★★★★⫯
Alc./Vol. 13.5%
Drink 2009
Closure Screwcap

As the name suggests, this is made in limited quantities but well worth seeking out. Pure perfumed nose, showing some cool edges from this Red Hill location, a red cherry-scented wine with stripes of oak throughout. The palate's bright and direct with brisk acid drive, quite edgy and backed by plenty of fine but firm tannin. Stamped with regional character, it unfurls nicely with some time in glass.

2006 Mandala Pinot Noir

Score **89**

YARRA VALLEY
Price $22.00
Quality ★★★⫯
Alc./Vol. 13%
Drink Now
Closure Screwcap

They've captured a more general impression of pinot here, toned back fragrance with ripe fresh red fruits and spice. The palate has slightly tart cherry fruit flavour across fine supple tannins, a splash of wood, finishing soft and approachable.

2006 Mandala Prophet Pinot Noir

Score **93**

YARRA VALLEY
Price $45.00
Quality ★★★★⫯
Alc./Vol. 13.5%
Drink 2010
Closure Screwcap

This single-vineyard wine is intense and generously weighted, ripe red cherries and some spicy nuances, there's some game meat in here too. The palate has richness and presence, fleshy cherry and red fruit flavours perch on supple tannins, smoky twist through the finish.

2007 Mayer Bloody Hill Pinot Noir

Score **94**

YARRA VALLEY
Price $30.00
Quality ★★★★⫯
Alc./Vol. 13.3%
Drink 2011
Closure Diam

Plenty of complex pinot characters and smoky meats, dark ripe cherries – the full spice cupboard is on offer here. The palate trades on sprightly acidity, sweet ripe cherry flavour and supple tannins to keep it anchored in place. A commanding wine with charm and finesse.

2007 Mayer Pinot Noir
Score **94**

YARRA VALLEY
Price $38.00
Quality ★★★★┤
Alc./Vol. 13.5%
Drink 2011
Closure Diam

Dressed like a full-blown Chambertin, Timo Mayer's flagship pinot means business. Ripe and attractive cherry fruits with some deeper toasty oak behind, meat, spice and subtle earthy complexity. Supple and smoky palate entry, building depth and weight, this has Yarra Valley elegance and precision. It is complex and looks every bit the part.

2007 Moorooduc Estate Devil Bend Creek Pinot Noir
Score **91**

MORNINGTON PENINSULA
Price $25.00 ✓
Quality ★★★★
Alc./Vol. 14%
Drink 2009
Closure Screwcap

This entry level wine from the McIntyre family has plenty of bright sweet red fruits, strawberry and cherry, very primary and fresh, with handy varietal definition. Taut tannins and brisk acidity keep the palate linear and focused; crisp, crunchy finish and tart cherries to close.

2006 Moorooduc Estate Wild Yeast Pinot Noir
Score **93**

MORNINGTON PENINSULA
Price $35.00
Quality ★★★★┤
Alc./Vol. 14%
Drink 2011
Closure Screwcap

Some depth, darker fruits and generally a riper impression than the Devil Bend Creek. Sweet spices, earth, florals and upbeat French oak all add up to convincing complexity. Great focus and supple pinot structure, fine dense tannins and straight-shooting acidity, long, even and elegant.

2007 Mount Majura Pinot Noir
Score **90**

CANBERRA DISTRICT
Price $20.00 ✓
Quality ★★★★
Alc./Vol. 12.2%
Drink Now
Closure Screwcap

This has plenty of Canberra's cool-climate spice and some whole-bunch fruit character; strawberry, cherry, meaty aromas and savoury spices too. A complex and exotic pinot. The palate has bright supple strawberry fruit and some dark chocolate flavour, fine dense tannins, finishing with a lighter flurry.

2006 Nepenthe Charleston Pinot Noir
Score **90**

ADELAIDE HILLS
Price $23.00
Quality ★★★★
Alc./Vol. 13.5%
Drink Now
Closure Screwcap

Named after one of the Hills' picturesque hamlets, this starts with ripe berry fruits – almost plums, some pine needles and gentle sweet spice. The palate packs red fruit flavour amid bright chewy tannins; simple and primary from top to toe, finishing with a sour cherry twist.

2005 Nepenthe The Good Doctor Pinot Noir
Score **91**

ADELAIDE HILLS
Price $38.00
Quality ★★★★
Alc./Vol. 14%
Drink Now
Closure Screwcap

Essentially a barrel selection of all pinot parcels in the winery, the top-shelf Nepenthe pinot has textbook cherry and earth aromas, ripe spices and nutty oak complexity. On the palate it has sweet cherry and musk, some bright Adelaide Hills acidity and an elegant soft tannin ride, finishing with musky afterburn.

2007 Ninth Island Pinot Noir
Score **91**

TASMANIA
Price $24.00 ✓
Quality ★★★★
Alc./Vol. 13.5%
Drink 2009
Closure Screwcap

This is a dense and spicy pinot that speaks of its cool-climate origin with some cooler herbs and cherries, fine bright fragrance and a hint of pepper. The tannins are taut and chewy, a distinctive regional Tasmanian pinot of good depth and density; bold and confident.

2006 Oakridge Pinot Noir
Score **94**

YARRA VALLEY
Price $32.00 ✓
Quality ★★★★ ⌐
Alc./Vol. 13.5%
Drink 2010
Closure Screwcap

A well-made pinot with the Yarra Valley's classic mix of elegance and power. Attractive sweet oak and complexity has been built in with a steady hand, ripe red cherry fruits and complementary spice. The palate is filled with fine tannin and has a juicy compact structure; tannins are wrapped in ripe red fruit flavour, finishing with measured richness and impressive balance.

2007 Over The Shoulder Pinot Noir
Score **89**

YARRA VALLEY
Price $20.00
Quality ★★★ ⌐
Alc./Vol. 12%
Drink Now
Closure Screwcap

Here's a simple but lovable pinot with red accented fruits, slightly confected, simple and bright. Tailor-made for up-front enjoyment – no prior knowledge required. The palate is as straightforward as the nose suggests: simple ripe fruits, a spray of oak and a musky finish.

2006 Paracombe Pinot Noir
Score **90**

ADELAIDE HILLS
Price $21.00 ✓
Quality ★★★★
Alc./Vol. 14%
Drink Now
Closure Screwcap

A real strawberries and cream style, very bright, sweet fruit aromas and simple fruit-driven appeal, the oak sweetens it up, adds some chocolate too. It fans out across a light bed of fine tannin, building cherry flavour and some more savoury notes on the palate, a balanced, early-drinking pinot.

2006 Paradigm Hill L'Ami Sage Pinot Noir
Score **91**

MORNINGTON PENINSULA
Price $45.00
Quality ★★★★
Alc./Vol. 14%
Drink 2009
Closure Diam

A big, ripe and juicy Mornington Peninsula pinot, shows plenty of spiced dark cherry fruit and a good serve of wood to one side. Fruit flavour rolls densely across the palate, plenty of rich texture and juicy cherry/plum flavour, this cuddly effort leaves a trail of toasty oak in its wake.

2006 Paringa Estate Reserve Pinot Noir
Score **95**

MORNINGTON PENINSULA
Price $90.00
Quality ★★★★⟩
Alc./Vol. 14.5%
Drink 2013
Closure Screwcap

There's plenty of everything here and it's hard to resist. Lindsay McCall always goes for full ripeness at his Red Hill location, capturing ripe brambly red berry aromas and savoury meaty complexity. Give the oak some time to integrate. Terrific density through the palate, impressive weight and richness, plenty of oak and strapping, supple tannins. This will age well given the chance.

2006 Penfolds Cellar Reserve Pinot Noir
Score **93**

ADELAIDE HILLS
Price $55.00
Quality ★★★★⟩
Alc./Vol. 14.5%
Drink 2011
Closure Cork

Could be that it's a pinot aimed at drinkers of Penfolds' bigger reds but this is amazingly dark in the glass – about twice the depth of most Adelaide Hills pinots when you line them up together. Big rich dark cherry aromas, ripe and dense, strawberries and brambly forest fruits, plenty of brand spanking new French oak too, cedary and attractive. The palate is dense but not heavy, has real weight and flesh, builds juicy cherry and berry flavour through dense fine tannins and finishes with smooth resolve.

2005 Picardy Pinot Noir
Score **92**

PEMBERTON
Price $30.00
Quality ★★★★
Alc./Vol. 14%
Drink 2009
Closure Cork

Having nailed their tribute to Bordeaux at Moss Wood, the Pannell family went to Pemberton in search of Burgundy. This opens with damp forest smells, gentle fragrance and some bright mixed berries, turning toasty with air. The palate arrives with fresh, smoky cherry fruits and fine tannins; even, long and smooth.

2006 Pike & Joyce Pinot Noir   *Score* 91

ADELAIDE HILLS	
Price	$32.00
Quality	★★★★
Alc./Vol.	13%
Drink	Now
Closure	Screwcap

Good purity, bright cherries and cooler pinot characters here. Elemental red florals, oak is complementary but not at all overt; some game meats and savoury complexity. Supple and juicy, deceptive power and a confident entry, cherry and liquorice flavour balls up through the middle, juicy and direct, good drive through the finish lightens and sweetens.

2006 Pipers Brook Estate Pinot Noir   *Score* 91

NORTHERN TASMANIA	
Price	$42.00
Quality	★★★★
Alc./Vol.	13.5%
Drink	2012
Closure	Screwcap

This ripe, meaty and brazen cool-climate pinot shows plenty of spice and attractive forest fruits, still shy and adjusting to its oak. The palate, a little squared off by wood, is distinctly savoury. It's a hearty wine riding on dense tannin.

2006 Pirie Estate Pinot Noir   *Score* 96

TAMAR VALLEY	
Price	$39.00 ✓
Quality	★★★★★
Alc./Vol.	14%
Drink	2010
Closure	Screwcap

Andrew Pirie's flagship pinot is from south of Launceston. Simple red cherries and cool brambly fruit aromas open to fine-pointed aromatics; sweet spicy oak laid in low lets the fine cherry fruit sit up nice and bright. The palate has brisk acid crunch and fine fruit-derived tannins, ripe red cherry flavour, cool shape and precise lines, long and fine.

2006 Port Phillip Estate Morillon Pinot Noir   *Score* 93

MORNINGTON PENINSULA	
Price	$45.00
Quality	★★★★ ╡
Alc./Vol.	13.5%
Drink	2011
Closure	Diam

This Port Phillip reserve wine is looking the part in 2006, showing complex spices, roasted meats and savoury oak. It digs in with plenty of bright red fruit flavour and fine tannins – an appealing mix of length and finesse. Well made and boasts terrific balance; the oak is slipped nicely below the fruit.

2006 Port Phillip Estate Pinot Noir   *Score* 92

MORNINGTON PENINSULA	
Price	$35.00
Quality	★★★★
Alc./Vol.	13.5%
Drink	2010
Closure	Diam

The lifted fragrance of this wine reflects its cool, elevated position at Red Hill. Smells of fine red cherries, red florals and a lick of savoury oak. The palate is all abut finesse and detail, lifted by bright acidity and carried by smooth easygoing tannins.

2007 Port Phillip Estate Pinot Noir

Score **92**

MORNINGTON PENINSULA
Price $35.00 ✓
Quality   ★★★★
Alc./Vol. 13.5%
Drink   2010
Closure   Diam

The 2007 boasts a darker colour than many from the region, showing cooler aromas of fine red cherry fruits, citrus oils, smoked meats and savoury notes. The palate is svelte and neatly crafted into shape, swirls briefly across the middle, then sets a course to a linear, fine-tannin finish, lifting and fanning out.

2006 Punch Lance's Vineyard Close Planted Pinot Noir

Score **95**

YARRA VALLEY
Price $90.00
Quality   ★★★★ ⌐
Alc./Vol. 13.5%
Drink   Now
Closure   Screwcap

Sweet and exotic, this is a complex, clever pinot noir – the brazen aromatics are captivating. A stunning wine that stops you in your tracks, some herbs and poached strawberry, almost Beaujolais-like. The palate has fine, precise shape, savoury tannins layered below sweet ripe red fruits, strawberry and raspberry, musky and elegant. From a small close-planted section of the Lance vineyard planted in 1989. Limited production.

2006 Punch Lance's Vineyard Pinot Noir

Score **93**

YARRA VALLEY
Price $44.00
Quality   ★★★★ ⌐
Alc./Vol. 12.5%
Drink   2012
Closure   Screwcap

The Diamond Valley vineyard's original vines deliver instant savoury appeal as toasty oak leads the wine, opening to plenty of smoky/meaty barrel-derived complexity, hard spices and sweet fragrant lift. The palate has supple sweet tannin, layers of delicate fine-sliced red cherry and strawberry fruits, and finishes juicy and fresh. Limited production.

2006 Punt Road Pinot Noir

Score **91**

YARRA VALLEY
Price $25.00 ✓
Quality   ★★★★
Alc./Vol. 13.5%
Drink   2009
Closure   Screwcap

Rich and ripe in the glass, this smells of savoury spices, dark yeasty complexity and grilled mushrooms; it's both earthy and fragrant. The palate has balance, resolve and purpose, zesty acidity keeps red fruit flavours bright, finishing with a light dusting of oak.

2006 Red Claw Pinot Noir

Score **89**

MORNINGTON PENINSULA
Price $28.00
Quality   ★★★ ⌐
Alc./Vol. 14%
Drink   Now
Closure   Screwcap

Yabby Lake's new junior label washes ripe, almost jammy pinot characters together with tobacco and undergrowthy complexity, the oak is assertive. Quite chunky and chewy in the mouth with greener tannin edges, shows some depth and density, needs time to settle.

2006 **Riposte The Sabre Pinot Noir** *Score* **93**

ADELAIDE HILLS
Price $27.00 ✓
Quality ★★★★ ⌐
Alc./Vol. 13.5%
Drink 2010
Closure Screwcap

From veteran Tim Knappstein's comeback label, this starts out shy on the nose, a more meaty and savoury wine with red fruits and spices; quite pure. The palate holds some complexity with layered tannins, bright cherry and wild raspberry flavour, freshening with crisp acidity and musky fragrance through the finish.

2007 **Salitage Pinot Noir** *Score* **93**

PEMBERTON
Price $44.00
Quality ★★★★ ⌐
Alc./Vol. 13%
Drink 2009
Closure Screwcap

One of the established Pemberton pinot crew. Ripe, smoky dark cherry fruits and some bright aromatic lift; really shows the gravelly ironstone soils with savoury/smoky mineral characters and meaty roasted game complexity. The palate has beautifully supple fine-grained tannins, musky red cherry flavour and more of the smoky mineral soil character, finishing fresh and upbeat.

2007 **Scorpo Noirien Pinot Noir** *Score* **91**

MORNINGTON PENINSULA
Price $28.00
Quality ★★★★
Alc./Vol. 13%
Drink 2010
Closure Diam

This is Scorpo's regional wine, sourcing fruit from a range of neighbours. Deep colour and rich, dark cherry fruits frame regional pinot style. The palate's brisk and youthful with an abundance of cherry flavour, soft supple tannins and enough savoury complexity to be taken seriously.

2006 **Scorpo Pinot Noir** *Score* **93**

MORNINGTON PENINSULA
Price $43.00
Quality ★★★★ ⌐
Alc./Vol. 13.5%
Drink Now
Closure Diam

The Scorpo estate pinot has moved into more elegant territory: lighter strawberry-scented fruits, well ripened with some darker cherries too. The palate plays an even hand of direct cherry flavour and fine sweeping tannins, subtly complex and laid-back, balanced and smart.

2006 **Scotchmans Hill Pinot Noir** *Score* **93**

GEELONG
Price $29.00
Quality ★★★★ ⌐
Alc./Vol. 14%
Drink 2010
Closure Screwcap

One of the better recent Scotchmans' pinots, it's dressed in plenty of savoury game meat aromas and assertive oak derived spice, with some fragrance behind. The palate is rich and weighty, superb fruit concentration, it nails itself down with deep-layered fruit and rich ripe tannin presence.

2007 Scotchmans Hill Swan Bay Pinot Noir

Score 91

GEELONG
Price $19.00 ✓
Quality ★★★★
Alc./Vol. 14%
Drink Now
Closure Screwcap

Scotchmans' junior label shows good varietal character, upbeat cherries and spice, a little confected with oak-derived savoury meaty characters behind, chocolate and subtle smoke too. Smoky cherry-flavoured palate, supple tannins make for enjoyable appeal.

2007 Shelmerdine Pinot Noir

Score 92

YARRA VALLEY
Price $33.00
Quality ★★★★
Alc./Vol. 12%
Drink 2009
Closure Screwcap

There's plenty of toasty oak folded into this Yarra pinot fruit adding a shroud of smoky complexity, grilled meats and spices, some cherry fruit rolling through. The palate's straight-edged with smoky cherry flavour and approachable tannins below.

2007 South Pinot Noir

Score 93

TAMAR VALLEY
Price $25.00 ✓
Quality ★★★★ ⌐
Alc./Vol. 13.5%
Drink 2010
Closure Screwcap

Tamar Valley fruit's fine aromatics and some chalky mineral edges, citrus peel, soft ripe red cherry fruit aromas and simple primary restraint. The palate folds out simple cherry and strawberry flavour, and crisp crunchy acid lays out soft and supple through the finish, fanning in fine pinot style. A balanced and approachable, elegant pinot.

2006 St Huberts Pinot Noir

Score 94

YARRA VALLEY
Price $26.00 ✓
Quality ★★★★ ⌐
Alc./Vol. 13.5%
Drink Now
Closure Screwcap

Feted by the wine show circuit, this smells of smoothly raked earth and wet forest floor, a classic savoury pinot with fragrant sweet fruit lift and spicy oak. The palate's balanced from the outset and carries impressive fruit weight, fresh and vibrant, toasty oak runs through the finish with a brush of tannin to close.

2007 Starvedog Lane Pinot Noir

Score 93

ADELAIDE HILLS
Price $28.50
Quality ★★★★ ⌐
Alc./Vol. 13.5%
Drink 2014
Closure Screwcap

This marks a step in the right direction for Adelaide Hills pinot, concentrated wild cherry fruits, violet perfume and spicy lift; it's had substantial work done in the winery. The palate rides on dense tannins with plenty of red fruit flavour and some musky lift, dense, long and delicious.

2006 Stefano Lubiana Estate Pinot Noir — *Score* 96

TASMANIA
Price $45.00 ✓
Quality ★★★★★
Alc./Vol. 13.5%
Drink 2011
Closure Cork

This 2006 edition is looking superb. Spiced fragrant cherry fruits lift in volume out of the glass, some gentle brambly notes below; alluring pinot. Superb flavour and clarity, really focused and elegant, ripe cherry flavours and spices here again. Tannins are finely etched and build with musky lift through the finish. Classic elegance and bright acid lines.

2007 Stonier Pinot Noir — *Score* 88

MORNINGTON PENINSULA
Price $28.00
Quality ★★★ ⅃
Alc./Vol. 13%
Drink 2009
Closure Screwcap

This is a wine of the variety – sound stupid? Simple and a little flat, not especially brawny or distinct – a light red-fruited pinot noir. The palate is a little crumpled and squeezed, perky acid crunch, even and supple, some musky tannin chew.

2006 Stonier Reserve Pinot Noir — *Score* 93

MORNINGTON PENINSULA
Price $50.00
Quality ★★★★ ⅃
Alc./Vol. 13.5%
Drink 2010
Closure Screwcap

Shy on opening, so give it some air. Framed by red cherry and berry fruits, soft fragrance, straightforward and gently earthy. Plenty of palate-weight, berries and cream, it builds in fine layers, nice line and length, elegant tannins with a fine line to the finish. Balanced, with a toasty aftertaste.

2007 T'Gallant Juliet Pinot Noir — *Score* 89

MORNINGTON PENINSULA
Price $20.00
Quality ★★★ ⅃
Alc./Vol. 12.5%
Drink 2010
Closure Screwcap

Terrific lift and lively fruit, very primary sweet dark berry and cherry aromas, some brambly forest-floor aromas, regional and ripe. There's a light savoury undercurrent through the palate, smooth tannins and attractive balance. Easy.

2006 T'Gallant Tribute Pinot Noir — *Score* 90

MORNINGTON PENINSULA
Price $29.00
Quality ★★★★
Alc./Vol. 13.5%
Drink Now
Closure Screwcap

Quite ripe, juicy and dense, this has some sweet baking spices, anise and cinnamon, dark cherry aromas and clove too. Bright, deep cherry-flavoured palate, ripe and dense, it's an easy style, finishing juicy and direct.

2007 Tamar Ridge Kayena Vineyard Pinot Noir — *Score* **93**

KAYENA	
Price	$28.00 ✓
Quality	★ ★ ★ ★ ⌐
Alc./Vol.	14%
Drink	2012
Closure	Screwcap

Here's a much richer expression, still in the cool-fruited style, but darker cherries and richer more muscular oak; attractive and assertive. The palate follows suit: punchy entry, cool resolve and bright acidity, plenty of toasty oak and accompanying tannins, it builds sweet rich cherry flavour through the finish, good length.

2007 Tapanappa Foggy Hill Pinot Noir — *Score* **91**

FLEURIEU PENINSULA	
Price	$50.00
Quality	★ ★ ★ ★
Alc./Vol.	13%
Drink	Now
Closure	Cork

From an elevated site on the Fleurieu Peninsula, this is Brian Croser's crack at seriously great pinot, and not a bad first effort. Plenty of vinous cherry fruit aroma and some briary forest characters here, earthy, the oak is spicy and sits up in the mix, strong anise, some clove too. Fine gentle tannins and ripe soft fruits, liquorice and flighty cherry fruit flavour. Musky balanced finish.

2006 TarraWarra Estate Reserve Pinot Noir — *Score* **92**

YARRA VALLEY	
Price	$50.00
Quality	★ ★ ★ ★
Alc./Vol.	13.8%
Drink	Now
Closure	Screwcap

Shows clever meaty barrel-derived characters that suit the juicy pinot fruit, plenty of spiced cherry and some light earthy complexity below. Fine even tannins and supple bright cherry fruit flavours, nicely matched here by savoury complexity, balanced and even.

2006 Ten Minutes By Tractor McCutcheon Vineyard Pinot Noir — *Score* **95**

MORNINGTON PENINSULA	
Price	$70.00
Quality	★ ★ ★ ★ ⌐
Alc./Vol.	13.8%
Drink	2009
Closure	Screwcap

A convincing wine from one of the most improved Mornington Peninsula producers, plenty of wild cherry and raspberry fruit aromas; there's some spice and lift, anise, violets and fresh French oak in there too. Supple, fine and even palate, cinnamon spiced cherries and smoothly textured tannins that ball up through the middle, finishing soft and elegant.

2005 Toolangi Estate Pinot Noir — *Score* **92**

YARRA VALLEY	
Price	$39.00
Quality	★ ★ ★ ★
Alc./Vol.	14%
Drink	2010
Closure	Screwcap

Shows impressive winemaking complexity and 2005-vintage richness, a savoury slant of oak and sweet spices splice through mouth-watering cherry fruit aromas. Plenty of supple charm and musky ripe cherry-flavoured fruit, milk chocolate, supple tannins, balance and length.

2006 Toolangi Pinot Noir   *Score* 93

YARRA VALLEY
Price $25.00 ✓
Quality   ★★★★ ⌐
Alc./Vol. 13%
Drink   2010
Closure   Screwcap

This speaks of its vintage; the '06 Yarra pinots are uplifting wines. Fine fragrance and lift, neat restraint and elegance, smelling balanced too, this is complex and well crafted. The palate boasts ripeness and weight, rich soft tannins flowing and curvaceous, staying light through the finish with a waft of smoky complexity.

2006 Treehouse Pinot Noir   *Score* 91

PEMBERTON
Price $22.00 ✓
Quality   ★★★★
Alc./Vol. 12.5%
Drink   2010
Closure   Screwcap

Salitage takes other fruit from around the region, crafting some complex pinot aromatics here. Clever winemaking has dressed strawberry and berry fruits nicely, with oak adding further spicy intrigue. The palate is softly textured, smoky and intense, superb tannins, ripe strawberry fruits, flowing and concentrated, layered and complete.

2007 The Wanderer Pinot Noir   *Score* 92

YARRA VALLEY
Price $32.00
Quality   ★★★★
Alc./Vol. 13.4%
Drink   2012
Closure   Screwcap

Andrew Marks' eye for making good pinot is in full effect here: cooler wild berry fruit characters, bright and really primary, with plenty of sweet musky spice dusted across the top. The palate, laid out across fine supple tannins, has attractive direct character; structure rules the roost, fanning fruit out along the line. Great balance and resolve.

2007 Three Wishes Pinot Noir   *Score* 93

TASMANIA
Price $35.00
Quality   ★★★★ ⌐
Alc./Vol. 13.5%
Drink   2011
Closure   Screwcap

Another striking pinot from Tasmania, this is a ball of bright cherry fruits and fragrant perfume; pomegranate makes an appearance too. Tannins slide through on supple tracks with bright acidity holding the fruit up high. Cherry flavours run from start to flourishing finish, dusted with spicy complexity.

2007 Weemala Pinot Noir   *Score* 90

ORANGE
Price $16.00 ✓
Quality   ★★★★
Alc./Vol. 13.5%
Drink   Now
Closure   Screwcap

Weemala is the junior label of Logan and this pinot is a fresh, fruit-driven beauty. It all sits in the mixed berry and cherry spectrum, ripe strawberries and some wild raspberry too. There's gentle spice and smooth, musky tannins throughout. Nice balance, very approachable and easy on the wallet.

2007 **Wignalls Pinot Noir** *Score* **90**

ALBANY
Price $31.00
Quality ★★★★
Alc./Vol. 15%
Drink 2010
Closure Screwcap

This is unmistakably pinot with sweet floral fragrant lift and some bright red fruits, kirsch, very fruit driven and ripe with a creamy oak overlay. The palate shows simple sweet cherry and light plum flavours, decent tannin density, a round alcohol-filled middle and some springy acid crunch.

2006 **William Downie Mornington Peninsula Pinot Noir** *Score* **95**

MORNINGTON PENINSULA
Price $45.00
Quality ★★★★⸴
Alc./Vol. 13.5%
Drink 2011
Closure Diam

This young talented pinot whiz kid has broadened his horizons and made a cool, restrained brambly Mornington pinot. Bright lifted aromatics, brambly fruits and orange zest; it shows great purity and precision. The palate is fine and svelte, finishing with a flurry of fragrance rather than a thunder of tannin, tightly wound and nicely balanced.

2006 **Willow Creek Vineyard Tulum Pinot Noir** *Score* **93**

MORNINGTON PENINSULA
Price $35.00
Quality ★★★★⸴
Alc./Vol. 14%
Drink 2011
Closure Screwcap

There's real brightness and fine red cherry lift about this wine, some musk and fine spices, the oak is well placed and adds savoury support; really impressive. The palate follows suit: fine tannins, bright musky cherry and raspberry fruit, plenty of fleshy juicy flavour. Good drive and balance.

2005 **Winbirra The Brigadier Pinot Noir** *Score* **92**

MORNINGTON PENINSULA
Price $35.00
Quality ★★★★
Alc./Vol. 14%
Drink 2011
Closure Diam

The combination of a warmer year and this cool location has delivered charming finesse and fragrance. It's an open and inviting pinot, showing red cherry aromas and sweet spices dusted across the top. Convincing weight and drive on the palate, some pencil-shaving oak and richer plum fruit flavour, just finishes a little square.

2006 **Yabby Lake Vineyard Pinot Noir** *Score* **90**

MORNINGTON PENINSULA
Price $60.00
Quality ★★★★
Alc./Vol. 14%
Drink 2009
Closure Screwcap

The oak is a bit obtrusive here – comes ahead of the fruit and blurs the clarity. There's dark regional brambly cherry fruit below and some smoked spice complexity building, needs time to breathe up. Plenty of ripe cherry flavour and ripe thick tannin, still a little raw, heading into dry red style. A big pinot that wants for elegance.

2007 Yarra Burn Pinot Noir   *Score* **92**

YARRA VALLEY
Price $28.00
Quality   ★★★★
Alc./Vol. 12.5%
Drink   2010
Closure   Screwcap

Sporting some really complex winemaking influence, the fruit smells cool and restrained: cherries, berries, some citrus peel and plenty of smoky/charry oak. Smoky palate, toasty oak stripes run from top to tail balanced aboard fleshy tannins and crisp acid, finishing fresh.

2006 Yering Station Reserve Pinot Noir   *Score* **92**

YARRA VALLEY
Price $75.00
Quality   ★★★★
Alc./Vol. 13.5%
Drink   Now
Closure   Screwcap

This flagship shows fine spicy fragrance and bright lifted fruit aromas; a young, brash and straightforward pinot with broad appeal and plenty of savoury oak complexity. The palate's supple and ripe, carrying cherry/berry flavours that roll smoothly through, light and easy, finishing with musky fragrant lift.

2006 Yeringberg Pinot Noir   *Score* **92**

YARRA VALLEY
Price $60.00
Quality   ★★★★
Alc./Vol. 14%
Drink   2011
Closure   Diam

Deeper blue fruits and some concentrated, almost candied aromas, this is complex and ripe with plenty of cedary oak dealt in deep. The palate has fine, taut, juicy tannins, really supple fleshy cherry fruit – they've picked it fresh and bright, some gentle chew and nice balance.

Pinot noir NZ

It may be the land of sauvignon but New Zealand's pinot noir is fast becoming the main event. It's an extremely young category and, although the story has just begun, international attention and surging interest in regions like Central Otago, Martinborough, Waipara, Waikari and Marlborough pinot noir is the envy of other pinot makers the world over. Predominantly very young vines are producing intensely fruited wines that are loaded with easy appeal – tannins are generally soft and easy, the acidity holds them bright, and styles are already maturing to even greater heights. A very exciting group of wines, any way you look at it. FOOD: As for Australian pinot, although acidity tends to be a little brighter in these wines. Again, look to game meats and a range of cuisines, from French to Chinese. Game birds always work superbly.

2006 **Alana Estate Pinot Noir**   *Score* **94**

MARTINBOROUGH	Made by Australian Chris Archer, this delivers bright
Price $60.00	fragrance, some strawberry fruits and pink musky perfume,
Quality ★★★★ᐟ	then into dark regional cherry aromas, earthy/smoky sweet
Alc./Vol. 14%	spices. Complex and engaging. The palate's supple and
Drink Now	superbly ripened, really intense regional cherry and earthy
Closure Screwcap	gravel fruits, bright acid lifts through the finish, tannins fan
	upwards.

2007 **Ata Rangi Crimson Pinot Noir**   *Score* **93**

MARTINBOROUGH	Be afraid, be very afraid – the Ata Rangi crew has delivered
Price $30.00 ✓	a knock-out punch with this '07 Crimson. Super-bright fruit
Quality ★★★★ᐟ	aromas here, really intense and subtly complex. There's
Alc./Vol. 15%	pure cherry flesh and gravelly mineral complexity, gentle
Drink 2010	savoury spice and haunting fragrance. The palate is supple
Closure Screwcap	and steadily balanced, elegant smooth tannins layer up in
	impressive formation, cherry flavour runs deep through the
	finish. A long and convincing young wine.

2007 The Aurora Vineyard Bendigo Pinot Noir — *Score* 93

CENTRAL OTAGO 🏷
Price $39.00 ✓
Quality ★★★★ ⌐
Alc./Vol. 13.5%
Drink 2010
Closure Screwcap

From out in the barren warmth of the Bendigo Hills, ripe, bright berry compote, superb concentration of fruit aromas, dark cherry and some sweet pastry too. The acid bites in through the entry, ripe and rich, supple flesh through the middle, tannins weigh in through the back, cherry pie finish. An authoritative pinot.

2007 Babich Marlborough Pinot Noir — *Score* 89

MARLBOROUGH
Price $23.00
Quality ★★★ ⌐
Alc./Vol. 13%
Drink Now
Closure Screwcap

Plenty of oak wedged into the nose of this Marlborough pinot, some sweet anise and liquorice spices, orange zest, ripe and juicy. The palate has bright primary appeal, and fine integrated tannins carry cherry flavours deep – some creamy oak through the finish.

2007 Babich Winemakers' Reserve Pinot Noir — *Score* 92

MARLBOROUGH
Price $33.00 ✓
Quality ★★★★
Alc./Vol. 13.5%
Drink 2010
Closure Screwcap

The winemakers certainly selected well: impressive concentration and ripe cherry fruits, orange zest and complex fine minerals across the top, gentle deli meat complexity below. The palate's fine and intensely packed, really crisp fruit crunch, fine tannin chew – a juicy young style, elegant and compact.

2007 Braided River Marlborough Pinot Noir — *Score* 89

MARLBOROUGH
Price $19.00 ✓
Quality ★★★ ⌐
Alc./Vol. 13.5%
Drink Now
Closure Screwcap

This well-priced Marlborough pinot looks the part with bright crimson colour, aromas sail out with sweet cherry fruit leading the charge, impressive lift and verve, some wild raspberries and sweet oak spice. Supple palate and simple light tannins. Easy-drinking style, very fruit driven.

2007 Burnt Spur Pinot Noir — *Score* 91

MARTINBOROUGH
Price $39.00
Quality ★★★★
Alc./Vol. 14.5%
Drink Now
Closure Screwcap

There's a big stamp of toasty oak here, a signature of the Martinborough Vineyards crew, smoked cherry fruits and sweet spices – a little milk chocolate and liquorice. The palate is dense and rich, smooth rounded red fruits roll through fine supple tannins, finishes with dark cherry and toasty flavour. Very ripe.

2007 Cape Campbell Pinot Noir   *Score* **92**

MARLBOROUGH
Price $30.00 ✓
Quality   ★★★★
Alc./Vol. 14%
Drink   2010
Closure   Screwcap

Sourced from the far south of the region near a remote surf break, this brings fine lighter aromas, more fragrant and pure cherry fruit appeal, some meaty winemaking and subtle complexity. The palate has decent density and weight, juicy twang and acid crunch too; long, fine and youthful.

2006 Carrick Pinot Noir   *Score* **94**

CENTRAL OTAGO
Price $50.00
Quality   ★★★★⭤
Alc./Vol. 14%
Drink   2011
Closure   Screwcap

One of the reliable names in Bannockburn, this has plenty of ripeness and richness, a pure cherry fruit nose – the oak is buried deep. The palate is savoury, structured and balanced, fine gravelly tannins draw cherry flavour long through the finish; it has superior poise and elegance, juicy acid crunch.

2007 Carrick Unravelled Pinot Noir   *Score* **92**

CENTRAL OTAGO
Price $30.00 ✓
Quality   ★★★★
Alc./Vol. 13.5%
Drink   Now
Closure   Screwcap

This junior Carrick label offers phenomenal value and style. Has a fragrant musky oak aroma, gentle spices too; there's some fresh mineral tones, fine spiced cherry and sweet pepper. It has handy shape and build through to the back palate where it launches delicate aromas on a fan of tannin. Long cherry flavour – superb.

2006 Churton Pinot Noir   *Score* **93**

MARLBOROUGH
Price $39.00
Quality   ★★★★⭤
Alc./Vol. 13.5%
Drink   Now
Closure   Cork

This small-winery pinot is nurtured into superbly complex shape. Impressive aromatic buzz, sweet and lifted whole-bunch aromas, bright cherry fruits. Very engaging. The palate is supple, rich and ripe, bright cherries, fine dense pinot tannins fanning through the finish, elegant and even.

2007 Clos de Ste Anne Pinot Noir   *Score* **93**

GISBORNE
Price $50.00
Quality   ★★★★⭤
Alc./Vol. 14%
Drink   2011
Closure   Cork

Sourced from the oldest plantings on the original vineyard, this offers bright cherry fruit, poached strawberry and gentle aromatics. A wine with reserved poise on opening, it unfurls a distinct pinot palate, cherry and spice. It really opens up with air, becomes supple and reveals textural swing; fine juicy tannin/acid finish, gentle smoky waft.

2007 Clos Henri Marlborough Pinot Noir   *Score* 94

MARLBOROUGH	
Price	$56.00
Quality	★★★★ ⅃
Alc./Vol.	13.5%
Drink	2011
Closure	Cork

This Franco-Kiwi pinot shows ripe, deep and bright cherry fruit aromas, terrific freshness and purity; there's old-world savoury aromas, winemaking has bound the fruit in tight. Superb palate texture, fine and dense, savoury tannins climb through the finish, dragging musky cherry fruit in their wake. Will build further weight in the medium term.

2006 Craggy Range Calvert Vineyard Pinot Noir   *Score* 93

CENTRAL OTAGO	
Price	$63.00
Quality	★★★★ ⅃
Alc./Vol.	14%
Drink	Now
Closure	Screwcap

One of a trio of high-quality producers making wine from this vineyard (the others being Felton Road and Pyramid Valley), the Craggy version is assertive and structured. Classic regional dark cherry aromas, gentle mountain herbs and sweet spice. The palate's supple on entry and builds to a structured finish, bright acidity and deep-seated tannins bring length and drive.

2007 Dashwood Pinot Noir   *Score* 89

MARLBOROUGH	
Price	$20.00 ✓
Quality	★★★ ⅃
Alc./Vol.	13%
Drink	Now
Closure	Screwcap

Sourced from the Awatere Valley, this has bright zesty cherry fruit aromas, some orange peel and light sweet pinot fragrance. The palate's an easygoing roll in the hay, light tannins, sweet cherry and a hint of earthy chocolate to close.

2006 Delta Vineyard Hatters Hill Pinot Noir   *Score* 93

MARLBOROUGH	
Price	$30.00 ✓
Quality	★★★★ ⅃
Alc./Vol.	13%
Drink	Now
Closure	Screwcap

This is essentially a reserve parcel, based on vineyard selection. It's a finer, lighter coloured and very delicate precise pinot; gently earthy with fine-faceted complexity and complementary (50% new) oak. The palate follows the same light, elegant path: bright acidity, pure cherry flavour and a fine-boned firm tannin finish.

2007 Delta Vineyard Pinot Noir   *Score* 91

MARLBOROUGH	
Price	$23.00 ✓
Quality	★★★★
Alc./Vol.	13%
Drink	Now
Closure	Screwcap

This offers a lot of pinot for the money, especially given the premium position most New Zealand offerings tend to take. Pure cherry-scented wine, bright spice and brambly complexity, very fragrant and varietal. Soft, easy palate with bright acidity, ripe red cherry flavour and supple, fine, light tannins.

2006 Dog Point Pinot Noir   *Score* **95**

MARLBOROUGH	
Price	$45.00 ✓
Quality	★★★★ ♪
Alc./Vol.	13.5%
Drink	2010
Closure	Cork

The Dog Point folks have a prime patch of Marlborough dirt, delivering sweet lifted fragrance and red-scented cool-climate pinot fruit. Add plenty of swanky oak, roasted game meats and sweet spices, and this has the full gamut of complexity. The palate delivers ripe cherry and cherry-pip flavour, smooth tannins and an innate sense of balance. A stylish, well-made pinot and a proven performer.

2006 Drylands Pinot Noir   *Score* **92**

MARLBOROUGH	
Price	$27.00
Quality	★★★★
Alc./Vol.	13.5%
Drink	2011
Closure	Screwcap

This is bristling with fine pinot fruits, some sweet spices and attractive oak lift, there's a haunting background of enticing perfume. Plenty of vibrant cherry flavour, more finely dusted spices and brisk acidity delivering a crunchy, assertive finish.

2007 Fairhall Downs Single Vineyard Pinot Noir   *Score* **93**

MARLBOROUGH	
Price	$29.00 ✓
Quality	★★★★ ♪
Alc./Vol.	14%
Drink	2011
Closure	Screwcap

From an elevated estate established in 1982, this has darker cherry aromas and deep colour in the glass, there's richness and ripeness here, moist earthy undergrowth. Sweet ripe dark cherry fruits, juicy and approachable, nice purity, the oak chimes in through the back, expansive finish.

2007 Felton Road Pinot Noir   *Score* **96**

CENTRAL OTAGO	
Price	$70.00 ✓
Quality	★★★★★
Alc./Vol.	14%
Drink	2011
Closure	Screwcap

Attractive savoury complexity and dense cherry/plum fruit aromas. Fine fragrance, plenty of deep fruit and light, fine-ground spices, sweet perfumed aromatics, minerals and a flash of oak char. The palate's supple and elegant, really refined, superb tannin climb to the finish, lifting bright cherry flavour on the finish. One of the greatest Felton pinots to date.

PENGUIN BEST NEW ZEALAND PINOT NOIR

2007 Felton Road Pinot Noir Block 3 — *Score* (96–98)

CENTRAL OTAGO
Price $120.00
Quality ★★★★★
Alc./Vol. 13.5%
Drink 2014
Closure Screwcap

The Block 3 has more brooding muscle and depth, aromas spin deeper into spicy ripe territory, very unevolved; there's a full array from violette perfume through to stony minerals, around pure dark cherry fruits. The palate's the thing though, impeccable drive and commanding tubular tannin shape, grand cru power and poise, toasty oak smoulders away, spiced fleshy dark cherry and long unrelenting flavour.

2007 Felton Road Pinot Noir Calvert Vineyard — *Score* (93–95)

CENTRAL OTAGO
Price $85.00
Quality ★★★★ ⌐
Alc./Vol. 14%
Drink Now
Closure Screwcap

The Calvert vineyard is managed by Felton Road and fruit is divided among three wineries. This is quite a savoury, laid-back fine pinot with a strong minerally side, lighter pink fragrance and some complex sweet baking spices, gentle citrus rind. Finely sheeted palate with bright pure fruit flavour, the oak adds sweeter spice, an elegant and very, very long finish.

2007 Felton Road Pinot Noir Cornish Point — *Score* (93–95)

CENTRAL OTAGO
Price $85.00
Quality ★★★★ ⌐
Alc./Vol. 14%
Drink 2010
Closure Screwcap

From Nigel Greening's original purchase: fine and savoury aromas, gravelly light fragrance, some wild herbs and bright cherry fruits; a more brazen nose than the home block. The palate's wrapped in an impressive ball of flavour, swirling tannins hold cherry and orange zest in a tight core, releasing toasty oak through the finish that will integrate in time. Brash and appealing.

2007 Framingham Pinot Noir — *Score* 91

MARLBOROUGH
Price $26.00 ✓
Quality ★★★★
Alc./Vol. 14%
Drink Now
Closure Screwcap

An excellent statement of the Marlborough region's attractive, easy-drinking pinot style, showing fine elegant ripe red cherry fruits and subtle spice. A gently meaty palate that has bright acidity and fine savoury mineral notes, upbeat finish.

2007 Gibbston Highgate Estate Soultaker Pinot Noir   *Score* 93

CENTRAL OTAGO
Price $40.00 ✓
Quality ★★★★ ꜛ
Alc./Vol. 13.5%
Drink Now
Closure Screwcap

A sensational new discovery of this year's tasting. It has superb density and swirling cherry fragrance, super-sweet spices and mountain herbs, sitting right in the regional zone. Tannins are fine and juicy, really smoky too, there's plenty of richness and fruit flesh, finishing with lightness, plums and dark cherry pip. Watch this space.

2007 Gibbston Valley Central Otago Pinot Noir   *Score* 94

CENTRAL OTAGO
Price $45.00
Quality ★★★★ ꜛ
Alc./Vol. 14.5%
Drink 2011
Closure Screwcap

Small berries and a minute crop make for attractive fine fragrance and some citrus rind here, dark plum and cherry, pomegranate and wild thyme. Rich dense palate, dark plum fruit and springy tannins, lifts through the finish, quite taut, bright acidity, superb concentration.

2007 Hunter's Pinot Noir   *Score* 91

MARLBOROUGH
Price $27.00
Quality ★★★★
Alc./Vol. 13.5%
Drink Now
Closure Screwcap

A nice marriage of dark spicy oak and rich pinot fragrance here, finer too; lovely aromatic lift and ripe dark cherry aromas. The palate is sweeping and supple, has smooth density and slide, ripe, supple and elegant balance, medium-weight. Plenty of juicy appeal.

2006 Jackson Estate Vintage Widow Pinot Noir   *Score* 92

MARLBOROUGH
Price $37.00
Quality ★★★★
Alc./Vol. 13.5%
Drink Now
Closure Screwcap

This quality-focused grower's pinot shows solid ripeness and aromatic density, dark cherry fruits and some dark woody spices. The palate is supple and swirling, has meaty toasty complexity, finishing vibrant and fresh. Nice balance between fruit quality and switched-on winemaking.

2006 Kumeu River Estate Pinot Noir   *Score* 90

AUCKLAND
Price $45.00
Quality ★★★★
Alc./Vol. 13.5%
Drink 2011
Closure Screwcap

Just a pitching wedge from downtown Auckland, the Brajkovich's upbeat pinot shows lifted fragrance and simple confected berry fruit aromas, with savoury oak in the background and some meaty funk. The palate is all elegant cherries and smoked spices with supple tannin below.

2007 Main Divide Marlborough Pinot Noir   *Score* **93**

MARLBOROUGH
Price $26.00 ✓
Quality ★★★★ ┨
Alc./Vol. 14.5%
Drink 2012
Closure Screwcap

The Donaldson family has their pinot house in perfect order. This is all savoury, cryptic complexity, and has plenty to give in the next couple of years as it builds aromatics and fragrance. Ripe and brambly, tannins sweep wide and deep, meaty supple complexity and decent depth here. Supple and intense.

2006 Main Divide Pinot Noir   *Score* **93**

MARLBOROUGH
Price $27.00 ✓
Quality ★★★★ ┨
Alc./Vol. 14.5%
Drink Now
Closure Screwcap

The junior pinot from Pegasus Bay shows cooler characters: darker fruits with herbal notes mixed through. It's got all the qualities of a proper complex pinot, terrific concentration and density, smoky dark cherry flavours and plush ripe tannins. A delicious easy-drinking wine.

2006 Main Divide TeHau Pinot Noir   *Score* **93**

WAIPARA
Price $37.00 ✓
Quality ★★★★ ┨
Alc./Vol. 14%
Drink 2010
Closure Screwcap

This shows some deeply ripe, darker fruit characters, black minerals, pepper and almost tarry fruit concentration. Gentle spices and dark cherry flavour, really rich liquorice and anise flavours, a little chocolate through the finish. Well made, brooding and super-cool style.

2006 Main Divide Tipinui Marlborough Pinot Noir   *Score* **93**

MARLBOROUGH
Price $37.00 ✓
Quality ★★★★ ┨
Alc./Vol. 14%
Drink 2010
Closure Screwcap

Donaldson family class and style on full show here: dark colour and really fresh ripe rich cherry fruit aromas. Almost heads into maraschino territory with fine spices and brooding meaty complexity. The palate packs plenty of dark cherry and spice too, really well-applied oak and supple tannin balance.

2007 Martinborough Vineyard Te Tera Pinot Noir   *Score* **89**

MARTINBOROUGH
Price $35.00
Quality ★★★ ┨
Alc./Vol. 14%
Drink Now
Closure Screwcap

This has a striking dark brooding colour – looks like a shiraz in the glass; super-ripe smoky spiced cherry fruits, quite complex, some plum and chocolate too, very rich. The palate is supple and packed with sweet meaty spices, complex and savoury, very ripe and fleshy, finishes with mahogany-like oak. A red wine lover's pinot.

2007 Maude Pinot Noir   *Score* **93**

CENTRAL OTAGO
Price $32.00
Quality   ★★★★ ┤
Alc./Vol. 14.2%
Drink   2011
Closure   Screwcap

Made by ex-Hunter winemakers Sarah-Kate and Dan Dineen, this shows deep colour and some handy ripeness, dark cherry and berry fruits, plenty of spice and gentle meaty richness. Supple swirling palate, acidity is a feature and tannins run in fine lines with gentle savoury drive. Compact, elegant and even with a sturdy structural core – a blend of grapes from Wanaka, Gibbston Valley, Bendigo and Alexandra.

2006 Mitre Rocks Central Otago Pinot Noir   *Score* **91**

CENTRAL OTAGO
Price $55.00
Quality   ★★★★
Alc./Vol. 14%
Drink   Now
Closure   Screwcap

A newer label that is making strong headway. Supple plum aromas here, really bright and rich, ripe and dense chocolate oak and some roasting herbs. There's rich flavour on the palate without overdoing the density and texture, swirling tannins, open-knit and ripe.

2007 MOMO Pinot Noir   *Score* **90**

MARLBOROUGH
Price $26.00
Quality   ★★★★
Alc./Vol. 13.5%
Drink   Now
Closure   Screwcap

This junior Seresin pinot needs some air to come alive, then releases fragrant dark cherry aromas and sweet vibrant spice. The palate has fine slippery tannin texture and plenty of ripe sweet cherry fruit – easy flavoursome enjoyment.

2007 Montana Terraces Pinot Noir   *Score* **91**

MARLBOROUGH
Price $36.00
Quality   ★★★★
Alc./Vol. 14%
Drink   Now
Closure   Screwcap

A distinctive bright cherry and brambly wild berry Montana pinot, very primary and showing some sweeter spices in the mix. The palate follows suit with a direct delivery of ripe juicy fruits and fine tannin slide, really even and gently earthy, red fruit finish.

2007 Mount Difficulty Pinot Noir   *Score* **93**

CENTRAL OTAGO
Price $55.00
Quality   ★★★★ ┤
Alc./Vol. 14%
Drink   2011
Closure   Screwcap

Mt Diff is perched in a prime riverbank position along the golden mile of Bannockburn. Compelling black cherry and dark spiced plum fruit, tobacco leaf, wild thyme and blue fruits; there's plenty of spicy lift here, sweet and rich, superb concentration. The palate has density and depth; thick striding tannin that arches long through the finish carrying plum and dark berry flavour all the way.

2007 Mount Michael Bessie's Block Pinot Noir   Score 92

CENTRAL OTAGO 🖉
Price $40.00
Quality ★★★★
Alc./Vol. 14.5%
Drink 2010
Closure Screwcap

Named after the vineyard dog, this single-vineyard wine is from the Cromwell Hills. It shows a lighter nose, more open-knit and has light, bright cherry aromas, fine fragrance and musky lift. The palate has terrific detail and finesse, musky fruits and superb bright flavours, fine tannins and zesty acidity, blueberry and griottes.

2007 Mud House Pinot Noir   Score 91

MARLBOROUGH
Price $22.00 ✓
Quality ★★★★
Alc./Vol. 13.3%
Drink Now
Closure Screwcap

Nothing muddy here, just bright, brambly fragrance, and ripe cherries, dark toasted spices and plenty of aromatic complexity on offer. The palate's rich and ripe, really big on bright fruit flavours and strong tannin stride, sweet dark cherry finish. Great balance.

2007 Mud House Swan Pinot Noir   Score 92

CENTRAL OTAGO
Price $35.00 ✓
Quality ★★★★
Alc./Vol. 14%
Drink 2010
Closure Screwcap

Swan, the Mud House reserve label, is showing class, clarity and richness, deep dark concentrated cherry fruit aromas, really pure and primary, gentle fragrance. The palate picks up with bright acidity and takes a fine tannin line to the finish, decent flesh through the middle, pure cherry flavour again, finishes juicy. Perfect for smaller birds like duck.

2006 Mystery Creek Pinot Noir   Score 89

WAIKATO
Price $25.00
Quality ★★★ ⫞
Alc./Vol. 13%
Drink Now
Closure Screwcap

This mystery hails from just near Hamilton and shows some mature, savoury characters, undergrowth, toasty oak and decent ripeness. The palate is smooth and has a glossy, ripe quality, very much a new-world riper style. Creamy finish, soft tannins.

2006 Neudorf Moutere Pinot Noir   Score 94

NELSON 🖉
Price $65.00
Quality ★★★★ ⫞
Alc./Vol. 13.5%
Drink 2009
Closure Screwcap

Consistently among the money, this edition of Moutere pinot is ripe and complete, showing plenty of high-class cedary French oak amid youthful cherry fruit. The palate is refined and compact, tannins are smooth and cherry flavours are tucked in neatly. Great length and innate balance.

2006 Neudorf Tom's Block Pinot Noir

Score **92**

NELSON
Price $38.00
Quality ★★★★
Alc./Vol. 13.5%
Drink Now
Closure Screwcap

Originally from their young vine cuvée, this now has a mix of the newer clones and shows impressive primary complexity, quite vinous and raw, some spicy cherry fruits and pointed aromatics. The palate mixes elegance and fruit power, the oak is slotted in behind, tannins are soft and lively, finishes with fresh balance.

2006 Nobilo Icon Pinot Noir

Score **90**

CENTRAL OTAGO
Price $29.00
Quality ★★★★
Alc./Vol. 14%
Drink 2012
Closure Twin top cork

This shows some bigger fruit aromas, typical Central Otago stuff with plenty of spice, some toasty oak, and undergrowthy forest floor. The palate follows with plenty of bright ripe fruits, fine tannins and some swanky oak; it's a modern wine with sturdy tannins and strident drive through the finish.

2006 Palliser Estate Martinborough Pinot Noir

Score **91**

MARTINBOROUGH
Price $40.00
Quality ★★★★
Alc./Vol. 14%
Drink 2011
Closure Screwcap

A brassy, juicy dark cherry-scented pinot noir with some rich earthy aromas, looking youthful and forthright, richness here. The palate has plenty of weight and flesh; there's a lot to sink the teeth into before a flurry of tannin at the finish.

2006 Pegasus Bay Pinot Noir

Score **95**

WAIPARA
Price $65.00
Quality ★★★★ ⌐
Alc./Vol. 14%
Drink 2011
Closure Screwcap

The Donaldson family's record with pinot is nothing short of superb. Dark, briary forest-floor aromas, game meats and wild berries, sweet oak sits among essence-like fruit. The palate is a swirling mix of dark cherry and mushroom flavours, thoroughly ripe dense tannins and bright acid cut, finishing with a smoky twist. Magnificent.

2005 Pegasus Bay Prima Donna Pinot Noir

Score **97**

CENTRAL OTAGO
Price $110.00
Quality ★★★★★
Alc./Vol. 13.5%
Drink 2012
Closure Screwcap

The *über* pinot from Pegasus Bay is worth every ounce of the fanfare it attracts. Dense, ripe, meaty and super-spiced pinot nose, this is superbly complex and has grounded earthy complexity. The palate is superior again, fine and precise, a smooth core of fine fruits and slick ripe cherry, really earthy/savoury – has burgundian layering and texture, a smoky finish. Orchestral.

2007 Peregrine Pinot Noir

Score **94**

CENTRAL OTAGO
Price $55.00
Quality ★★★★ ⁺
Alc./Vol. 13.5%
Drink 2013
Closure Screwcap

One of the stars of the 2007 Otago pinots, showing plenty of complexity and weight, impressive depth and fragrant aromatic lift. Striking spice and musky perfume, red florals and brambly edges, some glossy wood too. A supple and swirling palate, acidity is a feature and the tannins aren't exactly shrinking; they sheet compelling texture and tautness into the finish. Grapes are sourced from the Cromwell Basin (80%) and Gibbston Valley (20%).

2007 Peregrine Saddleback Pinot Noir

Score **89**

CENTRAL OTAGO
Price $30.00
Quality ★★★ ⁺
Alc./Vol. 13.5%
Drink Now
Closure Screwcap

This mini Peregrine pinot opens with really sweet baked berry aromas, ripe plum fruits, pastry and nutty/toasty oak spice. The palate makes a direct and slightly chewy fruit impression, finishing light and easy.

2007 Picnic By Two Paddocks Pinot Noir

Score **91**

CENTRAL OTAGO
Price $30.00 ✓
Quality ★★★★
Alc./Vol. 13%
Drink 2010
Closure Screwcap

This junior label delivers straightforward style with quite restrained fruit aromas, a little held-back and reserved, young and spicy. Plenty of verve and juicy fruit presence on the palate, saffron-flavoured oak, fine juicy tannins and raw appeal.

2006 Prophet's Rock Pinot Noir

Score **92**

CENTRAL OTAGO
Price $50.00
Quality ★★★★
Alc./Vol. 14%
Drink Now
Closure Cork

A blend of Bendigo and Pisa fruit (from either side of Lake Dunstan), this has intense red cherry fruit and some mountain herbs, gentle chocolate and perfume too. Fine, supple palate and gentle fanning tannins, terrific balance and grace, full of pinot charm.

2007 Pyramid Valley Growers Collection Calvert Vineyard Pinot Noir
Score **96**

CENTRAL OTAGO 🍃
Price $70.00 ✓
Quality ★★★★★
Alc./Vol. 14%
Drink Now
Closure Screwcap

They say pinot is sexy and here's why. Pristine, ripe and dense, impressive haunting complexity, super-fragrant and essence-like pinot aromas. The palate tastes like fresh cinnamon-dusted cherries, only better; it winds up with soft curving tannins, pitching deep through the finish, assertive acidity keeps it fresh and balanced to a fine edge. The gods are smiling, you will be too.

2007 Pyramid Valley Growers Collection Eaton Family Vineyard Pinot Noir
Score **96**

MARLBOROUGH 🍃
Price $70.00
Quality ★★★★★
Alc./Vol. 14%
Drink 2011
Closure Screwcap

From a steep clay hillside in the Omaka Valley, this boasts superb ripeness and fruit purity, smells super fresh and full of life. Juicy dark cherries, strong pinot character, the oak sits in behind, earthy, fragrant, perfumed and complex. The palate holds smoothly honed tannins and an abundant pure cherry fruit flavour, folding superior texture. This has the extra dimension of truly great wine. Brilliant!

2006 Quartz Reef Bendigo Estate Vineyard Pinot Noir
Score **96**

CENTRAL OTAGO 🍃
Price $95.00
Quality ★★★★★
Alc./Vol. 14.5%
Drink 2012
Closure Screwcap

Superb depth and doubled-up richness in this super cuvée from Rudi Bauer. Strong ripe cherry and spiced blueberry fruits, some savoury biscuit oak – very pure and direct. The palate's dense yet elegant and files tannins in ascending layers, a savoury commanding finish. Intensity with grace.

2006 Quartz Reef Pinot Noir
Score **92**

CENTRAL OTAGO 🍃
Price $50.00
Quality ★★★★
Alc./Vol. 14.5%
Drink 2012
Closure Screwcap

This is an unmistakable Otago pinot with rich dark cherries, forest berry fruits and some ripe dark plum aromas, a little orange peel too. Tannins are fleshy and supple, sweeping in thick waves through the palate, carrying ripe plum flavours and subtle spice. Deceptive acidity ensures its best is yet to come.

2007 Rabbit Ranch Pinot Noir
Score **89**

CENTRAL OTAGO 🍃
Price $30.00
Quality ★★★ ⸱
Alc./Vol. 13.5%
Drink Now
Closure Screwcap

This has riper fruit characters and undergrowthy aromas, aniseed spice and some sweeter oak in there too, a little candied. The palate has super-ripe mulberry fruits, slight musky lift, big rich flavour and chewy tannin glide.

2006 **Rippon Pinot Noir**   *Score* **96**

WANAKA	
Price	$75.00
Quality	★★★★★
Alc./Vol.	13%
Drink	2014
Closure	Diam

A deep, soulful and profound wine with spice and precise dark minerals. This is all about tannin texture and shows the inspired approach that winemaker Nick Mills has gathered through multiple vintages at some of Burgundy's greatest domaines. Oak is discreet and structural, and tannins are resolved and velveteen, layered in sheets that assemble and then peel away – there's a flurry of whole-bunch aroma and texture that launches out the finish. Superb pinot and worth every cent.

2007 **Roaring Meg Pinot Noir**   *Score* **90**

CENTRAL OTAGO	
Price	$35.00
Quality	★★★★
Alc./Vol.	14%
Drink	Now
Closure	Screwcap

Mt Difficulty's second label, named after some formidable local river rapids. A super-ripe, meaty nose, the fruit is herded into the deep end of the scale of plums, cassis aromas and jubes. The palate's dense and juicy, more spiced plum, tannins are soft and ripe, cascading out the finish.

2007 **Rockburn Pinot Noir**   *Score* **93**

CENTRAL OTAGO	
Price	$42.00
Quality	★★★★ ┤
Alc./Vol.	14.1%
Drink	2011
Closure	Screwcap

Attractive spicy aromatic complexity here, really juicy and complex, some game meats. Shows the full array of pinot possibilities – oak is well married and there's a soulful side on show. The palate's in terrific shape, glossy and enriched, smoothly textured and resolved with silky tannins; plenty of fruit presence and juicy brambly complexity.

2006 **Secret Stone Pinot Noir**   *Score* **90**

MARLBOROUGH	
Price	$20.00
Quality	★★★★
Alc./Vol.	13.5%
Drink	Now
Closure	Screwcap

Bright cherry fruits and lifted fragrant aromas, some cherry and brown spices, ripe dark fruits and chocolate too. The palate's pitched with serious acidity and richness, strong ripe cherry flavour and fine tannins to finish.

2007 Seresin Leah Pinot Noir *Score* **93**

MARLBOROUGH
Price $40.00 ✓
Quality ★★★★ ┤
Alc./Vol. 13.5%
Drink 2010
Closure Screwcap

One of the darkest coloured Marlborough pinot noirs, it has rich black cherry fruits, undergrowth and some dark toasted spices; a more brooding style. The palate delivers full dark fruit flavours and more toasted rich spices, chocolate and earth, brisk acidity sharpens up the finish. A striking and distinctive style.

2007 Spy Valley Pinot Noir *Score* **92**

MARLBOROUGH
Price $30.00 ✓
Quality ★★★★
Alc./Vol. 13.5%
Drink Now
Closure Screwcap

Dark colour and deep rich juicy cherry aromas here; this is a ripe style with impressive concentration, really pure – some wild earthy spices too. The palate is super smooth and supple, has an abundance of rich ripe fruits and soft flowing tannins, and draws fragrant lift through the finish. Impressive shape and build.

2006 Stoneleigh Pinot Noir *Score* **91**

MARLBOROUGH
Price $25.00
Quality ★★★★
Alc./Vol. 13%
Drink Now
Closure Screwcap

A well-made, sweetly spiced wine from the Montana stable has savoury oak pushing through forest berries, obvious and likeable. Plenty of flavour here too, vibrant red fruits and musky sweetness, tannins charm away below.

2007 Stoneleigh Pinot Noir *Score* **89**

MARLBOROUGH
Price $25.00
Quality ★★★ ┤
Alc./Vol. 13%
Drink Now
Closure Screwcap

Open cherry fruits, this is an access-all-areas style, full of appealing varietal character, straight-shooting and nicely dressed in gentle oak spice. Moves in a line across the palate with dark cherry flavour and fine tannin build. Direct and appealing.

2007 Stoneleigh Rapaura Series Pinot Noir *Score* **91**

MARLBOROUGH
Price $37.00
Quality ★★★★
Alc./Vol. 13%
Drink Now
Closure Screwcap

Named for the stony soils from whence the fruit is sourced, this shows some punchy oak and bright red cherry fruits. The palate is sweetly fruited with poached strawberry and mulberry flavours, the oak weighs in with spice through the finish – a supple rolling tannin finish.

2007 Te Mania Nelson Pinot Noir
Score **92**

NELSON
Price $28.00 ✓
Quality ★★★★
Alc./Vol. 13.5%
Drink Now
Closure Screwcap

This is as bright as a button, really lifted fresh wild strawberry fruit aromas, flinty river pebbles, earth and spice – complex. Smoky cherry flavours roll through some sweeter toasty oak influence, tannins sit smoothly throughout, balanced smooth and supple.

2007 Te Mania Nelson Pinot Noir Reserve
Score **94**

NELSON
Price $35.00 ✓
Quality ★★★★ ⸳
Alc./Vol. 14.5%
Drink Now
Closure Screwcap

This is one of the highlights of the NZ pinots on offer, really well made: superb bright ripe red and dark cherry fruits, earthy spice, the oak sits in a supporting role. A very supple and intensely flavoured palate, pink musky lift, smoky spice, pure dark cherry flavour and plenty to marvel at. Bright acid finish; elegant, superb!

2007 Trinity Hill Hawkes Bay Pinot Noir
Score **92**

HAWKES BAY
Price $19.00 ✓
Quality ★★★★
Alc./Vol. 13.5%
Drink 2011
Closure Screwcap

Unbelievably great pinot for under 20 bucks, and it's from Hawkes Bay, New Zealand! This has heady rich pinot fruit aromas, plenty of cherry and juicy sweet aromas, there's impressive concentration and deep fruit richness – stunning. Bright upbeat pinot fruit flavour and a fair stripe of toasty oak, meaty complexity and fine smooth tannins. Really pure, elegant and balanced.

2007 Trinity Hill High Country Pinot Noir
Score **93**

HAWKES BAY 🖉
Price $39.00
Quality ★★★★ ⸳
Alc./Vol. 14%
Drink 2010
Closure Diam

Who says pinot doesn't work in Hawkes Bay? Sourced from cooler sites in the southerly hills, this has deep crimson colour and really upbeat concentrated pinot aromas – symphonic. Toasty oak sits across ripe cherry and dark berry fruits. The palate is superbly crafted and even, with really smooth tannins and an innately elegant, rich balance. Engaging.

2007 Triplebank Awatere Valley Pinot Noir
Score **91**

MARLBOROUGH
Price $27.00
Quality ★★★★
Alc./Vol. 13%
Drink 2011
Closure Screwcap

Lovely finesse and fragrance here, this has some bright spice and fine, almost peppery characters; it shows its savoury Awatere Valley origins. The palate sits evenly on fine smooth tannins, bright cherry and mulberry fruits, some gravelly savoury flavours and neat balance.

2006 Two Paddocks Central Otago Pinot Noir   *Score* 92

CENTRAL OTAGO
Price $45.00
Quality   ★★★★
Alc./Vol. 13%
Drink   Now
Closure   Screwcap

This blend of all three vineyards in the region has some poise and complex style about it, ripe and fragrant, superb richness and dense dark minerals, earthy and soulful. The palate's a rich, ripe affair with soft dense tannins, raw dark cherry and plum fruit, easy finish, terrific fresh balance.

2007 Villa Maria Cellar Selection Pinot Noir   *Score* 94

MARLBOROUGH
Price $46.00 ✓
Quality   ★★★★ᴶ
Alc./Vol. 13.5%
Drink   2012
Closure   Screwcap

Another ever-reliable Villa pinot, showing fine spiced cherry fragrance, pomegranate and super-fine aromatics here, minerally river pebbles, savoury and precise. The palate has some chalky/musky flavour, crunchy savoury cherry fruits, passionfruit, fine and structured, gentle spices, subtle smoky oak and a long fine finish.

2007 Villa Maria Private Bin Pinot Noir   *Score* 93

MARLBOROUGH
Price $31.00 ✓
Quality   ★★★★ᴶ
Alc./Vol. 13.5%
Drink   Now
Closure   Screwcap

This packs some attractive varietal character and taps into the Marlborough region's aptitude for making ripe pinot with fragrance. Gravelly minerals, spiced cherry, chirpy oak aromas, supple cherry flavours and fine musky tannins. The acidity freshens and brings lift through the finish – young, balanced and confident style.

2006 Villa Maria Single Vineyard Taylors Pass Pinot Noir   *Score* 95

MARLBOROUGH
Price $46.00 ✓
Quality   ★★★★ᴶ
Alc./Vol. 13.5%
Drink   2011
Closure   Screwcap

This flagship pinot has bright resolve and intense ripe dark cherry fruit aromas, dark spices and complex earthy flavours. The palate delivers supple tannins amid bright acidity; they've lined this one up for the long haul. Supple swirling tannins through the finish, really pure and fine, terrific cut and glide.

2006 Vynfields Pinot Noir   *Score* 91

MARTINBOROUGH
Price $55.00
Quality   ★★★★
Alc./Vol. 14%
Drink   Now
Closure   Screwcap

This little organic producer has captured bright meaty notes and liquorice, the oak sits up slightly and makes a cedary impression, earthy too. In the mouth it's all fine breezy tannins and dense juicy dark cherry fruit, some plums, lots of liquorice and a lingering cherry-pip finish.

2007 Waimea Pinot Noir Barrel Selection

Score **92**

NELSON
Price $29.00
Quality ★★★★
Alc./Vol. 14.5%
Drink 2010
Closure Screwcap

From the top of the bottom island, this has Nelson-region depth and ripeness, a deeper colour, meat and spice aromas, sweetly smoked dark cherry fruits and impressive concentration. The palate has mouth-watering intensity and richness, dark toasted spices and long smooth fruit presence, pencil shavings at the finish.

2007 Waipara Hills Southern Cross Selection Pinot Noir

Score **93**

CENTRAL OTAGO
Price $30.00 ✓
Quality ★★★★↓
Alc./Vol. 14%
Drink Now
Closure Screwcap

This vineyard is perched in the northern corner of the Bendigo area. Here it shows bright ripe dark berry fruits and deep cherry aromas, really inviting and soft violetine fragrance, gentle spice, earthy minerals; a superb pinot nose. The palate has juicy upbeat style, real blueberry and baked cherry flavours, fine open-knit tannins that slide through the finish.

2007 Wild Rock Cupid's Arrow Pinot Noir

Score **90**

CENTRAL OTAGO
Price $28.00
Quality ★★★★
Alc./Vol. 13.5%
Drink Now
Closure Screwcap

This junior Craggy Range pinot has bright plum fruits and regional richness and ripeness, an attractive pinot with gentle brambly notes. Upbeat fruit flavours and light easy tannins, enough flesh and brambly berry fruit to carry it all off. Great value!

2007 Winegrowers of Ara Composite Pinot Noir

Score **91**

MARLBOROUGH
Price $28.00
Quality ★★★★
Alc./Vol. 13%
Drink 2010
Closure Screwcap

The best of several wines submitted under this banner, this has plenty of charming fine fragrant spices and bright juicy cherry fruit aromas, some musk, liquorice and supportive oak. The palate's a bright chirpy tannin and acid assembly, it frames up the cherry flavour nicely, finishing precise and fine.

2007 Wooing Tree Pinot Noir

Score **91**

CENTRAL OTAGO
Price $48.00
Quality ★★★★
Alc./Vol. 14.5%
Drink Now
Closure Screwcap

This has simple, rich ripe sweet dark cherry fruits and some sweet dark chocolate aromas, sweet earthy spices, smoky cherry notes too. The palate has an arresting tannin presence, punchy and direct, juicy acid and brambly cherry flavour.

Italian varietals

Italian red grapes have marched well beyond the borders of Italy, greatly enriching the world of red wine. These varieties hold a special place in our appreciation of wine and deserve their own chapter here. Sangiovese has been most widely adopted in Australia, spurred along by the Renaissance of Chianti and Tuscan wines. It delivers one of the great all-round styles: lighter colour, cherry fruits, bright acid and savoury tannins. The best examples place juicy flesh on the wine's fine structural bones. Nebbiolo, a relatively recent arrival in Australia, is showing some promising results, making perfumed spicy reds with powerful tannin. Barbera's easygoing appeal and ability to retain acidity in warm growing conditions has caught the eye of many Australian winemakers. FOOD: These wines can take food to a whole new dimension. Savoury tannins generally demand meat or game, and accompanying flavours include mushrooms, truffles, root vegetables, dried citrus peel and savoury spices. Needless to say, regional Italian cuisine is the way to go.

2006 Acrobat Sangiovese Shiraz
Score **89**

MUDGEE	
Price	$10.00 ✓
Quality	★★★ ╯
Alc./Vol.	13.5%
Drink	Now
Closure	Screwcap

It'll be easy to locate this vibrantly packaged wine if this review inspires you to seek it out. The blend works a treat, showing bright lifted aromas ahead of some older oak aromas. The palate is all ripe red fruits with simple soft tannins and easy balance; not a stretch at all.

2006 Cardinham Estate Sangiovese
Score **92**

CLARE VALLEY	
Price	$18.00
Quality	★★★★
Alc./Vol.	14.2%
Drink	2012
Closure	Screwcap

Sangiovese has shown some flashes of brilliance in the Clare Valley; nutty marzipan oak here, savoury dried berries and cedary oak too. It delivers really assertive palate structure, deep fine tannins placed savoury and even. Finishes with power and will benefit from time.

2004 **Casa Freschi La Signora**   *Score* **92**

LANGHORNE CREEK
Price $40.00
Quality ★★★★
Alc./Vol. 14%
Drink 2012
Closure Cork

A unique blend that's built on nebbiolo and cabernet sauvignon, there's a little shiraz and a tiny bit of malbec here too. It has a fresh leafy aroma and some sweet liquorice – herbal and intriguing. It swings into medium-weight territory on the palate, crisp acidity and fine juicy tannins hold it in tight, rose petals to close.

2006 **Catherine Vale Winifred Barbera**   *Score* **87**

HUNTER VALLEY
Price $18.00
Quality ★★★
Alc./Vol. 13.5%
Drink Now
Closure Screwcap

This Hunter barbera has lighter fruits, wild red berries and gentle spice, quite lifted. The palate's bright, light and easy to drink, trading on the assertive natural acidity of this variety, keeping red confected flavours nice and fresh. A lunch wine.

2006 **Chalk Hill Barbera**   *Score* **91**

McLAREN VALE
Price $26.00
Quality ★★★★
Alc./Vol. 15%
Drink 2011
Closure Screwcap

This northern Italian variety looks well suited to McLaren Vale where this stunner won an impressive four trophies at the 2007 wine show. Rich purple fruits, super ripe and concentrated with gentle background spice. The palate has impressive density and balance, jammed full of dark berry fruit flavour and approachable swirling tannins, finishing with acid-driven freshness.

2006 **Chalk Hill Sangiovese**   *Score* **90**

McLAREN VALE
Price $25.00
Quality ★★★★
Alc./Vol. 15%
Drink 2011
Closure Screwcap

Sangiovese grows pretty well in McLaren Vale. This shows light, red fruit aromas and simple primary charm, oak isn't really a part of the equation, some fine hard spices make for gentle complexity. The palate is all about light, dried red berry fruits, and displays more oak here, liquorice and fine easy tannins.

2005 **Chalmers Sagrantino**   *Score* **89**

MURRAY DARLING
Price $28.00
Quality ★★★⅃
Alc./Vol. 14.5%
Drink Now
Closure Diam

The Chalmers family has been an advocate of lesser-known grapes via their nursery business in the Murray Darling region. Sagrantino hails from Umbria where it can produce very powerful reds. Here it's sporting some meaty baked berry aromas, the palate's lightly flavoured, quite juicy, with drying tannins just trailing out beyond the fruit. Needs food.

2006 Chapel Hill il Vescovo Sangiovese

Score **90**

McLAREN VALE	
Price	$20.00 ✓
Quality	★★★★
Alc./Vol.	14.2%
Drink	2011
Closure	Screwcap

This has some assertive new wood just obscuring the ripe cherry fruit at this stage, brambly too with savoury spices. The palate is a typical medium-weight sangiovese with plenty of presence, taut tannins and simple red cherry flavours. Give the oak some time to integrate.

2007 Coriole Sangiovese

Score **93**

McLAREN VALE	
Price	$22.00 ✓
Quality	★★★★ ꜀
Alc./Vol.	14%
Drink	Now
Closure	Screwcap

The benchmark has once again re-asserted itself in the 2007 vintage. Sensational vibrant young purple colour, an instantly recognisable sangiovese with anise-spiced cherry fruits, easy on the oak. Beautifully ripe, it packs ripe berry and cherry flavour, a little chocolate oak here and a juicy kick of tannin through the middle – superb!

PENGUIN BEST ITALIAN VARIETAL

2007 Fermoy Estate Nebbiolo

Score **90**

MARGARET RIVER	
Price	$50.00
Quality	★★★★
Alc./Vol.	14%
Drink	Now
Closure	Diam

Nebbiolo is an incredibly versatile grape and can be steered into early drinking or cellar-worthy styles. Here it's the former, with bright cherry fragrance, some rose petal perfume and regional roasting herbs. Juicy cherry flavour and some toasty oak boost it along; almost crunchy it's so fresh.

2006 Gapstead Limited Release Barbera

Score **90**

KING VALLEY	
Price	$27.00
Quality	★★★★
Alc./Vol.	13.5%
Drink	Now
Closure	Screwcap

The combination of barbera's natural brightness and the cool alpine valleys where Gapstead source this fruit from makes a winning combination. Bright cherry fruit and red perfume, the palate has cherry and wild raspberry flavours, bright chirpy acidity, neatly honed tannins and a wash of sweet oak spice through the finish.

2006 Grove Estate Reserve Nebbiolo

Score **93**

HILLTOPS	
Price	$30.00 ✓
Quality	★★★★ ꜀
Alc./Vol.	15%
Drink	2011
Closure	Screwcap

The Grove Estate folks reckon that this Italian variety is a shoe-in for the Hilltops region. This reserve bottling from 2006 is all they need to show to convince any sceptics: musk and rose petals, rich cherry fruits and a fine dense array of chewy delicious tannin. Finishes long and fades slowly. Superb.

2005 **Hollick Hollaia**   *Score* **89**

WRATTONBULLY	
Price	$21.00
Quality	★★★ ⌐
Alc./Vol.	13%
Drink	2009
Closure	Screwcap

A playful take on the Super-Tuscan names Solaia, Sassicaia and Ornellaia, Hollaia offers simple sweet, ripe fruit aromas, toasty oak, dark briary complexity and some meaty, gamey funk. Plenty of tannin ripeness, plum and cherry fruits; this trades on rustic charm and is not to be taken too seriously.

2006 **Joseph Nebbiolo**   *Score* **95**

McLAREN VALE	
Price	$75.00
Quality	★★★★ ⌐
Alc./Vol.	14%
Drink	2012
Closure	Procork

One of Joe Grilli's finest to date, it sports anise and cassia bark aromas, cedary oak and earthy cherry fruits. Beautiful poise and grace on the palate, smooth from the very outset, it builds tannins and intensity in layers and loads sweet juicy cherry fruit into every corner of the mouth, baking spices to close. Very young, very balanced and very good.

2007 **Lark Hill Sangiovese**   *Score* **90**

CANBERRA DISTRICT	
Price	$30.00
Quality	★★★★
Alc./Vol.	13.5%
Drink	2010
Closure	Screwcap

Cool but ripe cherry fruits and some mocha-scented oak make for attractive aromas, a touch of ripe herb and mint too, gently spicy and a distinct sour cherry twist. The palate has fine perky tannins and bright acid, drops cherry and plum at the edges. Medium-weight, it begs for food.

2006 **Luke Lambert Nebbiolo**   *Score* **93**

HEATHCOTE	
Price	$38.00
Quality	★★★★ ⌐
Alc./Vol.	13.3%
Drink	2013
Closure	Diam

Although this wine will be hard to track down, it's a label to keep an eye on. Heathcote-sourced fruit delivers bright and pure red cherry aromas, gently dressed in toasty oak. Very lively palate, more red cherries here and some softer tannins thanks to an extended maceration, bright acid lifts the finish. Superb!

2006 **Margan Barbera**   *Score* **92**

HUNTER VALLEY	
Price	$25.00 ✓
Quality	★★★★
Alc./Vol.	14%
Drink	2011
Closure	Screwcap

Think of Italian red grape varieties and the Hunter Valley isn't one of the usual suspects, but this is a great example of savoury barbera. Dried dark berries and some cedary French oak mean business on the nose. There's terrific acidity in the mouth, a hallmark of the variety, plenty of ripe berry fruit and fine gently drying tannins through the finish.

2003 Pizzini Nebbiolo   *Score* 95

KING VALLEY

Price $56.00 ✓

Quality   ★★★★)

Alc./Vol. 14.5%

Drink   2011

Closure   Cork

The Pizzini family has been chipping away at nebbiolo for some time and with real determination. This bottle-matured beauty has impressive authentic characters: cherries and leathery/savoury notes, game meats and floral red perfume. Beautiful depth and complex tannin structure, mouth-watering tannin and acid combination, ripe cherry fruits and nutty/savoury flavours through the finish. One of the best Australian examples.

2006 Pizzini Sangiovese   *Score* 92

KING VALLEY

Price $28.00

Quality   ★★★★

Alc./Vol. 14%

Drink   2012

Closure   Screwcap

The Pizzini family has unravelled the sangiovese puzzle better than most. Quite a rich style, it smells ripe and juicy with some sweet spice drawn between oak and cherry-scented fruit. The palate confirms the richness: bright acidity lifts through ripe plum pudding fruits, followed by a decent slice of tannin. Balanced and convincing.

2006 Primo Estate Il Briccone Shiraz Sangiovese   *Score* 90

McLAREN VALE

Price $22.00 ✓

Quality   ★★★★

Alc./Vol. 14%

Drink   2009

Closure   Screwcap

A purple youthful wine; there's a good serve of glossy sweetly spiced oak laid across ripe plum and dark berry fruits, some sweet floral lift too. The palate has effortless supple charm with hints of peppery shiraz filling out the middle palate. Finishes with soft fine savoury tannins all swathed in sweetly spiced toasty oak. It's all about pure enjoyment, not challenging your perceptions.

2005 Primo Estate Zamberlan Cabernet Sauvignon Sangiovese *Score* 93

McLAREN VALE

Price $28.00 ✓

Quality   ★★★★)

Alc./Vol. 14.5%

Drink   2010

Closure   Screwcap

There's no mistaking the fact that cabernet is leading the march here, but it has a strong affinity with the anise-scented sangiovese bonded below some cedary oak aromas. The real point though is the tannins: super-fine chocolate-like tannins with terrific texture; an extra dimension of thickness and smoothness is added thanks to the technique of passing the fermented wine across the already pressed skins of another. This enriches the texture, making for a supple, plush dark-fruit flavoured wine that's as captivating as it is distinctive.

2007 Ravensworth Sangiovese

CANBERRA DISTRICT
Price $24.00 ✓
Quality   ★ ★ ★ ★ ﹢
Alc./Vol.   13.5%
Drink   2011
Closure   Screwcap

Lovely charming fragrance – striking in fact – with pristine fresh red fruits and purple florals. Very expressive of the variety, it draws on insight and some refined winemaking technique. The tannins are supple and fine grained, showing plenty of endearing sangiovese character; cherry flavour, balanced and just the right amount of savoury grip.

2005 S.C. Pannell Nebbiolo

Score 93

ADELAIDE HILLS
Price $50.00
Quality   ★ ★ ★ ★ ﹢
Alc./Vol.   14%
Drink   2013
Closure   Screwcap

Pannell's passion for this Italian variety is evident and it's given full voice here: earthy spiced cherry aromas, anise and sweet rose perfume. The palate is a duet of acidity and tannin, flavours fold through; it's juicy, demanding and engaging stuff. Bravo!

2006 Sutton Grange Giove

Score 93

BENDIGO
Price $38.00
Quality   ★ ★ ★ ★ ﹢
Alc./Vol.   15%
Drink   2012
Closure   Diam

It's a sign of success when a three-way blend (sangiovese, cabernet sauvignon and merlot) is so precisely stitched together that the components can barely be pulled apart. A resolved compact style, this smells of cherry and mountain herbs; the palate travels on fluid tannins that turn savoury through the finish. Central Victoria meets Central Italy.

2007 Tar & Roses Sangiovese

Score 92

HEATHCOTE
Price $23.00 ✓
Quality   ★ ★ ★ ★
Alc./Vol.   14%
Drink   Now
Closure   Screwcap

A partnership between Don Lewis and Narelle King, this is the best of their reds and shows promise for sangiovese in Heathcote. Bright fresh red cherry aromas, liquorice and gentle earthy spices, the palate is medium-weight and built across fine savoury tannins, oak is in check; they've balanced it up nicely.

2006 Vinea Marson Nebbiolo

Score 92

HEATHCOTE
Price $45.00
Quality   ★ ★ ★ ★
Alc./Vol.   13.5%
Drink   2011
Closure   Diam

Mario Marson's little slice of terra rossa in Heathcote is already showing promise for this variety, even with young vines. Light and bright wild red cherry aromas, the palate follows suit with some fragrance and perfume across a sturdy tannin base, finishes with a twist of spice.

2006 Vinea Marson Sangiovese

Score 91

HEATHCOTE

Price	$33.00
Quality	★★★★
Alc./Vol.	14%
Drink	Now
Closure	Diam

Mario Marson backed a winner with his pursuit of Heathcote sangiovese; a little shiraz-like, this has bright brambly cherry fruit, anise, background oak and earthy regional spice. The palate is fine and dense, light cherry flavours and earthy fine tannins work side by side to make this a handy everyday red.

2007 Zilzie Sangiovese

Score 90

SOUTH EASTERN AUSTRALIA

Price	$16.00 ✓
Quality	★★★★
Alc./Vol.	13%
Drink	2011
Closure	Screwcap

This represents terrific value and works well within the capacity of the grape source. Attractive ripe red fruits and some gentle red liquorice; nice varietal character. The palate is soft and easy, and builds rich through the middle, finishing soft, simple and easy. Some charry oak to close.

2007 Zonte's Footstep Sangiovese Barbera

Score 91

LANGHORNE CREEK

Price	$18.00 ✓
Quality	★★★★
Alc./Vol.	14.5%
Drink	Now
Closure	Screwcap

This is my pick of the Zonte's range, an innovative blend. The grapes are concentrated on the vine by cutting the canes and leaving them hanging to dehydrate before picking. Beautiful berry and cherry fruit nose, soft and dense mid-palate, finishing with plenty of flavour and convincing balance.

Emerging red wines

As with the emerging whites chapter, this is a collection of the more promising but lesser known varietals being made around the country. Italian varietals have been singled out for their own chapter, leaving this eclectic mix of wines, many made by the hands of the country's most esteemed winemakers. The Spanish grape tempranillo is a hot topic right now and shows real promise in a range of regions. Durif continues to impress with its hearty dark fruits, most notably from the region Rutherglen. There's malbec, graciano, zinfandel, gamay and even tannat on offer here; plenty to keep you busy. FOOD: With such a motley crew in one chapter it's hard to generalise. Pay attention to the structure of the wine and as a starting point look to find food styles that match the intensity and tannin profile.

2006 All Saints Estate Durif
Score **91**

NORTH EAST VICTORIA	Showing settled, balanced richness with deep berry
Price $23.00 ✓	and plum fruit aromas, and some rich spicy liquorice
Quality ★★★★	complexity – this is no shrinking violet, quite fragrant.
Alc./Vol. 14.8%	Super-rich palate, there's plenty of deep fruit-soaked
Drink 2013	tannins running supple and even, plum fruit and sweetly
Closure Screwcap	spiced oak fitted neatly around.

2006 All Saints Estate Family Cellar Durif
Score **92**

NORTH EAST VICTORIA	Typical dense, dark durif colour, the aromas sit in the ripe
Price $50.00	plum spectrum, some earthy complexity below and musky
Quality ★★★★	fragrant oak on top. Rich ripe tannins sweep deep dark fruit
Alc./Vol. 14.8%	flavour from start to finish, really long, ripe and intense,
Drink 2015	punchy oak after-burn. Needs time to integrate.
Closure Screwcap	

2005 Bleasdale Malbec
Score **90**

LANGHORNE CREEK	Outside of Argentina, malbec is more often a seen and
Price $15.00 ✓	not heard blender, used to fine-tune cabernet and other
Quality ★★★★	red wines. It has a strong affinity with Langhorne Creek,
Alc./Vol. 14.5%	showing rich, ripe dark fruits here and a wedge of bold
Drink 2010	oak. Round and mouth-filling, the tannins sweep wide,
Closure Screwcap	opening out plenty of flesh and mulberry flavour, oak
	nails the finish shut.

2006 **Brown Brothers Durif**   *Score* **90**

HEATHCOTE
Price $20.00 ✓
Quality   ★★★★
Alc./Vol. 14.5%
Drink   2010
Closure   Cork

This is parked in the cellar door release range and has terrific freshness, more than most durif wines are capable of. Ripe dark berry fruits, blackberry and plum are the mainstays, bright fragrance too. Tannins are sturdy but not over the top, it's a well-balanced full-bodied style, already drinking nicely.

2006 **Brown Brothers Graciano**   *Score* **90**

KING VALLEY
Price $20.00 ✓
Quality   ★★★★
Alc./Vol. 15%
Drink   2010
Closure   Cork

A medium-bodied red made from this native Spanish grape, most famously a lynchpin of rioja wines. It's fragrant here and carries sweet ripe cherry aromas, very primary. The palate's fine tannins are superb, as is the cassis and cherry fruit – kicks with a warming alcohol-driven finish.

2006 **Cape Mentelle Zinfandel**   *Score* **91**

MARGARET RIVER
Price $53.00
Quality   ★★★★
Alc./Vol. 15%
Drink   2013
Closure   Screwcap

Zin is a wine that's not for everyone but it tends to have its loyal followers, enthusiasts if you like. Cape Mentelle has made one of the best examples for many years, with better balance than most. Ripe spiced plums and some regional herbal edges, the palate is dressed in velvet tannins, quite juicy, and the cool '06 vintage has tightened the style right up.

2007 **Cascabel Tempranillo**   *Score* **92**

McLAREN VALE
Price $21.00 ✓
Quality   ★★★★
Alc./Vol. 13.5%
Drink   Now
Closure   Screwcap

The folks at Cascabel are passionate about all things wine, especially when it has a Spanish accent. This is their baby wine, an early-release fruit bomb and a homage to the young Spanish styles. Brilliant charm and seductive fragrance, bright cherry fruit that's built for immediate pleasure, all beautifully captured.

2007 **Chalk Hill The Procrastinator**   *Score* **91**

McLAREN VALE 🖋
Price $18.00
Quality   ★★★★
Alc./Vol. 14.5%
Drink   2012
Closure   Screwcap

Cabernet franc leads cabernet sauvignon here with sprightly, musky oak aromas lifting through brambly berry fruits; plenty of attractive fragrance. The palate is redolent with berries and some lifted violet-like flavour; elegant and flavoursome with sturdy tannin scooping around the finish. Will fill out the structure in no time at all.

2007 Chapel Hill il Vescovo Tempranillo

Score **89**

ADELAIDE HILLS
Price $22.00
Quality   ★★★ ┤
Alc./Vol. 14%
Drink   2011
Closure   Screwcap

The il Vescovo range is reserved for lesser-known varietals; here there are classic cherry and dark mineral characters of tempranillo, a little reduction suits the variety, some lifted fragrance too. The palate delivers simple cherry flavour and assertive chewy tannins, finishes with bright cranberry flavour.

2007 Cofield Durif

Score **90**

RUTHERGLEN
Price $22.00
Quality   ★★★★
Alc./Vol. 14.2%
Drink   2012
Closure   Diam

A trademark regional statement of very ripe dark plum fruits, some ripe glossy notes across the top, earthy depth below and silvery spice nuances. The tannins are juicy and deep, delivered in a modern style with purple fragrance through the finish and easy rich balance.

2006 Coldstone Tempranillo

Score **88**

VICTORIA
Price $13.00
Quality   ★★★ ┤
Alc./Vol. 12.5%
Drink   Now
Closure   Screwcap

Coldstone is reference to the alpine country in which this winery is set. Bright perfumed fruit-driven tempranillo here, cherry and some gentle blackcurrant. Light tannins, some crisp acidity and easy refreshing red fruit flavour.

2006 Fox Gordon By George Cabernet Tempranillo

Score **93**

BAROSSA VALLEY/
ADELAIDE HILLS
Price $20.00 ✓
Quality   ★★★★ ┤
Alc./Vol. 13.5%
Drink   2012
Closure   Screwcap

A clever inter-regional blend: cabernet from the Barossa meets tempranillo from the Adelaide Hills, and 'by George' . . . Attractive dark, toasted spices and warm berry aromas, a little leaf, purple berries and cedary oak float through. Terrific tannins, really dense and fine, carpeted from front to back, holding plenty of berry flavour. Fine, concentrated and elegant.

2007 Gemtree Bloodstone Tempranillo

Score **92**

MCLAREN VALE
Price $25.00 ✓
Quality   ★★★★
Alc./Vol. 14.5%
Drink   2009
Closure   Screwcap

Looking terrific in its youth with bright, upbeat aromas of fresh cherry fruit, cedary oak sits in nicely; there's a fragrant attractive side to the wine, modern and fresh. The palate has some musky red fruit flavour, plenty of fine tannin spread all over and crunchy red fruits through the finish. Great balance too. Ace.

2007 **Hardy's The Sage Shiraz Sangiovese** *Score* **90**

SOUTH AUSTRALIA
Price $13.00 ✓
Quality ★★★★
Alc./Vol. 14%
Drink 2010
Closure Screwcap

Terrific colour to this modern take on an alternative blend. The shiraz is sourced predominantly from McLaren Vale, but also Adelaide Hills, Fleurieu and the Limestone Coast, with Sangiovese from the Adelaide Hills. Plums and red fruits, cherries and spice, the oak sits in well. Some gentle peppery shiraz and plenty of fine tannin throughout. Terrific balance and shape. Stunning finish – superbly crafted. A hell of a lot of wine for the money. Why aren't there more like this?

PENGUIN BEST EMERGING RED WINE

2006 **Hare's Chase Tempranillo** *Score* **90**

BAROSSA VALLEY
Price $20.00 ✓
Quality ★★★★
Alc./Vol. 14%
Drink 2010
Closure Screwcap

An earthy Barossa-take on the tempranillo theme, made by a couple of guys who know exactly what they're doing. Sweet cinnamon spice and some older wood characters, musk aromatics and bright lifted fragrance. Cherry fruits sit medium-weighted across the palate, smoky to close.

2005 **Hastwell & Lightfoot Cabernet Franc** *Score* **91**

McLAREN VALE
Price $22.00 ✓
Quality ★★★★
Alc./Vol. 14.5%
Drink 2013
Closure Screwcap

The sighting of a straight cabernet franc in Australia is pretty darn rare. This one has a leafy edge to it and some mint too, earthy and savoury with a complex array of bright berry aromas. The palate shows plenty of oak and sweetly spiced plum fruit flavour, fine dense tannins, well crafted and long.

2006 **Hastwell & Lightfoot Tempranillo** *Score* **90**

McLAREN VALE
Price $22.00
Quality ★★★★
Alc./Vol. 14.5%
Drink 2010
Closure Screwcap

Another ringing endorsement for this Spanish native grown in McLaren Vale. A deeper expression here with darker berry fruits and wild cherry, some cassis too; straightforward youthful style and some regional liquorice. The palate's fine and zesty with depth and richness, balanced and supple, medium-weight, light but punchy tannins.

2006 Hewitson Cellar Reserve Tempranillo

Score **94**

McLAREN VALE
Price $70.00
Quality   ★★★★⭒
Alc./Vol. 14%
Drink   2012
Closure   Screwcap

Dean Hewitson backed this prize wine all the way to the top of his range. Terrific fragrance that draws you in, plenty of tempranillo's ripe cherries, savoury oak spice and an earthy undercurrent. Nicely judged in the mouth, more medium- than full-bodied, the tannins are supple and smoothly textured. Hewitson has played this like a charm.

2006 Hollick Wrattonbully Tempranillo

Score **90**

WRATTONBULLY
Price $21.00
Quality   ★★★★
Alc./Vol. 12.6%
Drink   2010
Closure   Screwcap

Hollick has tossed a few lines in the direction of nearby Wrattonbully; this tempranillo shows attractive cherry cola aromas, the fruit and wood work in together. Tannins are ripe and seem in balance, the flavours are a little toasty through the finish – grilled meats will do the trick.

2007 Juniper Crossing Tempranillo

Score **90**

MARGARET RIVER
Price $18.00 ✓
Quality   ★★★★
Alc./Vol. 14%
Drink   Now
Closure   Screwcap

Juniper make terrific wine across the board and the Juniper Crossing range is outstanding value. The tempranillo is an honest fruit-forward style with liquorice and cherry aromas, the palate's sprung with juicy acid crunch, fine tannins and vibrant berry flavours; balanced and ready to drink as a youngster.

2007 Kirrihill Companions Tempranillo Garnacha

Score **90**

CLARE VALLEY/ADELAIDE HILLS
Price $15.00 ✓
Quality   ★★★★
Alc./Vol. 14.5%
Drink   Now
Closure   Screwcap

This little blend really comes up trumps, throwing plenty of bright fragrant aromas – tempranillo plus garnacha (Spanish for grenache) makes a charming wine. Decent ripeness and richness, the palate is medium-weighted and has crisp cherry/berry flavour, fine tannins, musky through the finish. Delicious.

2005 McHenry Hohnen Tiger Country

Score **91**

MARGARET RIVER
Price $32.00
Quality   ★★★★
Alc./Vol. 14%
Drink   2010
Closure   Cork

The McLeod Creek vineyard where these grapes are grown is a favourite hangout for tiger snakes, hence the name. A blend of tempranillo, petit verdot and cabernet sauvignon – innovative and successfully matched up – it smells of ripe plum, cassis and berry fruits with an earthy/savoury side, some roasting herbs, sweet spices and super subtle oak. The palate is polished into smooth shape with soft easy fruits and some bounce through the finish.

2004 Morris Rutherglen Durif
Score **91**

RUTHERGLEN
Price $21.00 ✓
Quality ★★★★
Alc./Vol. 14%
Drink 2012
Closure Cork

Mick Morris is one of the pioneers of this hearty rich grape and this is a ripper. Really ripe plums and mulberry fruits, some oak sitting in behind, intense and concentrated. The palate's winched into place by fine dense tannin structure, holding ripe sweet berry flavour long through the finish.

2004 Mount Majura Dinny's Block
Score **90**

CANBERRA DISTRICT
Price $20.00
Quality ★★★★
Alc./Vol. 13.8%
Drink 2012
Closure Screwcap

A warmer vintage has edged this blend of cabernet franc, merlot and cabernet sauvignon into riper, berry fruit territory, smells soft and attractive with blue fruits and cassis. The palate is finely structured and simply fruited with a soft tannin, savoury twist through the finish.

2007 Mount Majura Tempranillo
Score **90**

CANBERRA DISTRICT
Price $30.00
Quality ★★★★
Alc./Vol. 13.4%
Drink Now
Closure Screwcap

This fiery young 2007 from Mount Majura's north-east facing slopes shows bright red fruits, raspberry leaf, smelling a little jumpy and assertive – angular. The wood has a sharpening effect on the fruit aromas, resin and dusty. Light raspberry flavour and bright musky tannins, very much an easy style that balances on fruit.

2007 Mount Trio Tempranillo
Score **89**

WESTERN AUSTRALIA
Price $16.00 ✓
Quality ★★★ ⸱
Alc./Vol. 13.5%
Drink Now
Closure Screwcap

This medium-bodied red is great in that it doesn't try too hard. It's a cherry-scented, fragrant quaffer that doesn't demand too much thinking; very drinkable. The palate is soft and supple with an easy tannin slide, plenty of cherry flavour here, finishing nice and fresh.

2006 Nashwauk Tempranillo
Score **92**

McLAREN VALE
Price $25.00 ✓
Quality ★★★★
Alc./Vol. 15.5%
Drink 2011
Closure Cork

This is the McLaren Vale project of the Barossa-based Kaesler crew. They've done a great job cutting the wood in here, some sweet spices, liquorice and rich dark cherry fruits. The fine tannins have also been massaged neatly into shape, fragrant lift through the finish, integrated and almost shiraz-like.

2005 Nepenthe Zinfandel
Score **90**

ADELAIDE HILLS	
Price	$30.00
Quality	★★★★
Alc./Vol.	15.5%
Drink	2010
Closure	Screwcap

Classic plum pudding nose here, ripe raisins and spicy complexity, a hint of chocolate too. The palate is all about sweet rich plum fruits, very ripe and slightly syrupy, but that's the variety – zinfandel certainly ain't wine for wimps.

2006 Peter Lehmann Tempranillo
Score **89**

BAROSSA VALLEY	
Price	$22.00
Quality	★★★ ⌐
Alc./Vol.	14.5%
Drink	Now
Closure	Screwcap

An honest to goodness medium-weighted Barossa tempranillo that doesn't get carried away with trying to do much. Sweet cherry and berry fruits, some regulation oak, all easy to handle. The palate lifts with fragrance and some chirpy red cherry flavour, bright light tannins, full of youthful appeal.

2008 Pfeiffer Gamay
Score **90**

RUTHERGLEN	
Price	$17.00
Quality	★★★★
Alc./Vol.	13%
Drink	Now
Closure	Screwcap

This youthful answer to 'beaujolais nouveau' (which itself has plenty to answer for) smells beautiful! Light colour and abundant lifted musky cherry and blueberry fruits, superb perfume. The palate's brightly stated and pure, flavours of raspberries and milk chocolate, soft and easy.

2006 Pondalowie MT Tempranillo
Score **93**

BENDIGO	
Price	$25.00 ✔
Quality	★★★★ ⌐
Alc./Vol.	14.5%
Drink	Now
Closure	Screwcap

This Central Victorian label has made a name for an unwooded, inky take on tempranillo. Incredibly vibrant and intense fruit here, cherries and cranberry, some sarsaparilla too; really intense. The palate delivers sweeping dense velvet tannin texture and bundles of rich purple fruit flavour. More delicious fruit than you would have thought possible.

2006 Quattro Mano La Reto Tempranillo
Score **91**

BAROSSA VALLEY	
Price	$27.00
Quality	★★★★
Alc./Vol.	14.5%
Drink	2013
Closure	Diam

Edgy cherry and tarry fruit aromas in this wild Barossan Spaniard, there's a wild meaty character, some fragrant lift, sweet oak and ripe cherry fruits. Sweet entry and charming middle-palate fragrance, sweet soft tannins and a core of fruit flavour running through the finish. Youthful and balanced.

2006 Rutherglen Estates Red Shiraz Durif
Score **90**

RUTHERGLEN
Price $13.00 ✓
Quality ★★★★
Alc./Vol. 14.5%
Drink 2012
Closure Screwcap

A shining example of the virtues of blending, this shows dense, ripe earthy plum fruits and rich tarry complexity, bright, well made and nicely measured oak. The palate is similarly well arranged with a juicy core of dark fruit flavour, deep berries and fine soft tannins.

2006 Samuel's Gorge Tempranillo
Score **92**

McLAREN VALE
Price $40.00
Quality ★★★★
Alc./Vol. 14.5%
Drink 2011
Closure Cork

Quite an earthy richly scented tempranillo in a hearty McLaren Vale style, ripe dark cherries and berries, some plums and sweetly spiced earthy tones. Plenty of ripe fruit packed into the palate, dense and juicy, some tarry tannins through the finish. Superb fruit richness, this has more on offer than most.

2005 Smidge Wines The Donald Zinfandel
Score **91**

BAROSSA VALLEY
Price $38.00
Quality ★★★★
Alc./Vol. 15.7%
Drink 2011
Closure Screwcap

Instantly recognisable as zin with its ripe plum pudding and fruit cake aromas, sweet earthy plum liqueur and red liquorice. The palate has smooth thick texture, carries the big alcohol with ease; it's a hedonist's wine, ripe, juicy and soft, warm through the finish.

2006 Spinifex D.R.S. Vineyard Durif
Score **93**

BAROSSA VALLEY
Price $48.00
Quality ★★★★⌐
Alc./Vol. 15%
Drink 2013
Closure Diam

Seems that whatever they turn their hand to the results are stunning; this is Spinifex's take on durif – made in tiny quantity. Plenty of spice and pepper, some roasted meats, rich ripe berry fruits and plush richness. The palate has really dense fruit flavour, dark berries and soft swirling tannins, a surprising spear of acid, finishing intense and long. Really opulent. Limited production.

2006 Spinifex Taureau
Score **93**

BAROSSA VALLEY
Price $24.00
Quality ★★★★⌐
Alc./Vol. 14.3%
Drink 2014
Closure Screwcap

A unique blend of carignan (41%), tempranillo (32%) and cabernet sauvignon (27%), this has striking savoury cherry and spiced plum compote aromas. Deep plum and dark berry flavour, and savoury soulful tannins – make sure you've got some red meat handy or let it brood in bottle for a spell.

2005 Symphonia Tannat
Score **92**

KING VALLEY
Price $24.00
Quality ★★★★
Alc./Vol. 14%
Drink   2012
Closure Screwcap

Tannat tastes like it sounds – typically tannic and pretty burly. This wine is striking, really unique: deep brambly plum fruits and rich, ripe spices, some orange rind and orange oil aromas too. The palate wrestles with chewy tannins; rich, tart plum fruits and upbeat acidity. It's a full-throttle experience and works best with hearty braised food.

2007 Tar & Roses Tempranillo
Score **90**

HEATHCOTE
Price $23.00
Quality ★★★★
Alc./Vol. 13.5%
Drink   Now
Closure Screwcap

This tempranillo seems to have found a happy home in Victoria's Heathcote where it's warm and dry. Attractive spicy fragrance and berry perfume here, light and breezy, it's all about the fruit. The palate is a succulent mouthful of cherry flavour and light tannins; an early-drinking style.

2006 Tscharke Only Son Tempranillo Graciano
Score **92**

BAROSSA VALLEY
Price $30.00 ✓
Quality ★★★★
Alc./Vol. 14.9%
Drink   2013
Closure Screwcap

This young artisan label has delivered an astute Aussie take on a classic Spanish blend. The dark fragrant cherries of tempranillo are bolstered by graciano's pretty fruit fragrance, with some sweeter oak toast in there too. Plenty of fruit flesh and fine, upbeat tannins give this wine undeniable youthful appeal.

2006 Westend 3 Bridges Durif
Score **89**

SOUTH EASTERN AUSTRALIA
Price $20.00 ✓
Quality ★★★ ┘
Alc./Vol. 15%
Drink   Now
Closure Cork

It's no shrinking violet but this durif is so fleshy it's a sure bet for early drinking. Ripe plum and berry fruits, some sweeter oak aromas well suited to the fruit. Fine gentle tannins and bright plum flavours make for a rich, flavoursome mouthful, some vanilla dusted across the finish.

Grenache, shiraz, mataro and blends

Grenache, one of the world's most widely planted wine grapes, suits some of Australia's best winegrowing regions. It is harvested late and ripe, making wines of vibrant colour and aroma with a fruit-filled palate. Shiraz has a familiar calling card and mataro (aka mourvèdre) is one of the most underrated red grapes in Australian soil. On its own, mataro shows intense savoury character thanks to its thick-skinned small berries, offering lots of spice and meaty flavour. When all three are combined, they make for some of the most soulful and consistently great Australian reds on offer today. FOOD: GSM blends are among the most rewarding wines to match with food; their complex aromas, flavours and supple palate textures are ideal for game meats, light red meats and tasty pork dishes.

2006 Australian Old Vine Collection Grenache   Score 94

McLAREN VALE
Price $110.00
Quality   ★★★★ ┤
Alc./Vol.   14.5%
Drink   2014
Closure   Cork

These vines were planted in 1908, so if the price tag worries you think of it as a dollar for every year, plus GST. Genuine depth, almost tarry, some boot leather and plenty of earth; spiced dark berries in abundance, plums too. There's an extra dimension of texture and richness here; although the innate balance of centenarian vines delivers it all with effortless charm. Additional richness, like a 12-string guitar.

2006 Blackbilly GSM   Score 90

McLAREN VALE
Price $22.00 ✓
Quality   ★★★★
Alc./Vol.   14.5%
Drink   Now
Closure   Screwcap

Plenty of McLaren Vale plum here, just moves into jammy territory, some blackberry too, gently spicy; really pure, good concentration. Grenache runs the show on the palate, bright blackberry fruit flavour and easygoing tannins, some darker more brooding flavours at the finish.

2006 Cape Barren Native Goose GSM   Score 91

McLAREN VALE
Price $25.00 ✓
Quality   ★★★★
Alc./Vol.   14.5%
Drink   2010
Closure   Screwcap

Ripe, sweet and attractive, this has sweet regional grenache aromas, sitting in the dark berry spectrum, a little plum in there too; nice and bright, some resiny oak. The palate's a swirling ball of ripe juicy dark berry flavour, spices chime in and tannins roll even and wide.

2006 Cape Mentelle Marmaduke Shiraz Grenache   *Score* 91

WESTERN AUSTRALIA
Price $19.50 ✓
Quality ★★★★
Alc./Vol. 13.5%
Drink Now
Closure Screwcap

This entry-level Cape Mentelle red blend is meant for early drinking and it delivers plenty of forward fruit character that ensures it will go down well. An array of berry fruit flavours, some toasty oak and meaty barrel-derived winemaking complexity. Strapping young and spicy.

2006 Chapel Hill Bush Vine Grenache   *Score* 93

McLAREN VALE
Price $30.00
Quality ★★★★⁴
Alc./Vol. 15%
Drink 2011
Closure Screwcap

This is the stuff that McLaren Vale should be famous for: super-rich, earthy red fruits, a decent dose of French oak and some fine nut and spice complexity. The palate is concentrated and mouth-filling, driving rich, ripe, wild red fruit flavour deep through the finish; supple tannins to close.

2006 Chapel Hill Shiraz Grenache   *Score* 91

McLAREN VALE
Price $20.00 ✓
Quality ★★★★
Alc./Vol. 14.5%
Drink 2011
Closure Screwcap

This wine created some contentious debate at the McLaren Vale wine show where it eventually got up for a slice of glory. Simple moist oak spices, spiced plums and savoury/earthy aromas. Supple, easygoing tannins, balanced enough, attractive chew and some regional liquorice to close.

2006 Coriole The Dancing Fig Shiraz Mourvèdre   *Score* 92

McLAREN VALE
Price $22.00 ✓
Quality ★★★★
Alc./Vol. 14.5%
Drink 2012
Closure Screwcap

This weighs in with sweet earthy aromas, it has real presence and makes a compelling case for this two-way blend; shiraz from the north of the Vale and mourvèdre from the south. Dark plums and spices, it's quite savoury and distinctive. The palate introduces rich regional liquorice shiraz flavour, some chocolate and savoury mourvèdre tannins, dark mineral finish. Perfect for grilled meat.

2006 d'Arenberg d'Arry's Original Shiraz Grenache   *Score* 92

McLAREN VALE
Price $20.00 ✓
Quality ★★★★
Alc./Vol. 14.5%
Drink Now
Closure Screwcap

This is one of the most 'natural' feeling red wines going – by that I mean it fits with the region's strengths and is a well-polished routine. It sports brambly red fruits, some plum and dark cherry, oak is just in support. Medium-weight palate, doesn't push too hard, laid-back tannins, smoothly balanced, eminently drinkable. Lasting berry flavour. Brilliant!

2005 d'Arenberg Sticks & Stones

Score **92**

McLAREN VALE
Price $30.00 ✓
Quality ★ ★ ★ ★
Alc./Vol. 14.5%
Drink 2012
Closure Screwcap

A less common combination of tempranillo, grenache and shiraz; grenache is the link to the rest of the d'Arenberg range. Tarry spices and gentle fragrant notes, anise, dark cherries and plum. A rich palate with plenty of flesh; tannins are buried deep below ripe fruit, finishing soulful and savoury with a kick of fragrance.

2006 d'Arenberg The Cadenzia GSM

Score **93**

McLAREN VALE
Price $25.00 ✓
Quality ★ ★ ★ ★ ⌐
Alc./Vol. 14.5%
Drink 2012
Closure Screwcap

There's some real resolve about this three-way blend, plenty of savoury dark berry fruit, the grenache lifts lighter red tones and mourvèdre punches down deeper into savoury territory. Powerful plum and cherry fruit on the palate, really superb blending has it evenly balanced and made for some cellaring potential. Solid tannins.

2006 d'Arenberg The Custodian Grenache

Score **91**

McLAREN VALE
Price $20.00 ✓
Quality ★ ★ ★ ★
Alc./Vol. 14.5%
Drink 2010
Closure Screwcap

This legendary McLaren Vale winery has a long history of producing exceptional grenache; sometimes blended, sometimes as a solo effort. A pure, ripe and earthy style, deep dark fruits and a waft of spice-cupboard aromas. Intense red and dark berry fruit flavours, fine tannins that build richness and power through the finish. Old-school style with a contemporary twist – works like a charm.

2006 d'Arenberg The Derelict Vineyard Grenache

Score **93**

McLAREN VALE
Price $30.00 ✓
Quality ★ ★ ★ ★ ⌐
Alc./Vol. 15%
Drink 2014
Closure Screwcap

Chester Osborn restores neglected old vines by cherished repair. Dark spiced plums and earthy/savoury notes, very direct, varietal and concentrated; some lighter red fruit perfume at the top. Superb impact, really grabs the middle palate with dark berry and cherry fruit flavour, surprising tannin grab. Youthful blue fruit finish; liquorice too.

2006 d'Arenberg The Ironstone Pressings

Score **96**

McLAREN VALE
Price $65.00 ✓
Quality ★ ★ ★ ★ ★
Alc./Vol. 14.5%
Drink 2020
Closure Screwcap

Of the three top-tier d'Arenberg reds, this one best represents all that's great and unique about the Osborn family's approach. Superb earthy nose, concentrated brambly dark fruits and savoury spice. The palate is superbly crafted, particularly given the concentration – flavours and texture match up in a complex layered style. Dark fruits, savoury tannin build and the promise of a couple of decades of enjoyment, maybe more.

2006 d'Arenberg The Stump Jump
Score **88**

McLAREN VALE
Price $12.00 ✓
Quality ★★★ ⅃
Alc./Vol. 14.5%
Drink Now
Closure Screwcap

There simply aren't too many McLaren Vale reds around at this price – a beaut blend of grenache, shiraz and mourvèdre, and terrific drinking. Sweet red fruit fragrance, light spices, dark berry fruits and juicy fresh texture – leaves a lively impression and makes an easygoing regional statement.

2006 d'Arenberg The Twenty-eight Road Mourvèdre
Score **93**

McLAREN VALE
Price $35.00 ✓
Quality ★★★★ ⅃
Alc./Vol. 14.5%
Drink 2016
Closure Screwcap

The steel-blue stripes that frame the label are well-chosen to represent mourvèdre's steely/savoury blue-fruited character. Earthy and ripe, plenty of savoury spice and well-applied oak. The palate's dense and juicy, tannins chime in with savoury compact solid force, taking the wine long and intense through the finish, some dried plum flavour too. Will reward cellaring.

2006 Deisen Grenache
Score **94**

BAROSSA VALLEY
Price $40.00
Quality ★★★★ ⅃
Alc./Vol. 15%
Drink 2012
Closure Cork

The Deisen grenache gets a little dose of shiraz in 2006. A ripe and enigmatic nose, showing strong character and plenty of deep brambly berry fruits, some plum in there too. The palate has almost unbridled sweet fruit, very fleshy through the middle and sweeps through the finish on fine basket-pressed tannins. Made in tiny quantity – well worth seeking out.

2006 Deisen Mataro
Score **94**

BAROSSA VALLEY
Price $40.00
Quality ★★★★ ⅃
Alc./Vol. 14.6%
Drink 2012
Closure Cork

Sourced from the Deisen vineyard out in Marananga, this shows ripe tarry plum fruits and earthy/savoury spice, liquorice and anise; soulful and savoury, really haunting. The palate is taut and fine, tannins are ripe and there's some really chewy dark plum flavour, long fine finish, restrained power.

2006 Dirty Bliss Grenache Shiraz
Score **92**

BAROSSA VALLEY 🌿
Price $20.00 ✓
Quality ★★★★
Alc./Vol. 14.5%
Drink 2014
Closure Screwcap

Despite any connotations the name may conjure up, this shows restraint and cool fruit characters, some savoury/earthy notes and sweet spice. An impressive flowing palate that drives liquorice flavour amid a bright core of red and purple berry flavour, sitting up on the palate with plum fruits to close.

2005 DogRidge Cadenzia
Score **90**

McLAREN VALE	
Price	$24.00
Quality	★★★★
Alc./Vol.	14%
Drink	Now
Closure	Screwcap

This earthy traditionally styled grenache is a part of the regional grenache promotion known as the Cadenzia. It's packing plenty of dark fruits and tarry oak complexity, the palate's rich and strapping with sturdy tannins and long berry/plum flavour.

2007 Domain Barossa Toddler GSM
Score **91**

BAROSSA VALLEY	
Price	$22.00 ✓
Quality	★★★★
Alc./Vol.	15%
Drink	Now
Closure	Screwcap

Made in a fruit-forward, early-bottled style, they've captured vivacious fresh fruits, delivering dark cherry and plums, gentle earthy spiced complexity too. The palate's deep and juicy and has some meaty berry and musk flavour, tannins are anchored neatly throughout; finishes up tidy.

2006 Eden Road Two Trees Grenache Shiraz
Score **93**

EDEN VALLEY	
Price	$75.00
Quality	★★★★↓
Alc./Vol.	15.5%
Drink	2012
Closure	Screwcap

A new label out of Eden Valley weighing in at the premium end of the field. Old-vine intensity and regional depth, plenty of spiced red fruits. Captivating palate texture, silken red fruit and blackberry flavours amid fine sweet tannins. Impressive balance and style.

2006 Gilligan Shiraz Grenache Mourvèdre
Score **92**

McLAREN VALE	
Price	$23.00 ✓
Quality	★★★★
Alc./Vol.	16.5%
Drink	2012
Closure	Diam

Well made and upbeat, there's roughly three-quarters shiraz in this blend; grenache adds some lifted red fruit aromas across the top, plenty of liquorice and plum. The palate's thick and swarthy, really deeply concentrated plum and chocolate flavour, dense tannins, dark chocolate and toasty oak linger on the palate.

2006 Glaetzer Wallace
Score **90**

BAROSSA VALLEY	
Price	$20.00 ✓
Quality	★★★★
Alc./Vol.	14.5%
Drink	2012
Closure	Screwcap

A 70/30 shiraz-grenache blend, sourced from the Ebenezer district. Dark peppered berry fruit aromas, some smoky oak and earthy/meaty complexity. Medium-weight palate with a whack of acid jutting out, tannins wrestle the tongue to the ground, finishing with solid dryness.

2005 Hanging Rock Shiraz Grenache Mourvèdre Pinot Noir   *Score* 89

SOUTH EASTERN AUSTRALIA	John Ellis steps out of his Macedon Ranges identity and
Price $14.00 ✓	crafts a handy four-way blend that gives terrific value and
Quality ★★★ ┤	drinkability. Plenty of rich, integrated sweet spices, red
Alc./Vol. 14%	fruits and dark berry flavours offer balance and juicy fruit
Drink 2012	appeal. Made for the backyard BBQ.
Closure Screwcap	

2006 Henschke Johann's Garden   *Score* 93

BAROSSA VALLEY	Grenache, mourvèdre and shiraz looking showy and ripe,
Price $38.00	there's plenty of creamy toasty oak, spice and fragrant
Quality ★★★★ ┤	red perfume. The palate has bright red fruit flavour and
Alc./Vol. 15.5%	an upbeat 2006-vintage character, plenty of ripeness and
Drink 2013	poise, some bright springy tannin, shapely and supple.
Closure Screwcap	

2006 Hentley Farm The Stray Mongrel   *Score* 90

BAROSSA VALLEY	An innovative blend of grenache, shiraz and zinfandel,
Price $28.00	sporting a modern swanky nose of ripe berry fruits, horse
Quality ★★★★	stalls and spicy sweet oak; there's a touch of the Sunday
Alc./Vol. 15%	races here. The fine palate has some compact, resolved
Drink Now	tannins running down the line, smoky/savoury plum fruits
Closure Screwcap	and even tannins.

2006 Hewitson Miss Harry Grenache Shiraz Mourvèdre   *Score* 91

BAROSSA VALLEY	This affordable modern take on the Barossa blend has
Price $22.00 ✓	plenty of fruit-derived complexity, dark spices and dark
Quality ★★★★	fruits; there's some toasty oak here too that also suits. The
Alc./Vol. 14.5%	palate's low-strung and even, dark berry flavours, tannins
Drink 2012	stitched seamlessly together, finishing with fleshy plum-skin
Closure Screwcap	bite.

2006 Hewitson Old Garden Mourvèdre   *Score* 96

BAROSSA VALLEY	With more than 150 years of vine age behind it, this wine
Price $50.00 ✓	is striking for its balance and consistency. Typical meaty
Quality ★★★★★	mourvèdre, smells of ripe plums, black minerals and citrus
Alc./Vol. 14.5%	peel. The palate delivers essence-like flavour, even and rich,
Drink 2018	it's very complete. Soulful silky tannins and some toasty
Closure Screwcap	oak to close; retrospective tastings reveal this is best with
	some bottle-age.

2005 Jamabro Bush Vine Grenache

Score **91**

BAROSSA VALLEY
Price $25.00 ✓
Quality ★★★★
Alc./Vol. 15.9%
Drink 2012
Closure Screwcap

A complex grenache from the western side of the Barossa Valley: fine sandy soil minerals, leathery notes, dusty dried plums and spicy dark berry fruits, light smoky oak behind. The palate has impressive density and deep ripeness, some alcohol texture fills it out through chocolate-like tannins; a ripe and thick, plum and coconut finish. Big, hearty soulful grenache.

2006 John Duval Wines Plexus

Score **93**

BAROSSA VALLEY
Price $39.00
Quality ★★★★⁺
Alc./Vol. 14.5%
Drink 2012
Closure Screwcap

Duval leads with shiraz ahead of grenache and mourvèdre, it's a bright, forthright wine in '06, showing regional blackberry shiraz fruits and earthy/savoury mourvèdre; perfectly ripe. Grenache weighs in with more red fruits in the mouth, supple and structured, impeccably balanced and seamlessly woven together.

2006 John Hongell Old Vine Grenache Shiraz

Score **93**

BAROSSA VALLEY
Price $19.00 ✓
Quality ★★★★⁺
Alc./Vol. 15%
Drink Now
Closure Screwcap

Composed of two-thirds grenache planted in the 1940s, the balance is younger shiraz. An old-school style with plenty of earthy ripe red fruits and blackberry, the oak is wedged in firm. Dense flavours follow in the red and dark berry spectrum, impressive depth and fine-sheeted tannin, some oak toast to sweeten the finish. A solid, hearty regional statement.

2006 Kaesler Avignon

Score **92**

BAROSSA VALLEY
Price $30.00
Quality ★★★★
Alc./Vol. 16%
Drink 2012
Closure Cork

This grenache, shiraz, mourvèdre blend sits up bright in the glass: lifted grenache-driven aromas with direct sweet spice, ripe berries and plums. The palate delivers rich ripe plum fruits, a backdrop of tarry regional characters and a smooth tannin slide through the finish.

2006 Kaesler Stonehorse Grenache Shiraz Mourvèdre

Score **92**

BAROSSA VALLEY
Price $18.00 ✓
Quality ★★★★
Alc./Vol. 15.5%
Drink 2012
Closure Screwcap

Astonishing wine for the money, displaying dense dark plum fruits, some blackberry and deeper brooding fruit aromas, a little earth and tar. Impresses with depth and weight on the palate, a layer of upbeat flavour, a little musk and fine supple tannins.

2007 Kalleske Clarry's Red
Score **91**

BAROSSA VALLEY
Price $18.00 ✓
Quality ★★★★
Alc./Vol. 14.5%
Drink Now
Closure Screwcap

The vineyard blend of grenache and shiraz from the Kalleske farm out in Greenock shows plenty of oak for its humble station, earthy/brambly grenache berry fruits, some grilled nuts and chocolate. The palate's creamy and ripe, decent structure and plum/berry flavour; bold yet charming.

2006 Kalleske Old Vine Grenache
Score **96**

BAROSSA VALLEY
Price $45.00 ✓
Quality ★★★★★
Alc./Vol. 15.5%
Drink 2015
Closure Cork

A single-vineyard plot planted in 1935 on the Kalleske estate out in Greenock, this has true old-vine soul. Dark ripe berries and some brambly fragrance, savoury oak and earthy notes, very unevolved at this stage. Old vines bring concentration with elegance and balance, and that's what the palate is all about; smooth, supple tannins and a deep scoop through the finish. Australian grenache at the top level and phenomenal value for money on a world stage.

2006 La Curio The Nubile Grenache Shiraz
Score **90**

McLAREN VALE
Price $22.00 ✓
Quality ★★★★
Alc./Vol. 15%
Drink 2012
Closure Cork

Not so much nubile, more an earthy, character-filled creature, leather and open-grained resinous oak sits layered across ripe dark berry fruits and cake dough. The palate has a wedge of oak driving down the middle, plenty of ripe tawny fruit to swerve through the finish, chewy and raw.

2005 Loose End GSM
Score **88**

BAROSSA VALLEY
Price $20.00
Quality ★★★ ⌐
Alc./Vol. 14.5%
Drink Now
Closure Screwcap

Careful here, as the M stands for *merlot*, not mataro. Plenty of liquorice spice, some chocolate and ripe dark plum fruits. The palate is light and bright, steps on simple tannins and delivers chirpy berry and plum flavours, underpinned by toasty oak that creeps out the finish.

2006 Marius Symposium Shiraz Mourvèdre
Score **93**

McLAREN VALE
Price $30.00
Quality ★★★★ ⌐
Alc./Vol. 14.7%
Drink 2013
Closure Screwcap

Wow, this is a dark modern wine with plenty of brooding mourvèdre fruits, shiraz's dark spiced plums and savoury/earthy regional notes below. Plenty of spice and richness, all balanced out neatly, plush even tannins, rich black fruit flavours ride on supple savoury tannins, finishing intense, long and fine.

2006 Massena The Moonlight Run — Score 92

BAROSSA VALLEY	
Price	$25.00 ✓
Quality	★★★★
Alc./Vol.	14.5%
Drink	2010
Closure	Cork

An impressive follow-up to the '05, this GSM gets a slice of cinsault too. Very fragrant with purple florals and spicy mataro notes poking through mixed berry fruits. Attractive savoury and earthy, the middle palate is super compact, showing skilled blending; it rolls through all charming, balanced and slick, with a chirpy acid finish.

2007 Maverick Greenock Rise GSM — Score 93

BAROSSA VALLEY	
Price	$30.00 ✓
Quality	★★★★ ↓
Alc./Vol.	15%
Drink	2013
Closure	Cork

Grenache takes the lion's share, a mix of late-1800s bush vines and some 1950s plantings, around 30% shiraz and a hatful of mourvèdre, all from out Greenock way. Bright red fruits and some gently meaty/earthy notes in behind, has the Greenock resolve, sweetly spiced too. Fine and svelte on the palate, red fruits and plenty of sweet spice, gently creamy oak. Very compact, very good.

2006 McHenry Hohnen 3 Amigos Shiraz Grenache Mourvèdre — Score 91

MARGARET RIVER	
Price	$22.00 ✓
Quality	★★★★
Alc./Vol.	14%
Drink	Now
Closure	Screwcap

A distinctly peppery expression; lead by cool spicy Margaret River shiraz, some sweet berries in behind and really attractive complexity. Grenache lifts the palate and mourvèdre keeps it anchored, letting the cool spicy/berry shiraz work away through the middle. Nice blend, well made.

2006 McPherson Basilisk Shiraz Mourvèdre — Score 90

CENTRAL VICTORIA	
Price	$18.00 ✓
Quality	★★★★
Alc./Vol.	14%
Drink	2013
Closure	Screwcap

Sourced from a range of Central Victorian vineyards, this cool spicy shiraz has been gently dosed with a splash of savoury mourvèdre. Bright, fragrant berry aromas, some peppery Rhône-ish characters, chocolate and earthy complexity. The palate is well strung with supple tannin and fine spiced plum flavours – all integrated and balanced.

2005 Mitchelton Crescent Mourvèdre Shiraz Grenache — Score 90

CENTRAL VICTORIA	
Price	$26.00
Quality	★★★★
Alc./Vol.	14.5%
Drink	2012
Closure	Screwcap

Original vineyard plantings at Mitchelton from 1969, this takes its name from the bend in this riverside Goulburn Valley vineyard. Some earthy/savoury notes, the fruit is ripe yet has its measure, spicy plums and some rich berry aromas. The palate has a savoury spice of gravelly tannin, building berry fruit through the sides, firm but balanced finish; decent oak impact too.

2005 Parri Estate Pangkarra Grenache   Score 90

McLAREN VALE
Price $24.00
Quality   ★★★★
Alc./Vol.   15%
Drink   Now
Closure   Cork

This straight grenache shows some extra depth – old vines perhaps – smoky, sweet earth and ripe dark fruits; well made with a dark spice overlay. The palate is easygoing and supple, mellow tannins carry dark fruit flavour. Light on oak, it trades on fruit richness and finishes with ripe plum flavour.

2007 Paxton AAA Shiraz Grenache   Score 92

McLAREN VALE
Price $23.00 ✓
Quality   ★★★★
Alc./Vol.   14%
Drink   2010
Closure   Screwcap

It may bear a borrowed triple-A rating but it's absolutely worthy. Attractive peppery fragrance, plenty of spice and rich dark berry fruits, with oak riding across on a smoky wave, some faint tar too. A dense and supple palate, well made and modern with plum and berry flavour, fine ferrous savoury tannins, finishing with resolve and balance.

2006 Penfolds Bin 138 Shiraz Grenache Mourvèdre   Score 93

BAROSSA VALLEY
Price $30.00
Quality   ★★★★ ꜰ
Alc./Vol.   14.5%
Drink   2014
Closure   Screwcap

Generally one of the standout wines in the Bin Series release, '06 wins with its ripe attractive sweet fruits, sweet toasty oak and fragrant lift. Charming stuff. The palate is supple yet it has plenty of raw vinous appeal, berry fruits and approachable fine tannins. Balance ensures it will mature well.

2006 Pertaringa Two Gentlemens Grenache   Score 92

McLAREN VALE
Price $20.00 ✓
Quality   ★★★★
Alc./Vol.   15%
Drink   Now
Closure   Screwcap

Attractive ripe red fruits, some citrus peel as well, the oak adds savoury backing, there are mountain herbs too. Superb clarity – a straight varietal statement. Superb fleshy entry, it's been creamed out through the middle with some swanky oak; a fleshy, balanced and fine tannin slide to the finish. Brilliant.

2005 Rosemount Show Reserve GSM   Score 91

McLAREN VALE
Price $20.00 ✓
Quality   ★★★★
Alc./Vol.   14.5%
Drink   2013
Closure   Screwcap

Plenty of toasty oak resources have been tossed at this ripe '05 blend, rich dark plum fruits, berries and regional liquorice accents. The palate is taut and balanced; it has real density and richness, the oak just slides out the back. Dense and long.

2006 Ross Estate Old Vine Grenache

Score **90**

BAROSSA VALLEY
Price $19.00 ✓
Quality ★★★★
Alc./Vol. 14.5%
Drink 2012
Closure Screwcap

From the original estate plantings, they were planted in 1912! This is exceptional value. Decent concentration of red fruits and dark berries, some honeyed ripe smells and dusty oak. Plenty of approachable fruit flavour, sturdy tannins and deft balance.

2005 Rudderless Grenache

Score **94**

McLAREN VALE
Price $40.00
Quality ★★★★⁺
Alc./Vol. 15.2%
Drink 2012
Closure Cork

This has some aromatic depth for grenache, ripe plums and dark berry fruits, some sweet cinnamon spice and sandy/earthy nuances, a little regional liquorice, pure and intense. The palate packs a core of rich, deep sweet fruit flavour, intense dark ripe berries, savoury tannins quench the finish. Terrific presence.

2005 Rudderless Grenache Shiraz Mataro

Score **94**

McLAREN VALE
Price $40.00
Quality ★★★★⁺
Alc./Vol. 15%
Drink 2014
Closure Cork

This is Doug Govan's masterpiece, the cream of the hillside vineyard perched behind his Victory Hotel on Sellick's Hill. It has superb complexity and ripe regional fruits – plums, spiced blackberry and rich dark cherries, some chocolate, black minerals and sweet liquorice. The palate's wound in tight and dense, plenty of oak support, earthy/berry fruits and thick savoury tannins.

2005 Rudderless Mataro

Score **93**

McLAREN VALE
Price $40.00
Quality ★★★★⁺
Alc./Vol. 16%
Drink 2013
Closure Cork

This straight mataro is full of darkly brooding complexity, peppered plums and spices, very ripe, very earthy and nicely met by savoury oak. Super-ripe palate with powerful deep plum and liquorice mataro flavour, full tannin sweep, soft and sweet, some tawny/leathery complexity through the finish. Hedonistic.

2006 S.C. Pannell Grenache

Score **93**

McLAREN VALE
Price $50.00
Quality ★★★★⁺
Alc./Vol. 14.5%
Drink 2011
Closure Screwcap

The nose shows terrific density and richness, plenty of ripe plum fruits – appealing, fresh and direct. Also much to admire about the even-handed palate, great weight and length, juicy red fruits, some sweet spices in the background; this is well made and balanced. Less obvious but more profound.

2006 S.C. Pannell Pronto
Score **90**

McLAREN VALE	
Price	$20.00 ✓
Quality	★★★★
Alc./Vol.	14%
Drink	Now
Closure	Screwcap

Based on a parcel of grenache from a 65-year-old vineyard, this is unbeatable value – delicious quaffing red. It's a romp through ripe berry and spice country, no oak to speak of, it equates to a regional everyday red that showcases superb balance.

2006 S.C. Pannell Shiraz Grenache
Score **96**

McLAREN VALE	
Price	$50.00
Quality	★★★★★
Alc./Vol.	14.5%
Drink	2016
Closure	Screwcap

Dark spices and rich dark fruit aromas speak of authentic regional McLaren Vale intensity, cloaked in charm and soft appeal. Supple palate texture, smooth weight and drive, spiced plum and some dark oak toast here too. The texture is where it really takes off, gripping intense flavour, completely balanced structure; a long even and authentic red.

2006 Samuel's Gorge Grenache
Score **92**

McLAREN VALE	
Price	$45.00
Quality	★★★★
Alc./Vol.	14.5%
Drink	2012
Closure	Cork

These Samuel's Gorge wines have improved leaps and bounds over the last two vintages; this grenache is a sweet-smelling, fragrant red fruit style, big on charm. The palate's smooth and concentrated – it sits on the riper side of the balance beam, finishing with toasty oak after-burn.

2007 Schild Estate GMS
Score **90**

BAROSSA VALLEY	
Price	$16.00 ✓
Quality	★★★★
Alc./Vol.	15%
Drink	Now
Closure	Screwcap

Roughly 50% grenache and the rest shared evenly between mataro and shiraz, the nose is superb: bright red berries, cherry and plum fruits, gently spicy and beautifully ripe. Texture is right on the money, soft and swirling, sweet red berry flavours, some darker fruits too, fine supple tannins dealt evenly throughout.

2006 Spinifex Esprit
Score **96**

BAROSSA VALLEY	
Price	$28.00 ✓
Quality	★★★★★
Alc./Vol.	14.5%
Drink	2014
Closure	Diam

Almost equal parts mataro, grenache and shiraz with a hatful of cinsault, this is a benchmark mod-Barossa blend. Ripe blackberry and deep blueberry fruit aromas, perfume and spice, plums and pepper, savoury/tarry notes make a hearty impression. Strapping and bold on the palate, driven by mataro's savoury liquorice and pepper, meaty and concentrated with long bold tannins. Definitive.

PENGUIN WINE OF THE YEAR

PENGUIN BEST GSM BLEND

2006 Spinifex Indigene

Score 93

BAROSSA VALLEY
Price $44.00
Quality ★★★★ ⁺
Alc./Vol. 14.8%
Drink 2014
Closure Diam

Shiraz and mataro team up here, a wine that's still building: plenty of dark fruit aromas and tarry blackberry, chocolate and spice; smells very ripe and very rich. The tannins are strapping, swathed in plum pudding flavours, really thickening up through the finish. It needs time.

2007 Spinifex Papillon

Score 92

BAROSSA VALLEY
Price $22.50 ✓
Quality ★★★★
Alc./Vol. 13.9%
Drink 2010
Closure Screwcap

Papillon leads with bright grenache fruits, berries and red floral lift; a simple attractive wine that's made for drinking young. Oak sits in the background, allowing plenty of room for briary fruit flavour, this grenache (46%), cinsault (28%), mataro (26%) blend trades on vivacious fruit, soft tannins and charming balance.

2007 St Hallett Gamekeeper's Reserve

Score 89

BAROSSA VALLEY
Price $15.00 ✓
Quality ★★★ ⁺
Alc./Vol. 14.5%
Drink Now
Closure Screwcap

An approachable, well-priced blend of Barossa shiraz and grenache; there's plenty of bright, light red and dark berry fruits and just a tickle of meaty spice, some pepper too. The palate's upbeat and juicy, light red-fruit flavours and easy tannins, musky finish.

2007 St Hallett GST

Score 93

BAROSSA VALLEY
Price $30.00 ✓
Quality ★★★★ ⁺
Alc./Vol. 14.5%
Drink 2011
Closure Screwcap

This unique grenache-shiraz-touriga blend shows impressive complexity and bright fruit aromas. Really attractive spicy fragrance and bright lift, ripe dark cherries and plum fruits; lovely stuff. The palate wields impressive power and is already knitted together; medium-weighted tannins with the oak buried deep below concentrated ripe plum and red fruit flavours. Brilliant.

2006 St John's Road A Motley Bunch

Score 92

BAROSSA VALLEY
Price $24.00 ✓
Quality ★★★★
Alc./Vol. 15%
Drink 2010
Closure Screwcap

Constructed from grenache planted in 1969 and a splash of estate-grown Greenock shiraz and mataro, this is a measured, soulful rendition of the GSM blend with a good balance of fleshy fruit and savoury tannin. From red fruit fragrance to soulful earthy flavours, this is a convincing wine. Best after 2010.

2006 Stanley Lambert Grenache Shiraz Mourvèdre   *Score* 90

BAROSSA VALLEY
Price $20.00
Quality   ★★★★
Alc./Vol. 13.5%
Drink   2010
Closure   Diam

The lighter colour in the glass points to grenache as the leading hand, quite lifted ripe red fruit aromas, some subtle spice too. Wild herbs join the fruit on the palate, simple red fruits, some low-end oak and supple, open tannin structure.

2006 Te-aro Estate GSM   *Score* 92

BAROSSA VALLEY
Price $20.00 ✓
Quality   ★★★★
Alc./Vol. 15.1%
Drink   Now
Closure   Screwcap

High-toned red fruits and fragrant red florals, it is equal parts grenache and shiraz with a smaller dose of mourvèdre. A fruit-forward style pitching brightness against earthy/savoury complexity. The palate packs a bigger punch than the nose suggests, darker fruits and fine juicy tannins run long through the finish.

2005 Torbreck The Pict Mataro   *Score* 95

BAROSSA VALLEY
Price $200.00
Quality   ★★★★ ↓
Alc./Vol. 14%
Drink   Now
Closure   Cork

The Pict makes a statement for mataro, masterfully conceived by the Torbreck crew. Fragrant engaging peppery aromas, ripe berries and dark chocolate on the nose. Well-matched oak brings attractive sweetness to this savoury variety; tannins are crafted with a steady hand, finishing with a flurry of deeply rooted flavour.

2006 Turkey Flat Butchers Block Shiraz Grenache Mourvèdre   *Score* 93

BAROSSA VALLEY
Price $30.00
Quality   ★★★★ ↓
Alc./Vol. 14.5%
Drink   2015
Closure   Screwcap

Turkey Flat's take on the Barossa red blend is a pleasing trade-off between sweet and savoury. Young and complex, it has plenty of ripe toasty oak, plenty of peppery plums, berries and spice. The palate wields savoury, grippy tannins and strong brooding flavour, finishing with chewy dark fruits.

2006 Turkey Flat Grenache   *Score* 91

BAROSSA VALLEY
Price $28.00
Quality   ★★★★
Alc./Vol. 15%
Drink   2013
Closure   Screwcap

The straight grenache from Turkey Flat has a more rustic style, deep dark berry fruits, nutty oak complexity, a little spice and earth. The palate is laid back, soft and easy, a wine with unpretentious drinkable appeal, just wagering some savoury tannin through the finish.

2006 Turkey Flat Mourvèdre

Score **94**

BAROSSA VALLEY 🖋
Price $35.00 ✓
Quality ★★★★ ↓
Alc./Vol. 14.5%
Drink 2012
Closure Cork

On the back of a stunning '05, this has the same trademark earthy/savoury notes with pepper-dusted dark fruits. The palate is a powerhouse, really thick and concentrated; toasty oak sweetens the fruit right the way through; tannins are sturdy, very ripe and long; dark plum finish. The only worry you'll have is the cork.

2007 Two Hands Brave Faces

Score **89**

BAROSSA VALLEY
Price $27.00
Quality ★★★ ↓
Alc./Vol. 15%
Drink Now
Closure Screwcap

A blend of roughly two-thirds shiraz and the balance shared equally between grenache and mataro, showing ripe regional blackberry shiraz aromas and some earthy complexity below. Juicy plum/berry flavours, there's a light toasty oak twist, moderate fruit concentration, plum-skin finish.

2005 Winter Creek Second Eleven Blend

Score **91**

BAROSSA VALLEY
Price $19.00 ✓
Quality ★★★★
Alc./Vol. 14%
Drink Now
Closure Screwcap

A reversal of the old Barossa formula: 75% shiraz and 25% grenache this time. Superb young plum fruits and dark berries, dark cherry too, they've captured this at full stride. Really smooth palate, fine tannins fan out across ripe dark berry and cherry fruit flavour. A balanced, superbly crafted wine.

2005 Winter Creek The Old Barossa Blend

Score **88**

BAROSSA VALLEY
Price $25.00
Quality ★★★ ↓
Alc./Vol. 14%
Drink Now
Closure Screwcap

This is a 75% grenache and 25% shiraz blend from Williamstown at the southern end of the region. Shows nice bright mixed berry fruits, gentle spice and plenty of ripeness, straightforward and appealing. Same story on the palate, light red fruits; undemanding and balanced.

Shiraz

Shiraz is as Australian as Holden motorcars, Hills hoists and barbecues. Although grown the world over, we have claimed it as our own and make wines that have captured the hearts and minds of drinkers everywhere. There is an enormous range of expressions, driven mostly by regional difference, and so suited is shiraz to Australia that almost every variation is a winner. It can be inexpensive and enjoyable, trumping the value-for-money stakes like no other red wine in Australia, or it can perform right at the upper limit of premium Australian red wine, fetching the highest prices – the scope is staggering. A recent surge in high-quality examples from our cooler regions is making the variety more interesting than ever before. FOOD: Bigger shiraz wines demand big slabs of red meat – grilled, served with red wine sauces, marinated and piled on with flavour! At the other end of the spectrum, the cool-climate styles will coax spices and game meats into new territory. Avoid sweet flavours.

2006 **Acrobat Shiraz** *Score* **88**

MUDGEE	This is the junior wine released by Prince Hill (see review for
Price $10.00 ✓	their '06 shiraz). Shows some simple bright fruit aromas,
Quality ★★★ ┤	confected jubes and young-vine lightness. Red fruits, sweet
Alc./Vol. 14%	raspberry flavours and simple light tannins, musky and
Drink Now	sweet finish. An easy-drinking ten-buck bottle.
Closure Screwcap	

2007 **The Aurora Vineyard Bendigo Syrah** *Score* **92**

CENTRAL OTAGO, NZ	I remember asking a few years back why shiraz wasn't
Price $28.00	carpeted across Central Otago's Bendigo Hills. Well, here's
Quality ★★★★	one of the first and it's a winner. Deep colour and attractive
Alc./Vol. 14%	meaty berry fruit aromas, sweet spiced oak and peppery
Drink 2012	appeal, some briary fragrance – young and exotic. The
Closure Screwcap	palate is finely pitched, superb tannins float dark berry
	flavour that lines up through the savoury mineral finish.

2005 Australian Old Vine Collection Barossa Shiraz
Score **95**

BAROSSA VALLEY

Price	$110.00 ✓
Quality	★★★★ ৴
Alc./Vol.	14.5%
Drink	2014
Closure	Cork

You've got to hand it to Rob Gibson for this old-vine concept. This Barossa wine comes from 100-plus-year-old plantings and really resonates with depth and complexity. Superb fruit integrity, ripe plums and dark berries and a decent dusting of fine spices. The palate's all elegance and finely etched tannins, flavours of liquorice and sweet earth; smoothly balanced and carries deceptive longevity below deck.

2005 Barossa Old Vine Company Shiraz
Score **93**

BAROSSA VALLEY

Price	$100.00
Quality	★★★★ ৴
Alc./Vol.	15.5%
Drink	2012
Closure	Cork

Something of a personal crusade for Carl Lindner, this fruit is sourced from centenarian vines in the heart of the Barossa Valley. It is super rich and ripe, packing concentrated peppery blackberry fruit aromas and some sweeter oak nuances. The palate is all bright berry fruit, tannins draw deep through the middle and some sweeter oak lingers through the finish. Formidable yet elegant.

2006 Barossa Vines By Grant Burge Shiraz
Score **90**

BAROSSA VALLEY

Price	$16.00
Quality	★★★★
Alc./Vol.	14.5%
Drink	Now
Closure	Screwcap

This knockabout Barossa shiraz has attractive fragrance and lifted bright young berry fruits, red and dark berries, some musky notes; modern and assertive. Super-crisp, crunchy palate, really bright and juicy young shiraz, vivacious, gentle berry fruits and chocolate flavours through the finish.

2006 Battle of Bosworth Shiraz Viognier
Score **93**

McLAREN VALE 🍃

Price	$24.00 ✓
Quality	★★★★ ৴
Alc./Vol.	14.5%
Drink	2011
Closure	Screwcap

Complex spiced blackberry fruits and background savoury oak, there's some earthy rawness that makes for a compelling wine; neat and powerful. Lovely supple texture in the mouth, plum fruits and layers of toasty oak complexity, fine soft tannins roll around on smooth wheels; curvaceous yet elegant, and well balanced.

2006 Binbilla Good Friday Shiraz
Score **89**

HILLTOPS

Price	$26.00
Quality	★★★ ৴
Alc./Vol.	14.5%
Drink	Now
Closure	Screwcap

A small operation making a bright style, trademark regional deep red and dark fruits, it also shows some brazen nutty oak across the nose. The palate pitches direct confected fruit flavours, red fruits and black jube berry flavour, some bright acid lift, finishing balanced and even. A fresh early-drinking style.

2006 Breheny Vineyards Brown Magpie Shiraz — Score 90

GEELONG
Price $27.00
Quality ★★★★
Alc./Vol. 14%
Drink 2011
Closure Screwcap

This estate gem from Geelong shows complex, peppery cool-climate style, finely ground spices sit across ripe mixed berries and meaty/savoury notes. The palate's a medium-weight affair, elegant and restrained, plum and spiced berry flavours, finishing meaty and tidy.

2006 Bremerton Selkirk Shiraz — Score 88

LANGHORNE CREEK
Price $22.00 ✓
Quality ★★★┤
Alc./Vol. 14.5%
Drink Now
Closure Screwcap

An approachable earthy, regional Langhorne Creek style; all estate grown, it shows typical ripeness and earthy depth, hearty ripe berry and plum fruits. Solid but supple palate with sweet berry jam and plum flavours, good density and drive.

2006 Bress Heathcote Shiraz — Score 93

HEATHCOTE 🍾
Price $40.00
Quality ★★★★┤
Alc./Vol. 13.5%
Drink 2014
Closure Screwcap

Adam Marks' gold chook Heathcote shiraz delivers plenty of fragrance, red fruits and berries, gently complex spices and some earthy notes too. The palate shows iron-like soil characters, nicely ripe, plenty of savoury berry and plum flavours, tannins lend ample support right through the plum-skin finish.

2006 Brokenwood Graveyard Vineyard Shiraz — Score 96

HUNTER VALLEY
Price $125.00
Quality ★★★★★
Alc./Vol. 13.5%
Drink 2016
Closure Screwcap

Graveyard is a shiraz that steps between generations; the '06 is a more modern wine. Cedary oak binds the fruit tight in its youth, faint dried plums and berries; very guarded at this stage, showing absolute Hunter regional earth and fresh leather. The palate's superbly crafted in a neatly layered stack of fine tannins and ripe shiraz fruit. It builds high and steady through the mouth and finishes with raw juicy power, fading slowly. Very young and very good.

2006 Brokenwood Hunter Valley Shiraz — Score 93

HUNTER VALLEY
Price $40.00
Quality ★★★★┤
Alc./Vol. 14%
Drink 2013
Closure Screwcap

Very much in the traditional Hunter style: sweet leather and brown dusty/earthy aromas, dried plums and redcurrant fruit, sweet berries and leather; quite ripe. The palate is supple and even, has terrific density, will live for a long time; lovely fine, dense drying tannin and an ashen finish.

2006 Brokenwood Verona Vineyard Shiraz — Score 94

HUNTER VALLEY	
Price	$45.00
Quality	★★★★⌐
Alc./Vol.	13.5%
Drink	2015
Closure	Screwcap

This shows the class of Brokenwood's signature style. Red–purple in the glass, it looks concentrated and rich, dried plums and some sweet dusty/earthy aromas, blackberry, chocolate and background earthy complexity. The palate's rich and juicy, terrific even-handed fruit and a long frame of fine savoury tannin from start to finish. Reserved power.

2004 Brown Brothers Patricia Shiraz — Score 93

VICTORIA	
Price	$45.00
Quality	★★★★⌐
Alc./Vol.	14.5%
Drink	2011
Closure	Cork

A lone Patricia was released in the 2008 round, this is a three-way assembly of Pyrenees, King Valley and Heathcote shiraz. Shows plenty of liquorice and ripe dark fruits, mocha and meaty barrel-ferment complexity. The palate follows with similar fruit flavours, savoury spices and dense but soft tannins, a hint of gum leaf to close.

2006 By Farr Shiraz — Score 94

GEELONG	
Price	$60.00
Quality	★★★★⌐
Alc./Vol.	14.5%
Drink	2012
Closure	Cork

A wine with several more dimensions of complexity than most. Attractive sweet spice, fragrant cool-climate lift, gentle whole-bunch characters, bright berry fruits, some dark chocolate and pepper. It all adds up to an alluring and enticing style, the oak draws fruit aroma upwards. Super dense, fine tannins and assertive acidity here, elegant and eminently drinkable. Deep spiced plum flavour; balanced, supple and delicious.

2006 Chandon Heathcote Shiraz — Score 91

HEATHCOTE 🍷	
Price	$31.00
Quality	★★★★
Alc./Vol.	14.5%
Drink	2011
Closure	Screwcap

Lovely fresh, bright blue fruits – ripe, regional and fragrant; some citrus peel and fine spices, this looks superbly youthful and complex. Terrific palate freshness and fruit ripeness, soft flowing tannins, simple blue fruits, finishing open and easy.

2007 Clonakilla Hilltops Shiraz — Score 93

HILLTOPS	
Price	$30.00 ✓
Quality	★★★★⌐
Alc./Vol.	15%
Drink	Now
Closure	Screwcap

This has become something of a staple in the Clonakilla range of reds. Decidedly different in shape to the estate and locally sourced wines, it delivers dark fruits, cassis and distinct anise spice. The link comes via texture; Kirk's trademark fine-dusted tannins are in full effect!

2007 Clonakilla O'Riada Shiraz
Score **94**

CANBERRA DISTRICT
Price $40.00 ✓
Quality ★★★★ ╕
Alc./Vol. 14%
Drink 2012
Closure Screwcap

Named after the cousin of Clonakilla founder, John Kirk, and Irish music legend, Sean O'Riada; this is a collection of several parcels from around the district. Shows lifted, playful whole-bunch aromatics, rose water, spice-dusted red fruits and plenty of pepper. The palate has youthful juicy appeal, some viognier richness, plenty of red berry flavour and fine open-knit tannins.

2007 Clonakilla Shiraz Viognier
Score **97**

MURRUMBATEMAN 🍃
Price $90.00
Quality ★★★★★
Alc./Vol. 14%
Drink 2017
Closure Screwcap

Tim Kirk's '07 flagship (made in tiny quantity due to severe frost, just 10% of average production) is a spicy array of fine fragrant red fruits, ginger, cinnamon, cloves and black minerals. A superbly crafted palate, it rolls through in layers of precise berry and plum flavour, tannins folded in sheets, with gently toasty oak below. Sourced from a lone amphitheatre block that was spared from the devastating freeze; it's finer, a more minerally and elegant slice of the estate, precise and deceptively powerful. Act fast, only 150 dozen made.
PENGUIN BEST SHIRAZ

2006 Clonakilla Syrah
Score **96**

MURRUMBATEMAN 🍃
Price $80.00
Quality ★★★★★
Alc./Vol. 14%
Drink 2015
Closure Screwcap

The first release of this viognier-free estate shiraz as a wine in its own right, and it makes a terrific partner for the shiraz viognier. Restrained aromatics, fine pepper, musk and earth complexity, savoury spice, orange zest and cedary oak. Superbly textured palate, tubular fine-grained tannin, sweet elegant plum fruits, dark minerals and chocolate, a waft of toast across the finish. Seamless!

2006 Collector MTR Shiraz
Score **92**

CANBERRA DISTRICT
Price $27.00 ✓
Quality ★★★★
Alc./Vol. 13.5%
Drink 2010
Closure Screwcap

This represents some terrific value and delivers polished style; Collector is certainly a project to keep an eye on. MTR is a cool-climate fragrant shiraz with ripe dark fruits, berries and spice – complex and engaging. The palate is elegant and suave; very measured. Tannins are lined up in fine sheets, drawing succulent bright fruit flavour long and even.

2006 Collector Reserve Shiraz
Score **94**

CANBERRA DISTRICT
Price $46.00
Quality   ★★★★ ⌐
Alc./Vol. 13.5%
Drink   2012
Closure   Screwcap

This Canberra District shiraz, sourced from Andrew McEwin's block near Murrumbateman, was the top-scoring Australian shiraz in a recent international comparative tasting. All the trimmings of pristine cool-climate origins, precise aromatics, red and dark fruit flavours, abundant spice and detailed tannin structure are present. Impressive presence and depth married with elegance and precision adds up to winning style.

2006 Coriole Shiraz
Score **92**

McLAREN VALE
Price $28.00 ✓
Quality   ★★★★
Alc./Vol. 14.5%
Drink   2010
Closure   Screwcap

A consistent performer in the McLaren Vale region, showing plenty of poise and not striving to be a hero – more a stalwart. Bristling with red and dark berry fruits, forthright and direct, it plays fine tannins to impeccable effect, superbly balanced. If only there were more like this.

2006 Coriole The Soloist Shiraz
Score **93**

McLAREN VALE
Price $38.00
Quality   ★★★★ ⌐
Alc./Vol. 14.5%
Drink   2012
Closure   Screwcap

This single-site offering from Coriole is a newie to the collection and a welcome addition indeed. It packs a good deal more flesh and swirling fruit than the standard edition, yet still retains the house hallmark of elegance and balance. Sensational sweet plum fruit, pure and compelling.

2006 CR Ebenezer Shiraz
Score **92**

BAROSSA VALLEY
Price $25.00 ✓
Quality   ★★★★
Alc./Vol. 15.8%
Drink   2009
Closure   Screwcap

Chris Ringland is building an expanding repertoire of mostly rich red wines – his area of special interest and talent. Here he's tapped into some terrific material in the Ebenezer district, making an impressive, ripe stallion-like shiraz that sports mouth-quenching dark berry and plum flavour, choc-coated tannins and a handy serve of freshly toasted oak. This looks, smells and tastes fantastic!

2005 Craggy Range Le Sol
Score 94

HAWKES BAY, NZ
Price $97.00
Quality ★★★★⌿
Alc./Vol. 14%
Drink   2012
Closure Screwcap

Super cool-climate nose with green peppercorns and lifted fragrant spices, peppermint and cardamom, sweet dark berries – very much in the modern Hawkes Bay style. Superb piercing and focused palate, crisp fresh acidity and fine fresh fruits roll through in a fine tannin cage, outstanding balance; just at the beginning of its journey. Now sealed under screwcap.

2006 d'Arenberg Dead Arm Shiraz
Score 94

McLAREN VALE
Price $60.00
Quality ★★★★⌿
Alc./Vol. 14.5%
Drink   2015
Closure Screwcap

This Dead Arm is rippling with intense fruit and still very much on the make. Ripe plums and dark berries, earth and liquorice, the palate twists like a tornado of richly structured fruit flavour, tannins are first grade; it's eaten the oak but still beckons to be buried for a few years before its enjoyed.

2006 d'Arenberg Love Grass Shiraz
Score 92

McLAREN VALE
Price $30.00 ✓
Quality ★★★★
Alc./Vol. 14.5%
Drink   2011
Closure Screwcap

Not sure about the name here, but the wine's a fine example of middle-weighted, charming McLaren Vale juice. Super-ripe plum and liquorice aromas, almost into boot-polish concentration; the palate rolls on soft wheels, supple, balanced and bright.

2007 d'Arenberg The Laughing Magpie Shiraz Viognier
Score 92

McLAREN VALE
Price $30.00
Quality ★★★★
Alc./Vol. 14.5%
Drink   2010
Closure Screwcap

This takes a step to the left of the rest of the d'Arenberg shiraz wines: distinctly softer and intensely perfumed. It dishes up a rush of fragrant aromas, all very youthful, which will build spice in time. Supple and curvaceous, the palate is chock-full of charming fruit and swerving tannins. Great young drinking.

2006 De Bortoli Estate Grown Shiraz Viognier
Score 93

YARRA VALLEY 🖉
Price $35.00
Quality ★★★★⌿
Alc./Vol. 14%
Drink   2014
Closure Screwcap

A very stylish, sophisticated and complex cool spicy shiraz: lovely fine spices and bright, dark mineral characters, some savoury plums, pepper and bright fragrance; smells cool and nervy. Bright fruit palate with fine intense dried plum and dark chocolate flavours, elegantly shaped tannins and deep, soulful style.

2006 De Bortoli Reserve Release Syrah — *Score* 96

YARRA VALLEY
Price $55.00 ✓
Quality ★★★★★
Alc./Vol. 14%
Drink 2014
Closure Screwcap

One of the most impressive Yarra shiraz and one that doesn't rely on smoke and mirrors to seduce. Super-fragrant nose, this has plenty of dark fruit aromas and some smoky nuances, really sweetly spiced; it's a well-made, distinctive style. The palate has more of the same class, almost burgundian texture, super-fine velvet tannins, enduring and balanced. Terrific cool-climate style.

2005 Deisen Shiraz — *Score* 93

BAROSSA VALLEY
Price $56.00
Quality ★★★★ ┤
Alc./Vol. 15.2%
Drink 2012
Closure Cork

Deisen is a label that has quickly started to cash in their potential, making vast improvements in the last three releases. This is a richly fruited, ripe and earthy shiraz from their western Barossa outcrop. Dark berry and plum fruits are strapped across ample tannins, 30 months in oak has given it plenty of time to marry with the fruit, finishing rich and convincing.

2006 Deisen Sweetheart Shiraz — *Score* 91

BAROSSA VALLEY
Price $42.00
Quality ★★★★
Alc./Vol. 15%
Drink 2012
Closure Cork

Sweetheart shiraz is the earlier release in the Deisen stable, given just 18 months in oak. It's a spicier shiraz than the regular estate bottling, more fragrant too. Fresh berry fruits and some cafe oak nuances, tannins are lightly sprung, it finishes spicy, juicy and fresh.

2006 DeLisio Shiraz — *Score* 93

McLAREN VALE
Price $70.00
Quality ★★★★ ┤
Alc./Vol. 15.5%
Drink 2013
Closure Cork

Tony DeLisio has made some superb wines in the McLaren Vale region, placing faith in the richness and robust nature of the region's fruit. This is a wine with serious substance and drive, the tannins have a double-edged quality of softness and density, there's an abundance of plum flavour; great juice!

2006 Dutschke GHR Shiraz — *Score* 91

BAROSSA VALLEY
Price $25.00 ✓
Quality ★★★★
Alc./Vol. 14.8%
Drink Now
Closure Screwcap

GHR stands for God's Hill Road, the address that Wayne Dutschke shares with a handful of grape-growing neighbours who supply the grapes for this reasonably priced Barossa shiraz. Dark plums and spices, rich ripe berry fruits too, some chocolate and musky fragrance in the mouth, all bundled up for immediate appeal. This punches well above its weight.

2006 **Dutschke Oscar Semmler** *Score* **94**

BAROSSA VALLEY	
Price	$50.00
Quality	★★★★ ┤
Alc./Vol.	14.8%
Drink	2014
Closure	Screwcap

Named in tribute to one of the doyens of the local wine industry through the 1960s and '70s, this is effectively the label reserved for the prime parcel from each vintage. It's dripping with ripe mixed berry aromas, smells sweet and fresh. The palate's built around a core of concentrated flavour and fine sturdy tannin, red fruits burst out the finish; this has many fine years ahead.

2006 **Dutschke St Jakobi Shiraz** *Score* **93**

BAROSSA VALLEY	
Price	$35.00 ✓
Quality	★★★★ ┤
Alc./Vol.	14.8%
Drink	2013
Closure	Screwcap

Always a staggering wine, really solid and flavour-packed but never overdone or extended too far. Wayne Dutschke has his eye in here, delivering earthy dark plum and berry fruit on sweet ripe tannins, some smoky nuances and tarry stripes cut through the finish. Balanced enough to drink anytime, but best given a few years.

2006 **Eden Road V06 Shiraz** *Score* **94**

EDEN VALLEY	
Price	$200.00
Quality	★★★★ ┤
Alc./Vol.	15%
Drink	2014
Closure	Screwcap

There's no question of the quality of this wine and the winemaker behind it, Mr Martin Cooper; he has a fine professional pedigree, most notably with McWilliams. But it is a first release and is pitched well into glamour territory at an audacious $220. If you like to back wines in *before* they become iconic, check into these superbly ripe dark fruits, red berries and freshly sprinkled Eden Valley spices. Tannins sit up in bright lines, taking flavours for the long haul – this has all the makings of a bright new star. STOP PRESS: Cooper has moved on following the 2008 vintage.

2005 **Fairbank Syrah** *Score* **92**

CENTRAL VICTORIA 🔖	
Price	$25.00 ✓
Quality	★★★★
Alc./Vol.	13.5%
Drink	2012
Closure	Diam

Winemaker Gilles Lapalus has worked plenty of complexity into this savoury/meaty syrah, one of the new bastions of elegant, complex Central Victorian red wine. Superb character and texture, red fruits and warm spices combine well. Elegant tannins, even and tidy right the way through.

2006 **Farr Rising Shiraz** *Score* **93**

GEELONG	
Price	$40.00
Quality	★★★★┤
Alc./Vol.	14.5%
Drink	2011
Closure	Cork

This has some higher-toned aromatics, lifted fragrant shiraz characters, neatly polished and set nicely against sweet oak aromas. The palate builds multi-dimensional texture and sweet spices, insightful winemaking is at play; tannins sit fine and approachable amid bright dark berry flavours that run long through the finish.

2005 **First Drop Fat Of The Land Ebenezer Shiraz** *Score* **94**

BAROSSA VALLEY	
Price	$75.00 ✓
Quality	★★★★┤
Alc./Vol.	15%
Drink	2015
Closure	Cork

One of a pair of single-vineyard shiraz that make their debut in the 2005 vintage (the other is from a Seppeltsfield vineyard); charming stuff, impossible to resist. Ripe blood plum and dark berry aromas, gentle earthy edges, it arches across the palate with bright fruit impact, really fresh red and dark berries; this looks supremely youthful and builds smoky tannins through the finish. The First Drop lads are mixing it up with the big boys here, showing flair and style.

2005 **First Drop Two Percent Barossa Shiraz** *Score* **93**

BAROSSA VALLEY	
Price	$35.00 ✓
Quality	★★★★┤
Alc./Vol.	14.5%
Drink	2010
Closure	Screwcap

Matt Gant and John Retsas (both ex-St Hallett) are in the pink with their First Drop project; they're making great wine and having a good time doing it. This flagship shiraz gets a 2% addition of albariño, used in much the same fashion as viognier. It's a rich result, plenty of black fruit, tarry and concentrated, yet delivered with a polished smooth-honed texture. So approachable it'll have you in raptures!

2006 **Five Shillings Shiraz** *Score* **92**

MUDGEE	
Price	$35.00
Quality	★★★★
Alc./Vol.	14.5%
Drink	Now
Closure	Screwcap

A selection of Prince Hill's finest – and well selected indeed. Greater ripeness and complexity here lifts fragrant fruit appeal, some meaty spices and attractive winemaking complexity. Sweet jube fruits, mixed berry flavours and bright balance, musky youthful tannins; very direct.

2006 **Fox Gordon Hannah's Swing Shiraz** *Score* **91**

BAROSSA VALLEY	
Price	$45.00
Quality	★★★★
Alc./Vol.	13.5%
Drink	2009
Closure	Screwcap

A lighter style, which makes a bright change to the deep, brooding Barossa shiraz fashion, it has lifted ripe dark cherry fruit and upbeat fresh plum-scented fragrance. A refreshing earlier-drinking style with impeccable, youthful structure and balance.

2006 **Gemtree Uncut Shiraz**
Score **91**

McLAREN VALE
Price $20.00 ✓
Quality ★★★★
Alc./Vol. 14.5%
Drink   Now
Closure Screwcap

An uncut and unhindered rich hearty shiraz from this diamond in the rough. There's some stiff competition for McLaren Vale shiraz around the 20-buck mark and this sails through to take line honours. Loaded up with ripe plum flavour and sweet earthy tannins, a little spice to add interest and there you have it – brilliant wine!

2006 **Giaconda Warner Vineyard Shiraz**
Score **96**

BEECHWORTH
Price $96.00
Quality ★★★★★
Alc./Vol. 13.5%
Drink   2018
Closure Cork

Stunning soil- and site-driven purity, graphite and dark minerals, some smoke, a little tar; this is a savoury and complex shiraz with intense dried dark plum – sanguine almost. Starts out supple and builds meaty complexity as plum flavours unfurl, minerals and spice, the tannins spiral through the finish. Striking and soulful.

2006 **Giant Steps Miller Vineyard Shiraz**
Score **94**

YARRA VALLEY
Price $32.00 ✓
Quality ★★★★ ⁌
Alc./Vol. 14%
Drink   2015
Closure Screwcap

Another wine to join the growing band of brooding, spicy Yarra shiraz, this has an earthy dark beetroot nose, ripe dark plum fruits, gentle spice and pipe tobacco; it opens with air. The palate starts out with some sweet cinnamon and eastern spices across bright red fruit flavour, supported with plenty of taut fine tannin, balanced, savoury and moody.

2005 **Gibson The Dirtman Shiraz**
Score **91**

BAROSSA
Price $27.00
Quality ★★★★
Alc./Vol. 15%
Drink   2011
Closure Screwcap

The Dirtman is a classic Barossa two-play of Valley floor and Eden fruit. Lovely depth and ripeness, tarry regional accents, plum and berries. The palate is fitted neatly together with fine tannins and ample berry fruit flavour, musky fragrant oak turns toasty through the finish.

2006 **Glaetzer Amon-Ra Shiraz**
Score **94**

BAROSSA VALLEY
Price $90.00
Quality ★★★★ ⁌
Alc./Vol. 14.5%
Drink   2014
Closure Cork

This king of the Glaetzer wine castle is an assertive, brash, concentrated Barossa shiraz; a real powerhouse of ripe juicy plum and blackberry fruit, backed by toasty oak sweetness and long sinewy rich tannins. There's plenty to work through, all presented with undeniable hedonistic appeal.

2006 Grant Burge Miamba Shiraz — Score 90

BAROSSA VALLEY
Price $24.00
Quality ★★★★
Alc./Vol. 14.5%
Drink Now
Closure Screwcap

Ripe blackberry fruits and some punchy chocolate oak aromas here, pitching into textbook Barossa shiraz style; well made and widely appealing. Some creamy oak spices, abundant berry flavour, dense chewy tannins, sweet oak and some savoury nuts through the finish.

2006 Greenstone Shiraz — Score 92

HEATHCOTE
Price $40.00
Quality ★★★★
Alc./Vol. 13.5%
Drink 2013
Closure Screwcap

From one of the newest and most cleverly established Heathcote vineyards, right on the golden mile of red Cambrian dirt. Shows integrated savoury complexity; fruit, oak and spice aromas swirl around together, some smoky toast, meaty notes and peppered plums. The palate has rich savoury tannin chew, long and fine, some dark fruits and mineral flavours, polished slate through the finish.

2007 Grove Estate The Cellar Block Shiraz Viognier — Score 94

HILLTOPS
Price $36.00 ✓
Quality ★★★★⁺
Alc./Vol. 14.5%
Drink 2016
Closure Screwcap

This fragrant shiraz viognier shows vision and insight in its making. Very complex fine spice and pepper aromas, some whole-bunch dark chocolate notes and dark cherry fruit. Savoury tannins back intense fruit presence, the palate's really focused and driven. Complex texture, dark minerals and meaty ferment characters; very young, dense and Cornas-like. Terrific.

2004 Hanging Rock Cambrian Rise Heathcote Shiraz — Score 92

HEATHCOTE
Price $27.00
Quality ★★★★
Alc./Vol. 14%
Drink 2013
Closure Diam

A regional blend of several vineyard parcels, showing savoury blue fruits and purple berries, the oak's a little dusty and there's sweet spice complexity below, gently meaty too. Tannins are commanding and savoury, some steely minerals wound tight – this will age neatly.

2004 Henschke Hill of Grace Shiraz

Score **96**

EDEN VALLEY
Price $550.00
Quality ★★★★★
Alc./Vol. 15%
Drink 2025
Closure Screwcap

This, fast becoming Australia's most famous and sought after wine, shows less artefact than most at this level. Intense cool-climate fruit displays terrific resolve, the oak is in check, mixed berries and cinnamon spice, finely detailed. Sweet fruit coats the palate in rich flavoursome layers, backed by chewy, dense old vine tannins that sit in compact formation – fine and elegant, yet uncompromising in their density and length. Smooth and integrated, long and supple.

2005 Henschke Mount Edelstone Shiraz

Score **96**

EDEN VALLEY
Price $90.00 ✓
Quality ★★★★★
Alc./Vol. 14.5%
Drink 2020
Closure Screwcap

This lights up in the glass with superb brightness, varietal and Eden Valley regional character; abundant ripe blackberry fruits and enticing spicy complexity, the oak wafts dusty across the fruit. Fully ripe shiraz in all its splendour, superb density, deep plum fruit flavour and impressive fruit weight. Tannins are layered up in soft, thick sheets; a luscious wine with a long, long future ahead.

2006 Hentley Farm Shiraz

Score **92**

BAROSSA VALLEY
Price $32.00 ✓
Quality ★★★★
Alc./Vol. 15%
Drink 2011
Closure Screwcap

Perched out Greenock way to the west of the Barossa floor, this is super dark with tarry regional plum aromas, really ripe, young and brooding. The palate has dense strapping style, rich blackberry fruit flavours, thick but supple tannins and some spiced chocolate through the finish. Plenty of wine for the money.

2006 Hentley Farm The Beauty Shiraz

Score **93**

BAROSSA VALLEY
Price $50.00
Quality ★★★★ ┤
Alc./Vol. 15%
Drink 2013
Closure Cork

This princess has had a bit of lipstick applied in the form of viognier (3%), making the fresh blackberry fruit lift even brighter. Superb ripeness and smoked earthy complexity, genuine concentration of both fruit flavours and tannins, reaching deep through the finish.

2005 Heritage Shiraz

Score **90**

BAROSSA VALLEY
Price $25.00
Quality ★★★★
Alc./Vol. 14.5%
Drink Now
Closure Cork

Big Steve Hoff has rolled together rich Greenock and Maranaga shiraz to great effect. Ripe fruits and punchy American oak here, really straightforward juicy plums – quite a meaty style for the Barossa; the tannins creep back up from the finish and build dry savoury texture.

2005 Hesketh The Protagonist Shiraz   *Score* **91**

BAROSSA VALLEY 🖺
Price $25.00 ✓
Quality   ★★★★
Alc./Vol. 15%
Drink   2012
Closure   Screwcap

They've sourced some handy material to make this sing in bright regional tune. Attractive plums and spices, tarry regional characters, plenty of weight and richness, really solid drive, like the oak and fruit match up, some chocolate. A classic rendition.

2006 Hewitson Ned & Henry's Shiraz   *Score* **91**

BAROSSA VALLEY
Price $24.00 ✓
Quality   ★★★★
Alc./Vol. 14.5%
Drink   2010
Closure   Screwcap

One of Hewitson's most consistent front-runner reds (named after his sons) shows bright blue fruits, plenty of fragrance and charm. The palate is supple and treads lightly for Barossa shiraz: red fruit and berry cola flavours, lively and exuberant, finishing balanced and fresh. Drink up!

2006 Hewitson The Mad Hatter Shiraz   *Score* **96**

McLAREN VALE
Price $50.00 ✓
Quality   ★★★★★
Alc./Vol. 15%
Drink   2015
Closure   Screwcap

Great McLaren Vale shiraz marries richness and softness in an irresistibly charming fashion. The brightness of this '06 is striking; it delves headlong into pure ripe dark berries and spicy lifted fruits, and has already eaten up the oak, shows terrific intensity and richness. The palate has great drive and direction, delivering deep plum and spice flavour with finesse, rolled out on plush ripe tannins; long, composed finish.

2006 Innocent Bystander Shiraz Viognier   *Score* **90**

YARRA VALLEY 🖺
Price $20.00 ✓
Quality   ★★★★
Alc./Vol. 14%
Drink   2011
Closure   Screwcap

Quite striking peppery/spicy aromas from this inexpensive approachable red; bright lifted fruits, an attempt at complex cool-climate style. The palate has fine tannins made in a savoury/meaty style, finishes with some plush plum flavour, blue and dark berries. Neat as a pin.

2006 Jamsheed Great Western Shiraz   *Score* **92**

GREAT WESTERN
Price $35.00 ✓
Quality   ★★★★
Alc./Vol. 14.5%
Drink   2013
Closure   Diam

Gary Mills makes a fine trio of Victorian shiraz; this intense parcel is sourced from a mature vineyard planted in the 1950s. Earthy fragrance and cool regional shiraz style, dark fruits, some mint and spice, the oak is assertive, tannins are sturdy and speak of vine age. Deceptively charming.

2005 John Duval Eligo Shiraz   *Score* **96**

BAROSSA VALLEY
Price $105.00
Quality ★★★★★
Alc./Vol. 14.5%
Drink 2012
Closure Cork

Duval has introduced this elite wine, a selection of the best shiraz he identified from the '05 vintage; it was given an additional spell in the finest French timber. Precise blackberry aromas, some tarry notes, it has eaten up the oak and smells quite elegant. Fruit has been sculpted with experienced hands and delivered in refined shape – plum and dark berry flavours, fine dense tannins, impeccable balance.

2006 John Duval Entity Shiraz   *Score* **93**

BAROSSA VALLEY
Price $48.00 ✓
Quality ★★★★ ⁴
Alc./Vol. 14.5%
Drink 2012
Closure Screwcap

Duval's latest Entity shiraz sits in a refined style, he's taken the best of Barossan shiraz fruit and crafted it into complex, layered shape. Dark berries, tar and plum fruit aromas, there's an essential freshness and vibrant heart to the palate that really impresses. Oak weighs in with chocolate flavour through sweeping waves of fruit-soaked tannins. A concentrated, elegant and thoughtful Barossa shiraz.

2006 John Forrest Collection Gimblett Gravels Syrah   *Score* **91**

HAWKES BAY, NZ
Price $50.00
Quality ★★★★
Alc./Vol. 14.7%
Drink Now
Closure Screwcap

This John Forrest syrah draws on Hawkes Bay's warmth, achieving impressive ripeness and deep sweet flavour. Rich plum fruits and boot polish, tar and spices, intense black cherry and minerals, almost Italianesque. The palate is soft and smooth, slips through the finish on a carpet or fine ripe tannins. Impressive style.

2005 John Hongell Shiraz   *Score* **90**

BAROSSA VALLEY
Price $20.00 ✓
Quality ★★★★
Alc./Vol. 14.5%
Drink 2012
Closure Screwcap

A whiff of sweet musky vanillin here, this has seen some punchy oak and it dominates the fruit aromas for now. The palate is more even-handed with ripe intense black fruit flavour, a little tar and deep stepping tannins. Lots here for the money.

2006 Kaesler Stonehorse Shiraz   *Score* **91**

BAROSSA VALLEY
Price $30.00
Quality ★★★★
Alc./Vol. 15.5%
Drink Now
Closure Cork

Kaesler have their eye in for juicy attractive Barossa shiraz. Straight-shooting ripe berries here, sets the mouth watering with perfectly pitched ripeness, some nutty oak complexity in the background. Bright palate with abundant ripe berry and plum fruits, attractive richness, supple and balanced; well played.

2006 Kaesler The Bogan Shiraz
Score **95**

BAROSSA VALLEY
Price $50.00 ✓
Quality ★★★★ ¹
Alc./Vol. 16%
Drink 2012
Closure Cork

One of the most impressive Barossa producers, the Kaesler approach is a 'give it everything it's got' style, and they've got the fruit to handle it. This is sourced from 1899 and 1965 plantings, it has impeccable bright blackberry and plum fruits – pristine. Tannins are supple, the palate is a rich, swirling ball of sweet ripe dark berry flavour and fine, melting tannins; fades slowly, superb!

2006 Kalleske Greenock Shiraz
Score **94**

BAROSSA VALLEY ✐
Price $40.00 ✓
Quality ★★★★ ¹
Alc./Vol. 15.5%
Drink 2012
Closure Cork

This is the Kalleske family's estate shiraz, grown on their Greenock property. It's a rich dense expression of dark plum fruits, chocolate and sweet earthy aromas. There's richness with harmony, seemingly endless ripe berry and plum fruits, fine tannins woven smoothly throughout. This is one easy wine to enjoy.

2006 Kalleske Johann Georg Old Vine Shiraz
Score **95**

BAROSSA VALLEY ✐
Price $100.00 ✓
Quality ★★★★ ¹
Alc./Vol. 15.5%
Drink 2016
Closure Cork

Sourced from the estate's original plantings, these gnarled old battlers date back to 1875. They were planted by Johann Georg Kalleske, the first of the family to settle in the Barossa. The aromas are haunting for their depth and complexity; very similar characters to the Greenock shiraz but it moves in an extra dimension. Ripe dark plum and sweet mocha-scented earthy nuances, some dark spice and pepper too. Astounding palate density and concentration, yet not at all overbearing – it scoops deep and soulful through the finish. This is a wine to marvel at!

2006 Kirrihill Baile an Gharrai Shiraz
Score **92**

CLARE VALLEY
Price $20.00 ✓
Quality ★★★★
Alc./Vol. 13.5%
Drink 2012
Closure Screwcap

From a plot of vines out in the Armagh sub-district, this shows power with elegance, bright lifted berry aromas, some musk, pomegranate and savoury/meaty oak influence. Achieves depth on the palate with supple style, musky red and dark fruit flavours and some chocolate through the finish.

2005 Kirrihill Estates Langhorne Creek Shiraz

Score **91**

LANGHORNE CREEK
Price $20.00 ✓
Quality ★★★★
Alc./Vol. 15%
Drink 2011
Closure Screwcap

Take some ripe hearty Langhorne Creek fruit, add some punchy oak – and here you have it. Oak leads the wine out amid vanillin and milky aromas, loamy Langhorne earthy fruits, ripe berries and some sweet bright characters behind. The palate is supple and sweet: ripe and juicy berry/plum flavours, soft tannin finish.

2006 Lethbridge Shiraz

Score **93**

GEELONG 🖉
Price $32.00 ✓
Quality ★★★★ ┥
Alc./Vol. 14.5%
Drink 2012
Closure Diam

Ray Nadeson and Maree Collis have charted a quick road to the front of the pack down in Geelong. This is a complex shiraz with dark toasted spices and ripe, peppery black fruits, smoky cinnamon and wave after wave of fine ground spices. The palate has bright acidity and black mineral flavours, more sweet spices dusted through plum fruit flavour. Will develop nicely.

2006 Lloyd Brothers Shiraz

Score **92**

McLAREN VALE
Price $22.00 ✓
Quality ★★★★
Alc./Vol. 14.5%
Drink Now
Closure Screwcap

This prime piece of vineyard has some special qualities when it comes to shiraz, making the first grade with its ripe juicy plum fruits and regional liquorice flavours. Tannins are open and welcoming, and the oak runs a toasty twist through the finish. Nicely played indeed!

2006 Logan Shiraz

Score **90**

ORANGE
Price $25.00
Quality ★★★★
Alc./Vol. 14.5%
Drink Now
Closure Cork

This is a well-stitched, smoothly fruited shiraz, showing really ripe dark fruits and a touch of tarry reduction, some fine sweeter spice lift too. Tannins are soft and easy, delivering plums and peppery flavour, toasty oak through the finish. A modern missionary-position style.

2006 Maglieri Shiraz

Score **88**

McLAREN VALE
Price $20.00
Quality ★★★ ┥
Alc./Vol. 14.5%
Drink Now
Closure Cork

You've got to respect a wine that comes in the cheapest bottle on earth, with a dried-out cork that spells bad warehouse storage and still tastes terrific! Hats off Maglieri, this has ripe dark fruits and plum aromas, medium-weight tannins, a little knocked around on the finish.

2006 **Marius Simpatico Shiraz**

Score **91**

McLAREN VALE
Price $24.00 ✓
Quality ★★★★
Alc./Vol. 14.5%
Drink Now
Closure Screwcap

The name says it all – this is about easy drinking and it shows, well, *simpatico* between the region and the variety. Ripe dark berries and plum fruits, gently supportive tannins that don't interrupt the flow of flavour or compromise the soft mouth-feel.

2005 **Marius Symphony Shiraz**

Score **93**

McLAREN VALE
Price $34.00 ✓
Quality ★★★★ ↓
Alc./Vol. 15%
Drink 2011
Closure Screwcap

This is the upper deck of the Marius shiraz range and offers plenty of value – a real gem. Ripe dark berry fruits, plums and liquorice; charming juicy smooth tannins from start to finish – a wine with style and grace, eminently balanced and beautifully delivered.

2006 **Maverick Greenock Rise Shiraz**

Score **94**

BAROSSA VALLEY
Price $55.00 ✓
Quality ★★★★ ↓
Alc./Vol. 15%
Drink 2014
Closure Cork

This dark, brooding Greenock shiraz hails from vines planted in the 1950s and has superb depth. It pushes the ripeness envelope with dark berry and plum fruits, toasted spices dress it up nicely and the oak is cast in a supporting role of structure and texture, adding toast through the finish. This juicy Barossa shiraz will cellar like a champ!

2005 **Maverick Trial Hill Eden Valley Shiraz**

Score **94**

EDEN VALLEY
Price $60.00
Quality ★★★★ ↓
Alc./Vol. 14.5%
Drink 2015
Closure Cork

Impressive colour – really vibrant; it packs a dense whack of bright red and dark berry fruits, dusted with fine spices, some plum in there too. The palate balances density with grace, tannins run deep and savoury, building weight towards the finish – the balance is spot-on. This is still very much on the ascent and deserves time in the cellar to reach its lofty best.

2007 **Mayer Big Betty Shiraz**

Score **91**

YARRA VALLEY
Price $35.00
Quality ★★★★
Alc./Vol. 14%
Drink 2011
Closure Diam

This clever Yarra shiraz is more on the beautiful side of big. It has ripe confected fruit aromas, black fruits and superb fragrant lift, cranberry and fine spice too; cleverly constructed. The palate travels on fine tannins delivering meaty barrel-derived complexity and light berry flavour. Easy and approachable.

2006 McKellar Ridge Shiraz Viognier

Score **90**

CANBERRA DISTRICT
Price $22.00
Quality ★★★★
Alc./Vol. 14%
Drink 2011
Closure Screwcap

Brian and Janet Johnston have played into the regional strength of this Rhône-inspired blend, plenty of ripeness and dark brambly fruits, youthful and lightly spiced. The palate packs dense sweet dark berry flavour into juicy tannins – shows promise.

2006 Meerea Park Hell Hole Shiraz

Score **94**

HUNTER VALLEY
Price $55.00
Quality ★★★★ ┥
Alc./Vol. 13.5%
Drink 2013
Closure Screwcap

This top-flight bottling delivers ripe dark berries and plum fruits, some lighter fragrant notes too; attractive and clean. Plenty of dark earthy complexity and oak spice in the mouth, medium-weight; dry dusty tannins dig in through the finish, dropping a wake of savoury liquorice complexity and dark minerals.

2007 Meerea Park Shiraz

Score **91**

HILLTOPS/HUNTER VALLEY
Price $15.00 ✓
Quality ★★★★
Alc./Vol. 14%
Drink 2012
Closure Screwcap

This regional pairing works well, Hilltops fruit adds bright fragrance and lift to ripe berries, with plenty of earthy Hunter notes below. The palate's forthright, delivering great density and supple savoury tannins, still in the medium-bodied league, finishing with elegant plum fruits.

2006 Meerea Park The Aunts Shiraz

Score **91**

HUNTER VALLEY
Price $26.00
Quality ★★★★
Alc./Vol. 13.5%
Drink 2012
Closure Screwcap

Named after two spinsters from way back, there's punchy overt oak sitting out from the fruit here, dark spiced fruit aroma and concentrated earthy presence. Dressed to impress, in the regional style, tannins are fine and savoury; finishes with dried berry and chocolate flavours.

2005 Michael Unwin One Goat Shiraz

Score **91**

CENTRAL VICTORIA
Price $14.00 ✓
Quality ★★★★
Alc./Vol. 14.5%
Drink Now
Closure Screwcap

Attractive bright ripe red and dark berry fruits here, this has some life and lift, purple florals and charming primary fruit characters. The palate moves into maraschino cherry and cassis territory, tannins are fine, finishes fresh.

2006 Mistletoe Shiraz

Score **93**

HUNTER VALLEY
Price $20.00 ✓
Quality ★★★★ ·
Alc./Vol. 13.5%
Drink 2014
Closure Screwcap

Bright blue fruits and nutty/leathery fruit aromas, intense and regional, the dusty dried berries are textbook Hunter; it smells savoury and ripe. The palate sits supple and bright, fine tannins ride across the tongue in dense formation, delivering spiced black fruit flavours, yet finishing fine and elegant. Has direction and style.

2006 Mount Horrocks Watervale Shiraz

Score **92**

CLARE VALLEY
Price $35.00
Quality ★★★★
Alc./Vol. 14%
Drink 2012
Closure Screwcap

One of the best of the recent Horrocks shiraz releases, showing attractive, ripe bright aromas. There's lifted blue fruits and berries, some gently savoury oak behind and a hint of pepper too. The palate has springy tannins through the middle, even and supple, elegant plum flavours, finishing fine and balanced.

2006 Mount Majura Shiraz

Score **93**

CANBERRA DISTRICT
Price $25.00 ✓
Quality ★★★★ ·
Alc./Vol. 14.1%
Drink 2012
Closure Screwcap

Delicious elegant shiraz and superb value. Super-fine, fragrant aromas, peppery and spicy Canberra District characters, bright dark berries and plums; complex and very much in the mod-Oz cool style. Plenty of supple fruit and sweet spice on the palate, the oak adds some sweetness and gentle toast, dried plums and dark chocolate to close.

2003 Mount Pleasant OP & OH Shiraz

Score **93**

HUNTER VALLEY
Price $39.00
Quality ★★★★ ·
Alc./Vol. 14.5%
Drink 2012
Closure Cork

A champion of the regional savoury/leathery Hunter shiraz characters (the good ones): dried earth and some dusty fruits, distinctly leathery nose and pine needles too. On entry, the palate has terrific chocolate and dried plum flavour that travels medium-bodied, then delivers a big tannin kick through the finish, still unfurling.

2006 Mountain X Shiraz

Score **92**

HUNTER VALLEY
Price $35.00
Quality ★★★★
Alc./Vol. 13.5%
Drink 2010
Closure Diam

A 100-case project conceived by wine scribe Campbell Mattinson and blogger Gary Walsh. They set out to make a traditional Hunter shiraz-pinot blend and, well, they did. Trademark dried berry fruits and dusty Hunter characters, dried berries and earth, the oak sits in tight. Medium-weighted palate with red fruits and citrus peel flavour, light dry tannins. Well done lads!

2006 Mr Riggs McLaren Vale Shiraz — Score 92

McLAREN VALE	
Price	$50.00
Quality	★★★★
Alc./Vol.	14.5%
Drink	2012
Closure	Cork

Well, Ben Riggs, big Ben Riggs, should know this region about as well as anyone, and clearly he's all over it if the quality of his 2006 shiraz is any indication. The wine has played right into the region's sweet spot of sweet ripe flavour and soft approachable tannins. It's dressed in weekend clothes, casual and comfortable, toasty oak and berry/plum flavours slide easily through from start to finish.

2006 Murdoch James Saleyards Syrah — Score 91

HAWKES BAY/ MARTINBOROUGH, NZ	
Price	$36.00
Quality	★★★★
Alc./Vol.	12.5%
Drink	2010
Closure	Screwcap

A 60/40 split between Hawkes Bay and Martinborough fruit, this elegant syrah makes a smokier and cryptic impression on the nose: pepper berries and some spiced roasted meats, gravelly notes below. The palate is a bright, juicy assembly of mainly savoury characters, some decent oak sliced in, and fine tannins, finishes with finesse.

2005 Oakridge 864 Shiraz — Score 93

YARRA VALLEY	
Price	$60.00
Quality	★★★★ ⊣
Alc./Vol.	14.5%
Drink	2013
Closure	Screwcap

864 is the top-rung bottling. Yet to reveal its full detail, showing bright open berry fruits, quite ripe with some measure, meaty winemaking, and spice in the background. Wins on palate texture and healthy tannin draw, moderate weight and fine cool balance; finishes with savoury/nutty flavours. A keeper.

2007 Oakridge Over The Shoulder Shiraz Viognier — Score 91

YARRA VALLEY	
Price	$22.00 ✓
Quality	★★★★
Alc./Vol.	13.5%
Drink	2011
Closure	Screwcap

The componentry is evident here; you can see the oak sitting beside the fruit, musky and powdery, some brambly dark berry shiraz characters. A serious attempt at seduction by winemaking. The palate has a more restrained dark fruit and mineral flavour, savoury too, the tannins are gentle and fine, peppery and spicy to close. Easy style.

2006 Oakridge Shiraz — Score 93

YARRA VALLEY	
Price	$32.00 ✓
Quality	★★★★ ⊣
Alc./Vol.	13.5%
Drink	2010
Closure	Screwcap

This is right in the zone, showing cool complex fine spices and bright red fruits, fragrant pepper, savoury minerals and some citrus peel – Rhône-like. The palate is an exercise in finesse and elegance: layered fine smoky tannins, ripe berry flavours stacked throughout in beautifully balanced formation.

2006 Off The Leash Max Shiraz Viognier   *Score* **93**

ADELAIDE HILLS	Strong peppery nuances, this has a cool accent, smoky and
Price $25.00 ✓	spicy, really striking dark fruit characters here. The palate
Quality ★★★★ ꜰ	is rich and supple, loaded with spice and lively Rhône-ish
Alc./Vol. 13.5%	dark fruits. Fine tannins that balance through the finish,
Drink 2012	even, supple and long, exotic saffron aftertaste.
Closure Screwcap	

2005 Paracombe Shiraz Viognier   *Score* **91**

ADELAIDE HILLS	The addition of viognier to Adelaide Hills shiraz works
Price $21.00 ✓	extremely well: sweet dark spices and rich ripe fruits, some
Quality ★★★★	liquorice and earthy complexity, brooding dark fruits and
Alc./Vol. 16%	spice. The palate's sweetly fruited with deep ripe flavours,
Drink 2011	plums and red berries, super-ripe tannins.
Closure Screwcap	

2006 Paradigm Hill Col's Block Shiraz   *Score* **90**

MORNINGTON PENINSULA	This is an open-knit, aromatic Mornington shiraz, showing
Price $38.00	fine brambly cool-climate berry fruits, some savoury earth
Quality ★★★★	and hints of pepper. The palate is defined by cool-climate
Alc./Vol. 14%	acidity, spiking up out of the middle palate, followed by
Drink 2011	fine tannins, finishing with soft fresh berry flavour.
Closure Diam	

2005 Penfolds Bin 28 Kalimna Shiraz   *Score* **91**

SOUTH AUSTRALIA	Attractive bright fragrant berry fruits, blackberry and red
Price $32.00	fruits too, really vivacious, the oak adds more lift. This is a
Quality ★★★★	well-pitched palate: fine dense tannins pack berry fruit in
Alc./Vol. 14.5%	deep and even – like the simplicity and balance.
Drink Now	
Closure Screwcap	

2003 Penfolds Grange Shiraz   *Score* **92**

SOUTH AUSTRALIA	Dark, brooding aromas, plenty of tarry/savoury smells, boot
Price $550.00	polish and trademark resinous American oak – one of its
Quality ★★★★	signatures. If the nose doesn't instantly win you over, the palate
Alc./Vol. 14.5%	displays some handy pedigree; the intensity is hard to fathom,
Drink 2013	ripe dark berry fruits, dark plums and chocolate, tannins are
Closure Cork	tucked in tight as a drum. It pulls everything in through the
	middle and makes a beeline for the finish. There's plenty more
	to come in the next few years, but it's not one of their finest.

2005 Penfolds Magill Estate

Score **93**

ADELAIDE
Price $100.00
Quality   ★★★★ ⸜
Alc./Vol. 14.5%
Drink   2013
Closure   Cork

This is usually one of the more restrained and elegant reds in the Penfolds line-up, but in 2005 it's in swanky, assertive form. Richly spiced plums and berry fruits, fine savoury tannins, toasty barrel fermentation is laid on meaty and thick, some berry cola to close. An attractive if atypical Magill Estate.

2005 Penfolds RWT Shiraz

Score **96**

BAROSSA VALLEY
Price $160.00
Quality   ★★★★★
Alc./Vol. 14.5%
Drink   2014
Closure   Cork

The RWT is in fine shape in 2005, delivering bright rich fruits in an elegant frame with impressive focus and clarity. Mixed berries are lifted by fragrant, understated French oak, the palate is supremely elegant and balanced – this has deceptive power and will be marked as one of the great RWT releases. Pure class.

2004 Penfolds St Henri Shiraz

Score **96**

SOUTH AUSTRALIA
Price $90.00
Quality   ★★★★★
Alc./Vol. 14.5%
Drink   2016
Closure   Cork

Penfolds' Peter Gago has the luxury of the entire portfolio to sip and swirl from but he claims a soft spot for St Henri. The 2004 is a classic rendition of fragrant, rich shiraz characters, dried berries and savoury/earthy notes. The palate travels on focused fruit flavour and fine elegant tannins that are anchored securely in line, ensuring an elegant life ahead in the cellar – this is one of the best ageing Penfolds reds.

2006 Penny's Hill Shiraz

Score **91**

McLAREN VALE
Price $27.00
Quality   ★★★★
Alc./Vol. 15%
Drink   2010
Closure   Cork

Penny's Hill sits in a plum position between the McLaren Vale township and Willunga. This is a bold, brassy style, big on plum and dark cherry fruits, a decent slice of toasty oak to sweeten the deal and smooth, supple tannins; all tuned up for racing!

2006 Pertaringa Undercover Shiraz

Score **91**

McLAREN VALE
Price $20.00 ✓
Quality   ★★★★
Alc./Vol. 15%
Drink   2014
Closure   Screwcap

This contains some of the prime parcels of McLaren Vale fruit, presided over by Geoff Hardy and Ian Leask. It's stacked to the roof with ripe juicy blackberry fruit, plums and toasty oak for good measure; the palate's still unfurling so give it a break in the cellar before you hop in.

2005 Pikes EWP Reserve Shiraz

Score **94**

CLARE VALLEY
Price $65.00
Quality ★★★★ ⌐
Alc./Vol. 14.5%
Drink 2015
Closure Screwcap

After riesling, shiraz is the next card played at this Polish Hill River stalwart. True reserve-wine style and intensity, it's built for the long haul and impresses with balance as well as intensity. Deep-seated plum and chocolate flavours, ripe thunderous tannins and the promise of great years ahead.

2006 Pirathon by Kalleske Shiraz

Score **90**

BAROSSA VALLEY ✎
Price $24.00
Quality ★★★★
Alc./Vol. 15%
Drink 2010
Closure Cork

Inky black in the glass, it has some tarry, very rich Barossa regional shiraz aromas and lots of sweet open-grained oak. There's plenty of tannin too, plums and sweet punchy coconut oak, finishing thick and toasty. Bit of a bruiser.

2006 Port Phillip Estate Rimage Syrah

Score **91**

MORNINGTON PENINSULA
Price $45.00
Quality ★★★★
Alc./Vol. 13.5%
Drink 2014
Closure Diam

This is a wine that will polarise opinion with its intense reduction and meaty/gamey aromas; really edgy and scintillating, ground pepper, dry spices and plums. The palate traces a twangy cool-climate shape with peppery dark fruit flavour and punchy tannin chew. Look forward to this one sweetening out in the next few years.

2006 Port Phillip Estate Shiraz

Score **91**

MORNINGTON PENINSULA
Price $35.00
Quality ★★★★
Alc./Vol. 13.5%
Drink 2012
Closure Diam

Plenty of peppery cool-climate shiraz fruit: spiced dried berries, savoury smoked meats, framed up in well-laid oak and some mealy/savoury notes. The palate delivers the same peppery, dried berry flavour, making a distinctly savoury impression; really tight and driven by bright acidity, it squares up through the finish. Straight to the cellar.

2006 Prince Hill Shiraz

Score **90**

MUDGEE
Price $25.00
Quality ★★★★
Alc./Vol. 14.5%
Drink Now
Closure Screwcap

Named in homage to one of the Mudgee district's pioneers, it's a riper wine with some deeper darker berry fruit aromas, more savoury earthy notes, brambly berries – enough complexity for now. The palate is supple and juicy with approachable blackberry flavours and some light, fine tannins. Balanced and young.

2007 Purple Hen Estate Shiraz   *Score* 92

GIPPSLAND
Price $26.00
Quality ★★★★
Alc./Vol. 13%
Drink   2010
Closure Screwcap

Sweet ripe aromatics, really attractive dark berries and spiced chocolate aromas, they've added a tiny splash (1%) of viognier as subtle seasoning. Lovely supple palate, fine soft tannins and brightly balanced acidity, the smooth texture rolls cherries and chocolate out through the finish. Approachable, even, good.

2007 Pyrette Shiraz   *Score* 92

HEATHCOTE
Price $40.00
Quality ★★★★
Alc./Vol. 13.5%
Drink   2012
Closure Diam

Michael Dhillon (of Bindi) satisfies his hankering to make shiraz with this parcel of Heathcote fruit. Very regional with cassis and brambly berry fruits, plenty of spice and a gentle twist of chocolate. The palate is elegant, although much fuller than the '06, it slides on fine tannins and brisk acidity, finishing crisp and juicy.

2005 Radford Dale Eden Valley Shiraz   *Score* 94

EDEN VALLEY
Price $32.00 ✓
Quality ★★★★ ⟩
Alc./Vol. 14.5%
Drink   2013
Closure Cork

Ben and Gill Radford make wines with vision and personal style, informed by the place the grapes are grown and the Radfords' experience of being there and making wine. Superb bright red fruits and complex pepper and roasted spices, terrific aromatic complexity here. The palate unfurls a silken textured, smoothly polished sheet of ripe red and dark berry flavour, sensational finesse and evenness. A star in the making.

2007 Ravenswood Lane Shiraz   *Score* 94

ADELAIDE HILLS
Price $39.00
Quality ★★★★ ⟩
Alc./Vol. 13.5%
Drink   2015
Closure Screwcap

A convincing, complex shiraz: plenty of rich ripe dark fruit aromas, sweet finely ground spices, there's plums and anise, some pepper too, and mocha-scented oak sits in the background. Tannins are fine and fan out evenly from start to finish, terrific grip and even weight, cool and balanced with a slow-burning finish.

2007 Ravensworth Hunter Valley Shiraz   *Score* 91

HUNTER VALLEY
Price $30.00
Quality ★★★★
Alc./Vol. 14%
Drink   2010
Closure Screwcap

Brian Martin took advantage of a fortuitous opportunity to snap up some Hunter shiraz in 2007. Good thing! Terrific lively purple colour, bright raspberry fruits, looks really together; fine aromatics, berry pudding and milk chocolate, young and primary. Medium-weight Hunter palate with blackberry jam flavours and supple dense tannins. A handsome young Hunter shiraz.

2007 Ravensworth Shiraz Viognier
Score **93**

MURRUMBATEMEN
Price $32.00
Quality ★★★★↓
Alc./Vol. 13.5%
Drink   2012
Closure Screwcap

Brian Martin's take on the shiraz-viognier theme has some savoury earthy notes and toasty grilled nut complexity; it's cool and measured. The palate reveals some terrific power and richness; fine tannins precipitate down through rich plum and cherry flavours, finishing with toasty oak char.

2005 Richmond Grove Limited Release Shiraz
Score **88**

BAROSSA VALLEY
Price $20.00
Quality ★★★↓
Alc./Vol. 14.5%
Drink   2010
Closure Screwcap

Reserve release is a rubbery term that we're seeing just a little too often these days. This is a workhorse 'fruit + oak = wine' Barossa shiraz, showing dark berries and earthy regional tannins alongside resiny, rugged oak. Starting to look a bit old-fashioned next to its competition.

2004 Ridgeline Shiraz
Score **91**

YARRA VALLEY
Price $35.00
Quality ★★★★
Alc./Vol. 13.5%
Drink   2011
Closure Diam

One of the best Ridgeline releases I've come across, this has fine, lifted, cool-climate shiraz berry fruits and spices. Light and bright palate with taut berry flavours and attractive dark mineral complexity, a little tar at the edges and fine tannins slide through the finish. Understated and elegant.

2005 Rolling Shiraz
Score **91**

CENTRAL RANGES
Price $17.00 ✓
Quality ★★★★
Alc./Vol. 13.5%
Drink   Now
Closure Screwcap

Clean, ripe berry and plum fruits, simple and direct, chewy and dense, the palate is bolstered by toasty oak, and some mocha flavours run through the finish. Light easy tannins make the brightness last; a safe style with a balanced plum skin finish.

2005 Ross Estate Shiraz
Score **92**

BAROSSA VALLEY
Price $26.00
Quality ★★★★
Alc./Vol. 14.5%
Drink   2011
Closure Cork

Like the earthy/tarry ripe plum fruits here, this has soulful red Barossa soil character, deep spices and concentration, the oak sits across the top in nutty roasted shape. Supple tannins and some sweet spicy toast, balanced and even; appealing richness, plush and symphonic with balance, blackberry flavour runs long through the finish.

2006 Rutherglen Estates Shiraz Viognier
Score **89**

RUTHERGLEN
Price $20.00
Quality   ★★★ ⊰
Alc./Vol. 14.5%
Drink   2010
Closure   Screwcap

A 5% dose of viognier brings lift and spice to brambly Rutherglen shiraz fruits. It's all about flavour, with deep tarry plums and juicy middle-palate texture. Tannins run savoury through the finish, compact and chewy.

2006 S.C. Pannell Shiraz
Score **94**

McLAREN VALE
Price $65.00
Quality   ★★★★ ⊰
Alc./Vol. 14.5%
Drink   2013
Closure   Screwcap

Super-youthful and understated McLaren Vale shiraz, this wine loves the air. Ripe precise plum fruits and liquorice, some nutty older oak characters and sweet earthy spice; it's settled and oozes harmony. Curvy, smooth palate, really compact and brightly concentrated plum fruit flavour, tannins are fanned out from front to back. A soulful McLaren Vale shiraz without the attitude.

2004 Saltram No.1 Shiraz
Score **93**

BAROSSA VALLEY
Price $70.00
Quality   ★★★★ ⊰
Alc./Vol. 14.5%
Drink   2012
Closure   Screwcap

This king of the Saltram castle is one smartly crafted, rich Barossa shiraz. It oozes ripe blackberry fruits and deep dense tarry regional character, vanillin oak lightens the impression. The palate packs chewy dark berry flavour, really strapping swarthy flesh through the middle, and then attention-grabbing structure to finish.

2006 Scorpo Shiraz
Score **93**

MORNINGTON PENINSULA
Price $43.00
Quality   ★★★★ ⊰
Alc./Vol. 13.5%
Drink   2014
Closure   Diam

A wine to buy and keep, this shows the restrained dark earthy fruits of past vintages, some gravelly aromas, fine pepper and spice. The palate is tightly wound, showing musky/berry flavour, locked away by guarding tannins and savoury winemaking influence. Full of promise.

2006 Scotchmans Hill Shiraz
Score **89**

GEELONG
Price $30.00
Quality   ★★★ ⊰
Alc./Vol. 14.5%
Drink   2010
Closure   Screwcap

Scotchmans have delivered an earthy/savoury shiraz, really soulful and approachable dark fruits, straight shooting and primary. Ripe blackberry flavour, assertive spice and bright acidity, some punchy tannin kick but the fruit wins the finish.

2006 Seppelt Benno Bendigo Shiraz

Score **94**

BENDIGO
Price $55.00
Quality ★★★★┐
Alc./Vol. 14%
Drink 2012
Closure Screwcap

A sensational follow-up to the stunning 2005 vintage, very deep but restrained. A haunting set of aromas: super-fine spices and peppery edges, earthy and dried dark berry fruits, dark liquorice and anise. Terrific depth and drive in the mouth, understated, thick dense tannins and cryptic complexity, taut and balanced, dark savoury liquorice finish.

2006 Seppelt Silverband Grampians Shiraz

Score **93**

GRAMPIANS
Price $35.00
Quality ★★★★┐
Alc./Vol. 14%
Drink 2014
Closure Screwcap

A ringing endorsement for the Grampians region's innate suitability to shiraz. Attractive fine fruit aromas here, some elegant star anise spice, savoury meats and dark mineral smells, dense dried plum fruits – very savoury and subtle. Fine supple tannins and a terrific even-handed palate, savoury here again, dark mineral and black liquorice finish.

2006 Seppelt St Peters Grampians Shiraz

Score **96**

GRAMPIANS
Price $60.00
Quality ★★★★★
Alc./Vol. 13.5%
Drink 2015
Closure Screwcap

This top Seppelt shiraz has asserted impressive superiority in 2006. Super-fine meaty complexity and sweet oak spices are laid across spicy cool-climate fruits, dark minerals, dried plums – all very compelling. Tannins are super fine and acidity backs the wine in across the palate; sprightly but savoury, dark intense dried berry and plum, deceptive tannin weight. Superb balance.

2006 Shaw & Smith Shiraz

Score **94**

ADELAIDE HILLS
Price $38.00
Quality ★★★★┐
Alc./Vol. 14%
Drink 2013
Closure Screwcap

Stripes of musky oak and ripe red fruits, quite perfumed and lifted, this is a forthright, modern style, overlaid by attractive mocha-scented oak toast. The palate is elegant and direct with fine dark fruit and mineral flavours, tightly integrated, and finishes purposefully. Cellar-worthy.

2005 Shingleback Shiraz

Score **90**

McLAREN VALE
Price $25.00
Quality ★★★★
Alc./Vol. 14.5%
Drink 2009
Closure Cork

The Davey family has made a name with their cabernet but John Davey rightly protests that the shiraz is also excellent! The Shingleback style is fine and luscious, drawing on the hearty soils to make hearty wine, soft tannins, ripe blood plum and a wedge of punchy oak.

2006 St Hallett Faith Shiraz

Score 89

BAROSSA VALLEY
Price $21.00
Quality ★★★ ↓
Alc./Vol. 14.5%
Drink Now
Closure Screwcap

This has an additional lifted fragrant side, some tar and dark chocolate edges and nutty oak, nice complexity and elegance, light meaty edges too. The palate is simpler and more straitlaced, oak sits out to the side a little, ripe and juicy.

2005 St Hallett Old Block Shiraz

Score 93

BAROSSA VALLEY
Price $80.00
Quality ★★★★ ↓
Alc./Vol. 14.5%
Drink 2013
Closure Cork

Old Block is delving into earthy, tarry blackberry country – a classic Barossa shiraz with some nutty oak influence edging across the nose. On the one hand there's a deep anchor of fruit through the base, and on the other sits fragrant lift. Plum fruits linger through the finish, ripe, juicy and promising to deliver handsomely with time in the cellar.

2006 St John's Road Blood and Courage Shiraz

Score 91

BAROSSA VALLEY
Price $20.00
Quality ★★★★
Alc./Vol. 14.5%
Drink 2010
Closure Screwcap

This creamy, spicy-smelling wine has had a fair leg up from the oak it's received along the way. Plenty of rich Greenock shiraz lurks below, steered into a fresh, vibrant style on the palate by winemaker Pete Schell, red and dark berries rule the roost here; really vibrant.

2005 St John's Road Julia Greenock Shiraz

Score 89

BAROSSA VALLEY
Price $33.00
Quality ★★★ ↓
Alc./Vol. 14.8%
Drink 2011
Closure Screwcap

This rockabilly style has plenty of toasty oak to warm up the crowd, nice and ripe too. Dark spiced berry fruits and rumbling earthy tannins make for a savoury palate, finishing with a firmer hand than its sibling, Blood and Courage.

2005 Starvedog Lane Shiraz Viognier

Score 91

ADELAIDE HILLS
Price $28.50
Quality ★★★★
Alc./Vol. 14%
Drink 2013
Closure Screwcap

Displays an overt nose of spicy fruits and obvious viognier influence, bringing bright appeal, primary and lifted. The palate is rich and ripe, slick dark fruit flavours, some meaty notes too, soft tannins through the finish, savoury and even.

2005 Sutton Grange Estate Syrah

Score 95

CENTRAL VICTORIA 🌿
Price $50.00
Quality ★★★★ɟ
Alc./Vol. 13.2%
Drink 2014
Closure Diam

This is a masterful statement of bright, complex vineyard-driven character and insightful winemaking. Freshly ground hard spices, a really elevated and expressive fragrance. Power meets finesse on the palate: the tannins are velveteen, flavours ride in the dark berry spectrum, finishes with grace.

2006 Syrahmi Petit Prière Shiraz

Score 93

HEATHCOTE
Price $45.00
Quality ★★★★ɟ
Alc./Vol. 14%
Drink 2015
Closure Screwcap

This has some terrific Rhône-like dark chocolate and cherry fruits, smells rich and juicy, there are dark spices too and the oak is neatly sliced in. Fine mid-earthy tannins wrap around a juicy core of dark fruit flavours, twisting through to a more savoury grip finish. Captures the richness of the region and makes a statement of elegance too. More please!

2003 Taltarni Cephas Shiraz Cabernet

Score 93

PYRENEES
Price $53.00
Quality ★★★★ɟ
Alc./Vol. 14%
Drink Now
Closure Screwcap

Essentially an estate-reserve red wine, released with time in bottle to soften and mellow. It shows plenty of rich ripe mixed berry fruits and soft earthy notes, gentle herbs and eucalypt. The palate is smooth and flowing, medium- to full-weight, balanced with some old school appeal. Charming.

2005 Taltarni Heathcote Shiraz

Score 91

HEATHCOTE
Price $42.00
Quality ★★★★
Alc./Vol. 14.5%
Drink 2012
Closure Screwcap

The nose shows attractive regional ripeness, the oak sits in all sweet and nutty, there are jubey red berries, and fresh primary characters. The palate has terrific supple texture and weight, deep dark berry flavours, quite ripe, finishing with smooth tannin glide.

2005 Taltarni T Series Shiraz

Score 90

VICTORIA
Price $15.00 ✓
Quality ★★★★
Alc./Vol. 14.5%
Drink 2011
Closure Screwcap

This blend of Pyrenees and Heathcote fruit is brimming with ripe blackberries and really bright attractive primary characters. The palate is fresh and lively too, riding on perky acidity, easygoing tannins and juicy fruit texture, a little regional mint and caramel oak through the finish.

2005 Tapestry The Vincent Shiraz
Score **91**

McLAREN VALE	
Price	$45.00
Quality	★★★★
Alc./Vol.	15%
Drink	2011
Closure	Cork

Tapestry sits in one of the best vantage points in the north of the Vale, looking out towards the Gulf from whence this wine's name originates. A striking nose of sarsaparilla, liquorice and ripe plums – super-rich palate, really ripe and dense, more plums and plum pudding flavours, raisins and toasty oak through the finish. Quite the blockbuster.

2006 Thomas Kiss Shiraz
Score **92**

HUNTER VALLEY	
Price	$50.00
Quality	★★★★
Alc./Vol.	14.3%
Drink	2012
Closure	Cork

This is one of the vanguards of the new Hunter school, unashamedly made in a modern style: deep colour, smelling very savoury ripe and dense, there's some musky oak and a twist of herbed meats. The palate starts out bright with plenty of dark fruit flavour, unfolding along ripe chewy tannins, finishing flavoursome and savoury.

2006 Thorn–Clarke Shotfire Shiraz
Score **90**

BAROSSA VALLEY	
Price	$20.00 ✓
Quality	★★★★
Alc./Vol.	14%
Drink	2009
Closure	Screwcap

Thorn-Clarke have this 20-buck shiraz pointed in the right direction; offering plenty of fruit and chunky toasty oak, it's built to please instantly. Abundant black fruits, the tannins are served in smooth sweet mouthfuls, finishing juicy and invigorating.

2005 Thorn–Clarke William Randell Shiraz
Score **93**

BAROSSA VALLEY	
Price	$50.00
Quality	★★★★ ↵
Alc./Vol.	15%
Drink	2013
Closure	Cork

The William Randell name is reserved for the very best of the Thorn-Clarke shiraz. It's an honest to goodness fruit and oak assembly in a traditional mould; ripe blackberry and plums, quite upbeat and expressive. The palate packs ripe mulberry and plum flavours, some gentle oak flavour, very ripe, very concentrated – finishes with a gentle tannin charge.

2004 3 Rings Reserve Shiraz
Score **93**

BAROSSA VALLEY	
Price	$65.00
Quality	★★★★ ↵
Alc./Vol.	16.5%
Drink	2012
Closure	Screwcap

Shiraz, dark and dense and lots of it. This is an extension of a highly successful export project and has unbridled opulent ripe fruit that manages to stay out of trouble. Must be some clever magic in the rings. Super-rich blackberry and spice, earthy, some grilled nuts and saddle leather; a wine to marvel at!

2006 **Torbreck Descendant** *Score* **94**

BAROSSA VALLEY

Price	$120.00
Quality	★★★★ ⌐
Alc./Vol.	14.5%
Drink	2015
Closure	Cork

There's a strong tarry stripe through the nose of this single-vineyard shiraz; distinct apricots, added spice and aromatics thanks to fermentation on viognier skins, plenty of ripe black fruits back it all in. Supple and elegant – the balance is striking, fine tannins carry plum and tar flavours long and true.

2005 **Torbreck Run Rig** *Score* **96**

BAROSSA VALLEY

Price	$240.00
Quality	★★★★★
Alc./Vol.	14.5%
Drink	2015
Closure	Cork

The finest release of this flagship to date, showing very ripe fruit aromas, raisins and fruitcake, plum pudding, earthy and rich, and the oak sits deep in the fruit. An opulent, hedonistic style, draped in black fruits and some tarry, oily richness. The palate is massive, more concentration than is comprehensible. You'll marvel as it fills the mouth with deep, dense plum and blackberry fruits, long and sweet through the middle, then toasty charry oak rolls through on smooth dense strapping tannins that carry long and even. Pause for breath, you'll need it!

2006 **Torbreck The Gask** *Score* **94**

EDEN VALLEY

Price	$80.00
Quality	★★★★ ⌐
Alc./Vol.	13.5%
Drink	2014
Closure	Cork

Sourced from a single grower, high up in the Eden Valley, this shows a precise side to shiraz that's distinctly different in shape from the rest of the Torbreck line-up. Dark spices and ripe black fruits, savoury fragrance. It runs a taut line across the palate on fine sturdy tannins, plenty of savoury dark fruit flavour and a convincing even-handed finish. Has the balance to improve with some age.

2006 **Torbreck The Struie** *Score* **96**

BAROSSA & EDEN VALLEYS

Price	$45.00 ✓
Quality	★★★★★
Alc./Vol.	14%
Drink	2014
Closure	Cork

This has impeccable spice and pepper, really lifted and impressive – the finest Struie since the outstanding '02. There's something haunting about the aromatics, the palate brings it all home to roost with dark berry flavour stretched across fine supple tannins, building through the finish, piercing and intense, all layered up in fine formation. Torbreck is in stunning form!

2006 Trevor Jones Boots Shiraz

Score **89**

BAROSSA VALLEY
Price $18.00 ✓
Quality   ★★★ ⸲
Alc./Vol.   14.5%
Drink   Now
Closure   Screwcap

A rockabilly boots-and-all offering from Trevor Jones with more superlatives on the back label than a bottle of Grange. It's a well-priced, fruit-forward shiraz showing ripe plum, berry, pepper and spice, light on tannins and long on drinkability.

2006 Trinity Hill Homage Syrah

Score **96**

HAWKES BAY, NZ
Price $120.00
Quality   ★★★★★
Alc./Vol.   14%
Drink   2012
Closure   Cork

The unchallenged king of the NZ syrah pile shows a superb richly fruited nose, really deep and open, inviting shiraz aromas of plums, berries and sweet fresh-ground spice – the small (3%) dose of viognier works a charm. Super-complex and multi-dimensional palate, smooth and flowing, dark minerals in abundance, textural and balanced, expands through the finish. A benchmark.

2006 Turkey Flat Shiraz

Score **93**

BAROSSA VALLEY
Price $45.00
Quality   ★★★★ ⸲
Alc./Vol.   14.5%
Drink   2016
Closure   Cork

The track record of this Barossa shiraz has been well and truly established; the '06 is a wine that's building steadily in bottle with real purpose. Savoury and tarry, it has a brooding palate with dried berry fruit and concentrated tannin build through the finish. Lip-smacking, savoury finish.

2006 Two Hands Bad Impersonator Shiraz

Score **91**

BAROSSA VALLEY
Price $45.00
Quality   ★★★★
Alc./Vol.   14.5%
Drink   2012
Closure   Screwcap

This juicy rich ball of Barossa shiraz fruit is a sweet ripe fruit bomb that packs some serious impact. Blackberry fruits and vanillin oak, some lifted red fragrant notes, super-expressive. The palate is sweetly fruited and leaves you wondering about nothing, other than what the original must be like.

2005 Tyrrell's Brokenback Shiraz

Score **90**

HUNTER VALLEY
Price $24.00
Quality   ★★★★
Alc./Vol.   13.7%
Drink   2012
Closure   Screwcap

This is a kind of modern classic. Made with delicate hands, it rests on the region's savoury shiraz style, layering toasty oak across bright ripe berry fruits. The palate dishes out some swanky oak flavour, dried plums and chewy tannins, finishing smoky and dry.

2006 Tyrrell's Rufus Stone Heathcote Shiraz
Score **91**

HEATHCOTE
Price $24.00 ✓
Quality ★★★★
Alc./Vol. 15.5%
Drink 2015
Closure Screwcap

Super-ripe nose, smells like boot polish and pencil shavings, sweet spices and some plum fruits, looks well made and quite tightly integrated. The palate has intense acid swathed in simple, fresh plum and berry fruit flavours. The alcohol runs a little warm, tannins trail fine and dense through the finish.

2006 Tyrrell's Vat 9 Shiraz
Score **91**

HUNTER VALLEY
Price $60.00
Quality ★★★★
Alc./Vol. 13%
Drink 2013
Closure Cork

This historic cuvée is looking quite muscular in '06. A slightly bigger more modern wine with some savoury density and weight, there's a lot of cedary French timber threaded in here, dried berries, slightly dusty. The palate's a classic medium-weight Hunter, led by savoury wind-blown tannins, black fruit finish.

2006 Villa Maria Cellar Selection Syrah
Score **91**

HAWKES BAY, NZ
Price $46.00
Quality ★★★★
Alc./Vol. 14%
Drink Now
Closure Screwcap

This riper Villa syrah trades on sweet, bright, lifted red fruit fragrance; really primary, really ripe with some musky oak overlay and smoked meats behind. Simple red fruit palate, very elegant and soft; it has an easy, well-made balance and soft tannin glide.

2006 Villa Maria Private Bin Syrah
Score **92**

HAWKES BAY, NZ
Price $31.00
Quality ★★★★
Alc./Vol. 13.5%
Drink 2010
Closure Screwcap

The quality on offer here is hard to beat for value in the NZ syrah stakes, sweet spice and complex toasty characters abound, there's a fine aniseed and pepper edge, plenty of bright, ripe berry aromas too. The palate has a core of sweet ripe purple berry flavour, oak adds sweet musky spices, nicely balanced and flows easily.

2006 The Wanderer Shiraz
Score **92**

YARRA VALLEY
Price $32.00
Quality ★★★★
Alc./Vol. 13.6%
Drink 2015
Closure Screwcap

Another super-fragrant Yarra shiraz, this has a keenly constructed nose of dark savoury fruits and plenty of oak – all well integrated. Attractive mocha and dark spice flavours, the palate has a svelte, savoury character and a fluid linear shape, leaves dried plum and dark choc flavours behind. Smooth finish.

2006 Water Wheel Bendigo Shiraz   *Score* 94

BENDIGO
Price $19.00 ✓
Quality ★★★★ ⅃
Alc./Vol. 15.5%
Drink 2011
Closure Screwcap

Fine berry fruit fragrance, cool and reserved, bright red and dark fruits and some gentle spices; very pristine and gently fragrant. Pleasurable texture and smooth tannins, red fruit flavours, some darker toasty notes, bright acidity and balance, dense and even. A mix of original plantings from the mid-'70s, and vines planted in the 1990s.

2006 Waurn Ponds Reserve Shiraz   *Score* 91

GEELONG
Price $30.00
Quality ★★★★
Alc./Vol. 15%
Drink 2010
Closure Cork

The commercial face of the winemaking course at Deakin University shows polished fragrance, nice spicy lift and dark meaty complexity, some cherry, cassis and chocolate oak, citrus, passionfruit and warm earthy smells. Plenty going on! The palate is smooth and supple, really svelte tannins and a fine, almost silty texture. Spicy plum finish.

2005 Whistler Shiraz   *Score* 92

BAROSSA VALLEY
Price $27.00 ✓
Quality ★★★★
Alc./Vol. 15%
Drink 2013
Closure Screwcap

Whistler's shiraz fruit comes from their vineyard in the Marananga district and has real power and intensity. It's still very youthful with ripe blackberry and spiced plum fruits, a lifted fragrance, nicely ripe and vivacious. Astounding flavour, superb richness and intensity, tannins thunder away below, holding the palate in fulsome yet balanced shape. Barossa shiraz at its finest!

2005 Wicks Estate Shiraz   *Score* 92

ADELAIDE HILLS
Price $19.00
Quality ★★★★
Alc./Vol. 14.5%
Drink 2012
Closure Screwcap

Super-fine fragrance, styled by its cool-climate origins: savoury and complex, some earthy notes and dark minerals, the oak twists nutty characters around ripe black fruit. Intense palate texture, smoky and spicy, long plush fruits and dense, ripe tannins.

2005 The Wilson Vineyard Shiraz   *Score* 90

CLARE VALLEY
Price $35.00
Quality ★★★★
Alc./Vol. 16%
Drink 2012
Closure Screwcap

From out in the Polish Hill River sub-district, where shiraz gets very ripe, this flips bright ripe berry fruits amid some brassy modern oak, fragrant spices too. Follows suit on the palate with mixed berry flavours and plenty of toasty oak, strong linear tannins run deep and warm. Big ripe style.

2006 Wirra Wirra RSW Shiraz

Score **94**

McLAREN VALE	
Price	$60.00
Quality	★★★★+
Alc./Vol.	14.5%
Drink	2012
Closure	Screwcap

This swanky top-shelf Wirra shiraz is an impressive international player; dressed in stylish toasty oak, the vivacious ripe fruit is a statement of the region's supple berry fruits and smooth tannin ride. A great ambassador for the irresistible charm of McLaren Vale shiraz.

2006 Wirra Wirra Woodhenge Shiraz

Score **90**

McLAREN VALE	
Price	$30.00
Quality	★★★★
Alc./Vol.	14.5%
Drink	Now
Closure	Screwcap

Making the very most of the late Greg Trott's persona, this wine takes its name from the oversized front fence he added to the winery entrance. Big and bold but still easygoing, there's deep berry and plum fruits, dark toasted spice, roasted meats and boot polish – all knitted up in fine juicy tannins. Plenty of oak! Enjoy this in its youth.

2004 Witchmount Shiraz

Score **91**

SUNBURY	
Price	$26.00
Quality	★★★★
Alc./Vol.	14.5%
Drink	2011
Closure	Screwcap

From a vineyard attached to a Sunbury restaurant and function venue not far from Melbourne, this shiraz is a complex savoury style with smoked meats and spicy berry fruits. The palate delivers juicy vibrant blackberry flavour, chocolate-like tannins and a brash, driving finish.

2006 Wolf Blass Grey Label Shiraz

Score **90**

McLAREN VALE	
Price	$40.00
Quality	★★★★
Alc./Vol.	15%
Drink	Now
Closure	Screwcap

This is right in the sweet spot of the Wolf Blass red wine range and takes the vivacious approach to McLaren Vale shiraz, keeping the wine really fresh and alive. It's smooth sailing from start to finish, tannins are easy and flavour falls in all directions.

2005 Wynns Michael Shiraz

Score **93**

COONAWARRA	
Price	$75.00
Quality	★★★★+
Alc./Vol.	14.5%
Drink	2012
Closure	Screwcap

This is a riper, softer smelling wine than the usual Coonawarra suspects; blue fruits, berries and some grilled-nut oak aromas – like the elegance. The palate holds bright berries and some lively middle-palate texture, it tastes as soft and charming as it smells, light pepper, chocolate and juicy, upbeat berries. Soft, easy tannins with enough structure to go the distance.

2006 Yering Station Reserve Shiraz Viognier   *Score* 94

YARRA VALLEY
Price $75.00
Quality ★★★★ ⌐
Alc./Vol. 14.5%
Drink 2016
Closure Screwcap

Made in Yering's established reserve style, some liquorice and sweet oak tend to dominate a little at this stage. Throws a seductive mix of ripe plum and chocolate, the palate is super-dense and ripe, really rich chocolate oak characters, sweet spices and dense fruit. Tannins are plush and even, terrific intensity and drive through the finish, show-stopping concentration.

2006 Yering Station Shiraz Viognier   *Score* 91

YARRA VALLEY
Price $24.00 ✓
Quality ★★★★
Alc./Vol. 14.5%
Drink 2011
Closure Screwcap

This shows cool restraint, dried plums and sweet spices, a little liquorice too, the oak sits savoury behind. Plenty of dark fruit and deep blackberry flavour; bright, fresh medium-weighted palate, with raspberry fruit flavour and light tannins, finishing fine and elegant.

2006 Yeringberg Shiraz   *Score* 92

YARRA VALLEY
Price $40.00
Quality ★★★★
Alc./Vol. 14.5%
Drink 2012
Closure Diam

This hillside Yarra stalwart carries a direct berry fruit core, and a clear viognier lift (2%) brings apricot kernel to the wine amid savoury nutty oak characters. Clear red berry fruit flavours placed through fine musky tannins, supported by juicy acid spring.

2007 Zonte's Footstep Shiraz Viognier   *Score* 89

LANGHORNE CREEK
Price $18.00
Quality ★★★ ⌐
Alc./Vol. 14.5%
Drink Now
Closure Screwcap

Viognier adds depth and complexity here; this has savoury spice and integrated meaty characters, bright berries and clear viognier fruits. The palate has soul and verve, purple and blue berries, some cassis, fine tannins and earthy rich appeal.

Shiraz cabernet blends

When cabernet makers looked around Australia several decades ago, seeking something to beef up the palate, shiraz was the natural partner. Similarly, a dose of cabernet to a fleshy shiraz adds structure and length. These two varieties have formed an all-Australian alliance and this blend – whichever way it is split – makes a balanced, flavoursome wine that has reliability and consistency as its hallmark. Spanning a range of price points with enduring success, you'll find terrific value and some of Australia's finest, most unique wines on offer today. FOOD: Like straight cabernet sauvignon, rich tannins make a strong case for richly flavoured meat dishes. Sweetness draws the tannins bitter so avoid sauces that tend this way, look instead for savoury demi-glace, and gentle spice will also work wonders.

2006 Bremerton Tamblyn Cabernet Shiraz Malbec Merlot   *Score* 90

LANGHORNE CREEK
Price $19.00 ✓
Quality   ★★★★
Alc./Vol. 14.5%
Drink   Now
Closure   Screwcap

A four-way split between cabernet, shiraz, malbec and merlot – more a regional red than anything else: ripe dark berries, cassis and minty wafts, oak is very understated. The palate's a rolling maul of berries, bundled up with gentle tannins, just a little chocolate through the finish.

2003 David Franz Alexander's Reward Cabernet Shiraz   *Score* 90

BAROSSA VALLEY
Price $36.00
Quality   ★★★★
Alc./Vol. 14.5%
Drink   2012
Closure   Cork

Plenty of toasty oak from the outset here and a tawny, mature character: vegemite, soy sauce, grilled nuts and cabernet's herbs and berries. The palate mixes mature flavours with some punchy tannins, more grilled nuts and sweet leathery richness, with a kick of Barossa tannin through the finish.

2006 Dutschke Willow Bend Shiraz Merlot Cabernet Sauvignon *Score* 93

BAROSSA VALLEY
Price $20.00 ✓
Quality   ★★★★ ⌐
Alc./Vol. 14.8%
Drink   2011
Closure   Screwcap

There's much to love about this throaty Barossa blend, smelling ripe and juicy, with blackberry, cassis and savoury oak chocolate. The palate delivers plenty of flavour too, ripe black fruits and a heart of deep, rich earthy tannin. Astonishing quality and value.

2006 Formby & Adams Cutting Edge Cabernet Shiraz — *Score* 90

LANGHORNE CREEK
Price $20.00
Quality ★★★★
Alc./Vol. 14.5%
Drink Now
Closure Screwcap

Cutting edge? More a classic Langhorne Creek rendition of the rockabilly Aussie cabernet-shiraz blend (85%/15%): earthy regional dark fruits, some fresh leaves and mint. Supple and smooth entry, dark fruit flavours, chocolate and earthy complexity, it lays up for the finish with fine savoury/tarry tannin.

2006 Fox Creek JSM Shiraz Cabernet Sauvignon Cabernet Franc *Score* 89

McLAREN VALE
Price $22.00
Quality ★★★ ⃕
Alc./Vol. 14.5%
Drink 2011
Closure Screwcap

The first impression of this deeply coloured shiraz, cabernet sauvignon, cabernet franc blend is nutty/savoury oak, sitting across liquorice and berry fruits. The palate is a direct juicy dose of plum fruit flavour, backed by fine dense tannins; young and brash.

2006 Glaetzer Anaperenna Shiraz Cabernet Sauvignon — *Score* 92

BAROSSA VALLEY
Price $55.00
Quality ★★★★
Alc./Vol. 14.5%
Drink 2012
Closure Cork

A swanky modern rendition of the shiraz-cabernet blend, showing ripe, sweet earthy Barossa berry fruits, some leathery/earthy complexity, liquorice and nutty oak toast. The palate has Glaetzer's trademark engineering: ripe fruits, chocolate and slow-flowing tannins, grazing thick and deep through the finish.

2005 Hamelin Bay Rampant Red — *Score* 90

MARGARET RIVER
Price $20.00
Quality ★★★★
Alc./Vol. 13.5%
Drink 2011
Closure Screwcap

Rampant it may be, but this blend works well to deliver a cooler accent of shiraz, cabernet and merlot, some spicy oak and wild leathery complexity. The oak adds sweet spice to the palate's dark berry fruits, there's some grippy tannin chew and it finishes with resolve.

2005 Hare's Chase Red Blend — *Score* 90

BAROSSA VALLEY
Price $15.00 ✓
Quality ★★★★
Alc./Vol. 14.5%
Drink 2009
Closure Screwcap

This brightly assembled bargain shows attractive primary fruit complexity; they've thrown shiraz, merlot, cabernet franc, cabernet sauvignon and tempranillo together and no one variety stands out. Starightforward, attractive red berry fruits and even tannins make for an approachable all-rounder.

271

2006 Henschke Keyneton Estate Euphonium

Score **93**

EDEN VALLEY
Price $46.00
Quality   ★★★★┧
Alc./Vol. 14.5%
Drink   2013
Closure   Screwcap

The 2006 vintage is shaping up very nicely in the Henschke red department; this is ripe with measure, clear berries, plums and some slightly resinous oak. The palate's bristling with lifted plum and berry flavours, some chocolate oak flavour leads a charge of sturdy ripe tannins through the finish. Brilliant medium-term cellaring.

2006 Hentley Farm Fool's Bay Beached Shiraz Cabernet

Score **90**

BAROSSA VALLEY
Price $14.00 ✓
Quality   ★★★★
Alc./Vol. 14.5%
Drink   2011
Closure   Screwcap

This toasty little blend snapped up gold at the Adelaide wine show with its direct black fruits and savoury oak toast. The savoury profile runs through the palate too, squaring off the fruit sweetness and accentuating the regional dusty tannin grip.

2005 Hollick Shiraz Cabernet

Score **91**

WRATTONBULLY/COONAWARRA
Price $21.00 ✓
Quality   ★★★★
Alc./Vol. 14%
Drink   Now
Closure   Screwcap

This blend of Wrattonbully and Coonawarra fruit, a well-crafted mid-week BBQ red, has some bright brambly berries and gentle oak influence. The palate is driven by a succinct core of fine tannins carrying ripe blackberry flavours, finishing with fragrant lift and concise balance.

2005 Lake Breeze Bernoota Shiraz Cabernet

Score **90**

LANGHORNE CREEK
Price $22.00 ✓
Quality   ★★★★
Alc./Vol. 14.5%
Drink   2012
Closure   Screwcap

This rockabilly Langhorne Creek blend is a regular fixture on the best-value lists. It has unmistakable berry, chocolate and mint characters – true to its region and grape varieties, some dark brooding oak too. There's dark olives and deep choc-berry flavour on the palate, curvy tannin shape and plenty of American oak through the finish. Loamy and rich.

 ## 2004 Mildara Coonawarra Cabernet Shiraz

Score **96**

COONAWARRA
Price $29.00 ✓
Quality   ★★★★★┧
Alc./Vol. 14.5%
Drink   2018
Closure   Screwcap

When this classic Australian blend works it *really* works. Deeply coloured, plenty of richness, bright berry fruit, and some cooler minted aromas pin it to the region. A wine of real intensity and resolve. Liquoricey cabernet cassis flavours, anise and briary plums, with a wall of fine tannin that will serve this wine well for many years. Dense, even and long.

PENGUIN BEST SHIRAZ CABERNET BLEND

2005 Mr Frog Cabernet Shiraz Merlot

Score **88**

YARRA VALLEY
Price $15.00
Quality ★ ★ ★ ⟩
Alc./Vol. 14.5%
Drink 2011
Closure Screwcap

Yering Station's discount label offers plenty of berries, aromas are just a little stifled by damp-smelling oak. The palate is simple and lightweight, it's made for quaffing not pondering, and tannins are fine boned right the way through to the soft, even finish.

2005 Penfolds Bin 389

Score **93**

SOUTH AUSTRALIA
Price $50.00
Quality ★ ★ ★ ★ ⟩
Alc./Vol. 14.5%
Drink 2015
Closure Screwcap

First thing to say about this is shop around, there's a huge variation in RRP in the Australian market. The wine is stamped with unmistakable American oak character, sweet deep berry fruits, ripe plums and vanillin. Looks, smells and tastes like Penfolds. As a youngster the oak sits a little thick on the palate, tannins are chunky and drying, but 389 is always best served with age and this '05 will cellar sweetly.

2006 Penfolds Koonunga Hill Shiraz Cabernet

Score **89**

SOUTH AUSTRALIA
Price $15.00 ✓
Quality ★ ★ ★ ⟩
Alc./Vol. 13.5%
Drink 2012
Closure Screwcap

This workhorse Penfolds blend is a successful each-way bet of bright fragrant berry fruits and some lifted fragrance. The palate is balanced and looks well constructed (a Penfolds specialty), plenty of sweet spicy oak and briary flavour, savoury tannins to close; even and balanced.

2007 Penfolds Rawson's Retreat

Score **87**

SOUTH EASTERN AUSTRALIA
Price $12.50
Quality ★ ★ ★ ⟩
Alc./Vol. 13.5%
Drink Now
Closure Screwcap

A youthful amalgam of raw ripe fruits, made to shine bright; plums, blackberries, blackcurrant, a little pepper and musky spice too. The palate's simply phrased with ripe plum and berry fruits framed in easygoing tannins.

2006 Penley Estate Condor Coonawarra Shiraz Cabernet

Score **90**

COONAWARRA
Price $19.00 ✓
Quality ★ ★ ★ ★
Alc./Vol. 15%
Drink 2011
Closure Screwcap

Smells of raw wood and has some dense rich fruits, tannins are a little high-strung, smoky to close. It has some weight and density – ripe fruit but the oak has too much mocha finish.

2007 Plain Jane Cabernet Shiraz
Score **89**

MARGARET RIVER/SWAN VALLEY
Price $15.00
Quality ★★★ ꜀
Alc./Vol. 13.8%
Drink Now
Closure Screwcap

A bright, youthful blended red with milk chocolate, musk, some roasting herbs and bright sweet berry fruit aromas from Jane Brook Estate Wines. Peppery fruit flavours, more berries and gentle liquorice, soft open-knit tannins and an easy glide through the finish.

2005 Tapanappa Cabernet Shiraz
Score **94**

WRATTONBULLY
Price $78.00
Quality ★★★★ ꜀
Alc./Vol. 13.5%
Drink 2017
Closure Cork

This Franco-Australian partnership (led by none other than Brian Croser) brings together a polished technique and innate fruit potential. Oak is applied with Bordeaux-like charm, across cassis and dark cherry fruits, mint and chocolate. Handsomely integrated, its well-crafted tannins fan out evenly across the palate, delivering plenty of berry flavour; elegant and defined.

2006 Tatachilla Partners Cabernet Shiraz
Score **89**

LANGHORNE CREEK/
McLAREN VALE/KING VALLEY
Price $11.00 ✓
Quality ★★★ ꜀
Alc./Vol. 14.5%
Drink Now
Closure Screwcap

Drawing on Langhorne Creek, McLaren Vale and the King Valley grapes, this is a straight-up bright berry style, well made and certainly over-delivering for the price. The palate, built on fine tannins, has an even-handed, smooth shape, more berry and cherry flavour here, soft and easy.

2006 Te-aro Estate Shiraz Cabernet
Score **91**

BAROSSA VALLEY
Price $18.00 ✓
Quality ★★★★
Alc./Vol. 15.5%
Drink 2011
Closure Screwcap

This plays in a swashbuckling style: hearty ripe Barossa fruit bursts from the glass, blackberry and some earthy, brambly cabernet aromas. Dense, chewy and ripe, plenty of richness and a handy balance between the varieties, plenty of density and a warm deep choc-berry finish.

2006 Thorn-Clarke Sandpiper The Blend
Score **89**

BAROSSA VALLEY
Price $15.00 ✓
Quality ★★★ ꜀
Alc./Vol. 15%
Drink Now
Closure Screwcap

There's plenty of ripeness in this complex blend: roughly half shiraz, the rest is shared between petit verdot and cabernet sauvignon. Blackberry fruit aromas, some earthy/savoury notes below and subdued oak. Juicy blackberry flavours and fine easy tannins, toasty oak to close; this is a smooth complete red.

2004 Tyrrell's Vat 8 Shiraz Cabernet

Score **92**

HUNTER VALLEY/MUDGEE	
Price	$45.00
Quality	★★★★
Alc./Vol.	13.5%
Drink	Now
Closure	Cork

Predominantly Hunter shiraz with a small percentage (13%) of Mudgee cabernet, this is an old-school beauty. Plenty of bright cherry fruits and dried raspberry aromas, some old woody complexity and fine savoury, berry-flavoured tannins. Balanced and even, it's more about elegance than impact.

2006 Water Wheel Memsie

Score **92**

BENDIGO	
Price	$12.00 ✓
Quality	★★★★
Alc./Vol.	14.5%
Drink	Now
Closure	Screwcap

A balanced, highly drinkable estate blend of mostly shiraz with a splash each of cabernet sauvignon and malbec – one of *the* great bargains going. Plenty of attractive oak, plums, pepper, spice and berries, lots to hold your interest. Soft tannins, really supple and balanced with a strong thread of regional Central Victorian style.

2006 Wirra Wirra Church Block

Score **89**

McLAREN VALE	
Price	$20.00 ✓
Quality	★★★ ┧
Alc./Vol.	14.5%
Drink	Now
Closure	Screwcap

The bread-and-butter red of the Wirra stable, Church Block weighs in with structure and oak, savoury cabernet drives the style with earthy berries, herbs, leaves, cassis and mint. The palate is softly fruited and runs a gently sweet line of berry flavour, some plums in there too, simple and easy.

2007 Wirra Wirra Scrubby Rise Shiraz Cabernet Petit Verdot

Score **88**

FLEURIEU PENINSULA/	
ADELAIDE HILLS	
Price	$15.00
Quality	★★★ ┧
Alc./Vol.	14.5%
Drink	Now
Closure	Screwcap

Wirra delivers this reliably each year with bright ripe berry fruits and plenty to draw you in, attractive, straightforward and with a bit of fragrant lift. The palate's bursting with ripe plum and berry fruits, soft tannins and a clean exit.

2006 Wynns Coonawarra Estate Cabernet Shiraz Merlot

Score **91**

COONAWARRA	
Price	$18.00 ✓
Quality	★★★★
Alc./Vol.	14%
Drink	2010
Closure	Screwcap

There's a line of fine Wynns red blends made over many decades; this is painted in regional tones, showing ripe cassis fruits, red berries and background mint. Still very young, the palate delivers direct primary fruits, charming supple tannins and a stripe of toasty oak through the finish. Will reward medium-term cellaring.

Cabernet sauvignon

Although it's been squeezed into the shadows of shiraz's unbridled success in the last ten years, cabernet sauvignon is on the comeback trail, making one very convincing case for greatness. There's been a flurry of effort and meticulous attention to detail in cabernet vineyards to get things tuned up perfectly; winemakers are working around the clock and the results are flooding in – a wealth of great cabernet around the $30 price-point, some of the best-value reds in the country. And if you're into cellaring, remember that great cabernet matures gracefully, providing years of enjoyment. FOOD: The best Australian cabernets, such as those from Coonawarra and Margaret River, possess deep blackcurrant fruit, mint, liquorice, herbs, spice and an elegant tannin structure. Rich meat dishes suit this kind of wine, and, as with shiraz, stay away from sweet foods that can react with cabernet's assertive tannin, creating bitter flavours.

2006 **Balnaves Cabernet Sauvignon**　　　　　　　*Score* **94**

COONAWARRA	Showing some greener edges, light methoxy and mint aromas, this builds cassis and berries with air, some herbs and purple florals here too. The palate looks intensely balled up and young, quite savoury, always the last of the Balnaves cabernets to unfurl. Tannins are dense and chewy; definitely decant.
Price $35.00 ✓	
Quality ★★★★⅃	
Alc./Vol. 15%	
Drink 2011	
Closure Procork	

2006 **Balnaves The Tally Reserve Cabernet Sauvignon**　　*Score* **96**

COONAWARRA	This makes a hat-trick of outstanding consecutive releases: The Tally has really asserted its position at the top tier of Coonawarra cabernets. Cloaked in plenty of new French oak, it's a cedary, regal cabernet, the blackcurrant and dark berry fruit soaks the wood up fast. Terrific density and palate structure, deep and intense, it rolls smoothly from start to finish. Swanky, youthful cabernet at its finest.
Price $95.00	
Quality ★★★★★	
Alc./Vol. 15%	
Drink 2016	
Closure Procork	

PENGUIN BEST CABERNET SAUVIGNON

2005 Big R Cabernet Sauvignon

Score **93**

BAROSSA VALLEY
Price $35.00 ✓
Quality ★★★★ ⌐
Alc./Vol. 15.7%
Drink 2015
Closure Screwcap

Chris Ringland's stamp of rustic ripe sturdy fruit, dark oily aromas and some oak punch is unmistakably Australian, unmistakably Barossa, unmistakably cabernet and unmistakably Ringland. Big, sweet, juicy cabernet fruits and a nutty twist through the finish, tannins are plush and soft; this is complex, hedonistic wine, beautifully executed and finishing with a flurry of toasty oak.

2005 Binbilla Special Steps Cabernet Sauvignon

Score **92**

HILLTOPS
Price $26.00 ✓
Quality ★★★★
Alc./Vol. 13.8%
Drink 2011
Closure Screwcap

This newcomer weighs in with attractive cassis and blackcurrant cabernet fragrance, it smells ripe yet reserved and has a briary herb and leaf aroma; really varietal, a slightly stony/gravelly edge too. The palate is juicy, intense and eminently balanced, treads a steady line of sturdy tannins, all ripened up nicely, finishing smooth and dry. Terrific cool cabernet.

2006 Bowen Estate Cabernet Sauvignon

Score **94**

COONAWARRA
Price $30.00 ✓
Quality ★★★★ ⌐
Alc./Vol. 14.5%
Drink 2012
Closure Cork

The best Bowen cabernet for some time, sporting a bright set of ripe berry and musky oak aromas, wet concrete; well crafted in a modern concentrated style. Geez it looks the part. Love the palate's freshness and tannin draw, pulling rich deep berry flavour and great balance – finesse and elegance with power. Superb.

2004 Cape Mentelle Cabernet Sauvignon

Score **96**

MARGARET RIVER
Price $80.00
Quality ★★★★★
Alc./Vol. 14.5%
Drink 2012
Closure Screwcap

This has some real depth and richness: deep brooding aromas, almost oily liquorice smells, plenty of rich brambly berry fruits, roasting herbs and nutty oak. The palate is carpeted with thick smooth tannins, fine and ripe, dense and even. Rich dark berry flavours marry through the finish with sweet cedary oak, smoothly honed and assertive.

PENGUIN BEST CABERNET SAUVIGNON

2005 Capel Vale Regional Series Cabernet Sauvignon

Score **93**

MARGARET RIVER
Price $23.00 ✓
Quality ★★★★ ⌐
Alc./Vol. 14.5%
Drink 2015
Closure Screwcap

This really looks the part: settled and integrated, a measured cabernet with ripe cassis fruits, plenty of cedary oak and bright sweet spices, framed in dried leaf smells. Soft tannins swing nice and deep through the palate, mixed dark berry flavours – balanced, youthful and impressively elegant.

2006 Chapel Hill Cabernet Sauvignon

Score 92

McLAREN VALE
Price $30.00
Quality ★★★★
Alc./Vol. 14.5%
Drink 2012
Closure Screwcap

Faint herbs, mint and cassis cabernet aromas join with meaty winemaking complexity and cedary oak. The palate has some real depth and rolls out fine tannins, richly concentrated purple fruit flavours, terrific depth and slow-burning chocolate plum finish.

2005 Clairault Cabernet Sauvignon

Score 93

MARGARET RIVER
Price $44.00
Quality ★★★★ ⌐
Alc./Vol. 15%
Drink 2011
Closure Screwcap

Another suave, effortlessly balanced cabernet from the northern end of Margaret River, showing some green herbs and leaves, ripe berries and chocolate. On the palate it stretches across finely sprung acidity, tightly coiled and balanced, with more leaf and herb amid cassis fruit flavour, fine tannins. Powerful and compact.

2005 Coldstream Hills Reserve Cabernet Sauvignon

Score 93

YARRA VALLEY
Price $50.00
Quality ★★★★ ⌐
Alc./Vol. 14%
Drink 2013
Closure Screwcap

With pinot and chardonnay where they want it, the team at Coldstream Hills has turned their efforts towards the more challenging task of promoting cabernet. This should be an easy sell with its bright cassis aromas, some mint and herbs, distinctly floral cabernet with cedary oak influence. The palate sits balanced and plush, plenty of ripe berry flavour, lively acidity, fine tannins and some toasty oak through the finish.

1998 David Franz Georgie's Walk Cabernet Sauvignon

Score 94

BAROSSA VALLEY
Price $120.00
Quality ★★★★ ⌐
Alc./Vol. 14.6%
Drink Now
Closure Cork

Showing plenty of mature bottle-developed characters, some dark demi glace and roasted meats, earthy dried berries; it freshens with air to reveal more dried fruits and liquorice. Rich, ripe supple fruits and some dense middle-palate sweetness, reflecting the ripeness and juicy fruit that '98 delivered. Not a blockbuster, balanced and balled up nicely in fine ripe tannins, a swathe of oak toast, all balanced and kindly cellared on your behalf by the maker. Well worth the considerable spend.

2006 De Bortoli Estate Grown Cabernet Sauvignon   *Score* **92**

YARRA VALLEY
Price $36.00
Quality   ★★★★
Alc./Vol. 14%
Drink   2012
Closure   Screwcap

A solid performance from 2006, showing bright blueberry and brambly black fruits, some cassis and earthy aromas with nutty savoury oak wedged in. It lifts gracefully across the palate: fine tannins backed by plenty of toasty oak, acidity strings it tight. Certainly at the cooler, edgier end of the regional spectrum.

2006 Evil Cabernet Sauvignon   *Score* **89**

SOUTH EASTERN AUSTRALIA
Price $12.00 ✓
Quality   ★★★ ┤
Alc./Vol. 15%
Drink   2010
Closure   Screwcap

This hearty knockabout cabernet smells of ripe cassis, aniseed and brambly dark berry fruits – not too evil at all. There's incredible ripeness on the palate, smoothed out by rich fruit and some beefy alcohol, it delivers a sweeping fan of silky tannin where cabernet would usually dig its heels in. Plenty of wine for 12 bucks!

2005 Grant Burge Shadrach Cabernet Sauvignon   *Score* **94**

EDEN VALLEY
Price $55.00
Quality   ★★★★ ┤
Alc./Vol. 15%
Drink   2018
Closure   Cork

A dense and juicy Barossa Valley cabernet that hails from the Corryton Park property up in Eden Valley. Plenty of strapping dark fruits and deep-seated intensity, some spicy oak weighs in and there's a hint of green mint and herb – a true cabernet! Long and resounding finish, delicious now, even better in a few years.

2005 Hamelin Bay Five Ashes Vineyard Cabernet Sauvignon   *Score* **93**

MARGARET RIVER
Price $29.00 ✓
Quality   ★★★★ ┤
Alc./Vol. 13.5%
Drink   2012
Closure   Screwcap

The Five Ashes vineyard is down at Karridale in the cool southerly end of the region. This has peppery aromas, fine dark berry fruits, gentle herbal complexity and gravelly notes too. The palate is handsomely integrated and really settled into stride, the tannins sweep through in fine layers; an elegant medium-weight wine that finishes with balanced grace.

2005 Hastwell & Lightfoot Cabernet Sauvignon   *Score* **89**

McLAREN VALE
Price $22.00
Quality   ★★★ ┤
Alc./Vol. 14%
Drink   2014
Closure   Screwcap

Makes an impact with brassy oak characters, some mocha and ripe dark berry fruits, a little nut skin – a very punchy fruit-plus-oak style. The palate packs impressive density and intense berry flavour, deep drying tannins, very ripe.

2005 Hay Shed Hill Cabernet Sauvignon *Score* **94**

MARGARET RIVER
Price $23.00 ✓
Quality ★★★★ᐧ
Alc./Vol. 14%
Drink 2012
Closure Screwcap

This is terrific cabernet: fine bright fragrant fruits married with musky wood, floral red berries and light spices, some gravelly regional notes below. Tannins are thick and chewy, runs on a spine of fine tannin and bright acidity, giving classic, elegant cabernet shape. Plenty of oak and a big tannin kick through the finish; savoury cassis aftertaste.

2005 Henschke Cyril Cabernet Sauvignon *Score* **96**

EDEN VALLEY 🖋
Price $110.00
Quality ★★★★★
Alc./Vol. 15%
Drink 2020
Closure Screwcap

This is the least evolved of the top-flight 2005 Henschke reds released this year; super young, raw and appealing, with ripe red and black fruits, the oak sits glazed across the top. The palate is thick and sturdy, although superbly balanced, and the depth and weight makes a fine case for ageing. Fine musky tannins and some bright floral flavours ahead of intense dark berry fruits and gently toasty oak building through the finish. Whilst there's Eden Valley finesse and precision built in the vineyard, it's a wine that will make some fine transitions in the cellar.

2004 Juniper Estate Cabernet Sauvignon *Score* **94**

MARGARET RIVER
Price $36.00 ✓
Quality ★★★★ᐧ
Alc./Vol. 14%
Drink 2012
Closure Screwcap

A complex, deeply spiced and measured cabernet that has some resolve and class about it; leafy/savoury cassis fruits, regal cedary oak and some gravelly notes below. Fine supple tannins, a bright and even palate, it drives through the finish with slick tannin shape, ending with poise.

2005 Kirrihill Tulach Mor Cabernet Sauvignon *Score* **92**

CLARE VALLEY
Price $20.00 ✓
Quality ★★★★
Alc./Vol. 14%
Drink 2014
Closure Screwcap

Kirrihill has harnessed the Clare Valley's affinity for making cabernet sauvignon, sourcing a select parcel of grapes from an elevated vineyard (450 metres) for this single-site release. With brambly dark-berry fruits, some florals, cedary French timber and regional gum leaf, the palate is balanced but forthright, delivering plenty of ripe black-fruit flavour and juicy texture. A textbook Clare Valley cabernet.

2006 Little r Cabernet Sauvignon
Score **91**

SOUTH AUSTRALIA
Price $15.00 ✓
Quality ★★★★
Alc./Vol. 14%
Drink 2013
Closure Screwcap

This shows ripe, juicy aromas but also some reserved characters; a little leaf and mint, some oak char and attractive sweet cassis, certainly ticks all the cabernet boxes. Same story on the palate, measured and resolved with taut compact fruit, toned-back powdery tannins, blackcurrant and plum flavour.

2005 Mac Forbes 'Hugh' Cabernet Sauvignon
Score **92**

YARRA VALLEY
Price $40.00
Quality ★★★★
Alc./Vol. 12.5%
Drink 2014
Closure Screwcap

This has Mac Forbes' trademark brassy nose with plenty of meaty barrel-ferment characters, berries and leaves sit cool below, some spice and vanillin. Still very youthful. Crisp crunchy palate with terrific depth, chocolate and sweet berry fruits, sheets of fine savoury tannin glide through the finish – a terrific young cabernet.

2006 Mac Forbes 'Hugh' Cabernet Sauvignon
Score **94**

YARRA VALLEY
Price $40.00 ✓
Quality ★★★★ ┤
Alc./Vol. 12.5%
Drink 2014
Closure Screwcap

This has some downright Euro style and elegance, pencil shavings and cedary, attractive florals, purple berries and lifted complex fragrance. The palate is measured, balanced and driven by fine tannin. Sporting length and fresh acid life, it finishes compact. Brilliant!

2006 Mildara Cabernet Sauvignon
Score **91**

COONAWARRA
Price $28.00
Quality ★★★★
Alc./Vol. 15%
Drink 2011
Closure Screwcap

The oak sits forward a little here and tends to accentuate the mint and green-herb aromas, pushing the berry fruits to one side. It's a wine with strongly regional Coonawarra character; the oak's just a little dominant. The palate is taut and tightly strung, flavoursome but not especially weighty and framed up in neat tannin. Needs time.

2006 Moss Wood Amy's Cabernet Sauvignon
Score **91**

MARGARET RIVER
Price $32.00 ✓
Quality ★★★★
Alc./Vol. 13.5%
Drink Now
Closure Screwcap

A good result for the extremely cool 2006 vintage, albeit a little lighter on, showing attractive toasty oak and brambly berry fruit, a little earth and handy freshness. The palate continues along the theme of elegance, delivering a lighter than usual, approachable luncheon claret.

2005 Oakridge Cabernet Sauvignon
Score 93

YARRA VALLEY
Price $32.00
Quality ★★★★⟩
Alc./Vol. 14.5%
Drink 2012
Closure Screwcap

Fine cool-region cabernet aromas on show, not at all green: measured, savoury cassis fruit aromas and dried leaves, autumnal, the oak sits nicely in beside. Plenty of savoury berry fruits and liquorice here, really pure and concentrated cassis flavours, ripe fine tannins, all balanced up neatly, chocolate flavoured finish. A regal cabernet.

2005 Parker Coonawarra Estate Terra Rossa Cabernet Sauvignon
Score 93

COONAWARRA
Price $40.00
Quality ★★★★⟩
Alc./Vol. 15%
Drink 2015
Closure Screwcap

This shows the ripeness of the '05 Coonawarra vintage and some attractive swanky oak. Mixed berries and a little sweet-spice lift, smells creamy and soft. The palate is built around ripe tannins, aniseed and some chocolate, just the faintest hint of herbs, smoothly textured and ripe with elegance.

2005 Parker Coonawarra Estate Terra Rossa First Growth
Score 94

COONAWARRA
Price $110.00
Quality ★★★★⟩
Alc./Vol. 15%
Drink 2012
Closure Screwcap

This reserve bottling certainly shows ripeness and depth, some intense fruit, black olives and boot polish, warm berry fruits with assertive charry oak sweetening the fruit aromas. The palate is an action-packed assembly of rich fruit and punchy oak, which are starting to integrate; settling into savoury cassis flavour, it reveals its hand with balanced resolve through the finish.

2005 Penfolds Bin 407 Cabernet Sauvignon
Score 92

SOUTH AUSTRALIA
Price $45.00
Quality ★★★★
Alc./Vol. 14.5%
Drink 2013
Closure Screwcap

In a line-up, this shows as a more swanky style. Toasty oak and hazelnuts lead, mocha and chocolate, some berries too; it's savoury, complex and smart. The palate's all supple tannins, plush berry fruits and even-paced weight, garnished with toasty oak and finishing with soft berry flavour. The benefit of cross-regional blending is on full show.

2005 Penfolds Bin 707 Cabernet Sauvignon
Score 94

MULTI-REGIONAL
Price $175.00
Quality ★★★★⟩
Alc./Vol. 14.5%
Drink 2017
Closure Cork

A convincing top-flight cabernet in this 2005 vintage, showing trademark Penfolds forthright oak impact. Plenty of ripe dark berries, cassis, mint, dried roasting herbs and gentle oak spice. The palate's seamlessly structured, ripe and juicy; plenty of oak char registers here too, the vanillin runs through dark berries, with a smooth svelte trail of tannin. Impressive.

2006 **Penley Estate Phoenix Cabernet Sauvignon**   *Score* **93**

COONAWARRA
Price $19.00 ✓
Quality   ★★★★ ┤
Alc./Vol. 15%
Drink   2016
Closure   Screwcap

Kym Tolley consistently makes a great wine under this Phoenix label. Rich cabernet aromas, regal and defined, have the full array of berries, leaves and mint, with fragrant French oak lifting the purple florals. The palate delivers a core of ripe berry flavour with fine leafy edges; the oak adds some frame and the tannins are soft and fine. Punches well above its weight.

PENGUIN BEST-VALUE RED WINE

2004 **Peter Douglas Chime Hoop Cabernet Sauvignon**   *Score* **92**

COONAWARRA
Price $25.00
Quality   ★★★★
Alc./Vol. 14.2%
Drink   2011
Closure   Screwcap

A man with considerable form in Coonawarra has hung his own shingle out in impressive form. Fine cabernet leaf and mint, gentle restrained red fruits and mixed berries, fresh and understated, vibrant and clear. Medium-weight palate with plenty of cassis fruit and a solid core of dark berry flavour, fine supple tannins, balanced and elegant. Fondly honours the outer-most metal hoop on barrels.

2005 **The Poplars Reserve Cabernet Sauvignon**   *Score* **93**

COONAWARRA
Price $30.00 ✓
Quality   ★★★★ ┤
Alc./Vol. 14.5%
Drink   2010
Closure   Cork

Looks as if 2005 brought some nice ripe fruit to the gate at Poplars Winery in Coonawarra. This reserve bottling has vibrant cassis and berry fruit, fine savoury oak sitting quietly behind, leaves and mint too. The palate's super smooth and elegant, truly medium-weighted; more ripe berries here, tannins sit even, building savoury through the finish. Elegant and approachable.

2006 **Punch Cabernet Sauvignon**   *Score* **91**

YARRA VALLEY
Price $44.00
Quality   ★★★★
Alc./Vol. 13%
Drink   2014
Closure   Screwcap

The Lance family's cabernet has a healthy dose of oak swathed across cranberry fruit, very toasty with mocha cafe smells and dried red berries. The palate is a savoury affair, very meaty and charry, fruit tannins are tightened up by the wood. There's plenty on offer – it just needs time to integrate.

2005 Punt Road Cabernet Sauvignon   Score 92

YARRA VALLEY
Price $25.00 ✓
Quality   ★★★★
Alc./Vol.   14%
Drink   2014
Closure   Screwcap

Cloaked in the complete ripeness of the vintage, this '05 Punt Road blend smells of sweet-berry compote, bright leaf and herb cabernet aromas, some dusty earth too. Charming supple tannins, black fruits and chocolate, aniseed and a savoury twist of meaty tannin; this has plenty to offer.

2004 Redman Cabernet Sauvignon   Score 91

COONAWARRA
Price $30.00
Quality   ★★★★
Alc./Vol.   13.5%
Drink   2012
Closure   Cork

Break out the tongs and the thongs for this deeply ripe cabernet. Dark fruits and berry cola aromas, fruit and oak are nicely matched up, with dark olives and roasting herbs, liquorice too. The palate packs some rock-solid weight, black tea leaf flavours, deep berry and liquorice, and a formidable, chewy tannin finish.

2005 Rymill Cabernet Sauvignon   Score 92

COONAWARRA
Price $30.00
Quality   ★★★★
Alc./Vol.   13.5%
Drink   2012
Closure   Diam

Rymill's cabernet is always in the elegant, medium-bodied part of the field. This edition shows attractive plum, blackberry and cassis fruits, a touch of mint and fragrant musky oak. The palate is strung on fine tannins that carry cassis-flavoured fruit, finishing fine and dusty.

2005 Sandalford Cabernet Sauvignon   Score 93

MARGARET RIVER
Price $34.00
Quality   ★★★★⁺
Alc./Vol.   14.5%
Drink   2014
Closure   Screwcap

This shows distinct regional leaf and herbs, bright cassis and blackberry fruit, with some wet concrete and subtle savoury gravel, the oak sits in tight. Precise cassis fruit flavour, tannins are assertive and grainy. A sturdy wine with savoury resolve that should develop nicely.

2005 Sandalford Prendiville Reserve Cabernet Sauvignon   Score 94

MARGARET RIVER
Price $89.00
Quality   ★★★★⁺
Alc./Vol.   14.5%
Drink   2013
Closure   Screwcap

The flagship Sandalford cabernet shows bay leaf and roasting herbs, plenty of bright new oak across cool-fruit aromas, cassis, bramble and a touch of mint. The oak drives through the palate forming a stripe of berry cola flavour, ripe tannins sit soft and fine, finishing savoury and serious. Still on the ascent.

2006 Stonehaven Father Woods Cabernet Sauvignon   *Score* **96**

COONAWARRA
Price $55.00 ✓
Quality   ★★★★★
Alc./Vol.   12.6%
Drink   2016
Closure   Screwcap

A newie from the Stonehaven stable and a brilliant addition to the range. It's dripping with intensely bright cabernet aromas, cassis and dark-berry fruits, wet concrete, graphite and high-class savoury oak. The palate shows forthright youthful power, rich thick tannins and plenty of draw through the finish. Brilliant.

2005 Suckfizzle Cabernet Sauvignon   *Score* **94**

MARGARET RIVER
Price $50.00
Quality   ★★★★ ⌐
Alc./Vol.   14%
Drink   2014
Closure   Screwcap

This striking wine hails from the deep south of Margaret River, wearing plenty of ripe roasting herbs, brambly fruits and gravelly complexity, the oak dips in as the wine breathes some air. Bright berry fruits and a spine, this is a class act and will reward some time in the cellar. Assertive and precise.

2005 Vasse Felix Cabernet Sauvignon   *Score* **94**

MARGARET RIVER
Price $35.00 ✓
Quality   ★★★★ ⌐
Alc./Vol.   14.5%
Drink   2015
Closure   Cork

A classic Vasse cabernet. Deep purple colour and a full array of aromas: herbs, bay leaf and spices, assertive cedary oak, ripe purple fruits and regional wet gravelly earth. Sweeping waves of sweet fruit-soaked tannins and concentrated rich ripe berry flavours; this impresses with its density and sturdy structural frame, all lined up in the right direction.

2005 Vasse Felix Heytesbury Cabernet Sauvignon   *Score* **95**

MARGARET RIVER
Price $75.00
Quality   ★★★★ ⌐
Alc./Vol.   14.5%
Drink   2015
Closure   Cork

Here's some real power and ripeness, classic Vasse style: deep cassis and cedary oak characters, sweet spices, it's bursting with verve and ripeness. The cassis-flavoured palate is swathed in juicy tannins that wrap around the finish in impressive formation. Regal, powerful cabernet.

2005 Watershed Awakening Cabernet Sauvignon   *Score* **90**

MARGARET RIVER
Price $50.00
Quality   ★★★★
Alc./Vol.   13.5%
Drink   2011
Closure   Cork

This bright medium-bodied cabernet shows some leafy regional characters, coolly restrained cassis aromas and a decent wedge of toasty oak. The palate is smoothly fruited and cloaked in sweet vanillin oak, fine tannins run below. Give it a couple of years to fully integrate.

2005 Woodside Baudin Cabernet Sauvignon

Score **94**

MARGARET RIVER
Price $56.00
Quality ★★★★ ⅃
Alc./Vol. 14%
Drink 2014
Closure Diam

From the northern end of Margaret River, leafy aromas and assertive oak run ahead of ripe brambly blackcurrant fruits and earthy root vegetable notes, some gentle spice there too. The palate is compact and finely phrased offering up attractive dark fruit flavours, some mocha oak toast and fine ripe tannins – an overall impression of innate balance and elegance.

2005 Wyndham Estate Bin 444 Cabernet Sauvignon

Score **87**

SOUTH EASTERN AUSTRALIA 🍃 This old-school classic is one of the softest, most
Price $15.00
Quality ★★★ ⅃
Alc./Vol. 14%
Drink Now
Closure Screwcap

approachable cabernets going. Some varietal leafy aromas, cassis and brambly edges. The palate is impossibly soft, attractive blackcurrant flavour, just sweet through the finish. They've worked hard on this.

2006 Wynns Cabernet Sauvignon

Score **93**

COONAWARRA
Price $32.00 ✓
Quality ★★★★ ⅃
Alc./Vol. 14%
Drink 2011
Closure Screwcap

Looks very confident and polished: bright sweetly spiced modern oak sits across ripe berry fruits, elegant and regal, some regional mint at the edges. Fine tannins and plenty of richness on the palate, the vanillin kicks into gear, really taut and elegant, finishing chewy and convincing.

2005 Wynns John Riddoch Cabernet Sauvignon

Score **94**

COONAWARRA
Price $75.00
Quality ★★★★ ⅃
Alc./Vol. 14%
Drink 2013
Closure Screwcap

This Riddoch is in terrific form, showing what seems to be an emerging house-style, swanky oak approach. Assertive purple floral aromas run across pristine ripe berry fruits; plenty of richness and ripeness on the palate, dark deep tannins quench the fruit sweetness, it slides through to the finish with balance and finesse. Still very young.

2005 Wynns Messenger Cabernet Sauvignon

Score **93**

COONAWARRA
Price $39.00 ✓
Quality ★★★★ ⅃
Alc./Vol. 13.5%
Drink 2012
Closure Screwcap

From 20-year-old vines at the southern end of the cigar, this is the first time it's been bottled as a single release. Custard spices and sweet oak overlay across juicy elegant berries; cedary, regal and médoc-like. The palate holds deceptive power, really fine, elegant and linear, terrific shape, fine dense tannins that carry long and deep, crisp acidity and a musky upbeat finish.

2005 Xanadu Cabernet Sauvignon

Score **91**

MARGARET RIVER

Price $25.00
Quality ★★★★
Alc./Vol. 14%
Drink 2012
Closure Screwcap

This is showing terrific lift and nerve for an '05, which tend to be richer and more opulent in Margaret River. Very primary berry fruits, some fragrant musky oak, nutty nuances, herbs and a waft of dry brick dust. Tannins are chewy and still untamed, flavours sit in the berry fruit spectrum, plenty of oak here too; needs to settle.

2006 Yering Station Cabernet Sauvignon

Score **91**

YARRA VALLEY

Price $24.00 ✓
Quality ★★★★
Alc./Vol. 14.5%
Drink 2012
Closure Screwcap

Neat, fine and brambly fruits that speak in regional voice; cassis, some red liquorice and some cooler, more reserved red fruits, cedary oak too. Elegant, but there's complete ripeness here: juicy fruit presence, lightly strung tannins and a fresh, lively finish. Medium-bodied and harmonious.

2005 Zema Estate Cabernet Sauvignon

Score **91**

COONAWARRA

Price $25.00 ✓
Quality ★★★★
Alc./Vol. 14.5%
Drink 2012
Closure Cork

A brightening of sorts at Zema with a more intense dose of oak, some sweet baking spices and fine ripe fragrant fruits, cassis and rich berries. The palate is medium-weight and soft, oak spice complements dark berry flavours, tannins are fine for the most part, running a little wild through the finish.

Cabernet merlot blends

Although cabernet sauvignon is one of the finest of all grape varieties, making wines of noble structure and great ageing potential, it is often blended with one or more other grapes. Cabernet's sturdy structure and abundance of tannin can be overbearing in young wines and merlot makes a handy softener to fill in the middle ground, leaving cabernet's tannins to work away below. Again, there is incredible value to be found in this section, especially either side of the $20 price-point, and there's superb class at the top end. FOOD: These wines have classic structure and balance, they're not too heavy and will respond to most meat dishes really well. Lamb is a banker here, especially with a sauce that's flavoured with roasting herbs and some juniper berries.

2006 **Balnaves Cabernet Merlot**   *Score* **92**

COONAWARRA	Attractive cedary, fresh oak aromas that peel back with
Price $24.00 ✓	air, revealing fine redcurrant and cassis fruits, a little mint
Quality ★★★★	too. It's certainly from Coonawarra. The palate is soft and
Alc./Vol. 14.5%	supple, like a good cab merlot should be, it rolls around
Drink 2012	casually with bright berry and cassis fruit flavour, squaring
Closure Procork	up for a structured finish.

2006 **Balnaves The Blend**   *Score* **91**

COONAWARRA	This baby of the Balnaves cabernet arsenal has a good dose
Price $19.00 ✓	of merlot, showing fresh berry and mint aromas, it's driven
Quality ★★★★	by regionally phrased cabernet, some hazelnut and vanillin
Alc./Vol. 14.5%	oak on the side. Tannins are placed in fine chewable
Drink 2011	layers – youthful, dense and ripe. Staggering value.
Closure Screwcap	

2006 **Bethany Cabernet Merlot**   *Score* **91**

BAROSSA VALLEY	This sits nicely in the glass, ripe and clean; a neatly
Price $27.00	assembled array of berries, cassis and purple florals. The
Quality ★★★★	palate has a terrific approachable feel, soft supple tannins
Alc./Vol. 14%	are rolled out in all directions, plenty of plum, berry and
Drink Now	cassis flavour, finishing toasty and warm.
Closure Cork	

2006 Cape Mentelle Trinders Cabernet Merlot   *Score* 90

MARGARET RIVER
Price $35.00
Quality ★★★★
Alc./Vol. 14%
Drink 2012
Closure Screwcap

Smoky aromas and briary blackcurrant and berry fruits, cedary oak sits in nicely – all very youthful and integrated, sweet and ripe. The palate reveals cooler vintage angles, a little jumpy in the acid department but tannins are softer with medium-weighted fruitjube flavours.

2005 Capel Vale Cellar Exclusive Cabernet Blend   *Score* 93

MARGARET RIVER
Price $27.00
Quality ★★★★ ┤
Alc./Vol. 14.5%
Drink 2013
Closure Screwcap

A four-way blend of cabernet sauvignon, merlot, petit verdot and malbec, shows ripe blackberry and cassis fruits, some leafy notes, all settled and integrated with sweetly spiced background oak. The palate starts out with sweetly ripe berry flavour, neatly placed, sits easily over the palate with balance and resolve, fine tannins carry flavour evenly. An elegant ambassador for the art of blending.

2006 Clonakilla Ballinderry   *Score* 94

CANBERRA DISTRICT
Price $40.00
Quality ★★★★ ┤
Alc./Vol. 14.5%
Drink 2014
Closure Screwcap

Only a tiny 280 cases of this blend were made; it's roughly a third each of cabernet sauvignon, cabernet franc and merlot and has a cool restrained fruit character, cassis and blue fruits – elegant. The palate has supple smooth tannins and a rush of sweet cassis flavour through the middle. Trademark finesse, Kirk's a master when it comes to texture.

2005 Devil's Lair Cabernet Merlot   *Score* 92

MARGARET RIVER
Price $60.00
Quality ★★★★
Alc./Vol. 14%
Drink 2010
Closure Screwcap

A ripe and forward-leaning blend, plays into anise and liquorice territory, mirepoix vegetables, cabernet's cassis and some blue-fruited merlot. The tannins start out soft and forward, sweet berry flavour rides through beside a nudge of oak, finishing with savoury chew.

2006 Dividing Range Cabernet Merlot   *Score* 87

SOUTH EASTERN AUSTRALIA
Price $10.00 ✓
Quality ★★★ ┤
Alc./Vol. 14%
Drink Now
Closure Screwcap

Plenty of wine here for the dough: ripe mulberry and slightly soapy purple fruits, florals and plums too. The palate starts out easy and soft, juicy berry flavours with some spice – it builds some decent weight and structure.

2007 Ferngrove Symbols Cabernet Merlot
Score **89**

FRANKLAND RIVER
Price $16.00 ✓
Quality ★★★ ꜞ
Alc./Vol. 13.5%
Drink Now
Closure Screwcap

A bright and breezy cabernet merlot from this reliable producer, dark spicy oak sliced across some ripe plum and dark berry fruits, earthy too. Medium-weight palate has chirpy acidity, light tannins and simple fruit flavour.

2005 Fire Gully Cabernet Sauvignon Merlot
Score **90**

MARGARET RIVER
Price $25.00 ✓
Quality ★★★★
Alc./Vol. 14.5%
Drink Now
Closure Cork

A straightforward commercial style, there's oak and meaty/savoury characters across the fresh leaves and berry fruits. The palate is medium-weight and has fine stringy tannins, not especially concentrated but a thoroughly decent everyday quaffing cabernet.

2007 Flying Fish Cabernet Merlot
Score **90**

MARGARET RIVER
Price $22.00 ✓
Quality ★★★★
Alc./Vol. 14.5%
Drink 2016
Closure Screwcap

Very bright, raw cassis aromas, really direct and primary; you'll make no mistake about the varieties at work here – berries, purple florals and musky wood. Plenty of juicy fruit presence in the mouth, purple and black fruit flavours, sturdy tannins and a soft blueberry finish.

2005 Freycinet Cabernet Merlot
Score **90**

TASMANIA
Price $35.00
Quality ★★★★
Alc./Vol. 14%
Drink Now
Closure Screwcap

Well, this Tassie stalwart has come up trumps in '05: some vivid redcurrant fruit and lifted violet florals, bright and attractive primary fruits lead the way, still looking youthful. The palate has a breezy cool red berry flavour and musky tannins. A balanced, elegant style.

2006 Gemtree Tatty Road
Score **90**

McLAREN VALE
Price $18.00 ✓
Quality ★★★★
Alc./Vol. 14.5%
Drink 2009
Closure Screwcap

Half cabernet sauvignon, the rest is a mix of petit verdot, merlot and cabernet franc. Named after their Tatachilla Road vineyard, this has cooler maritime cabernet aromas and some savoury/cedary oak. The palate's a varietal quilt: a little mint and chocolate laced through berry fruits and herbs, fine soft tannins, finishing plush and supple.

2005 Happs Cabernet Merlot
Score **91**

MARGARET RIVER
Price $22.00 ✓
Quality ★★★★
Alc./Vol. 13.5%
Drink 2013
Closure Cork

Roasting herb aromas and freshly swept leaves show a cooler side of cabernet here; quite regional and a touch meaty. The palate is medium-weight to start and builds some juicy tannin chew as it goes, finishing with cedary oak and savoury cassis.

2006 Higher Plane Cabernet Merlot
Score **91**

MARGARET RIVER
Price $22.00 ✓
Quality ★★★★
Alc./Vol. 13.5%
Drink 2010
Closure Screwcap

Higher Plane is a southerly vineyard recently acquired by the owners of Juniper Estate, whose property is in the northern end of the region. Cooler berries and almost peppery nuances on the palate, leaves and herbs, fine tannin finish – a good result for the chilly '06 vintage.

2005 Jacob's Creek Cabernet Merlot
Score **88**

SOUTH EASTERN AUSTRALIA
Price $11.00 ✓
Quality ★★★ ꜀
Alc./Vol. 13%
Drink Now
Closure Screwcap

At the bargain end of the red wine pool, blended products often do better than the single varietals. This takes the best of merlot's charming fruits and cabernet's reliable structure. Soft plums and cassis, tannins build gently through the finish. Very approachable.

2006 Joseph Moda Cabernet Merlot
Score **93**

McLAREN VALE
Price $55.00
Quality ★★★★ ꜀
Alc./Vol. 15%
Drink 2016
Closure Twin top

Punchy, smoky oak characters open to some deeply concentrated plums and ripe berries, nutty/savoury notes at the edge. Very young and concentrated. The palate sits strong, ripe and juicy, more plums and dried berry flavours, a good serve of toasty/cedary oak and some dried fruits. Straight to the cellar, it's a proven campaigner!

2005 Juniper Crossing Cabernet Sauvignon Merlot
Score **93**

MARGARET RIVER
Price $20.00 ✓
Quality ★★★★ ꜀
Alc./Vol. 13.5%
Drink Now
Closure Screwcap

A terrific wine from the ever-reliable Juniper, looking ripe and tidy here in 2005, plenty of savoury berry aromas, dried herbs and superbly stated oak. Amazing concentration and sweeping flavours, dark berry fruits, plums and chocolate, all wrapped neatly together in a supple tannin package. Brilliant!

2006 Kirrihill Companions Cabernet Merlot

Score 90

CLARE VALLEY/ADELAIDE HILLS
Price $15.00 ✓
Quality ★★★★
Alc./Vol. 14.5%
Drink Now
Closure Screwcap

Companions indeed, this Clare Valley–Adelaide Hills double teamer has some assertive oak laid across straight-shooting cassis fruit aromas, gentle leaf and mint. Full of charm and elegance on the palate, merlot has built additional flesh, cabernet carries it through. Nicely nicely.

2004 Lake Breeze Arthur's Reserve Cabernet Sauvignon Petit Verdot Malbec

Score 93

LANGHORNE CREEK
Price $34.00
Quality ★★★★ꜰ
Alc./Vol. 14.5%
Drink 2011
Closure Cork

One of the stellar regional blends, and a fine tribute to Arthur John Follett who established the family vineyards way back in the 1880s. Deeply earthy and full of dark olive, black fruits and cedary oak. The palate is intense, commanding and balanced, the tannins roll with pace and length. Hearty stuff.

2003 Leeuwin Estate Prelude Cabernet Merlot

Score 90

MARGARET RIVER
Price $29.00
Quality ★★★★
Alc./Vol. 13%
Drink 2010
Closure Screwcap

A prelude indeed. Showing laid-back cabernet-merlot style with ripe berry fruits, plenty of creamy oak influence, some roasted meats and baking spices – nutty/savoury oak too. Starts out all taut and a little twangy then fades to a soft-centred easygoing palate, ripe fruit flavours and unobtrusive tannins.

2005 Little Rebel Cabernet Sauvignon Merlot

Score 89

YARRA VALLEY
Price $17.00
Quality ★★★ꜰ
Alc./Vol. 14%
Drink 2013
Closure Screwcap

This little rebel's showing plenty of sun-drenched fruit, really ripe with some strapping toast oak, liquorice and bright-blue merlot fruits. The two varieties fill out the palate into evenly shaped berry and chocolate flavours. Loads of raw appeal.

2006 Logan Cabernet Merlot

Score 91

ORANGE
Price $25.00
Quality ★★★★
Alc./Vol. 15%
Drink 2012
Closure Cork

This impresses with an overlay of slick swanky oak, spices and fragrant vanilla, fresh brambly berries are working below. The palate follows suit with musky oak and sweet bright berry fruits, some vanillin across the finish; elegant, young and bright, it makes a modern impression.

2006 Maverick Twins Cabernet Sauvignon Merlot Petit Verdot Cabernet Franc

Score **91**

BAROSSA VALLEY	
Price	$28.00
Quality	★★★★
Alc./Vol.	14.5%
Drink	2011
Closure	Screwcap

A raw, youthful myriad blend of varieties presents as a rich regionally driven red, plenty of earthy berry fruits and some oak punch. Terrific palate texture and density, ripe berries in all directions here, supple tannins bundle out the finish in youthful form.

2006 Mount Trio Cabernet Merlot

Score **89**

GREAT SOUTHERN	
Price	$16.00
Quality	★★★ ↝
Alc./Vol.	13.5%
Drink	2010
Closure	Screwcap

Gavin and Gill Berry's home vineyard near Mount Barker delivers cool dark berries and a nutty/savoury oak overlay; some mulberry, meats and chocolate too. A direct and compact palate structure: the tannins are fine-cut and wrapped tight around plum fruits, pencil-shaving oak to close.

2005 Over The Shoulder Cabernet Merlot

Score **92**

YARRA VALLEY	
Price	$20.00 ✓
Quality	★★★★ ↝
Alc./Vol.	14.5%
Drink	2015
Closure	Screwcap

What a pleasant surprise this wine was when, following the tasting, I discovered it was a mere twenty bucks! Showing some bright fruit and stylishly applied oak, purple fruit flavours, liquorice and leafy edges; it has great depth, weight and balance, with a sweet oak spice aftertaste. Effortless, easy-drinking style.

2004 Paracombe The Reuben

Score **91**

ADELAIDE HILLS	
Price	$21.00 ✓
Quality	★★★★
Alc./Vol.	15%
Drink	Now
Closure	Screwcap

This pitches cool-climate style, and some savoury bottle-derived maturity adds interest. Not exactly Rubenesque: rhubarb and dried cassis, liqueured fruits, leaves and mint. Very supple palate, more mint and berries here, subtle spices and a dense, resolute finish. Like a ripe luncheon claret!

2005 Petaluma Coonawarra

Score **95**

COONAWARRA	
Price	$60.00
Quality	★★★★ ↝
Alc./Vol.	13.5%
Drink	2014
Closure	Cork

This is a class act, smelling warm, soft and decidedly claret-like. Bright musky oak helps lift cabernet's purple florals, berries and merlot's blue fruits. It layers up nicely across the palate, flavours follow aromas; the tannins are supple and run in fine lines that stretch the length of the palate. Already settled and, cork willing, set to age with grace.

2006 Philip Shaw No.17 Merlot Cabernet Franc Cabernet   *Score* 92

ORANGE
Price $25.00 ✓
Quality   ★★★★
Alc./Vol. 13.8%
Drink   2011
Closure   Screwcap

A high-altitude take on the Bordeaux right-bank varieties, all ripened up nicely with plenty of fragrance intact; brambly ripe mulberry and blue fruits, cassis and meaty complexity in behind. The palate's a modern, slickly structured affair, loads of bright plum and cassis flavour, finishing toasty, a fine tannin trail.

2004 Pierro Reserve Cabernet Sauvignon Merlot   *Score* 93

MARGARET RIVER
Price $65.00
Quality   ★★★★ ⁄
Alc./Vol. 13%
Drink   2012
Closure   Cork

Initially shy on opening, decant and give it plenty of air. Opens to soft ripe berries, gentle savoury regional leaf, and merlot's more charming soft berry-fruit aromas. The palate is elegant and understated, has a gentle soft tannin ride, liquorice and cassis flavours, finishing even and fine.

2005 The Poplars Cabernet Merlot   *Score* 90

COONAWARRA
Price $24.00
Quality   ★★★★
Alc./Vol. 13.5%
Drink   Now
Closure   Screwcap

A ripe, chocolate-scented Coonawarra cabernet merlot that's guaranteed to bring smiles right around the table with its berry and plum fruits, and gentle earthy complexity below. The palate's smooth, round and made for early drinking enjoyment, supple tannins, ripe berry flavour and some sweet vanillin to boot.

2005 Redman Cabernet Sauvignon Merlot   *Score* 90

COONAWARRA
Price $35.00
Quality   ★★★★
Alc./Vol. 14.5%
Drink   2015
Closure   Twin top

This shows some classic Coonawarra cassis and purple olive aromas, the oak smells porous and resiny and it's already starting to show some bottle maturation. The palate is wrapped around a core of fine dense drying tannins, elegantly shaped with plenty of berry flavour to carry through the finish.

2004 Reschke Bull Trader Cabernet Merlot   *Score* 91

COONAWARRA
Price $18.00 ✓
Quality   ★★★★
Alc./Vol. 14%
Drink   2010
Closure   Screwcap

Plenty of trademark Coonawarra mint and chocolate; this 2004 has settled nicely, very integrated and right in the zone showing cool berry-fruit, ripe herbs and smoky oak complexity. The palate rolls in supple and soft with blackcurrant fruit, some mint and sturdy chewy tannins.

2004 Rymill MC²

Score **91**

COONAWARRA
Price $17.00 ✓
Quality ★★★★
Alc./Vol. 13%
Drink 2010
Closure Screwcap

A boon to have this '04 still available, Rymill's everyday red, made with balance and grace in mind. Reserved cassis and berry aromas, some mint and cedary oak in there too. Very supple and suave, medium-weight, dried berry flavours, fine tannins and juicy, compact acid balance. Superb.

2004 Shaw Vineyard Estate Cabernet Merlot

Score **90**

CANBERRA DISTRICT
Price $22.00 ✓
Quality ★★★★
Alc./Vol. 14%
Drink 2013
Closure Screwcap

Super lifted violette florals, very cool cassis cabernet aromas with some gravel and roasting herbs too. The palate switches between ripe fruits and bracing acidity, plenty of dark blackcurrant and berry flavour, assertive fine tannins and a crunchy flavoursome finish. Youthful and fiercely intense.

2005 Taltarni 3 Monks Cabernet Merlot

Score **91**

VICTORIA
Price $22.00 ✓
Quality ★★★★
Alc./Vol. 14%
Drink Now
Closure Screwcap

One of the great value wines getting around in the cabernet merlot category, this has attractive fragrance and life, fresh berry fruits, blueberries and attractive floral lift. Oak's a little dusty, there's boot polish and a stripe of dark minerals; lovely balance.

2006 Te Mata Estate Awatea Cabernet Merlot

Score **94**

HAWKES BAY, NZ 🖋
Price $46.00 ✓
Quality ★★★★ᶴ
Alc./Vol. 13.5%
Drink 2013
Closure Cork

Always a strong performer, it nearly upstages the Te Mata red line-up in 2006 – nearly. Shows subdued aromas of gravelly earth, ripe blackcurrant fruits and sweeter florals too; merlot's blue fruits, a little leathery oak influence, peppery almost. The palate is dense and has terrific savoury depth: graphite, liquorice and sweet berry flavour, long fine tannins – regal and smooth. The blend is 38% merlot, 36% cabernet sauvignon, 15% cabernet franc, 11% petit verdot.

2006 Te Mata Estate Coleraine

Score **96**

HAWKES BAY, NZ 🖋
Price $90.00
Quality ★★★★★
Alc./Vol. 13.5%
Drink 2012
Closure Cork

A rich blend of 49% merlot, 43% cabernet sauvignon and 8% cabernet franc, it shows terrific elegance and complexity. Dense brambly berry and chocolate aromas, vanillin and savoury/gravelly earthy notes. The palate is classy: some dense fine tannins, super smooth, almost St Emilion-like; the overall impression is supple with the grace, power and elegance to age handsomely.

2006 Te Mata Estate Merlot Cabernet

Score **91**

HAWKES BAY, NZ
Price $25.00 ✓
Quality ★★★★
Alc./Vol. 13.5%
Drink Now
Closure Screwcap

The baby of the range has bright fine berry fruits and soft milky oak aromas – simple and forthright. The palate has a peppery edge, cool and reserved, the tannins are medium thick, driving through the palate with good direction and harmony, even and balanced. Light, elegant and polished.

2004 Thompson Estate Cabernet Merlot

Score **89**

MARGARET RIVER
Price $28.00
Quality ★★★⸒
Alc./Vol. 14%
Drink Now
Closure Screwcap

Nice to see this '04 wine developing some bottle-derived complexity. Demi-glace and brambly cassis berries, some cedary oak, all nicely integrated. The palate is open and approachable, already developing brown savoury flavours.

2006 Thorn–Clarke Quartage

Score **92**

BAROSSA VALLEY
Price $20.00 ✓
Quality ★★★★
Alc./Vol. 14%
Drink 2010
Closure Screwcap

A five-way cabernet sauvignon, cabernet franc, malbec, merlot and petit verdot blend that represents staggering quality and value. Ripe Barossa berry fruit aromas, mixed berry flavours, some spice and a wedge of attractive oak. All delivered on fine, smooth tannins, plum skin and sweetly spiced oak to close.

2004 Voyager Estate Cabernet Merlot

Score **96**

MARGARET RIVER
Price $60.00 ✓
Quality ★★★★★
Alc./Vol. 14.2%
Drink 2015
Closure Screwcap

Consistent with past form, Voyager has made one of the most soulful, balanced '04 Margaret River reds. Fine cassis and berry fruits sit fresh and ripe amid sweet cedary oak and berry fruits, almonds and savoury nuances, berry pudding. Very precise. The palate is an exercise in fine craftsmanship, sweet berry flavours stretch across fine layered tannins, convincing balance and regal. A benchmark.

PENGUIN BEST CABERNET MERLOT BLEND

2006 Voyager Estate Girt By Sea Cabernet Merlot

Score **91**

MARGARET RIVER
Price $24.00 ✓
Quality ★★★★
Alc./Vol. 14%
Drink 2010
Closure Screwcap

Characterised by the cool year, this has cool green beans, gently smoky oak and some lighter cassis fruit aromas. The palate has the same slight green tinges to it, making a lighter impression and sitting up in the mouth, jumpy with cooler greenish edges.

2004 Watershed Cabernet Merlot

Score **92**

MARGARET RIVER	
Price	$25.00
Quality	★★★★
Alc./Vol.	14%
Drink	2012
Closure	Cork

Showing ripe mixed-berry aromas and a touch of tomato leaf, deeper demi-glace and meaty roasting juices with savoury oak nuances, there's depth and drive. It's a commanding but elegant style, well balanced with fine tannins that persist in even shape.

2004 Watershed Shades

Score **91**

MARGARET RIVER	
Price	$17.00
Quality	★★★★
Alc./Vol.	14%
Drink	2012
Closure	Cork

A cabernet, merlot and shiraz blend displays a lovely array of ripe fruits, deep bramble and spiced mixed berries, some chirpy oak and plenty of polish. The palate folds out on fine soft tannins coated in sweet fruit, all three varieties sitting in tune. An easy-drinking style.

2005 Wine By Brad Cabernet Merlot

Score **90**

MARGARET RIVER	
Price	$18.00 ✓
Quality	★★★★
Alc./Vol.	13.5%
Drink	Now
Closure	Screwcap

Nicely assembled by Brad; Brad Wehr, that is. He's brought this classic blend together from 2005, and it shows charming ripe berry/plum fruits, gentle leafy edges and some smooth savoury oak. Very tidy. There's ample soft, easy tannin through the palate, cassis and berry flavour, balanced, easy finish.

2004 Xabregas Cabernet Merlot

Score **91**

MOUNT BARKER	
Price	$15.00 ✓
Quality	★★★★
Alc./Vol.	14.5%
Drink	2011
Closure	Screwcap

A well-priced blend of three vineyards in the Great Southern region, this has a good spread of roasting herbs and bay leaf characters, some cassis and peppery plum fruit below, cedary oak too. Tannins are fine and grainy with depth and drive, a savoury cabernet boot-polish finish.

2006 Xanadu Dragon Cabernet Merlot

Score **89**

MARGARET RIVER	
Price	$16.00
Quality	★★★ ⌐
Alc./Vol.	14%
Drink	Now
Closure	Screwcap

From the cool '06 vintage, Xanadu have this Dragon all warmed up and firing. Aromas of brambly cassis and plum fruits, ripe leaf and herbs in the background. Smooth open juicy tannins roll through easily, ripe plum and purple berry flavours trail off gently, building some grip through the finish.

Merlot and blends

'Quaffable, but . . . uh, not transcendent' is the famous opinion of the wine-loving geek, Miles, in the hit film *Sideways*. Miles really gave merlot a flogging, the first time a wine was targeted on the big screen with such a convincing effect on the market; sales plummeted around the globe, especially in the US. Merlot is an appealing soft and simple grape, capable of making structured and complex wine when grown in very specific areas, yet it has been planted here, there and everywhere. It typically makes a decent medium- to full-bodied red wine with soft plum and mulberry fruit, sometimes floral in cooler areas, relatively easygoing tannins and the ability to drink well on release. FOOD: Merlot's soft structure and generous fruit make it an ideal marriage with simple meat dishes like pork loin or veal sausages.

2005 **Brand's Laira Merlot**   *Score* **92**

COONAWARRA	Bright, lively and varietal, primary fruit leads this affordable
Price $23.00 ✓	merlot, the oak is cut in with a good eye, adding punchy
Quality ★★★★	sweet complexity. The palate is still folding together, grainy
Alc./Vol. 15%	tannins are wrapped in flavour; it just needs a little time.
Drink 2011	
Closure Screwcap	

2002 **Brookland Valley Merlot**   *Score* **90**

MARGARET RIVER	The wood sits across the top of this wine in regal fashion;
Price $44.00	it's savoury and cedary with cassis and blackberry fruits,
Quality ★★★★	some leafy/brambly complexity in the mix too. The palate
Alc./Vol. 14%	is a fine savoury arrangement of brambly berry flavours,
Drink 2013	savoury tannins, some herbal leafy notes and a firm,
Closure Cork	business-like finish.

2005 **Burnbrae Merlot**   *Score* **92**

MUDGEE	A classic Australian merlot with attractive berry fruits and
Price $23.00 ✓	a greenish stripe running throughout, cool and elegant
Quality ★★★★	with some fragrant oak lift. The palate is a chewy, savoury
Alc./Vol. 14.5%	affair, well made and balanced, tannins are fine but dense,
Drink 2014	delivering a medium-weight wine with a crunchy fruit
Closure Screwcap	finish.

2006 Craggy Range Gimblett Gravels Merlot   *Score* **93**

HAWKES BAY, NZ	
Price	$45.00
Quality	★★★★ ⫞
Alc./Vol.	13.5%
Drink	2011
Closure	Cork

Hawkes Bay is prime merlot country and the folks at Craggy Range have a great handle on just how to deliver it. Ripe berry fruits, attractive floral lift and some sweeter cedary spiced oak; bright and modern. The palate is terrific: smooth swirling tannins glide across the tongue carrying svelte elegant plum and some savoury oak alongside. Impressive.

2005 Craggy Range Sophia   *Score* **94**

HAWKES BAY, NZ	
Price	$70.00
Quality	★★★★ ⫞
Alc./Vol.	14%
Drink	2013
Closure	Cork

You'll recognise Sophia by her hulking great bottle, bend at the knees when lifting it to the glass. She's a beauty: roughly two-thirds merlot, the rest cabernet franc with a tiny splash of cabernet sauvignon. A superb rendition of a right-bank Bordeaux-inspired style with its concentrated savoury/earthy aromas and ripe dark berry fruits. There's concentration with smooth balance and effortless style, sweet oak spice and some black minerally edges, fine deeply arching tannins, finishing long and elegant. Will cellar for some time.

2006 Craggy Range Te Kahu   *Score* **93**

HAWKES BAY, NZ	
Price	$45.00 ✓
Quality	★★★★ ⫞
Alc./Vol.	13.5%
Drink	2012
Closure	Cork

Predominantly merlot (58%) with the balance composed of cabernet sauvignon, cabernet franc and malbec, this proprietary single-vineyard red is a stylish foray into elegance. Blue fruits, cassis and sweet cedary oak spice – it shows depth with finesse, crafted into stylish balance. Mannerly and impeccable.

2006 Deakin Estate Merlot   *Score* **87**

SOUTH EASTERN AUSTRALIA	
Price	$10.00
Quality	★★★ ⫞
Alc./Vol.	13.5%
Drink	Now
Closure	Screwcap

You'd be hard pressed to find a better 10-buck bottle of merlot; they've tuned this one up just right. Perfumed berry fruit aromas smell nice and sweet, blackcurrant and a little oak in there too. Very soft, easy palate, bright blue fruit finish.

2005 Dominique Portet Merlot

Score **92**

YARRA VALLEY
Price $26.00
Quality ★★★★
Alc./Vol. 14.5%
Drink 2012
Closure Screwcap

One of the best examples from out in the Yarra Valley: soft, swirling berry fruits and some brambly ripe plums, gently tickled up with cedary oak. Smooth berry flavour and a juicy core of ripe tannins, spicy oak peeks through the finish, all balanced and tidy.

2007 Dowie Doole Merlot

Score **90**

McLAREN VALE
Price $25.00
Quality ★★★★
Alc./Vol. 13.5%
Drink 2012
Closure Screwcap

McLaren Vale makes a good fist of supple rich merlot and here it's showing bright lifted purple floral aromas, some fine spice and a twist of savoury funk. The palate is medium-weight with a strong earthy flavour, dense black fruits and rolling soft tannins.

2007 Ferngrove Merlot

Score **91**

FRANKLAND RIVER
Price $19.00 ✓
Quality ★★★★
Alc./Vol. 13.5%
Drink Now
Closure Screwcap

Tucked up in the middle of nowhere, Frankland River seems to suit this elusive grape. Plenty of earthy liquorice and dark berry fruit aromas, some savoury cedary oak in there too. The palate sits in the medium-bodied spectrum, fine tannins and bright, breezy flavour.

2005 Gapsted Merlot

Score **89**

SOUTH EASTERN AUSTRALIA
Price $25.00
Quality ★★★ ⌐
Alc./Vol. 14.5%
Drink Now
Closure Screwcap

Attractive, modern choc-berry aromas, this is an appealing style made to deliver in its youth; liquorice and mint in there too. The palate is really soft and easy to take, light tannins and ripe berry flavours, gently fading finish.

2005 Gibson Reserve Merlot

Score **90**

**BAROSSA VALLEY/
ADELAIDE HILLS**
Price $35.00
Quality ★★★★
Alc./Vol. 14.6%
Drink Now
Closure Screwcap

A welcoming all-rounder, just as merlot should be when it's done well, earthy spiced plum fruits, cinnamon and some briary/leafy complexity; oak sits in the chocolate spectrum. The palate's a supple, sweetly oaked, soft tannin affair; easy and smooth.

2006 Grant Burge Hillcot Merlot

Score **87**

BAROSSA VALLEY	
Price	$21.00
Quality	★★★ ┤
Alc./Vol.	14.5%
Drink	Now
Closure	Screwcap

Very straightforward berry fruits and bright approachable plums – varietal and direct. The palate is supple and has soft tannin glide, plenty of plum, cassis and violet flavours, juicy, even and easy.

2004 Highbank Merlot

Score **92**

COONAWARRA	
Price	$59.00
Quality	★★★★
Alc./Vol.	13.5%
Drink	Now
Closure	Cork

Perched in a prime Riddoch Highway location, Highbank has always been a bastion of quality and pride. This is a sweet, complex-smelling merlot, really lifted purple florals, ripe mulberry and plums. Some smooth tannins tube around ripe plum fruit flavour; even, elegant and neatly balanced. Already building mature character.

2007 Jacob's Creek Merlot

Score **86**

AUSTRALIA	
Price	$11.00
Quality	★★★
Alc./Vol.	13.5%
Drink	Now
Closure	Screwcap

Very simple blue fruits and some liquorice too, this everyday quaffer delivers in easy-to-love shape. Gentle brambly flavours; oak isn't a part of the picture – just supple purple berry flavour and easy soft tannins.

2005 Jones The Winemaker Merlot

Score **91**

NORTH EAST VICTORIA	
Price	$20.00 ✓
Quality	★★★★
Alc./Vol.	15%
Drink	Now
Closure	Procork

Mandy Jones has judged this beautifully, it takes another step up in complexity with attractive toasty oak and gentle spice. The palate's well made, delivering straightforward berry fruit flavour, fine tannins and juicy, easy-drinking appeal.

2006 Juniper Crossing Merlot

Score **92**

MARGARET RIVER	
Price	$20.00 ✓
Quality	★★★★
Alc./Vol.	13.5%
Drink	Now
Closure	Screwcap

Nice bright crimson–red colour, this shows the coolness of the 2006 vintage in Margaret River: plenty of herbs and leaves, fragrant berry fruits below. The palate looks in shape though, light pepper and spice, bouncy berry flavour and finely sprung tannins. Medium-bodied and an approachable easy drinker.

2006 Logan Weemala Merlot

Score **90**

CENTRAL RANGES	
Price	$16.00 ✓
Quality	★★★★
Alc./Vol.	14.5%
Drink	Now
Closure	Screwcap

Logan has their eye in here, this junior label has some attractive ripe berry-pie aromas and gentle plums in beside nice oak spice – it's all there. A super-fresh palate, moves into brambly territory, soft fine tannins; it leaves a fresh impression.

2006 McWilliam's Hanwood Estate Merlot

Score **90**

SOUTH EASTERN AUSTRALIA	
Price	$13.00 ✓
Quality	★★★★
Alc./Vol.	13.5%
Drink	Now
Closure	Screwcap

Startling quality is often found in this workhorse McWilliam's label, plenty of merlot's brambly berry fruits and sweetly spiced complexity. Impressive varietal blue fruits on the palate, some floral fragrance, medium-weighted, with a gentle twist of savoury tannin.

2007 Millamolong Isabelle's Ghost Merlot

Score **91**

ORANGE	
Price	$20.00 ✓
Quality	★★★★
Alc./Vol.	13.9%
Drink	Now
Closure	Screwcap

Lovely bright mulberry and cassis nose, ripened into the right varietal zone; the oak sits in the background and allows the fruit to take centre-stage. Plenty of cassis on the palate too, some light purple berries and gentle fine tannins run full length.

2005 Murdock Merlot

Score **91**

COONAWARRA	
Price	$23.00 ✓
Quality	★★★★
Alc./Vol.	14.5%
Drink	2011
Closure	Screwcap

A reserved, medium-weight merlot, shows strong regional heritage with its dried brambly berries, cassis and gentle mint aromas. A supple and unpretentious palate, delivers plenty of flavour, stretched across fine savoury tannins, with cedary oak sitting just under the radar; it finishes fresh and elegant.

2006 Penley Estate Gryphon Merlot

Score **94**

COONAWARRA	
Price	$19.00 ✓
Quality	★★★★ ᛃ
Alc./Vol.	15%
Drink	2012
Closure	Screwcap

Kym Tolley, take a bow! A masterfully delivered Coonawarra merlot for under 20 bucks, showing attractive brambly blue fruits, some earthy aromas, a hint of mint, and barrel-derived spice; it looks complex and complete. Very plush and bending in the direction of a charming St Emilion with fine savoury tannins. Superb!

PENGUIN BEST MERLOT AND BLENDS

2004 **Petaluma Merlot**   *Score* **93**

COONAWARRA	This more discreet stablemate of the Petaluma Coonawarra
Price $60.00	shows plenty of '04 vintage power and richness, the oak
Quality ★★★★ ᕯ	sits a little bit proud but it's nothing a brief spell in the
Alc./Vol. 14.5%	cellar won't fix. Offers plenty of middle-palate flesh, purple
Drink 2012	berry flavours, some regional mint and toasty oak through
Closure Cork	the back.

2007 **Primo Estate Merlesco**   *Score* **88**

McLAREN VALE	One from Joe Grilli's suite of quaffable junior wines,
Price $15.00	impressive integration and resolve at such a tender
Quality ★★★ ᕯ	age. Grilli has set humble goals for this wine and more
Alc./Vol. 13%	than met them. The palate is all about light berry fruits,
Drink Now	unpretentious and direct, with medium-weight tannins.
Closure Screwcap	Easily enjoyed.

2006 **Prince Hill Merlot**   *Score* **92**

MUDGEE	Seems that Mudgee does merlot better than most, here it
Price $25.00 ✓	shows sweet spice and some deeper boot-polish aromas,
Quality ★★★★	bright dark berry fruits; modern and clean. The palate is
Alc./Vol. 14.5%	right in the zone with medium-weight structure, direct
Drink 2014	berry and plum fruit flavours, complementary oak and a
Closure Screwcap	sturdy smoky finish.

2006 **Printhie Merlot**   *Score* **91**

ORANGE	Nice bright fragrant expression thanks to the cool climes of
Price $17.00 ✓	the Orange region, some chocolate-scented oak and gentle
Quality ★★★★	spice. Great colour too: bright red–purple in the glass.
Alc./Vol. 15%	Boot polish, almost olive-like with plenty of purple berry
Drink 2010	flavour, fine tannins, elegant and measured.
Closure Screwcap	

2005 **Robert Channon Merlot**   *Score* **88**

GRANITE BELT	One of the most successful Queensland producers, Robert
Price $20.00	Channon's merlot shows typical green-edged blue fruits
Quality ★★★ ᕯ	and berries with some milk chocolate–scented oak that
Alc./Vol. 14%	suits the fruit nicely. The palate is a quaffable medium-
Drink Now	weight affair, not especially deep but has some tidy balance
Closure Screwcap	and springy light tannins.

2006 Ross Estate Single Vineyard Merlot — Score 88

BAROSSA VALLEY
Price $23.00
Quality ★★★ ⟩
Alc./Vol. 15%
Drink Now
Closure Screwcap

An attractive brambly Barossa merlot with ripe berry fruit aromas and some bright lifted purple florals; it has some light sweet spice too, quite vibrant. Straight-shooting ripe berries on the palate, light tannins and a purple musky, blackcurrant finish.

2005 Schild Estate Merlot — Score 90

BAROSSA VALLEY
Price $20.00
Quality ★★★★
Alc./Vol. 14.5%
Drink Now
Closure Screwcap

This has regional earthy Barossa depth, ripe plum and berry fruits, sweet florals, oak here too; it sits well. The palate has sweeping soft tannins, berry and cassis flavours, some floral lift and plum-skin flavour through the finish.

2005 Tapanappa Merlot — Score 93

WRATTONBULLY
Price $75.00
Quality ★★★★ ⟩
Alc./Vol. 14%
Drink 2012
Closure Cork

A slick, modern and decidedly cedary oak-enhanced style, heading into classic, Bordeaux-inspired territory (not surprising given that one of the partners in the project hails from there), some plums and mulberry too. Lovely sweet tannins carrying fruit in three dimensions, more of the same ripe fruits here; length and class.

2007 3 Drops Merlot — Score 90

MOUNT BARKER
Price $24.00
Quality ★★★★
Alc./Vol. 14%
Drink 2011
Closure Screwcap

This shows quite assertive ripe fruit and some spicy sweet oak, it's attractive and well made with rich dark fruits and bright direct appeal. The palate has smoky notes, it starts out supple and tightens through the finish, balanced and full of youthful juicy charm.

2006 Wild Rock Gravel Pit Red — Score 89

HAWKES BAY, NZ
Price $22.00 ✓
Quality ★★★ ⟩
Alc./Vol. 13%
Drink Now
Closure Screwcap

This little scrapper from the Craggy Range team is a brilliant medium-bodied wine you can sip on all day long. Blended between merlot and malbec, it has ripe approachable berry fruits, a little fennel seed and it needs little else, such is its charm. The palate rolls through on supple tannins and deft balance.

Imported red wines

Australia now has a group of busy importers making impressive headway into all corners of the winegrowing globe. There are more wines from more countries than ever before – you'll find an astounding range if you go searching. This chapter offers a range of the more widely available imported reds, mixing up some classics like chianti and Côtes du Rhône with modern Portuguese and Spanish reds that are taking the wine world by storm. And, in a number of cases, these imported wines offer impressive value and drinkability. FOOD: In general, they all deliver a more savoury palate than the average Australian red, with firmer tannins and brighter acid. Savoury dishes are the answer; take culinary inspiration from the country of origin and you'll discover just how food-friendly these wines can be.

2006 Alvaro Castro Dão D.O.C.   *Score* **90**

DÃO, PORTUGAL	
Price	$32.00 ✓
Quality	★★★★
Alc./Vol.	13%
Drink	2010
Closure	Cork

This easy-drinking, medium-weight red opens with really savoury aromas, some black berries and cassis, dark minerals and perfume too. The palate is a rockabilly-styled quaffing red with plenty of juicy flavour, quite crunchy; then stripes of open-knit tannins run down through the finish, some chocolate on the tail.

2006 Cerro del Masso Chianti   *Score* **90**

CHIANTI, ITALY	
Price	$25.00 ✓
Quality	★★★★
Alc./Vol.	12.5%
Drink	Now
Closure	Diam

This Italian all-rounder shows plenty of ripe cherry fruits. It's from a good recent vintage with classic spiced, marinated cherry fruits, liquorice and fairly punchy oak that's well matched. Supple and intense with zesty acidity, the tannins fan out evenly across the medium weight palate. Shows a good mix of fruit and savoury tannin drive; cherries to close.

2006 Cillar de Silos Tempranillo Joven Ribera del Duero D.O.   *Score* **93**

RIBERA DEL DUERO, SPAIN	
Price	$33.00 ✓
Quality	★★★★ ⸴
Alc./Vol.	13.5%
Drink	Now
Closure	Cork

Purity is the all-important ingredient in young reds that rely on their fruit, and this wine sets the benchmark high. It showcases rich ripe red and dark cherry fruits, fragrant and uncluttered, moving into curvaceous silky tannins that bring shape and poise to the palate – impeccably balanced.

2006 Concha Y Toro Casillero del Diablo Cabernet Sauvignon *Score* 89

VALLE CENTRAL, CHILE	Chilean wine is making annual leaps and bounds and this
Price $15.00 ✓	is one of the stars of the Concha Y Toro Diablo 2006 reds.
Quality ★★★ɔ	Understated and neatly ripe cassis, liquorice and briary
Alc./Vol. 13.5%	leaves. The palate is polished and finely balanced, really
Drink Now	even and elegant, fine smooth tannins and berry/plum
Closure Cork	flavour. Sensational value.

2006 Concha Y Toro Casillero del Diablo Carmenere *Score* 90

VALLE DE RAPEL, CHILE	Carmenere is a native of Chile and has some similar
Price $15.00 ✓	qualities to merlot – soft blue fruit aromas, cranberry and
Quality ★★★★	tobacco leaf, gentle smoky spice. The palate is soft, fine
Alc./Vol. 13.5%	and supple, round and easy in the middle, sweetened by
Drink Now	some oak through the finish. Slides down effortlessly, have
Closure Cork	a second bottle at the ready!

2005 Cosme Palacio Rioja Cosecha *Score* 93

RIOJA, SPAIN	One of the great bargain Spanish red wines getting
Price $21.00 ✓	around, this has modern swagger and confident style –
Quality ★★★★ɔ	there's plenty to admire here. Creamy oak spices sit across
Alc./Vol. 13.5%	fragrant ripe dark cherry fruits, pure and engaging, gentle
Drink Now	liquorice in the background. Scintillating juicy palate that
Closure Cork	packs ripe cherry and plum flavours into upbeat tannins –
	very youthful, very good.

2004 Damana Ribera del Duero *Score* 92

RIBERA DEL DUERO, SPAIN	The baby brother of the monolithic Tábula, it has the same
Price $35.00 ✓	clarity and purity; 100% tempranillo brings fragrant cherry
Quality ★★★★	fruits, backed by savoury tight-grained oak. Terrific pure
Alc./Vol. 14%	cherry and dark minerals on the palate, slate and spice,
Drink 2011	dense tannins ride through the finish at pace.
Closure Cork	

2005 Eric & Joel Durand Cornas Empreintes *Score* 93

RHÔNE VALLEY, FRANCE	The 2005 vintage was a cracker for shiraz in the Northern
Price $75.00	Rhône Valley; this is a superb example. Fragrant dark
Quality ★★★★ɔ	fruits, light spices and pepper, roasted meat, black granite
Alc./Vol. 13.5%	minerals, and some well-delivered oak – very complex.
Drink 2014	Supple smooth tannins and a great play between
Closure Cork	concentrated flavour and elegant structure. Long
	savoury berry and spice flavour.

2006 Fattoria Zerbina Ceregio Sangiovese Di Romagna   *Score* **92**

EMILIA ROMAGNA, ITALY	
Price	$24.00 ✓
Quality	★★★★
Alc./Vol.	13%
Drink	2011
Closure	Cork

Gosh this is good! Ripe cherry fruit aromas swirl around the glass and push fragrant sweet spices into play, there's intensity here. Wild berries and cherry fruits, superb juicy flesh running through the mid-palate, sailing out the finish in fine tannins and bright acid, deep balance and great build.

2006 Fonterutoli Chianti Classico   *Score* **93**

TUSCANY, ITALY	
Price	$46.00
Quality	★★★★ ┤
Alc./Vol.	13.5%
Drink	2011
Closure	Cork

One of the most modern and convincing bottles of chianti on Australian shelves, dark purple colour and classic rich cherry fruits, spice, earth and just the right dose of oak. Ripe and sassy. The palate is supple with a savoury tannin undercurrent, building juicy deep cherry flavour and finishing with a terrific follow-through.

2004 Guigal Côtes du Rhône   *Score* **92**

RHÔNE VALLEY, FRANCE	
Price	$25.00 ✓
Quality	★★★★
Alc./Vol.	13%
Drink	Now
Closure	Cork

It's staggering to see just how consistently this is delivered, given the quantity produced. Guigal is a phenomenal producer and this is their world-conquering everyday drink. A myriad dark berries and gentle spice, the palate is smooth, round and juicy, balanced up a treat.

2005 Guigal Côtes du Rhône   *Score* **93**

RHÔNE VALLEY, FRANCE	
Price	$25.00 ✓
Quality	★★★★ ┤
Alc./Vol.	13%
Drink	Now
Closure	Cork

The legend continues! This is a supple, ripe, balanced and thoroughly convincing 2005 red blend. Fresh and all settled into stride, there's an abundance of ripe red and dark berry fruit packed in amidst gentle peppery spice. The palate's pitched into medium weight territory and has plenty of supple swirling fruit flesh. Tannins gather through the finish, building lengthy flavour before fading smoothly. Brilliant!

PENGUIN BEST IMPORTED RED WINE

2006 Henri Fessy Beaujolais–Villages   *Score* **88**

BEAUJOLAIS, FRANCE	
Price	$15.50
Quality	★★★ ┤
Alc./Vol.	12.5%
Drink	Now
Closure	Screwcap

A modern, ripe and sweetly scented light red from near Lyon, one of the most picturesque French wine regions. Super-fragrant strawberry fruits and red musky perfume. The palate is as light as a feather, plenty of sweet musky strawberry flavour, soft and easy. Serve at room temperature or with a light chill during summer. Great to see screwcap here too.

2005 La Braccesca Sabazio Rosso di Montepulciano
Score **91**

TUSCANY, ITALY
Price $22.00 ✓
Quality ★★★★
Alc./Vol. 13%
Drink Now
Closure Cork

Forget the long name, it's a lot easier to drink than it is to say and offers terrific presence, not to mention value. Classic sour cherry sangiovese fruits, some tobacco and earthy complexity – plenty of flavour, open and approachable tannins; you'd better have a second bottle on stand-by.

2005 La Montesa Rioja
Score **92**

RIOJA, SPAIN
Price $38.00
Quality ★★★★
Alc./Vol. 14%
Drink 2011
Closure Cork

This is a restrained, understated style, measured and balanced. Black cherry fruits, sweet earth and gentle spices, there are some grey minerals here too. The palate is svelte and rides on bright acidity; tannins are young and strung tight, the cherry-flavoured fruit has an evenly weighted fleshy presence through the middle. Elegant, with some punch.

2006 LZ Tempranillo Rioja D.O.
Score **92**

RIOJA, SPAIN
Price $25.00 ✓
Quality ★★★★
Alc./Vol. 14%
Drink Now
Closure Cork

This is the pick of Telmo Rodriguez's entry-range wines in '06. Modern, ripe and rich, with some whole-bunchy complexity giving fragrant lift and another dimension of spice. Terrific supple palate, even and vibrant with plenty of flavour and a savoury twist through the finish.

2006 Mac Forbes Blaufrankisch
Score **90**

CARNUNTUM, AUSTRIA
Price $28.00
Quality ★★★★
Alc./Vol. 12.5%
Drink 2010
Closure Screwcap

Don't freak out if you've never heard of this variety, it ain't exactly taking the world by storm. It makes a light red with soft fruits; here it's cloaked in a savoury oak shroud, some brambly red fruits below and peppery spice. The palate sits up bright and lively, plenty of power, ripe cherry flavour and punchy earthy tannins; superb drive through the finish.

2005 Maison Champy Bourgogne Pinot Noir
Score **89**

BURGUNDY, FRANCE
Price $25.00
Quality ★★★⁺
Alc./Vol. 13%
Drink Now
Closure Screwcap

Sealed under screwcap, this hails from one of the greatest recent vintages. Bright red fruits and cherries, some subtle undergrowth and spice. Chirpy acidity holds cherry flavour up nice and high, tannins are soft and there's a savoury rush of acidity through the finish. Nicely balanced bargain burgundy.

2006 **Poderi Ruggeri Corsini Dolcetto d'Alba**   *Score* **90**

PIEDMONT, ITALY
Price $24.00
Quality   ★★★★
Alc./Vol.   13.5%
Drink   Now
Closure   Cork

Impressive vibrant purple colour, this fleshy everyday northern Italian red oozes charm with its spiced blue fruits, dark minerals and gentle earthy spices. The palate sits up on a fine acid spine with perky bright berry flavours and light tannins. A juicy little fruit bomb.

2006 **Poliziano Chianti**   *Score* **90**

TUSCANY, ITALY
Price $24.00 ✓
Quality   ★★★★
Alc./Vol.   13.5%
Drink   Now
Closure   Cork

2006 is a much-anticipated vintage for Tuscan red wines and this is one of the best-value early arrivals. Bright sangiovese aromas of red cherry and very subtle spice. The palate is elegantly poised on fine savoury tannins and snappy acid crunch. Refreshing and balanced.

2006 **Prunotto Barbera d'Alba**   *Score* **90**

PIEDMONT, ITALY
Price $22.00 ✓
Quality   ★★★★
Alc./Vol.   13.5%
Drink   Now
Closure   Cork

A light and easy style, made for lunchtime drinking, an easy drop to tackle. Plenty of up-front red fruit aromas and brambly herbal complexity, the palate is super fresh and lively, soft and juicy through the middle, juicy red berry flavours bounce through the finish on chirpy acidity, a soft tannin landing.

2005 **Quinta do Vallado Douro D.O.**   *Score* **92**

DOURO, PORTUGAL
Price $33.00 ✓
Quality   ★★★★
Alc./Vol.   13.5%
Drink   2011
Closure   Cork

This medium-bodied Portuguese red is grown on the steep terraced vineyards along the Douro river. It has intense, bright purple cherry and perfume, really bright fruit that opens up beautifully with some time in the glass. Decanting is a good option too. Rich cherry flavour, liquorice and impeccable interplay between tannin and acidity, balanced and refined. Superb value too.

2006 **Saint Cosme Côtes du Rhône**   *Score* **92**

RHÔNE VALLEY, FRANCE
Price $17.00 ✓
Quality   ★★★★
Alc./Vol.   13.5%
Drink   Now
Closure   Cork

One of the more solid Côtes du Rhône styles, a quality statement with ripe dark berry and some plum fruits, gentle oak – all neatly styled and balanced. Smooth juicy palate with impeccably fine tannins, fleshy texture and even shape; berry fruit from start to finish. Delicious!

2004 Tábula Ribera del Duero

Score **94**

RIBERA DEL DUERO, SPAIN
Price $67.00
Quality ★★★★┤
Alc./Vol. 15%
Drink 2012
Closure Cork

This inky, muscular red is mostly tempranillo with a handful of cabernet sauvignon, no doubt helping the deep dark colour. Plenty of oak spice and earthy/savoury aromas, there's smoky cherry fruit in behind. Superb concentration and depth, flinty smouldering cherry fruit flavours and long, fine tannins building in intensity through the finish. Will age beautifully.

2004 Vidal-Fleury Côtes du Ventoux

Score **88**

RHÔNE VALLEY, FRANCE
Price $15.50
Quality ★★★┤
Alc./Vol. 13%
Drink Now
Closure Extruded synthetic

A chipper southern Rhône red blend, this has ripe dark berries and earthy complexity, some liquorice and mountain herbs. Supple and soft palate, quite sanguine and savoury, light tannins, gentle liquorice-flavoured finish – a handy knockabout BBQ red.

2006 Vietti Barbera d'Asti Tre Vigne

Score **93**

PIEDMONT, ITALY
Price $45.00 ✓
Quality ★★★★┤
Alc./Vol. 14%
Drink 2010
Closure Cork

Vietti may well be the world's #1 barbera producer. This wine has electric appeal, superbly concentrated; it's built on complex structure that's driven by acidity and tannin. Distinctly earthy, smells Italian, savoury dried berry fruits and gentle liquorice spice. Red fruit flavours, musky spices and linear, direct impact, pushing deep and fresh through the finish.

2006 Vietti Dolcetto d'Alba Tre Vigne

Score **91**

PIEDMONT, ITALY
Price $35.00 ✓
Quality ★★★★
Alc./Vol. 14.5%
Drink Now
Closure Cork

My god this is an outstanding wine! Intense wet black minerals, blue and dark berry fruits, light spice – really concentrated. Oozing rich ripe fruit flavour across the palate, delivered on smooth fine tannins that travel long and even – punches well above its weight.

2005 Vietti Perbacco Nebbiolo

Score **94**

PIEDMONT, ITALY
Price $45.00 ✓
Quality ★★★★┤
Alc./Vol. 13.5%
Drink 2011
Closure Cork

This is one of the terrific little Italian wines getting around our shelves (albeit in limited supply); the grapes are sourced from within the Barolo area of Piedmont and blended together. Savoury dried cherries and grilled meats, anise and minerals. Terrific freshness and acid crunch on the palate, musky red fruit flavours and a long commanding tannin finish.

Sweet wines

There are many, many styles of sweet wine in Australia that can be enjoyed with a sweet course, before or after the meal, or simply on their own. Styles include gently sweet, late-harvest through to the very late-picked wines, and then into botrytis-affected wines. Almost any grape can be made in a sweeter style, but in Australia riesling, semillon and sauvignon blanc are the main players. Although in one sense it's all about sugar, it's also all about balance, especially when matching these up with food. FOOD: Sweet wines partner exquisitely with desserts such as apple tarte tatin, passionfruit custard and pineapple upside-down cake. Make sure the wine is slightly sweeter than the dessert for the best results. Cheeses and foie gras (pâté) also love these wines.

2006 Brown Brothers Patricia Botrytis Riesling   *Score* **94**

MILAWA	Harvested in autumn mists that drift across the vineyard until mid-morning, this is an intense botrytised style with glace citron and essence-like lemon and lime oil flavours. The texture is luscious, really opulent, with terrific concentration and crystalline purity.
Price $35.00 (375 ml)	
Quality ★★★★ ͐	
Alc./Vol. 8.5%	
Drink 2010	
Closure Screwcap	

2006 Craggy Range Noble   *Score* **94**

MARTINBOROUGH	A refreshing difference here; this is a botrytis-infected sweet wine made from two-thirds sauvignon blanc and one-third riesling, all sourced from Craggy's Te Muna Road vineyard in Martinborough. Tropical fruits, gentle grassy notes and plenty of fine gravelly minerals, the balance is superb, finishing pristine, crisp and juicy.
Price $51.00 (375 ml)	
Quality ★★★★ ͐	
Alc./Vol. 11%	
Drink 2010	
Closure Cork	

2007 d'Arenberg The Noble Riesling   *Score* **92**

McLAREN VALE	One of the quiet little stars in the d'Arenberg arsenal, this packs plenty of riesling character, spicy and chock-full of botrytis characters – apricot and floral honey. Concentrated candied orange-rind flavours, some ginger, iced tea and apricot nectar on the palate, super-rich unctuous texture, all pulled into balance.
Price $25.00 ✓ (375 ml)	
Quality ★★★★	
Alc./Vol. 11.5%	
Drink Now	
Closure Screwcap	

2006 De Bortoli Noble One Botrytis Semillon

Score 96

RIVERINA
Price $34.00 (375 ml)
Quality ★★★★★
Alc./Vol. 10%
Drink 2011
Closure Screwcap

Australia's benchmark botrytis semillon is alive and well in the '06 vintage, showing plenty of dried apricot, lime rind and candied cumquat aromas. The palate rolls smooth and deep, very polished, juicy and intense, peach fruits here, lime through the finish, gentle grilled nuts close it off; fresh, intense and impeccably balanced.

2006 Domaine des Bernardins Muscat de Baumes de Venise

Score 92

RHÔNE VALLEY, FRANCE
Price $35.00 (375 ml)
Quality ★★★★
Alc./Vol. 15%
Drink Now
Closure Cork

A striking deep pink–gold colour, this style is a richer, more alcoholic proposition than most sweet styles. It trades on the fragrant qualities of the muscat grapes from which it is made. Sweet rose water, musk, quince and lychee flavours sweep through on rich but clean texture. Serve well chilled.

2007 Heggies Botrytis Riesling

Score 97

EDEN VALLEY
Price $27.00 (375 ml)
Quality ★★★★★
Alc./Vol. 10%
Drink Now
Closure Screwcap

Beautiful gold-tinged botrytis colour, this has intensity almost beyond belief; ripe, rich stone fruits and some chalky minerals, honeyed and symphonic, very intense and gently grassy. Massive fruit flavour – limes and lemons, more nectarine and apricot too – pulled into line by crystal clear acidity, taking flavour long through the finish. Superb balance, striking length, world-class!

PENGUIN BEST SWEET WINE

2007 Josef Chromy Botrytis Riesling

Score 96

TASMANIA
Price $24.00 (375 ml)
Quality ★★★★★
Alc./Vol. 12%
Drink Now
Closure Screwcap

As clean as it gets, superb purity in a concentrated late-picked style. Plenty of intense riesling citrus fruits, superb fragrance and aromatic lift. Smooth palate with impeccable sugar–acid balance; even and complete, an elegant and stylish wine.

2006 Lou Miranda Leone Botrytis Semillon

Score 90

RIVERINA
Price $17.00 ✓ (375 ml)
Quality ★★★★
Alc./Vol. 11%
Drink Now
Closure Diam

Classic candied citrus rind and dried peach fruits here, some gentle grassy edges, honeysuckle and apricots. The palate is richly flavoured with dried apricot, peach and honey, decent concentration and balance, smooth and complete.

2007 Pegasus Bay Aria Riesling

Score **95**

WAIPARA
Price $48.00
Quality   ★★★★ ┤
Alc./Vol.   15%
Drink   Now
Closure   Screwcap

Very well made, shows Pegasus Bay style with its concentrated mandarin fruits and impeccably executed fine florals that swirl in spirals from the glass. The palate is spellbinding for its concentrated, luscious fruit flavour and texture, cut into shape by sizzling acidity; it stays crunchy and finishes with long bold cumquat flavour.

2006 Pirie Clark's Botrytis Riesling

Score **93**

TASMANIA
Price $32.00 ✓ (375 ml)
Quality   ★★★★ ┤
Alc./Vol.   7.5%
Drink   Now
Closure   Screwcap

This is one of the Australia's best sweet wines and best-kept secrets; Andrew Pirie captures intensity like few others and balances it all up superbly. Fresh stone fruits and some tropical aromas, lime citrus and gentle lime blossom florals – pristine and delicate. Incredible sugar-driven density, elixir-like honey flavour and cleansing acidity; marvellous.

2006 Yalumba Hand Picked Botrytis Viognier

Score **90**

WRATTONBULLY
Price $26.00 ✓ (375 ml)
Quality   ★★★★
Alc./Vol.   12%
Drink   Now
Closure   Cork

Viognier lends itself well to the complexity that botrytis brings to this sweet golden wine; plenty of apricot and peach fruit, honey and orange aromas. Richly textured palate, with concentrated peach and apricot flavours, there's a core of intense luscious flavour that carries long and smooth.

Fortified wines

Given the quality and value in the top end, and the fact that these treasured drops are sipped in small doses, I'm commending the very best of Australian fortified wine to you. The range of style varies considerably, so pay close attention to make sure you're selecting the one you're after. The percentage of high-pointed wines is greater in this chapter than any other in the book, as these really deliver outstanding quality at the top end. There are some outstanding, inexpensive fortifieds, largely due to the steep decline in their popularity. Beware, the rest of the world has discovered the rare beauty of Australian fortified wines and they're snapping them up at a rate of knots. FOOD: Cheese is the first thing that comes to mind with these wines, but due to the range of styles and concentrations they are versatile options for matching with dessert (especially chocolate dishes), and sherry styles are handy partners to savoury courses.

NV Baileys of Glenrowan Winemakers Selection Old Tokay   Score 93

GLENROWAN
Price $55.00 (375 ml)
Quality   ★★★★⇥
Alc./Vol.   16.5%
Drink   Now
Closure   Cork

Amber with yellow edges, there's some old material in this deliciously rich and malty tokay from Ned Kelly country. Creamed caramel, mocha and dried raisin tea cake, the palate has fine intensity, shadows of lightly grilled cashew nut rancio, bright malted butterscotch flavour and elegant balance.

NV Baileys of Glenrowan Winemakers Selection Old Muscat   Score 92

GLENROWAN
Price $55.00 (375 ml)
Quality   ★★★★
Alc./Vol.   17%
Drink   Now
Closure   Cork

Dried raisins and dark citrus marmalade aromas, dried candied peel and gentle sweet unctuous perfume. Moves into treacle flavours on the palate, more orange rind here too, brightly structured and neatly balanced.

NV Chambers Grand Muscat

Score **98**

RUTHERGLEN

Price	$50.00 ✓ (375 ml)
Quality	★★★★★
Alc./Vol.	18%
Drink	Now
Closure	Cork

The highest pedigree in Rutherglen muscat rests at the Rosewood Vineyards of the Chambers family. This, their almost top-tier wine, is a thoroughbred that balances richness and intensity with fragrance and elegance. Deeply fragrant, moist rose petals and superb freshness balance this profound sticky liquid. Intense raisined flavours fan out in a stunning layered form, rancio builds up through the finish in perfect pace; haunting, clean and fragrant.

PENGUIN BEST FORTIFIED WINE

NV Chambers Old Vine Muscadelle

Score **96**

RUTHERGLEN

Price	$40.00 ✓ (375 ml)
Quality	★★★★★
Alc./Vol.	18%
Drink	Now
Closure	Cork

A blend of material graded as Classic and Grand and a style that shows concentration with elegance. Intense malt, tea leaf and burnt caramel aromas, candied citrus rind, some toasted nuts too. Soft, fine palate, precise honeyed flavour, some toffee and not at all cloying, this is great tokay packed with character.

NV De Bortoli Show Liqueur Muscat

Score **94**

RIVERINA

Price	$18.00 ✓
Quality	★★★★ ⌐
Alc./Vol.	18%
Drink	Now
Closure	Cork

A serious bargain in a (750 ml) bottle, this has plenty of rich raisin aromas, deeply concentrated, bright muscat fragrance and gentle toasty complexity. Dark toasty flavours on the palate, some deep chocolate through the middle, concentrated raisined fruit, it sails up on a rush of rancio through the finish, toasty fade. Unbelievable value!

NV Dutschke 'The Tawny' 22 Year Old

Score **96**

BAROSSA VALLEY

Price	$35.00 ✓ (375 ml)
Quality	★★★★★
Alc./Vol.	20%
Drink	Now
Closure	Screwcap

This deep amber-coloured tawny is a private passion of winemaker Wayne Dutschke. He's established a solera of old base wines from numerous varieties and every year he adds in some younger material to take out some of the complex older stuff; bottled in small format and screwcapped for your enjoyment. Savoury/nutty rancio character, dried raisins and butterscotch, there's terrific balance between this wine's sweet luscious texture and the cleansing long finish that twists towards dryness.

NV Grant Burge 20 Year Old Tawny

Score **96**

BAROSSA VALLEY
Price $62.00 ✓
Quality ★★★★★
Alc./Vol. 20%
Drink Now
Closure Cork

Grant Burge has a strong family tradition of fortified winemaking in the Barossa Valley, and he upholds the lineage with a determined sense of pride and craftsmanship. This 20-year-old tawny is staggering in its concentration, complexity and completeness. Super-intense rancio aromas, grilled nuts, leather and sweet old woody notes. The palate packs incredible power and drive, dense dried fruit peel and savoury/nutty flavours, finishing with a crisp, virtually dry resolve. A liquid national treasure.

NV Jones Apero

Score **90**

RUTHERGLEN
Price $25.00 (500 ml)
Quality ★★★★
Alc./Vol. 20%
Drink Now
Closure Cork

A well-conceived white port style making the most of some trebbiano and pedro ximinez in the vineyard. Shows honeyed white figs, gentle oak influence and nice freshness. Lovely nutty rancio flavours run right through the palate, sugar is balanced and it retains freshness. Works well with a light chill.

2005 Jones Vintage Fortified

Score **91**

RUTHERGLEN
Price $25.00 (500 ml)
Quality ★★★★
Alc./Vol. 19.3%
Drink Now
Closure Cork

Showing plummy shiraz richness, some deeply ripe fruit has been steered into this wine, aromas of prunes and raisins, spice and liquorice, oak toast sits atop it all. Decent weight and drive, the oak registers strongly on the palate and will mature in time; plum flavours, anise and a lifted spirity finish.

2006 Kalleske J.M.K. Shiraz VP

Score **96**

BAROSSA VALLEY
Price $24.00 ✓ (375 ml)
Quality ★★★★★
Alc./Vol. 19%
Drink Now
Closure Cork

Dedicated by sixth-generation winemaker Troy to his father John Malcolm Kalleske and packaged in a grenade-sized bottle. It has all the regional and varietal hallmarks of Greenock shiraz, super-ripe blackberries, sweet earth and dark spices; the oak is tucked neatly below. There's terrific textural richness and flavour concentration, a slice of toasty oak, well-chosen spirit and trademark Kalleske balanced opulence.

NV Morris of Rutherglen Old Premium Amontillado Sherry   *Score* 93

RUTHERGLEN
Price $50.00 ✓ (500 ml)
Quality ★★★★ ⸵
Alc./Vol. 21.5%
Drink   Now
Closure Cork

Pale amber and intense rancio character here, this amontillado gives an incredible array of complexity – the best of many worlds in one glass. Some fresh toasty oak on the palate, piercing and intense, with a long trail of savoury grilled nut flavour.

NV Morris of Rutherglen Old Premium Liqueur Muscat   *Score* 96

RUTHERGLEN
Price $70.00 ✓ (500 ml)
Quality ★★★★★
Alc./Vol. 17.5%
Drink   Now
Closure Cork

Mahogany coloured with mustard-green edges, intense dried raisins, Christmas spices and plum pudding aromas, some earthy dark toasted nuts too. Supreme concentration and complexity. A no-holds-barred textural experience, deep raisin flavour, mocha and earthy chocolate and a super slow-fading toasted nut finish.

NV Morris of Rutherglen Old Premium Liqueur Tokay   *Score* 97

RUTHERGLEN
Price $70.00 ✓ (500 ml)
Quality ★★★★★
Alc./Vol. 18%
Drink   Now
Closure Cork

Dark, deep brown in the glass. Very malty, toasted chocolate bread and spiced tea-cake aromas, this is super-intense. Full and luscious palate, the texture is like treacle with grilled nuts rolled through; there's a waft of smoke and pipe tobacco through the finish. Staggering concentration, this has to be tasted to be believed.

2006 Noon Winery VP   *Score* 95

McLAREN VALE
Price $18.00 ✓ (500 ml)
Quality ★★★★ ⸵
Alc./Vol. 18%
Drink   Now
Closure Cork

Sourced from old bush-vine grenache (Noon have a special little plot), showing mixed dark berries and plums, ripe fragrant lift and liquorice aniseed spices. Delivers lively dark liquorice and blackberry flavours, soft supple tannins, shows terrific integration, concentration and balance. Will cellar nicely. This is the cellar door price; expect to pay more than twice this humble amount on the secondary market.

NV Pfeiffer Old Distillery Classic Rutherglen Tokay   *Score* 91

RUTHERGLEN
Price $24.00 ✓ (500 ml)
Quality ★★★★
Alc./Vol. 17.5%
Drink   Now
Closure Cork

This has real freshness about the nose, lifted honeyed aromas and some dried apricot fruits, deeper loose leaf tea and malty edges – classic indeed. Soft honeyed palate with nutty rancio and candied orange rind through the finish. Finishes clean and fresh, nice balance in this everyday style.

2003 Pondalowie Vintage Port — Score 94

BENDIGO	
Price	$30.00 (500 ml)
Quality	★★★★ ⫪
Alc./Vol.	19.5%
Drink	Now
Closure	Cork

Ripe black fruits, cherry and plum, some regional Bendigo mint at the edges, nicely settled and integrated. Depth and drive, shiraz shines through and underscores the dark cherry flavour of tinta roriz, tannins are sturdy and well shaped, drawing long and soulful through the finish.

NV Ramos Pinto Adriano 6 Year Old Tawny Port — Score 92

OPORTO, PORTUGAL	
Price	$39.00
Quality	★★★★
Alc./Vol.	19.5%
Drink	Now
Closure	Cork

This is the real deal from a Portuguese producer with their house in order; still showing dusty red hues in the glass, it's a young, elegant tawny that's lighter and drier than most Australian styles. Only gentle rancio at this stage (it won't develop in bottle), some dried cherry and earthy/savoury notes; the palate is supple and open-knit, strong on acidity, it leaves a lingering dried cherry flavour.

2006 Scion Sweet Durif — Score 90

RUTHERGLEN	
Price	$22.00 (500 ml)
Quality	★★★★
Alc./Vol.	18.5%
Drink	Now
Closure	Procork

Striking dark durif colour, youthful purple tinges and classic cassis fruit aromas, a little liquorice too; very primary and could certainly be dropped in the cellar for a spell. Intense berry-fruited palate, sturdy ripe tannins, plum skin and a flurry of spirit to close.

NV Seppelt DP63 Grand Muscat — Score 96

RUTHERGLEN	
Price	$30.00 ✓
Quality	★★★★★
Alc./Vol.	17%
Drink	Now
Closure	Screwcap

This wine has amassed a distinguished trophy and medal count over many years, it has the trademark alluring rose petal and raisin aromas, savoury dark grilled nuts too. The palate is superbly rich, luscious and completely balanced; fulsome raisin flavour, a steady build of rancio. Winemaker James Godfrey's keen eye for the right spirit makes for compelling sipping.

NV Stanton & Killeen Classic Rutherglen Tawny Port — Score 95

RUTHERGLEN	
Price	$27.00 ✓ (500 ml)
Quality	★★★★ ⫪
Alc./Vol.	18%
Drink	Now
Closure	Cork

This tawny claims the best of both worlds: making a statement of the old and the new, with an average age of 12 years. A 50/50 split between shiraz and touriga, it has riches and fragrance, there's some dried berry fruit still in the mix, stylish oak and a sweep of rancio. The palate's built with fortitude and grace, truly brilliant – if there was just one tawny port to stock the bar, this would have to be it!

NV Stanton & Killeen Grand Muscat   Score **96**

RUTHERGLEN
Price $75.00 ✓ (500 ml)
Quality ★★★★★
Alc./Vol. 18.5%
Drink   Now
Closure Cork

One of the deeper Grand Rutherglen muscats in the line-up, with an average age of 25 years there's plenty of raisiny concentration, rolled rose petal and toasted nut rancio. Very concentrated: dark raisins, coffee and toasty rancio intensity through the finish. A brooding sweet dark style with a modern oak twist and superb powerful impact.

NV Stanton & Killeen Ruby Port   Score **91**

RUTHERGLEN
Price $16.50 ✓ (500 ml)
Quality ★★★★
Alc./Vol. 18%
Drink   Now
Closure Cork

Ruby port refers to a style that's fresh and ready to drink now, made here from shiraz, cabernet and touriga. The spirit draws fruit fragrance upwards, accentuating red fruits and florals; this is quite rich and complex for a ruby style. Bright supple red fruits, currants and raisin flavours laid across soft tannins.

2003 Stanton & Killeen Vintage Fortified   Score **96**

RUTHERGLEN
Price $27.00 ✓
Quality ★★★★★
Alc./Vol. 18.5%
Drink   Now
Closure Cork

Dark deep colour, haunting fragrance and complexity, this is a masterpiece from one of Rutherglen's finest, most dedicated vintage-style fortified makers. Cassis and mixed berries shine through a sheen of fragrance and perfectly matched spirit; sweet, juicy and intense palate, terrific integration and build, cherry liqueur and berries, some cassis rolls through and lifts at the finish. Majestic yet measured, with a delicious plum skin aftertaste.

NV Valdespino Pedro Ximinez   Score **90**

JEREZ, SPAIN
Price $25.00
Quality ★★★★
Alc./Vol. 17%
Drink   Now
Closure Cork

Pedro ximinez, or PX as it is fondly referred to, is a dark, sweet sticky brown sherry that is famous for its thick texture and symphonic complexity. Rich aromas of sweet warm blueberry pie, orange peel, pastry dough and dark raisins. Flavours run in the same vein through super-luscious texture – this can be served chilled or at room temperature and (just quietly) it's a winner when poured over a bowl of your finest vanilla ice-cream.

Wine terms

The following are commonly used winemaking terms.

Acid There are many acids that occur naturally in grapes and it's in the winemaker's interest to retain the favourable ones because these promote freshness and longevity.

Agrafe A metal clip used to secure champagne corks during secondary bottle fermentation.

Alcohol Ethyl alcohol (C_2H_5OH) is a by-product of fermentation of sugars. It's the stuff that makes people happy and it adds warmth and texture to wine.

Alcohol by volume (A/V) The measurement of the amount of alcohol in a wine. It's expressed as a percentage, e.g. 13.0% A/V means there is 13.0% pure alcohol as a percentage of the total volume.

Aldehyde An unwanted and unpleasant organic compound formed between acid and alcohol by oxidation. It's removed by sulphur dioxide.

Allier A type of oak harvested in the French forest of the same name.

Aperitif A wine that stimulates the appetite.

Aromatic A family of grape varieties that have a high terpene content. Riesling and gewürztraminer are examples, and terpenes produce their floral qualities.

Autolysis A Vegemite or freshly baked bread taste and smell imparted by spent yeast cells in sparkling wines.

Back blend To add unfermented grape juice to wine or to add young wine to old wine in fortifieds.

Barrel fermentation The process of fermenting a red or white wine in a small barrel, thereby adding a creamy texture and toasty or nutty characters, and better integrating the wood and fruit flavours.

Barrique A 225-litre barrel.

Baumé The measure of sugar in grape juice used to estimate potential alcohol content. It's usually expressed as a degree, e.g. 12 degrees Baumé juice will produce approximately 12.0% A/V if it's fermented to dryness. The alternative brix scale is approximately double Baumé and must be divided by 1.8 to estimate potential alcohol.

Bentonite A fine clay (drillers mud) used as a clarifying (fining) agent.

Blend A combination of two or more grape varieties and/or vintages. *See also* Cuvée.

Botrytis cinerea A mould that thrives on grapevines in humid conditions and sucks out the water of the grapes thereby concentrating the flavour. Good in white wine but not so good in red. (There is also a loss in quantity.)

Breathing Uncorking a wine and allowing it to stand for a couple of hours before serving. This introduces oxygen and dissipates bottle odours. Decanting aids breathing.

Brix *see* Baumé.

Brut The second lowest level of sweetness in sparkling wine; it does not mean there is no added sugar.

Bush vine   Although pruned the vine is self-supporting in a low-to-the-ground bush. (Still common in the Barossa Valley.)

Carbonic maceration   Fermentation in whole (uncrushed) bunches. This is a popular technique in Beaujolais. It produces bright colour and soften tannins.

Charmat process   A process for making sparkling wine where the wine is fermented in a tank rather than in a bottle.

Clone (clonal)   A recognisable subspecies of vine within a varietal family, e.g. there are numerous clones of pinot noir and these all have subtle character differences.

Cold fermentation   (Also Controlled Temperature Fermentation) Usually applied to white wines where the ferment is kept at a low temperature (10–12 degrees Centigrade).

Cordon   The arms of the trained grapevine that bear the fruit.

Cordon cut   A technique of cutting the fruit-bearing arms and allowing the berries to dehydrate to concentrate the flavour.

Crush   Crushing the berries to liberate the free-run juice (*q.v.*). Also used as an expression of a wine company's output: 'This winery has a 1000-tonne crush'.

Cuvée   A Champagne term meaning a selected blend or batch.

Disgorge   The process of removing the yeast lees from a sparkling wine. It involves freezing the neck of the bottle and firing out a plug of ice and yeast. The bottle is then topped up and recorked.

Dosage   Sweetened wine added to a sparkling wine after disgorgement.

Downy mildew   A disease that attacks vine leaves and fruit. It's associated with humidity and lack of air circulation.

Drip irrigation   An accurate way of watering a vineyard. Each vine has its own dripper and a controlled amount of water is applied.

Dryland vineyard   A vineyard that has no irrigation.

Esters   Volatile compounds that can occur during fermentation or maturation. They impart a distinctive chemical taste.

Fermentation   The process by which yeast converts sugar to alcohol with a by-product of carbon dioxide.

Fining   The process of removing solids from wine to make it clear. There are several methods used.

Fortify   The addition of spirit to increase the amount of alcohol in a wine.

Free-run juice   The first juice to come out of the press or drainer (as opposed to pressings).

Generic   Wines labelled after their district of origin rather than their grape variety, e.g. Burgundy, Chablis, Champagne etc. These terms can no longer legally be used on Australian labels. *Cf.* Varietal.

Graft   Changing the nature/variety of a vine by grafting a different variety onto a root stock.

Imperial   A 6-litre bottle (contains eight 750-ml bottles).

Jeroboam   A 4.5-litre champagne bottle.

Laccase   A milky condition on the surface of red wine caused by noble rot. The wine is usually pasteurised.

Lactic acid   One of the acids found in grape juice; as the name suggests, it's milky and soft.

Lactobacillus   A micro-organism that ferments carbohydrates (glucose) or malic acid to produce lactic acid.

Lees   The sediment left after fermentation. It consists mainly of dead yeast cells.

Malic acid   One of the acids found in grape juice. It has a hard/sharp taste like a Granny Smith apple.

Malolactic fermentation   A secondary process that converts malic acid into lactic acid. It's encouraged in red wines when they are in barrel. If it occurs after bottling, the wine will be fizzy and cloudy.

Mercaptan   Ethyl mercaptan is a sulphur compound with a smell like garlic, burnt rubber or asparagus water.

Méthode champenoise   The French method for producing effervescence in the bottle; a secondary fermentation process where the carbon dioxide produced is dissolved into the wine.

Methoxypyrazines   Substances that give sauvignon blanc and cabernet sauvignon that added herbaceousness when the grapes aren't fully ripe.

Mousse   The froth or head on sparkling wines.

Must   *see* Free-run juice.

Negociant   A French word that describes a person or organisation that produces and sells wine from grapes and/or bulk wine bought-in from other people.

Noble rot   *see* Botrytis cinerea.

Non-vintage   A wine that is a blend of two or more years.

Oak   The least porous wood, genus *Quercus*, and used for wine storage containers.

Oenology   The science of winemaking.

Organic viticulture   Growing grapes without the use of pesticides, fungicides or chemical fertilisers. Certain chemicals, e.g. copper sulphate, are permitted.

Organic wines   Wines made from organically grown fruit without the addition of chemicals.

Oxidation   Browning and dullness of aroma and flavour caused by excessive exposure to air.

pH   The measure of the strength of acidity. The higher the pH the higher the alkalinity and the lower the acidity. Wines with high pH values should not be cellared.

Phenolics   A group of chemical compounds which includes the tannins and colour pigments of grapes. A white wine described as 'phenolic' has an excess of tannin, making it taste coarse.

Phylloxera   A louse that attacks the roots of a vine, eventually killing the plant.

Pigeage   To foot-press the grapes.

Pressings   The juice extracted by applying pressure to the skins after the free-run juice has been drained.

Pricked   A wine that is spoilt and smells of vinegar, due to excessive volatile acidity. *Cf.* Volatile.

Puncheon   A 500-litre barrel.

Racking   Draining off wine from the lees or other sediment to clarify it.

Saignée   French for bleeding: the winemaker has run off part of the juice of a red fermentation to concentrate what's left.

Skin contact   Allowing the free-run juice to remain in contact with the skins; in the case of white wines, usually for a very short time.

Solero system   Usually a stack of barrels used for blending maturing wines. The oldest material is at the bottom and is topped up with younger material from the top barrels.

Solids   Minute particles suspended in a wine.

Sulphur dioxide (SO₂)   (Code 220) A chemical added since Roman times to wine as a preservative and a bactericide.

Sur Lie   Wine that has been kept on lees and not racked or filtered before bottling.

Taché   A French term that means 'stained', usually by the addition of a small amount of red wine to sparkling wine to turn it pink.

Tannin   A complex substance derived from skins, pips and stalks of grapes as well as the oak casks. It has a preservative function and imparts dryness and grip to the finish.

Terroir   Arcane French expression that describes the complete growing environment of the vine, including climate, aspect, soil, etc., and the direct effect this has on the character of its wine.

Varietal   An industry-coined term used to refer to a wine by its grape variety, e.g. 'a shiraz'. *Cf.* Generic.

Véraison   The moment when the grapes change colour and gain sugar.

Vertical tasting   A tasting of consecutive vintages of one wine.

Vigneron   A grapegrower or vineyard worker.

Vinegar   Acetic acid produced from fruit.

Vinify   The process of turning grapes into wine.

Vintage   The year of harvest, and the produce of a particular yeast.

Volatile   Excessive volatile acids in a wine.

Yeast   The micro-organism that converts sugar into alcohol.

Tasting terms

The following terms refer to the sensory evaluation of wine.

Aftertaste   The taste (sensation) after the wine has been swallowed. It's usually called the finish.

Astringent (astringency)   Applies to the finish of a wine. Astringency is caused by tannins that produce a mouth-puckering sensation and coat the teeth with dryness.

Balance   'The state of . . .'; the harmony between components of a wine.

Bilgy   An unfortunate aroma like the bilge of a ship. Usually caused by mouldy oak.

Bitterness   A sensation detected at the back of the tongue. It's not correct in wine but is desirable in beer.

Bouquet   The aroma of a finished or mature wine.

Brettanomyces (Brett)   A spoilage yeast that produces chemical compounds that are present in most red wines but usually at small concentrations. In large doses, these cause aromas reminiscent of bandaids, sweaty horses and other unappetising things, as well as a metallic taste and bitter tannins on the palate.

Broad   A wine that lacks fruit definition; usually qualified as soft or coarse.

Burnt match   A sulphide-related odour, often associated with wild or indigenous yeast fermentations in chardonnay. In small doses, can be a positive factor.

Cassis   A blackcurrant flavour common in cabernet sauvignon. It refers to a liqueur produced in France.

Chalky   An extremely dry sensation on the finish.

Cheesy   A dairy character sometimes found in wine, particularly sherries.

Cigar box   A smell of tobacco and wood found in cabernet sauvignon.

Cloudiness   A fault in wine that is caused by suspended solids that make it look dull.

Cloying   Excessive sweetness that clogs the palate.

Corked   Wine that has reacted with a tainted cork, and smells like wet cardboard.

Creamy   The feeling of cream in the mouth, a texture.

Crisp   Clean acid on the finish of a white wine.

Depth   The amount of fruit on the palate.

Dry   A wine that does not register sugar in the mouth.

Dull   Pertaining to colour; the wine is not bright or shining.

Dumb   Lacking nose or flavour on the palate.

Dusty   Applies to a very dry tannic finish; a sensation.

Earthy   A loamy/mineral character that can add interest to the palate.

Finesse   The state of a wine. It refers to balance and style.

Finish   *see* Aftertaste.

Firm   Wine with strong, unyielding tannins.

Flabby   Wine with insufficient acid to balance ripe fruit flavours.

Fleshy   Wines of substance with plenty of fruit.

Flinty   A character on the finish that is akin to sucking dry creek pebbles.

Flor yeast   A yeast that grows on the surface of young sherry in partly filled barrels, producing aldehydes that are a key part of the flavour and aroma of fino and manzanilla sherries.

Garlic   *see* Mercaptan (in Wine Terms).

Grassy   A cut-grass odour, usually found in semillon and sauvignon blancs.

Grip   The effect on the mouth of tannin on the finish; a puckering sensation.

Hard   More tannin or acid than fruit flavour.

Herbaceous   Herbal smells or flavour in wine.

Hollow   A wine with a lack of flavour in the middle palate.

Hot   Wines high in alcohol that give a feeling of warmth and a slippery texture.

Hydrogen sulphide   A rotten-egg-like character, usually created by yeasts during fermentation.

Implicit sweetness   A just detectable sweetness from the presence of glycerin (rather than residual sugar).

Inky   Tannate of iron present in a wine which imparts a metallic taste.

Integrated (well)   The component parts of a wine fit together without gaps or disorders.

Jammy   Ripe fruit that takes on the character of stewed jam.

Leathery   A smell like old leather, not necessarily bad if it's in balance.

Length (long)   The measure of the registration of flavour in the mouth. (The longer the better.)

Lifted   The wine is given a lift by the presence of either volatile acid or wood tannins.

Limpid   A colour term usually applied to star-bright white wine.

Madeirised   Wine that has aged to the point where it tastes like a madeira.

Mouldy   Smells like bathroom mould; dank.

Mouth-feel   The sensation the wine causes in the mouth; a textural term.

Musty   Stale, flat, out-of-condition wine.

Pepper   A component in either the nose or the palate that smells or tastes like cracked pepper.

Pungent   Wine with a strong nose.

Rancio   A nutty character found in aged fortifieds that is imparted by time on wood.

Reductive   *see* Hydrogen Sulphide.

Residual sugar   The presence of unfermented grape sugar on the palate; common in sweet wines.

Rough   Unpleasant, aggressive wines.

Round   A full-bodied wine with plenty of mouth-feel (*q.v.*).

Sappy   A herbaceous character that resembles sap.

Short   A wine lacking in taste and structure. *See also* Length.

Sous-bois   The French word for undergrowth. Used in describing some pinot noirs, especially those made with stalks included in the fermentation.

Spicy   A wine with a high aromatic content; spiciness can also be imparted by wood.

Stalky   Exposure to stalks, e.g. during fermentation, leaving a bitter character.

Tart   A lively wine with a lot of fresh acid.

Toasty   A smell of cooked bread.

Vanillin   The smell and taste of vanilla beans; usually imparted by oak ageing.

Varietal   Refers to the distinguishing qualities of the grape variety used in the wine.

Principal wine regions

WESTERN AUSTRALIA
1 Swan Valley
2 Perth Hills
3 Geographe
4 Margaret River
5 Pemberton/Manjimup
6 Great Southern

SOUTH AUSTRALIA
7 Riverland
8 Clare Valley
9 Barossa Valley
10 Eden Valley
11 Adelaide Hills
12 McLaren Vale
13 Langhorne Creek
14 Coonawarra

TASMANIA
15 Tamar Valley
16 Derwent Valley
17 Coal River
18 East Coast
19 Piper's River

VICTORIA
20 Henty/Drumborg
21 Murray Valley
22 Sunraysia
23 Gippsland
24 Mornington Peninsula

25 Yarra Valley
26 Sunbury
27 Geelong/Bellarine
      Peninsula
28 Grampians/Great Western
29 Macedon Ranges
30 Heathcote
31 Bendigo
32 Pyrenees
33 Rutherglen
34 Beechworth
35 King Valley
36 Goulburn Valley

NEW SOUTH WALES
37 Murray Valley
38 Tumbarumba
39 Riverina
40 Canberra District
41 Hilltops/Young
42 Cowra
43 Shoalhaven
44 Southern Highlands
45 Orange
46 Mudgee
47 Hunter Valley
48 Hastings Valley

QUEENSLAND
49 Granite Belt
50 South Burnett

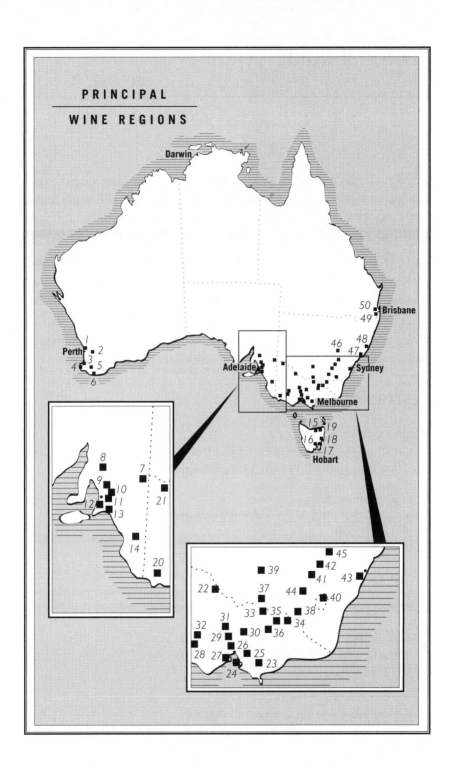

PRINCIPAL
WINE REGIONS

Darwin

Perth

Adelaide

Sydney

Melbourne

Brisbane

Hobart

1
2
3
4
5
6

7
8
9
10
11
12
13
14
20
21

15
16
17
18
19

0

22
23
24
25
26
27
28
29
30
31
32
33
34
35
36
37
38
39
40
41
42
43
44
45

46
47
48
49
50

Regional guide

The regional guide is one of this year's new inclusions. The regions covered here are an essential collection of the most popular and accessible of Australia's 60-odd regions; easy to reach and, with a few simple pointers, easy to enjoy. I've visited all the places recommended and endorse them as ones you need to know about in order to experience the best each region has to offer.

There's enough information here to get you through a great weekend: which wines to look out for, where best to taste them, where to eat, sleep, take a cleansing ale and get a reliable dose of caffeine. If you are planning to stay longer than a weekend, ask for further recommendations at the suggested cellar doors and check in with the regional information centres.

WESTERN AUSTRALIA

Margaret River
From Perth, allow three hours to drive to this stunning coastal region, where you'll find the cream of Western Australia's whites and reds.

i **Regional Information**
Margaret River Wine, 33 Tunbridge St, Margaret River WA 6285
(08) 9757 9330
margaretriverwine.org.au

Wines
Cabernet sauvignon, cabernet merlot, chardonnay, semillon-sauvignon blanc blends.

Top Cellar Doors
Voyager Estate, Stevens Rd, Margaret River WA 6285
(08) 9757 6354
voyagerestate.com.au

Cullen Wines, Caves Rd, Cowaramup WA 6284
(08) 9755 5277
cullenwines.com.au

Cape Mentelle Vineyards, 331 Wallcliffe Rd, Margaret River WA 6285
(08) 9757 0888
capementelle.com.au

Pierro, Caves Rd, Wilyabrup WA 6280
(08) 9755 6220
pierro.com.au

Vasse Felix, cnr Caves Rd & Harmans Rd South, Cowaramup WA 6284
(08) 9756 5000
vassefelix.com.au

Eat

Wino's, 85 Bussell Highway, Margaret River WA 6285
(08) 9758 7155

Voyager Estate, Stevens Rd, Margaret River WA 6285
(08) 9757 6354
voyagerestate.com.au

Cullen, Caves Rd, Cowaramup WA 6284
(08) 9755 5277
cullenwines.com.au

Pub

Settlers Tavern, 114 Bussell Hwy, Margaret River WA 6285
(08) 9757 2398
settlerstavern.com

Coffee

Wino's (as above)

Stay

Posh – Cape Lodge, Caves Rd, Yallingup WA 6282
(08) 9755 6311

Budget – beachside cabins are a great alternative to hotels and conventional accommodation.

Tip

If you're into rugged coastal scenery and surfing, add a couple of extra days to your trip. This region has some of the wildest surf breaks in Australia and is home to world champion Taj Burrow.

SOUTH AUSTRALIA

Coonawarra

If you head out on the road from either Adelaide or Melbourne, you'll arrive at Coonawarra four to five hours later. It's a long way from anywhere, which is perhaps why the hospitality here is renowned. The wines are in better shape than ever, there are some brilliant restaurants and a spectacular stretch of nearby coastline.

i **Regional Information**
coonawarra.org

Wines
Cabernet sauvignon, merlot, shiraz and blends thereof, sauvignon blanc.

Top Cellar Doors
Wynns, Memorial Dve, Coonawarra SA 5263
(08) 8736 2226
wynns.com.au

Balnaves, Main Rd, Coonawarra SA 5263
(08) 8737 2946
balnaves.com.au

Hollick, Ravenswood Lane, Coonawarra SA 5263
(08) 8737 2318
hollick.com

Rymill, Riddoch Hwy, Coonawarra SA 5263
(08) 8736 5001
rymill.com.au

Eat
Pipers of Penola, 58 Riddoch St, Penola SA 5277
(08) 8737 3999
pipersofpenola.com.au

Red Fingers, Memorial Dve, Coonawarra SA 5263
(08) 8736 3006

Upstairs at Hollick, cnr Riddoch Hwy & Ravenswood Lane, Coonawarra SA 5263
(08) 8737 2752
hollick.com/upstairs

Pub
Not much out of the ordinary, so head to Penola for a cleansing ale.

☕ **Coffee**
Better pack the thermos!

🛏 **Stay**
Posh – Chardonnay Lodge, Riddoch Hwy, Coonawarra SA 5263
(08) 8736 3309
chardonnaylodge.com.au

Budget – Must at Coonawarra, 126 Church St, Penola SA 5277
(08) 8737 3444
mustatcoonawarra.com.au

💡 **Tip**
The best times of year to visit are when the crayfish at Robe are in season
(October to May) or during the running of the Coonawarra Cup in January.

McLaren Vale

Just tipping the southern edge of the Adelaide suburbs, this quiet region
is possibly the easiest to visit. It is Australia's answer to the central Italian
coastline and you'll find olives scattered throughout the carpet of vineyards
on the plain. The sheltered beaches are terrific for families, and getting
around is made easy by the compact layout of cellar doors.

ℹ **Regional Information**
mclarenvale.info

🍷 **Wines**
Grenache, shiraz, mourvèdre and blends thereof, cabernet sauvignon and a
growing number of well-made Italian and Spanish varietals.

🍾 **Top Cellar Doors**
d'Arenberg, Osborn Rd, McLaren Vale SA 5171
(08) 8329 4848
darenberg.com.au

Samuel's Gorge, Lot 10, Chaffeys Rd, McLaren Vale SA 5171
(08) 8323 8651
gorge.com.au

Penny's Hill, Willungal Rd, McLaren Vale SA 5171
(08) 8556 4460
pennyshill.com.au

Oliver's Taranga, Seaview Rd, McLaren Vale SA 5171
(08) 8323 8498
oliverstaranga.com

Lloyd Brothers, Warners Rd, McLaren Vale SA 5171
(08) 8323 8792
lloydbrothers.com.au

Wirra Wirra, McMurtie Rd, McLaren Vale SA 5171
(08) 8323 8414
wirra.com.au

Eat
d'Arry's Verandah, Osborn Rd, McLaren Vale SA 5171
(08) 8329 4848
darenberg.com.au

Victory Hotel, Main South Rd, Sellicks Beach SA 5174
(08) 8556 3083
victoryhotel.com.au

Star of Greece, cnr Esplanade & Port Rd, Port Willunga SA 5172
(08) 8557 7420

Penny's Hill, Main Rd, McLaren Vale SA 5171
(08) 8556 4460
pennyshill.com.au

Pub
Victory Hotel – one of Australia's finest regional pubs.
Main South Rd, Sellicks Beach SA 5174
(08) 8556 3083
victoryhotel.com.au

Coffee
Tin Shed Cafe, 225 Main Rd, McLaren Vale SA 5171
(08) 8323 7343
tinshedcafe.com.au

Market 190, 190 Main Rd, McLaren Vale SA 5171
(08) 8323 8558
market190.com.au

🛏 **Stay**

Posh – Chapel Hill Gourmet Retreat, cnr Chapel Hill & Chaffeys Rds,
McLaren Vale SA 5171
(08) 8323 8429
chapelhillwine.com.au

Budget – the Victory Hotel's new cottages, perched high on the hill with
stunning views, are fully self-contained.
Main South Rd, Sellicks Beach SA 5174
(08) 8556 3083
victoryhotel.com.au

💡 **Tip**

The local whiting and squid, caught just out in the Gulf, are worth watching out
for on menus. The region also wins many awards for its olive oil.

Barossa Valley

Steeped in history and boasting a dynamic contemporary edge, the Barossa
is an amazing wine region to visit. No other Australian region offers such a
diverse and convincing wine experience; from the wines to the people and
places, this is unbeatable. Famous names, big and small, are tucked around
every corner; whether you're down on the Valley floor or perched up in the
hills of the Eden Valley, you'll find great wines in abundance.

ℹ️ **Regional Information**

barossa.com

🍷 **Wines**

Shiraz, grenache, mataro and blends thereof, cabernet sauvignon, rosé styles,
riesling, viognier, semillon, frontignac.

🍾 **Top Cellar Doors**

Rockford, Krondorf Rd, Tanunda SA 5352
(08) 8563 2720
rockfordwines.com.au

Charles Melton, Krondorf Rd, Tanunda SA 5352
(08) 8563 3606
charlesmeltonwines.com.au

Peter Lehmann, off Para Rd, Tanunda SA 5352
(08) 8563 2100
peterlehmannwines.com

Yalumba, Eden Valley Rd, Angaston SA 5353
(08) 8561 3200
yalumba.com

Torbreck, Roennfeldt Rd, Marananga SA 5352
(08) 8562 4155
torbreck.com

Eat

Vintners Bar & Grill, Lot 51, Nuriootpa Rd, Angaston SA 5353
(08) 8564 2488
vintners.com.au

Appellation at Peppers, cnr Seppeltsfield & Stonewell Rds, Marananga SA 5355
(08) 8562 4144
peppers.com.au/thelouise

1918 (Tanunda), 94 Murray St, Tanunda SA 5352
(08) 8563 0405
1918.com.au

Lou Miranda, Barossa Valley Way, Rowland Flat SA 5352
(08) 8524 4537
loumirandaestate.com.au

Pub

Eden Valley Hotel – the only pub in the region that hasn't been taken over by pokies and parmigianas.
Main St, Eden Valley SA 5235
(08) 8564 1072
evhotel.com.au

Coffee

Blond Coffee, 60 Murray St, Angaston SA 5353
(08) 8564 3444

Stay

Posh – Peppers Vineyard Resort, cnr Seppeltsfield & Stonewell Rds, Marananga SA 5355
(08) 8562 4144
peppers.com.au

Budget – choose one of the many cottages for rent around the district.

Tip
The region, which was settled in large part by German immigrants, has a strong tradition of locally smoked meats. The bacon is famous, either from Schultz's in Angaston or Linke's in Nuriootpa, depending on your tastes.

Clare Valley

A good two-hour drive north of Adelaide will bring you to this famous series of valleys that run along a line from Auburn in the south to the Clare township in the north. This is noted riesling country and has the potential to deliver reds of impressive structure and weight that are capable of long cellaring.

i **Regional Information**
clarevalley.com.au

Wines
Riesling, shiraz, cabernet sauvignon and grenache.

Top Cellar Doors
Pikes, Polish Hill River Rd, Sevenhill SA 5453
(08) 8843 4370
pikeswines.com.au

Grosset, 164 Stanley St, Auburn SA 5451
(08) 8849 2175
grosset.com.au

Mount Horrocks, The Old Railway Station, Curling St, Auburn SA 5451
(08) 8849 2243
mounthorrocks.com

Leasingham, 7 Dominic St, Clare SA 5453
(08) 8842 2555
leasingham-wines.com.au

Mitchell, Hughes Park Rd, Sevenhill South SA 5453
(08) 8843 4258
mitchellwines.com

Sevenhill Cellars, College Rd, Sevenhill SA 5453
(08) 8843 4222
sevenhillcellars.com.au

Eat
Skillogalee, Trevarrick Rd, Sevenhill SA 5453
(08) 8843 4311

Mount Horrocks, The Old Railway Station, Curling St, Auburn SA 5451
(08) 8849 2243
mounthorrocks.com

Pub
Sevenhill Hotel – offers the most lively local bar scene; food is serviceable.
Main North Rd, Sevenhill SA 5453
(08) 8843 4217

Coffee
Epic, Shop 4, 260 Main North Rd, Clare SA 5453
(08) 8842 2917

Stay
Posh – Thorn Park, College Rd, Sevenhill SA 5453
(08) 8843 4304
thornpark.com.au

Budget – Rising Sun Hotel, Main North Rd, Auburn SA 5451
(08) 8849 2015

Tip
Head out to Mintaro for a look at some local history. It's famous for its slate; the same slate runs beneath many of the region's vineyards and gives the wines a pronounced mineral character. The Riesling Trail that meanders nearby is also a fun bike ride for the actively minded.

Adelaide Hills
Choose one of the many winding entries from the Adelaide Plain and head up to higher altitudes, and some of the most picturesque rolling wine country. The hills are now a rich source of cool-climate grapes and home to some premium names in Australian wine. Cellar doors are dotted throughout the many towns and there are myriad places to stop and browse.

Regional information
visitadelaidehills.com.au

Wines
Sauvignon blanc, chardonnay, shiraz and riesling.

Top Cellar Doors
Shaw & Smith, Lot 4, Jones Rd, Balhannah SA 5242
(08) 8398 0500
shawandsmith.com

Petaluma, Mt Barker Rd, Bridgewater SA 5155
(08) 8339 9200
petaluma.com.au

Ashton Hills, Tregarthen Rd, Ashton SA 5137
(08) 8390 1243

Longview Vineyard, Pound Rd, Macclesfield SA 5153
(08) 8388 9694
longviewvineyard.com.au

Tilbrook Estate, 17/1 Lobethal Rd, Lobethal SA 5241
(08) 8389 5318

Golding Wines, Western Branch Rd, Lobethal SA 5241
(08) 8389 5120
goldingwines.com.au

Eat

Bridgewater Mill, Mount Barker Rd, Bridgewater SA 5155
(08) 8339 9200
bridgewatermill.com.au

The Lane, Ravenswood Lane, Hahndorf SA 5245
(08) 8388 1250
thelane.com.au

Pub

There are many great pubs throughout the Hills: the Three Brothers Arms and the Uraidla Hotel both offer a reliable feed, and the balcony of the Scenic is a great place for an afternoon ale.

Three Brothers Arms, 40–42 Venables St, Macclesfield SA 5153
(08) 8388 9265

Uraidla Hotel, 1198 Greenhill Rd, Uraidla SA 5142
(08) 8390 3029

Scenic Hotel, Old Norton Summit Rd, Norton Summit SA 5136
(08) 8390 1705

Coffee

Organic Market, 5 Druids Ave, Stirling SA 5152
(08) 8339 4835

🛏 **Stay**
Posh – Mount Lofty House, 74 Mount Lofty Summit Rd, Crafers SA 5152
(08) 8339 6777
mtloftyhouse.com.au

Budget – many bed & breakfast options.

🔆 **Tip**
Grapes, apples, figs and cherries are planted right throughout the Hills area and
you can go picking in season. Pick-your-own cherries as you pass through or take
on some seasonal work and experience vineyard/orchard life.

TASMANIA

The Apple Isle may one day be known as the Isle of Wine, such is the intense
buzz and interest surrounding this part of Australia. There are many reasons
to visit Tasmania and the produce is every bit as stunning as the wines.
Either Hobart or Launceston will give you an abundant choice of wineries,
cellar doors, restaurants and spectacular scenery.

ⓘ **Regional Information**
taswines.net

🍷 **Wines**
Riesling, pinot noir, chardonnay, sparkling, pinot gris, gewürztraminer, sauvignon
blanc.

🍾 **Top Cellar Doors**
Josef Chromy, 370 Relbia St, Relbia Tas. 7258
(03) 6335 8700
josefchromy.com.au

Meadowbank Estate, 699 Richmond Rd, Cambridge Tas. 7170
(03) 6248 4484
meadowbankwines.com.au

Bay of Fires Vineyard, 40 Baxters Rd, Pipers River Tas. 7252
(03) 6382 7622
bayoffireswines.com.au

Freycinet Vineyard, 15919 Tasman Hwy, Bicheno Tas. 7215
(03) 6257 8574
freycinetvineyard.com.au

Jansz Tasmania, 1216B Pipers Brook Rd, Pipers Brook Tas. 7254
(03) 6382 7066
jansztas.com

Eat
Stillwater Cafe, Richies Mill, Paterson St, Launceston Tas. 7250
(03) 6331 4153
stillwater.net.au

Fee & Me, 190 Charles St, Launceston Tas. 7250
(03) 6331 3195
feeandme.com.au

The Source (Moorilla Estate), 655 Main Rd, Berriedale Tas. 7011
(03) 6277 9900
moorilla.com.au/thesource/

Pub
Too many to mention – Hobart and Launceston are home to some of Australia's oldest operating pubs.

Coffee
Croplines, Brisbane Court, Shop 1, 76 Brisbane St, Launceston Tas. 7250
(03) 6331 4023

Oomph, 60 Liverpool St, Hobart Tas. 7000
(03) 6234 5991
oomphcoffee.com

Stay
Posh – Henry Jones Art Hotel, 25 Hunter St, Hobart Tas. 7000
(03) 6210 7700
thehenryjones.com

Islington Hotel, 321 Davey St, South Hobart Tas. 7004
(03) 6220 2123
islingtonhotel.com

The Pavilions at Moorilla Estate, 655 Main Rd, Berriedale Tas. 7011
(03) 6277 9900
moorilla.com.au/pavilions/

Tip
Brewing is another of Tasmania's specialties, and both Cascade and James Boag have informative tours and tastings. For something really unique, though, check out beer scribe Willie Simpson's Seven Sheds brewery in Railton.

VICTORIA

Yarra Valley

Just over one hour from the centre of Melbourne, the Valley is an ideal day trip, although you may find you want to spend more time exploring the myriad wineries and other attractions.

This region has everything to make for a complete experience, and will be particularly appealing to those interested in fine food as well as wine.

ℹ️ Regional Information
yarravalleywine.com

🍷 Wines
Chardonnay, pinot noir, shiraz, cabernet blends and sparkling.

🍾 Top Cellar Doors
Giant Steps, 336 Maroondah Hwy, Healesville Vic. 3777
(03) 5962 6111
giant-steps.com.au

Yering Station, 38 Melba Hwy, Yarra Glen Vic. 3775
(03) 9730 1107
yering.com

De Bortoli, Pinnacle Lane, Dixons Creek Vic. 3775
(03) 5965 2271
debortoli.com.au

TarraWarra, 311 Healesville–Yarra Glen Rd, Yarra Glen Vic. 3775
(03) 5962 3311
tarrawarra.com.au

🍴 Eat
De Bortoli, Pinnacle Lane, Dixons Creek Vic. 3775
(03) 5965 2271
debortoli.com.au

Healesville Hotel, 256 Maroondah Hwy, Healesville Vic. 3777
(03) 5962 4002
healesvillehotel.com.au

Giant Steps, 336 Maroondah Hwy, Healesville Vic. 3777
(03) 5962 6111
giant-steps.com.au

Pub
Healesville Hotel, 256 Maroondah Hwy, Healesville Vic. 3777
(03) 5962 4002
healesvillehotel.com.au

Coffee
Giant Steps roast and blend their own coffee (it's quite dark and rich); Healesville Harvest is also a reliable cup.

Giant Steps, 336 Maroondah Hwy, Healesville Vic. 3777
(03) 5962 6111
giant-steps.com.au

Healesville Harvest (cafe at Healesville Hotel), 256 Maroondah Hwy,
Healesville Vic. 3777
(03) 5962 2044

Stay
Posh – Chateau Yering, 42 Melba Hwy, Yering Vic. 3770
1800 237 333
chateauyering.com.au

Budget – Healesville Hotel, 256 Maroondah Hwy, Healesville Vic. 3777
(03) 5962 4002
healesvillehotel.com.au

RACV Healesville Country Club, Yarra Glen Rd, Healesville Vic. 3777
(03) 5962 4899

Tip
The Yarra Valley Pasta Shop in Healesville is a source of delicious traditional take-home pasta.

Mornington Peninsula
Definitely the posh side of the bay, this is where many well-heeled Melburnians head in the summer months to take up residence in the sought-after beachside havens of Portsea and Sorrento. The vineyard backdrop to the spectacular bay and surf beaches makes for an excellent region to visit.

Regional Information
mpva.com.au

Wines
Chardonnay, pinot noir, shiraz and pinot gris.

Top Cellar Doors

Paringa Estate, 44 Paringa Rd, Red Hill South Vic. 3937
(03) 5989 2669
paringaestate.com.au

Ten Minutes By Tractor, 1333 Mornington–Flinders Rd, Main Ridge Vic. 3928
(03) 5989 6455
tenminutesbytractor.com.au

Moorooduc Estate, 501 Derril Rd, Moorooduc Vic. 3933
(03) 5971 8506
moorooduc-estate.com.au

Port Phillip Estate, Red Hill Rd, Red Hill Vic. 3937
(03) 5989 2708
portphillip.net

Eat

Kazu Japanese – a little-known gem.
35 Main St, Mornington Vic. 3931

Ten Minutes By Tractor, 1333 Mornington–Flinders Rd, Main Ridge Vic. 3928
(03) 5989 6455
tenminutesbytractor.com.au

Montalto, 33 Shoreham Rd, Red Hill South Vic. 3937
(03) 5989 8412
montalto.com.au

Salix at Willow Creek, 166 Balnarring Rd, Merricks North Vic. 3926
(03) 5989 7640
willow-creek.com.au

The Long Table in Red Hill, 159 Shoreham Rd, Red Hill South Vic. 3937
(03) 5989 2326
thelongtable.com.au

Vines of Red Hill, 150 Red Hill Rd, Red Hill Vic. 3937
(03) 5989 2977
vinesofredhill.com.au

Jill's at Moorooduc, Derril Rd, Moorooduc Vic. 3933
(03) 5971 8507

Pub
Flinders Hotel – decent pub fare and wine list.
Cook St, Flinders Vic. 3929
(03) 5989 0201

Coffee
Page Eight, Main St, Mornington Vic. 3931
(03) 5973 4888

Stay
Posh – Peppers Moonah Links Resort, Peter Thomson Dve, Fingal Vic. 3939
(03) 5988 2000

Budget – The Royal Hotel, Esplanade, Mornington Vic. 3931
(03) 5975 5466

Tip
Some of Victoria's most famous golf courses are dotted along the Mornington Peninsula, so pack the sticks.

Geelong

One of the many maritime wine regions in Victoria, this has a history dating back to the 1840s. The modern face is one of soulful, soil-driven wines that are starting to make an ascent to the top echelons of quality. The scenery makes for spectacular touring – an easy day trip from the heart of Melbourne and a refreshing coastal getaway.

Regional Information
winegeelong.com.au

Wines
Chardonnay, pinot noir, shiraz.

Top Cellar Doors
Lethbridge Wines, 74 Burrows Rd, Lethbridge Vic. 3332
(03) 5281 7279
lethbridgewines.com

Pettavel Winery, 65 Pettavel Rd, Waurn Ponds Vic. 3216
(03) 5266 1120
pettavel.com

Shadowfax, K Rd, Werribee Vic. 3030
(03) 9731 4420
shadowfax.com.au

Clyde Park Vineyard, 2490 Midland Hwy, Bannockburn Vic. 3331
(03) 5281 7274
clydepark.com.au

¶ Eat

Pettavel Winery, 65 Pettavel Rd, Waurn Ponds Vic. 3216
(03) 5266 1120
pettavel.com

Clyde Park Vineyards, 2490 Midland Hwy, Bannockburn Vic. 3331
(03) 5281 7274
clydepark.com.au

Hey Leroy, 61A Gheringhap St, Geelong Vic. 3220
(03) 5221 0019
heyleroy.com.au

Chris's at Beacon Point, 280 Skenes Creek Rd, Apollo Bay Vic. 3233
(03) 5237 6411
chriss.com.au

Shadowfax – wood-fired pizzas on weekends.
K Rd, Werribee Vic. 3030
(03) 9731 4420
shadowfax.com.au

¶ Pub

Cremorne Hotel – simple reliable pub fare.
336 Pakington St, Newtown Vic. 3351
(03) 5221 2702

☕ Coffee

Pakington Street is home to many a good cup.

🛏 Stay

Posh – Sofitel Mansion & Spa, K Rd, Werribee Vic. 3030
(03) 9731 4000

Budget – Head to the surf coast and check out one of the many motels and holiday cabins.

☼ Tip

If you're a fan of hanging the toes on the nose, grab a surfboard and head to one of the famous local surf beaches for a few waves. Torquay and 13th Beach are better for beginners, Bells is definitely for the experienced surfer only.

Macedon Ranges

If you fly into Melbourne and are approaching from the north, look out for a few vines dotted below. This rugged cool-climate region is home to some of the most intense and edgy chardonnay, pinot and sparkling wines in Victoria. The vignerons here are a dedicated bunch, working hard to create the very best-quality wines.

i **Regional Information**
macedonrangeswine.com

Wines
Chardonnay, pinot noir, sparkling, riesling, shiraz.

Top Cellar Doors
Hanging Rock Winery, 88 Jim Rd, Newham Vic. 3442
(03) 5427 0542
hangingrock.com.au

Knight's Granite Hills, 148 Burke and Wills Track, Baynton Vic. 3444
(03) 5423 7264
granitehills.com.au

Bindi Wine Growers (by appointment – the best wines in the region by far)
343 Melton Rd, Gisborne Vic. 3437
(03) 5428 2564

Cobaw Ridge Winery, 31 Perc Boyer's Lane, Pastoria East Vic. 3444
(03) 5423 5227
cobawridge.com.au

Ellender Estate Winery, 260 Green Gully Rd, Glenlyon Vic. 3461
(03) 5348 7785
ellenderwines.com.au

Eat
Campaspe House, Goldies Lane, Woodend Vic. 3442
(03) 5427 2273
campaspehouse.com.au

Lake House, King St, Daylesford Vic. 3460
(03) 5348 3329
lakehouse.com.au

Annie Smithers Bistrot, 72 Piper St, Kyneton Vic. 3444
(03) 5422 2039

Pub
Royal George Hotel, 24 Piper St, Kyneton Vic. 3444
(03) 5422 1390

Coffee
Mad Gallery, 19 High St, Lancefield Vic. 3435
(03) 5429 1432
madgallery.com.au

Stay
Posh – Lake House, King St, Daylesford Vic. 3460
(03) 5348 3329
lakehouse.com.au

Budget – Rectory Bed & Breakfast, Ebden St, Keyneton Vic. 3444

Tip
In winter, pack the woollies and even a toboggan – this is truly cool-climate country!

Grampians

There's some commitment involved in visiting this south-western Victorian area; allow four hours from Melbourne at a relaxed pace. There's a great deal of history dating back to the gold rush, and the soils really drive the wine styles made today. The scenery is spectacular and the wines are scintillating.

Regional Information
grampianswine.com.au

Wines
Shiraz and riesling are the undisputed champions.

Top Cellar Doors
Best's Wines, 111 Best's Rd, Great Western Vic 3377
(03) 5356 2250
bestswines.com

Seppelts Great Western, Moyston Rd, Great Western Vic. 3377
(03) 5361 2239
seppelt.com.au

Mount Langi Ghiran Vineyards, 80 Vine Rd, Buangor Vic. 3377
(03) 5354 3207
langi.com.au

Eat
Royal Mail Hotel, Glenelg Hwy (Parker St), Dunkeld Vic. 3294
(03) 5577 2241

Pub
Royal Mail Hotel, Glenelg Hwy (Parker St), Dunkeld Vic. 3294
(03) 5577 2241

Coffee
Pack the thermos.

Stay
Posh – Royal Mail Hotel, Glenelg Hwy (Parker St), Dunkeld Vic 3294
(03) 5577 2241

Budget – camping, Grampians National Park
Enquiries & Booking: Grampians Rd (cnr Bucklere St), Halls Gap Vic. 3381
(03) 5356 6221

Tip
The Grampians National Park is one spectacular piece of Australian landscape.
A favourite of bushwalkers and rock climbers, it's definitely worth a look, no
matter how unadventurous you may be.

NEW SOUTH WALES

Hunter Valley
The Hunter Valley is dear to the heart of Sydneysiders and a leisurely
two-plus hours drive away, depending on your pace and Sydney's traffic.
The region is well established and boasts an impressive history, which is just
being rewritten with the new generation of winemakers approaching their
apogee.

Regional Information
winecountry.com.au

Wines
Semillon and shiraz rule this part of Australia's wine country, hands down.

Top Cellar Doors
Brokenwood, 401–427 McDonalds Rd, Pokolbin NSW 2320
(02) 4998 7559
brokenwood.com.au

Tempus Two Winery, cnr McDonalds Rd & Broke Rd, Pokolbin NSW 2320
(02) 4993 3999
tempustwowinery.com.au

Tyrrell's Wines, Broke Rd, Pokolbin NSW 2320
(02) 4993 7000
tyrrells.com.au

Margan Family Winegrowers, 266 Hermitage Rd, Pokolbin NSW 2320
(02) 6574 7004
margan.com.au

Eat

Margan Restaurant, 1238 Milbrodale Rd, Broke NSW 2330
(02) 6579 1372
margan.com.au

Esca, Bimbadgen Estate, 790 McDonalds Rd, Pokolbin NSW 2320
(02) 4998 7585
bimbadgen.com.au

Wine House and Kitchen, Pokolbin Village, 188 Broke Rd,
Pokolbin NSW 2320
(02) 4998 7670

Pub

Blaxlands Inn, Broke Rd, Pokolbin NSW 2320
(02) 4998 7550

Blue Tongue Brewery – offer an impressive range of their own beers and a great place to stop and enjoy them.
917 Hermitage Rd, Pokolbin NSW 2320
(02) 4998 7777
hunterresort.com.au

Coffee

Wine House and Kitchen, Pokolbin Village, 188 Broke Rd,
Pokolbin NSW 2320
(02) 4998 7670

Bliss, Shop 2, Hunter Valley Gardens Village, Broke Rd, Pokolbin NSW 2320
(02) 4998 6700
blisscoffee.com.au

Stay

Posh – Tower Lodge, Halls Rd, Pokolbin NSW 2320
(02) 4998 7582
towerestate.com

Peppers Guest House, Ekerts Rd, Pokolbin NSW 2320
(02) 4993 8999
peppers.com.au/Guest-House

Budget – Mercure Hunter Valley Gardens, Vintage Dve, Rothbury NSW 2320
(02) 4998 2222
grandmercurehuntervalley.com.au

Tip

Golf is well-catered for in the Hunter and the winter days are crisp and clear –
so pack the kit.

Directory of wineries

Abbey Vale
Wildwood Rd
Yallingup WA 6282
(08) 9755 2121
abbeyvale.com.au

Abercorn
Cassilis Rd
Mudgee NSW 2850
(02) 6373 3106
abercornwine.com.au

Affleck Vineyard
RMB 244
Millynn Rd
(off Gundaroo Rd)
Bungendore NSW 2651
(02) 6236 9276

Ainsworth Estate
Ducks Lane
Seville Vic. 3139
(03) 5964 4711
ainsworth-estate.com.au

Alan & Veitch
(see Robert Johnson
Vineyards)

Albert River Wines
1–117 Mundoolun
Connection Rd
Tamborine Qld 4270
(07) 5543 6622
albertriverwines.com.au

Alkoomi
Wingebellup Rd
Frankland WA 6396
(08) 9855 2229
alkoomiwines.com.au

All Saints Estate
All Saints Rd
Wahgunyah Vic. 3687
(02) 6035 2222
allsaintswine.com.au

Allandale
Lovedale Rd
Pokolbin NSW 2320
(02) 4990 4526
allandalewinery.com.au

Allanmere
(see First Creek)
allanmere.com.au

Allinda
119 Lorimers Lane
Dixons Creek Vic. 3775
(03) 5965 2450
allindawinery.com.au

Alta Wines
(not open to public)
0434 077 059

Amberley Estate
Wildwood & Thornton Rds
Yallingup WA 6282
(08) 9755 2288
amberleyestate.com.au

Amulet
Wangaratta Rd
Beechworth Vic. 3747
(03) 5727 0420
amuletvineyard.com.au

Anderson Winery
Lot 13 Chiltern Rd
Rutherglen Vic. 3685
(03) 6032 8111
andersonwinery.com.au

Andraos Bros. Wines
150 Vineyard Rd
Sunbury Vic. 3429
(03) 9740 9703
andraosbros.com.au

Andrew Harris
Sydney Rd
Mudgee NSW 2850
(02) 6373 1213
andrewharris.com.au

Angove's
Bookmark Ave
Renmark SA 5341
(08) 8580 3100
angoves.com.au

Annie's Lane
Main North Rd
Watervale SA 5452
(08) 8843 0003
annieslane.com.au

Antcliffe's Chase
RMB 4510
Caveat
via Seymour Vic. 3660
(03) 5790 4333

Anvers
(no cellar door)
(08) 8374 1787
annvers.com.au

Apsley Gorge
'The Gulch'
Bicheno Tas. 7215
(03) 6375 1221

Arakoon
229 Main Rd
McLaren Vale SA 5171
(08) 8323 7339

Arlewood
Harmans South Rd
Wilyabrup WA 6284
(08) 9755 6267
arlewood.com.au

Armstrong Vineyards
(not open to public)
(08) 8277 6073

Arrowfield
Golden Hwy
Jerry's Plains NSW 2330
(02) 6576 4041
arrowfieldwines.com.au

Ashton Hills
Tregarthen Rd
Ashton SA 5137
(08) 8390 1243

Ashwood Grove
(not open to public)
(03) 5030 5291

Audrey Wilkinson Vineyard
Oakdale, De Beyers Rd
Pokolbin NSW 2320
(02) 4998 7411
audreywilkinson.com.au

Auldstone
Booth's Rd
Taminick via Glenrowan
Vic. 3675
(03) 5766 2237
auldstone.com.au

Austins Barrabool
870 Steiglitz Rd
Sutherlands Creek Vic. 3331
(03) 5281 1799
abwines.com.au

Australian Old Vine Wine
Farm 271, Rossetto Rd
Beelbangera NSW 2680
(02) 6963 5239
australianoldvine.com.au

Avalon
4480 Wangaratta–Whitfield Rd
Whitfield Vic. 3733
(03) 5729 3629
avalonwines.com.au

Baileys of Glenrowan
Taminick Gap Rd
Glenrowan Vic. 3675
(03) 5766 2392
baileysofglenrowan.com.au

Baldivis Estate
(see Palandri)

Balgownie
Hermitage Rd
Maiden Gully Vic. 3551
(03) 5449 6222
balgownieestate.com

Balnaves
Main Rd
Coonawarra SA 5263
(08) 8737 2946
balnaves.com.au

Bannockburn
(not open to public)
Midland Hwy
Bannockburn Vic. 3331
(03) 5243 7094
bannockburnvineyards.com

Banrock Station
(see Hardys)

Barak's Bridge
(see Yering Station)

Barambah Ridge
79 Goschnicks Rd
Redgate via Murgon
Qld 4605
(07) 4168 4766
barambahridge.com.au

Barossa Old Vine Company
Para Road
Tanunda SA 5352
(08) 8563 3733

Barossa Valley Estate
Seppeltsfield Rd
Marananga SA 5355
(08) 8562 3599
brlhardy.com.au

Barratt
Uley Vineyard
Cornish Rd
Summertown SA 5141
(08) 8390 1788
barrattwines.com.au

Barwang
(see McWilliams)

Barwick Wines
Yelverton North Rd
Dunsborough WA 6281
(08) 9755 7100
barwickwines.com

Bass Phillip
(by appointment)
cnr Tosch's & Hunts Rds
Leongatha South Vic. 3953
(03) 5664 3341

Batista
Franklin Rd
Middlesex WA 6258
(08) 9772 3530

Battle of Bosworth
(by appointment)
Edgehill Vineyards, Gaffney Rd
Willunga SA 5172
(08) 8556 2441
battleofbosworth.com.au

Bay of Fires Vineyard
(see Hardys)

Beresford
26 Kangarilla Rd
McLaren Vale SA 5171
(08) 8323 8899
beresfordwines.com.au

Berrys Bridge
633 Carapooee Rd
St Arnaud Vic. 3478
(03) 5496 3220
berrysbridge.com.au

Best's Great Western
Western Hwy
Great Western Vic. 3377
(03) 5356 2250
bestswines.com

Bethany
Bethany Rd
Bethany
via Tanunda SA 5352
(08) 8563 2086
bethany.com.au

Bianchet
187 Victoria Rd
Lilydale Vic. 3140
(03) 9739 1779
bianchet.com

Bidgeebong
(no cellar door)
PO Box 5393
Wagga Wagga NSW 2650
(02) 6931 9955
bidgeebong.com

Binbilla Wines
(no cellar door)
binbillawines.com

Bindi Wine Growers
(not open to public)
(03) 5428 2564

Bird in Hand
Pfeiffer & Bird In Hand Rds
Woodside SA 5244
(08) 8389 9488
olivesoilwine.com

Birdwood Estate
Mannum Rd
Birdwood SA 5234
(08) 8263 0986

Blackbilly Wines
(by appointment)
Kangarilla Rd
McLaren Vale SA 5171
0419 383 907
blackbilly.com

Blackjack Vineyard
Calder Hwy
Harcourt Vic. 3452
(03) 5474 2355
blackjackwines.com.au

Bleasdale
Wellington Rd
Langhorne Creek SA 5255
(08) 8537 3001
bleasdale.com.au

Blewitt Springs
Recreational Rd
McLaren Vale SA 5171
(08) 8323 8689
hillsview.com.au

Bloodwood Estate
4 Griffin Rd
via Orange NSW 2800
(02) 6362 5631
bloodwood.com.au

Blue Pyrenees Estate
Vinoca Rd
Avoca Vic. 3467
(03) 5465 3202
bluepyrenees.com.au

Bookpurnong Hill
Bookpurnong Rd
Loxton SA 5333
(08) 8584 1333
salenaestate.com.au

Boston Bay
Lincoln Hwy
Port Lincoln SA 5605
(08) 8684 3600
bostonbaywines.com.au

Botobolar
Botobolar Lane
PO Box 212
Mudgee NSW 2850
(02) 6373 3840
botobolar.com

Bowen Estate
Riddoch Hwy
Coonawarra SA 5263
(08) 8737 2229

Boyntons of Bright
Great Alpine Rd
Porepunkah Vic. 3740
(03) 5756 2356

Brand's Laira Coonawarra
Riddoch Hwy
Coonawarra SA 5263
(08) 8736 3208
mcwilliams.com.au

Brangayne
49 Pinnacle Rd
Orange NSW 2800
(02) 6365 3229
brangaynewines.com

Bremerton
Strathalbyn Rd
Langhorne Creek SA 5255
(08) 8537 3093
bremerton.com.au

Bress
3894 Calder Hwy
Harcourt Vic. 3453
(03) 5474 2262
bress.com.au

Briagolong Estate
Valencia–Briagolong Rd
Briagolong Vic. 3860
(03) 5147 2322
briagolongestate.com.au

Brian Barry
(not open to public)
PO Box 128
Stepney SA 5069
(08) 8363 6211
brianbarrywines.com

Briar Ridge
593 Mount View Rd
Mt View NSW 2321
(02) 4990 3670
briarridge.com.au

Bridgewater Mill
(see Petaluma)

Brindabella Hills
156 Woodgrove Rd
via Hall ACT 2618
(02) 6230 2583
brindabellahills.com.au

Broke Estate
(see Ryan Family Wines)

Brokenwood
McDonalds Rd
Pokolbin NSW 2321
(02) 4998 7559
brokenwood.com.au

Brookland Valley
Caves Rd
Wilyabrup WA 6280
(08) 9755 6042
brooklandvalley.com.au

Brothers in Arms
(not open to public)
brothersinarms.com.au

Brown Brothers
Meadow Crk Rd
(off the Snow Rd)
Milawa Vic. 3678
(03) 5720 5500
brownbrothers.com.au

Brown Magpie Wines
125 Larcombes Rd
Modeware Vic. 3240
(03) 5261 387
brownmagpiewines.com

Browns of Padthaway
PMB 196
Naracoorte SA 5271
(08) 8765 6040
browns-of-padthaway.com

Buller & Sons, R.L.
Three Chain Rd
Rutherglen Vic. 3685
(02) 6032 9660
rlbullerandson.com.au

Burge Family Winemakers
Barossa Hwy
Lyndoch SA 5351
(08) 8524 4644
burgefamily.com.au

Burnbrae
Hargraves Rd
Erudgere
Mudgee NSW 2850
(02) 6373 3504

By Farr
(no cellar door)
101 Kelly Lane
Bannockburn Vic. 3331
(03) 5281 1733
byfarr.com.au

Calais Estate
Palmers Lane
Pokolbin NSW 2321
(02) 4998 7654

**Caledonia Australis
Estate**
(not open to public)
PO Box 626
North Melbourne Vic. 3051
1800 225 287
caledoniaaustralis.com

Cambewarra Estate
520 Illaroo Rd
Cambewarra NSW 2541
(02) 4446 0170

Campbells
Murray Valley Hwy
Rutherglen Vic. 3685
(02) 6032 9458
campbellswines.com.au

Cannibal Creek
260 Tynong North Rd
Tynong North Vic. 3813
(03) 5942 8380

Canobolas-Smith
Boree Lane (off Cargo Rd)
Orange NSW 2800
(02) 6365 6113

Canonbah Bridge
Merryanbone Station
Warren NSW 2824
(02) 6833 9966
canonbah.com.au

Cape Barren Wines
(by appointment)
Lot 20, Little Rd
Willunga SA 5172
(08) 8556 4374
capebarrenwines.com.au

**Cape Mentelle
Vineyards**
Wallcliffe Rd
Margaret River WA 6285
(08) 9757 0888
capementelle.com.au

Capel Vale
Lot 5 Capel North West Rd
Capel WA 6271
(08) 9727 0111
capelvale.com

Capercaillie
Londons Rd
Lovedale NSW 2325
(02) 4990 2904
capercailliewine.com.au

Carlei Green Vineyards
1 Albers Rd
Upper Beaconsfield Vic. 3808
(03) 5944 4599
carlei.com.au

Carlyle
(see Pfeiffer)

Cartwheel
(no cellar door)
cartwheelwines.com.au

Casa Freschi
Ridge Rd
Summertown SA 5141
(08) 8536 4569
casafreschi.com.au

Cascabel
Rogers Rd
Willunga SA 5172
(08) 8557 4434

**Casella Carramar
Estate**
Wakley Rd
Yenda NSW 2681
(02) 6961 3000
casellawines.com.au

Cassegrain
Fern Bank Crk Rd
Port Macquarie NSW 2444
(02) 6583 7777
cassegrainwines.com.au

Castagna
(by appointment)
88 Ressom Lane
Beechworth Vic. 3747
(03) 5728 2888
castagna.com.au

Castle Rock Estate
Porongurup Rd
Porongurup WA 6324
(08) 9853 1035
castlerockestate.com.au

Centennial Vineyards
Centennial Rd
Bowral NSW 2076
(02) 4861 8700
centennial.net.au

Chain of Ponds
Main Adelaide Rd
Gumeracha SA 5233
(08) 8389 1415
chainofpondswines.com.au

Chalk Hill
(not open to public)
chalkhill.com.au

Chalkers Crossing
387 Grenfell Rd
Young NSW 2594
(02) 6382 6900
chalkerscrossing.com.au

Chambers Rosewood
Corowa–Rutherglen Rd
Rutherglen Vic. 3685
(02) 6032 8641

Chapel Hill
Chapel Hill Rd
McLaren Vale SA 5171
(08) 8323 8429
chapelhillwine.com.au

Charles Cimicky
Hermann Thumm Dve
Lyndoch SA 5351
(08) 8524 4025

Charles Melton
Krondorf Rd
Tanunda SA 5352
(08) 8563 3606
charlesmeltonwines.com.au

Charles Sturt University
Boorooma St
North Wagga Wagga
NSW 2678
(02) 6933 2435
csu.edu.au/winery

Chateau Leamon
5528 Calder Hwy
Bendigo Vic. 3550
(03) 5447 7995
chateauleamon.com.au

Chatsfield
O'Neill Rd
Mount Barker WA 6324
(08) 9851 2660
chatsfield.com.au

Chatto
(see First Creek)

Chestnut Grove
Perup Rd
Manjimup WA 6258
(08) 9772 4255
chestnutgrove.com.au

Cheviot Bridge
(no cellar door)
(03) 9820 9080
cheviotbridge.com.au

Chrismont
Upper King Valley Rd
Cheshunt Vic. 3678
(03) 5729 8220
chrismontwines.com.au

Clair de Lune Vineyard
8805 Gippsland Hwy
Kardella South Vic. 3951
(03) 5655 1031
clairdelune.com.au

Clairault Estate
via Caves Rd
Wilyabrup WA 6280
(08) 9755 6225
clairaultwines.com.au

Clarendon Hills
(not open to public)
(08) 8364 1484
clarendonhills.com.au

Classic McLaren
PO Box 245
McLaren Vale SA 5171
(08) 8323 9551

Cleveland
Shannons Rd
Lancefield Vic. 3435
(03) 5429 9000
clevelandwinery.com.au

Clonakilla
Crisps Lane
Murrumbateman NSW 2582
(02) 6227 5877
clonakilla.com.au

Cloudy Bay
(see Cape Mentelle)

Clover Hill
(see Taltarni Vineyards)

Clyde Park Vineyard
2490 Midland Hwy
Bannockburn Vic. 3331
(03) 5281 7274
clydepark.com.au

Cobaw Ridge Winery
Perc Boyer's Lane
East Pastoria
via Kyneton Vic. 3444
(03) 5423 5227
cobawridge.com.au

Cockatoo Ridge
Barossa Valley Way
Tanunda SA 5352
(08) 8563 6404 or
(08) 8563 6408
cockatooridge.com.au

Cockfighter's Ghost
(see Poole's Rock)

Cofield
Distillery Rd
Wahgunyah Vic. 3687
(03) 6033 3798
cofieldwines.com

Coldstone
(see Victorian Alps Winery)

Coldstream Hills
31 Maddens Lane
Coldstream Vic. 3770
(03) 5964 9410
coldstreamhills.com.au

Collector Wines
(02) 6116 8722
collectorwines.com.au

Connor Park
59 Connor Road
Leichardt Vic. 3516
(03) 5437 5234
bendigowine.com.au

Constable Estate
205 Gillards Rd
Cessnock NSW 2320
(02) 4998 7887
constablevineyards.com.au

Cookoothama
(see Nugan Estate)

Coolangatta Estate
1355 Bolong Rd
Shoalhaven Heads NSW 2535
(02) 4448 7131
coolangattaestate.com.au

Coombend
(see Tamar Ridge)

Cope-Williams
221 Ochiltrees Rd
Romsey Vic. 3434
(03) 5429 5595
copewilliams.com.au

Coriole
Chaffeys Rd
McLaren Vale SA 5171
(08) 8323 8305
coriole.com

Cowra Estate
Boorowa Rd
Cowra NSW 2794
(02) 6342 3650

Crabtree of Watervale
North Tce
Watervale SA 5452
(08) 8843 0069

Craig Avon
Craig Avon Lane
Merricks North Vic. 3926
(03) 5989 7465

Craigie Knowe
80 Glen Gala Rd
Cranbrook Tas. 7190
(03) 6257 8252

Craiglee
Sunbury Rd
Sunbury Vic. 3429
(03) 9744 4489

Craigmoor
Craigmoor Rd
Mudgee NSW 2850
(02) 6372 2208

Craigow
Richmond Rd
Cambridge Tas. 7170
(03) 6248 4210
craigow.com.au

Craneford
Moorundie St
Truro SA 5356
(08) 8564 0003
cranefordwines.com

Crawford River
(by appointment)
741 Upper Hotspur Rd
Condah Vic. 3303
(03) 5578 2267
crawfordriverwines.com

Crittenden at Dromana
25 Harrisons Rd
Dromana Vic. 3936
(03) 5981 8322

Crofters
(see Houghton)

Cullen Wines
Caves Rd
Cowaramup WA 6284
(08) 9755 5277
cullenwines.com.au

Cumulus Wines
Euchareena Rd
Molong NSW 2866
(02) 6369 6236
cumuluswines.com.au

Curly Flat Vineyard
263 Collivers Rd
Lancefield Vic. 3435
(03) 5429 1956
curlyflat.com

Currency Creek
Winery Rd
Currency Creek SA 5214
(08) 8555 4069
currencycreekwines.com.au

Cuttaway Hill Estate
(not open to public)
cuttawayhillwines.com.au

Dal Zotto
Main Rd
Whitfield Vic. 3678
(03) 5729 8321
dalzotto.com.au

Dalfarras
(see Tahbilk)

Dalrymple
Pipers Brook Rd
Pipers Brook Tas. 7254
(03) 6382 7229
dalrymplevineyards.com.au

Dalwhinnie
Taltarni Rd
Moonambel Vic. 3478
(03) 5467 2388
dalwhinnie.com.au

d'Arenberg
Osborn Rd
McLaren Vale SA 5171
(08) 8323 8206
darenberg.com.au

Darling Park
232 Red Hill Rd
Red Hill 3937
(03) 5989 2324
darlingparkwinery.com

David Franz
(not open to public)
david-franz.com

David Hook Wines
cnr Broke Road & Ekerts Rd
Pokolbin NSW 2320
(02) 4998 7121
davidhookwines.com.au

David Traeger
139 High St
Nagambie Vic. 3608
(03) 5794 2514

De Bortoli
De Bortoli Rd
Bibul NSW 2680
(02) 6966 0100
or
Pinnacle Lane
Dixons Creek Vic. 3775
(03) 5965 2423
debortoli.com.au

De Iuliis
1616 Broke Rd
Pokolbin NSW 2320
(02) 4993 8000
dewine.com.au

Deakin Estate
(not open to the public)
deakinestate.com.au

Deisen
(not open to public)
deisen.com.au

Delamere
4238 Bridport Rd
Pipers Brook Tas. 7254
(03) 6382 7190
delamerevineyards.com.au

Delatite
Stoney's Rd
Mansfield Vic. 3722
(03) 5775 2922
delatitewinery.com.au

Dennis
Kangarilla Rd
McLaren Vale SA 5171
(08) 8323 8665
denniswines.com.au

Devil's Corner
(see Tamar Ridge)

Devil's Lair
(not open to public)
PO Box 212
Margaret River WA 6285
(08) 9757 7573
devilslair.com.au

Diamond Valley Vineyards
Kinglake Rd
St Andrews Vic. 3761
(03) 9722 0840
diamondvalley.com.au

Dirty Bliss
(see Hentley Farm Wine)

Dividing Range
(see Victorian Alps Winery)

DogRidge Vineyard
(by appointment)
RSD 195 Bagshaws Rd
McLaren Flat SA 5171
(08) 8383 0140
dogridge.com.au

Domaine Chandon
(see Green Point)

Domaine Day
(by appointment)
24 Queen St
Williamstown SA 5351
(08) 8524 6224
domaindaywines.com

Dominion Wines
Upton Rd, via Avenel
Strathbogie Ranges Vic. 3664
(03) 5796 2718
dominionwines.com

Dominique Portet
870–872 Maroondah Hwy
Coldstream Vic. 3770
(03) 5962 5760
dominiqueportet.com

Doonkuna Estate
Barton Hwy
Murrumbateman NSW 2582
(02) 6227 5811
doonkuna.com.au

Dowie Doole
182 Main Rd
McLaren Vale SA 5171
(08) 8323 8875
dowiedoole.com

Drayton's Bellevue
Oakey Creek Rd
Pokolbin NSW 2320
(02) 4998 7513
draytonswines.com.au

Dromana Estate
555 Old Moorooduc Rd
Tuerong Vic. 3933
office (03) 5974 4400
dromanaestate.com.au

Dutschke Wines
(not open to public)
dutschkewines.com

Eden Road Wines
(by appointment)
Hamilton Rd
Springton SA 5235
(08) 8568 1766
edenroadwines.com.au

Elderton
3 Tanunda Rd
Nuriootpa SA 5355
(08) 8568 7878
eldertonwines.com.au

Eldridge Estate
120 Arthurs Seat Rd
Red Hill Vic. 3937
(03) 5989 2644
eldridge-estate.com.au

Element Chardonnay
(see Sandalford)

Elgee Park
(no cellar door)
Junction Rd
Merricks Nth Vic. 3926
(03) 5989 7338
elgeeparkwines.com.au

Ellender Estate Winery
260 Green Gully Rd
Glenlyon Vic. 3461
(03) 5423 5227
ellenderwines.com.au

elgo Estate
(by appointment)
Upton Rd
Longwood Vic. 3665
(03) 5798 5563
elgoestate.com.au

Eppalock Ridge
(by appointment)
633 North Redesdale Rd
Redesdale Vic. 3444
(03) 5443 7841
eppalockridge.com

Evans & Tate
Lionel's Vineyard
Payne Rd
Jindong WA 6280
(08) 9755 8855
evansandtate.com.au

Evans Family
(not open to public)
Broke Rd
Pokolbin NSW 2320
(02) 4998 7237

Even Keel
(no cellar door)
evenkeelwines.com.au

Evoi Wines
(not open to public)
evoiwines.com

Fairbank
(see Sutton Grange Winery)

Farr Rising
(see By Farr)

Fergusson's
84 Wills Rd
Yarra Glen Vic. 3775
(03) 5965 2237
fergussonwinery.com.au

Fermoy Estate
Metricup Rd
Wilyabrup WA 6284
(08) 9755 6285
fermoy.com.au

Fern Hill Estate
Ingoldby Rd
McLaren Flat SA 5171
(08) 8323 9666
fernhillestate.com.au

Ferngrove
Ferngrove Rd
Frankland WA 6396
(08) 9855 2378
ferngrove.com.au

Fettler's Rest
(see Jindalee)

Fire Gully
(see Pierro)

First Creek
Monarch Wines
McDonalds Rd
Pokolbin NSW 2320
(02) 4998 7293
firstcreekwines.com.au

First Drop Wines
(not open to public)
firstdropwines.com

Flaxman Wines
(by appointment)
Lot 535, Flaxmans Valley Rd
Angaston SA 5353
0411 668 949
flaxmanwines.com.au

Fleur de Lys
(see Seppelt)

Flinders Bay
Bussell Hwy
Metricup WA 6280
(08) 9755 7103
flindersbaywines.com.au

Flying Fish Cove
Caves Rd
Wilyabrup WA 6284
(08) 9755 6600
flyingfishcove.com

Fontys Pool
(see Cape Mentelle)

Forest Hill Vineyard
cnr Myers Rd and South
Coast Hwy
(4 kms west of Denmark)
Denmark WA 6333
(08) 9848 2199
foresthillwines.com.au

Formby & Adams
(see Brothers in Arms)

Foster's Group
77 Southbank Blvd
Southbank Vic. 3006
(03) 9633 2000
fosters.com.au

Fox Creek
Malpas Rd
Willunga SA 5172
(08) 8556 2403
foxcreekwines.com.au

Fox Gordon
(not open to public)
foxgordon.com.au

Fox River
(see Goundrey)

Frankland Estate
Frankland Rd
Frankland WA 6396
(08) 9855 1544
franklandestate.com.au

Fraser Gallop Estate
(by appointment)
547 Merricup Rd
Wilyabrup WA 6280
(08) 9755 7553
fgewines.com.au

Freeman Vineyards
(by appointment)
101 Prunevale Rd
Prunevale NSW 2587
(02) 6384 4299
freemanvineyards.com.au

Freycinet Vineyard
Tasman Hwy
Bicheno Tas. 7215
(03) 6257 8574
freycinetvineyard.com.au

Frog Rock Wines
Edgell Lane
Mudgee NSW 2850
(02) 6372 2408
frogrockwines.com

Gabriel's Paddocks
Deasy's Rd
Pokolbin NSW 2321
(02) 4998 7650
gabrielspaddocks.com.au

Galafrey
Quangellup Rd
Mount Barker WA 6324
(08) 9851 2022
galafreywines.com

Galli Estate
1507 Melton Hwy
Rockbank Vic. 3335
galliestate.com.au

Gapsted Wines
Great Alpine Rd
Gapsted Vic. 3737
(03) 5751 1383
gapstedwines.com

Garden Gully
Western Hwy
Great Western Vic. 3377
(03) 5356 2400
gardengully.com.au

Gartelmann
Lovedale Rd
Lovedale NSW 2321
(02) 4930 7113
gartelmann.com.au

Gembrook Hill
(not open to public)
Launching Place Rd
Gemrook Vic. 3783
(03) 5968 1622
gembrookhill.com.au

Gemtree
Kangarilla Rd
McLaren Vale SA 5171
(08) 8323 8199
gemtreevineyards.com.au

Geoff Merrill
291 Pimpala Rd
Woodcroft SA 5162
(08) 8381 6877
geoffmerrillwines.com.au

Geoff Weaver
(not open to public)
2 Gilpin Lane
Mitcham SA 5062
(08) 8272 2105
geoffweaver.com.au

Giaconda
(not open to public)
Beechworth Vic.
(03) 5727 0246
giaconda.com.au

Giant Steps
(see Innocent Bystander)
giant-steps.com.au

Gibson Barossavale
Willows Rd
Light Pass SA 5355
(08) 8562 3193
barossavale.com

Gilbert Wines
Albany Hwy
Kendenup WA 6323
(08) 9851 4028
(08) 9851 4021

Gilligan
(not open to public)
gilligan.com.au

Glaetzer
34 Barossa Valley Way
Tanunda SA 5352
(08) 8563 0288
glaetzer.com

Glenara
126 Range Rd Nth
Upper Hermitage SA 5131
(08) 8380 5277
glenara.com.au

Glenguin Estate
Boutique Wine Centre
Broke NSW 2330
(02) 4998 7474
glenguinestate.com.au

Golden Grove Estate
Sundown Rd
Ballandean Qld 4382
(07) 4684 1291
goldengrove.com.au

Golding Wines
Western Branch Rd
Lobethal SA 5241
(08) 8389 5120
goldingwines.com.au

Goona Warra
790 Sunbury Rd
Sunbury Vic. 3429
(03) 9740 7766
goonawarra.com.au

The Gorge
(see David Hook Wines)

Goundrey
Muir Hwy
Mount Barker WA 6324
(08) 9892 1777
goundrey.com

Gramp's
(see Orlando)

Grand Cru Estate
Ross Dewell's Rd
Springton SA 5235
(08) 8568 2378

Granite Hills
Burke and Wills Track
Baynton
via Kyneton Vic. 3444
(03) 5423 7273
granitehills.com.au

Grant Burge
Jacobs Creek
Barossa Valley Hwy
Tanunda SA 5352
(08) 8563 3700
grantburgewines.com.au

Green Point
Maroondah Hwy
Coldstream Vic. 3770
(03) 9738 9200
greenpointwines.com.au

Greenock Creek
Radford Rd
Seppeltsfield SA 5360
(08) 8562 8103

Greenstone Vineyard
(not open to public)
greenstoneofheathcote.com

Grosset
King St
Auburn SA 5451
(08) 8849 2175
grosset.com.au

Grove Estate
Murringo Rd
Young NSW 2594
(02) 6382 6999
groveestate.com.au

The Growers
(see Abbey Vale)
thegrowers.com

Gulf Station
(see De Bortoli)

Hainault
255 Walnut Road
Bickley WA 6076
(08) 9293 8339
hainault.com.au

Half Mile Creek
(see Foster's Group)

Hamelin Bay
McDonald Rd
Karridale WA 6228
(08) 9758 6779
hbwines.com.au

Hamilton
Willunga Vineyards
Main South Rd
Willunga SA 5172
(08) 8556 2288
hamiltonwinegroup.com.au

Hamilton's Ewell
Barossa Valley Way
Nuriootpa SA 5355
(08) 8562 4600
hamiltonewell.com.au

Hanging Rock Winery
Jim Rd
Newham Vic. 3442
(03) 5427 0542
hangingrock.com.au

Hanson Wines
'Oolorong'
49 Cleveland Ave
Lower Plenty Vic. 3093
(03) 9439 7425

Happs
Commonage Rd
Dunsborough WA 6281
(08) 9755 3300
happs.com.au

Harcourt Valley
Calder Hwy
Harcourt Vic. 3453
(03) 5474 2223
harcourtvalley.com.au

Hardys
Reynella Rd
Reynella SA 5161
(08) 8392 2222
hardys.com.au

Hare's Chase
(not open to public)
hareschase.com

Harewood Estate
Scotsdale Rd
Denmark WA 6333
(08) 9840 9078
harewoodestate.com.au

Haselgrove Wines
Sand Rd
McLaren Vale SA 5171
(08) 8323 8706
haselgrove.com.au

Hastwell & Lightfoot
(by appointment)
Foggos Rd
McLaren Vale SA 5171
(08) 8323 8692
hastwellandlightfoot.com.au

Hat Rock Vineyard
(not open to public)
hatrockvineyard.com.au

Hay Shed Hill
Harmans Mill Rd
Wilyabrup WA 6285
(08) 9755 6046
hayshedhill.com.au

Hazard Hill
(see Plantagenet Wines)

Heathcote Winery
183 High St
Heathcote Vic. 3523
(03) 5433 2595
heathcotewinery.com.au

Heathfield Ridge
Caves Rd
Naracoorte SA 5271
(08) 8363 5800
heathfieldridgewines.com.au

Heggies
(see Yalumba)

Helm Wines
Butts Rd
Murrumbateman NSW 2582
(02) 6227 5953
helmwines.com.au

Henschke
Moculta Rd
Keyneton SA 5353
(08) 8564 8223
henschke.com.au

Hentley Farm Wines
(not open to public)
hentleyfarm.com.au

Heritage Wines
106a Seppeltsfield Rd
Marananga SA 5355
(08) 8562 2692
heritagewinery.com.au

Hesketh Wine Company
(not open to public)
heskethwinecompany.com.au

Hewitson
16 McGowan Ave
Unley SA 5061
(08) 8271 5755
hewitson.com.au

Hickinbotham
Nepean Hwy
Dromana Vic. 3936
(03) 5981 0355
hickinbotham.biz

Highbank
Riddoch Hwy
Coonawarra SA 5263
(08) 8736 3311
highbank.com.au

Higher Plane
(no cellar door)
higherplanewines.com.au

Hill Smith Estate
Flaxman's Valley Rd
Eden Valley SA 5235
(08) 8561 3200
hillsmithestate.com

Hillstowe Wines
104 Main Rd
Hahndorf SA 5245
(08) 8388 1400
hillstowe.com.au

Hoddles Creek Estate
(by appointment)
505 Gembrook Rd
Hoddles Creek Vic. 3139
(03) 5967 4692
hoddlescreekestate.com.au

Hollick
Racecourse Rd
Coonawarra SA 5263
(08) 8737 2318
hollick.com

Holm Oak
11 West Bay Rd
Rowella, Tas. 7270
(03) 6394 7577
holm-oak.com

Home Hill
38 Nairn St
Ranelagh Tas. 7109
(03) 6264 1200
homehillwines.com.au

Homes
(see Massoni)

Honeytree
130 Gillards Rd
Pokolbin NSW 2321
(02) 4998 7693
honeytree.wines.com

Hope Estate
Broke Rd
Pokolbin NSW 2320
(02) 4993 3555
hopeestate.com.au

Horseshoe Vineyard
Horseshoe Rd
Horseshoe Valley
Denman NSW 2328
(02) 6541 3512

Houghton
Dale Rd
Middle Swan WA 6056
(08) 9274 5100
houghton-wines.com.au

Howard Park
Scotsdale Rd
Denmark WA 6333
(08) 9848 2345
howardparkwines.com.au

Hugh Hamilton Wines
McMurtrie Rd
McLaren Vale SA 5171
(08) 8323 8689
hamiltonwines.com.au

Hugo
Elliott Rd
McLaren Flat SA 5171
(08) 8383 0098

Hungerford Hill
(see Cassegrain)

Ingoldby
Kangarilla Rd
McLaren Vale SA 5171
(08) 8383 0005
beringerblass.com.au

Innisfail
(by appointment only)
Cross St
Batesford Vic. 3221
(03) 5276 1258

Innocent Bystander
336 Maroondah Hwy
Healesville Vic. 3777
(03) 5962 6111
innocentbystander.com.au

Ivanhoe
Marrowbone Rd
Pokolbin NSW 2320
(02) 4998 7325
ivanhoewines.com.au

Jacob's Creek
Barossa Valley Way
Rowland Flat SA 5352
(08) 8521 3000
jacobscreek.com

Jamabro Wines
(not open to public)
jamabro.com.au

James Irvine
Roeslers Rd
Eden Valley SA 5235
(08) 8564 1046
irvinewines.com.au

Jamiesons Run
(see Foster's Group)

Jamsheed
(not open to public)
jamsheed.com.au

Jane Brook
229 Toodyay Rd
Middle Swan WA 6056
(08) 9274 1432
janebrook.com.au

Jansz
Pipers Brook Rd
Pipers Brook, Tas. 7254
(03) 6382 7066
jansz.com.au

Jasper Hill
Drummonds Lane
Heathcote Vic. 3523
(03) 5433 2528
jasperhill.com

Jeanneret
Jeanneret Rd
Sevenhill SA 5453
(08) 8843 4308
ascl.com/j-wines

Jeir Creek Wines
Gooda Creek Rd
Murrumbateman NSW 2582
(02) 6227 5999

Jenke Vineyards
Jenke Rd
Rowland Flat SA 5352
(08) 8524 4154
jenkevineyards.com

Jim Barry
Main North Rd
Clare SA 5453
(08) 8842 2261

Jindalee
(not open to public)
(03) 5276 1280
jindaleewines.com.au

Jingalla
Bolganup Dam Rd
Porongurup WA 6324
(08) 9853 1023
jingallawines.com.au

John Duval Wines
(not open to public)
johnduvalwines.com

John Gehrig
80 Gehrig's Lane
Oxley Vic. 3678
(03) 5727 3395
johngehrigwines.com.au

Jones Winery
61 Jones Rd
Rutherglen Vic. 3685
joneswinery.com

Josef Chromy
370 Relbia Rd
Relbia Tas. 7258
(03) 6335 8700
josefchromy.com.au

Joseph
(see Primo Estate)

Juniper Estate
Harmans Rd Sth
Cowaramup WA 6284
(08) 9755 9000
juniperestate.com.au

Kaesler Wines
Barossa Valley Way
Nuriootpa SA 5355
(08) 8562 4488
kaesler.com.au

Kalleske
(not open to public)
kalleske.com

Kangarilla Road Winery
Kangarilla Rd
McLaren Flat SA 5171
(08) 8383 0533
kangarillaroad.com.au

Kanta Wines
kantawine.com

Kara Kara
Sunraysia Hwy
St Arnaud Vic. 3478
(03) 5496 3294
pyrenees.org.au/karakara.htm

Karina Vineyards
35 Harrisons Rd
Dromana Vic. 3936
(03) 5981 0137

Karrivale
Woodlands Rd
Porongurup WA 6324
(08) 9853 1009

Karriview
RMB 913
Roberts Rd
Denmark WA 6333
(08) 9840 9381
karriviewwines.com.au

Katnook Estate
Riddoch Hwy
Coonawarra SA 5263
(08) 8737 2394
katnookestate.com.au

Kays Amery
Kay's Rd
McLaren Vale SA 5171
(08) 8323 8201
kaybrothersamerywines.com

Keith Tulloch
Hunter Ridge Winery
Hermitage Rd
Pokolbin NSW 2320
(02) 4998 7500
keithtullochwine.com.au

Kies Estate
Barossa Valley Way
Lyndoch SA 5351
(08) 8524 4110
kieswines.com.au

Kilikanoon
PO Box 205
Auburn SA 5451
(08) 8843 4377
kilikanoon.com.au

Killawarra
(see Foster's Group)

Killerby
Minnimup Rd
Gelorup WA 6230
(08) 9795 7222
killerby.com.au

Kingston Estate
Sturt Hwy
Kingston-on-Murray SA 5331
(08) 8583 0500
kingstonestatewines.com

Kirrihill Estates
Farrell Flat Rd
Clare SA 5453
(08) 8842 1233
kirrihillestates.com.au

Knappstein Wines
2 Pioneer Ave
Clare SA 5453
(08) 8842 2600
knappsteinwines.com.au

Knight's Granite Hills
1481 Burke and Wills Track
Newham Vic. 3442
(03) 5427 0542
granitehills.com.au

Kooyong
110 Hunts Rd
Tuerong Vic. 3933
(03) 5989 7355
kooyong.com

Koppamurra
(no cellar door)
PO Box 110
Blackwood SA 5051
(08) 8271 4127
koppamurrawines.com.au

Krinklewood Biodynamic Vineyard
712 Wollombi Rd
Broke NSW 2330
(02) 6579 1322
krinklewood.com

KT & The Falcon
(not open to public)
ktandthefalcon.com.au

Kulkunbulla
Brokenback Estate
1595 Broke Rd
Pokolbin NSW 2320
(02) 4998 7140
kulkunbulla.com.au

Kyeema
(not open to public)
PO Box 282
Belconnen ACT 2616
(02) 6254 7557

La Curio
(not open to public)
lacuriowines.com

Laanecoorie
(by appointment)
RMB 1330
Dunolly Vic. 3472
(03) 5468 7260

Lake Breeze
Step Rd
Langhorne Creek SA 5255
(08) 8537 3017
lakebreeze.com.au

Lake's Folly
Broke Rd
Pokolbin NSW 2320
(02) 4998 7507
lakesfolly.com.au

Lalla Gully Vineyard
(see Taltarni Vineyards)

Lamont's
Bisdee Rd
Millendon WA 6056
(08) 9296 4485
lamonts.com.au

364

The Lane
Ravenswood Lane
Hahndorf SA 5245
(08) 8388 1250
ravenswoodlane.com.au

Langmeil
cnr Langmeil & Para Rds
Tanunda SA 5352
(08) 8563 2595
langmeilwinery.com.au

Lark Hill
521 Bungendore Rd
Bungendore NSW 2621
(02) 6238 1393
larkhillwine.com.au

Laurel Bank
(by appointment)
130 Black Snake Lane
Granton Tas. 7030
(03) 6263 5977
laurelbankwines.com.au

Leabrook Estate
4/3 Rochester St
Leabrook SA 5068
(08) 8331 7150
leabrookestate.com

Leaping Lizard
(see Ferngrove)

Leasingham
7 Dominic St
Clare SA 5453
(08) 8842 2555
leasingham-wines.com.au

Leconfield
Riddoch Hwy
Coonawarra SA 5263
(08) 8737 2326
leconfield.com.au

Leeuwin Estate
Stevens Rd
Margaret River WA 6285
(08) 9757 0000
leeuwinestate.com.au

Leland Estate
PO Lenswood SA 5240
(08) 8389 6928
lelandestate.com.au

Lengs & Cooter
24 Lindsay Tce
Belair SA 5052
(08) 8278 3998
lengscooter.com.au

Lenswood Vineyards
3 Cyril John Crt
Athelstone SA 5076
(08) 8365 3766
knappsteinlenswood.com.au

Lenton Brae
Caves Rd
Wilyabrup WA 6280
(08) 9755 6255
lentonbrae.com

Leo Buring
(see Foster's Group)

Lethbridge Wines
74 Burrows Rd
Lethbridge Vic. 3332
(03) 5281 7279
lethbridgewines.com

Liebich Wein
Steingarten Rd
Rowland Flat SA 5352
(08) 8524 4543
liebichwein.com.au

Lillydale Vineyards
Davross Crt
Seville Vic. 3139
(03) 5964 2016
mcwilliams.com.au

Lillypilly Estate
Farm 16, Lilly Pilly Rd
Leeton NSW 2705
(02) 6953 4069
lillypilly.com

Lindemans
McDonalds Rd
Pokolbin NSW 2320
(02) 4998 7501
fosters.com.au

Little Rebel
Yarra Hill Winery
10 St Huberts Rd
Coldstream Vic. 3770
(03) 9739 0666
littlerebel.com.au

The Little Wine Company
824 Milbrodale Rd
Broke NSW 2330
(02) 6579 1111
thelittlewinecompany.com.au

Lloyd Brothers
Warners Rd
McLaren Vale SA 5171
(08) 8323 8792
lloydbrothers.com.au

Logan
Castlereagh Hwy
Apple Tree Flat
Mudgee NSW 2850
(02) 6373 1333
loganwines.com.au

Long Gully
Long Gully Rd
Healesville Vic. 3777
(03) 5962 3663
longgullyestate.com

Longview Vineyard
Pound Rd
Macclesfield SA 5153
(08) 8388 9694
longviewvineyard.com.au

Loose End Wines
(no cellar door)
(08) 8563 2507
looseend.com.au

Lou Miranda Estate
Barossa Valley Way
Rowland Flat SA 5352
(08) 8524 4537
loumirandaestate.com.au

Lovegrove
Heidelberg–Kinglake Road
Cottlesbridge Vic. 3099
(03) 9718 1569
lovegrovewinery.com.au

Lowe Family
Ashbourne Vineyard
Tinja Lane
Mudgee NSW 2850
(02) 6372 0800
lowewine.com.au

Mac Forbes
(not open to public)
macforbes.com

McGuigan
cnr Broke & McDonalds Rds
Pokolbin NSW 2320
(02) 4998 7700
mcguiganwines.com.au

McHenry Hohnen Vintners
(not open to public)
mchv.com.au

McIvor Estate
80 Tooborac-Baynton Rd
Tooborac Vic. 3522
(03) 5433 5266
mcivorestate.com.au

McKellar Ridge Wines
Point of View Vineyard
2 Euroka Ave
Murrumbateman NSW 2582
(02) 6258 1556
mckellarridgewines.com.au

McPherson Wines
(not open to public)
mcphersonwines.com

McWilliams
Hanwood NSW 2680
(02) 6963 0001
mcwilliams.com.au

Madew
Westering Vineyard
Federal Hwy
Lake George NSW 2581
(02) 4848 0026
madewwines.com.au

Madfish
(see Howard Park)

Maglieri
RSD 295 Douglas Gully Rd
McLaren Flat SA 5171
(08) 8383 2211
fosters.com.au

Main Ridge
80 William Rd
Red Hill Vic. 3937
(03) 5989 2686
mre.com.au

Majella
Lynn Rd
Coonawarra SA 5263
(08) 8736 3055
majellawines.com.au

Malcolm Creek
(open weekends and public holidays)
Bonython Rd
Kersbrook SA 5231
(08) 8389 3235

Mandala Wines
1568 Melba Hwy
Dixons Creek Vic. 3775
(03) 5965 2016
mandalawines.com.au

Margan Family
1238 Milbrodale Rd
Broke NSW 2330
(02) 6579 1317
margan.com.au

Maritime Estate
Tucks Rd
Red Hill Vic. 3937
(03) 5989 2735

Marius Wines
(not open to public)
PO Box 545
Willunga SA 5172
(08) 8556 2421
mariuswines.com.au

Massena Vineyards
(by appointment)
PO Box 54
Tanunda SA 5352
(08) 8564 3037
massena.com.au

Massoni
Level 1
414 Lonsdale St
Melbourne Vic. 3000
1300 131 175
massoniwines.com

Maverick Wines
Lot 141, Light Pass Rd
Vine Vale, Moorooroo SA 5352
(08) 8563 3551
maverickwines.com.au

Maxwell
cnr Olivers & Chalkhill Rds
McLaren Vale SA 5171
(08) 8323 8200
maxwellwines.com.au

Mayer
(by appointment)
66 Miller Rd
Healesville Vic. 3777
(03) 5967 3779
timomayer.com.au

Meadowbank Estate
Denholms Rd
Cambridge Tas. 7170
(03) 6248 4484
meadowbankwines.com.au

Meerea Park
Lot 3 Palmers Lane
Pokolbin NSW 2320
(02) 4998 7006
meereapark.com.au

Merricks Creek
(by appointment)
44 Merricks Rd
Merricks Vic. 3916
(03) 5989 8868
merrickscreek.com

Merricks Estate
cnr Thompsons Lane &
Frankston–Flinders Rd
Merricks Vic. 3916
(03) 5989 8416

Miceli
60 Main Creek Rd
Main Ridge Vic. 3928
(03) 5989 2755

Michael Unwin Wines
2 Racecorse Rd (Western Hwy)
Beaufort Vic. 3373
(03) 5349 2021
michaelunwinwines.com.au

Middleton Estate
Flagstaff Hill Rd
Middleton SA 5213
(08) 8555 4136

Mildara
(see Foster's Group)

The Mill
(see Windowrie Estate)

Millamolong Estate
Millamolong Rd
Mandurama NSW 2792
0429 635 191
millamolong.com

Mintaro Wines
Leasingham Rd
Mintaro SA 5415
(08) 8843 9150
mintarowines.com.au

Miramar
Henry Lawson Dr.
Mudgee NSW 2850
(02) 6960 3000
miramarwines.com.au

Miranda Wines
57 Jordaryan Ave
Griffith NSW 2680
(02) 6960 3000
mirandawines.com.au

Mirrool Creek
(see Miranda Wines)

Mistletoe Wines
771 Hermitage Rd
Pokolbin NSW 2320
(02) 4998 7770
mistletoewines.com.au

Mitchell
Hughes Park Rd
Sevenhill via Clare SA 5453
(08) 8843 4258
mitchellwines.com

Mitchelton Wines
Mitcheltstown
Nagambie 3608
(03) 5736 2222
mitchelton.com.au

Mitolo Wines
(not open to public)
mitolowines.com.au

Molly Morgan
Talga Rd
Lovedale NSW 2321
(02) 4930 7695
mollymorgan.com

Monichino
70 Berrys Rd
Katunga Vic. 3640
(03) 5864 6452
monichino.com.au

Montalto
33 Shoreham Rd
Red Hill South Vic. 3937
(03) 5989 8412
montalto.com.au

Montara
Chalambar Rd
Ararat Vic. 3377
(03) 5352 3868
montara.com.au

Montrose/Poets Corner
Henry Lawson Dr.
Mudgee NSW 2850
(02) 6372 2208
poetscornerwines.com.au

Moondah Brook
(see Houghton)

Moorilla Estate
655 Main Rd
Berridale Tas. 7011
(03) 6277 9900
moorilla.com.au

Moorooduc Estate
Derril Rd
Moorooduc Vic. 3933
(03) 5971 8506
moorooducestate.com.au

Mornington Estate
(see Dromana Estate)

Morris
off Murray Valley Hwy
Mia Mia Vineyards
Rutherglen Vic. 3685
(02) 6026 7303
morriswines.com

Moss Brothers
Caves Rd
Wilyabrup WA 6280
(08) 9755 6270
mossbrothers.com.au

Moss Wood
Metricup Rd
Wilyabrup WA 6284
(08) 9755 6266
mosswood.com.au

Mount Avoca
Moates Lane
Avoca Vic. 3467
(03) 5465 3282
mountavoca.com

Mount Horrocks
Curling St
Auburn SA 5451
(08) 8849 2202
mounthorrocks.com

Mount Hurtle
(see Geoff Merrill)

Mount Ida
(see Foster's Group)

Mount Langi Ghiran
Warrak Rd
Buangor Vic. 3375
(03) 5354 3207
langi.com.au

Mount Majura Vineyard
RMB 314 Majura Rd
Majura ACT 2609
(02) 6262 3070
mountmajura.com.au

Mount Mary
(not open to public)
(03) 9739 1761
mountmary.com.au

Mount Pleasant
Marrowbone Rd
Pokolbin NSW 2321
(02) 4998 7505
mcwilliams.com.au

Mount Prior Vineyard
cnr River Rd & Popes Lane
Rutherglen Vic. 3685
(02) 6026 5591

Mount Trio Vineyard
(by appointment)
2534 Porongurup Rd
Mount Barker WA 6324
(08) 9853 1135
mounttriowines.com.au

Mount William Winery
Mount William Rd
Tantaraboo Vic. 3764
(03) 5429 1595
mtwilliamwinery.com.au

Mountadam
High Eden Ridge
Eden Valley SA 5235
(08) 8564 1900
mountadam.com

Mr Frog
(see Yering Station)

Mr Riggs Wine Co. Ltd
'Ingleburne'
Main Road
McLaren Vale SA 5171
(08) 8556 4460

Mulyan
North Logan Rd
Cowra NSW 2794
(02) 6342 1336
mulyan.com.au

Murchison Wines
Old Weir Rd
Murchison Vic. 3610
(03) 5826 2294
murchisonwines.com.au.

Murdock
(by appointment)
Riddoch Hwy
Coonawarra SA 5263
(08) 8737 3700
murdockwines.com

Murrindindi Vineyard
RMB 6070 Cummins Lane
Murrindindi Vic. 3717
(03) 5797 8217

Narkoojee
170 Francis Rd
Glengarry Vic. 3854
(03) 5192 4257
narkoojee.com

Nashwauk
(not open to public)
nashwaukvineyards.com.au

Nazaaray
266 Meakins Rd
Flinders Vic. 3929
(03) 5989 0126
nazaaray.com.au

Neagle's Rock
Main North Rd
Clare SA 5453
(08) 8843 4020
neaglesrock.com

Nepenthe Vineyards
(not open to public)
(08) 8389 8218
nepenthe.com.au

Nicholson River
Liddells Rd
Nicholson Vic. 3882
(03) 5156 8241
nicholsonriverwinery.com.au

Ninth Island
(see Pipers Brook)

Noon
Rifle Range Rd
McLaren Vale SA 5171
(08) 8323 8290
noonwinery.com.au

Nugan Estate
Kidman Way
Wilbriggie NSW 2680
(02) 6968 5311
nuganestate.com.au

Oakridge Winery
864 Maroondah Hwy
Coldstream Vic. 3770
(03) 9739 1920
oakridgeestate.com.au

Oakvale Winery
1596 Broke Rd
Pokolbin NSW 2320
(02) 4998 7088
oakvalewines.com.au

Ocean Eight
(by appointment)
271 Tucks Road
Shoreham Vic. 3916
(03) 5989 6471
oceaneight.com

Off the Leash
(see The Lane)

Old Kent River
Turpin Rd
Rocky Gully WA 6397
(08) 9855 1589

Old Mill Estate Wines
(not open to public)
oldmillestatewines.com

Old Station
PO Box 40
Watervale SA 5452
(02) 9144 1925

O'Leary Walker
Main Rd
Leasingham SA 5452
(08) 8843 0022
olearywalkerwines.com

Oliver's Taranga
Seaview Rd
McLaren Vale SA 5171
(08) 8323 8498
oliverstaranga.com

Orlando
Barossa Valley Way
Rowland Flat SA 5352
(08) 8521 3111
orlandowyndhamgroup.com

Osborns
166 Foxeys Rd
Merricks North Vic. 3926
(03) 5989 7417

Over The Shoulder
(see Oakridge Winery)
overtheshoulder.com.au

Padthaway Estate
Riddoch Hwy
Padthaway SA 5271
(08) 8765 5235
padthawayestate.com

Palandri
cnr Boundary Rd & Bussell
Hwy
Margaret River WA 6285
(08) 9756 5100
palandri.com.au

Palmer Wines
Caves Rd
Wilyabrup WA 6280
(08) 9756 7388

Pankhurst Wines
Woodgrove Rd
Hall ACT 2618
(02) 6230 2592
pankhurstwines.com.au

Panorama
1848 Cygnet Coast Rd
Cradoc Tas. 7109
(03) 6266 3409
panoramavineyard.com.au

Paracombe
Paracombe Rd
Paracombe SA 5132
(08) 8380 5058
paracombewlnes.com

Paradigm Hill
26 Merricks Rd
Merricks Vic. 3916
(03) 5989 9000
paradigmhill.com.au

Paradise Enough
Stewarts Rd
Kongwak Vic. 3951
(03) 5657 4241
paradiseenough.com.au

Paringa Estate
44 Paringa Rd
Red Hill South Vic. 3937
(03) 5989 2669
paringaestate.com.au

Parker Coonawarra Estate
Riddoch Hwy
Coonawarra SA 5263
(08) 8737 3525
parkercoonawarraestate.com.au

Parri Estate
Sneyd Rd
Mount Compass SA 5210
(08) 8554 9660
parriestate.com.au

Passing Clouds
Powlett Rd
via Inglewood
Kingower Vic. 3517
(03) 5438 8257

Pattersons
St Werburghs Rd
Mount Barker WA 6324
(08) 9851 2063

Paul Conti
529 Wanneroo Rd
Woodvale WA 6026
(08) 9409 9160
paulcontiwines.com.au

Paul Osicka
Majors Creek Vineyard
Graytown Vic. 3608
(03) 5794 9235

Paulett Wines
Polish Hill River Rd
Sevenhill SA 5453
(08) 8843 4328
paulettwines.com.au

Paxton
Wheaton Rd
McLaren Vale SA 5171
paxtonvineyards.com

Peel Estate
Fletcher Rd
Baldivis WA 6171
(08) 9524 1221
peelwine.com.au

Pendarves Estate
110 Old North Rd
Belford NSW 2335
(02) 6574 7222

Penfolds
(see Foster's Group)

Penley Estate
McLean's Rd
Coonawarra 5263
(08) 8736 3211
penley.com.au

Penny's Hill
Main Rd
McLaren Vale SA 5171
(08) 8556 4460
pennyshill.com.au

Pepper Tree Wines
Halls Rd
Pokolbin NSW 2320
(02) 4998 7539
peppertreewines.com.au

Pepperjack
(see Foster's Group)

Peppers Creek
cnr Ekerts & Broke Rds
Pokolbin NSW 2321
(02) 4998 7532

Pertaringa
cnr Hunt Rd & Rifle Range Rd
McLaren Vale SA 5171
(08) 8323 8125
pertaringa.com.au

Petaluma
Mt Barker Rd
Bridgewater SA 5155
(08) 8339 9200
petaluma.com.au

Peter Douglas Wines
(not open to public)
peterdouglaswines.com.au

Peter Lehmann
Para Rd
Tanunda SA 5352
(08) 8563 2500
peterlehmannwines.com.au

Petersons
Lot 21 Mount View Rd
Mount View NSW 2325
(02) 4990 1704
petersonswines.com.au

Pettavel Winery
65 Pettavel Rd
Waurn Ponds Vic. 3216
(03) 5266 1120
pettavel.com

Pewsey Vale
Eden Valley Rd
Angaston SA 5353
(08) 8561 3200
pewseyvale.com

Pfeiffer
Distillery Rd
Wahgunyah Vic. 3687
(02) 6033 2805
pfeifferwines.com.au

Philip Shaw Wines
Koomooloo Vineyard,
Caldwell Lane
Orange NSW 2800
(02) 6365 2334
philipshaw.com.au

Phillip Island Wines
Lot 1 Berrys Beach Rd
Phillip Island Vic. 3922
(03) 5956 8465
phillipislandwines.com.au

Pibbin Farm
Greenhill Rd
Balhannah SA 5242
(08) 8388 4794

Picardy
(not open to public)
(08) 9776 0036
picardy.com.au

Pierro
Caves Rd
Wilyabrup via Cowaramup
WA 6284
(08) 9755 6220
pierro.com.au

Pike & Joyce
(not open to public)
pikeandjoyce.com.au

Pikes
Polish Hill River Rd
Seven Hill SA 5453
(08) 8843 4370
pikeswines.com.au

Pipers Brook
3959 Bridport Hwy
Pipers Brook Tas. 7254
(03) 6332 4444
pbv.com.au

Pirie Estate
(not open to public)
(03) 6334 7772

Pirramimma
Johnston Rd
McLaren Vale SA 5171
(08) 8323 8205
pirramimma.com.au

Pitchfork Wines
(see Hay Shed Hill)

Pizzini
King Valley Rd
Whitfield Vic. 3678
(03) 5729 8278
pizzini.com.au

Plantagenet Wines
Albany Hwy
Mount Barker WA 6324
(08) 9851 2150

Plunkett's
cnr Lambing Gully Rd &
Hume Fwy
Avenel Vic. 3664
(03) 5796 2150
plunkett.com.au

Pondalowie Vineyards
6 Main St
Bridgewater-on-Loddon
Vic. 3516
(03) 5437 3332

Poole's Rock
McDonalds Rd
Pokolbin NSW 2320
(02) 4998 7501
poolesrock.com.au

The Poplars Winery
Riddoch Hwy
Coonawarra SA 5263
(08) 8736 3130
chardonnaylodge.com.au

Port Phillip Estate
261 Red Hill Rd
Red Hill Vic. 3937
(03) 5989 2708
portphillip.net

Portree Vineyard
72 Powell's Track
Lancefield Vic. 3435
(03) 5429 1422
portreevineyard.com.au

Pothana Vineyard
(see David Hook Wines)

Preece
(see Mitchelton Wines)

Prentice
(see Tuck's Ridge)

Preston Peak
31 Preston Peak Lane
Preston Qld 4352
(07) 4630 9499
prestonpeak.com

Primo Estate
cnr Old Port Wakefield &
Angle Vale Rds
Virginia SA 5120
(08) 8380 9442
primoestate.com.au

Prince Albert
Lemins Rd
Waurn Ponds Vic. 3221
(03) 5243 5091

Prince Hill Wines
1220 Sydney Rd
Mudgee NSW 2850
(02) 5373 1245
princehillwines.com

Printhie Wines
489 Yuranigh Rd
Molong NSW 2866
(02) 6366 8422
printhiewines.com.au

Provenance
(by appointment)
PO Box 74
Bannockburn Vic. 3331
(03) 5265 6055
provenancewines.com.au

Providence
236 Lalla Rd
Lalla Tas. 7267
(03) 6395 1290
providence-vineyards.com.au

Punch
(not open to public)
punched.com.au

Punt Road
St Huberts Rd
Coldstream Vic. 3770
(03) 9739 0666
puntroadwines.com.au

Punters Corner
cnr Riddoch Hwy &
Racecourse Rd
Coonawarra SA 5263
(08) 8737 2007
punterscorner.com.au

Purple Hen
96 McFees Rd
Rhyll (Phillip Island) 3923
(03) 5956 9244
purplehenwines.com.au

Quattro Mano
(no cellar door)
quattromano.com.au

Queen Adelaide
(see Foster's Group)

Radenti
(see Freycinet Vineyard)

Radford Wines
(not open to public)
radfordwines.com

Ralph Fowler
Lot 101 Limestone Coast Rd
Mount Benson SA 5275
(08) 8768 5008
ralphfowlerwines.com.au

Ravenswood Lane
(see The Lane)

Ravensworth
(not open to public)
ravensworthwines.com.au

Red Claw
(see Yabby Lake)

Red Edge
(not open to public)
Heathcote Vic. 3523
(03) 9337 5695

Red Hill Estate
53 Shoreham Rd
Red Hill South Vic. 3937
(03) 5989 2838
redhillestate.com.au

Redbank Winery
1 Sally's Lane
Redbank Vic. 3478
(03) 5467 7255
sallyspaddock.com.au

Redgate
cnr Caves & Boodjidup Rds
Margaret River WA 6285
(08) 9757 6488
redgatewines.com.au

Redman
Riddoch Hwy
Coonawarra SA 5263
(08) 8736 3331

Renmano
Renmark Ave
Renmark SA 5341
(08) 8586 6771
hardywines.com.au

Reschke Wines
(not open to public)
reschke.com.au

Reynell
(see Hardys)

Ribbon Vale Estate
(see Moss Wood)

Richmond Grove
(see Orlando)

Riddoch
(see Katnook Estate)

Ridgeline
(no cellar door)
ridgelinewines.com.au

Rimfire
via Bismarck St
Maclagan Qld 4352
(07) 4692 1129
rimfirewinery.com.au

Riposte
(not open to public)
(08) 8389 8149

Robert Channon Wines
32 Bradley Lane
Stanthorpe Qld 4380
(07) 4683 3260
robertchannonwines.com

Robinvale Wines
Sealake Rd
Robinvale Vic. 3549
(03) 5026 3955
organicwines.com

Rochford
cnr Maroondah Hwy & Hill Rd
Coldstream Vic. 3770
(03) 5962 2119
rochfordwines.com.au

Rockford
Krondorf Rd
Tanunda SA 5352
(08) 8563 2720

Rolling Wines
(see Cumulus Wines)

Rosabrook Estate
Rosa Brook Rd
Margaret River WA 6285
(08) 9758 2286
rosabrook.com

Rosemount
Rosemount Rd
Denman NSW 2328
(02) 6549 6450
rosemountestate.com.au

Rosevears
1A Waldhorn Dve
Rosevears Tas. 7277
(03) 6330 1800
rosevears.com.au

Rosily Vineyard
Yelverton Rd
Wilyabrup WA 6280
(08) 9755 6336
rosily.com.au

Ross Estate Wines
Barossa Valley Way
Lyndoch SA 5351
(08) 8524 4033
rossestate.com.au

Rothbury Estate
Broke Rd
Pokolbin NSW 2321
(02) 4998 7555
fosters.com.au

Rothvale
Deasy's Rd
Pokolbin NSW 2321
(02) 4998 7290
rothvale.com.au

Rudderless Wines
Main South Rd
Sellicks Beack SA 5174
(08) 8556 3083
rudderlesswines.com.au

Rufus Stone
(see Tyrrell's)

Rumball
(no cellar door)
(08) 8332 2761

Rutherglen Estates
cnr Great Northern Rd &
Murray Valley Hwy
Rutherglen Vic. 3685
(02) 6032 7999
rutherglenestates.com.au

Ryan Family Wines
Broke Estate
Broke Rd
Broke NSW 2330
(02) 6579 1065
ryanwines.com.au

Ryecroft
Ingoldby Rd
McLaren Flat SA 5171
(08) 8383 0001
rosemountestate.com.au

Rymill
The Riddoch Run Vineyards
(off Main Rd)
Coonawarra SA 5263
(08) 8736 5001
rymill.com.au

Saddlers Creek
Marrowbone Rd
Pokolbin NSW 2321
(02) 4991 1770
saddlerscreekwines.com.au

Salisbury
(see Evans & Tate)

Salitage
Vasse Hwy
Pemberton WA 6260
(08) 9776 1771
salitage.com.au

Saltram
Nuriootpa Rd
Angaston SA 5353
(08) 8564 3355
saltramwines.com.au

Sam Miranda of King Valley
1019 Snow Rd
Oxley Vic. 3678
(03) 5727 3888
sammiranda.com.au

Samuel's Gorge
Lot 10, Chaffeys Rd
McLaren Vale SA 5171
(08) 8323 8651
gorge.com.au

Sandalford
West Swan Rd
Caversham WA 6055
(08) 9374 9374
sandalford.com

Sandhurst Ridge
156 Forest Dve
Marong Vic. 3515
(03) 5435 2534
sandhurstridge.com

Sandstone Vineyard
(by appointment)
Caves & Johnson Rds
Wilyabrup WA 6280
(08) 9755 6271

Savaterre
(not open to public)
PO Box 337
Beechworth Vic. 3747
(03) 5727 0551
savaterre.com

S.C. Pannell
(not open to public)
(08) 8299 9256

Scarborough Wines
Gillards Rd
Pokolbin NSW 2321
(02) 4998 7563
scarboroughwine.com.au

Scarpantoni
Scarpantoni Dve
McLaren Flat SA 5171
(08) 8383 0186
scarpantoni-wines.com.au

Schild Estate Wines
cnr Barossa Valley Way &
Lyndoch Valley Rd
Lyndoch SA 5351
(08) 8524 5560
schildestate.com.au

Schinus
(see Crittenden at Dromana)

Scion Vineyard & Winery
74 Slaughterhouse Rd
Rutherglen Vic. 3685
(02) 6032 8844
scionvineyard.com

Scorpo Wines
(by appointment)
23 Old Bittern-Dromana Rd
Merricks North Vic. 3926
scorpowines.com.au

Scotchmans Hill
Scotchmans Rd
Drysdale Vic. 3222
(03) 5251 3176
scotchmanshill.com.au

Seaview
Chaffeys Rd
McLaren Vale SA 5171
(08) 8323 8250
fosters.com.au

Seppelt
Seppeltsfield
via Tanunda SA 5352
(08) 8562 8028
fosters.com.au

Seven Hill Cellars
College Rd
Sevenhill
via Clare SA 5453
(08) 8843 4222
sevenhillcellars.com.au

Seville Estate
Linwood Rd
Seville Vic. 3139
(03) 5964 2622
sevilleestate.com.au

Shadowfax
K Road
Werribee Vic. 3030
(03) 9731 4420
shadowfax.com.au

Shantell
Melba Hwy
Dixons Creek Vic. 3775
(03) 5965 2155
shantellvineyard.com.au

Sharefarmers
(see Petaluma)

Shaw & Smith
Lot 4, Jones Rd
Balhannah SA 5242
(08) 8398 0500
shawandsmith.com

Shaw Vineyard Estate
34 Isabel Dve
Murrumbateman NSW 2582
(02) 6227 5865
shawvineyards.com.au

Shelmerdine Vineyards
Merindoc Vineyard,
Lancefield Rd
Tooborac Vic. 3522
(03) 5433 5188
shelmerdine.com.au

Shingleback
1 Main Rd
McLaren Vale SA 5171
(08) 8323 7388
shingleback.com.au

Shottesbrooke
1 Bagshaws Rd
McLaren Flat SA 5171
(08) 8383 0002
shottesbrooke.com.au

Simon Hackett
(not open to public)
(08) 8331 7348

Skillogalee
Skillogalee Rd
via Sevenhill SA 5453
(08) 8843 4311
skillogalee.com.au

Smidge Wines
(not open to public)
smidgewines.com

Smithbrook
(not open to public)
(08) 9772 3557
smithbrook.com.au

Smiths Vineyard
Croom Lane
Beechworth Vic. 3747
0412 475 328
smithsvineyard.com.au

Sorrenberg
Alma Rd
Beechworth Vic. 3747
(03) 5728 2278
sorrenberg.com

Spinifex
(not open to public)
(08) 8564 2059
spinifexwines.com.au

St Hallett
St Halletts Rd
Tanunda SA 5352
(08) 8563 7000
sthallett.com.au

St Huberts
Maroondah Hwy
Coldstream Vic. 3770
(03) 9739 1118
sthuberts.com.au

St John's Road
(not open to public)
stjohnsroad.com

St Leonards
St Leonard Rd
Wahgunyah Vic. 3687
(02) 6033 1004
stleonardswine.com.au

St Mary's Vineyard
V and A Lane
via Coonawarra SA 5263
(08) 8736 6070
stmaryswines.com.au

St Matthias
(see Moorilla Estate)

Stanley Lambert Wines
Barossa Valley Way
Box 459, Tanunda, SA 5352
(08) 8563 3375
stanleylambert.com.au

Stanton & Killeen
Murray Valley Hwy
Rutherglen Vic. 3685
(02) 6032 9457
stantonandkilleenwines.com.au

Starvedog Lane
Reynell Rd
Reynella SA 5161
starvedoglane.com.au

Stefano Lubiana
60 Rowbottoms Rd
Granton Tas. 7030
(03) 6263 7457
slw.com.au

Stein's Wines
Pipeclay Rd
Mudgee NSW 2850
(02) 6373 3991

Stella Bella
(no cellar door)
PO Box 536
Margaret River WA 6285
(08) 9757 6377
stellabella.com.au

Stephen John Wines
Government Rd
Watervale SA 5452
(08) 8843 0105

Stonehaven
(see Hardys)

Stoney Vineyard/ Domaine A
Teatree Rd
Campania Tas. 7026
(03) 6260 4174

Stonier
362 Frankston–Flinders Rd
Merricks Vic. 3916
(03) 5989 8300
stoniers.com.au

Stumpy Gully
1247 Stumpy Gully Rd
Moorooduc Vic. 3933
(03) 5978 8429

Suckfizzle
(see Stella Bella)

Summerfield
Main Rd
Moonambel Vic. 3478
(03) 5467 2264
summerfieldwines.com.au

Sutton Grange Winery
Carnochan's Lane
Sutton Grange Vic. 3448
(03) 5474 8277
suttongrangewines.com

Symphonia Wines
(see Sam Miranda of King Valley)

Syrahmi
(not open to public)
0407 057 471

Tahbilk
Tahbilk Vic. 3607
via Nagambie
(03) 5794 2555
tahbilk.com.au

Talijancich
26 Hyem Rd
Herne Hill WA 6056
(08) 9296 4289

Tallarook
(not open to public)
(03) 9818 3455
tallarook.com

Taltarni Vineyards
Taltarni Rd
Moonambel Vic. 3478
(03) 5459 7900
taltarni.com.au

Talunga
Lot 101 Adelaide-Mannum Rd
Gumeracha SA 5233
(08) 8389 1222
talunga.com.au

Tamar Ridge
Auburn Rd
Kayena Tas. 7270
(03) 6394 1114
tamarridgeestates.com.au

Tamburlaine Wines
McDonalds Rd
Pokolbin NSW 2321
(02) 4998 7570
tamburlaine.com.au

Tanglewood Downs
Bulldog Creek Rd
Merricks North
(03) 5974 3325
tanglewoodestate.com.au

Tapanappa
(not open to public)
tapanappawines.com.au

Tapestry
Merrivale Wines
Olivers Rd
McLaren Vale SA 5171
(08) 8323 9196
merrivale.com.au

Tar & Roses/Trust
(not open to public)
trustwines.com.au

TarraWarra
Healesville Rd
Yarra Glen Vic. 3775
(03) 5962 3311
tarrawarra.com.au

Tatachilla Winery
151 Main Rd
McLaren Vale SA 5171
(08) 8323 8656
tatachillawinery.com.au

Taylors
Mintaro Rd
Auburn SA 5451
(08) 8849 1111
taylorswines.com.au

Te-aro Estate
(by appointment)
Lot 501, Fromm Square Road
Williamstown SA 5351
(08) 8524 6116
te-aroestate.com

Temple Bruer
Angas River Delta
via Strathalbyn SA 5255
(08) 8537 0203
templebruer.net.au

Tempus Two
(see McGuigan)

Ten Minutes by Tractor
1333 Morning–Flinders Rd
Main Ridge Vic. 3928
(03) 5989 6455
tenminutesbytractor.com.au

Terra Felix
(not open to public)
terrafelix.com.au

T'Gallant
1385 Mornington–Flinders Rd
Main Ridge Vic. 3928
(03) 5989 6565
tgallant.com.au

Thalgara Estate
De Beyers Rd
Pokolbin NSW 2321
(02) 4998 7717
thalgara.com.au

Thomas Wines
PO Box 606
Cessnock NSW 2325
(02) 6574 7371
thomaswines.com.au

Thompson Estate
Harmans Road South
Wilyabrup WA 6284
(08) 9386 1751
thompsonestate.com

Thorn-Clarke
PO Box 402
Angaston SA 5353
(08) 8564 3373
thornclarkewines.com.au

3 Drops
(not open to public)
3drops.com

Three Wishes Vineyard
655 Craigburn Rd
Hillwood Tas. 7252
(03) 6331 2009
threewishesvineyard.com

Tilbrook Estate
17/1 Lobethal Rd
Lobethal SA 5241
(08) 8389 5120
marketsatheart.com/
tilbrookestate

Tim Adams
Warenda Rd
Clare SA 5453
(08) 8842 2429
timadamswines.com.au

Tim Gramp
Mintaro/Leasingham Rd
Watervale SA 5452
(08) 8843 0199
timgrampwines.com.au

Tim Smith Wines
(not open to public)
(08) 8563 0939

Tintilla
Hermitage Rd
Pokolbin NSW 2335
(02) 6574 7093
tintilla.com

Tisdall
Cornelia Creek Rd
Echuca Vic. 3564
(03) 5482 6058

Toolangi Vineyards
(not open to public)
toolangi.com

Torbreck
Roennfeldt Rd
Marananga SA 5360
(08) 8562 4155
torbreck.com

Torresan Estate
Estate Dve
Flagstaff Hill SA 5159
(08) 8270 2500

Tower Estate
cnr Broke & Halls Rds
Pokolbin NSW 2321
(02) 4998 7989
towerestatewines.com.au

377

Trentham Estate
Sturt Hwy
Trentham Cliffs
via Gol Gol NSW 2738
(03) 5024 8888
trenthamestate.com.au

**Trevor Jones/
Kellermeister**
Barossa Valley Hwy
Lyndoch SA 5351
(08) 8524 4303
kellermeister.com.au

Tscharke
(no cellar door)
tscharke.com.au

Tuck's Ridge
37 Shoreham Rd
Red Hill South Vic. 3937
(03) 5989 8660
tucksridge.com.au

Turkey Flat
Bethany Rd
Tanunda SA 5352
(08) 8563 2851
turkeyflat.com.au

Turramurra Estate
295 Wallaces Rd
Dromana Vic. 3936
(03) 5987 1146
turramurraestate.com.au

24 Karat Wines
(not open to public)
24karat.com.au

Two Hands
Neldner Rd
Marananga SA 5355
(08) 8562 4566
twohandswines.com

Two Rivers
2 Yarrawa Rd
Denman NSW 2328
(02) 6547 2556
tworiverswines.com

Tyrrell's
Broke Rd
Pokolbin NSW 2321
(02) 4993 7000
winefutures.com.au

Vasse Felix
cnr Caves & Harmans Rds
Cowaramup WA 6284
(08) 9756 5000
vassefelix.com.au

Veritas
cnr Seppeltsfield & Stelzer Rds
Dorrien SA 5355
(08) 8562 3300
veritaswinery.com

Victorian Alps Winery
cnr Great Alpine Road &
Snow Road
Gapsted Vic. 3737
(03) 57511383
victorianalpswinery.com.au

Virgin Hills
(not open to public)
(03) 5422 3032
virginhills.com.au

Voyager Estate
Stevens Rd
Margaret River WA 6285
(08) 9757 6354
voyagerestate.com.au

The Wanderer
(see Gembrook Hill)

Wandin Valley Estate
Wilderness Rd
Lovedale NSW 2320
(02) 4930 7317
wandinvalley.com.au

Wantirna Estate
(not open to public)
(03) 9801 2367
wantirnaestate.com.au

Warburn Estate
700 Kidman Way
Tharbogang NSW 2680
(02) 6963 8300
warburnestate.com.au

Wards Gateway Cellars
Barossa Valley Hwy
Lyndoch SA 5351
(08) 8524 4138

Warrabilla
Murray Valley Hwy
Rutherglen Vic. 3687
(02) 6035 7242
warrabillawines.com.au

Warramate
27 Maddens Lane
Gruyere Vic. 3770
(03) 5964 9219

Warrenmang
Mountain Ck Rd
Moonambel Vic. 3478
(03) 5467 2233
bazzani.com.au/warrenmang

Water Wheel
Raywood Rd
Bridgewater Vic. 3516
(03) 5437 3060
waterwheelwine.com

Watershed Wines
cnr Bussell Hwy & Darch Rd
Margaret River WA 6285
(08) 9758 8633
watershedwines.com.au

Wedgetail
40 Hildebrand Rd
Cottles Bridge Vic. 3099
(03) 9714 8661
wedgetailestate.com.au

Weemala
(see Logan)

Wellington
(Hood Wines)
489 Richmond Rd
Cambridge Tas. 7170
(03) 6248 5844

Wendouree
Wendouree Rd
Clare SA 5453
(08) 8842 2896

West Cape Howe Wines
678 South Coast Hwy
Denmark WA 6333
(08) 9848 2959
westcapehowewines.com.au

Westend
1283 Brayne Rd
Griffith NSW 2680
(02) 6964 1506

Westfield
Memorial Ave
Baskerville WA 6056
(08) 9296 4356

Wetherall
Naracoorte Rd
Coonawarra SA 5263
(08) 8737 2104

Whistler Wines
Seppeltsfield Rd
Marananga SA 5355
(08) 8562 4942
whistlerwines.com

Wicks Estate Wines
(not open to public)
wicksestate.com.au

Wignalls
Chester Pass Rd
Albany WA 6330
(08) 9841 2848
wignallswines.com.au

Wild Duck Creek
(by appointment)
Springflat Rd
Heathcote Vic. 3523
(03) 5433 3133

Wildwood
St Johns Lane
via Wildwood Vic. 3428
(03) 9307 1118
wildwoodvineyards.com.au

Will Taylor
1 Simpson Pde
Goodwood SA 5034
(08) 8271 6122

Willespie
Harmans Mill Rd
Wilyabrup WA 6280
(08) 9755 6248
willespie.com.au

William Downie
(not open to public)
williamdownie.com.au

Willow Creek
166 Balnarring Rd
Merricks North Vic. 3926
(03) 5989 7448
willow-creek.com

The Willows Vineyard
Light Pass Rd
Barossa Valley SA 5355
(08) 8562 1080
thewillowsvineyard.com.au

The Wilson Vineyard
Polish Hill River
via Clare SA 5453
(08) 8843 4310
wilsonvineyard.com.au

Winbirra Vineyard
173 Point Leo Rd
Red Hill South Vic. 3937
(03) 5989 2109
winbirra.com.au

Winchelsea Estate
c/- Nicks Wine Merchants
(03) 9639 0696

Windowrie Estate
Windowrie Rd
Canowindra NSW 2804
(02) 6344 3598
windowrie.com.au

Wine By Brad
(no cellar door)
PO Box 475
Margaret River WA 6285
0409 572 957
winebybrad.com.au

Winstead
Winstead Rd
Bagdad Tas. 7030
(03) 6268 6417

Winter Creek Wine
(by appointment)
(08) 8524 6382
wintercreekwine.com.au

Wirilda Creek
Lot 32 McMurtrie Rd
McLaren Vale SA 5171
(08) 8323 9688

Wirra Wirra
McMurtrie Rd
McLaren Vale SA 5171
(08) 8323 8414
wirra.com.au

Witchmount Estate
557 Leakes Rd
Rockbank Vic. 3335
(03) 9747 1055
witchmount.com.au

Wolf Blass
Sturt Hwy
Nuriootpa SA 5355
(08) 8568 7300
wolfblass.com.au

Wood Park
Kneebones Gap Rd
Bobinawarrah Vic. 3678
(03) 5727 3367
woodpark.com.au

Woodside Valley Estate
(not open to public)
woodsidevalleyestate.com.au

Woodstock
Douglas Gully Rd
McLaren Flat SA 5171
(08) 8383 0156
woodstockwine.com.au

Woody Nook
Metricup Rd
Metricup WA 6280
(08) 9755 7547
woodynook.com.au

Wyanga Park
Baades Rd
Lakes Entrance Vic. 3909
(03) 5155 1508

Wyndham Estate
Dalwood Rd
Dalwood NSW 2321
(02) 4938 3444
wyndhamestate.com.au

Wynns
Memorial Dve
Coonawarra SA 5263
(08) 8736 3266
wynns.com.au

Xabregas
(by appointment)
cnr Spencer Rd & Hay River Rd
Narrikup WA 6326
xabregas.com.au

Xanadu
Boodjidup Rd
Margaret River WA 6285
(08) 9757 2581
xanaduwines.com

Yabby Lake
(no cellar door)
(03) 9667 6644
yabbylake.com

Yaldara
Gomersal Rd
Lyndoch SA 5351
(08) 8524 0200
yaldara.com.au

Yalumba
Eden Valley Rd
Angaston SA 5353
(08) 8561 3200
yalumba.com

Yarra Burn
Settlement Rd
Yarra Junction Vic. 3797
(03) 5967 1428
yarraburn.com.au

Yarra Ridge
Glenview Rd
Yarra Glen Vic. 3775
(03) 9730 1022
beringerblass.com.au

Yarra Valley Hills
(see Dromana Estate)

Yarra Yering
Briarty Rd
Gruyere Vic. 3770
(03) 5964 9267

Yarrabank
38 Melba Hwy
Yarra Glen Vic. 3775
(03) 9730 0100
yering.com

YarraLoch
(not open to public)
11 Range Rd
Coldstream Vic. 3770
(03) 9525 4275
yarraloch.com.au

Yarraman Estate
700 Yarraman Rd
Wybong NSW 2333
(02) 6547 8118
yarramanestate.com.au

Yellow Tail
(see Casella)

Yellowglen
White's Rd
Smythesdale Vic. 3351
(03) 5342 8617
yellowglen.com.au

Yering Station
Melba Hwy
Yering Vic. 3775
(03) 9730 0100
yering.com

Yeringberg
(not open to public)
(03) 9739 1453

Zarephath
Moorialup Rd
East Porongurup WA 6324
(08) 9853 1152
zarephathwines.com

Zema Estate
Riddoch Hwy
Coonawarra SA 5263
(08) 8736 3219
zema.com.au

Zilzie
Lot 66 Kulkyne Way
Karadoc Vic. 3496
(03) 5025 8100
zilziewines.com

Zonte's Footstep
PO Box 53
Langhorne Creek SA 5255
(08) 8537 3334
zontesfootstep.com.au

Index

Acrobat Sangiovese Shiraz 202
Acrobat Shiraz 233
Alana Estate Pinot Noir 184
Alana Estate Sauvignon Blanc 73
Alkoomi Riesling 96
Alkoomi Sauvignon Blanc 64
Alkoomi Unwooded Chardonnay 126
All Saints Chardonnay Viognier 119
All Saints Estate Durif 209
All Saints Estate Family Cellar Durif 209
All Saints Family Cellar Marsanne 119
Alta for Elsie 153
Alta Pinot Grigio 107
Alta Sauvignon Blanc 64
Alvaro Castro Dão D.O.C 305
Amisfield Sauvignon Blanc 73
Andrew Thomas Braemore Semillon 83
Andrew Thomas The O.C. Semillon 83
Angove's Nine Vines Viognier 120
Apsley Gorge Pinot Noir 160
Arras 47
Ashton Hills Estate Pinot Noir 160
Ashton Hills Piccadilly Valley Pinot Noir
    160
Ata Rangi Crimson Pinot Noir 184
Audrey Wilkinson Chardonnay 126
The Aurora Vineyard Bendigo Pinot Noir
    185
The Aurora Vineyard Bendigo Syrah
    233
Australian Old Vine Collection Barossa
    Shiraz 234
Australian Old Vine Collection Grenache
    218
Ayala Rosé Nature 56
Ayala ZD 56

Babich Marlborough Pinot Noir 185
Babich Winemaker's Reserve Pinot Noir
    185
Baileys of Glenrowan Winemakers
    Selection Old Muscat 314
Baileys of Glenrowan Winemakers
    Selection Old Tokay 314
Balnaves Cabernet Merlot 288
Balnaves Cabernet Sauvignon 276
Balnaves The Blend 288
Balnaves The Tally Reserve Cabernet
    Sauvignon 276
Bannockburn Chardonnay 127
Bannockburn Pinot Noir 161
Bannockburn Riesling 96
Bannockburn Sauvignon Blanc 64
Bannockburn Serré Pinot Noir 161
Bannockburn Stuart Pinot Noir 161
Barossa Old Vine Company Shiraz 234
Barossa Vines By Grant Burge Shiraz
    234
Barratt Picadilly Sunrise Rosé 153
Barratt Picadilly Valley Chardonnay 127
Barratt The Bonython Pinot Noir 161
Barwang Chardonnay 127
Barwang Sauvignon Blanc 65
Barwick Estate The Collectables Pinot
    Noir 162
Basa Verdejo 150
Bass Phillip 21 Pinot Noir 162
Battle of Bosworth Shiraz Viognier 234
Bay of Fires Pinot Noir 162
Bay of Fires Pinot Noir Chardonnay 47
Bay of Fires Riesling 96
Bay of Fires Tigress Pinot Noir
    Chardonnay 48
Bay of Fires Tigress Rosé 48

Bell Echo Marlborough Sauvignon Blanc 73
Bethany Cabernet Merlot 288
Bethany Semillon 84
Big R Cabernet Sauvignon 277
Billecart Brut Rosé 56
Billecart Cuvée Nicholas François-Billecart 57
Binbilla Good Friday Shiraz 234
Binbilla Special Steps Cabernet Sauvignon 277
Bindi Block 5 Pinot Noir 162
Bindi Composition Chardonnay 127
Bindi Composition Pinot Noir 163
Bindi Macedon Cuvée V 48
Bindi Quartz Chardonnay 127
Blackbilly GSM 218
Blackbilly Sauvignon Blanc 65
Bleasdale Malbec 209
Blind River Sauvignon Blanc 74
Boizel Blanc de Blancs 57
Bollinger La Grande Année 57
Bowen Estate Cabernet Sauvignon 277
Braided River Marlborough Pinot Noir 185
Brand's Laira Merlot 298
Breheny Vineyards Brown Magpie Pinot Noir 163
Breheny Vineyards Brown Magpie Shiraz 235
Bremerton Selkirk Shiraz 235
Bremerton Tamblyn Cabernet Shiraz Malbec Merlot 270
Bress Heathcote Shiraz 235
Bridgewater Mill Chardonnay 128
Brokenwood Graveyard Vineyard Shiraz 235
Brokenwood Hunter Valley Shiraz 235
Brokenwood Indigo Vineyard Chardonnay 128
Brokenwood Verona Vineyard Shiraz 236
Brookland Valley Merlot 298
Brookland Valley Reserve Chardonnay 128
Brown Brothers Durif 210
Brown Brothers Graciano 210
Brown Brothers Patricia Botrytis Riesling 311
Brown Brothers Patricia Shiraz 236
Brown Brothers Pinot Noir Chardonnay Pinot Meunier 48
Brown Brothers Zibibbo Rosa 48
Burnbrae Merlot 298
Burnbrae Sauvignon Blanc Semillon 88
Burnt Spur Pinot Noir 185
By Farr Chardonnay 128
By Farr Farrago 116
By Farr Pinot Noir 163
By Farr Sangreal Pinot Noir 163
By Farr Shiraz 236
By Farr Viognier 120

Cape Barren Native Goose GSM 218
Cape Campbell Pinot Noir 186
Cape Mentell Chardonnay 128
Cape Mentelle Cabernet Sauvignon 277
Cape Mentelle Marmaduke Shiraz Grenache 219
Cape Mentelle Trinders Cabernet Merlot 289
Cape Mentelle Wallcliffe Vineyard Sauvignon Blanc Semillon 88
Cape Mentelle Zinfandel 210
Capel Vale Cellar Exclusive Cabernet Merlot 289
Capel Vale Cellar Exclusive Viognier 120
Capel Vale Pemberton Sauvignon Blanc 65
Capel Vale Regional Series Cabernet Sauvignon 277
Capel Vale Regional Series Semillon Sauvignon Blanc 89
Cardinham Estate Sangiovese 202
Carrick Pinot Noir 186
Carrick Unravelled Pinot Noir 186
Cartwheel Semillon Sauvignon Blanc 89
Casa Freschi La Signora 203
Cascabel Tempranillo 210
Cascineta Vietti Moscato d'Asti 150
Catalina Sounds Sauvignon Blanc 74

Catherine Vale Winifred Barbera 203

Cattier 57

Cerro del Masso Chianti 305

Chalk Hill Barbera 203

Chalk Hill Sangiovese 203

Chalk Hill The Procrastinator 210

Chalmers Sagrantino 203

Chambers Grand Muscat 315

Chambers Old Vine Muscadelle 315

Chandon Barrel Selection Chardonnay 129

Chandon Brut 49

Chandon Heathcote Shiraz 236

Chapel Hill Bush Vine Grenache 219

Chapel Hill Cabernet Sauvignon 278

Chapel Hill il Vescovo Sangiovese 204

Chapel Hill il Vescovo Sangiovese Rosé 154

Chapel Hill il Vescovo Tempranillo 211

Chapel Hill Shiraz Grenache 219

Charles Heidsieck Blanc des Millénaires 57

Charles Heidsieck Brut Reserve 58

Charles Heidsieck Rosé 58

Charles Melton Rose of Virginia 154

Churton Pinot Noir 186

Churton Sauvignon Blanc 74

Cillar de Silos Tempranillo Joven Ribera del Duero D.O. 305

Clair de Lune Pinot Noir 164

Clairault Cabernet Sauvignon 278

Clairault Chardonnay 129

Clairault Estate Chardonnay 129

Clairault Semillon Sauvignon Blanc 89

Clonakilla Ballinderry 289

Clonakilla Hilltops Shiraz 236

Clonakilla O'Riada Shiraz 237

Clonakilla Riesling 97

Clonakilla Shiraz Viognier 237

Clonakilla Syrah 237

Clonakilla Viognier 120

Clos de Ste Anne Pinot Noir 186

Clos Henri Marlborough Pinot Noir 187

Clos Henri Sauvignon Blanc 74

Clyde Park Pinot Noir 164

Cockatoo Ridge Sauvignon Blanc 65

Cockfighter's Ghost Semillon 84

Cofield Durif 211

Coldstone Pinot Grigio 107

Coldstone Tempranillo 211

Coldstream Hills Chardonnay 129

Coldstream Hills Pinot Noir 164

Coldstream Hills Reserve Cabernet Sauvignon 278

Coldstream Hills Reserve Chardonnay 129

Collector MTR Shiraz 237

Collector Reserve Shiraz 238

Concha Y Toro Casillero del Diablo Cabernet Sauvignon 306

Concha Y Toro Casillero del Diablo Carmenere 306

Coombend Sauvignon Blanc 65

Coriole Nebbiolo Rosé 154

Coriole Sangiovese 204

Coriole Shiraz 238

Coriole The Dancing Fig Shiraz Mourvèdre 219

Coriole The Optimist Reserve Chenin Blanc 116

Coriole The Soloist Shiraz 238

Cosme Palacio Rioja Cosecha 306

CR Ebenezer Shiraz 238

Crabree Watervale Riesling 97

Craggy Range Avery Vineyard Sauvignon Blanc 74

Craggy Range C3 Kidnappers Vineyard Chardonnay 130

Craggy Range Calvert Vineyard Pinot Noir 187

Craggy Range Fletcher Vineyard Riesling 97

Craggy Range Gimblett Gravels Merlot 299

Craggy Range Le Sol 239

Craggy Range Noble 311

Craggy Range Old Renwick Vineyard Sauvignon Blanc 75

Craggy Range Sophia 299

Craggy Range Te Kahu 299

Craggy Range Te Muna Road Vineyard
Sauvignon Blanc 75
Crittenden Estate Geppetto Pinot Noir
164
Crittenden Geppetto Chardonnay 130
Croser 49
The Crossings Marlborough Sauvignon
Blanc 75
Crowded House Pinot Gris 107
Crowded House Sauvignon Blanc 75
Cullen Mangan Vineyard Semillon
Sauvignon Blanc 89
Cullen Vineyard Sauvignon Blanc
Semillon 89
Cuttaway Hill Pinot Gris 108
Cuttaway Hill Sauvignon Blanc 66
Cuttaway Hill Semillon Sauvignon Blanc
90

d'Arenberg Dead Arm Shiraz 239
d'Arenberg Love Grass Shiraz 239
d'Arenberg Sticks & Stones 220
d'Arenberg The Cadenzia GSM 220
d'Arenberg The Custodian Grenache
220
d'Arenberg The Derelict Vineyard
Grenache 220
d'Arenberg The Hermit Crab Viognier
Marsanne 120
d'Arenberg The Ironstone Pressings 220
d'Arenberg The Last Ditch Viognier 121
d'Arenberg The Laughing Magpie Shiraz
Viognier 239
d'Arenberg The Money Spider Roussanne
121
d'Arenberg The Noble Riesling 311
d'Arenberg The Stump Jump 221
d'Arenberg The Twenty-eight Road
Mourvèdre 221
Damana Ribera del Duero 306
d'Arenberg d'Arry's Original Shiraz
Grenache 219
d'Arenberg The Stump Jump White 117
Darling Point Pinot Noir 164
Dashwood Pinot Noir 187

David Fransz Red Rosé 154
David Franz Alexander's Reward
Cabernet Shiraz 270
David Franz Georgie's Walk Cabernet
Sauvignon 278
David Hook Old Vines Semillon 84
David Hook The Gorge Pinot Grigio 108
De Bortoli Emeri Pink Moscato 49
De Bortoli Estate Grown Cabernet
Sauvignon 279
De Bortoli Estate Grown Pinot Noir 165
De Bortoli Estate Grown Sauvignon 66
De Bortoli Estate Grown Shiraz Viognier
239
De Bortoli Noble One Botrytis Semillon
312
De Bortoli Reserve Release Chardonnay
130
De Bortoli Reserve Release Pinot Noir
165
De Bortoli Reserve Release Syrah 240
De Bortoli Rococo Blanc de Blancs 49
De Bortoli Sacred Hill Brut Cuvée 49
De Bortoli Show Liqueur Muscat 315
De Bortoli Viognier 121
De Bortoli Windy Peak Pinot Grigio 108
De Bortoli Windy Peak Pinot Noir 165
De Bortoli Windy Peak Pinot Noir
Chardonnay 50
De Bortoli Yarra Valley Reserve Release
Sauvignon 66
Deakin Estate Merlot 299
Deisen Grenache 221
Deisen Mataro 221
Deisen Shiraz 240
Deisen Sweetheart Shiraz 240
Delamotte Blanc de Blancs 58
Delamotte Brut 58
Delatite Polly Sparkling Gewürztraminer
50
DeLisio Shiraz 240
Delta Vineyard Hatters Hill Pinot Noir
187
Delta Vineyard Pinot Noir 187
Devaux Cuvée D 58

Devil's Corner Chardonnay 130

Devil's Corner Pinot Grigio 108

Devil's Corner Pinot Noir 165

Devil's Lair Cabernet Merlot 289

Devil's Lair Chardonnay 130

Devil's Lair Fifth Leg Rosé 154

Devil's Lair Fifth Leg White 90

Devil's Lair Sauvignon Blanc 66

Dirty Bliss Grenache Shiraz 221

Dividing Range Cabernet Merlot 289

Dividing Range Sauvignon Blanc
Colombard Chardonnay 90

Dog Point Pinot Noir 188

Dog Point Sauvignon Blanc 75

Dog Point Section 94 76

DogRidge Cadenzia 222

Dom Perignon 59

Domain Barossa Toddler GSM 222

Domain Day Garganega 117

Domaine des Bernardins Muscat de
Baumes de Venise 312

Domaine Zind Humbrecht Riesling
Turckheim 150

Dominique Portet Fontaine Rosé 155

Dominique Portet Merlot 300

Dominique Portet Sauvignon Blanc 66

Dowie Doole Merlot 300

Drylands Pinot Noir 188

Dutschke 'The Tawny' 22 Year Old 315

Dutschke GHR Shiraz 240

Dutschke Oscar Semmler 241

Dutschke St Jakobi Shiraz 241

Dutschke Willow Bend Shiraz Merlot
Cabernet Sauvignon 270

Eden Road Two Trees Grenache Shiraz
222

Eden Road V06 Shiraz 241

Element Chardonnay 131

Eric & Joel Durand Cornas Empreintes
306

Evans & Tate Classic 90

Even Keel Chardonnay 131

Evil Cabernet Sauvignon 279

Evoi Reserve Chardonnay 131

Fairbank Syrah 241

Fairbank Viognier 121

Fairhall Downs Single Vineyard Pinot
Noir 188

Fairhall Downs Single Vineyard
Sauvignon Blanc 76

Falveys Sauvignon Blanc 76

Farr Rising Geelong Pinot Noir 165

Farr Rising Saignée 155

Farr Rising Shiraz 242

Fattoria Zerbina Ceregio Sangiovese Di
Romagna 307

Felton Road Pinot Noir 188

Felton Road Pinot Noir Block 3 189

Felton Road Pinot Noir Calvert Vineyard
189

Felton Road Pinot Noir Cornish Point
189

Fermoy Estate Nebbiolo 204

Ferngrove Cossack Riesling 97

Ferngrove Diamond Chardonnay 131

Ferngrove Merlot 300

Ferngrove Symbols Cabernet Merlot 290

Ferngrove Symbols Sauvignon Blanc
Semillon 90

Fire Gully Cabernet Sauvignon Merlot
290

Fire Gully Sauvignon Blanc Semillon 90

First Drop Fat Of The Land Ebenezer
Shiraz 242

First Drop Two Percent Barossa Shiraz
242

Five Shillings Shiraz 242

Flaxman Riesling 97

Flying Fish Cabernet Merlot 290

Fonterutoli Chianti Classico 307

Forest Hill Block 1 Riesling 98

Forest Hill Block 8 Chardonnay 131

Forest Hill Chardonnay 132

Formby & Adams Cutting Edge Cabernet
Shiraz 271

Forrest Estate Sauvignon Blanc 76

Fox Creek JSM Shiraz Cabernet
Sauvignon Cabernet Franc 271

Fox Gordon Abby Viognier 121

Fox Gordon By George Cabernet
 Tempranillo 211
Fox Gordon Hannah's Swing Shiraz
 242
Fox Gordon Princess Fiano 117
Framingham Pinot Noir 189
Framingham Sauvignon Blanc 76
Frankland Estate Isolation Ridge Vineyard
 Chardonnay 132
Frankland Estate Isolation Ridge Vineyard
 Riesling 98
Fraser Gallop Estate Chardonnay 132
Freeman Fortuna 117
Freycinet Cabernet Merlot 290
Freycinet Chardonnay 132
Freycinet Louis Pinot Noir 166
Freycinet Riesling 98
Freycinet Vineyard Pinot Noir 166
Frog Rock Pinot Gris 108
Frog Rock Semillon Sauvignon Blanc 91

Gail Estate Artigiano Viognier 122
Galli Estate Artigiano Pinot Grigio 109
Gapstead Limited Release Barbera 204
Gapstead Valley Selection Sauvignon
 Blanc Semillon 91
Gapsted Merlot 300
Gapsted Petit Manseng 117
Gembrook Hill Chardonnay 132
Gembrook Hill Pinot Noir 166
Gembrook Hill Sauvignon Blanc 67
Gemtree Bloodstone Tempranillo 211
Gemtree Tatty Road 290
Gemtree Uncut Shiraz 243
Giaconda Chardonnay 133
Giaconda Nantua Vineyard Pinot Noir
 166
Giaconda Warner Vineyard Shiraz 243
Giant Steps Miller Vineyard Shiraz 243
Giant Steps Sexton Vineyard Chardonnay
 133
Giant Steps Sexton Vineyard Pinot Noir
 166
Giant Steps Tarraford Vineyard
 Chardonnay 133

Giant Steps Tarraford Vineyard Pinot
 Noir 167
Gibbston Highgate Estate Soultaker Pinot
 Noir 190
Gibbston Valley Central Otago Pinot Noir
 190
Gibson Reserve Merlot 300
Gibson The Dirtman Shiraz 243
Giesen Marlborough Sauvignon Blanc
 77
Gilligan Shiraz Grenache Mourvèdre 222
Glaetzer Amon-Ra Shiraz 243
Glaetzer Anaperenna Shiraz Cabernet
 Sauvignon 271
Glaetzer Wallace 222
Glenguin Estate The Old Broke Block
 Semillon 84
Gosset Brut Excellence 59
Gosset Grande Reserve 59
Grant Burge 20 Year Old Tawny 316
Grant Burge East Argyle Pinot Gris 109
Grant Burge Hillcot Merlot 301
Grant Burge Miamba Shiraz 244
Grant Burge Shadrach Cabernet
 Sauvignon 279
Grant Burge Zerk Semillon Viognier 91
Greenstone Shiraz 244
Greystone Sauvignon Blanc 77
Grosset Polish Hill Riesling 98
Grove Estate Reserve Nebbiolo 204
Grove Estate The Cellar Block Shiraz
 Viognier 244
Grove Estate The Wombat Way Viognier
 122
The Growers' Reward Chardonnay 133
Guigal Côtes Du Rhône 307

Hamelin Bay Five Ashes Vineyard
 Cabernet Sauvignon 279
Hamelin Bay Five Ashes Vineyard
 Chardonnay 133
Hamelin Bay Rampant Red 271
Hamelin Bay Rampant White 91
Hanging Rock Cambrian Rise Heathcote
 Shiraz 244

Hanging Rock Cuvée VII LD 50

Hanging Rock Macedon Cuvée XII 50

Hanging Rock Rosé Brut 51

Hanging Rock Shiraz Grenache
Mourvèdre Pinot Noir 223

Hanging Rock The Jim Jim Pinot Gris
109

Hanging Rock The Jim Jim Sauvignon
Blanc 67

Happs Cabernet Merlot 291

Hardy's The Sage Shiraz Sangiovese 212

Hare's Chase Red Blend 271

Hare's Chase Tempranillo 212

Hastwell & Lightfood Tempranillo 212

Hastwell & Lightfoot Cabernet Franc
212

Hastwell & Lightfoot Cabernet
Sauvignon 279

Hat Rock Pinot Noir 167

Hay Shed Hill Block 1 Semillon
Sauvignon Blanc 92

Hay Shed Hill Block 6 Chardonnay 134

Hay Shed Hill Cabernet Sauvignon 280

Hay Shed Hill Chardonnay 134

Hay Shed Hill Sauvignon Blanc Semillon
92

Hazard Hill Semillon Sauvignon Blanc 92

Heggies Botrytis Riesling 312

Henri Fessy Beaujolais-Villages 307

Henriot Blanc de Blancs 59

Henry Pellé Menetou-Salon 151

Henschke Coralinga Sauvignon Blanc 67

Henschke Croft Chardonnay 134

Henschke Cyril Cabernet Sauvignon 280

Henschke Giles Pinot Noir 167

Henschke Hill of Grace Shiraz 245

Henschke Johann's Garden 223

Henschke Joseph Hill Gewürztraminer
98

Henschke Julius Riesling 99

Henschke Keyneton Estate Euphonium
272

Henschke Louis Semillon 84

Henschke Mount Edelstone Shiraz 245

Henschke Tilly's Vineyard 92

Henshke Innes Vineyard Pinot Gris 109

Hentley Farm Fool's Bay Beached Shiraz
Cabernet 272

Hentley Farm Shiraz 245

Hentley Farm The Beauty Shiraz 245

Hentley Farm The Stray Mongrel 223

Heritage Shiraz 245

Herzog Sauvignon Blanc 77

Hesketh Hidden Garden Sauvignon Blanc
77

Hesketh The Protagonist Shiraz 246

Hewitson Cellar Reserve Tempranillo 213

Hewitson Gun Metal 99

Hewitson Miss Harry Grenache Shiraz
Mourvèdre 223

Hewitson Ned & Henry's Shiraz 246

Hewitson Old Garden Mourvèdre 223

Hewitson The Mad Hatter Shiraz 246

Highbank Merlot 301

Higher Plane Cabernet Merlot 291

Hoddles Creek Chardonnay 134

Hoddles Creek Estate Pinot Noir 167

Hollick Hollaia 205

Hollick Shiraz Cabernet 272

Hollick Wrattonbully Tempranillo 213

Howard Park Chardonnay 134

Hugel Pinot Blanc 151

Hunter's Pinot Noir 190

Hunter's Sauvignon Blanc 78

Innocent Bystander Chardonnay 135

Innocent Bystander Moscato 51

Innocent Bystander Pinot Gris 109

Innocent Bystander Pinot Noir 167

Innocent Bystander Shiraz Viognier 246

Isabel Estate Sauvignon Blanc 78

Jackson Estate Sauvignon Blanc 78

Jackson Estate Vintage Widow Pinot Noir
190

Jacob's Creek Cabernet Merlot 291

Jacob's Creek Merlot 301

Jacob's Creek Reserve Sauvignon Blanc
67

Jacob's Creek Reserve Shiraz Rosé 155

Jacob's Creek Steingarten Riesling 99
Jacquesson Rosé 60
Jamabro Bush Vine Grenache 224
Jamsheed Great Western Shiraz 246
Jansz Brut LD 51
Jansz Premium Cuvée 51
Jansz Premium Rosé 51
Jansz Premium Vintage Rosé 52
Jansz Vintage Cuvée 52
Jim Barry Lodge Hill Riesling 99
John Duval Eligo Shiraz 247
John Duval Entity Shiraz 247
John Duval Wines Plexus 224
John Forrest Collection Gimblett Gravels
  Syrah 247
John Hongell Old Vine Grenache Shiraz
  224
John Hongell Shiraz 247
Jones Apero 316
Jones The Winemaker Merlot 301
Jones Vintage Fortified 316
Josef Chromy Botrytis Riesling 312
Josef Chromy Pepik Pinot Noir 168
Joseph Moda Cabernet Merlot 291
Joseph Nebbiolo 205
Joseph Sparkling Red 52
Juniper Crossing Cabernet Sauvignon
  Merlot 291
Juniper Crossing Chardonnay 135
Juniper Crossing Merlot 301
Juniper Crossing Tempranillo 213
Juniper Estate Cabernet Sauvignon
  280
Juniper Estate Chardonnay 135
Juniper Estate Semillon 85

Kaesler Avignon 224
Kaesler Stonehorse Shiraz 247
Kaesler Stonehourse Grenache Shiraz
  Mourvèdre 224
Kaesler The Bogan Shiraz 248
Kalleske Clarry's Red 225
Kalleske Clarry's White 92
Kalleske Greenock Shiraz 248
Kalleske J.M.K. Shiraz VP 316

Kalleske Johann Georg Old Vine Shiraz
  248
Kalleske Old Vine Grenache 225
Kanta Riesling 99
Katnook Estate Founder's Block
  Sauvignon Blanc 67
Katnook Estate Sauvignon Blanc 68
Kilikanoon Mort's Block Riesling 100
Kirrihill Baile an Gharrai Shiraz 248
Kirrihill Companions Cabernet Merlot
  292
Kirrihill Companions Tempranillo
  Garnacha 213
Kirrihill Estates Langhorne Creek Shiraz
  249
Kirrihill Tulach Mor Cabernet Sauvignon
  280
Kooyong Clonale Chardonnay 135
Kooyong Estate Chardonnay 135
Kooyong Estate Pinot Noir 168
Kooyong Farrago Chardonnay 136
Kooyong Faultline Chardonnay 136
Kooyong Ferrous Pinot Noir 168
Kooyong Haven Pinot Noir 168
Kooyong Massale Pinot Noir 168
Kooyong Meres Pinot Noir 169
Kooyong Pinot Gris 110
Krinklewood Francesca Rosé 155
Krinklewood Semillon 85
Krinklewood Verdelho 118
Krinklewood Wild White 118
KT & The Falcon Watervale Riesling 100
Kumeu River Estate Chardonnay 136
Kumeu River Estate Pinot Noir 190
Kumeu River Maté's Vineyard
  Chardonnay 136
Kumeu River Village Chardonnay 136

La Braccesca Sabazio Rosso di
  Montepulciano 308
La Curio The Nubile Grenache Shiraz
  225
La Montesa Rioja 308
Lake Breeze Arthur's Reserve Cabernet
  Sauvignon Petit Verdot Malbec 292

Lake Breeze Bernoota Shiraz Cabernet 272
Lalla Gully Pinot Gris 110
Lalla Gully Sauvignon Blanc 68
Langmeil SWH Viognier 122
Lark Hill Pinot Noir 169
Lark Hill Sangiovese 205
Lawson's Dry Hills Sauvignon Blanc 78
Leabrook Estate Pinot Gris 110
Leaping Lizard Semillon Sauvignon Blanc
    93
Leasingham Classic Clare Riesling 100
Leeuwin Estate Art Series Chardonnay
    137
Leeuwin Estate Art Series Sauvignon
    Blanc 68
Leeuwin Estate Prelude Cabernet Merlot
    292
Leeuwin Estate Prelude Chardonnay 137
Leeuwin Estate Siblings Sauvignon Blanc
    Semillon 93
Leo Buring Eden Valley Leonay 100
Leo Buring Leopold Riesling 101
Lethbridge Pinot Noir 169
Lethbridge Shiraz 249
Liebich Tempranillo Rosé 155
Lillydale Estate Chardonnay 137
Lillydale Estate Pinot Noir 169
Lindemans Premier Selection Brut Cuvée
    52
Little r Cabernet Sauvignon 281
Little Rebel Cabernet Sauvignon Merlot
    292
Little Rebel Chardonnay 137
Little Rebel Pinot Noir 170
Lloyd Brothers Shiraz 249
Logan Apple Tree Flat Chardonnay 137
Logan Cabernet Merlot 292
Logan Chardonnay 138
Logan Pinot Noir 170
Logan Shiraz 249
Logan Weemala Merlot 302
Loose End GSM 225
Loose End Rosé 156
Lou Miranda Leone Botrytis Semillon
    312

Louis Jadot Saint-Veran 151
Louis Roederer Cristal 60
Luke Lambert Nebbiolo 205
LZ Tempranillo Rioja D.O. 308

Mac Forbes 'Hugh' Cabernet Sauvignon
    281
Mac Forbes Blaufrankisch 308
Mac Forbes Coldstream Pinot Noir 170
Mac Forbes Riesling rs9 101
Mac Forbes Woori Yallock Pinot Noir 170
Mac Forbes Yarra Valley Pinot Noir 170
McHenry Hohnen 3 Amigos Marsanne
    Chardonnay Roussanne 122
McHenry Hohnen 3 Amigos Shiraz
    Grenache Mourvèdre 226
McHenry Hohnen Calgardup Brook
    Chardonnay 138
McHenry Hohnen Tiger Country 213
McIvor Estate Marsanne Roussanne 123
McKellar Ridge Shiraz Viognier 251
McPherson Basilisk Shiraz Mourvèdre
    226
McWilliam's Hanwood Estate Merlot 302
Maglieri Shiraz 249
Magnetic Hill Pinot Noir 171
Mahi Marlborough Sauvignon Blanc 78
Main Divide Marlborough Pinot Noir
    191
Main Divide Pinot Noir 191
Main Divide Sauvignon Blanc 79
Main Divide TeHau Pinot Noir 191
Main Divide Tipinui Marlborough Pinot
    Noir 191
Main Ridge Half Acre Pinot Noir 171
Maison Champy Bourgogne Pinot Noir
    308
Mandala Pinot Noir 171
Mandala Prophet Pinot Noir 171
Mantra Sauvignon Blanc 68
Margan Barbera 205
Marius Simpatico Shiraz 250
Marius Symphony Shiraz 250
Marius Symposium Shiraz Mourvèdre
    225

Martin Codax Burgans Albariño 151

Martinborough Vineyards Te Tera
Sauvignon Blanc 79

MartinboroughVineyard Te Tera Pinot
Noir 191

Massena Rosé 156

Massena The Moonlight Run 226

Massena The Surly Muse Viognier 123

Matua Valley Hawkes Bay Sauvignon
Blanc 79

Maude Pinot Noir 192

Maverick Greenock Rise GSM 226

Maverick Greenock Rise Shiraz 250

Maverick Trial Hill Eden Valley Shiraz
250

Maverick Twins Cabernet Sauvignon
Merlot Petit Verdot Cabernet Franc
293

Mayer Big Betty Shiraz 250

Mayer Bloody Hill Chardonnay 138

Mayer Bloody Hill Pinot Noir 171

Mayer Pinot Noir 172

Meerea Park Epoch Semillon 85

Meerea Park Hell Hole Semillon 85

Meerea Park Hell Hole Shiraz 251

Meerea Park Shiraz 251

Meerea Park The Aunts Shiraz 251

Meerea Park Viognier 123

Michael Unwin One Goat Shiraz 251

Mildara Cabernet Sauvignon 281

Mildara Coonawarra Cabernet Shiraz
272

Millamolong Isabelle's Ghost Merlot 302

Minchinbury Private Cuvée Brut de Brut
52

Mistletoe Home Vineyard Semillon 85

Mistletoe Reserve Semillon 86

Mistletoe Shiraz 252

Mitchell McNicoll Riesling 101

Mitchell Semillon 86

Mitchelton Airstrip Marsanne Viognier
Roussanne 123

Mitchelton Crescent Mourvèdre Shiraz
Grenache 226

Mitchelton Viognier 123

Mitolo Jester Rosé 156

Mitre Rocks Central Otago Pinot Noir
192

Moët et Chandon Grand Vintage 60

Molly Morgan Semillon 86

MOMO Pinot Noir 192

Montana Terraces Pinot Noir 192

Moorooduc Estate Devil Bend Creek
Pinot Noir 172

Moorooduc Estate Wild Yeast Pinot Noir
172

Morris of Rutherglen Old Predium
Amontillado Sherry 317

Morris of Rutherglen Old Premium
Liqueur Muscat 317

Morris of Rutherglen Old Premium
Liqueur Tokay 317

Morris Rutherglen Durif 214

Moss Brothers Jane Moss Semillon
Sauvignon Blanc 93

Moss Wood Amy's Cabernet Sauvignon
281

Mount Difficulty Pinot Gris 110

Mount Difficulty Pinot Noir 192

Mount Horrocks Semillon 86

Mount Horrocks Watervale Riesling
101

Mount Horrocks Watervale Shiraz 252

Mount Majura Dinny's Block 214

Mount Majura Pinot Noir 172

Mount Majura Riesling 101

Mount Majura Rosé 156

Mount Majura Shiraz 252

Mount Majura Tempranillo 214

Mount Michael Bessie's Block Pinot Noir
193

Mount Nelson Sauvignon Blanc 79

Mount Pleasant Cellar Release Elizabeth
Semillon 86

Mount Pleasant Lovedale Semillon 87

Mount Pleasant OP & OH Shiraz 252

Mount Trio Cabernet Merlot 293

Mount Trio Chardonnay 138

Mount Trio Sauvignon Blanc 68

Mount Trio Tempranillo 214

Mountadam Estate Chardonnay 138
Mountadam Pinot Gris 110
Mountain X Shiraz 252
Mr Frog Cabernet Shiraz Merlot 273
Mr Riggs McLaren Vale Shiraz 253
Mud House Pinot Noir 193
Mud House Sauvignon Blanc 79
Mud House Swan Pinot Noir 193
Mumm de Cremant 60
Murdoch James Saleyards Syrah 253
Murdock Merlot 302
Mystery Creek Pinot Noir 193

Nashwauk Tempranillo 214
Nazaaray Pinot Gris 111
Nepenthe Charleston Pinot Noir 172
Nepenthe Pinot Gris 111
Nepenthe Sauvignon Blanc 69
Nepenthe The Good Doctor Pinot Noir
 173
Nepenthe Zinfandel 215
Neudorf Brightwater Riesling 102
Neudorf Moutere Chardonnay 139
Neudorf Moutere Pinot Noir 193
Neudorf Moutere Riesling 102
Neudorf Sauvignon Blanc 80
Neudorf Tom's Block Pinot Noir 194
Ninth Island Chardonnay 139
Ninth Island Pinot Grigio 111
Ninth Island Pinot Noir 173
Nobilo Icon Pinot Noir 194
Noon Winery VP 317

O'Leary Walker Blue Cutting Road
 Semillon Sauvignon Blanc 93
O'Leary Walker Polish Hill River Riesling
 102
O'Leary Walker Sauvignon Blanc 69
O'Leary Walker Watervale Riesling 102
Oakridge 864 Chardonnay 139
Oakridge 864 Shiraz 253
Oakridge Cabernet Sauvignon 282
Oakridge Chardonnay 139
Oakridge Over The Shoulder Sauvignon
 Blanc 69

Oakridge Over The Shoulder Shiraz
 Viognier 253
Oakridge Pinot Noir 173
Oakridge Shiraz 253
Ocean Eight Grande Chardonnay 140
Ocean Eight Pinot Gris 111
Ocean Eight Verve Chardonnay 140
Off The Leash Max Shiraz Viognier 254
Old Coach Road Sauvignon Blanc 80
Old Mill Estate Rosé 156
Over The Shoulder Cabernet Merlot 293
Over The Shoulder Chardonnay 140
Over The Shoulder Pinot Grigio 111
Over The Shoulder Pinot Noir 173
Overstone Sauvignon Blanc 80

Palliser Estate Martinborough Pinot Noir
 194
Palliser Estate Pinot Gris 112
Palliser Estate Sauvignon Blanc 80
Paracombe Chardonnay 140
Paracombe Pinot Gris 112
Paracombe Pinot Noir 173
Paracombe Sauvignon Blanc 69
Paracombe Shiraz Viognier 254
Paracombe The Reuben 293
Paradigm Hill Col's Block Shiraz 254
Paradigm Hill L'Ami Sage Pinot Noir 174
Paringa Estate Reserve Pinot Noir 174
Parker Coonawarra Estate Terra Rossa
 Cabernet Sauvignon 282
Parker Coonawarra Estate Terra Rossa
 First Growth 282
Parri Estate Pangkarra Grenache 227
Pascal Jolivet Sancerre 151
Paxton AAA Shiraz Grenache 227
Paxton PG Pinot Gris 112
Pegasus Bay Aria Riesling 313
Pegasus Bay Dry Riesling 102
Pegasus Bay Pinot Noir 194
Pegasus Bay Prima Donna Pinot Noir
 194
Pegasus Bay Riesling 103
Pegasus Bay Sauvignon Semillon 93
Pencarrow Sauvignon Blanc 80

Penfolds Bin 138 Shiraz Grenache Mourvèdre 227

Penfolds Bin 28 Kalimna Shiraz 254

Penfolds Bin 389 273

Penfolds Bin 407 Cabernet Sauvignon 282

Penfolds Bin 51 Riesling 103

Penfolds Bin 707 Cabernet Sauvignon 282

Penfolds Cellar Reserve Pinot Noir 174

Penfolds Grange Shiraz 254

Penfolds Koonunga Hill Shiraz Cabernet 273

Penfolds Magill Estate 255

Penfolds Rawson's Retreat 273

Penfolds RWT Shiraz 255

Penfolds St Henri Shiraz 255

Penley Estate Condor Coonawarra Shiraz Cabernet 273

Penley Estate Gryphon Merlot 302

Penley Estate Over The Moon Rosé 157

Penley Estate Phoenix Cabernet Sauvignon 283

Penny's Hill Shiraz 255

Peregrine Pinot Noir 195

Peregrine Saddleback Pinot Noir 195

Perrier-Jouet Belle Epoque Blanc 60

Perrier-Jouet Grand Brut 61

Pertaringa Two Gentlemens Grenache 227

Pertaringa Undercover Shiraz 255

Petaluma Chardonnay 140

Petaluma Coonawarra 293

Petaluma Merlot 303

Peter Douglas Chime Hoop Cabernet Sauvignon 283

Peter Lehmann Clancy's 94

Peter Lehmann Eden Valley Riesling 103

Peter Lehmann Semillon 87

Peter Lehmann Tempranillo 215

Peter Lehmann Wigan Eden Valley Riesling 103

Pewsey Vale Contours Riesling 104

Pewsey Vale Eden Valley Gewürztraminer 104

Pewsey Vale Eden Valley Riesling 104

Pewsey Vale Prima Riesling 104

Pfeiffer Gamay 215

Pfeiffer Old Distillery Classic Rutherglen Tokay 317

Pfeiffer The Carson Gewürztraminer 104

Philip Shaw No. 19 Sauvignon Blanc 70

Philip Shaw No.17 Merlot Cabernet Franc Cabernet 294

Philippe Portier Quincy 152

Picardy Pinot Noir 174

Picnic By Two Paddocks Pinot Noir 195

Pierre Gimonnet Cuis 1er Cru 61

Pierro Chardonnay 141

Pierro Reserve Cabernet Sauvignon Merlot 294

Pike & Joyce Pinot Gris 112

Pike & Joyce Pinot Noir 175

Pike & Joyce Sauvignon Blanc 70

Pikes EWP Reserve Shiraz 256

Pikes The Bleedings Pinot Noir Rosé 157

Pikes The Merle Reserve Riesling 105

Pipers Brook Chardonnay 141

Pipers Brook Estate Pinot Noir 175

Pirathon by Kalleske Shiraz 256

Pirie Clark's Botrytis Riesling 313

Pirie Estate Chardonnay 141

Pirie Estate Gewürztraminer 105

Pirie Estate Pinot Noir 175

Pirie South Chardonnay 141

Pirie South Pinot Gris 112

Pirie South Riesling 105

Pitchfork Chardonnay 141

Pitchfork Pink 157

Pitchfork Semillon Sauvignon Blanc 94

Pizzini Nebbiolo 206

Pizzini Rosetta 157

Pizzini Sangiovese 206

Plain Jane Cabernet Shiraz 274

Poderi Ruggeri Corsini Dolcetto d'Alba 309

Pol Roger Blanc de Blancs 61

Pol Roger Brut Vintage 61

Poliziano Chianti 309

Pommery Brut Royal 61

Pommery Grand Cru Vintage 62
Pondalowie MT Tempranillo 215
Pondalowie Vintage Port 318
Port Phillip Estate Chardonnay 142
Port Phillip Estate Morillon Pinot Noir
    175
Port Phillip Estate Pinot Noir 175
Port Phillip Estate Rimage Syrah 256
Port Phillip Estate Shiraz 256
Primo Estate Il Briccone Shiraz
    Sangiovese 206
Primo Estate Merlesco 303
Primo Estate Zamberlan Cabernet
    Sauvignon Sangiovese 206
Prince Hill Merlot 303
Prince Hill Shiraz 256
Printhie Merlot 303
Prophet's Rock Pinot Noir 195
Prunotto Barbera d'Alba 309
Punch Cabernet Sauvignon 283
Punch Lance's Vineyard Chardonnay 142
Punch Lance's Vineyard Close Planted
    Pinot Noir 176
Punch Lance's Vineyard Pinot Noir 176
Punt Road Cabernet Sauvignon 284
Punt Road Chardonnay 142
Punt Road Pinot Gris 113
Punt Road Pinot Noir 176
Purple Hen Estate Shiraz 257
Pyramid Valley Growers Collection
    Calvert Vineyard Pinot Noir 196
Pyramid Valley Growers Collection Eaton
    Family Vineyard Pinot Noir 196
Pyrette Shiraz 257

Quartz Reef Bendigo Estate Vineyard
    Pinot Noir 196
Quartz Reef Pinot Gris 113
Quartz Reef Pinot Noir 196
Quattro Mano La Reto Tempranillo 215
Quinta do Ameal Loureiro 152
Quinta do Vallado Douro D.O. 309

R osé McLaren Vale Cabernet Sauvignon
    Rosé 157

Rabbit Ranch Pinot Noir 196
Radenti Chardonnay Pinot Noir 53
Radford Dale Eden Valley Riesling 105
Radford Dale Eden Valley Shiraz 257
Ramos Pinto Adriano 6 Year Old Tawny
    Port 318
Ravenswood Lane Chardonnay 142
Ravenswood Lane Pinot Gris 113
Ravenswood Lane Sauvignon Blanc 70
Ravenswood Lane Semillon Sauvignon
    Blanc 94
Ravenswood Lane Shiraz 257
Ravensworth Hunter Valley Shiraz 257
Ravensworth Sangiovese 207
Ravensworth Semillon 87
Ravensworth Shiraz Viognier 258
Ravensworth Viognier 124
Red Claw Chardonnay 142
Red Claw Pinot Noir 176
Redman Cabernet Sauvignon 284
Redman Cabernet Sauvignon Merlot
    294
Reschke Bull Trader Cabernet Merlot
    294
Reschke Fumé Sauvignon Blanc 70
Richmond Grove Limited Release Shiraz
    258
Richmond Grove Pinot Grigio 113
Richmond Plains Nelson Sauvignon Blanc
    81
Ridgeline Shiraz 258
Riposte The Foil Sauvignon Blanc 70
Riposte The Sabre Pinot Noir 177
Rippon Pinot Noir 197
Roaring Meg Pinot Noir 197
Robert Channon Merlot 303
Rockburn Pinot Noir 197
Roederer Blanc de Blancs 62
Roederer Brut Premier 62
Roederer Brut Vintage 62
Rolling Shiraz 258
Rosemount Show Reserve GSM 227
Ross Estate Old Vine Grenache 228
Ross Estate Shiraz 258
Ross Estate Single Vineyard Merlot 304

Rudderless Grenache 228
Rudderless Grenache Shiraz Mataro 228
Rudderless Mataro 228
Ruinart Blanc de Blancs 62
Ruinart R de Ruinart 63
Rutherglen Estates Marsanne Viognier 124
Rutherglen Estates Red Shiraz Durif 216
Rutherglen Estates Shiraz Viognier 259
Rymill Cabernet Sauvignon 284
Rymill MC² 295
Rymill Sauvignon Blanc 71

S.C. Pannell Grenache 228
S.C. Pannell Nebbiolo 207
S.C. Pannell Pronto 229
S.C. Pannell Shiraz 259
S.C. Pannell Shiraz Grenache 229
Saint Clair Pioneer Block 2 Swamp Sauvignon Blanc 81
Saint Clair Pioneer Block 4 Sawcut Sauvignon Blanc 81
Saint Clair Sauvignon Blanc 81
Saint Cosme Côtes Du Rhône 309
Salitage Pinot Noir 177
Salitage Treehouse Chardonnay 143
Salon Cuvées Blanc de Blancs 63
Saltram No.1 Shiraz 259
Samuel's Gorge Grenache 229
Samuel's Gorge Tempranillo 216
Sandalford Cabernet Sauvignon 284
Sandalford Estate Reserve Chardonnay 143
Sandalford Estate Reserve Sauvignon Blanc Semillon 94
Sandalford Prendiville Reserve Cabernet Sauvignon 284
Schild Estate GMS 229
Schild Estate Merlot 304
Schild Estate Semillon Sauvignon Blanc 94
Scion Sweet Durif 318
Scorpo Aubaine Chardonnay 143
Scorpo Chardonnay 143
Scorpo Noirien Pinot Noir 177

Scorpo Pinot Gris 113
Scorpo Pinot Noir 177
Scorpo Shiraz 259
Scotchmans Hill Pinot Noir 177
Scotchmans Hill Sauvignon Blanc 71
Scotchmans Hill Shiraz 259
Scotchmans Hill Swan Bay Pinot Noir 178
Seaview Brut de Brut 53
Secret Stone Pinot Noir 197
Secret Stone Sauvignon Blanc 81
Seppelt Benno Bendigo Shiraz 260
Seppelt Coborra Pinot Gris 114
Seppelt DP63 Grand Muscat 318
Seppelt Fleur de Lys 53
Seppelt Grampians Chardonnay 144
Seppelt Jaluka Chardonnay 143
Seppelt Silverband Grampians Shiraz 260
Seppelt St Peters Grampians Shiraz 260
Seresin Leah Pinot Noir 198
Seven Hill Lost Boot Rosé 158
Seven Hill Riesling 105
Seven Hill White Spider Semillon Chardonnay 95
Shaw & Smith M3 Chardonnay 144
Shaw & Smith Sauvignon Blanc 71
Shaw & Smith Shiraz 260
Shaw Vineyard Estate Cabernet Merlot 295
Shelmerdine Chardonnay 144
Shelmerdine Pinot Noir 178
Shelmerdine Sauvignon Blanc 71
Shingleback Shiraz 260
Shottesbrooke Adelaide Hills Sauvignon Blanc 71
Shottesbrooke Sauvignon Blanc 72
Sir James Pinot Noir Chardonnay 53
Sir James Tumbarumba Cuvée 54
SmidgeWines The Donald Zinfandel 216
Smithbrook Sauvignon Blanc 72
Smithbrook The Yilgarn Blanc 95
Sorriso Rosé 158
South Pinot Noir 178
Spinifex D.R.S. Vineyard Durif 216

Spinifex Esprit 229
Spinifex Indigene 230
Spinifex Papillon 230
Spinifex Taureau 216
Spy Valley Pinot Noir 198
Spy Valley Sauvignon Blanc 82
St Hallett Eden Valley Riesling 106
St Hallett Faith Shiraz 261
St Hallett Gamekeeper's Reserve 230
St Hallett GST 230
St Hallett Old Block Shiraz 261
St Hallett Rosé 158
St Hallett Semillon 87
St Huberts Chardonnay 144
St Huberts Pinot Noir 178
St Huberts Roussanne 124
St John's Road A Motley Bunch 230
St John's Road Blood and Courage Shiraz 261
St John's Road Julia Greenock Shiraz 261
Staete Landt Estate Grown Marlborough Sauvignon 82
Stanley Lambert Grenache Shiraz Mourvèdre 231
Stanton & Killeen Classic Rutherglen Tawny Port 318
Stanton & Killeen Grand Muscat 319
Stanton & Killeen Ruby Port 319
Stanton & Killeen Vintage Fortified 319
Starvedog Lane Adelaide Hills Chardonnay Pinot Moir Pinot Meunier 54
Starvedog Lane Pinot Noir 178
Starvedog Lane Shiraz Viognier 261
Stefano Lubiana Estate Pinot Noir 179
Stella Bella Chardonnay 144
Stella Bella Pink Muscat 158
Stella Bella Sauvignon Blanc 72
Stella Bella Semillon Sauvignon Blanc 95
Stonehaven Father Woods Cabernet Sauvignon 285
Stoneleigh Pinot Noir 198
Stoneleigh Rapaura Series Pinot Noir 198
Stoneleigh Sauvignon Blanc 82

Stonier Chardonnay 145
Stonier Pinot Noir 179
Stonier Reserve Pinot Noir 179
Suckfizzle Cabernet Sauvignon 285
Suckfizzle Sauvignon Blanc Semillon 95
Sutton Grange Estate Rosé 158
Sutton Grange Estate Syrah 262
Sutton Grange Fairbank Rosé 159
Sutton Grange Giove 207
Symphonia Tannat 217
Syrahmi Petit Prière Shiraz 262

T'Gallant Grace Pinot Grigio 114
T'Gallant Juliet Pinot Noir 179
T'Gallant Tribute Pinot Noir 179
Tábula Ribera del Duero 310
Taittinger Comtes de Champagne 63
Taltarni 3 Monks Cabernet Merlot 295
Taltarni Brut Taché 54
Taltarni Cephas Shiraz Cabernet 262
Taltarni Heathcote Shiraz 262
Taltarni T Series Chardonnay Pinot Noir Pinot Meunier 54
Taltarni T Series Shiraz 262
Taltarni Vintage Brut 55
Tamar Ridge Gewürztraminer 106
Tamar Ridge Kayena Vineyard Pinot Noir 180
Tamar Ridge Pinot Gris 114
Tamar Ridge Research Series 83-1 Viognier 124
Tamar Ridge Research Series Albariño 118
Tapanappa Cabernet Shiraz 274
Tapanappa Foggy Hill Pinot Noir 180
Tapanappa Merlot 304
Tapanappa Tiers Vineyard Chardonnay 145
Tapestry The Vincent Shiraz 263
Tar & Roses Pinot Grigio 114
Tar & Roses Sangiovese 207
Tar & Roses Tempranillo 217
TarraWarra Estate Reserve Pinot Noir 180
TarraWarra Reserve Chardonnay 145

Tatachilla Partners Cabernet Shiraz 274
Taylors Gewürztraminer 106
Te Mania Nelson Pinot Noir 199
Te Mania Nelson Pinot Noir Reserve 199
Te Mata Elston Chardonnay 145
Te Mata Estate Awatea Cabernet Merlot 295
Te Mata Estate Coleraine 295
Te Mata Estate Merlot Cabernet 296
Te Mata Woodthorpe Vineyard Viognier 124
Te-aro Estate GSM 231
Te-aro Estate Shiraz Cabernet 274
Ten Minutes By Tractor 10X Chardonnay 145
Ten Minutes By Tractor 10X Pinot Gris 114
Ten Minutes By Tractor McCutcheon Vineyard Pinot Noir 180
Ten Minutes By Tractor Wallis Vineyard Chardonnay 146
Terra Felix Viognier 125
The Lane Viognier 122
The Poplars Cabernet Merlot 294
The Poplars Reserve Cabernet Sauvignon 283
Thomas Kiss Shiraz 263
Thompson Estate Cabernet Merlot 296
Thorn-Clarke Quartage 296
Thorn-Clarke Sandpiper Chardonnay 146
Thorn-Clarke Sandpiper The Blend 274
Thorn-Clarke Shotfire Chardonnay 146
Thorn-Clarke Shotfire Pinot Gris 115
Thorn-Clarke Shotfire Shiraz 263
Thorn-Clarke William Randell Shiraz 263
3 Drops Merlot 304
3 Rings Reserve Shiraz 263
Three Wishes Pinot Noir 181
Tiefenbrunner Pinot Grigio 152
Tim Smith Viognier 125
Toolangi Chardonnay 146
Toolangi Estate Chardonnay 146
Toolangi Estate Pinot Noir 180
Toolangi Pinot Noir 181

Toolangi Reserve Chardonnay 147
Torbreck Descendant 264
Torbreck Run Rig 264
Torbreck The Gask 264
Torbreck The Pict Mataro 231
Torbreck The Struie 264
Treehouse Pinot Noir 181
Trevor Jones Boots Shiraz 265
Trinity Hill Hawkes Bay Pinot Noir 199
Trinity Hill High Country Pinot Noir 199
Trinity Hill Homage Syrah 265
Triplebank Awatere Valley Pinot Noir 199
Tscharke Only Son Tempranillo Graciano 217
Turkey Flat Butcher's Block Marsanne Viognier 125
Turkey Flat Butchers Block Shiraz Grenache Mourvèdre 231
Turkey Flat Grenache 231
Turkey Flat Mourvèdre 232
Turkey Flat Rosé 159
Turkey Flat Shiraz 265
24 Karat Chardonnay 147
Two Hands Bad Impersonator Shiraz 265
Two Hands Brave Faces 232
Two Paddocks Central Otago Pinot Noir 200
Tyrell's Vat 8 Shiraz Cabernet 275
Tyrell's Vat 9 Shiraz 266
Tyrrell's Belford Chardonnay 147
Tyrrell's Brokenback Shiraz 265
Tyrrell's Rufus Stone Heathcote Shiraz 266
Tyrrell's Vat 47 Chardonnay 147

Valdespino Pedro Ximinez 319
Vasse Felix Cabernet Sauvignon 285
Vasse Felix Heytesbury Cabernet Sauvignon 285
Vasse Felix Heytesbury Chardonnay 147
Vasse Felix Semillon 87
Vidal-Fleury Côtes Du Ventoux 310
Viette Barbera d'Asti Tre Vigne 310

Viette Dolcetto d'Alba Tre Vigne 310

Viette Perbacco Nebbiolo 310

Viette Roero Arneis 152

Villa Maria Cellar Selection Pinot Noir
200

Villa Maria Cellar Selection Syrah 266

Villa Maria Private Bin Pinot Noir 200

Villa Maria Private Bin Syrah 266

Villa Maria Single Vineyard Taylors Pass
Pinot Noir 200

Vinea Marson Nebbiolo 207

Vinea Marson Sangiovese 208

Voyager Estate Cabernet Merlot 296

Voyager Estate Chardonnay 148

Voyager Estate Girt By Sea Cabernet
Merlot 296

Vynfields Pinot Noir 200

Waimea Pinot Noir Barrel Selection 201

Waipara Hills Souther Cross Selection
Pinot Noir 201

The Wanderer Pinot Noir 181

The Wanderer Shiraz 266

Water Wheel Bendigo Shiraz 267

Water Wheel Memsie 275

Watershed Awakening Cabernet
Sauvignon 285

Watershed Cabernet Merlot 297

Watershed Shades 297

Watershed Viognier 125

Waurn Ponds Reserve Shiraz 267

Weemala Pinot Noir 181

West Cape Howe Styx Gully Chardonnay
148

Westend 3 Bridges Durif 217

Whistler Shiraz 267

Wicks Estate Shiraz 267

Wignalls Pinot Noir 182

Wild Rock Cupid's Arrow Pinot Noir 201

Wild Rock Gravel Pit Red 304

William Downie Mornington Peninsula
Pinot Noir 182

William Fevre Chablis 152

Willow Creek Vineyard Tulum Pinot Noir
182

The Wilson Vineyard Shiraz 267

Winbirra The Brigadier Pinot Noir 182

Windowrie Estate Deep River
Chardonnay 148

Windowrie Estate The Mill Verdelho
118

Wine By Brad Cabernet Merlot 297

Wine By Brad Semillon Sauvignon Blanc
95

Winegrowers of Ara Composite Pinot
Noir 201

Winter Creek Second Eleven Blend 232

Winter Creek The Old Barossa Blend 232

Wirra Wirra Church Block 275

Wirra Wirra RSW Shiraz 268

Wirra Wirra Scrubby Rise Shiraz Cabernet
Petit Verdot 275

Wirra Wirra Woodhenge Shiraz 268

Witchmount Shiraz 268

Wolf Blass Grey Label Shiraz 268

Woodside Baudin Cabernet Sauvignon
286

Wooing Tree Pinot Noir 201

Wyndham Estate Bin 444 Cabernet
Sauvignon 286

Wynns Cabernet Sauvignon 286

Wynns Coonawarra Estate Cabernet
Shiraz Merlot 275

Wynns John Riddoch Cabernet
Sauvignon 286

Wynns Messenger Cabernet Sauvignon
286

Wynns Michael Shiraz 268

Xabregas Cabernet Merlot 297

Xanadu Cabernet Sauvignon 287

Xanadu Chardonnay 148

Xanadu Dragon Cabernet Merlot 297

Yabby Lake Vineyard Pinot Noir 182

Yalumba FDW[7c] Chardonnay 148

Yalumba Hand Picked Botrytis Viognier
313

Yalumba The Virgilius Viognier 125

Yarra Burn Pinot Noir 183

Yarra Burn Pinot Noir Chardonnay Pinot Meunier 55

Yarra Burn Third Light Pinot Noir Chardonnay 55

Yarrabank LD Sauvage 55

YarraLoch Arneis 118

YarraLoch Rosé 159

Yering Station Cabernet Sauvignon 287

Yering Station Chardonnay 149

Yering Station Reserve Chardonnay 149

Yering Station Reserve Pinot Noir 183

Yering Station Reserve Shiraz Viognier 269

Yering Station Shiraz Viognier 269

Yeringberg Chardonnay 149

Yeringberg Pinot Noir 183

Yeringberg Shiraz 269

Zema Estate Cabernet Sauvignon 287

Zilzie Sangiovese 208

Zonte's Footstep Pinot Grigio 115

Zonte's Footstep Sangiovese Barbera 208

Zonte's Footstep Shiraz Viognier 269

The Penguin Bloody Mary

If the door to the cellar gets jammed in the open position and you over-indulge, then here's a reliable tonic to get you back on the right track the next morning (bearing in mind that if you have several of these, you're heading back down the wrong track). The acidity stimulates alkaline stomach juices, the vodka kick-starts the breakdown of impurities in the blood and the spices fire the metabolism. Best taken either with or instead of breakfast.

Ingredients

50 ml freshly squeezed lemon juice
15 ml Worcestershire sauce
a good pinch each of salt, celery salt, sweet paprika and smoked paprika
plenty of freshly ground pepper
2 teaspoons of fresh horseradish
a few shakes of Tabasco (add to taste)
250 ml tomato juice

Method

Thoroughly mix lemon juice, Worcestershire sauce, salts, spices, pepper, horseradish and Tabasco in a small glass. Fill a cocktail shaker with plenty of ice, add mixture and tomato juice, and shake thoroughly. Pour contents into a large wine glass. Garnish with a stick of fresh celery and a slice of lemon.

The Age Good Food Guide 2009

John Lethlean & Necia Wilden

The Age Good Food Guide, Melbourne's most respected guide to eating out, reviews more than 400 of the best restaurants in and outside town. In this 29th edition, food critics John Lethlean and Necia Wilden reveal the most exciting new places to visit, as well as the award-winners.

They also note some intriguing trends: from traditional fine dining to more casual establishments that bend that rules but remain dedicated to the highest quality food and wine; the use of the freshest seasonal produce from kitchen gardens; and the impact of prices rises on the industry. Despite the hardships, many establishments are doing an incredible job, raising the bar for good food in a committed, understated and exceptional way. 2009 will be a great year to dine out in Victoria.

The 2009 Guide is fearless, compelling and new – and we loved every minute of putting it together. – John Lethlean and Necia Wilden

The Sydney Morning Herald Good Food Guide 2009

Simon Thomsen & Joanna Savill

For over two decades, *The Sydney Morning Herald Good Food Guide* has provided expert advice on negotiating Sydney's restaurant scene, keeping residents and visitors in touch with the best, the most interesting and the most innovative places to dine in the city and suburbs, and further afield in regional New South Wales.

In this expanded 2009 edition, food connoisseurs Simon Thomsen and Joanna Savill and their team review over 400 restaurants, numerous bars and cafes, and over 50 'Global Gems' in a new section that recognises interesting and exciting eateries across the city that do not necessarily rate on the fine-dining scale.

Setting down their impressions with the flair, insight and razor-sharp wit for which the guide has become known, the team also reveal the winners of the coveted *Good Food Guide* awards in various categories; restaurants that will go on to set the standards by which others are judged in the coming year.